red dot
design yearbook
红点
国际设计年鉴
2005/2006

red dot design yearbook 2005/2006
By Peter Zec (Editor)
Translated by Zhao Xin, Dong Honglan
First Published by red dot GmbH & Co. KG, Essen, Germany, in 2005,

ISBN-13: 978-988-99251-7-8
ISBN-10: 988-99251-7-6

Cover Photo:
The photo by Pia Mingels shows an Akashi bag of the BREE Collection GmbH & Co. KG, Isernhagen, designed by Studio Vertijet (Kirsten Hoppert, Steffen Kroll) in Halle, Germany. (See page 94)

封面照片：
由皮亚·明格斯拍摄的封面展现了伊塞尔哈根的博瑞公司的阿卡时包系列。
由Kirsten Hoppert， Steffen Kroll组成的Vertijet工作室设计。（见第94页）

The "red dot award:product design" competition is the continuation of the Design Innovations competition.
“红点奖：产品设计”大赛的前身是“设计创新”大赛。

出版发行：安基国际印刷出版有限公司
地址：香港湾仔轩尼诗路200号恒生湾仔大厦3层301-2室
印刷：恒美印务（番禺南沙）有限公司
幅面尺寸：295mm×302mm
印张：44
出版时间：2006年8月第1版
印刷时间：2006年8月第1次印刷
出版人：柳战辉
责任编辑：郭欣
责任校对：石方
封面设计：宝一设计
版式设计：晨丽

定价：428.00元
（您所购买的每一本图书都会有人民币壹元捐赠给西藏协庆慈善孤儿学校）

大连设计制作中心地址：大连市沙河口区软件园绘春街2号3-1102室，邮编116020
电话: +86-411-6291 5001，6291 5002
传真: +86-411-6291 5003
E-mail: info@archi-china.com
www.archi-china.com

red dot
design yearbook
红点
国际设计年鉴
2005/2006

中文网址
www.xq-school.net
English website
www.shechen-school.org

协庆慈善孤儿学校——藏族孤儿的希望

Shechen Charity Orphan School
A home and education for the orphans of Tibet

这些孩子都生活在中国四川省甘孜藏族自治州——80万康巴藏族人的故乡。而他们只是孤儿中的一小部分，大概有1000多名孤儿或者单亲儿童生活在这里。家庭是当地人唯一的生存保障。而教育、 医疗等生活水平的落后导致许多孩子生活孤苦无依。

These children live in Ganzi Tibetan Autonomous (TAR) Prefecture in West Sichuan Province in China, the home to more than 800,000 Khampa Tibetan people. They are not alone; it is estimated that more than 1,000 orphans and even more semi-orphans - children who have lost one of their parents - in the area still live in conditions of extreme poverty. Families are the only social security people have. The levels of literacy, basic education and medical care among this population are extremely low.

如何帮助孩子们?
A. 捐款
捐赠银行、帐户、地址
开户银行：中国农业银行甘孜县支行营业部
名称：协庆慈善孤儿学校
账 号：22-581101040003934
海外捐赠银行、帐户、地址
收款方行名：中国银行四川省成都市武侯支行洗面桥储蓄所
地址：四川省成都市洗面桥横街14号
快速入帐码：BKCH CN BJ570
收款人姓名：贡夏
帐号（A/C NO）：840584020002313
B. 捐物
捐物地址：四川省甘孜州甘孜县呷拉乡自贡村 德所 转协庆慈善孤儿学校
邮 编：626700
电 话：0836-7522013
敬请善心人士在捐赠后联系我们，以便我们及时反馈和查询
联系我们
E-mail: gongxia_2004@163.com
gongxia21@yahoo.com.cn

How can you help?
Bank account
ACCOUNT WITH INSTITUTION:
BANK OF CHINA WU HOU SUB-BRANCH XI MIAN QIAO SAVING OFFICE CHENG DU CITY, SICHUAN PRO
ADDRESS: 14 HENG ROAD XI MIAN QIAO BRIDGE CHENG DU CITY, SICHUAN PRO CHINA
SWIFT: BKCH CN BJ570
BENIFICIARY CUSTOMER: GONG XIA(NAME)
(A/C NO): 840584020002313
Please inform us if you donate.
Contact us
E-mail: info@shechen-school.org
gongxia21@yahoo.com.cn

四川省德格县教育体育局文件

四川省德格县教育体育局文件
Support letter from Dege county government

德格县人民政府民政局文件

德格县人民政府民政局文件
Support letter from Dege county government

甘孜藏族自治州民政局

甘孜藏族自治州民政局文件
Support letter from Ganzi Tibetan Autonomous Prefecture government

reddot design award

product design

“红点设计”奖项

产品设计

product design

10 前言
Preface by the editor

13 创新与质量铸就的五十年
Essay "50 years marked by innovation and quality"

23 红点：2005 设计团队
red dot: design team of the year

24 阿迪达斯—品牌与传奇
迈克尔・迈克斯凯
和阿迪达斯设计团队
adidas – brand and legend
Michael Michalsky
and the adidas design team

38 红点：精品中的精品
red dot: best of the best

40 最佳设计质量奖
Awards for the highest design quality

106 红点奖：精品中的精品——获奖设计师
The designers of the "red dot: best of the best"

108 帕特丽夏・乌古拉
Patricia Urquiola
109 弗罗瑞恩・佩特里
Florian Petri
110 罗南・蒲胡莱克与伊万・蒲胡莱克兄弟
Ronan und Erwan Bouroullec
111 托马斯・瑞特、蒂诺・多普勒
Thomas Ritt, Tino Töppler
112 莱茵哈德・亚茨克、伯诺・萨阔博士
Reinhard Zetsche, Dr. Bruno Sacco
113 Speziell produktgestaltung（西贝尔・弗莱肯斯坦、希洛・斯沃尔和与詹斯・普尔曼）和芭芭拉・施密特
speziell produktgestaltung (Sybille Fleckenstein, Thilo Schwer, Jens Pohlmann), Barbara Schmidt
114 克里斯汀・豪斯
Christian Hosse
115 Topeak设计团队
Topeak-Designteam
116 爱恬・莱杜因、尼古拉・哈摩依根
Etienne Redouin, Nicolas Hamoignon
117 艾伦・洛松齐
Áron Losonczi
118 Pinc设计团队（乔汉・莱恩内尔、简・鲁特恩斯克、玛丽亚・鲁特恩斯克）
Pinc-Designteam (Johan Lionell, Jan Rutensköld, Maria Rutensköld)
120 简・克莱夫曼
Jan Kleffmann
121 卡罗琳・施密特、简・克莱夫曼
Karoline Schmidt, Jan Kleffmann
122 斯蒂芬・斯达克、安东尼・海特、迈克尔・摩尔
Stefan Stark, Anthony Hatter, Michael Mauer
123 宝马集团设计团队
Designteam BMW Group
124 罗伯特・艾伦有限责任公司Z-Tech设计团队（罗伯特・G・艾伦、肯尼斯・D・哈佛德、胡旭辉、德怀特・D・奥根、斯科特・H・科蒂斯、威斯纳・克里帕）
Z-Tech-Designteam, Robert Allan Ltd. (Robert G. Allan, Kenneth D. Harford, Xuhui [Bill] Hu, Dwight D. Organ, Scott H. Curtis, Vesna Klipa)
125 迈克尔・摩尔
Michael Mauer
126 菲利普・斯达克
Philippe Starck
127 安东尼奥・奇特里奥
Antonio Citterio
128 安斯嘎・柽瑙
Ansgar Graw
129 亚历山大・万・阿瑟贝格、赫尔穆特・瓦格纳尔
Alexander von Ascheberg, Helmut Wagner
130 佛瑞德・海德、托马斯・马兹克
Fred Held, Thomas Märzke
131 彼得・马力、卡斯藤・戈尔尼克
Peter Maly, Carsten Gollnick
132 塞斯・格林
Seth Green
133 埃德蒙德・恩格力克、凤凰设计事务所（汤姆・逊合尔、安德雷亚斯・迪米特利亚迪斯和安德雷亚斯・浩克）
Edmund Englich, Phoenix Design (Tom Schönherr, Andreas Dimitriadis, Andreas Haug)
134 苹果设计团队，苹果电脑有限公司
Apple Design Team, Apple Computer, Inc.
135 宫下伸
Shin Miyashita
136 垂直喷射工作室（柯尔丝汀・霍派特和斯蒂芬・克罗尔）
Studio Vertijet (Kirsten Antje Hoppert, Steffen Kroll)
137 洛斯・拉古路夫
Ross Lovegrove
138 彼得・科瓦里
Peter Kövari
139 埃斯基耳・特莫尼、维斯・贝哈、肖恩・森约克
Eskil Tomozy, Yves Béhar, Shawn Sinyork
140 欧若・依图
ORA-ÏTO
141 让・米歇尔・维尔莫特
Jean-Michel Wilmotte

红点：
高品质设计奖（12个行业）
Awards for high design quality

142 客厅与卧室
Living rooms and bedrooms

164 家居用品和厨房用具
Households and kitchens

244 休闲、运动、健康、外出度假
Leisure, sports, wellness and caravaning

270 建筑和室内设计
Architecture and interior design

284 工业与工艺
Industry and crafts

314 交通
Transports

328 浴室、取暖、卫生清洁设备和空调
Bathrooms, heatings, sanitary installations and air-conditioning

356 生命科学与医药
Life science and medicine

376 商业与行政办公设备
Offices and administration

390 多媒体与家用电器
Media and home electronics

462 珠宝、服装、首饰、纺织品设计和新材料
Jewellery, fashion, accessories, textile design and new materials

472 照明与灯具
Lighting and lamps

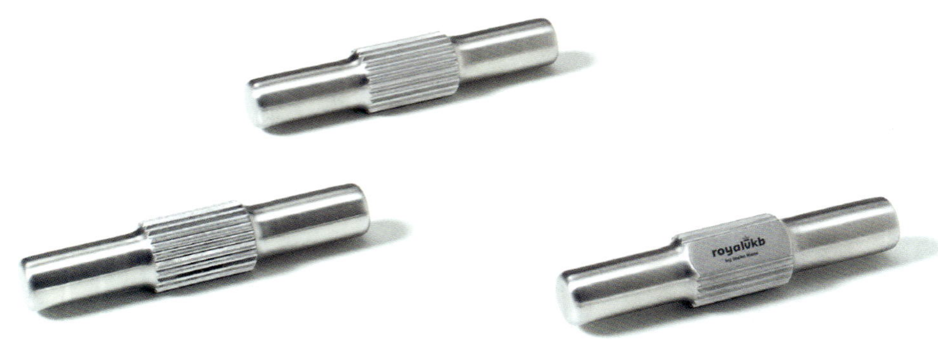

486 "红点奖：产品设计"的评委
The specialist jurors of the "red dot award: product design"

488 华纳・艾司令格
Werner Aisslinger
489 阿部真代
Masayo Ave
490 马丁・伯格曼
Martin Bergmann
491 马汀・克莱森
Mårten Claesson
492 毕勇・达尔斯特姆
Björn Dahlström
493 约西姆・H.浮士德
Joachim H. Faust
494 路易吉 ・发拉拉
Luigi Ferrara
495 安德里亚・芬克–安劳夫
Andrea Finke-Anlauff
496 深泽直人
Naoto Fukasawa
497 肯尼斯・格兰奇
Kenneth Grange
498 弗莱明・汉森
Flemming Bo Hansen
499 塔帕尼・海万恩
Tapani Hyvönen
500 金哲昊
Chul-ho Kim
501 奥杜・克洛斯
Odo Klose
502 安妮特・朗
Annette Lang
503 克瑞斯汀娜・拉萨斯
Kristiina Lassus
504 斯坦梵・伦吉尔
Stefan Lengyel
505 沃弗岗・K・梅尔–亥兹
Wolfgang K. Meyer-Hayoz
506 弗朗塞斯科・米拉尼
Francesco Milani
507 裘连诺・莫利那瑞
Giuliano Molineri
508 马尔切罗・莫然迪尼
Marcello Morandini
509 朗・纳巴罗
Ron Nabarro
510 丹尼・维勒特
Danny Venlet
511 海伦・亚勒
Helen Yardley

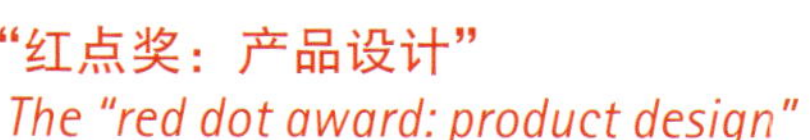

“红点奖：产品设计”
The “red dot award: product design”

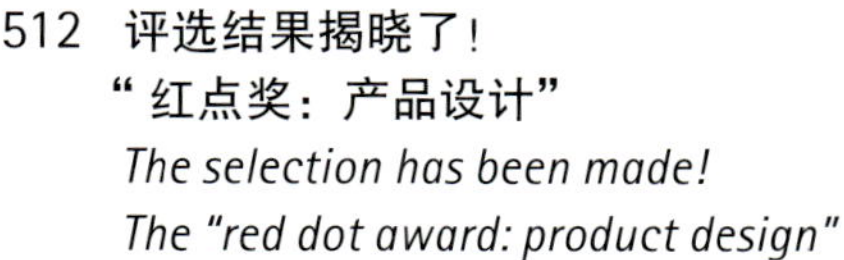

512 评选结果揭晓了！
“红点奖：产品设计”
The selection has been made!
The “red dot award: product design”

516 德国设计协会的赞助商
The Sponsors of the Design Zentrum Nordrhein Westfalen

索引：地址索引
Appendix: address index

517 生产厂商
Manufacturers

521 经销商
Distributors

522 设计师
Designers

前言

——彼得·柴克（Peter·Zec）教授（博士）

Foreword by Prof. Dr. Peter Zec

亲爱的读者们：

设计是我们生活中很重要的一部分。每天我们的生活都或多或少地被各种产品所包围着，这些产品无疑会让我们的生活变得更容易、更美好。然而，产品的种类愈是繁多，区分和辨别这类“好”的设计就显得愈为重要。我们不能说只有闻名世界的经典才称得上是杰出设计。设计有许多不同的表现形式，如果产品“仅仅”使用起来效果就很好，这个产品就可以说是设计得不错，或者，产品经得起推敲，并展示了一种具有创新意义的发展方向，这同样也是好的设计。

红点设计年鉴收录了所有主要行业里的最新产品，在这些行业里，设计扮演了一个很重要的角色。本书展示了来自当今各个领域的产品：家具行业、休闲和运动、建筑与室内设计、卫生与健康行业、生命科学与医疗、工程与工艺、汽车行业、媒体和家用电器、还有珠宝和时装业。所有的这些产品都凭借自身的设计水准获得了举世闻名的“红点设计奖”，全书对这些产品的特点进行了各种详细的介绍，并配有大量的图片。这些产品在关注细节和强调视觉效果方面，都十分令人惊叹一它们都在自己的领域里迈出了新的一步。

Dear Readers,

Design is a part of our life. Everyday we are surrounded by many, more or less useful, products that are all meant to make our lives easier and more beautiful. However, the wider the variety of products, the more important it becomes to make distinctions and to recognise "good" design as such. It is not only the world-famous classics that constitute good design. Design comes in many different forms, and something can be said to be well designed if it "simply" functions well, or if it shows an innovative new direction only on closer inspection.

The red dot design yearbook documents the latest in product developments from all major industries in which design plays a role today. It presents current products from the furniture industry, from leisure and sports, from architecture and interior design, the sanitary and wellness industries, life science and medicine, engineering and crafts, the automobile industry, media and home electronics, as well as from the jewellery and fashion industries. All of the products featured, shown throughout the book in numerous illustrations, have collected awards in the world-renowned "red dot design award" competition for their design quality. Often these products can be surprising, with careful attention to detail and great visual impact – and as such they are all new in their own way.

►

每个产品的背后都有其创造者和他们的故事。因此，红点设计年鉴不仅仅是一本书，它也讲述了设计幕后的故事。杰出设计师的自传细致地展现了设计的发展以及设计师本人对他们产品的看法。红点设计年鉴使人们清楚地认识到人与设计之间的紧密联系。比如，阿迪达斯公司的全球创意总监迈克尔・迈克斯凯在担当公司的总设计师时说到，阿迪达斯公司在全球范围内取得成功就证明了多年来，对他们来说，设计一直是成功的最重要的因素。从二十世纪五十年代起，对设计的理解及其发展中的精彩的点点滴滴戏剧性地向我们展现了世界是如何迅速地变成了一个设计的世界。

红点设计年鉴为读者提供了一个良机，使您能够从主要行业中了解到更多最新最棒的产品。无论您是浏览此书，观看插图描写还是阅读任意一篇精彩的文章，我们都希望它能对您有所裨益，了解到有关设计的创新之处。

彼得・柴克

Behind every product are the people who created it and a story. Thus, the red dot design yearbook is above all also a book that provides the background and tells the story. Detailed biographies of the best designers show how design develops and how the designers see their own products. The red dot design yearbook makes clear the close connection between people and design. The essay on the globally successful adidas company, for instance, demonstrates how for them over many years design has become the most important factor for success, with Global Creative Director Michael Michalsky talking about his role as Chief Designer. The detailed and engaging piece on the development and understanding of design since the 1950s dramatically traces how our world has rapidly changed into a world of design.

The red dot design yearbook gives you the opportunity to learn more about the latest and most exciting products from the major industries. Whether you browse through the book, looking at the illustrations, or read any of the fascinating essays, we hope you will always learn something new about design.

Sincerely
Peter Zec

创新与质量铸就的五十年

从一个国内的设计展成长为一个国际领先的大赛

From a national performance show to a leading international competition

50 years marked by innovation and quality

克劳黛·温尼格 *by Claudia Wanninger*

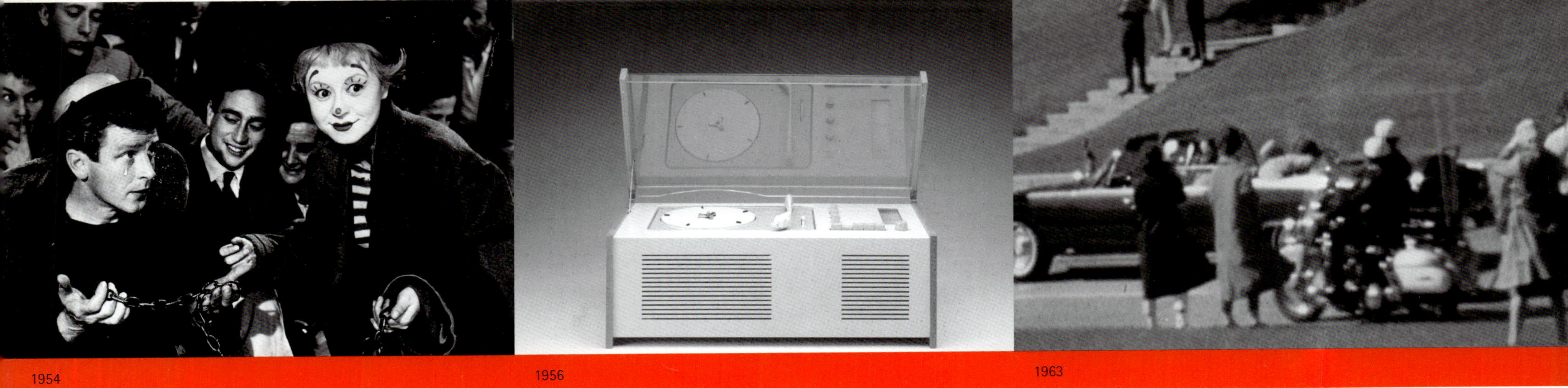

1954 1956 1963

1954：费德里科·费里尼“大路”；1956：布劳恩牌“白雪公主的棺材”SK4（留声机），由汉斯·古格洛特和迪特•拉姆斯设计；1963：肯尼迪总统遇刺；1969：人类登月；1970：乌兹托克纪实；1972：慕尼黑奥运会；1974：德国大众“高尔夫”汽车下线

(from left to right) 1954: "La Strada" by Federico Fellini; 1956: "Cinderella's coffin" SK4 by Braun, designed by Hans Gugelot and Dieter Rams; 1963: John F. Kennedy's assassination; 1969: Moon landing; 1970: Woodstock; 1972: Olympic Games in Munich; 1974: The "Golf" rolls off the line at VW

德国设计协会已有五十年的历史。五十年来，它一直致力于提升设计水平并嘉奖好的设计。五十，在给我们一个理由去庆祝的同时，也给了我们一个机会，我们可以通过回顾过去来准确定位未来。回顾历史，我们清楚的意识到设计是多么地依赖于周围变化的环境。设计不仅反映了个人的时尚意识；它通过各种新产品，通过设计交流模型与媒体，通过人与机器之间的界面，以及一直在变化的美学表现形式来体现一定的社会需求。在新材料和新技术结合的同时，产品和品牌也融合在一起。随着变化的速度日益加快，当要推广应用的时候，设计就显得尤为重要。环境和生活方式的改变给我们带来了好的设计，同时让我们跟上创新的步伐，从而满足新的需求。

The Design Zentrum Nordrhein Westfalen has turned 50 – and with it the Essen tradition to evaluate design performances and to honour them with prizes. 50 years – this is not only a reason to celebrate but also an opportunity to obtain a clear position for future perspectives by looking back. In retrospect we clearly see how much design lives on changes. It is not only the expression of a personal feeling for style; it also points out social needs: by using new kinds of products and functions, by designing communication models and media, interfaces between man and machine, and of course by ever changing forms of an aesthetic expression. New materials, new technologies are integrated; product and brand sectors are brought together. With the accelerating speed of changes, design gains in importance when it communicates new applications. When environment and life style are changing good design takes you along; it helps to grasp innovations and makes new requirements manageable.

埃森设计大赛是展示这些变化的一面镜子——每年的比赛都记录了这些创新设计发展的精彩片断，并且这个协会从1955年在位于克虏伯庄园的“小剧场”举办第一次展览会开始，就经历了深刻的变化。从开始的“工业造型”协会（成立于1954年）到“豪斯工业造型”（1955年后）再到“德国设计协会”（1990年至今），它经历了一条坎坷的发展道路。但恰恰也证明了这个协会的关联性和稳定性，就好比贯穿历史的一条红线。这是一条完全的靠质量去找寻有效设计标准的探索之路。大赛坚持在设计领域里不断提高质量标准。这不仅增强了竞争力，而且还提高了团体创始人以及当今大赛组织者的生活质量。随着这个团体的成熟，其观念也逐渐发生变化：每年一度的“工业产品最佳外形”奖的评选最初是作为工业的展示窗口而设立的，尤其是为德国工业而设的，其初衷是要培养一种对工业产品设计精妙的质量意识，同时，这种年度评选的国际影响力日益增强，并在世界范围内确立了新的标准。设计大赛的历史可以追溯到剥削时代。在德国“战后经济奇迹”的

The Essen design competition is a mirror of these changes – this is not only the continuing result of annual events documenting the highlights of creative developments but it is also an institution which has undergone a profound change since its first exhibition at the "Kleines Haus" on Villa Hügel in 1955. The road from the association "Industrieform" (founded in 1954) and "Haus Industrieform" (since 1955) to the "Design Zentrum Nordrhein Westfalen" (since 1990) had been a rough one. But it is precisely this fact which shows its relevance and stability, running like a red thread through its history. It is the search for valid design standards by means of a thoroughgoing alignment of quality. The conviction that the advancement of quality standards in the field of design not only improves the competitiveness but also the quality of life of a community unites initiators and today's organisers of competitions. The perspective, however, is a different one since the community has grown: The annual selection of "industrial products perfect in form" was originally introduced as a showcase of the industry, especially the German industry. It was the intention to establish an elaborate consciousness of quality for the design of industrial products. In the meantime this annual selection has developed competitive

1969 1970 1972 1974

最初几年里，首要问题是解决人们对香肠、巧克力和尼龙的需求。但是补偿自己品牌的缺乏仍然是个问题。就在这个时候，关注西方的德国人发现了一个绚烂多彩的世界。美国工业设计大师雷蒙德·洛伊设计的流线型的外型席卷了整个世界，他通过自己的流水线型设计，使我们的日常用品看起来赏心悦目，并成为高质量的美国生活方式的象征。作为一个在才智和感性上都有所欠缺的国家，德国极快地做出了反应。

从外部来看，产品设计关系到品牌形象是否适合出口。从内部来看，甚至是五十年前，设计主要是身份的问题。德国设计师曾尝试靠“忠实”于产品的功能来抵抗无约束浪漫主义的“肾形”桌子。在这点上，德国设计师深受德国乌尔姆造型学院“精美外形”思想的影响。（德国乌尔姆造型学院；

dimensions of growing international importance and is setting new standards worldwide.

The history of the design competition has its roots in a time of deprivation. In the first years of the "Wirtschaftswunder" first of all the urgent demand for sausage, chocolate and nylons was satisfied. But it was also a question of compensating a lack of own models. The Germans looking westwards saw a glittering and colourful world. The streamlined form, spread all over the world by Raymond Loewy, valorised all everyday items by a pleasing style and became the symbol of the belief in progress according to the American way of life. Being a country which was intellectually and sensuously depleted Germany was only too prone to it.

Outwardly product design was a matter of brand image with regard to the suitability for exports. Inwardly, even 50 years ago, design had mainly been a matter of identity. German designers

从“豪斯工业形式”再到“德国设计中心”的蜿蜒历程恰恰证明了这个协会的关联性和稳定性，它好比贯穿历史的一条红线，这也是一条完全地靠对质量的永不妥协而去找寻有效设计标准的探索之路。

The winding way of the Haus Industrieform and the Design Zentrum Nordrhein Westfalen proves how sustainable and constant the red thread of its history is: the search for valid design standards by an uncompromising quality focussing.

1953年开始授课，1955年正式办学）。这种观点认为设计是用途的一种形式，并且解除了关于正统美学的教条原则。产品外形主要是为产品服务。德国设计成功的关键在于他们对设计标准发展的尝试，最早着手于此标准的是魏玛和德绍，他们带有很强烈的理想主义色彩。此后乌尔姆造型学院对设计标准进行了透彻的分析和研究，并在设计中心得到了实际应用性的延续。凭借德国汉莎航空，德国博朗和Co这些品牌，这些设计标准在世界上享有盛名，直到今天仍然是同行业的榜样。

二十世纪五十年代，设计还是一株脆弱的幼苗，需要精心的培育和灌溉。甚至可以说，工业制造消费品的设计还是一项道德任务。为了提高生活水平和促进民主文化进步，艺术家和工业要联手打造一片天地。在这里消费

tried to counter the rampant romanticism of kidney-shaped tables through the functionality of "honest" products. In this they were significantly influenced by the idea of the "Good Form" which was developed at the Ulm Hochschule für Gestaltung (hfg Ulm – Ulm School of Design; teaching since 1953, official opening 1955). This concept conceived design as the form of use and relieved the discipline of the dogma of a formal aestheticism. Form was primarily committed to the object's purpose. Crucial for the success of the design model in Germany was the attempt to develop design standards, which started in Weimar and Dessau with so much idealism. Later it was thoroughly analysed in Ulm and has found its practical continuation in the design centres. These design standards became known worldwide due to brands like Lufthansa, Braun and Co. They still are exemplary today.

（从左到右）1982：“7.000 棵橡树”，第七届国际当代艺术展（Documenta 7）,约瑟夫·博伊斯（Joseph Beuys）；1989：柏林墙的倒塌；1991：欧洲之星（城际高速快车）“试验号”,采取德国高速轮轨列车国际公司列车；1996：克隆羊“多利”的诞生；1997：毕尔包·古根海姆艺术馆，法兰克·盖里(Frank O. Gehry)；2001：9.11创伤，纽约；2004：火箭喷气式太空船一号升天，开始了人类的探索太空之旅。

(from left to right) 1982: "7,000 oaks" by Joseph Beuys at the documenta 7· 1989: Fall of the Berlin wall; 1991: ICE "Experimental" takes the Transrapid course; 1996: Clone sheep "Dolly"; 1997: Guggenheim Museum Bilbao by Frank O. Gehry; 2001: The trauma of September 11, NY ; 2004: With the flight of the rocket jet SpaceShipOne the space tourism is beginning

代表了选择的自由。1954年在埃森工人阶级地区的鲁尔区中心建立了一个协会，专门为促进这种新文化的形成。这个中心曾经因所谓的“盖尔森基兴巴洛克”败笔而声名狼藉。协会的创始人包括弗里德里克·克虏伯公司的维地亚工厂的总裁，卡尔· 洪德豪森博士和来自杜塞尔多夫的建筑师保罗·马赫博格博士。

同时，这个协会的建立直接关系到一部分人的切身利益。这些有影响力的工业界的创始者绝对不会空手而归。除了在1953年成立的德意志制造联盟和德国设计委员会之外，德国工业联邦协会的“工业设计研究集团”在整个项目中也起到了决定性作用。克虏伯公司——就好比一个大家庭——不仅提供住所，而且在克虏伯王朝的家庭所在地——克虏伯庄园别墅的“小剧场”里对其进行了翻修，使之成为一个现代化的展览机构。

1955年10月5日，“工业造型——美观工业产品的永久展览”在克虏伯庄园别墅的“小剧场”举行了开幕典礼。评委会由十二个成员组成，他们将评选出的模范工业产品展示给参观者：参展的不只有瓷器，还有搅拌器、熨斗、小型家用物品以及窗帘、壁纸等装饰性用品，还有打字机和电话、炉子、燃气罐、电炉、洗衣机和收音机。从正式设计的角度来看，甚至是轧钢机、钢铁框架建筑物、涡轮和电动摩托车这样的产品都要拿来参展，但是只能以产品图片和模型的形式展出。从现今的观点来看，很显然这只是一场德国工业的表演秀，而不是以竞争和对话为名的提高设计质量的公正舞台。

豪斯工业造型的总经理洪德豪森是德意志联邦共和国最早的公共关系专家之一。他和设计的赞助机构一起遵循美国基础原料工业承诺的样本。根据“精美外形”的原则：只有当设计与原材料保持一致，并忠实于原材料才可以被称之为现代、真实、美观的设计，最后重要一点就是同时要促进钢材料的推广。人们越来越清楚地意识到人造材料被排除于“完美工业产品收藏”之外并不可信，在这个问题上，展览者保罗·马赫博格和评判委员会仍然坚持他们的观点，这样，汉斯工业丧失了在克虏伯公司的特权地位，不得不向公司历史的博物馆屈服。1961年，协会从克虏伯庄园别墅总部迁出，在埃森城内几次移址，直到最后寻觅到最佳位置——前矿业同盟煤矿所在地。在德国设计协会和红点设计博物馆里，收藏了1000多件现代设计品，使它成为新的设计区域中心。后来它又搬到由诺曼·福斯特爵士改建的克塞大楼，从2001年起，克塞汉斯隶属于被联合国科教文组织指定为世界文化遗产的矿业同盟。

处身于限制性行业内，“德国第一个此类的设计中心”，其评选原则最终却以失败而告终。然而，如果把这样一个独立的评奖活动作为一个公正公平的评选机构而进行创建，如今天我们所熟悉的红点设计奖，它还有很长的路要走。起先的年度特别展中所评选出来的产品和那些后来入围永久展览的产品都无法构成一个有代表性的总体，只能说那是一个有准备的筛选。当然，

In the 1950s design was regarded to be a delicate plantlet that needed fostering and nurturing. Even more – the designing of industry-manufactured consumer goods was a moral task. Artists and industry were to make common cause in order to raise the living standard and to advance a democratic culture where consumption stood for individual freedom of choice. To foster this new culture an association was founded in Essen in 1954 – in the centre of the Ruhrgebiet as a working-class region, notorious for the bloomers of the so called "Gelsenkirchen baroque." Among the initiators were the head of the Widia factory of the Friedrich Krupp AG, Professor Dr. Carl Hundhausen and the architect Dr. Paul Mahlberg from Düsseldorf.

At the same time tangible interests were linked to the foundation of the association. The founding members didn't come from influential industrial circles for nothing. In addition to the Deutscher Werkbund and the German Design Council, founded in 1953, the "Research Group for Industrial Design" of the Federal Association of the German Industry played a decisive role in the project. The Krupp Company – that is the family – not only provided the accommodation but also the means for structural conversions of the "Kleines Haus" on Villa Hügel, the family residence of the Krupp dynasty, to become a modern house of exhibition.

On October 5th, 1955 the "Industrial Form – Permanent Exhibition of Shapely Industrial Products" was inaugurated in the "Kleines Haus" on Villa Hügel. "Exemplary" industrial products, selected by a jury of twelve members, were exhibited: Not only porcelain and smaller household items such as mixers, flat irons and decorative furnishing such as curtains and wall paper were displayed but also typewriters and telephones, furnaces, gas and electric stoves, washing machines and radios. Even rolling mills, steel framework construction, turbines and electric motors were presented from the aspect of formal designing – however, only in the form of pictures or models. From today's point of view it is obvious that it was rather a performance show of the German industry than a neutral stage for promoting design quality by means of competition and discourse.

Hundhausen, managing director of Haus Industrieform, was one of the first PR-professionals in the Federal Republic of Germany. With the design sponsoring institution he followed the example given by the commitment of the American basic material industries. The principle of the "Good Form," according to which only a design corresponding with the material and being "honest with the material" could be considered as modern, "true" and beautiful, last but not least served the promotion of the material steel. When it became clear that synthetic material could not credibly be excluded from the "Collection of Ideal Industrial Products" – in this point the exhibitor Paul Mahlberg and the jury stuck to their belief – the Haus Industrieform lost its preferential position for the Krupp Company and had to yield to a museum for the company's history. In 1961 it left its headquarters at Villa Hügel and moved from one domicile to the next within the city of Essen before it acclimatised in the former Zollverein colliery. Here the Design Zentrum Nordrhein Westfalen together with the red dot design museum has allocated more

1996 1997 2001 2004

自由主义和个人主义促使在美学方面的决定中多少包含着一种“随意性”。同时，世界是如此的丰富多彩，我们更需要一些有质量的评判。

Liberalism and individualism promote a certain "randomness" in all decisions on aesthetics, at the same time there is a growing need for a qualitative judgement on the diversity which is offered us throughout the world.

从制造商的角度来说，他们可以询问其的产品是否在考虑的范围之内，但其中大多数获奖产品都是由评委会提名的，这与从十九世纪八十年代开始采用的方法——从大量的参赛产品中进行评选大为不同了。不仅如此，由于运输费用的问题，原作是不参加评选的。评委们最后所作的决定是根据那些宣传册的文字材料——直到今天许多比赛的组织者也常常使用这种方法。然而，这并不是一个能靠得住的评选基础，因为它往往传达了一些既定的观点。与今天的红点设计奖项的作品质量水平相比，评选过程的操作确是差强人意的。

虽然评选机构和评选大赛的自我形象都经历了根本性的改变，令人惊讶的是，评估标准却保持不变，甚至可以说是变得有些保守。除了产品的新颖性和功能性，在产品的外形和使用性上，也要让人容易理解，这一点也是授予“汉斯工业外形奖”奖章的决定性因素。生产商将这一奖章当作营销和公共关系的工具。在二十世纪七十年代和八十年代初期，人类工程学和社会伦理因素也被吸纳到这一标准中来。同时，另一质量标准——持续性——已逐步占据了重要的地位。唯一真正导致后来对大赛和展览重新命名的决定性变化在八十年代中期明朗起来：最能标明产品质量和产品的设计的创新特征变得越来越重要。

这就是竞争对需求持续饱和所做地回应。虽然满足了人们对新产品的基本需求，但是“真正”的创新却难得一见。交流产品的优点变得格外困难，因为产品之间以越来越快的速度互相追随效仿，所以我们只能对它们的功能进行一定的评判。如果把销售和设计联系到一起的话，能凸现工效学、美学和高品质加工方面的设计就会变得格外珍贵。我们评估设计时更加注重的是其创新价值。“创新设计”名下的年度评选也就是官方所说的“竞赛”最早始于1987年。评估必要性的决定不仅从根本上对产品进行重新诠释，也逐步提升了产品的实用价值，并且为全球营销策略划定了路线——竞争的权威性与建立在永久进步和变化基础上的市场经济相吻合，这一决定也培养了牢固永久的价值观念。这些标准除了在一些术语上有一定地修改，其它的至今仍然没有大的变动。（参见486页）

上述观点也被公司接受了，它们进一步提高了对质量的要求。市场上新问世的产品由原来的需要等三年才可以参加竞赛，而缩减到现在的两年。二

than 1,000 objects of modern design and thus constitutes the core of the new design location. Later it moved into the Kesselhaus which was reconstructed by Lord Norman Foster and which has belonged to the Zollverein UNESCO World Heritage Site since 2001.

As Closed Shop System the selection principle of the "first design centre of its kind in Germany" proved to be a failure. However, it was a long way until an independent competition could be established as neutral qualification centre, as it is represented today by the red dot design award. At the beginning the selection of the products for the annual special show and their following admission to the permanent exhibition therefore did not constitute a representative overview but only a deliberate selection. Of course, there are indeed inquiries on the part of the producers whether their products are taken into consideration, but the majority of the prized products were proposed by jury members; they had not been selected, as is customary today, out of a big pool of entries for the competition. This method was applied until the 1980s. Moreover, due to the logistic expenditure no originals were appraised. Decisions were rather made on the basis of brochure material – as is common practice still today with many other competition organisations. This however is hardly a really reliable basis for examination since it always conveys an arranged view. This is a situation unimaginable with today's quality level of the red dot design award.

While the organisation and the self-image of the competition underwent a fundamental change the valuation criteria remained astonishingly constant or even conservative. Beside originality functionality, whose form and use were comprehensible, was decisive for the conferment of the seal "Awarded with a prize by the Haus Industrieform." Producers used this seal as a marketing and PR instrument. During the 1970s and early 1980s ergonomic and social-ethical aspects were added; and also another quality criterion – sustainability – gained importance. The only real parameter change, which was to lead to a renaming of the competition and the exhibition in the following years, became apparent during the mid-1980s: The innovative character, as evidence for the quality of products and their design became increasingly important.

That was how competition responded to the increasing saturation of demand. The basic need for new products was satisfied. "Real" innovations became infrequent. It was troublesome to communicate the advantages of product generations, which followed each other faster and

十世纪八十年代中期，位于埃森的德国工业协会就已经意识到区分奖项和产品范围的必要性。红点奖中引进了“优秀品质”和“最佳设计品质”奖项（现称：‘红点：精品中的精品’）给大赛和获奖产品塑造了一个鲜明的形象。年鉴的引入进一步提高了评委会的评定和评审资料的透明度。评委在任命上也有很大的变化。二十世纪九十年代，评委组成变得国际化起来，因为这就是红点设计奖的标准，现在百分之八十的评委来自于国外，其侧重点不仅在欧洲，还延伸到美洲和亚洲。

生产商要得到消费者对其产品的品牌认可，就必须要通过权威的设计评估。随着生产商对此热情的逐渐高涨，评选和认证的过程就变得更具独立性和专业化了。这不仅关系到大赛的主办方和设计师，还关系到评委们最终的决定。未来的开发升级到以具体设计需求为导向的不同产品种类之间的划分。尽管在大赛历史发展的最初阶段，设计只是一项工程所必需的工作，而现在几乎遍布社会生活的各个领域，变得愈发重要起来。在红点设计奖项里，我们几乎可以在各个领域内找到设计的踪影：从古典家具设计、娱乐行业、商业界、健康器械到技术产品，建筑、仪器、甚至还包括移动通讯和界面设计。

领工资的时代、缺乏个性及创新的外形已经成为昔日黄花。在美学问题上，自由主义和个人主义造就了决定的随意性。但同时，对于我们生存环境多元化的专业评判需求也呈上升趋势。经济的发展导致了在消费者和工业生产之间形成了一种对抗，同样，也使我们的生活充满了各种外形设计及其多样化的功能。设计这一适宜在寂静中沉思的花园已经演变成为多姿多彩的复杂丛林。

然而，不仅消费者需要产品定位，企业同样需要渠道来评估设计，这不单是为了他们的公共关系，产品发展和设计理念，也是为了发掘优秀设计师和他们的一些自我理念。设计可以被看成一种所谓的“软性”因素，但是它不能完全避开经济规则的检验。然而为什么市场不能单独发挥这一功效呢？那是因为对一种成功的产品来说，设计同产品整个形象是不可分割的，这一点同样适用于品牌的外观和功用。只有那些在设计和流通领域里的专家才能在监督设计的过程中提供一定的帮助。也只有在大赛中对设计进行评估的时候，人们才有可能理解产品和设计与成败之间的关系。

制造行业和金融业的行业语言是建立在可测性原理之上的，因此我们现代文明的世界范围内基础就是所有事物的可测性。然而设计代表的既不是一种建立在可测性基础上的语言，也不是一种能做出是与否决定的语言，而是这些作品与我们的生活环境之间的情感联系。因此，由于它带有情感因素并且十分主观，我们无法证明设计的评判是否正确。这样一来，关于设计品质的说法也大相径庭。唯一一个可测量因素的替代物就是我们所说的惯例——在经过一系列所谓的沟通之后达成的品质上的评判，这恰好是那些专业化组织大赛的原则。一场大赛的质量评定结果不仅取决于评委的能力，也取决于企业的介入——只有在大量高质量产品参赛的情况下，所做出的评判才是具有代表性的。从这点来看，红点设计奖无疑是个最好的例子，因为它得到了国际上的赏识。

因此，红点设计奖是一种传播媒介——用来达成设计标准的共识。然而，使用这些传播知识既要适度，也要有责任感，而这点是许多年轻的参赛选手所做不到的。埃森的大赛组织者们有着多年的经验、遍布全球的网络再加上精湛的专业技术使他们的评审非常具有影响力。他们评价参赛作品不是依据

（从左至右）
1. 宝马 705iL汽车车身，慕尼黑宝马公司，设计者：宝马（克劳斯・卢梭负责）。
2. 3MIX Krups搅拌器，Krups设计部，1960年，照片提供：Krups。
3. AB310ts,勃朗石英表，勃朗产品设计，1982年10月（设计发明年鉴1985），照片提供：Braun公司。
4. Vorwerk Kobold 120,室内设计，Rolf Strohmeyer,1983（设计发明年鉴1985），照片提供：德国福维克公司。

(from left to right)
1. Automobile car body BMW 705 iL, BMW AG, Munich, Design: BMW (in charge: Claus Luthe)
2. Krups mixer 3 MIX, Krups design department, about 1960, photo: Krups
3. Braun quartz AB 310 ts, Braun product design, October 1982 (Design Innovations yearbook 1985), photo: Braun GmbH
4. Vorwerk Kobold 120, in-house design, Rolf Strohmeyer, 1983 (Design Innovations yearbook 1985), photo: Vorwerk & Co. KG

faster, with arguments merely referring to their functionality. Selling arguments relating to design, which pointed out the ergonomic, aesthetic and high-quality processing aspects became the more valuable. When design was assessed the innovative value also came the more to the fore. The annual selection under the title “Design-Innovationen,” which in the meantime is officially termed “competition,” has taken place since 1987. The basic decision about the necessity to evaluate not only fundamental reinterpretations of a product but also the gradual improvements of its practical value set the course for a global marketing instrument – a competition authority corresponding well to a market economy based on permanent progress and change, but which cultivates permanently valid conceptions of value. Apart from modifications of terms the catalogue of criteria has not generally changed until today (cf. page 486).

As this was accepted by companies the demands on quality increased. The period during which a product, which was new on the market, could participate in the competition was reduced from originally three years to two years. Already in the mid-1980s the necessity to distinguish between prize and product range was realised in Essen. The awards “High” and “Highest Design Quality” (today: “red dot: best of the best”) were introduced and contributed to a distinctive image of the competition and the awarded products. With the introduction of yearbooks the transparency of the juries' decisions and their public documentation was deepened. There was also a greater fluctuation in the appointment of jury members. In the 1990s the jury became international as it is standard for the red dot design award. Today 80 per cent of the jury members come from abroad. The emphasis lies not only in Europe but also in America and Asia.

The increasing interest of the producers in achieving brand recognition of their products through a qualified design evaluation led to more independence and professionalism in the processes of selection and qualification. This concerned organisers of the competition and its designers as well as the jury's decision making. For the future the development points to a further increasing differentiation of branches which are characterised by specific design requirements. Whereas at the beginning of the competition's history design was merely an engineering discipline it has now acquired a stable position in all spheres of life. Correspondingly all fields of applications find their expression in the red dot design award, from classic furniture design, the recreation sector, business world, machines for health and production technology, architectonic equipment, to mobility and even interface design.

实用主义为获得国际化的成功铺平了道路：诸如勃朗、Krups和宝马等品牌都是世界上公认的设计标准楷模，这个标准是由德国开发的，这些产品也都是在德国设计协会上获奖的产品。

Functionalism paves the way towards international success: Brands like Braun, Krups and BMW contributed to the worldwide acknowledged model of design standards developed in Germany and ranked among products that won an award in Essen.

某个人的标准，而是寻找最优秀的评委并建立最优化的评估标准（比如说，请设计者提供原始设计）。必要的物流运输由专业的组织者进行管理。这样一来，即使像MAN的“lyon's Regio L”大型旅行车以及保时捷的Carrera C2（参见326页和72页）这样的庞然大物也能够原样呈现在评委面前。然而，这么做只能初步确保比赛的高度关联性，因为评委们还需要依据时下的标准，对参赛作品进行独立评判。

企业获得“红点设计奖”，不仅是对该企业产品和品牌的认可，同时也是一个可灵活利用的营销工具。获奖为企业提供了与外界交流的机会，为多样化的选择奠定了基础。这包括通过贸易伙伴所创造的企业的公众影响力，以及由红点通过网络、年鉴和红点设计博物馆而合力打造的综合性平台，这些平台都是业内人士经常光顾的地方。最重要的是，红点奖作为设计证书而授予了该设计全球范围内的良好的信誉。

从长远的眼光来看，设计发起者最伟大的成就在于他们推动并在全球宣扬了一种全新的评判文化。乌尔姆造型学院（乌尔姆为德国南部城市）已经开发了一整套分析标准，目的是为了获得在审美过程中对概念上控制。正是应用这套分析标准而在埃森建立起了一种新的评判文化，并且得到了全世界的认可。曾经获得过“红点设计奖”的跨国大公司以及一些小型企业表示，他们不仅积极与全球的市场标准接触，而且还积极参与到标准发展过程中来。“红点设计奖”不仅是由某一特定行业的参赛者参加的论坛或是商品博览会，而是人人都有可能获得的极其重要的资格证书。这就是为什么全世界会有那么多的合作者加入到这种设计推广模式当中来，以此来传播一种质量意识，（例如通过“红点设计中心”的形式）。在欧洲的一些邻国，设计中心及合作模式已经建立起来并在不断扩大。同时，在充满活力的亚洲市场，“红点奖：设计理念”的新理念主要针对公司、设计师以及学生,且对亚洲文化和市场的需求反应尤其迅速。不论这些理念能否实现，如何实现，这些新颖的理念本身都受到好评并且获奖，而终端产品的情况却非如此。红点设计奖通过大赛发掘了一片新天地，将视线转移至有远见卓识的时尚活动中去。“红点奖：设计理念”欲建立属于自己的国际论坛，以便充分展示其创意和才华。

完成这项事业的主要途径是红点设计奖。埃森的设计赞助商们正是通过

The time of compensation and the lack of independent and ambitious forms is history long since. Liberalism and individualism have fostered arbitrary decisions in aesthetic questions but at the same time there is an increasing need for expert judgement about the diversity in our environment. The economic development resulted in a confrontation of consumers and industry likewise with an abundance of forms and functions. The contemplative front garden for design products has become a complex jungle of manifold forms and styles.

However, not only consumers need orientation, enterprises need clues to evaluate design as well – for their PR, for their product development, for their design policy, for their search for designers, for their own self-conception. Design may be considered to be a so-called "soft" factor, but it cannot elude the economic principle of benchmarking completely. The market alone cannot fulfil this function, though. Why? Because the share of design in the success of a product cannot be separated from the overall image. The same applies to the appearance and the performance of a brand. Help comes only from a separated examination of the design by experts, who have fundamental knowledge in matters of design and of trade as well. Only when design is evaluated in a competition it is possible to understand the relation between a product and its design with regard to success or failure.

The language of the producing industry and finance is based on the principle of measurability. The measurability of all things is therefore a worldwide basis of our modern civilisation; whereas design represents a language which is not based on measurability or yes/no decisions but on our emotional relationship to the objects of our environment. Therefore, judgement on design cannot be proved since it is emotional and subjective. Accordingly statements on design quality vary. The only possible substitute for a measurable factor is convention – a judgement on quality agreed upon in a process of communication. That is precisely the principle of a professionally organised competition. The quality rating of a judgement in a competition not only depends on the competence of the jury but also on the commitment of the enterprises – the judgement will be representative only when a wide and high-quality participation is achieved. Particularly from this point of view the red dot design award surely is an exceptional case due to its broad international appreciation.

Hence, the red dot design award is nothing else but a communication media – a means to agree on design standards. However, to make proper and responsible use of this means

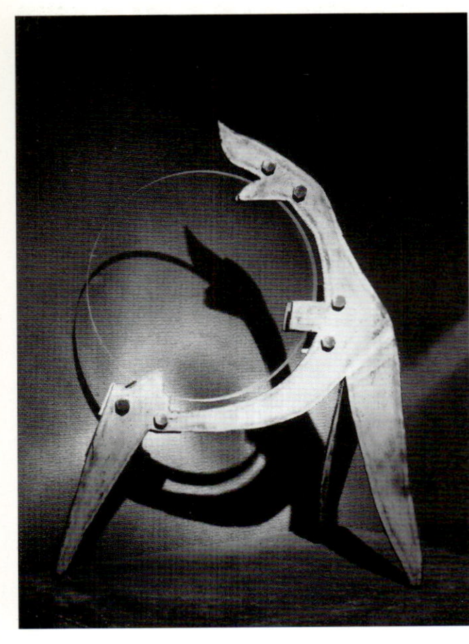

从最初的以精密产品为标志的工业到高科技含量的设计：红点奖不仅反映了设计产品日益地变得复杂，也展示了开发过程中的设计技术之间的相关性。

From the primary industry via complex products to intelligent design: The awards reflect the increasing complexity of design products and the technical relevance of design in the field of development.

这一奖项，引领了一场有关国际设计质量标准起草及实施的运动。它们不仅具备一定的经济标准，以便可测量设计质量，还要让全部设计方向的基本标准保持一致，即，把人类作为核心价值。未来产品的沟通价值注定要比产品的实际价值重要的多；其中，后者是指产品如何传达品牌效应、媒体宣传、公共效应，以及产品本身所附加的文化内涵。当然，设计不是一成不变的，红点设计奖也不会停滞不前。我们正在经历着一个过程，在这个过程中，我们生活的环境与设计之间的关系越来越紧密；这也就意味着设计任务变得愈加复杂，专业技术要求更加细致，即，设计是一个从产品到沟通设计，再到设计应用的基本项目的过程。随着设计过程的不断发展，设计最初的整体观念将被划分为许多不同的领域。评估标准中也包括了不断变化的生产要求，尤其在互动设计领域里，采用新的表现形式来满足需求，取得了显著的成就。同样，“红点：智慧设计”奖恰恰匹配了设计业内的急剧变革。在未来设计中，最大挑战将来自于跨领域的作品。在这种趋势下，设计大赛需要把不同水平的作品聚拢起来，指出互相得益的一致性和可能性。单人设计师办公室里绝对不会出现整体性思想，而这种整体性思想都会在设计对话和设计竞赛上有所体现。通过比较“红点奖：产品设计”和“红点奖：沟通设计”的相似性（作为“德国沟通设计奖”1993年在埃森登台亮相），对产品外围和品牌设计的垂直性，以及对类似网络设计这种沟通平台的统一性的检查，红点正好代表了为数不多并且可以提供此种服务的机构之一。因此，红点设计不仅给予国际设计组织一个公正中心的资格，也创造了一定的公众效应和对话平台，有助于促进和评估设计的发展。

最初的假说认为设计的特征是捉摸不定的。因为这种坚定的观点，作为一种思想表达工具，在世界范围内，红点设计奖并没有带着刻板的思想和一副固定的形象，而是对时下产品的质量，功能和设计世界情感做到了有效的理解，因此，红点设计奖的组织者们特意挑选地球仪作为他们品牌标识的象征。最终，设计不仅反映变化，也赋予了变化一种形式。正因为好的设计与好的质量紧密相连，因此，设计也被看成是好质量的担保。

of communication know-how is required which many young contestants are unable to achieve. Decades of experience, international networking and professional competence of the competition organisers in Essen have an effect: not by applying one's own standard to the submitted products but by finding the most competent jurors and by creating optimum evaluation criteria, e.g. by providing original products. The necessary logistic input is managed by the organisers with professional routine so that even big products like the huge station bus "Lyon's Regio L" by MAN or the spectacular Porsche Carrera C2 (cf. page 326 and 72) could be presented to the jury in the original. The high relevance of the competition, however, is primarily granted because the jury demands an independent judgement strictly related to the present and in accordance with actual and contemporary criteria.

When enterprises are awarded the red dot they do not only get a confirmation of their product and brand policy but also a marketing instrument which they can make use of actively. To get an award is an occasion for communication and forms the basis for a colourful selection of measures, from one's own PR efforts via publicity effects created by a trading partner to the integration of platforms which are offered by red dot in the Internet, with its yearbook and the red dot design museum and which are intensely frequented by the professional world. Above all, however, the red dot as design certificate bestows a credibility of worldwide significance.

From a future point of view the greatest achievement of the design promoters may be seen in the development and international promulgation of a new evaluation culture. The hfg Ulm (Ulm School of design) has developed analytic criteria in order to gain a conceptual control of aesthetic processes. Their application has established an evaluation culture in Essen which is acknowledged throughout the world. Having acquired a red dot the global player but also smaller companies demonstrate that they do not only meet with the standards of the global market but also participate in the process of their development. The red dot design award is far more than a forum of the competitors of a certain branch, or who are present at a trade fair – it is a vital qualification instrument accessible for everybody. That is why partners throughout the world join this model of design promotion to spread a consciousness of quality e.g. in the form of a "red dot design centre." In our European neighbour countries where design centres and cooperation models are already built up or enlarged but also on the dynamic Asian markets the

（左面）
物镜，是制造各种镜片最基本的产品
(德国蔡斯－耶拿光学仪器公司)
参展:1955
摄影: 李斯洛特・斯特罗

自行车液压制动器HS 77
1973年红点最高设计质量奖
摄影: 玛勒公司

引用自2002年FORM杂志
机器人AIBO ERS-111,索尼公司
摄影:汉斯・汉森

（右图）
奥迪A8轿车车身
红点设计博物馆斯书乐礼堂
摄影:西蒙・贝尔沃德

(left)
Object-glass, which serves as base product
for the manufacture of lenses
(Jenaer Glaswerk Schott & Gen.)
Exhibited: 1955
Photo: Liselotte Strelow

Hydraulic bicycle brake HS 77
Red Dot for the Highest Design Quality 1973
Photo: Gustav Magenwirth GmbH & Co.

Form quotation of the year 2002:
robot AIBO ERS-111, Sony Corporation
Photo: Hans Hansen

(right)
Car body of the Audi A8
in the Schürer hall of the red dot design museum
Photo: Simon Bierwald

red dot is an increasingly recognised factor. The new dimensions of the "red dot award: design concept" are particularly responsive to the needs of the Asian culture and market – addressing companies, designers and students as well. The original concepts are appraised and awarded, not the final products – no matter whether and how they were realised. With the competition the red dot design award breaks new ground and draws attention to visionary trend events. Moreover the "red dot award: design concept" wants to establish an international forum of its own to present ideas and talents.

Central instrument is the red dot design award with which the design sponsors in Essen are in the lead of a movement striving for the wording and implementation of international quality standards for design. They do not only want to meet the economic demand for a measurability of design qualities but also to preserve the basic standard in all questions of design – the human being – as a central value. In future it will be less a question for the practical value of a product than a question for its communication value; that is to say the way how it is communicated with reference to brand, media and publicity and what kind of cultural meaning is attached to it.

Certainly, neither does design remain static nor does the red dot design award stagnate. We experience a process in which more and more aspects of our environment blend with design; in which its tasks become more and more complex and its professional skills more sophisticated – going from the product and communication design to the design of fundamental programmes for the application of design. The more this process is advancing, the more the originally integrated concept of design will be fragmented into disparate special disciplines. The changing requirements of production are included into the assessment criteria. Explicitly appreciated are special achievements in the field of interactive design with its demands to adopt new ways of behaviour. The corresponding award "red dot: intelligent design" matches a general radical change in the design community. The real challenge for the design of the future lies in the interdisciplinary work. Against this background the design competition assumes the task to bring together these different levels and to point out the convergence and the chances of mutual enrichment. Holistic thinking no longer takes place in the office of a single designer but on the level of design discourse and design competition. Through the parallelism and comparability of the "red dot award: product design" and the "red dot award: communication design" (introduced as "German award for communication design" in Essen in 1993), the inspection of product periphery and the verticality of brand design as well as the integration of communication platforms such as web design, red dot represents one of the few institutions which are able to offer such a performance. Thus, red dot does not only offer the international design community a neutral qualification centre but it also creates publicity and a discourse forum in order to promote and evaluate design developments.

The initial hypothesis characterised design as something which is on the move. With this fundamental conviction the red dot design award, as an instrument of articulation, does not carry an inflexible image of a formal ideal around the world but the currently valid understanding of product quality, of functionality and of the emotional feeling of the designed world. The globe in turn has been chosen with good reason by the organisers of the red dot design award as a rotating symbol of their brand logo. Eventually design not only mirrors changes, it may also give them a form. And since (good) design is closely attached to (good) quality design may be considered as guarantor for the persistence of quality.

红点设计奖的目标是建立国际设计质量标准。

It is the objective of the red dot design award to establish international quality standards for design – as the community has grown.

克劳黛·温尼格是本书的作者之一

Claudia Wanninger is co-author of the book

（“红线——寻找最优秀的设计”）

("the red line – in search of outstanding design achievements")

我们在年鉴上第18次刊登出一个设计团队，这个设计团队所取得的成就吸引了大家的注意。它踏着前17个知名设计团队的脚印：莱宝公司（Leybold AG），博朗公司（Braun AG），斯拉尼（Slany）设计，瑞那·摩尔（Reiner Moll）与他们的技术工程师，纽梅斯特设计，青蛙设计，梅赛得斯–奔驰，西门子，IDEO产品开发、德鲁切（De Lucchi）工作室，飞利浦，奥迪，索尼，费斯托（Festo），苹果，诺基亚设计团队和平宁法利那（Pininfari–na）。今年的“年度设计团队”奖的获得者是阿迪达斯设计团队。

每年“Radius”奖杯都易主。这个奖杯是受弗雷登·尼辛珠宝（Niessing of Vreden）的委托，并由Weinstadt – Schnaidt的设计师西蒙·彼得·艾柏（Simon Peter Eiber）设计的。在“红点奖：产品设计”的颁奖仪式上，这个奖杯被授予了迈克尔·迈克斯凯(Michael Michalsky)和阿迪达斯设计团队，作为2005年“红点奖：年度设计团队”的标志。

For the eighteenth time in the Yearbook we are presenting a design team whose special achievements have captured attention. Following in the footsteps of the design teams of Leybold AG, Braun AG, Slany Design, moll design reiner moll und partner, Neumeister Design, frogdesign, Mercedes-Benz, Siemens, IDEO Product Development, Studio De Lucchi, Philips, Audi, Sony, Festo, Apple, the Nokia Design Team and Pininfarina this year's winner of the "design team of the year" award is the adidas design team.

Every year the "Radius" trophy changes hands. The sculpture was commissioned by Niessing of Vreden and created by the designer Simon Peter Eiber of Weinstadt-Schnaidt. At the "red dot award: product design" ceremony the trophy is passed on Michael Michalsky and the adidas design team as a symbol of the "red dot: design team of the year" in 2005.

红点: 2005 设计团队
red dot: design team of the year 2005

红点: 2005设计团队
迈克尔·迈克斯凯
和阿迪达斯设计团队

red dot: design team of the year 2005
Michael Michalsky
and the adidas design team

Michael Michalsky by Karl Lagerfeld

阿迪达斯——品牌与传奇

adidas – brand and legend

在一片呼喊声和口哨声中,他起跑了。这就是迪克·福斯伯里(Dick Fosbury),一位美国反叛青年,一心想要对跳高运动进行革命。多年来,就因为他非正统的跳高技术,他一直都是各种田径运动会上的笑柄。甚至连他的教练开始时对他也没有多少信心。现在他迅速取得动力,起跳比以往任何人跳得都高。他创造了1986年墨西哥奥运会的新纪录。他穿的鞋是制造商——阿迪·达斯勒(Adi Dassler)专门为配合他新的跳高技巧而设计的。许多这样的传奇故事,证明了在阿迪达斯悠久的历史上,这种对自己绝对的自信和无穷的胜利意志都一直存在着。这些故事引起了情感上的共鸣,使得人们喜欢用"三条白道"作为身份的标志。人们逐渐地把这个故事加以丰富,赋予了阿迪达斯这个品牌传奇以实际内涵。

To the sound of shouting and whistling he begins his run. Dick Fosbury, a young American rebel who was about to revolutionise the high jump, had been the joke of every track and field athletics meeting for many years due to his unorthodox jumping technique; even his coach had had little confidence in him at the start. He now quickly gains momentum, takes off – and jumps higher than anyone else has ever done before. A new world record at the 1968 Olympics in Mexico. In shoes tailor-made by Adi Dassler especially for Fosbury's new high jump technique. Many such legends, testifying to an absolute belief in one's self and a boundless will to win, are to be found in the long adidas company history. They create an emotional response, promote identification with the "Three Stripes" and are fostered, told and retold, giving substance to the adidas brand legend.

渊源：1926年，阿迪·达斯勒和他的第一双跑鞋。这是他亲手做成的一双鞋底全皮的跑鞋。阿迪·达斯勒制作的鞋在1928年阿姆斯特丹奥运会上第一次登场。

The origins: Adi Dassler and his first track shoe, with all-leather sole and hand-forged spikes in 1926. Shoes by Adi Dassler are worn for the first time at Olympic Games in 1928 in Amsterdam.

今天的阿迪达斯， 在竞争如此激烈的运动用品行业里依然居于领先地位，不能简单地归因于创造了一个奇迹——但也不能说和奇迹一点关系也没有。阿迪达斯是个很有实力的品牌。“品牌”现象， 不仅仅是它的经济意义,大多数人会把某些事物和一个名字联想到一起，所以当他们听到这个名字或是看到某个标志时，他们已经有了一个特殊的印象，头脑中就联想到这个品牌，这可以说已经超出了物体本身。正是人们头脑中所存在的产品形象，才使得一个公司的名字能够发展成一个品牌。就像迪克·福斯伯里（Dick Fosbury）或者“伯尔尼奇迹”那样的故事一样，回到1954年，阿迪·达斯勒通过使用他新发明的螺旋饰钉，为德国国家足球队特意制作了适合在下雨天湿滑的足球场地所穿用的球鞋。这给这个队带来了巨大的优势，使他们战胜了人们普遍看好的匈牙利队——正是这些传奇的故事在人们头脑中打下了一个烙印，然后用一个特殊的方式塑造了形象。

阿迪达斯这一品牌是基于这种英雄般的故事，它本身也成为传奇的一部分。公司的创始人阿迪·达斯勒，很久以前就是个英雄形象。对于阿迪达斯公司来说，必须在产品内涵和产品外形上都赋予品牌一定的意义，才能引导这个品牌向前发展。这也就是说通过把阿迪达斯的产品和英雄主义、完美的场上表现、永不停息的进取者阿迪·达斯勒联想到一起，一定的品牌价值已经长期被稳固下来，而且直到今天还在延续：对于运动和场上表现的热情和执著，对技术和美学上的细节的热爱以及对成就一段光辉历史的热爱。

1978年，阿迪·达斯勒逝世，九年以后，他儿子霍斯特也离开了这个世界，要带领这个品牌和这段公司历史走向未来，这个重任对任何人来说都是个有难度的。虽然开始有些迷惘，经济上还出现严重亏损现象，然而他们做到了。他们选择了唯一可行的方式——有目的地进行设计和营销，通过完善内部和把品牌价值向产品转移来提升整个品牌的形象。因为正是这些努力体现了品牌的价值，才得到了无数的运动爱好者的认同。

“简单的阿迪达斯”

迈克尔·迈克斯凯，起先是德国里维·史特劳斯的员工，1995年他接受新经理罗伯· 路易·德莱福的邀请，加入阿迪达斯，任运动服装的总设计师。那个时候，服装设计部门还没有自己的设计团队，他们只有几名业余设计师。每位设计师都把他自己的观念和创意，通过三条白道结合到一体；这也是证明它们是阿迪达斯服装的唯一途径。迈克斯凯还要面对核心事业之外的更大的挑战——不但要为运动员提供高品质的服装，还要给品牌一个更年轻的形象，才能更好的顺应时代潮流：越来越多的年轻人开始穿阿迪达斯运动鞋、运动衫、夹克，并不只是在运动场上，在大街上也可随处觅到它们的踪影。八十年代欧洲的Hip-hop组合如Run-D.M.C.，掀起了阿迪达斯运动鞋的复古风潮。现在，来自英国工业小镇的年轻球迷和流行乐队组合都开始在舞台上穿着阿迪达斯的帆布面胶底运动鞋和球衫，这样一来，人们普遍接受了运动装。如果忽视了这个趋势，就意味着忽视了一个很大的目标群体。于是迈克斯凯组建了一个设计团队开始工作，他深深地明白品牌的声誉和可信度必须要在服装上有所体现。在对品牌根源的研究中，他从厚厚的资料中发掘出大量地有价值的东西。五年以后，该服装部门取得前所未有的成功。

2000年，赫伯特·海纳，和全球营销总监艾瑞克·斯坦明格，担当起了公司的重任。海纳宣布了他的中期业务规划，这个计划是要带领公司在营业额和利润上都有大幅度的增长，该计划主要针对营销和设计而开展。随着设计变成一种行政功能，其结构也开始发生变化。33岁的迈克斯凯被任命为“全球创意总监”，负责确保所有产品的设计主题都能保持一致，并且他直接对全球营销总监负责。这样一来，设计与营销就站在了同等重要的位置。迈克斯凯回忆说：“我最初在阿迪达斯工作的时候，情况是很不一样的，设计部门被看作是一个附加物，当营销部门下达指示后，设计部门就在图纸上画几笔。许多营销人员都认为他们之所以需要设计师是因为他们自己画得不太好。现在这种局面已经有很大的改观，我们部门在公司的影响力也已大大提高。”

That adidas, today, again ranks among the leaders in the highly competitive sporting goods industry cannot be ascribed simply to the making of legends – even though it may not be entirely separated from it either. adidas is a strong brand. And the "brand" phenomenon, not least in its economic significance, develops first of all from the fact that many people associate something with a name, so that when they hear the name or see the logo they already have a specific image, an association with the brand in mind, something that goes far beyond the physical products themselves. It is the product images, which people have in their heads, that allow a company name to develop into a brand. Stories such as the one about Dick Fosbury or the "Miracle of Bern," when back in 1954, Adi Dassler himself had adapted the shoes of the German national soccer team to the ground conditions by using his newly developed screw-in studs, thus giving the team the probably crucial advantage on the rain-soaked field, an advantage that was to lead them to victory against the favoured Hungarians – it is these kinds of legends that evoke certain images and then shape them in a specific way.

The adidas brand is based on such heroic tales and has, thus, itself become part of the legend, with Adi Dassler, the company founder, long since styled a hero. For the adidas company, which has to fill the brand with both spirit and products in order to drive it forward, this means that because of associations of adidas products with heroism, peak performance, and with the ceaseless innovator Adi Dassler, certain brand values have long been established and continue to this day: passion and commitment to sports and performance, a love of technical and aesthetic details, and a prestigious history.

This was a somewhat difficult heritage for all those who, after the deaths of Adi Dassler in 1978 and, only nine years later, of his son Horst, were to carry the brand and the history of the company into the future.

They managed this, despite some initial disorientation and heavy economic losses, in the only possible way: by the targeted implementation of design and marketing to strengthen the brand image through the integration and translation of brand values into products. Because it is these that embody and communicate the brand with which so many sports enthusiasts identify.

"Simply adidas"

When Michael Michalsky, who previously worked for Levi Strauss Germany, is asked to join adidas as Chief Designer for sports apparel by the new manager Robert Louis-Dreyfus in 1995, the apparel department does not yet have a design team. It consists of several freelance designers who create the collection. Each designer brings in his own concepts and ideas, tied together by the three stripes as the only common element; the only thing that makes it possible to identify it as adidas apparel. A further challenge Michalsky has to face beyond the core business – producing quality apparel for athletes – is to give the brand a more youthful image to respond to the fact that more and more young people are wearing sports shoes, sports shirts and jackets not just on the field, but also on the street. Following the adidas footwear revival in the 1980s that came to Europe with hip-hop groups such as Run-D.M.C., it is now young football enthusiasts and Brit-pop bands from industrial English towns, who wear adidas trainers and adidas football shirts on stage and who, by reaching cult status, make sportswear socially acceptable. This trend, if ignored, would mean neglecting a large target group. Michalsky forms a team of fashion designers and sets to work. He knows that it is credibility and authenticity of the brand that has to be reflected in the apparel. Mining the depths of the archives in his search for the roots of the brand, he discovers a lot. Five years later, the apparel department is more successful than ever before.

In 2000, Herbert Hainer, together with Erich Stamminger as Head of Global Marketing, takes responsibility for the company. Hainer announces his mid-term business plan, which

“不论是公园里的足球赛还是雅典上的百米跑——我们过去在、现在在、将来也在！”

"Whether it's football in the park or the 100 meters in Athens – we have been there, we are there now, and we will always be there."

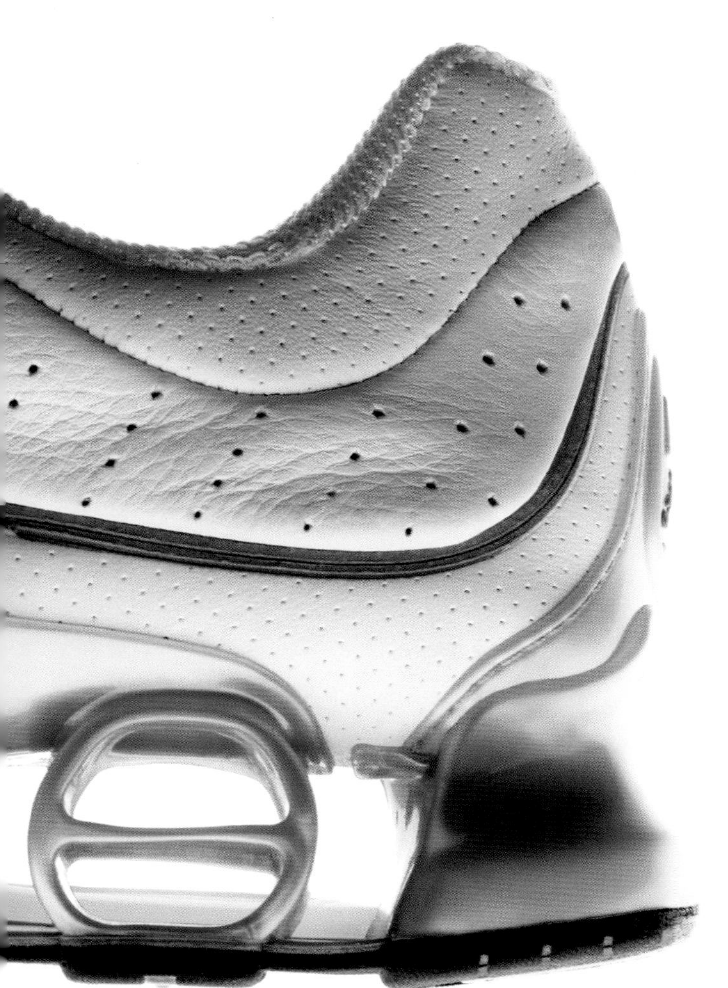

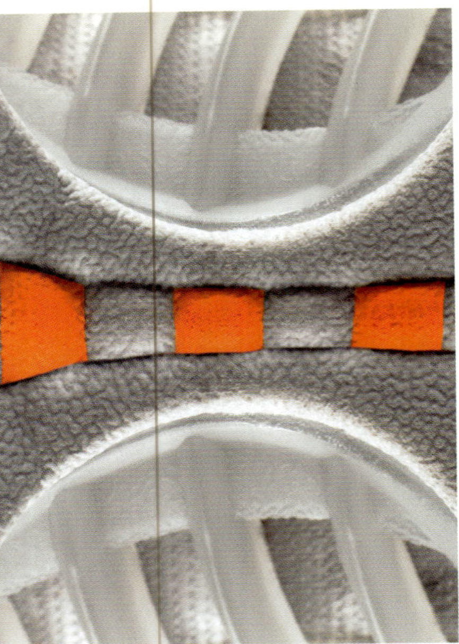

"阿迪达斯就是这样——简单而高效率。这个品牌本身就有一定的魔力。在这里工作过一段时间的人感觉特别敏锐，很容易看出来一种产品是不是阿迪达斯的。"

"It simply and effectively always has to be adidas. That certain magic of the brand. Those who have been working here for a long time have acquired a keen sense of whether a product is adidas or not."

迈克斯凯和他新的管理方法所面临的任务是强化阿迪达斯品牌，给阿迪达斯一个统一的形象，还肩负着它走向未来的使命。当谈到总体设计理念的时候，迈克斯凯说道："阿迪达斯就是这样——简单而高效率。这个品牌本身就有一定的魔力，在这里工作过一段时间的人感觉特别敏锐，很容易看出来一种产品是不是阿迪达斯的。"究竟什么是阿迪达斯？是什么构成了阿迪达斯的设计？人们看到阿迪达斯能联想到什么？公司又要给阿迪达斯品牌塑造一个什么样的未来形象？要同时做到上述这些，便是迈克斯凯和艾瑞克·斯坦明格所要完成的任务。

阿迪达斯的"品牌使命"肯定了它的责任，它的梦想是"要做世界上最顶级的运动品牌"。更重要的是："我们是以消费者为导向的，也就是说我们一直在产品的质量、外观、感觉和形象上进行改进。我们要优化公司的结构以便更好地满足甚至超过消费者的期望值，给他们以最高品质的享受。"最后，"我们是创新和设计领域的先行者。我们所要做得就是尽一切可能，使我们带给市场的所有产品都可以帮助不同技术层次上的运动员，使他们可以有最出色的表现."

所谓的"品牌展望"也就是 "热情"，对运动的热情成就了阿迪达斯。我们一直在把阿迪达斯的热情传递给每一种运动，无论何时，无论何地，不论是公园里的足球赛还是雅典赛场上的百米跑——我们曾经在，现在在，将来也在。"

迈克斯凯和艾瑞克·斯坦明格共同创立的《视觉语言守则》是他们俩的指导原则，这也是阿迪达斯内部所有员工的指导原则，上面列着最重要的品牌价值，还给美学标准下了定义，还通过实例在服装、鞋类、装饰物，销售和各种活动的沟通和广告中对它们进行了诠释。它不仅包括核心品牌、品牌使命、品牌展望、公司历史，也包括了质量、可信度和创新等价值体系。如克斯凯所说的："我们是想通过这个《视觉语言守则》来建立起一套体系。它的确立在某种程度上缩小了对阿迪达斯品牌的理解范围，让我们更清楚什么对阿迪达斯重要，什么不重要。阿迪达斯是一家拥有15,000名员工的企业，是一个拥有人文主义内涵的品牌。正因为如此，我们才更加有必要去设计一个工具，来定义品牌的界限，而且这种定义的准绳是放之四海而皆准的。"

服装总设计师托斯滕·霍赫施泰特尔在谈到"守则"对日常工作的重要性的时候说到："《视觉语言守则》就好比是根基，在这种根基上必须要有独立的设计。"所有代表品牌的特性都能够在《视觉语言守则》上体现出来，比如说真实、创新、运动、简单、真诚、明快——这些是任何一位阿迪达斯的设计师在动笔之前所必须了解的，因为我们要设计的是阿斯达斯的产品。"

这样，一个阿迪达斯品牌统一的外形基础就会建立。无论是理事会和营销团队，还是设计和沟通部门，它们都会以同样的语言，齐心合力地传达着同样的价值，广告和产品。无论是内部还是外部，阿迪达斯品牌都建立了一个清晰的轮廓。阿迪达斯公司已经打下了很稳固的基础，并且重新加足了马力，正准备着明天的起飞。

三个部门，三条白道—— 一个品牌

阿迪达斯，是从一个制作鞋类的小公司发展到当今世界上数一数二的大品牌的。在阿迪达斯历史上任何一个时期内，它都把运动员的需求放在第一位，为他们提供最好的技术解决办法。就这样，阿迪达斯才在过去的几十年里，真正地发

is intended to lead the company to substantial growth in turnover and profit. The plan focuses on marketing and design. The structures begin to change, with design becoming an executive function and the 33 year-old Michalsky appointed "Global Creative Director," responsible for all product areas and maintaining a consistent design theme. He reports directly to the Head of Global Marketing. Design stands on equal footing with marketing. Michalsky remembers: "When I started at adidas, things were very different. The Design Department was considered as something of an accessory. Briefs came down from marketing and the designers made a few pretty sketches. Many marketing people at the time were of the opinion that they were only in need of designers because they themselves could not draw particularly well. This has changed entirely and today we have a lot of influence within the company."

Michalsky, together with the new management, thus, faces the task of strengthening the adidas brand, giving it a consistent image and, at the same time, leading it into the future. Answering the question of an overall design philosophy, Michael Michalsky today says: "It simply and effectively always has to be adidas. That certain magic of the brand. Those who have been working here for a long time have acquired a keen sense of whether a product is adidas or not." But what is adidas? What constitutes adidas design? What do people associate with adidas? And what kind of future image of the adidas brand does the company want to communicate? To establish this once and for all is the task that Michalsky and Erich Stamminger address.

The adidas "Brand Mission" affirms its commitment, its desire "to be the leading sports brand in the world." And further: "We are consumer focused. That means we continuously improve the quality, look, feel and image of our products and our organisational structures to match and exceed consumer expectations and to provide them with the highest value." Finally: "We are innovation and design leaders who seek to help athletes of all skill levels achieve peak performance with every product we bring to the market."

The "Brand Vision" in turn is "Passion," "Passion for Sport. This is adidas. We consistently bring our passion to every single sport, wherever and whenever it is played. Whether it's football in the park or the 100 meters in Athens – we have been there, we are there now, and we will always be there."

These guidelines serve Michalsky and Stamminger as the basis for the "Visual Language Guide," which they develop together. It is an in-house set of guiding principles for all adidas staff and lists the most important brand values, defines aesthetic standards and, by giving examples, translates them for communications and advertising, for apparel, footwear and accessories, and for distribution and events. Alongside the core brand, the brand mission, the brand vision, and the company history, it also includes, among other things, values such as quality, authenticity and innovation. Michalsky: "With the Visual Language Guide we wanted to create a document that somehow narrows down the scope of interpretation of what counts as adidas, and what does not. adidas is a company with 15,000 employees – a kind of people's brand – and simply because of this it was vital that we create a tool that defines the parameters of the brand, a universally valid common thread."

Torsten Hochstetter, Head of Apparel Design, on the importance of the Guide for daily work: "The Visual Language Guide is something like the fundamental basis on which each

展成为一个世界品牌。

但是，运动世界一直在变化中。当今社会中，激增的媒体使运动在当今世界中无处不在；全球几百万人都在观看F1赛车、足球比赛、田径锦标赛。运动员变成了媒体上的明星，脱口秀的嘉宾，以及娱乐报纸的当红人物。运动不再仅仅关乎运动员和运动会，它还涉及到这些运动员是谁，他们所代表的是什么？他们穿的是什么？今天，运动也是一种生活方式，运动装也代表了流行趋势——同时也成为了一种文化的体现。既要对消费者不断变化的需求做出及时的回应，还要继续生产保质保量的服装，为此，迈克斯凯为这个品牌规划了三个部门，每个部门都专门负责一个目标群体，并且有它都自己的标志，分别为：运动经典，专业运动和运动时尚。

阿迪达斯运动经典是对hip-hop、英国流行乐队和俱乐部所掀起的早期阿迪达斯产品复兴运动所做出的回应。它不仅代表了极具技巧性的市场开发和新的销售策略，也是对市场需求的有效回应。聪明的年轻人可以从跳蚤市场，或者是二手商店购买，从而绕开阿迪达斯正常的销售渠道。在这个分支上，阿迪达斯传奇获得了一种新生。一般来说受欢迎的产品都是因为它们与某种运动传奇或者是某个运动盛事有联系，这些产品在复古系列中风靡一时，受到人们狂热的推崇。像“Samba”、“Copa Mundial”、“Gazelle” 或者是阿迪达斯第一批篮球鞋之一的“Superstar（超级明星）”这样的运动鞋产品，去年用35种特殊的样式组成的系列庆祝了其问世35周年。曾经一度它们在市场上也是最具有新意的产品，可是今天这些经典系列所代表的是真材实料，诚信和可靠。现在，“Streetstyle（街头时尚）”这一款把品牌形象与时尚连接到了一起，超出了运动的界限，把年轻的目标群体在他们年龄尚小时就和阿迪达斯品牌联结在了一起。对25岁以上的人来说，怀旧情结也起到了一定的作用，吸引他们去买这些经典产品。迈克斯凯说到：“当我去参加一个派对，提到我在阿迪达斯工作，即使我不问他们，人们也会告诉我有关他们和阿迪达斯的故事，说他们认为阿迪达斯是很了不起的。比如说，一些人现在还怀念着他们的第一双球鞋——一般都是“Mondial”或是“Predator”的。说到鞋，就勾起了很多人的回忆。”

这一系列的象征就是著名的三叶草标志了，当时是为了1972年慕尼黑奥运会而设计的。正如我们在地理书上学到的那样，其中两个叶子象征着地球的两面，三条白道把大陆连接起来。

阿迪达斯专业运动是品牌的核心——无论是在商业销售上还是在品牌理念上。它既是对传统的继承，又体现了巨大的创新。这部分延续了阿迪·达斯勒的理念——产品最初是为运动而设计，在技术上却是应该与时俱进的，这样就可以为任何一种运动训练提供一些创新的解决办法，不论是瑜伽还是拳击，跑步还是足球，仅仅穿上阿迪达斯的产品就可以让运动员的表现更为出色。正是运动员在训练或者比赛中无数次磨破过的这些产品，几乎被所有的团队在大型的运动赛事上都选用。在此之中最新的，具有轰动效应的应该算是“阿迪达斯1——世界上第一双智能鞋，”它的内部安装有感应技术，可以自动地提供减震，是一种可以持续进行自我调节的跑鞋。其标志是三条白道，于1990年首次使用。这个标志的灵感来源于从侧面看一双阿迪达斯鞋（在鞋的左面），这个由三条白道组成的三角形，代表着一座高山，同时象征着无穷的挑战。

阿迪达斯运动时尚系列，是与日本时尚设计师山本耀司合作，最终发展成为著名的Y-3系列。它以一种独特的方式把运动和时尚结合到一起，与其说它是运

individual design must be created. In the Visual Language Guide all attributes the brand stands for are listed, such as authentic, innovative, sporting, simple, honest, clear – these are things that an adidas designer has to know before sketching a single line, because it is after all an adidas product that needs to be designed."

Thus, the basis for a uniform appearance of the adidas brand is established. Executive Board and marketing team, design and communication departments work closely together, all communicating the same values, advertisements and products speak the same language. The adidas brand gets a clear, sharply defined profile – both internally and externally. Having established a firm basis and regaining its momentum, the company is ready to take off for the future.

Three divisions, three stripes – one brand

Since its beginnings as a small company producing footwear, adidas has developed into one of the best-known brands in the world. At any time in its history, adidas focused on the needs of athletes, always providing them with the best technical solutions for many kinds of sports. Thus, adidas has grown over the last few decades, developing into a true global player.

However, the world of sports has also changed. Due to our increasingly "media-abundant" society, today sport is omnipresent; millions of people all around the globe watch every Formula One race, every football game, every track and field championship. Sportspersons become media stars, populating talk shows and the tabloid press. Sport is no longer about the athletes and the events. It is also about who the sportspersons are, what they stand for – and what they wear. Today, sport is also lifestyle; sports apparel sets trends – and everything taken together is part of our culture. In order to respond to changes in consumer demands, yet at the same time continuing to supply sports apparel with the same familiar quality, Michalsky initiated a three-division structure for the brand. Each division addresses a particular target group and has its own logo: Sport Heritage, Sport Performance, and Sport Style.

adidas Sport Heritage is the answer to the revival of old adidas products adopted by hip-hop and Brit pop bands, and the club scene. It thus represents not only a skilful marketing manoeuvre and a new sales strategy, but also a response to the demands of the market and to what smart young people would otherwise pick up from flea markets and second hand shops, bypassing the usual channels of distribution used by adidas. In this division, adidas legends gain a new lease of life. Often it is exactly those goods that gained popularity due to their association with a sporting legend or a certain sporting event, which now enjoy cult status in their reincarnation: Products such as the sports shoes "Samba," "Copa Mundial," "Gazelle" or the "Superstar," one of the first adidas basketball shoes, which last year celebrated its 35th anniversary and was honoured by a collection of 35 special edition styles. At one time innovative products on the market, today these classics stand for authenticity, credibility and reliability. The result is Streetstyle, which fashions the brand image beyond the sports ground, linking the target group of young buyers to the brand

动装倒不如说是休闲装。虽然运动时穿着也合适，可它更大程度适合那些有一定经济基础、具有时尚意识的人当作休闲服去穿。阿迪达斯运动时尚发现了完全不同的新的目标群体，他们是一群具有时尚意识的运动精英，可以说，Y-3系列是一种生活方式的宣言。国际服装周上全部展出了这一系列产品，这使阿迪达斯成为所有大型服装杂志关注的焦点。阿迪达斯运动时尚圆满结束了对该品牌的组合，也成功地试验了未来有潜力的发展方向。这部分的标志是有三条极具动感的白道组成的球体，暗示了球总是在旋转，还象征着一直在变化着的世界——阿迪达斯借着三条白道覆盖全球，与世界保持同步。

阿迪达斯品牌已经具有很高的知名度，并且变得更加多样化了。海纳的“增长和效率”项目把设计和营销放在了主要地位，取得了很好的效果。

“多亏了和理事会以及全球营销部门的密切合作，我才可以实现这么多的愿望——尽管我的想法层出不穷，比我们实际上可以付诸实践的要多得多。” 迈克斯凯概括地说道，他的想法包括与山本耀司的合作和“阿迪达斯原创系列”作为独立品牌的发布。

迈克斯凯的另一想法是让年轻的时尚设计师斯特拉・麦卡托尼为阿迪达斯工作，通过与她的密切合作，让“阿迪达斯专业运动”恢复生机。“斯特拉・麦卡托尼的阿迪达斯”从某种程度上说是沿着Y-3的足迹，却又十分清楚的被划分在专业运动之列。麦卡托尼是从古典主义角度来设计运动服装的，就是说运动服只是在运动的时候穿，不仅功能多而且穿着舒服，但同时很具有女性化色彩。迈克斯凯说：“我们一直有点忽视女性的存在，尤其是和设计有关的时候。前两个季度与斯特拉・麦卡托尼和合作已经证明了我们的事业正在正确的轨道里运行。这一系列产品很受市场欢迎，很快就销售一空。“阿迪达斯 – 斯特拉・麦卡托尼”系列把运动与时尚相结合。让比赛的世界，顶级的运动员的世界与设计的世界齐头并进。事实上这两个领域一般很少有接触。我们的产品也按照和阿迪达斯其它所有的运动产品一样的检验方式，把产品在运动场上的表现作为衡量标准，所有的为运动员设计的阿迪达斯的产品都必须符合这一标准。服装设计总监尼克・高威说道：“与斯特拉・麦卡托尼的合作和与山本耀司的合作有很大的区别，因为我们与山本耀司合作追求的是时尚，而我们和斯特拉所追求的目标是完全不同的——它是关于女性体育运动，考虑到世界上所有女运动员的着装。”

对于阿迪达斯的设计师来说，与斯特拉・麦卡托尼的合作是向未来又迈进了一大步，更让人们坚信运动和时尚将会在未来的世界里联系得更加紧密。

于是，阿迪达斯将会不断地超越自我，延伸核心品牌，发展新的目标群体，寻找新的市场，逐步地扩大品牌组合。

品牌形象的创造者，设计师和管理者：迈克斯凯和他的团队

阿迪达斯依然名副其实，尽管迈克斯凯和他的设计团队完成了品牌重组，他们还是保证所有部门生产出来的产品所传递的设计语言是一致的，时刻都体现着阿迪达斯的精神。他们立足于《视觉语言守则》，很好地平衡了运动与生活方式、时尚和高科技之间的关系。其实在这期间，近年来新的设计方法已经崭露头角，即：“复杂产品简单化。” 这种观点就是告诉我们产品是不该繁杂的，而是应依靠新的材质或是技术上的改进。公司的目标是要制造那些没有过多装饰的综合性产品。拿鞋类来说，通过在不同层面上使用不同的原料，让面料和加工技术显而易见，以此来创造新的视觉效果，这就可以体现出鞋的质量好坏，而不是像以前那样的仅凭鞋的样式就给质量下定义。“复杂产品简单化”的理念产生自与日

from an early age on. With the over 25s, however, nostalgia also comes into play, enticing them to choose these classics. Michalsky: "When I go to a party and mention that I work for adidas, people often start telling me stories about why they think adidas is great, even without me asking. For instance, someone might still be dreaming about the first soccer boots they owned – usually the "Mondial" or "Predator" models. Especially with footwear, a lot is coupled with personal memories."

The symbol for this line is the famous trefoil logo, created for the 1972 Olympic Games in Munich. The foils bring to mind the two-dimensional representation of the Earth as we all know it from geography books. The three stripes connecting the continents.

adidas Sport Performance is the core of the brand – in terms of both economics and ideals. It covers the traditional aspects of the portfolio and, at the same time, represents its greatest innovations. This division continues Adi Dassler's heritage – with products that were originally designed for sports, that are technologically up-to-date, and that provide innovative solutions for every sporting discipline, be it yoga or boxing, running or football. Simply using this equipment helps to push the limits of performance. It is these products, worn by athletes in training and competition, with which adidas equips many teams at all the larger sporting events. One of the most recent and sensational coups of this division was the "adidas 1 – The world's first intelligent shoe," a running shoe equipped with sensor technology to provide intelligent cushioning by automatically and continuously adjusting itself. The logo is the three-stripes mark, used for the first time in 1990. The logo is inspired by the three stripes as they are perceived when looking at an adidas shoe (with the shoe pointing to the left) from the side. The triangle, which is formed by the three stripes, simultaneously stands for a mountain, symbolising challenge.

adidas Sport Style is a collaboration with world-famous Japanese fashion designer Yohji Yamamoto, resulting in the prestigious Y-3 collections. It combines sport with fashion in what was a unique way at the time and is less sportswear but rather casual fashion wear. Suitable for sports, and yet in large part meant rather as clothes that well-off and fashion-aware people would wear on their way there. Exclusive casual wear. adidas Sport Style develops an entirely new target group, a fashion-aware sporting elite. Y-3 is a statement. The collection is presented at the international Fashion Weeks and helps adidas get featured in all the big fashion magazines. adidas Sport Style rounds off the brand portfolio and, at the same time, is a highly successful experiment that shows a promising future direction. The logo of the division is a globe with three dynamic stripes that suggest the globe's rotation. It symbolises the constantly changing world – with adidas keeping pace in the form of the three stripes that span the globe.

The brand has gained a higher profile, it has become more diverse. Hainer's Growth and Efficiency Program, in which design and marketing play the leading role, pays off.

"Thanks to close collaboration with the Executive Board and Global Marketing I am able to realise many ideas – even though I often come up with more ideas than we can actually put into practice," Michael Michalsky says, summing it up. Among the ideas Michalsky has been able to realise are both the collaboration with Yamamoto and the launch of "adidas Originals" as a distinct brand.

It has also been one of Michalsky's ideas to get the young fashion designer Stella McCartney to work with adidas and, in close collaboration with her, to reinvigorate the "adidas Sport Performance" line. "adidas by Stella McCartney" follows to some extent in the footsteps of Y-3, yet it is clearly grounded in the Sport Performance division. McCartney designs sports apparel in the classical sense, that is sportswear to be worn exclusively for sports, functional and comfortable, but at the same time highly feminine. Michalsky: "We have always been

"……当时，许多营销人员认为他们只是因为自己画画不好，所以才需要设计师。现在这种想法已经全面改观，我们在公司里也具有很大的影响力。"

"... many marketing people at the time were of the opinion that they were only in need of designers because they themselves could not draw particularly well. This has changed entirely and today we have a lot of influence within the company."

本设计师山本耀司的合作中，他主张少用色彩，倡导简洁的外形，但选材十分优良。在与山本耀司的合作中，迈克斯凯和他的团队逐渐意识到，色彩的减少对产品的核心表述和产品的选料都是十分有效的。它使"简单的阿迪达斯"这一理念得以真正体现。

今天,在迈克斯凯的手下工作的设计师有200多名，他们来自十多个国家,这些人主要的任务就是用产品来诠释品牌理念。但在1992年，阿迪达斯在全世界范围内只有21名设计师，而现在却发展到了三个团队，一个在公司总部德国的赫尔佐根奥拉赫，另一个在波特兰开发美国市场，第三个在东京开发日本和亚洲市场。想要充分满足某个特定市场的个性化需求，设计团队"本土化"是非常重要的。例如，要充分考虑到亚洲市场的尺码与西方的区别，或是在美国占据重要地位的篮球等这些因素。然而，设计师的工作也不仅仅局限于设计产品。

今天,在迈克斯凯的手下工作的设计师有200多名，他们来自十多个国家,这些人主要的任务就是用产品来诠释品牌理念。但在1992年，阿迪达斯在全世界范围内只有21名设计师，而现在却发展到了三个团队，一个在公司总部德国的赫尔佐根奥拉赫，另一个在波特兰开发美国市场，第三个在东京开发日本和亚洲市场。想要充分满足某个特定市场的个性化需求，设计团队"本土化"是非常重要的。例如，要充分考虑到亚洲市场的尺码与西方的区别，或是在美国占据重要地位的篮球等这些因素。然而，设计师的工作也不仅仅局限于设计产品。

设计是构成产品的主导元素。截至目前，新产品中有三分之二的理念都是在设计部门与阿迪达斯创新团队和公司发展部的密切合作中创造的。这就要求设计师对各种体育项目的最新发展，最新技术可能性以及总体的产品发展趋势都有深层次的把握。因此，一名设计师，只负责一种专门产品，这样可以使他有针对性地把经验和知识做到最大限度的利用。阿迪达斯平均每年都会向市场投放500多种新产品，如果是有大型的运动赛事，比如说是奥运会、足球世界杯，这个数字还会增加。

在被问到" 什么样的一周才算是你具有代表性的工作周" 这个问题的时候，迈克斯凯回答："这个问题很难回答，我事实上并没有这么典型的一周。对我来说，每个星期都是很不一样的，因为我同时在三个完全不同的地方都有家，这里我指的是那三个部门，因为理所应当地我要对这个部门都负责，当然也包括要对与之相应的市场负责。我几乎就是住在飞机上，随时会飞往欧洲、美国和亚洲。"作为全球创意总监，迈克斯凯不仅仅负责阿迪达斯产品的设计，他还负责确保公众可以看见的所有阿迪达斯产品总是都与"阿迪达斯"形象一致。从广告促销资料到网络平台，从广告营销到商业报道，甚至到公司的建筑，迈克斯凯同时扮演着创造者、设计师、和品牌形象监督人的角色。

专业运动的过去、现在和未来。

在今天，阿迪达斯之所以能仍然处于运动世界的领先地位，要归功于品牌的持续影响力和设计策略。尽管在不同部门之间和不同合作之间存在着差异，但品牌本身却从内到外都所在塑造着一个一致的形象。在公司内部，设计其实肩负着一个极其艰巨的责任；它把品牌的价值以形象和产品来表现，并一直向纵深方向延伸。设计好像是一条纽带，它连接着品牌的过去和未来，时尚和技术，沟通和目标群体，产品和消费者。公司的根基总是反映在品牌和品牌的持续价值上。因为我们的目标群体也可以在新部门中重新发现他们与品牌之间的联系，阿迪达斯品牌一直都那么名副其实，精心的协调沟通会给人们带来安全感和认同感，因为品牌不会仅仅对销售额感兴趣，品牌是没有过多负荷的，畅想未来，阿迪达斯一

neglecting women a little bit, especially when it comes to design. The first two seasons of collaboration with Stella McCartney have shown that we are now on the right track. The collection made an amazing impact on the market, selling all by itself." The "adidas by Stella McCartney" collection combines sport with style. The world of competition, of top athletes, is paired with the world of fashion – two areas that generally have few points of contact. The products are tested in the same way as all other sports products for their sports-use performance – the standard, which all adidas products for athletes have to meet, must also be ensured in this line. Nic Galway, Head of Apparel Design: "The work with Stella McCartney differs significantly from the collaboration with Yamamoto, because our goal with Yamamoto is fashion. The goal we pursue with Stella is completely different – it is about women sports, taking into account the whole world of the female athlete who wears the apparel."

For the adidas designers, the collaboration with Stella McCartney is a further step forward into the future, convinced as they are that sport and fashion will be connected more closely in the future.

adidas thus outperforms itself, reaches beyond its core brand, develops new target groups, seeks out new markets, and gradually expands its brand portfolio.

Creator, designer and custodian of the brand image: Michalsky and his team

That adidas has remained authentic despite the brand restructure is in no short measure down to Michael Michalsky and his design team. They guarantee that the products from all divisions speak the same language of design, embodying adidas at all times. Taking the Visual Language Guide as their basis, they manage a fine balancing act between sports and lifestyle, between fashion and high tech. And, in doing so, a new approach to design has emerged in recent years: "The Complexity of Product Simplicity." Behind this stands the insight that products should not be overloaded. New materials or technical improvements should speak for themselves. The goal is to create comprehensive products without gratuitous adornment. With shoes, for instance, new visual effects are created by using the materials in the different layers in such a way as to leave the fabrics and the processing techniques visible. This allows for combinations with which shoes can communicate quality, without the styling that was usual in former times. The philosophy "Complexity of Simplicity" goes back to the collaboration with Yohji Yamamoto, who is a virtuoso of reduced colour use, an advocate of clear forms, while using cloth of very high quality. In collaborating with Yamamoto, Michalsky and his team have come to realise how effective a reduction can be for both the product's core statement and for the materials used to make the product. "Simply adidas" – in the truest sense of the word.

Today, approximately 200 designers from ten nations are working under the guidance of Michael Michalsky on the translation of the brand philosophy into products – in 1992, it was just 21 designers worldwide. Today, there are three teams, one at the company's headquarters in Herzogenaurach, another one in Portland for the American market, and a third one in Tokyo for Japan and Asia. The "local" design teams are considered important in order to effectively cater to the characteristics of individual markets, such as, for instance, the difference of size and fit in the Asian market or the unique importance of basketball in the USA. The work of the designers, however, is not limited merely to designing products.

阿迪·达斯勒在1920年做第一双鞋的时候，它是受到了一个灵感的启发：每位运动员都有为他们专门设计的最好的球鞋。从左到右：迪克·福斯伯里，威玛·鲁道夫，大卫·贝克汉姆。

Adi Dassler was inspired by a single idea when he made his first shoes in 1920: Every athlete was to be provided with the best footwear for his respective discipline. From left to right: Dick Fosbury, Wilma Rudolph, David Beckham.

定会取得更大的进步。

在赫尔佐根奥拉赫的阿迪达斯中心礼堂的入口处，有一个监控器。黑底上的红字一次次地滚动着。用一句话来代表阿迪达斯的理念，那就是：阿迪达斯的运动世界——过去，现在和未来都随心所欲。

指挥和管弦乐队——对阿迪达斯设计团队的采访

被采访对象：迈克尔·迈克斯凯(全球创意总监)，斯特凡·迪特里希（鞋类设计总监)，托斯滕·霍赫施泰特尔（服装设计总管)，尼克·高威（分类设计师)和托马斯·威尔格（鞋类设计总监)。

迈克尔·迈克斯凯，您可不可以首先用几个词来描写一下您作为总设计师的工作？

迈克尔:总设计师……——事实上，可能不只这些。当然了，我也是总设计师，但我更倾向于把我自己看做是管弦乐队的一名指挥。我想我有幸可以自己挑选设计部门合适的管理人员，但我并不是那种痴迷于控制别人的人。也就是说，如果我挑选某个人来担任领导的角色，我就真地希望看到他能担任起这个领导职位。一般我都是在我了解了很长时间的员工里挑选，我确定他是某个领域里最适合这个工作的人选。我自己更喜欢那种有很多见解和思想的团队，可以有效地做事情。任何一个项目刚开始的时候，我会对其进行有力的管理，并在这个时期寻找我可以与之共事的人，一段时间之后，我就可以把整个项目交给他， 那样我的大脑就可以接受新事物了。从那一刻起，我就只参与到决策中去。

像Y-3系列或者是把“经典”产品作为街头服饰品牌这样的创意，都需要与营销密切合作……

迈克尔：我喜欢和营销部门一起工作。阿迪达斯与很多其它公司的主要区别也在于五年来，设计一直与营销甚至全球营销并驾齐驱。在我看来，重组是公司经济转型的成功因素之一。

最初的阿迪达斯，根据创始人阿迪·达斯勒的理念，是集优异表现、完美品质和高新技术于一体的运动产品。而您把它越来越多地推向更专业化的领域。这又与核心品牌有什么联系呢？

迈克尔：阿迪达斯最初的涉及领域是运动。但此外，它还能把人们吸引到品牌中，使他们成为品牌的一部分，这些人骨子里也就是爱好运动的人。我们品牌的核心创始人，阿迪·达斯勒就是个百分百的运动狂，星期天他经常坐在长凳上，和那些运动员们聊天。不仅仅是那些奥运会冠军，也包括当地足球俱乐部的人。他每个星期天都会去问他们新的螺旋饰钉是否好用。阿迪·达斯勒全身心投入到了运动中，他的眼里只有运动。不同的人，不同水平的表现都令他着迷。他制作的鞋帮助杰西·欧文斯赢得了1936年奥运会的冠军，还让儿童时期曾经患有小儿麻痹症的女运动员威玛·鲁道夫，通过运动战胜了病魔，并在1960年的奥运会上

Design is a leading constituent element in many product ranges in so far as two-thirds of all new product concepts are created in the design department – in close collaboration with the adidas Innovation Team, the corporation's development department. This requires designers to have extensive knowledge of recent developments in individual sports, of new technological possibilities, and of product developments in general. This is also why each designer specialises in a particular product segment, allowing him to use his experience and knowledge optimally. Thus, adidas launches an average of more than 500 new products each year. Years in which there is a large sporting event, such as the Olympic Games or the football World Cup, see that number increase further still.

On being asked about a typical working week, Michalsky answers: "Difficult. I do not actually have a typical working week as such. For me each week is different, because I am at home in three different worlds at the same time, both with regard to the divisions, because naturally I am responsible for all three of them, and with regard to continents. I almost live on the airplane, somewhere between Europe, America and Asia." As Global Creative Director, however, Michalsky is not only responsible for the design of adidas products; it is also his responsibility to ensure that everything with which adidas is seen in public indeed always represents "adidas." Ranging from press kits to Internet presence, through advertising campaigns and business reports, all the way to the Corporate Architecture, Michalsky simultaneously is the creator, designer and custodian of the brand image.

The past, present and future of Sport Performance

Thanks to its ongoing brand and design strategy, today, adidas is again at the very top. Despite the diversity among the different divisions and various collaborations, the brand is communicating a consistent image outwardly and inwardly. Within the corporation, design serves a highly complex function; it translates the brand values into images and products, constantly developing them further. Design is the link between the brand's past and future, between fashion and technology, communication and target groups, products and consumers. Due to the fact that the company's roots are always reflected in the brand, its consistent brand values, and because the target groups can also rediscover their association with the brand in the new divisions, the adidas brand has remained authentic. With the help of its carefully coordinated communications, which offer people security and identification, and because the brand does not disappear behind a mere interest in sales, because it is not overloaded, adidas is making further progress as it looks to the future.

There is a monitor in the entrance hall of the adidas Centre in Herzogenaurach, on which – red on black – the same words run again and again. In one sentence they epitomise the adidas philosophy in the corporate wording of the brand: adidas world of sports – where the past, present and future of performance will feel at home.

阿迪达斯的胜利者：在2000年悉尼奥运会上，澳大利亚游泳名将科比（Lan Thorpe）勇夺3枚金牌。1971年，穆罕默德·阿里（Muhammad Ali）在"世纪之战"中击败"弗雷泽(Joe Frazier)"。

Winners in adidas: The Australian swimmer Ian Thorpe takes 3 gold medals at the Olympic Games in Sydney in 2000. Muhammad Ali after his victory against Joe Frazier in the "Fight of the Century" in 1971.

获得三枚金牌。对阿迪·达斯勒来说，最重要的就是运动和参与运动的人——这是独一无二的，这也是直到今天，我们的设计团队仍然关注的。

阿迪达斯就是要鼓励人们参加运动，它在意的并不是仅仅要完美的场上表现。阿迪达斯就是运动，它也要为赢得优秀的场上表现去开发产品，但不仅仅局限于此。

在针对业余爱好者和专业运动员的目标群体设计方面，阿迪达斯在设计方法上有什么不同呢？

托马斯：我遇见过很多运动员，并曾为世界顶级运动员设计过网球鞋和足球鞋。和他们谈话很有意思，你可以了解到什么对他们是真正有价值的。但是，从一个顶级运动员那里得到的第一手反馈信息是极其有限的。有一次我在德国菲尔德斯塔特的德国大师赛上遇见了马蒂娜·辛吉斯和安娜·库尔尼科娃，她们抱怨我们标准的网球鞋抓地性不够好，他们需要有更大抓地性的球鞋，因为法国网球公开赛的网球场很硬，上面还有一层细沙。如果你穿普通的网球鞋在上面滑倒了一次，你很可能会接连不断的滑倒。但是比赛是如此激烈，扣人心弦，要停的时候必须马上停稳，接球，转身，向另一个方向跑去……在得到这样的反馈信息的时候，我觉得如获珍宝：我们可以按照这些信息一对一的逐个对产品加以修改。除了这一点，遇到大明星也是件大好事——可以晚上回家的时候把这故事骄傲地讲给老婆孩子们听。

斯特凡：即使在方法上有所不同——在原理上，对两类目标群体来说，最重要的就是预见他们的渴望和梦想，设计的产品正好符合他们的胃口。不论产品是不是会出现在很脏的跑道、足球场、或是别的环境，它们都是作为运动产品而使用的——这就是我们在产品上所提出的要求，而不去管它们最后被用在何处。

未来怎么样呢？你脑海中有没有新的目标群体呢？

迈克尔：我不觉得我们有必要去寻找新的目标群体。未来注重的那些产品，实际上，现在还不是那么必需的,但我们还是会把同样的感觉灌注到那些产品设计和风格里去。当然不同的运动是有区别的,每种规则都有自己的文化，自己的粉丝圈，所以我们用不同的标准来对待。这也是为什么我们需要一段时间才能对所有领域做出一致地回应。比如说，一幅手球手套。最近这种产品很是流行，但是五年前，没有人对这种手套感兴趣。这种发展是十分缓慢但却一定能在不知不觉中蔓延到所有领域。

在"阿迪达斯经典系列"，我们还没有达到我们想要达到的境界，但是在这方面我们有越来越多的店面做得十分成功。我们目前在专业运动中心就是这么做的，在这里我们可以按照我们自己的理念，展出并销售我们自己的专业运动产品。直到最近，销售人员觉得时机成熟，才又把阿迪达斯的产品放到零售商店。目前，我们在马赛、法兰克福、纽伦堡、伦敦都有运动中心，纽约的那个马上就要开始营业……这不仅仅可以提升我们的企业形象，同时对商业销售起到了一定作用。换句话说，我们并不单纯地像同行们那样把这个中心看作是一个"展览馆"，我们更是把它看作是一个很重要的销售渠道。

Conductor and orchestra – an interview with the adidas design team

Being interviewed are: Michael Michalsky (Global Creative Director), Stephan Dietrich (Design Director Footwear), Torsten Hochstetter (Head of Apparel Design), Nic Galway (Category Designer) and Thomas Weege (Head of Footwear Design)

Michael Michalsky, could you first describe to us in a few words your work as Design Manager.

MM: *Design Manager... – actually it is a little more than that. Of course, I am also the Design Manager, but I see myself rather as the conductor of an orchestra. I guess I am lucky in being able to pick all the people for the leading roles within the design department myself. I am not one of those people who are obsessed with exercising control. Meaning that if I choose someone for a leading position, then I do want to see that person take leadership. I usually pick someone from the staff who I have known for a long time, someone I am sure is the right person for the job in a certain area. I myself rather belong to that group of people that have many ideas, that get things rolling. At the start of a project, I manage it very intensely, and in this phase I am already searching for people that I want to work together with, people to whom I can hand over the project after a certain period, so that I can keep my head clear for new things. From that moment onward, I am only involved in the decision-making processes.*

Ideas such as the Y-3 line or the idea of positioning the "Originals" products as a streetwear brand, require close coordination with marketing...

MM: *I enjoy working together with marketing. What distinguishes adidas from many other companies is that for five years now design is standing on absolutely equal ground with Marketing and Global Marketing. From my point of view, this restructure has been one of the success factors in the economic turnaround of the company.*

The original world of adidas, according to the philosophy of the founder, Adi Dassler, is sport in terms of performance, perfection and technique. You are pushing forward more and more into specialised fields. How does that relate to the core brand?

MM: *The original world of adidas is sport. Beyond that, however, adidas is a brand that in its communication invites people to be part of the brand, people who are, at root, sports enthusiasts. The core, the origin of our brand, Adi Dassler, was an absolute sports fanatic, who on Sundays used to sit on a bench somewhere, talking with average sportsmen. Not just with Olympic Champions, but also with people from the local football club. He would come back every Sunday to ask whether the new screw-on studs worked. Adi Dassler was into sport – only sport. He was fascinated by the many different people and the different levels of performance. He made the shoes that carried Jesse Owens to victory at the 1936 Olympic Games and also the shoes for women athletes such as Wilma Rudolph, who had suffered from polio as a child and who, conquering the disease through sports, took three*

“我自己也做运动，在我的记忆里，想到的总是阿迪达斯。对我来说，就感觉我在为我自己的品牌而工作。”

“I do sports myself, for as long as I can remember. And it has always been adidas. For me it is like working for my own brand.”

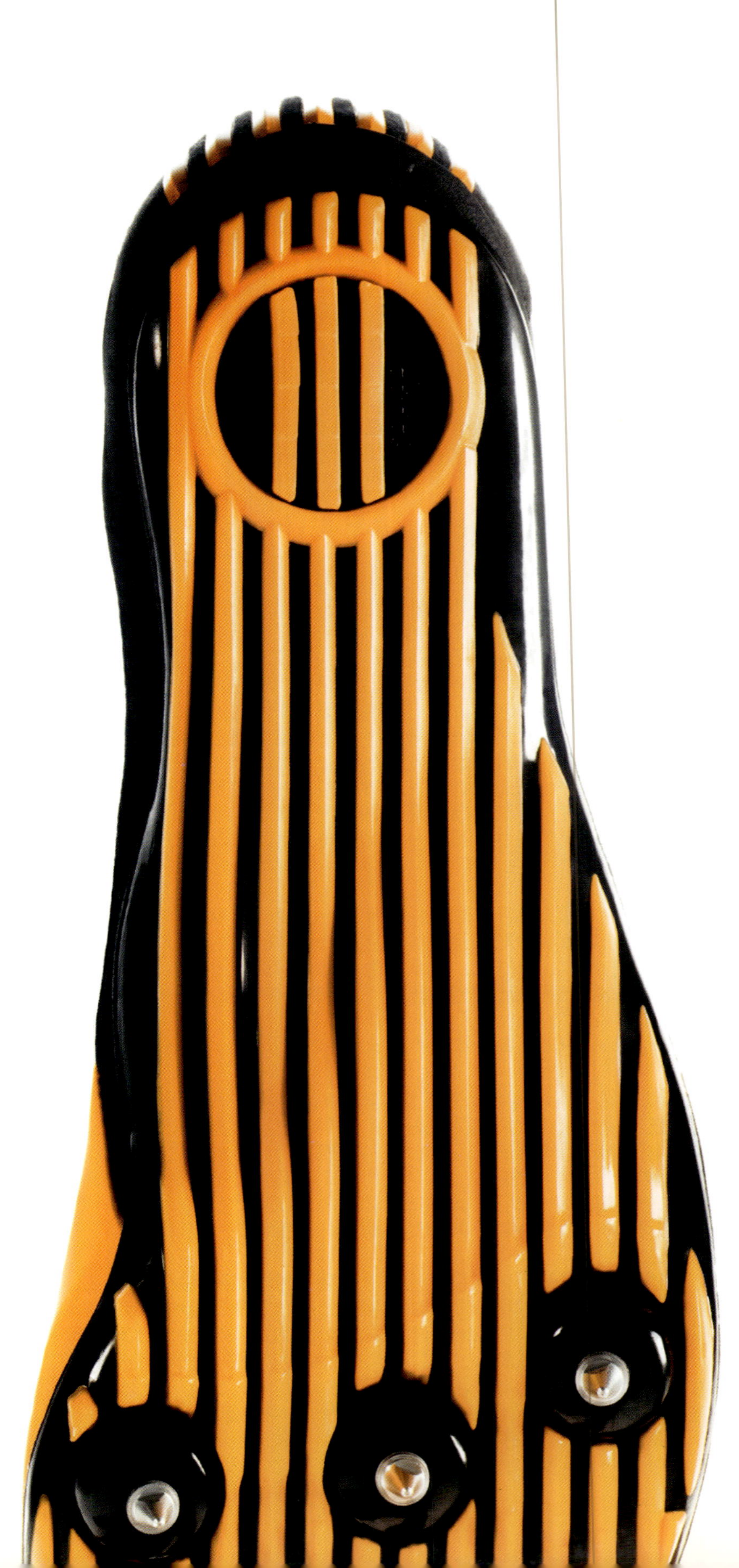

“阿迪达斯就是要鼓励人们参加运动，它在意的并不是仅仅要完美的场上表现。阿迪达斯就是运动，它也要为赢得优秀的场上表现去开发产品，但不仅仅局限于此。”

“adidas wants to encourage people to participate in sports, beyond the idea of high performance. adidas is sports. It is also about developing products for peak performance, but not exclusively so.”

斯特凡：这是“1”的未来[暗指“阿迪达斯1”——编者]。这款鞋本身就把运动与时尚相结合，但是要比今天做得更加巧妙和自然，因为人们都会认为它本该就是这个样子的。可能更多的电子产品要加入到这个行列。运动、时尚、电子产品可以相互补充，然后创造出全新的产品。目前最吸引人的是我们有像“阿迪达斯 1”这样的项目，因此我们可以做出别人所做不了的产品。相信在时尚与电子产品，运动与电子产品之间的相互作用的引导下，我们一定会创造出更多新产品，新造型。

托马斯：我们现在就已经生活在未来。我们团队中的绝大多数人都已经领先时代两年了，了解这个对我们至关重要。

托斯滕：通过了解某种运动背后的文化也可以激发我们的灵感，看看那些运动迷们，他们穿什么样子的衣服，或者是他们为什么对某种运动情有独钟。

阿迪达斯有没有一个整体的设计理念？你可以用一句或两句话来概括一下？

迈克尔：我觉得就两个词，简单和自然。这就是阿迪达斯这个牌子本身所具有的魔力。那些一直使用我们产品的消费者可以很敏锐地判断出一种产品是不是阿迪达斯的。

斯特凡：这个最重要的，也是最基本的，我想把它概括成“简单中的复杂”。过去，我们只是考虑到产品的复杂性了，结果把什么东西都放到一种产品里去增加它的价值。和山本耀司关于Y-3的合作，那绝对是个转折点。从那个时候开始，我们就开始懂得选择合适的材料来制作简单的产品，这样的成品就会比任何东西都更有价值。今天，可以用“简单中的复杂”来概括我们开发新产品的方法。它不仅仅只是一个公式，而更为原料、手工艺和细节的结合。这种结合体现了整体的设计，促使我们去设计简单和具有整体性的产品——但却具有很高的价值。其实创造简单的产品远远比创造那些有很多装饰的产品要难得多。我们想要简单，但绝不仅仅是把什么东西都去掉，让它们看起来很纯粹，让我来讲一个简单的故事。我要告诉您的是一个关于产品的什么样的故事呢？我们不需要给一个产品加15个说明，其实只需一个说明就能让它足够简单——这句话就是我要讲的故事。因此我们的方法就是设计产品的时候先确定题目，产品的故事内容，发展步骤是怎样通过线条、设计、产品信息得以成功体现。这才是我们创造了简单性的方式。

你们的团队是怎样组成的呢？一个设计师需要具备什么资格才可以为阿迪达斯工作呢？

迈克尔：到这里来工作的人必须喜欢这个品牌。还有很重要的一点，就是他们和我们的目标消费群要融为一体。我们已经有成型的专业的运动设计师，还有一些人是健康和运动爱好者，还有的是青年俱乐部的一员。他们的共同点就是都很年轻。阿迪达斯人的平均年龄是30岁，在阿迪达斯的平均时间是六年——对年轻人来说，六年的时间已经够长的了。尤其是在赫尔佐根奥拉赫这样的小城镇里——我们不能和伦敦、柏林、或者纽约那样的大城市竞争。而且，我们的董事们来自不同种族。这也使我们与众不同，也是过去这么多年我们的设计一直做的那么好的原因之一。

在鞋类产品的设计上，我们只雇佣工业设计师；一些是学汽车设计的，还有的甚至是为船舶制造商工作过，曾设计过快艇。服装设计师都是学服装的，是经过培训的裁缝——这点是我比较强调的。在这个领域我们有很多国外大学的毕业生，因为在面料设计课程上，德国还有很长的路要走。

[对其他的设计师说到]最后，我想问一下，你们为阿迪达斯这样一个品牌工作有什么特别的地方吗？

托斯滕：三条白道的十年——不会觉得厌烦，一点也不。在这里你会变成经典的一部分，很重要的事业的一分子。

托马斯：从我记事起，我就做运动，想到的总是阿迪达斯。对我来说好像我在为我自己的品牌而工作着。此外，我们是足球、网球和室内运动领域内的头号品牌，只要我认为合适的，我们都可以去做。我们可以对市场上的服装款式造成影响。总的来说，最好的事情莫过于我们具有一定的控制力度，对运动世界有一定的影响。

尼克：我六年前开始在这里工作的时候，“阿迪达斯运动经典”还不存在，没有与山本耀司的合作，没有Y-3系列，没有斯特拉·麦卡托尼，没有“阿迪达斯1”——所有的这些都是那个时候开始发展的，能够伴随着这个过程一路走来，真的是很快乐。

斯特凡：我们有个很优秀的团队，在这里的工作真是乐在其中。每隔两年，我太太就问我什么时候我们才能搬到北方去。每次我都这么回答她：如果你发现

gold medals in the 1960 Olympics. What mattered to Adi Dassler was simply sport and its participants – this is very unique, something that our design team still reflects today. adidas wants to encourage people to participate in sports, beyond the idea of high performance. adidas is sports. It is also about developing products for peak performance, but not exclusively so.

What are the differences in approach between designing for the lifestyle target group and for professionals?

TW: *I have met with many athletes and designed tennis shoes and football boots for the top players in the world. It is interesting to talk with them and to learn about what is really important for them. However, real first-hand feedback from a top athlete is quite rare. Once I met with Martina Hingis and Anna Kournikova at the German Masters in Filderstadt. They complained that the normal profile of our tennis shoes no longer offered sufficient grip; they needed more aggressive profiles, because the tennis court in Roland Garros is very hard and covered with a fine layer of sand. If you slip on it with a normal tennis shoe, you will continue to slide. But the match itself has become so powerful and fast that it is crucial to come to a full stop immediately, play the ball, turn around and dive for it in the other direction. If you get this kind of feedback, it is like getting a pearl: You can translate it one-to-one into a product. And apart from that, it is always a big plus to meet the big stars – you can proudly tell the story to your wife and children in the evening!*

SD: *Even though there would seem to be a difference in approach – in principle with both target groups it is a question of anticipating their desires and dreams and designing the right product for their needs. No matter whether a product will ever see a dirt track, a football field or any other conditions: They are all aimed at being used in sports – that is the demand we place on our products, regardless of where they finally end up.*

How about the future? Do you have further new target groups in mind?

MM: *I do not believe that we have to look for further target groups. The future will rather lie in applying the same feeling for design and style to those product ranges in which up to now it has been less necessary. This of course differs with the various kinds of sport; each discipline has its own culture, its own specific circle of fans, so we treat them according to different standards. That is also the reason why it takes a little while until one can respond equally well to all areas. Take, for instance, a pair of handball gloves. These days, they have become really trendy products, whereas only five years ago nobody at all had any interest in what handball gloves looked like. And this development is slowly but surely creeping into all areas.*
With "adidas Originals" we have not yet arrived at where we should be, but in that respect too we have an increasing number of stores that are highly successful. We are doing the same now with the Sport Performance Centres, where we can showcase and sell our Sport Performance goods following our own concept. Until recently, products created by adidas were only positioned in retail stores by salespeople as they saw fit. Currently, we have Performance Centres in Marseille, in Frankfurt, in Nuremberg, in London; the one in New York will open soon... This is not only important for boosting our image, it has simultaneously become a large economic factor. In other words, we do not consider a Centre to be a mere "showcase," as some of our competitors do, but rather a highly important channel of distribution.

SD: *There is "1" future [an allusion to the "adidas 1," – Ed]. It will indeed be a matter of combining sport and fashion, though in a more natural way than it is done today, because everyone will be taking it for granted. Then, possibly, more electronics will also come into play. Sport, fashion and electronics will complement one other, creating completely new products. Most interesting right now is that we have projects such as "adidas 1" and that we are capable of creating combinations that nobody else could do. This interplay between fashion and electronics, between sport and electronics, leads to new products, to new forms for the future.*

TW: *We are already living the future here. It is vital for us to know that most of us in our work are already two years ahead of time.*

TH: *We also get inspiration by dealing with the culture behind a certain sport, by looking at what the fan communities are like, what kind of clothes they wear, and why they are interested in that particular kind of sport.*

了一个和阿迪达斯一样好的牌子，我就走。但在此之前，绝对不离开。我们在这里呆了13年了，我希望日子就这样一直持续下去。因为，目前没有任何一个品牌可以比阿迪达斯更能激发我的创造力。

谢谢您接受我们的采访。

（采访者阿斯特丽德・史布莱格尔）

Is there an overall design philosophy at adidas? Something that you could summarise in one or two sentences?

MM: *It always has to be adidas, plain and simple. That certain magic that this brand has. Those that have been with us for a long time do have a keen sense of whether a product is adidas or not.*

SD: *What is also at the bottom of this is what I would summarise as "Complexity of Simplicity." In the past, it had rather been complexity alone, as a result of packing everything one had into a product, in order to add value. The collaboration with Yamamoto for Y-3 definitely marked a turning point: From then on, we were able to create products safe in the knowledge that simple products made from the right materials have more value than anything else. Today, "Complexity of Simplicity" sums up our approach to new products; it is not simply a formula, it is the combination of materials, of craftsmanship and details that embodies the whole design and which helps create a simple, holistic product - with high value. Simplicity is actually far more difficult to create than embellishing everything. And the idea in our approach to simplicity is not merely to reduce everything, to take away things to make them "pure"; rather the idea is about coming up with a simple story. What kind of story do I want to tell about the product? You do not need 15 statements for one product. Just one statement is enough in order to keep it simple – and that one is the story I want to tell. So, our approach when designing a product is to specify what the topic, what the story of the product is, how rhythm is achieved through lines, through design, a focus on the product message. This is how we create simplicity.*

How is your team put together, and what kind of qualifications does a designer need to be able to work for adidas?

MM: *The people who come to work here must love the adidas brand. It is also important that they identify with our target group. We have fully-fledged sports professionals, as well as people who simply do sport in order to feel well, or people who are part of youth and club culture. What they all have in common is that they are relatively young. The average age at adidas is about thirty, the average length of stay, however, is six years – which is quite unusually long for such young people. And especially in a small town such as Herzogenaurach – we cannot really compete with cities such as London, Berlin or New York. Furthermore, we have every kind of ethnic group on board. This makes us unique and it is probably also one of the reasons why, over the past few years, our designs have become so good.*
In Footwear Design we employ only industrial designers; some have studied automobile design, others have even worked for ship builders, designing yachts. The apparel designers have studied fashion and are trained tailors – I do insist on this. In this area especially we have many graduates from overseas universities, because when it comes to textile design courses, Germany still has a lot of catching up to do.

左图：商店也吸收了品牌重组的理念：专业运动，运动经典和运动时尚。运动经典商店（左侧，位于大阪）通过干净、简单的建筑和室内布置把阿迪达斯标志的清晰完整地传达出来。专业运动中心（右侧的伦敦）把对运动的热情通过极具现代感的室内建筑和高品质的材质一一展现出来。

右图：Y-3以它特别的方式把运动和时尚合为一体。这个系列的产品将在国际时装周上闪亮登场，目标锁定为极具时尚意识和热爱运动的精英群体。

left: The restructure of the brand into the three divisions Sport Performance, Sport Heritage and Sport Style is also taken up in the Shop concepts. The Sport Heritage Stores (in Osaka on the left) communicate the authenticity of the label through a clear, simple architecture and interior fittings, the Sport Performance Centres (in London on the right) communicate passion for sport and performance through innovative interior architecture and high-quality materials.

right: Y-3 combines sport with fashion in a unique way. The collection is presented at the international Fashion Weeks and is targeted at a fashion-aware sporting elite.

[Addressing the other designers] In the end, what is special for you about working for a brand such as adidas?

TH: *A decade of three stripes – and not boring yet, not at all. You are part of a legacy here, part of something really big.*

TW: *I do sports myself, for as long as I can remember. And it has always been adidas. For me it is like working for my own brand. Besides, we are the number one brand in football, in tennis and indoor sports, and I can do what I think appropriate. I can influence style in the market. And the greatest thing of all is that in general we can set so many things in motion and actually have an influence on the sports world.*

NG: *When I started here about six years ago, the "adidas Sport Heritage" did not yet exist, there was no collaboration with Yamamoto, no Y-3, no Stella McCartney, no "adidas 1" – all these things have developed since then and it is great to be part of that.*

SD: *We have a great team and it is really fun to be working here. About every two years my wife asks me when we will eventually be moving back to the North. Each time I answer: When you find a brand that is as good as adidas, then I might go. But not before that. We have been here for thirteen years and I hope things will continue the way they are. Because, at present, there is no other brand that could be more inspiring to me than adidas.*

Thank you very much for talking to us today.

(Interviewed by Astrid Sprenger)

Fotos: Alexander Gnädiger und adidas
Photography: Alexander Gnädiger and adidas

红点：精品中的精品
red dot: best of the best

每年，评委们都会从12个行业门类中选取比较有创意的产品。这些奖项最后都会落到那些不同寻常的、品质出色的设计上。每个产品种类中有三种产品可以获得评委提名入选 “红点：精品中的精品 ”奖。今年，评委会向33个杰出的设计作品颁发了“红点：精品中的精品 ”奖。

Each year, the jury can select *particularly innovative products from the twelve different categories. These awards go to design with unusual and outstanding qualities. The jury can nominate three products from each product group for the "red dot: best of the best" award . This year, the "red dot: best of the best" was awarded thirty-three times.*

红点：精品中的精品
red dot: best of the best

钻石桌子，2004

Molteni & C, Giussano, Italien
Design: Patricia Urquiola,
Mailand, Italien
www.molteni.it

水晶般的形状——符号与感悟。对于安伯托·埃柯来说，世界就是一个象征与符号所构成的体系。符号学家与名著作者们，例如《玫瑰之名》的作者，认为人类在其所生活的各个领域中，总是在他们那个时代创造出一系列由特殊的代码组成的符号体系，我们用世界本身的规则创造了我们自己的世界。正如设计师乌古拉所设计的钻石桌子那样，该设计具有某种符号特征，因为一些为人所熟知的结构和理念都受到了挑战。该设计是以“颜色、造型和人类工程学”为主旋律而创造的一个作品。桌腿与桌面设计成与众不同的造型，就像雕塑一般。看起来像被扭曲了的桌腿令人想起钻石那精致切割的角度，给人一种朦胧的怀旧感。水晶般的形状似乎让整个房间都变得缥缈起来，然后却在它的内部映衬出来。钻石桌子设计目标之一是凸现一种多功能的理念，桌子可以有多种摆放方式，而且有多种用途，而它的另一目标是创造出一件有品位的家具。它除了相当实用外，还可“过滤”思想。这个系列的桌子可做成矩形或正方形，桌面可用玻璃或木头做成，桌子的框架可以是黑色的阳极氧化铝或是有光泽的铝，也可以由天然的橡树、银橡树或乌木做成。这也是该理念的另一种体现方式：这些要素构筑了一种特殊的交流形式，同时为一种新的感悟提供了一套符号体系。

Crystalline forms – of signs and perceptions. *For Umberto Eco the world is a system of signs and symbols. The semiotician and author of famous books such as e.g. "The Name of the Rose" is of the opinion that areas of human life always produce sign systems with special codes in their time. We create our own worlds with their own rules. The design of the Diamond tables, which has been created by the designer Patricia Urquiola, has the characteristics of a sign, because known forms and perception are at least questioned. The design is a play with "colours, forms and ergonomics". The legs as well as the tabletops have unusual forms. They appear like sculptures. The form of the table legs, which appear twisted in themselves, is faintly reminiscent of the cut of a diamond. Crystalline forms seem to resolve the room and to be reflected in it. The aim of the Diamond table design was to create a multi-functional concept – the tables can be arranged and used in many variations. Another aim was to create a piece of furniture with an "identity". Apart from a high degree of functionality, they also imply the opportunity of a "filtered" perception. The series consists of square and rectangular tables with a thin glass or wooden top. The table structure is available in black, anodised aluminium or glossy aluminium as well as natural oak, grey oak and wenge. This is also an aspect of the concept: The elements enter into a specific form of communication and form a sign system for a new perception.*

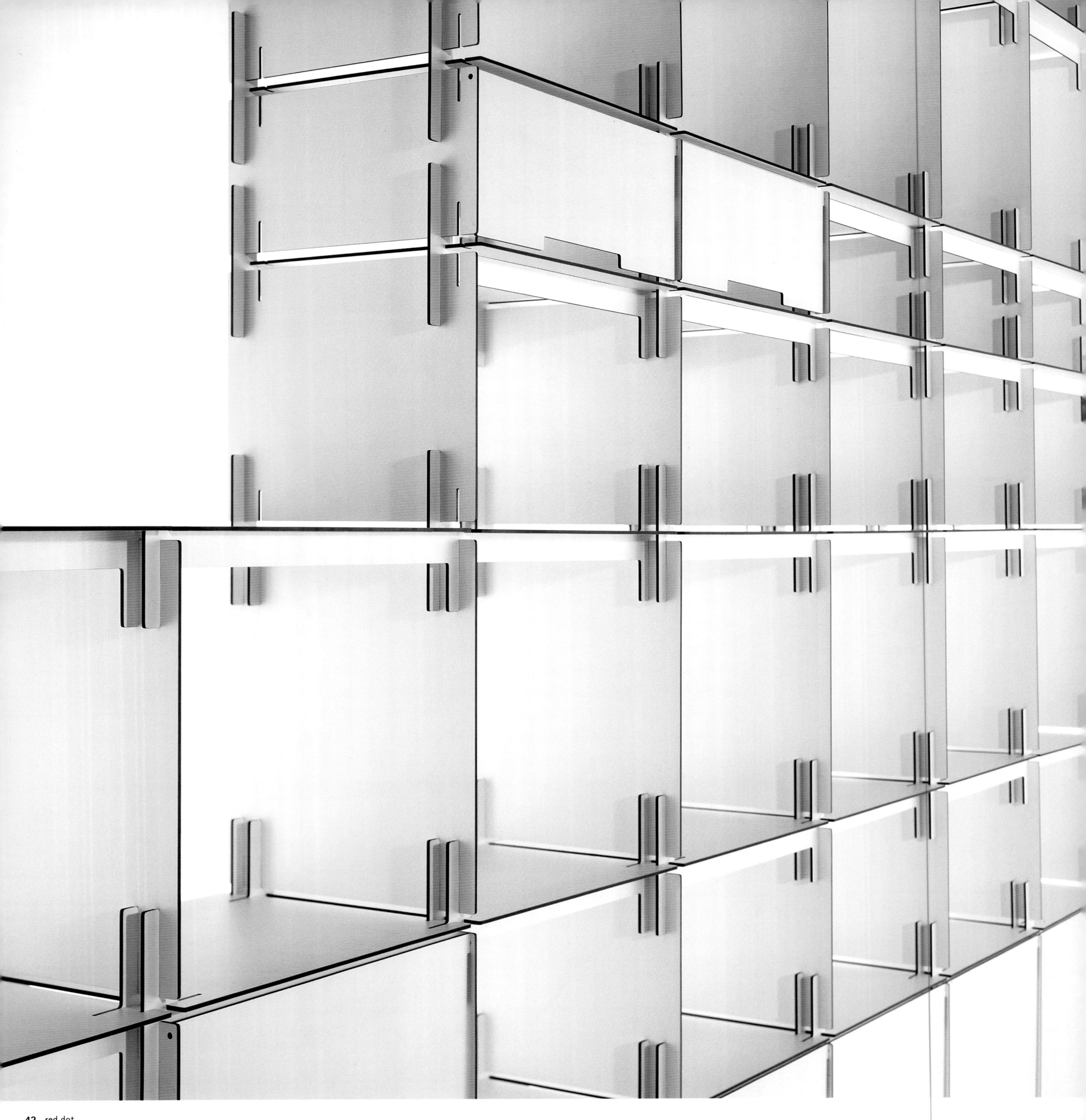

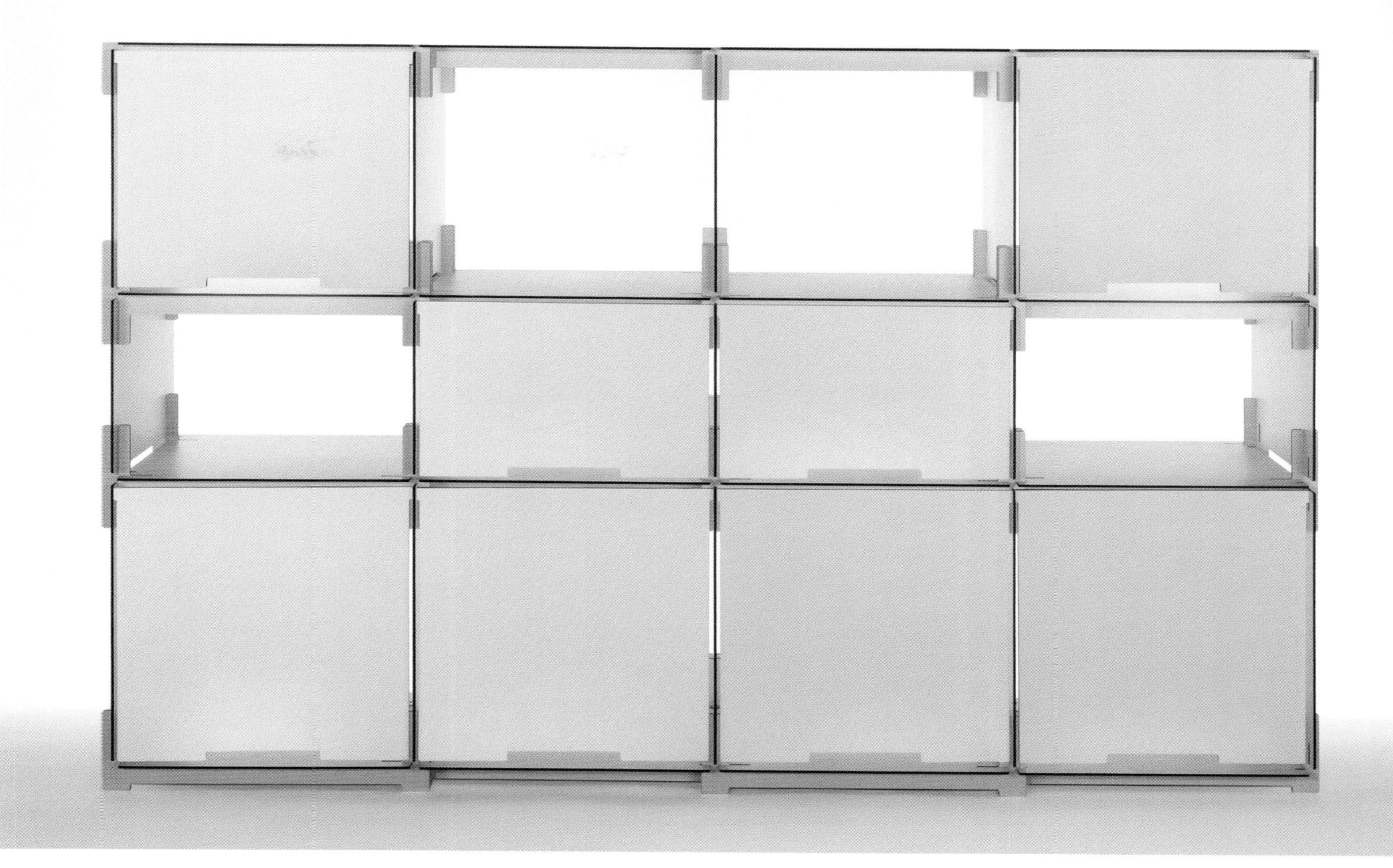

板式组合储物架，2004

möbelbau kaether & weise, Lamspringe
Design: Florian Petri, Berlin
www.kaetherundweise.de
www.fpid.de

品味更高，变化更快，更具有开放性的个性房间。在家具设计上，各种题材的设计以各种方式表现着新千年的到来，这些表现几乎涉及方方面面。在个人居住空间的装饰中，“个性”可以说是扮演了一个重要角色。家具已成为享受自己生活方式的一种途径。Platten-bau整合了储物架的结构，还使人们的储藏变得趣味十足，花样百出，极大地满足了人们对高度个性化家具的要求。Platten-bau，这个名字让人联想到20世纪50年代的民主德国的混凝土建筑。储物架采用一种轻型材料设计，轻巧灵活：架子在各个方面和方向都可以调整，可以相互叠加，可以单独组合，还可以重组。架子的每个单元都有许多部分组成，每一部分在长度和高度上都可以做相应调整。每一块组成材料都是相互嵌插在一起的，不需要借助任何工具。整个储物架结构中有四个不同高度的架子：两个宽架和两个长架，这样的构造可以提供不同的空间，以便来储藏不同的东西，如：CD、平装书、文件夹或大开本的书。Platten-bau整个构造都采用4毫米的HPL板制成，然而，尽管材料很轻，但却有很强的承载能力，而且非常稳固。该设计充分地利用CNC机械技术，在用同一种材料制作架子及其连接部分上，创造了极大的可能性。同时该设计理念使得前面敞开的物架仅用几扇合叶铰合的门和后挡板就能关闭上成为可能。就这方面而言，Platten-bau整合的架子结构为个人生活文化创造了一个富有情趣的空间。

Higher, faster and more open – rooms for individuals. *In furniture design, the still young millennium finds its expression particularly in the variety of stylistic approaches, akin to "Anything goes". The aspect of "self" in the individual furnishing of one's living space plays an important role. Furniture has become a means to indulge in one's own lifestyle. The platten_bau assembly shelving system satisfies the demand for a highly personal piece of furniture by offering interesting possibilities and interpretations. The name platten_bau also brings to mind associations with the concrete architecture of the GDR in the 1950s. The shelving system is designed using a lightweight construction to keep it flexible: it is adjustable in all aspects and directions, and it can be built on, built up and rebuilt. Each unit is made up of several parts – individually adjustable in both width and height. The individual shelf components slot together without the use of tools. The entire platten_bau system offers four different shelf heights, two shelf widths and two shelf depths, providing space to store different items such as CDs, paperback books, folders or oversized books. platten_bau is entirely made out of 4mm HPL boards. Yet, despite the lightness of the material, the construction has a high load-bearing capacity and is very stable. In order to use the same material for both the shelves and the connecting parts, the design has made the most of the possibilities of CNC-machine technology. The design concept also provides the possibility to close the open shelves with front top-hinged doors and back panels. In this respect, too, the platten_bau assembly shelving system creates an interesting spatiality for an individual culture of living.*

多面体扶手椅, 2005

Roset S.A., Briord, Frankreich
Design: Ronan & Erwan Bouroullec, St. Denis, Frankreich
Vertrieb: Roset Möbel GmbH, Gundelfingen
www.ligne-roset.com
www.bouroullec.com

新型“多面体”产品。新产品与某种几乎是一闪而过的灵感结合在一起是很平常事情。有时候重新审视一下已经知道的东西，就能感触到它，这一幕就发生在了“多面体”扶手椅的发展过程中。在拜访法国“写意空间”室内装潢工作室时，罗南与伊万兄弟俩看到了一台机器，该机器可以把多层棉织物切割成很复杂的形状。于是，在他们不断寻求新产品外形的过程中，他们在这台机器上找到了把手工艺与现代技术结合的新方法。在设计师们看来，“多面体”系列扶手椅是“前卫视觉与公司基本理念的综合”。极简与整体上的朴素的有机结合给“多面体”系列扶手椅带来一种独具特色的气息。同时，装潢工作室曾用过的有趣的生产方法也很有意义，许多布块经过多层缝合后拼接在一起的棉织物，既蕴涵着一种对精致钻石切割技术的怀旧情结，也是对日本折纸的复杂折叠技术的缅怀。脚凳的设计非常实用，在作为配套设置的同时，该脚凳装置在扶手椅的正下方，这样扶手椅又成了躺椅。此外还有一条毯子，毯子也是这一系列产品之一，坐直时，脚凳可以做靠背，而躺下时，它又可以做枕头。在整个“多面体”系列产品中，所有能被利用上的功用全都被考虑过了，而且由于他们尺寸小，可以舒适地放在各种大小的房间里。所以无论是在宽敞的阁楼里还是在小城市中的公寓里，你都可以轻而易举地体会到它们的美。

Facets of the new. *It is not unusual for innovations to emerge with a certain lightness, almost in passing. Sometimes they come about by taking a fresh look at something already known. This is what happened in the development of the Facett armchair. Whilst on a visit to the Ligne Roset upholstery studio, brothers Ronan and Erwan Bouroullec saw a machine capable of cutting multiple layers of fabric into ever more intricate shapes. In their constant search for new product forms they saw in the machine a novel approach combining craftsmanship with modern technology. According to the designers, what came out of this – the armchair of the Facett collection – is a "synthesis of an avant-garde vision and a return to the company's roots." The combination of minimalist simplicity with monolithic austerity lends a distinctive air to the Facett collection. Also significant is the interesting way the upholstery has been processed. The patches and seams of the multiple-stitched fabric are reminiscent of the precise art of diamond cutting or the intricate folding techniques of Japanese origami. The design of the footrest is highly functional. Forming a kind of kit, it fits beneath the front of the armchair, transforming it into a chaise longue. Furthermore, the footrest, in combination with one of the carpets from the collection, can be used as a backrest when sitting upright or as a headrest when lying down. The possible usage of the whole Facett collection has been functionally thought out, and due to their compact dimensions, they fit comfortably into rooms of various sizes. Their aesthetics unfold as easily in a spacious loft as in a small city apartment. Facets of the new.*

Varino II, 可变式厨具收纳组合，2005

Miele & Cie. KG, Werk Warendorf
Werksdesign
www.miele-kuechen.de

精密的设计工序。厨房是一处有自己特色的空间。家庭主妇，“家庭主夫”和要求苛刻的美食大师们对于如何设计他们的厨房，都有自己相当个性化的想法。设计可以帮助他们优化各个过程，使得厨房工作既有趣又简便。作为一个有一百多年历史的德国米勒公司，它在很多领域上都充当了开拓者的角色。1929年，米勒公司在欧洲市场上投放了第一台家用电子洗碗机，它的一整套精美的厨房设施使厨房在美观与功效方面定下了基调。Varino II是一套厨房组合系统，第二代设计是对Varino I系统的改进。在第一代的经验和基础上，第二代设计对第一代进行了改良，增加了一些新的而且有趣的功能。这套装置只适用于米勒厨房，各种大小的抽屉和活页设计得很灵活。它的创新方面体现在细节处和各种要素的组合上：作为一种简单的模块组合体系，它由一些可折叠的硬木柜组成，这些木柜可以被灵活地拆分，上面还有不同的插口和零件以便按顺序组装。组装系统主要的特色在于其具有强大的功能，当然还得考虑到它组装的逻辑性和要能经久耐用。既然该系统不要求每个木柜都有各自的功能，那么两个木柜之间的空间就可以同样被规划地井井有条以便加以利用，节约了成本。除此之外，其连接的部件可以在任何两个硬木柜之间插进去，辅之用不锈钢螺钉。因此，没有双层墙，这套厨房设施仍旧运转自如，并且最大化地使厨房空间变得井然有序，在厨房门前看这个储藏空间都能做到一目了然。如果说天天生活在这样一个功能齐全，极具秩序美感和清晰的逻辑性的厨房里，相信柴米生活也会变得赏心悦目起来。

Sophisticated – designing order. *The kitchen is a world of its own. Housewives, house husbands and avid gourmet cooks all have highly individual ideas of how their kitchens should be organised. Design can help optimise the organisation, making work in the kitchen both fun and easy. With a history of more than 100 years, the Miele company has been a pioneer in many areas. In 1929, Miele launched the very first electric dishwasher for the home on the European market, and Miele's fully fitted kitchen also set standards in terms of aesthetics and functionality. Varino II is an organisation system for the kitchen. The design of the second generation modifies the Varino I system and expands it with a new and interesting functionality that is based on the experiences and strength of the first generation system. The system is for use in a Miele kitchen only and flexibly organises drawers and pull-outs of all widths and heights. The innovation lies in the detail and in the arrangement of the elements: as an easy-to-understand modular assembly system it consists of stackable solid wood chests that can be flexibly subdivided with many different inserts and elements to create order. The organisation system features a functional and, with regard to its logical arrangement, certainly long-lasting innovation, since it does not require a wood chest for each single function as the space between two chests can be used in a systematic and even cost-saving way. Bridging elements are inserted between any two solid wood chests, using stainless steel bolts as special organising aids. Thus, the system does without double walls, creating a maximum of orderliness and easy overview in the storage space behind the kitchen front. Sophisticated functionality with a highly specific aesthetics of order and an intelligent logic for everyday life in the kitchen.*

Miele

Hansacanyon
单柄盥洗龙头, 2005

Hansa Metallwerke AG, Stuttgart
Design: octopus productdesign (Reinhard Zetsche), München; Bruno Sacco, Sindelfingen
www.hansa.de

水或者最初的设计。水是一种对人类极为重要的东西，寻找新的对水的诠释和利用水的方法越来越变成人们讨论的热门话题。对纯净的水和“纯度和净化”的本质的探索分别占据了健康和浴室设计问题的核心。在探索新的水的表达方式过程中，设计师莱因哈德和伯诺·萨阔把水演绎成为一种纯净的，不可或缺的物质，于是，一个“溪流在家中”的一套装置在他们的手里新鲜出炉了，它拥有光滑而又优美的轮廓。一体化的设计上的敞开的水道设置似乎在传达着这样的主题：“设计并没有到此结束，而是被有意识而又大胆的简化了，而又恰恰展示了一种体验：水这种元素最本质的精神在于，当它与物体相遇时，它会明智的为自己搭桥铺路，然后在自由空间里展示着自己最美丽的身姿。”此外，“溪流在家中”装置同时还增加了对水元素更深层次的诠释：它凸现了人文意识，由丁利用发光二极管制造灯光氛围，水喷头可以根据水的温度逐渐改变它的颜色。人们可以根据颜色来判断水温高低，这些都是由一电子控制系统来完成，通过传感按钮可以精确调节水温；照明带可以对正确的操作给出精确的反应。灯光的使用不仅使生活充满情调，还很实用。在设计师看来，“溪流在家中”的装置恰恰证明了这样的事实：“基本的创造性和技术的新颖性并不相互排斥，而是相辅相成的。”

Aqua or the design of the elementary
The search for new approaches and interpretations of water, an element so vital for human beings, has recently become a highly important issue. The search for primal "pure" water and for the essential nature of "purity and purification" is located at the centre of wellness and bathroom design. In their search for new forms of expression, the designers Reinhard Zetsche and Bruno Sacco have interpreted water as something pure and very elementary. They designed the Hansacanyon fittings series with smooth, defined contours. Its monolithically shaped fixture with an open watercourse system visualises the message "that here design is not an end in itself, rather it is consciously and boldly reduced. What is presented is an experience: The watery element in its original spirit encounters a material, ingeniously begins to carve a path for itself, and unfolds its surprisingly multi-dimensional appeal." The Hansacanyon fitting also adds a further aspect to this interpretation of the elementary: it addresses the human senses, since by means of LEDs the atmospheric lighting of the water jet gradually changes its colour depending on the water temperature. One can see whether the water is hot or cold. This is facilitated by an electronic control system. The water temperature is precisely adjustable via a sensor button; illuminated strips give precise feedback for accurate operation. The light, thus, acquires an additional highly interesting and functional meaning. According to the designers, the Hansacanyon fitting is an expression of the fact "that elementary ingenuity and technical innovation do not at all have to contradict one another, rather they can even form a coherent symbiosis."

触摸！丝绒瓷器，2004

KAHLA/Thüringen Porzellan GmbH, Kahla
Werksdesign: Barbara Schmidt, Regina Hadersbeck
Design: speziell produktgestaltung, Offenbach
www.kahlaporzellan.com
www.speziell.net

一定要触摸—为感官而设计。当中国第一个瓷器经过新的贸易之路到达欧洲的时候，就像是一个新生的婴孩，她的表面好像天鹅绒一样柔软，半透明而且非常精致。一种迄今从未有过的感官体验，它对人们来说是一种全新的事物。在十七世纪，一种新的“令人愉悦的饮料”——咖啡、茶和巧克力就是盛在这些昂贵易碎的瓷器里被人享用的，因此它们的样式也受到人们的宠爱，几乎都对它们大加赞美，那是一种格调多么的高雅的设计啊！瓷器外面的涂层也让人们有一种既精致又新颖的体验。该涂层把瓷器与纺织物表面结合在一起，当使用者触摸时，能够激起他们的独特的触觉感受。另外，软似天鹅绒的涂层可用作隔热层，并且即防滑又可以吸音。鉴于以上这些特点，三维表面就不仅是用来装饰的了，而是和使用者之间又建立了新的联系：三种产品系列都可以抵挡洗碗机的腐蚀。表面涂层，每一系列都体现出其独特的美感。例如，“五种感觉”系列，它不仅有带有涂层的把手，而且在碗，酒水器皿和杯子下面还有软垫。该系列中的别的产品还配上了绘画，看起来更加完美了。在最新的情侣系列产品中，咖啡碗和杯子上也涂有涂层，这样一来，当里面盛有热咖啡时，人们就可以舒服地端着杯子了。还有是在咖啡玛妮娅系列(五种感觉)系列产品中，显现出一个重要的设计要素，即杯子的放置位置常常由于涂层的存在而背离中心，并且被涂层强调了其背离。把瓷杯放在柔软的抗噪音的瓷杯垫上可以带来一种全新的感受。可以说，它们是为感官而设计的。

Please do touch – design for the senses
When the first Chinese porcelain reached Europe via the new trade routes, it was like a revelation: its surface felt as soft as velvet; it was translucent and delicate. A sensual experience that had been hitherto unknown, it was something completely new to people. In the 17th century, the new "pleasure drinks" of coffee, tea and chocolate were thus served in these valuable and fragile porcelain cups so that they could be enjoyed in style – almost celebrating them. The design of the touch! porcelain coating also embodies a delicate and novel sensual experience. It combines porcelain with a textile surface stimulating the user's tactile senses when touching it. In addition, the velvet-soft coating serves as thermal insulation, is anti-skidding and sound-absorbing as well. Due to these properties, the three-dimensional surface turns into more than just decoration: it establishes a new connection with the user. Three product ranges have been supplemented with the dishwasher-resistant touch! coating, each range emerging with its own specific aesthetics. The Five Senses range, for instance, comes with coated handles as well as padded grips on the bowls, the carafe and the mugs. The other items of the range are integrated by a matching graphic element. In the Update Twin Sets range, the café au lait bowl and mugs are also coated so that even when filled with hot liquid one can comfortably hold them. Last but not least, in the Coffeemania Collection (Five Senses) an important design element, the area where the cups are placed, has been de-centred and emphasised by the coating. Setting the porcelain cup down onto the soft, noise-reduced porcelain coaster produces a completely new sensation. Designed for the senses.

silverfish

银鱼摄像机水下防护罩, 2004

RWE Mechatronics GmbH, Mechernich
Werksdesign: Christian Hosse
Vertrieb: AVD Videoproduktion GmbH, Troisdorf
www.silverfish.info

为魅力而设计。奥地利人汉斯·哈斯是专业的水下摄像方面的先行者。在二十世纪四十年代，他就成为最早能够拍摄有关于鲨鱼，鲸鱼和海蛇的精彩壮观的水下活动场景的人物之一。汉斯·哈斯是一位务实的人，他倾向于使用简单装置：在很长一段时间里，他仅用一台透镜为16毫米的摄像机，还曾经让一位锁匠为这台摄影机做了一个防护外壳。“银鱼”装置是一种为摄影机设计的水下防护层，该设计打破了传统，即一些知名的水下防护层只适用于一些专业摄影机或者仅适用于一些专门的摄影机型号。因此，这个新型防护外壳的开发目标就是为带有LANC控制的摄像机制造一种大众化的、可以灵活使用的水下防护壳。“银鱼”可以与将近100个不同型号的摄影机相匹配。该设计既适合业余电影制作人又适合专业的电影制作人。它是通过利用液压形成理论来运作的，在这个过程中，水在高压下使得钢管膨胀，钢管表面与铸模内部相挤压，这样它们的几何原理就被体现出来了。这个装置的外层的防护壳和所有的金属部分都是用特种钢制成的。由于这种钢内含有大量的铬和镍，可以很好地防止海水腐蚀。该防护壳装有根据人机工程学原理设计的固体手握垫，可以在水下很容易移动。在下水之前，摄影机要固定在一个被打了孔的杆子上，通过一个三角支架，把这个杆子装在中心控制组件上面。由于装有一台900克的摄影机，“银鱼”防护壳就有一些浮力了。磁制的按钮使你戴着手套时也可以很容易的操作。着实是魅力无穷的功能性设计。

Design for fascination. *The Austrian Hans Hass ranks among the pioneers of professional underwater photography, and back in the 1940s he was one of the first to shoot spectacular, gorgeous underwater films featuring sharks, whales and sea snakes. Hans Hass was a pragmatic person who believed in simple equipment: For quite a long time he used only a 16 mm film camera, for which he had commissioned a locksmith to build a waterproof housing. SILVERFISH is an underwater housing for camcorders, designed against the trend of the well-known underwater housings that are only suitable for specialist camcorders, or for only a few specific models. Thus the objective in developing this innovative housing was to create a universal and flexibly applicable underwater housing for camcorders with LANC control: SILVERFISH is compatible with approximately a hundred different camcorder models. It is designed for amateur and professional film-makers alike. It was shaped using hydro-forming, a process in which water under high pressure distends a steel tube and presses its surface against the insides of a mould, so that its geometry is precisely depicted. The housing and all metal parts located on the outer surface are made of special-purpose steel, sea water resistant due to its high chromium and nickel content. With its ergonomic design of the solid double-hand grip, the housing is easy to manoeuvre under water. Before submersing in water, the camcorder is fastened on the punched bar, located at the control module, by means of a tripod screw. SILVERFISH is buoyancy-neutral with a camcorder weight of 900 grammes; the magnetic push-button elements are easy to operate even when wearing gloves. Functional design for fascination.*

TOPEAK自行车帐篷，2005

Topeak, Inc., Taichung, Taiwan
Design: Topeak Design Team &
Lutz Scheffer
Vertrieb: RTI Sports GmbH, Urmitz
www.topeak.com

纯自然的美学功能。骑自行车是人类设计出来的最自然的运动方式之一。骑车去领略一下乡村风光,到任何想要去的地方野营，这是许多自行车爱好者对完美的自由的最真挚的表达。既然自带帐篷有很有用处，那么精心设计的装备就变得非常重要了。在这样的背景下，TOPEAK设计出一种式样新颖并有创新性功能的自行车露营帐篷，以便能够解决方方面面的需求。自行车本身被作为主要的结构要素来扎帐篷，这种单人帐篷利用自行车框架和前轮来代替帐篷支撑杆，这样以来，帐篷不仅体积小、重量轻、还易于装卸。因此，TOPEAK自行车帐篷是对紧凑轻巧的帐篷设计的重新诠释。TOPEAK自行车帐篷所利用的材料结合的也很有趣，它是用45D防破裂，防水，轻巧耐用的尼龙做成，两个做工精细的网状窗户用来通风，还可以在美丽的夜晚遥望星空幻想。帐篷的两翼由70D防裂尼龙制成，完全防水，并提供额外的保护层，顶棚和两翼都能够打包以节省空间，体积仅有(14 x 26厘米)，包括所有的附件总重量仅有1200克。帐篷的设计整合了简单与复杂，营造了一种非常独特而且纯粹的功能的美感。

Pure nature – the aesthetics of functionality. *Cycling is one of the most natural forms of mobility ever devised. To enjoy the countryside touring by bicycle and to camp wherever one wishes is the ultimate expression of pure freedom for many cycling enthusiasts. And since carrying space is at a premium, well-designed equipment is of the utmost importance. Against this backdrop, the Topeak Bikamper tent has been designed with an interesting and innovative functionality, providing solutions to several needs at once. The bicycle itself serves as the main structural element for pitching the tent. The one-person tent utilises the bicycle frame and front wheel in place of tent poles. Consequently the tent is extremely small and light, and easily stowed. As such, the Topeak Bikamper is also a reinterpretation of compact, lightweight tent design. The combination of materials used in the Topeak Bikamper is also interesting. The canopy is constructed of light, durable and waterproofed 45D ripstop nylon. It features two sophisticated mesh windows for ventilation that also invite stargazing on pleasant nights. The separate fly is made of a fully waterproofed 70D nylon construction, offering an additional layer of protection from the elements. Canopy and fly together pack down to a compact size (14 x 26cm), with a total weight of just 1,200 grammes, all accessories included. The design of the tent merges simplicity with sophisticated interpretation, producing a highly specific and very pure functional aesthetic.*

Initech Geologic 弓, 2004

Decathlon Sportartikel GmbH, Herne
Werksdesign: Decathlon
(Etienne Redouin, Nicolas Hamoignon),
Villeneuve d'Ascq, Frankreich
www.decathlon.com

箴言与传统的结合。射箭艺术与人类的文明紧密相连。哲学家孔子曾高度赞扬射箭艺术，因为它不但可以形成，并且展示了一个人的性格。他曾说到："在一个人拉弓的时候，你就可以识别出这个人有什么样的品德和行为举止。" 因此，孔子坚决支持要求青少年必须学习弓箭。Initech Geologic是一种现代弓箭，它使得初学者更容易入门。在设计这一款弓箭的时候，设计师考虑到了多种要求：弓箭必须得让人们买得起，必须在材料和形状上不同于其它弓箭，而且必须满足初学者在功能性方面的要求。Initech Geologic弓箭的性能与一种新型材料（一种注入了30%玻璃纤维的聚酰胺）的特性紧密相连，这使得手柄的各个组成部分都用同一种材料组成，并且很容易能达到弓箭要求的很大的张力。选择这种材料可以使弓箭简单，耐用，同时降低了成本。此外，Initech Geologic被制造成一种较硬的弓，这样可以提高弓箭的发射速度以及射击的准确度和稳定性。由于它的造型结合了人体工程学原理，它能够很稳的被握在手中，使射箭这一过程变得更加具有艺术性。Initech Geologic弓箭的设计用现代科技进一步发展了这种传统的体育器械，一切都是依据当今先进的材料和理念，才使它的功能变得更为强大，不断跟上了时代的步伐。

Maxims and traditions. *The art of archery has a close link with human civilisation. The philosopher Confucius praised the art of archery highly, since it formed as well as showed a person's character: "While pulling the bow one can recognise a person's virtue and behaviour." Confucius was therefore a strong advocate of the idea that it should be obligatory for any adolescent to learn archery. The Initech Geologic is a "modern" bow, which makes it particularly easy for beginners to take up this sport. The demands on the design were manifold. The bow had to be affordable, had to differ from others in terms of form and material and meet the functional requirements of a beginner. The design of the Initech Geologic bow is closely linked with the characteristics of a new innovative material (a polyamide injection with 30 per cent glass fibre). This material allows forming all the components of the handle out of one piece and makes it easier to create the large openings required for a bow. The choice of material makes the bow simple and durable as well as reducing the cost. The Initech Geologic has been formed as a stiff bow, which raises the firing speed of the arrow as well as the precision and stability of the shot. Due to its ergonomic form, it sits well in the hand, thus making the art of archery easier. The design of the Initech Geologic bow has managed to further develop this traditional piece of sports equipment in a modern way. Today's materials and ideas create a clear and contemporary functionality.*

Pinc House 预制住宅, 2003

Pinc AB, Nacka, Schweden
Werksdesign: Pinc Designteam
www.pinchouse.se

设计大师的构思——当代生活的平台。 是什么构成了现代生活的设计？或者当今的民族设计传统要表达什么意思？这些重要的问题也摆在斯堪的纳维亚半岛的Pinc House的设计师们的面前。作为家具的设计师，他们一直在寻求能够与他们斯堪的那维亚经典设计相匹配的新房型。这些经典设计如阿尔托扶手椅 400，小书架Mathson Mi 1200 和雅格布森AJ 餐具. 这些设计师们——来自后来的Pinc House工作室，一直没有找到一个能够满足他们需要的预制房子，因此，他们很快就开始寻找一种积极、健康、有趣的生活方式：一个为现代人创造的完整的生活平台。因此，他们把想法集中到寻找一种全面的理念上来，这种理念既代表了至关重要的过去又代表了现在。依靠他们的运气和技术，他们很快就创造出了他们的第一个模型——Pinc House Sport 70。作为一种带有斯堪的纳维亚设计风格的新颖的房子，它经久耐用，并且尚在人们经济许可范围之内。它把经典和设计师们的设计语言紧紧地连在了一起，而且，它巧妙地融技术性和需求性为一体。对空间的合理运用，大块的透明空间，外带它那可以饱览全景的落地窗都使它与众不同。The Pinc House Sport 70 的基本理念已被进一步地发展，其类型也在慢慢丰富并完善。虽然说每一种设计都是为某种特定的生活方式量身定做的，但几乎所有的设计都与文化建立了某种联系。可以说，在当代生活的文化中体现了设计大师级设计理念。

In the spirit of the old masters – platforms for contemporary living. *What constitutes living design? Or what meaning can a national design tradition acquire today? These are important questions that also arose for the Scandinavian designers of the Pinc House when, as furniture designers, they had been looking for a new house to go with their Scandinavian design classics, the Aalto Armchair 400, the small book stand Mathson Mi 1200 and the Jacobsen AJ cutlery. The designers from what was later to become the design studio Pinc House could not find a prefabricated house that would fulfil their needs. They soon set out on a search for an active, healthy and enjoyable lifestyle: the complete living platform created for the people of today. Thus, they had centred their approach on finding an overall concept that could be representative of both a vital past and the present. Relying on their own fate and skills, they soon realised their first model, the Pinc House Sport 70. As an innovative and timeless, yet affordable house with a Scandinavian design, it ties in with the design classics and their language of forms. Yet it also creates a felicitous connection to current needs and technologies. Its design features an intelligent use of space, a transparent concept as well as panoramic windows. The basic concept of the Pinc House Sport 70 has been further developed and modified for further types of houses, each tailored for a specific lifestyle, but all establishing a relationship to human culture. Designed in the spirit of the old masters – in a contemporary living culture.*

LiTraCon™ – 透光混凝土, 2005

LiTraCon Bt., Csongrád, Ungarn
Werksdesign: Áron Losonczi
www.litracon.hu

Lichtwände – Faszination eines Materials

光墙——有趣的材料

作为材料，混凝土——这个包含了许多种成分的混合物，已经激起了全世界建筑师的想象。或许让人们印象最深刻，并且能够证明这种材料的可能性的一个例子，就在巴西的首都巴西利亚，是由城市规划师们和城市建筑师们共同创建完成。在巴西利亚，有许多类似雕刻的建筑物，整座城市就像是一处用混凝土建造的令人印象深刻的建筑景观。“透光水泥”是一种新型的建筑材料，该材料由光纤玻璃纤维和优质的混凝土混合而成,具有半透明的特点。这种有趣的材料的主要特点就是把玻璃融合进去：数以万计的光纤玻璃纤维平行组成一个巨大的矩阵，其两头连接在每一个建筑块料的两个主要对立面上，这样纤维材料就和混凝土融为一体了，像是一种“不严格的”添加剂，但是表面仍然是一种均质的混凝土。材料是半透明的，因为玻璃纤维可以把光以小光点的形式从建筑材料的一面传到另一面。由于玻璃纤维是平行排列的，光信号可以由比较明亮的一端传输到比较暗的一端而不发生任何改变。然而，这种现象最有趣的一点是它的清晰度，这使得物体的影子在墙的另一面都可以被看到，甚至穿过它的光的颜色也不会改变。“透光水泥”在建筑方面有多种用途，如预制块料或者预制板。既然玻璃纤维可以在厚达20米的材料中传输光信号，并且在亮度方面不会有任何大的减弱，那么，从理论上讲一个墙体甚至可以有数米厚。这些建筑材料可以用来建造承重墙和建筑框架，而且还可以起到隔热的作用。这种材料以其新颖有趣的特点，成为创建建筑景观的基础，相信建成的景观定会有一个崭新的，明快通透的魅力空间——未来的建筑。

Light walls – fascinating material

As a material, concrete – a mixture of several components – has excited the fantasy of architects all over the world. Probably one of the most impressive examples, demonstrating the possibilities of this material, is Brasília – the capital of Brazil, created by urban architects and city planners. With its sculptural buildings, the city resembles an impressive architectural vision in concrete. LiTraCon™ – Light-Transmitting Concrete is an innovative building material with translucent characteristics – a mixture of optical glass fibre and fine concrete. The main idea behind this interesting material was the integration of glass: thousands of optical glass fibres create a matrix of lines that run in parallel, connecting the two opposing main faces of each block. The fibres integrate into the concrete as a kind of "undemanding" additive and the surface still reminds one of homogenous concrete. The material is translucent because the glass fibres carry light in the form of little dots from one face of the block to the opposite one. Due to the parallel arrangement, the light information from the brighter side of such a wall appears on the darker side without any changes. However, the most interesting aspect of this phenomenon is the sharpness with which shadows become visible on the other side of the wall. Even the colours of the light coming through do not change. LiTraCon™ can be used in architecture in many ways – as pre-cast blocks or in the shape of panels. Theoretically, a wall structure can even be several metres thick, since the fibres carry light through blocks with a thickness of up to 20 metres without significant loss in brightness. These blocks can be used to erect supporting walls and building structures and they provide thermal insulation as well. This material with its innovative and fascinating characteristics thus serves as the basis for architectural visions to create new aesthetic spaces filled with light – for the architecture of the future.

Druckluftaufbereitungseinheit MS12, 2004

Festo AG & Co. KG, Esslingen
Werksdesign: Jan Kleffmann
www.festo.com

压缩空气的美学原则。气体力学的物理特性在设计领域不断着开拓新的道路。其工作原理很简单,但却非常有趣。使用压力下降,压缩空气所储存的能量在空气成分的帮助下转化为运动。MS12气源处理单元是最大的系列，该系列是由德国费斯托设计的具有新的模块化结构。其设计遵循了传统气动系统，该产品差不多适合所有行业。它具有过滤、清洁、干燥和润滑压缩空气，使用安全性能高。这些非常大的单元的高流量在气体力学领域几乎是独一无二的。它非常适用于流量较大的集中和分散式气源处理应用场合，使用时要消耗很多的空气，可广泛应用在大型机器、完善的车间、自动装配线和用在厂房局部空间之中。MS12气源处理单元的一个重要优势是其空气供应器安装方便，模块易于安装、重建或补充。MS12的气源处理单元为该产品树立了新的美学原则。该设计突出了各个组成部分并且通过颜色来强调各要素之间的联系。功能模块被放置在了顶部，底部放置了看上去非常紧凑的模块系统。MS12气源处理单元各部分精巧结合的设计元素在视觉上与现代厂房建筑达成了完美统一。

Aesthetics for compressed air. *The physical particularities of pneumatics constantly open up new ways in the field of design. The working principle is simple but nevertheless highly fascinating. Utilising the pressure drop, the stored energy of the compressed air is converted into movement with the help of pneumatic components. The MS12 air supply unit is the largest series and belongs to the new modular standard service unit series by Festo. Its design follows that of traditional pneumatic systems. The unit is suitable for almost any industry. It filters, cleans, dries and oils the compressed air and also provides safety functions. The high flow rate of these very large units is almost unique in the field of pneumatics. They are used for centralised and decentralised compressed air supply and for applications with very high air consumption. This includes larger machines, complete plants, assembly lines and parts of factory halls. An important aspect of the MS12 air supply unit is its installation-friendliness. The modules are easy to install, rebuild or supplement. The MS12 air supply unit creates a new aesthetics for this product. The design accentuates the individual components and emphasises the connection elements between the components by means of colour. The uniform modules with platforms for functional units located at the top and the bottom turn it into a compact-looking modular unit. The neatly arranged components visually integrate well into modern plant construction.*

FESTO

HSW操作模具, 2005

Festo AG & Co. KG, Esslingen
Werksdesign: Karoline Schmidt, Jan Kleffmann
www.festo.com

情感——机器的语言形式。一种统一的完美表现形式在机械工程领域中扮演着越来越重要的角色。想要拥有“几合一”功能的产品，的确不是一件容易的事。德国费斯托公司把创新的型技术与独特的造型结合了起来，使产品看起来非常地小巧精致。这个新的操作模具可用于小型组件生产线,并进行自动嵌入操作，重新定位并且以90度的角度把各种机件连接起来。由于HSW制造的是小的组件，因此可以在很短的周期内制造出理想水平的产品，这常常是大型线性生产单元难以达到的。通过操控进行连续垂直和水平运动，设计达到了人们对重复的精准性和可高频率循环的要求，且能运转平稳。此外，由于旋转角度合适，因而组件可以对角移动，再回来重复下一过程，这就极大地提高了该过程的可靠性。盖子不仅保证了安全，而且盖子上的弯曲的金属边缘的设计，沿着一个规定的外向路径运动，更凸现了它具有高度动态操作的特点。所有的设置都易于操作，如果打开盖子，它还会变得更加灵活。用于终端传感的邻近传感器的发光二极管通过两个显示窗来发光，设计成棱镜形状的显示窗表面使光折射得更亮。发光二极管的构造仍以90度的角运动，这种简洁的设计可以由气动旋转和电力来驱动。这个装置系列共有三种尺寸，且安装简单快捷。它代替了必须要单独安装和调试的产品。这个操作模块设计把传统机械设计和人们的情感表达联系在了一起。

Emotion – language of forms for machines
A uniform and aesthetic language of forms plays an increasingly important role in the field of mechanical engineering. Not an easy task in the face of the plurality of uses. The Festo company combines innovative technologies with a distinct use of forms, which seems almost subtle. The new handling module is used in the line production of small components and provides automatic insertion, repositioning and joining of work pieces at an angle of 90 degrees. The HSW builds small components, thus creating the desired level of production with short cycles that is often not reached by large linear units. The design meets the high demands on repetition accuracy, running performance, and achievable cycle frequency. This is achieved through a guided vertical and horizontal motion sequence. The swivel angle is adjustable so that components can be, for example, removed diagonally and then re-fed into the process. This significantly increases process reliability. The cover provides safety and emphasises the product's highly dynamic operating characteristics with its curved sheet metal edge. It shows the outward path of the forced guidance. All settings are easily accessible and can be activated after removal of the cover. The LEDs of the proximity sensor for end-position sensing shine through two display windows with prism-shaped surfaces designed to increase luminosity. The configuration of the LEDs continues the 90-degree angle of movement. This compactly designed unit can be driven by a pneumatic rotary drive and an electrical drive. This line of devices, available in three sizes, can be quickly and easily mounted. It replaces units that must be individually mounted and adjusted. The handling module's design provides traditional mechanics with an emotional expression.

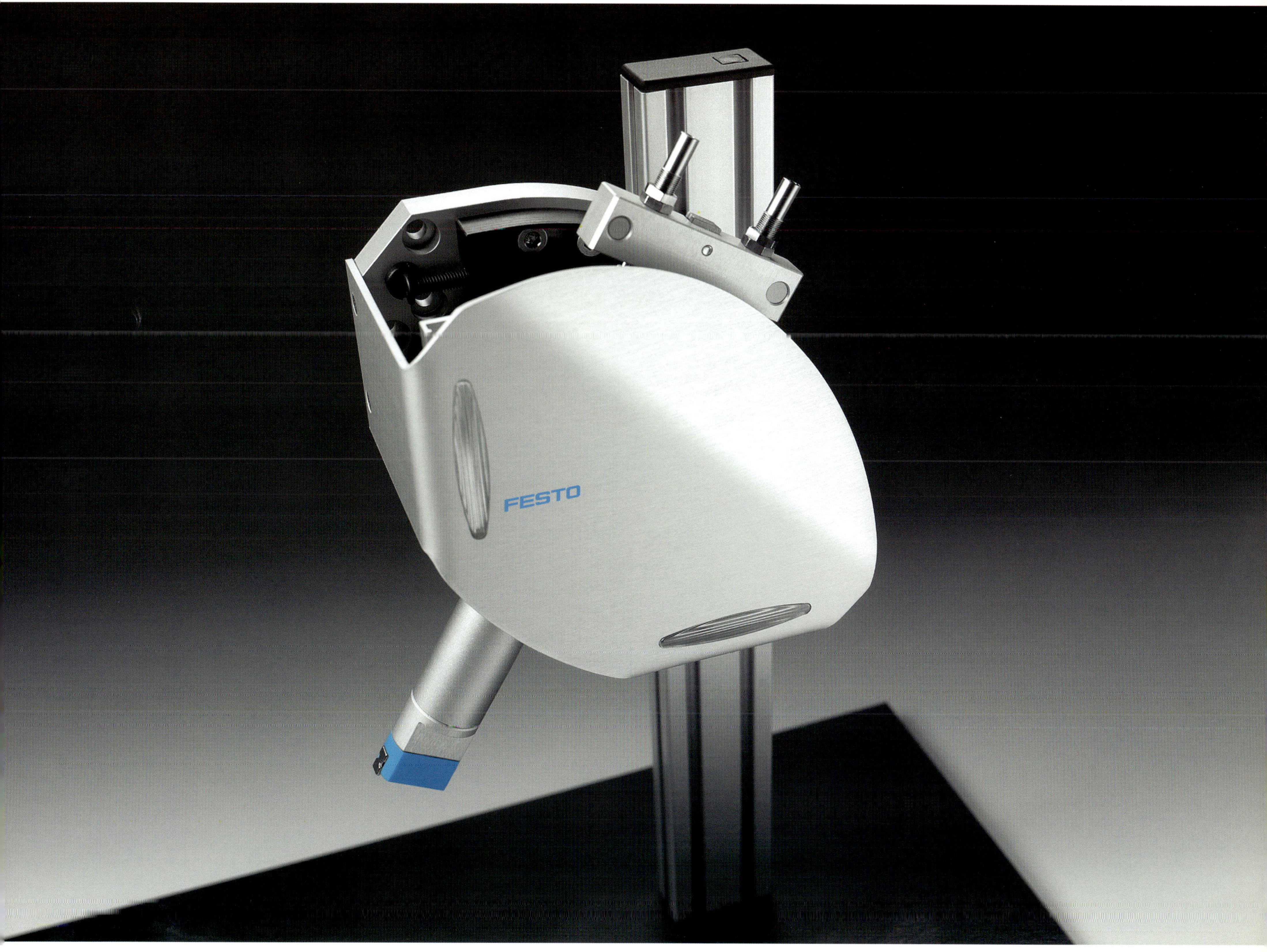
FESTO

Linde
T20

林德T20/T24 SP型电动站式码垛车，2005

Linde AG, Aschaffenburg
Design: Dr. Ing. h.c. F. Porsche AG
(Stefan Stark, Michael Mauer, Anthony Hatter), Weissach
www.linde-stapler.de
www.porsche-design.com

关于工作和规则。人类工程学这个术语是一个合成词，来源于希腊语“ergon”（工作）和“nomos”（法令、规则）。作为一个对人类工作研究很感兴趣的跨学科的研究组织，成立于1949年的人类工程学研究学会创造了这个词。从那时候开始，它就能很容易地被人记住。研究会的目标旨在改进并提高人及其工作环境之间的关系。当今，人类工程学已经成为在设计方面的一个国际性的指标和考虑因素，T20 / T24 SP站立式的电动码垛车就是一个例子，它可以很好地说明一个成熟的设计是怎样有效地改善了工作环境。这种设计就是基于对人类工程学的研究，这种研究的结果是建立了所谓的SP理念。卡车连接着一种有效的运转装置，它是一种新型的运转装置，被称为电子驱动器，这同时还是一个安全舒适的操作间。在实际操作中它意味着操作者能够在操作仓内以一个放松而又舒适的站姿下方便地控制他的工作环境。不管向前还是向后操作，T20 / T24 SP都能给操作者一个45度的操作位置，这使得他可以不受身体条件的束缚，在各个方向上扩大了操作者的视野，同时还让操作者可以俯瞰整个工作环境。这种方便可行的电子控制装置除了适应45度的操作位置之外，还能够毫不费力让操作者只使用一只手操作，左手就可以自由地从事其他工作。此外，20 / T24 SP外观的设计给它披上了一个动态的外衣，暗示着它极为灵巧高效。精准的控制，低噪音，智能的建造标准，所有的一切都结合了人类工程学，对于这种密切结合工作环境的经典设计，同时也体现了一种新的美学理念。

On ergon and nomos. *The term ergonomics is a hybrid word, derived from the Greek "ergon" (work) and "nomos" (law or rule). The word was meant to be catchy as it was postulated by the Ergonomics Research Society founded back in 1949, an interdisciplinary group interested in the study of human work. The objective of the Society was defined as the improvement of the relationship between man and his working environment. Today, ergonomics is an internationally valid maxim in design, and the T20 / T24 SP stand-on electric pallet truck is just another example of how sophisticated design can effectively improve the working environment. The design is based on an ergonomic study, the results of which are built into the so-called SP concept. The truck combines an optimised driving position, an innovative drive control called e-Driver, as well as a safe and comfortable operator's compartment. For real-world use this means that the operator can easily control his working environment from a relaxed and comfortable standing position in the cockpit. Whether driving forward or backwards, the T20 / T24 SP provides the operator with a 45-degree driving position. This removes physical constraints and widens the operator's view in every direction, giving him good overview of his working environment. The easily accessible e-Driver drive control has been adapted to the 45-degree driving position and can be controlled effortlessly with one hand. The left-hand is then left free for other tasks. The exterior design of the T20 / T24 SP lends the vehicle a dynamic appeal, suggesting agility and efficiency. In its combination of precision control, low running noise and an intelligent construction principle, all paired with an ergonomic approach, the truck also embodies a new aesthetic for the classic pallet fork-lift truck, designed for the working environment.*

K 1200 S 摩托赛车

BMW Group, München
Werksdesign: Designteam der BMW Group / Designteam Motorrad
www.bmw.com

路上小巧的外形。摩托车视觉语言的塑造隶属于它的整个历史发展过程。它总是试图把新技术与品牌的内在含义连接在一起。同样的，宝马汽车boxer引擎的每一个创新设计都以它自己的特色而令人着迷。当今宝马K1200 S摩托赛车最有意思的特征就是它长长的轴距，这对于这种类型的摩托车来说是令人吃惊的。尽管如此，这种专门定制的被命名“Duolever”的前轮悬挂技术有一种超乎寻常的机动性和灵活性，从而让机车更稳定安全。另一个显著的设计特征是以一定角度设在汽车底盘的同轴四汽缸引擎，配合着简洁的车身给人一种紧凑的视觉效果。真正吸引人的是一个有机设计的车尾灯和设有金银丝的轮胎，这是为这种车特别设计的。同其他的宝马组系生产的车一样，在K1200 S的设计中，空气动力起着举足轻重的作用。简单的外壳已经历了反复的实验，并在风洞中试验中完善，摩托车的外壳上没有大的阻碍其功能的排气管道，车身侧面也没有灯光装置。K1200 S结合精巧的设计以及其醒目流畅的外形于一身，其形式上的自由和外形的简练旨在提升宝马品牌的主旨——它是如此完美，以至于精致到了每一个细节。

Tight shapes for the road. *The visual language of a motorcycle was subject to numerous evolutionary developments throughout its history. It was always attempted to combine new technologies with the personal message of the brand. As such, each innovative redesign of the BMW boxer motors was spectacular in its own way. The most interesting feature of the current BMW K 1200 S on-road motorcycle is the long wheelbase, surprising for a motorcycle of this particular class. However, the specially developed front wheel suspension with the name "Duolever" allows an unusually good manoeuvrability, resulting in the motorcycle gaining stability and safety. Another outstanding design feature is the four-cylinder in-line motor built in at right angles to the chassis, translating to a tight visual language together with the slim body of the machine. Real eye-catchers are an organically designed backlight and filigree wheels, which have specially been developed for this particular bike. As with any other vehicle of the BMW Group, the aerodynamics aspect played a dominant role in the design of the K 1200 S; the plain exterior shell was repeatedly tested and optimised in the wind tunnel in such a way that, for example, no large air ducts disturb functions or optics of the lateral body parts. The K 1200 S is deliberately designed with a striking and eye-catching, yet authentic profile. The formal autonomy and the compressed shape are also intended to promote the mission of the BMW brand – it does so successfully without getting lost in details.*

BMW
K1200S

Z-Tech 气垫拖轮, 2004

PSA Marine (Pte) Ltd, Singapur
Design: Robert Allan Ltd., Vancouver, Kanada
Produktion: Cheoy Lee Shipyards Ltd., Hongkong
www.ztechtug.com

海上风景线——集美观性和移动性于一身的轮船。对于大多数贸易国家而言，海路是最重要的货物交换途径。有超过90%的世界贸易是通过海路完成的。大吨位的运输轮船在近海及港口海域自由移动并能到达停泊地点，港口拖轮的牵引作用显得至关重要。Z-Tech这一全新系列的港口拖轮是由世界著名的加拿大籍轮船设计师罗伯特・艾伦（Robert Allan）先生设计的。这一设计的主要目的是提高港口拖轮的日常工作效率、作业效果及其安全可靠性。罗伯特・艾伦先生代表新加坡港务集团海事公司设计这些港口拖轮，而新加坡港务集团则拥有亚洲最大的现代拖船船队。Z-Tech拖轮主要是设计应用在主要港口和能源设施码头进行作业的。该船舷弧较低且向前倾斜，甲板仓和驾驶室偏向船尾，这样的设计使得拖轮在轮船极端摇晃的条件下也能够应付自如。远航时，Z-Tech系列拖轮可以在海上船后身拖拽模式下进行全方位作业。所以，这一部分船体的设计与一般的典型ASD设计相比要更显圆滑。前方甲板处（龙骨上方）的舷弧较低且趋于平坦，从而形成一块宽敞、平坦，没有任何铰链阻碍的安全的工作甲板。船员无需担心是否会在陡峭倾斜的甲板上滑倒，或者是被其它的障碍物绊倒。舷窗的尺寸尽力做到了最大化，从而尽可能地拓宽了拖轮周围视野。为了避免视觉失真，窗户的朝向都以驾驶员的主要视线方向为准。Z-Tech系列拖轮设计的最根本目的是要在其中达到一种严格的美学意义上的高度平衡，同时也集技术、性能和人体工程学设计于一身。由于Z-Tech的设计特点独树一帜，从而吸引了全世界的目光。到2006年底，Z-Tech系列拖轮将会在包括中北美、中东、亚洲及太平洋地区在内的世界各地被广泛投入使用。

Marine aesthetics – defined mobility
For most trading nations, the sea is the most important route of transport for exchange of goods. More than 90 per cent of the total world trade is handled via sea routes. To enable bulky transport ships to manoeuvre in coastal waters and ports, harbour tugs are of great importance to tow the ships on the spot. The Z-Tech is a new category of harbour tugs designed by world-renowned Canadian naval architect, Mr. Robert Allan. Primarily, the design is aimed to improve daily operational efficiency and performance as well as reliability. The tugs were designed on behalf of PSA Marine, the owner of the leading fleet of modern tugs in Asia. Z-Tech tug is designed primarily for operations in major ports and energy terminals. It has a low sheer forward, coupled with the aft bias of the deckhouse and wheelhouse even to function under the extreme flares of modern ships. Z-Tech can be used for omni-directional performance to work astern in tractor mode when sea-going. Therefore, the shape of the part of the hull is more rounded than would typically be seen in any common ASD design. The forward deck (over the skeg) has a low, flat sheer, creating a spacious, relatively flat and safe working deck without any obstructive anchor chains. Crews do not have to worry about losing their footing on a steeply sloped deck, or falling over any steps or other discontinuities. To achieve optimum visibility all around the tug the window size is maximised, and the orientation of windows is oriented to the operator's primary sight lines to minimise sight distortion. An essential aim of the design of the Z-Tech tug is a high degree of balance in proportion and lines to create a stringent and determined aesthetics. This feature comprises at its best with a perfected technology, functionality and ergonomics. The Z-Tech design has drawn a worldwide appeal for its many unique features. By end 2006, Z-Tech tugs will be operating in various parts of the world including the North and Central America, Middle East, Asia and the Pacific regions.

保时捷 911 Carrera 跑车, 2004

Dr. Ing. h.c. F. Porsche AG, Stuttgart
Werksdesign
www.porsche.com

保时捷911 Carrera型跑车——外型与连贯性的体现。长久以来，保时捷911型跑车的设计已成为一个经典。车型最初的设计创意来自于亚力山大·保时捷,他是德国斯图加特"保时捷"跑车品牌的创立者费利·保时捷的儿子。作为二十世纪六十年代初的一位年轻设计师，亚历山大将保时捷911设计成对保时捷356的继承。1963年9月，这款新车在法兰克福汽车展首次亮相，不久之后，"Elfer"以它的后轮驱动和清晰的产品线管理成为了跑车的典范，同时还被应用在第六代车的生产中。以著名的基本车型为基础，现在的保时捷 911 Carrera秉承了911系列一贯的视觉表现。设计遵循了"明晰，紧凑和精确"的原则，以力争把这一原则体现在车的各个细节为目标。明朗的外形，突出的细节特征与光滑紧凑的表面和边缘设计相结合。保时捷 911 Carrera的设计人员十分重视外观、空间和细节的精确设计。整体外部的形象的设计也经过了深思熟虑：宽大的两翼与轻薄的车顶和车门形成了对比。几何形状的大灯、尾灯，造型特别的后窗和车篷对比强烈。保时捷 911 Carrera前半部分车身最令人瞩目的特点是由大气的前照灯和雾灯、指示灯搭配组成的灯组设计。从侧面看，整体布局紧凑，从后面看，动感十足。它那连贯性的设计方式，既成功地继承了911 Carrera的传统，又不失自己的特色。

Porsche 911 Carrera – language of forms and consistency. *The Porsche 911 has become a design classic long since. The typical shape is the design idea of Ferdinand Alexander Porsche, son of the founder of the Stuttgart-based sports car brand, Ferry Porsche. As a young designer at the beginning of the 1960s, he drew the 911 as successor of the Porsche 356. In September 1963, the new car celebrated its premiere at the Frankfurt Auto Show. Soon after, the "Elfer" with its rear-wheel drive and its clear line management became the epitome of a sports car, meanwhile built in the sixth generation. On the basis of the well-known basic shape, the current Porsche 911 Carrera consistently continues the visual language of the 911. The design follows the maxim of "clarity, tension and precision" with the aim to consistently continue this in all the car's details. Clearly defined forms and features combine with a taught and maximised tension of the surfaces and the gap lines. The designers of the Porsche 911 Carrera placed high value on the precise design of the visible surfaces, gaps and details. The overall image of the exterior is also characterised by deliberate contrasts: The wings are wide and create a contrast to the slim roof and doors. Further contrasts are formed by the geometrically designed headlights and rear lights with the independently shaped rear side windows and the hood gap. The most striking characteristic of the Porsche 911 Carrera's front is the arrangement of the lights with large main headlights and an extra front light unit with indicators and fog lights. From the side view the tension of the surfaces becomes apparent and especially from the back view the Porsche 911 Carrera has a powerful look. It has been designed consistently – in order to continue the 911 Carrera tradition successfully without leaving its clear lines.*

S GO 135

雅生・斯达克X单杆盥洗龙头，2005

Hansgrohe AG, Schiltach
Design: Philippe Starck,
Paris, Frankreich
www.hansgrohe.com

设计的力量——以丰富为原则。流水从不按规矩行事，它会尽可能的另辟新径。像亚马逊河与尼罗河这样的大河流，他们会以洪水的形式完全淹没一片地区，从而为自己创造新的生存空间。然而，现在的农田灌溉和堤坝建设，往往使得流水丧失了这种力量。阿瑟・斯达克X型单杆水龙头可调式盥洗台就是被设计用来模仿水流的这种不受束缚的力量，并且在设计过程中特意用“以丰富为准则”这一理念作为设计准则。这一可调式盥洗台的外形设计极富雕塑感，同时具有硬朗简洁的特征。铬合金制造的平坦光滑的表面与纯几何外形的水龙头浑然一体。盥洗台外表高贵且富有质感，这使得富有生气的水流与纯几何形状的外观形成了鲜明的对比。“以丰富为准则”这一理念在产品的制造品质上也有体现。高品质的磨光表面加以精确的边缘设计，将其基本部件都隐匿在里面的大气的水龙头设计看起来就好像是“悬浮于好似平川的盥洗台之上”。简洁的外形加以近乎“奢华”的表现形式，营造出一种生动迷人,充满戏剧性的氛围，同时这也是整个阿瑟・斯达克X系列产品的共同特点。而且，考虑到水的流动，盥洗台的设计还遵循了一种刻意的，但却十分得体的“丰富”原则。水流如同从岩石裂缝中涌出，倾斜而下流入洗脸池。这样一来，我们将会再一次真切地体验到用活水清洗这一洗浴的真正意义所在，这种体验甚至能被你真真切切地“握在手中”。

Designed power – abundance as a principle
Water does not obey rules. It looks for new ways with all its force. Large rivers such as the Amazon or the Nile constantly create new living spaces by flooding complete areas. As a result of cultivation and embankments water has often lost its force today. The design of the Axor Starck X single-lever washstand mixer attempts to model this aspect of water's ungovernable force and "abundance as a principle" has deliberately been chosen as a design maxim. The mixer has been designed with a sculptural and at the same time stark and reduced language of forms. The planar, smooth surface made of chrome corresponds with the pure geometry of the faucet body. The washstand mixer has a luxurious and uncompromising appearance – the organic aspect of water forms a contrast to the geometrical forms. Abundance as a principle is also reflected in the manufacturing quality. The surfaces have a high-quality finish with precise edges. The large faucet, which conceals its base, seems to "hover above the washstand like a plateau". The reduced language of forms and the expression of an "extravagant" abundance create a fascinating, dramatic tension, which is characteristic of the complete collection Axor Starck X. Also with regards to the flow of the water, the design of the washstand mixer follows the maxim of an intended, but nevertheless appropriate abundance. The water pours out in a wide gush like out of a rock crevasse into the washbasin. Thus, the ritual character of washing oneself with the life elixir water shall again become a conscious experience, which can be "grasped".

雅生·奇特里奥浴缸盥洗台组合
卫浴, 2003

Hansgrohe AG, Schiltach
Design: Antonio Citterio,
Mailand, Italien
www.hansgrohe.com

设计的各个方面。对于罗马人来说，洗浴是一种习俗。花时间好好地休息一下是他们日常生活重要的一部分。如今洗浴则变得更加重要了，因为它已成为我们放松身心最后的世外桃源。将欲望抛到九霄云外，远离周围环境中的嘈杂与喧嚣，人们在浴缸中能够重归宁静。在现代社会中，能够有属于自己的休闲时间已经成为一种"奢侈"。阿瑟·奇特里奥浴缸和盥洗台组合系列为我们设计了一个大面积的休闲空间。这种浴缸和盥洗台组合简化了盥洗和洗浴之间的转换，可以使之变得一气呵成，从而使盥洗和洗浴融为一体。这种自然的转换是通过延长浴池边缘并将盥洗台至于其上这种设计方式得以实现的。原来两种各自独立的要素被组合在一起，从而创造出一个集功能性与美观性于一身的全新的区域空间。这种奢华的表达方式同样明显的体现在材料的选择上，因为这种浴缸和盥洗台组合的另一个特点是材质体现出来的动态质感。它是由亚光聚合混凝土制成,这种材料表面质感柔和，因此，它与浴室通常所采用的其他表面富有光泽的材料有所不同，你尽可以舒适地仰卧于浴池之中，将肩膀靠在浴池的边缘，在65cm深的池水中尽情洗浴。黑色的盥洗台和它白色的底座与光滑的白色浴缸形成鲜明的对比，外表看上去很有陶土的质感。雅生·奇特里奥浴缸和盥洗台组合是一种全新的产品系列，相信这样的浴缸一定会为你尽情舒展身心提供一个好地方。

Dimensions of design. *For the Romans, the bath was an institution. It was part of daily life to take time to relax on a large scale. Today, the bath is more important than ever, since it is one of the last bastions of relaxation. Free from the demands, the daily hustle and bustle, and the noise of the environment one searches for calmness in the bath – having time for yourself and your body is the "modern luxury". The Axor Citterio bathtub and washstand combination creates a design of relaxation with large dimensions and newly interpreted transitions. As a combination of a washstand and a bathtub, this tub has reduced, flowing transitions. Washing and taking a bath merge into one action. This has formally been solved by an extended tub edge, on which the washstand sits. Two previously separate elements can be united and create a functionally as well as aesthetically newly dimensioned room. This interpretation of luxury also becomes evident in the choice of materials, because another important aspect of the bathtub and washstand combination is its kinaesthetic qualities. It is made of a matt shining polymer concrete (Christalplant). The material's surface feels soft and thus differs from the otherwise common high-gloss look, which often dominates bathrooms. You can comfortably lean back, rest your shoulders on the tub and take a bath in the 65cm deep water. The black washstand with its white insert forms an interesting contrast to the smooth white tub, which almost has a clay look. The Axor Citterio bathtub and washstand combination belongs to a new product class. The bathtub becomes the centre of the staging of the body.*

SIEMENS
c.cam
SIEMENS
c.cam
c.cam

c.cam SPECT 扫描仪, 2003

Siemens Medical Solutions USA,
Hoffman Estates, USA
Werksdesign
www.medical.siemens.com

服务于医师和患者的开放式设计。医疗场所的设计要遵循其自身的规则。由于这些场所的设计通常是与特殊情况联系在一起的，所以往往会让患者感到不适。因此，一个好设计的宗旨就是要达到形式、功能以及选材上的平衡，这体现在在日常的医疗活动中就是医师和患者在使用医疗器械时必须要感到舒适和从容。心脏SPECT摄影仪是用来检查心脏状况的，以往像这样的检查项目只可以在传统的病床上得以实施，而如今，这套检查设备加上它那经过精心设计，完全符合人体工程学特点的座椅则确确实实可以称得上是一项革新了。当座椅靠背处于垂直位置时，病人可以很舒适地坐上去，座椅倾斜度的可调节功能尤其适用于老人和不方便的患者。实际中，这样的设计不仅可以使医生的工作流程更加省时有效，同时还可以让患者有一种不受打扰被尊重的感觉。此外，医疗检查中更重要的一点是它的精确性。由于SPECT检查要花30分钟时间，其间患者可能会由于不适而移动身体，从而造成影像模糊。为了避免这种情况，让患者放松就显得至关重要。这套由摄影仪和座椅组成的设备不仅尺寸小，而且色彩亮丽。柔和的外形不仅使它外表看起来既开放又友好，而且也可以使患者能亲眼看见整个设备，摒弃了那种传统的，让人一看就会望而生畏的环形托台式的设计，这样有助于减少患者的焦虑及对密闭空间的恐惧。无论从哪一方面说，这都是医疗场所中的开放式的美学设计。

Open – design for physicians and patients
The design for medical spaces follows its own laws. Because design here is always part of an extreme situation, it usually is a discomfort for patients. An essential aspect of good design, thus, is the balance of form, function and material. In dealing with medical devices, both physicians and patients have to feel comfortable and at ease while using these devices in medical everyday life. The cardiac SPECT camera serves to examine the human heart. Since examinations like these have so far only been possible on conventional flat patient tables, now the design of this examination unit with its ergonomically well thought-out chair is a genuine innovation. When in the upright position, the chair allows for easy access for the patient. A tilting function is particularly helpful for the elderly and for ill persons. It makes the workflow more efficient in practice and, at the same time, gives the patient a sense of independence and dignity. A further important aspect in this context is the precision during the medical study. Since SPECT studies require up to 30 minutes, a relaxed patient position is important in order to avoid blurred images due to the patient moving when he or she feels uncomfortable. As an entity of camera and chair, the c.cam is designed with small dimensions and pleasant colours. Soft shapes yield an open and friendly appearance, making the unit also visually accessible for patients. The open design without the typically large ring gantry is less intimidating and helps reduce patient anxiety and claustrophobia. An open design – in all senses – for an adequate aesthetics in medical spaces.

单侧关节系统, 2004

Otto Bock HealthCare GmbH, Duderstadt
Werksdesign: Helmut Wagner, Alexander von Ascheberg
www.ottobock.com

自然式设计——远离行动障碍。矫形器的设计必须要符合特定的要求，它不仅要能够帮助使用者完成日常生活的动作，而且还要能恰当地满足他们各自特定的需要。矫形器的设计把其自身的设计概念直接传递到使用者的身上，从而使日常生活中设计与“机械辅助”的关系变得重要起来。另外，设计还会同样深刻地影响使用者对自己行动障碍的认知，但单侧关节支撑器可以通过自身的设计来改变使用者的这种认知。这种器械是专为有腿部肌肉病症的患者而开发的。自十九世纪六十年代开始就已经出现了类似的矫形器械，其部件可以根据个体需要进行调节。这种器械有效地提高了腿部肌肉乏力患者的行动能力，做到了功能与设计的和谐统一。它向我们证实了，卓越的功能与高品质的设计在现代整形外科技术中是可以得到完美结合的。该设计遵循了“极尽简洁”的原则，虽然深知设计这种关节支撑系统要以器械的安全性考虑为主，但单侧关节支撑器的开发者们却并不仅仅局限于把其安全性能做到最大化。其它的支撑器需要从两侧对关节施以支撑，与此不同的是，这种支撑器只须从单侧便可达到支撑作用，因此其设计也会有所不同。这种支撑器不但重量上更轻，同时比它的两侧支撑器前辈们具有更多的功能上的优势。它的纤细外形可以让使用者按自己的风格来打扮自己，这样的设计从某种程度上说，可以使具有行动障碍的人看起来更加大方自然。

Something natural – design without handicap. *The design of orthoses has to fulfil very specific demands, as it has to do with supporting the natural courses of motions and fitting the orthoses precisely according to the wearers' individual needs. The self-conception of the design is directly carried over to the users, exerting a significant influence on how these get along with such "mechanical aids" in everyday life. The design also has a large impact on how the wearer perceives him- or herself with their handicap. The unilateral jointsystem can also change perception through its design. It has been developed for people with unstable leg musculature. Since the 1960s there have been similar orthosis systems with individually adjustable modules. They provide people with unstable leg musculature with a higher mobility. The unilateral jointsystem adds a harmonious unity of function and design, thus showing, that high quality of function and design can go together in modern orthopaedic technology. The design follows the maxim of reduction. While known joint systems above all optimise the safety of the systems, the developer of the unilateral jointsystem wanted more than just maximum safety. In contrast to other systems, which support the joint from both sides, this joint system only needs a lateral support. Thus the design could also be altered. It is lighter and has many functional advantages compared to the bilateral predecessors. A slim design enables the wearer to dress in their personal style. Such a design can make the handicap somewhat more natural.*

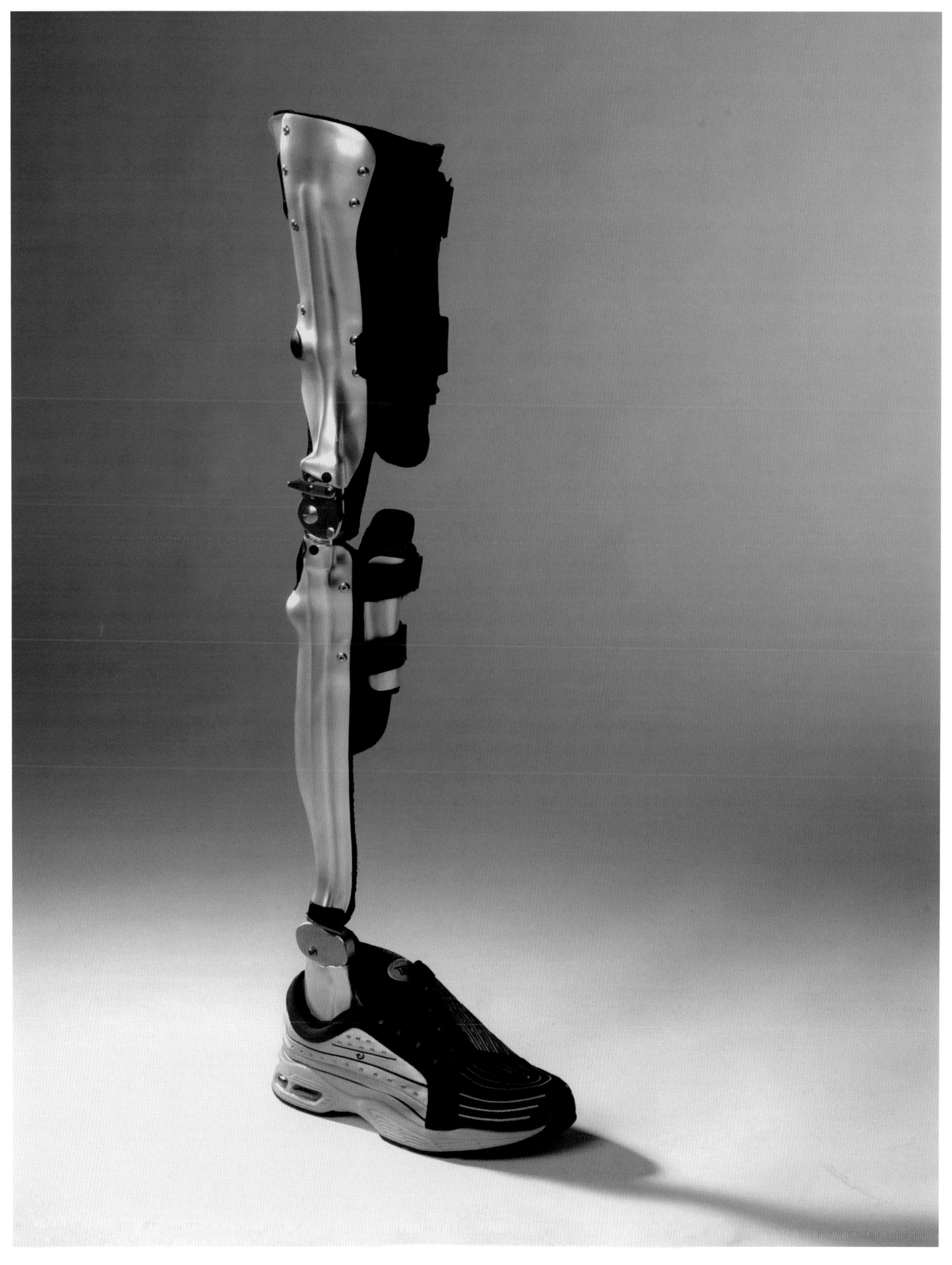

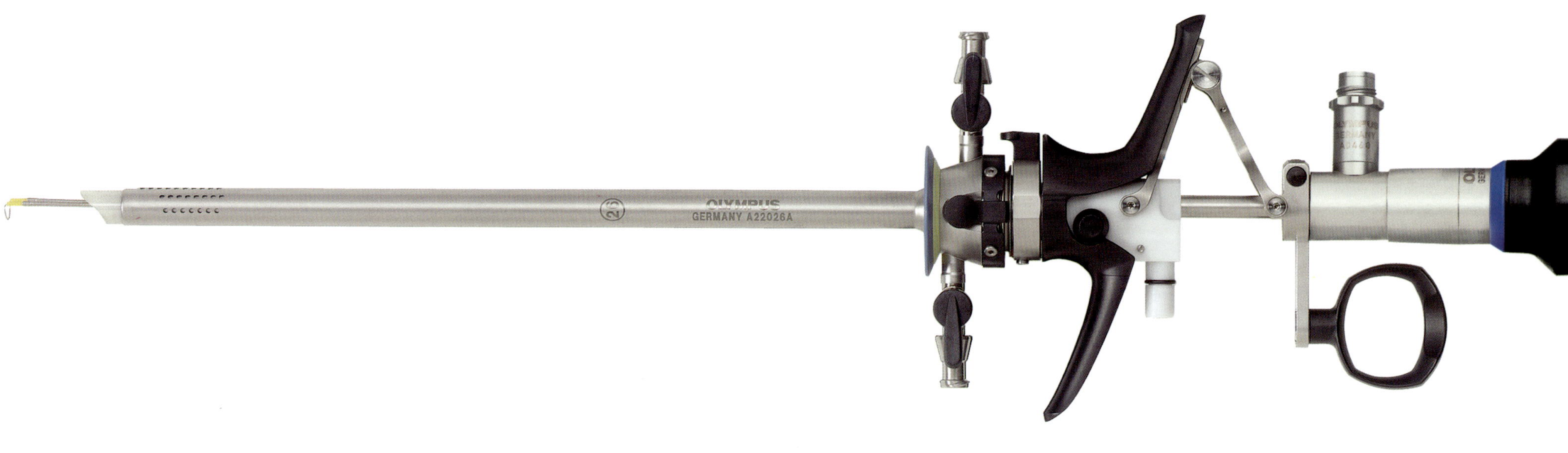
GERMANY A22026A

OES Pro-2 前列腺切除仪, 2005

Olympus Winter & Ibe GmbH, Hamburg
Design: Held + Team (Fred Held, Thomas Märzke), Hamburg
www.olympus-owi.com
www.heldundteam.de

精密。当征服者西班牙神父狄亚哥·迪兰达号令烧毁玛雅人有关于医疗知识方面的文献时，他们并没有意识到所烧毁的东西将会从此一去不复返。玛雅人是进行外科手术的大师。他们可以很熟练地进行高难度的手术。如今，在许多医疗领域中，"手工作业"仍然扮演者着重要的角色。其中的一个领域就是泌尿学中的前列腺肥大切除术。在这一手术过程中，医生会将前列腺重新切割，并用高频电线一点点使其变小。其间医生仅仅是用一根拇指来操纵前列腺切除仪。外观极具美感的OES Pro-2型前列腺切除仪的设计特点主要体现在它的中心拇指环上。这是因为合适的拇指环不会伤到医生的手，而医生只有在合适的拇指环的帮助下才能工作得更加出色。OES Pro-2型前列腺切除仪的拇指环有两种尺寸可供选择，所以它可以更好地根据使用者的拇指尺寸进行调节。无论手的尺寸如何，都可以很容易地接触到该仪器的操纵杆，这样就避免了手被困在手柄和操纵杆之间的情况。该设计突出了操纵杆的宽度和角度，从而使这套仪器操纵起来更为顺手。由于采用了全新的（而且兼容的）固定装置，OES Pro-2型前列腺切除仪的复杂程度和组装过程被大大简化了。所有的部件都可以通过一个固定装置连接起来，若想拆除的话则只需按一个按钮便可完成。装有按钮的部件包括：操纵手柄、传送器、光学镜以及电极。这种安装和拆卸方式尤为重要，因为它可以确保仪器的组装方式是正确的，从而保证仪器的可靠性和稳定性。

Delicate. *When the Spanish bishop and conqueror Diego de Landa ordered to burn the records on the medical knowledge of the Mayas, he did not know that he was destroying something irretrievable. The Mayas were masters of surgery and could skilfully perform highly complicated operations. Today, there are still many medical fields, in which "manual" work plays a great role. One of these fields is the resection of an enlarged prostate in urology. In this process, the prostate is redissected and made smaller in small steps with a high-frequency wire. The doctor operates the so-called resectoscope only with a thumb. The aesthetically appealing design of the OES Pro-2 resectoscope optimised this central thumb ring, because a doctor can work particularly well with a well-fitting thumb ring, which does not cause bruises. Thanks to the choice between two sizes, the OES Pro-2 thumb ring can be better adjusted to the thumb of the user. The instrument's handle is easily reachable for all hand sizes, thus avoiding the important problem of getting caught between the shaft and the handle. The design optimises the width as well as the angle of the handle and creates an instrument that operates particularly smoothly. The complexity of the OES Pro-2 and its assembly were significantly simplified by using new (but compatible) catch mechanisms. All elements can be connected by an automatic catch mechanism and disconnected by a pushbutton (shafts, transporting device, optics, electrodes). This is particularly important, because it ensures that the device is always assembled in the right way and thus reliable as well as durable.*

Sqr 网络织毯, 2004

Carpet Concept Objekt-Teppichboden GmbH, Bielefeld
Design: Carsten Gollnick, Berlin; Peter Maly, Hamburg
www.carpet-concept.de

三维编织技术：编织成形。Sqr使编织技术获得了新生。织毯外表朴实无华，乍一看并没有什么特别之处，可当你再一瞥的时候，会发现富于变化的毛束装饰使织毯更为美观。而这一效果的基础就是式样各不相同的丝线。经线和纬线相互交错，构成了织毯匀称结构的主要基调。笔直和卷曲的毛束装饰相互衬托，共同构成了雅致的地面装饰。这种设计集传统和创新于一体，使编织的艺术成为人们关注的焦点。由于毛束装饰以自己特有的方式改变了光线，所以光和影就好像从网格滤过一般。而且，织毯清晰的几何网格图案使得这种自然效果更加逼真。在交替变化的毛束装饰图案中的线条和正方形图案是这一设计的关键。Sqr基础是比较单调的，而Sqr细微差别则加强了交替变化的毛束与其亮丽色调之间相互映衬的效果。Sqr接缝技术则强调了网格与金属色泽的接缝在暗淡背景下的效果。统一的美学思想下的三种不同的表现形式在人们的家居中交相辉映。该设计力求简单，然而它对材料的准确运用却在外观上达到了一种意想不到的效果。通过缤纷的色彩，Sqr运用协调和对比两种方式突出了房间的内部效果。另还有不同的色调，包括经典的灰色和最近流行的夜蓝色、沙黄色、暖陶土色以及深褐色。

Three-dimensional weaving technique: weaving shapes. *Sqr revitalises the technique of weaving. The woven carpet makes a discreet appearance only revealing how special it is with a second glance. Varying tufts make for fine effects. And the basis of it all is different threads. In the network of warp and weft, the pile thread is supreme. It creates the tone for the rhythm of the structure. Straight and kinky tufts complement each other to form an elegant floor covering. They move the art of weaving into the limelight combining tradition with innovation. Light and shade appear to be filtered through a grid. Because the varying structures of the tufts vary the light in their own special way. A natural effect which is convincing in its clear geometric grid. Stripes and squares in the alternating tuft pattern are the key to this design. Sqr Basic is plain and Sqr Nuance intensifies the interplay of the alternating tuft pattern with fine shades of colour. Sqr Seam emphasises the grid with a metallic seam on a plain background. Three variations of consistent aesthetics which complement each other in any room. Minimalist in design, the delicate play of materials is surprising in its formality. The special colourfulness of Sqr highlights the interior with either harmony or contrast. The range includes classic grey tones and the latest night blue, shades of sand, warm terracotta and deep brown.*

妙韵音乐设备, 2004

Bose Corp., Framingham, USA
Werksdesign: Bose Corp. Design Team
Vertrieb: Bose GmbH, Friedrichsdorf
www.bose.de

迷宫中的电波——赋予声音以形状。Nada Brahma——世界即声音。由乔奇姆・恩斯特・贝伦特主持的德国广播节目在二十世纪八十年代着实掀起了一阵热潮，并被译成许多不同语言。主持人在节目中创造了一个声音的世界，在使人们听力变得更加敏锐的同时，也为人们带来前所未有的听觉体验。让声音变得直观，赋予声音以形状，这一直是设计历史上的一个重要课题。由博士公司设计制造的全新妙韵音乐设备是对其十年前开发的早期产品的重新诠释，但即使是在那时，该产品也已迅速跻身于高档产品之列。设计小巧美观的机身只有笔记本电脑大小，但它的声音效果可以与当时高保真音响相媲美。该产品在音质和设计上的创新是建立在一种叫做电波引导技术的基础之上的。这一技术使得人们在使用它时如同是在演奏一件体积小巧的乐器，其技术创意是经过多年研究所得出的结果：机体内置的中程和远程扩音器不仅向前方发出声音，而且还可以在机体内产生无线电波，这些电波会穿过一系列计算精确的，立体的通道所组成的迷宫，这样有利于将声音处理得更加有力和有节奏感，而且不会产生低音失真。现在的系统进一步优化了原来清晰的全面音质处理，并采用了两个最新开发的6.3厘米防磁全程控制单位，这样即使在高声量时也不会产生声音失真。这款设备秉承了时下流行的紧凑式设计，简单明了，操作简便，显现出它独特的魅力。大尺寸的显示器代替了原来前端的操作面板，使操作一目了然，更加方便，并且可以提供更多的设备信息。Wave音响设备优化了收音机/CD播放器的声音效果，同时，创造性地诠释了什么是“音箱”——即赋予声音以形状。

Waves in a labyrinth – giving shape to sound

Nada Brahma – the world is sound. The German radio feature by Joachim-Ernst Berendt had caused a real stir in the 1980s and was translated into numerous languages. The author had created a cosmos of sounds, presenting something that had never been heard before and which sharpened people's sense of listening. To make sound visible in design, giving it shape – this has also been a very important subject in the history of design. The new Wave Music System by Bose is a reinterpretation of a predecessor that had been developed ten years ago and which, back then, had quickly advanced to become a classic – the aesthetically designed small housing (with the basic measurements of a laptop) had featured a sound that until then had only been known from large hi-fi systems. The basis of this innovation both in terms of music quality and design is the so-called Wave Guide technology, which makes it possible to use a compact, very small housing in the same way as the corpus of a musical instrument. The basic idea of this technology is the outcome of many years of research: the sound of the two built-in mid-/high-range speakers does not only come straight out of the front, the speakers also generate air waves inside the housing. These waves are then guided through a labyrinth of precisely calculated and dimensioned channels. This allows for a powerful and dynamic sound reproduction without generating distorted bass. The current system optimises the clear and full-range sound reproduction even further, using two newly developed, magnetically shielded 6.3cm full-range drivers, capable of reproducing high-volume sound without any acoustic distortions. The design of the new system follows the well-known compact shape: it is appealing and user-friendly – with a simple and clear arrangement. The user interface at the front was replaced by a larger display that is easier to read, offering expanded text information. The Wave Music System optimises the sound of a radio/CD player and, simultaneously, creates an amazing interpretation of a "sound box" – giving a new shape to sound.

Spheros R 37 经典版 LCD电视机, 2004

Loewe AG, Kronach
Werksdesign: Loewe Design
Design: Phoenix Design, Stuttgart
www.loewe.de
www.phoenixdesign.de

Skulpturen der Kommunikation. Die ersten

媒体雕塑。人们常常把第一个电视当作家具来看待，对其爱护有加。因此，在二十世纪五十年代早期，对于要购买电视的人来说，电视表面抛光的颜色要比它整体的造型设计更加重要。时代变了，但人们的对电视机的热度依旧不减，与此同时却对电视机提出了更高的要求。现在,电视机的设计是购买的决定性因素。如今，一台“现代化”的电视机不仅要在外观上使人眼前一亮，还要有创新的技术，并且要和其设计达到和谐统一。Spheros R37经典版电视机的设计外观成功地与其技术融为一体。宽大的屏幕，加上覆盖了整个电视前端的一整块玻璃，使它具有引人注目的雕塑般的效果。电视机在细节设计上力求一致，在材料选择上也是如此：其材料均是采用玻璃及打磨后的铝片，从而使电视机的设计与技术上的创新相互协调，十分吸引眼球。然而，这一设计特点并没有使操作界面复杂化，反而使其更加变得简单明了。电视机的数字录像功能可以让使用者延时观看电视节目，电视机内置了一块可录制100个小时节目的硬盘，这使录制节目的过程变得非常简便。另一个技术创新是它的数码照片浏览功能，有了这一功能，使用者可以用观看幻灯片的方式浏览照片（如假日期间拍摄的照片）。Spheros R37 经典版电视机的设计使其看起来就好像是一座具有视觉信息沟通功能的雕塑。这座充满自信的雕塑与整个建筑融为一体，交相辉映。

Sculptures of communication. *The first television sets were carefully treated pieces of furniture. Therefore, in the early 1950s the colour of the finish was more important to the future owner than the overall design. Today, just like in the 1950s, the television is a cult object, but the requirements are completely different. Today, the design of the television set plays a decisive role. It is important for the design of a "modern" TV set to appeal to the emotions and implement innovative technologies in such a way that they harmonise with the design. The design of the Spheros R 37 Masterpiece TV set manages the difficult task of finding a form that is appropriate for its technology. A large screen has been combined with a sheet of glass, which covers the complete front of the set. This creates an interesting sculptural character. The design is consistent down to the details and as such is continued in the choice of materials, which are glass and brushed aluminium. The design aesthetically harmonises with the technical innovations. These do not overload the user interface; they are easy to operate and self-explanatory. The Digital RecorderPlus function allows deferred viewing of TV programmes. Due to the built-in hard drive with its 100-hour capacity programmes can be recorded easily. Another innovative feature is the Digital PhotoViewer with which slide shows can be created (e.g. of holiday photos). The Spheros R 37 Masterpiece has been designed like a sculpture of visual communication. This self-confident sculpture becomes part of the architecture – and interacts with it.*

苹果影院电脑, 2004

Apple, Cupertino, USA
Werksdesign: Apple Design Team
www.apple.com

办公桌上的影院——结构与外形的结合。 把显示器和主机结合在一起的设计在一时间，比比皆是。二十世纪九十年代，色彩多样、半透明的苹果电脑将显示器集成在一个设计小巧简洁的外壳之上。这对于苹果电脑来说绝对算不上什么新鲜事，但2004年这款机器再一次向我们证明了，电脑并不一定要局限于某种已知的外形——它的设计表现形式可以十分自由，也可以日新月异。苹果桌上影院系列包括三款：20英寸显示器，23英寸高清晰显示器和大尺寸的30英寸高清晰显示器。它们的设计与Power苹果电脑和Power Book苹果笔记本电脑的阳极氧化铝制外壳十分匹配。这些分辨率极高的显示器看上去简洁明快。由于这些显示器只包含有一块铝片，而且没有明显的底座，所以看起来没有什么重量。由于采用了轻薄式结构设计，所以几个显示器叠放在一起也不足为奇——这一特点在其他系列产品中也很重要。影院系列显示器的另一个创新是它功能卓越，操作灵活的折叶设计，这使得我们在不经意间就可以改变显示器的姿态。显示器设计的可视角度为-5度到+25度。影院显示器的操作界面和插件程序设计十分巧妙，简单明了，毫无累赘，其中最重要的操作部件都安置在屏幕的侧面，触手可及。电缆线安置在屏幕后方，使其有较大的走线空间。通过DVI接口，苹果影院系列显示器可以简便快捷地连接到其它个人电脑和笔记本电脑上，如苹果Power Book笔记本电脑，这样便形成了一种高度统一的外观表现形式。影院系列显示器的外观极具美感，设计集功能卓越和操作简便等特点于一身，并为电脑外形设计创造了一个新的形式。

Cinema for the desktop – of frames and forms. *Suddenly it was everywhere. In the 1990s, the translucent and colourful iMac integrated the screen in a compact and organically designed casing. This was definitely no novelty for Apple design, but it once again demonstrated that a computer is not necessarily defined by any known form – its design can be freely interpreted and can change completely from one day to the next. The Apple Cinema Display line consists of a 20-inch display, a 23-inch high-definition display and a very large 30-inch high-definition display. Their design matches the anodised aluminium casings of the Power Mac and the PowerBook. These extremely high-resolution displays have a fine and simple look. They appear to be almost weightless, because they consist of a single piece of aluminium without a visible mounting. Due to this very slim frame design several of these displays can be placed next to one another – an aspect that is important in many different types of work. Another innovative feature of the Cinema Displays is the functionally designed, smoothly operating hinge. With a hardly noticeable movement the monitor's position can be altered. The display design also creates a visibility angle ranging from –5 to +25 degrees. The Cinema Displays' interfaces and plug-ins are cleverly thought out; they are self-explanatory and reduced to the essentials. The most important operating elements are located on the side of the screen where they are easily accessible and the single cable at the back of the screen enables an elegant cable route. Via their DVI connector, the Apple Cinema Displays can be quickly and easily connected to other personal computers as well as mobile computers such as for example the Apple PowerBook. This results in an expression of an extremely consistent language of forms. The Cinema Displays have a fine aesthetic appearance, which is functional as well as self-explanatory. It creates a new framework for the form of a computer.*

Finder File Edit View Go Window Help
Mon 10:32 AM

HDR-FX1 HDV1080i-便携式摄像机，2004

Sony Corporation, Tokio, Japan
Werksdesign: Shin Miyashita
Vertrieb: Sony Deutschland GmbH, Köln
www.sony.net

精致。录影带是一种有趣而且十分受欢迎的传播方式。随着二十世纪七十年代传媒的发展和进化，与之相关的媒体存储技术也取得了长足的进步，出现了Beta-max、压V8、Hi-8以及DV等格式。现在的DV格式卡带可以进行分辨率的调整，这在二十世纪七十年代是不可想象的。HDR-FX1型摄像机是HDV1080i系列可兼容式数字高清家庭便携摄像机中的第一款可在DV卡带上进行录制和回放视频的摄像机。这一设计成果是在专业的工作室中，经过大量摄影设备实践所得出的。这款摄像机的大尺寸镜头、取景器和3.5英寸液晶监视器无一不在体现着它的功能卓越，操纵简单的设计特点。一次性压铸的镁合金外壳加上均匀的重量分配使摄像机的携带、运输和操作都变得更加容易。由于摄像机在录制高清晰画面时需要有稳固的支撑，因此便携式摄像机的电子取景器（EVF）并没有和其部件设计在一起，而是安置在手柄的后方。这样一来，即使是在拍摄长镜头时也可以将摄像机举起，舒适地进行操作。另一个方便使用者的设计是监视器的新位置：监视器被移至与手柄水平线相齐的顶端，这样使用者就可以在取景器和监视器里同时看到所录制的内容。监视器的角度可以调节，这样即便使用者在拍摄低角度镜头时也能够看到监视器。最常使用的功能键和操作键被尽可能地分开设置，这样就使得操作变得更加简便。摄像机机体和操纵杆上都分别设有录制的开始/停止键。而且手柄上另外有专为进行低角度拍摄而装配的镜头调焦操纵杆。作为一款分辨率极高的摄像机，HDR-FX1型摄像机的设计是“精致”的完美体现。

Well defined. *Video is an interesting and very popular means of communication. Parallel to the evolution and development of this communications medium in the 1970s, the development of relevant storage media also advanced, with formats such as Betamax, the compact Video 8, the Hi-8 and the DV format. The current format of the DV cassette allows resolution figures, which would have been unthinkable back in the 1970s. The HDR-FX1 is the first HDV1080i-compatible digital high-definition home video camcorder that allows recording and playback of high-definition videos on these DV cassettes. The design is the result of many experiences made in the operation of professional studio equipment. The functional as well as self-explanatory design focuses on a large objective lens, a viewfinder and a 3.5-inch LCD monitor. The die-cast magnesium housing together with the well-balanced weight distribution allow for easy handling, transport and operation. As a camera needs a firm support when recording high-definition images, the design of the camcorder separates the electronic viewfinder (EVF) from the main unit of the camera and places it behind the handle. Thus, the camera can be held and operated comfortably, even when shooting longer sequences. An additional user-friendly aspect of the design is the new position of the LCD monitor. It has been moved to the tip of the handle lever, enabling the user to view the recording through both the viewfinder and the LCD display simultaneously. The angle of this monitor is adjustable so that it can be seen even when doing low-angle shots. To facilitate the operation even further, the most commonly used function and operating buttons were isolated wherever possible. The start/stop button for recording is located not only on the camera itself, but also on the handle. This handle is additionally equipped with a functional zoom lever suitable for low-angle shots. As a camcorder with extremely high resolution, the HDR-FX1 is an expression of a "well-defined" design.*

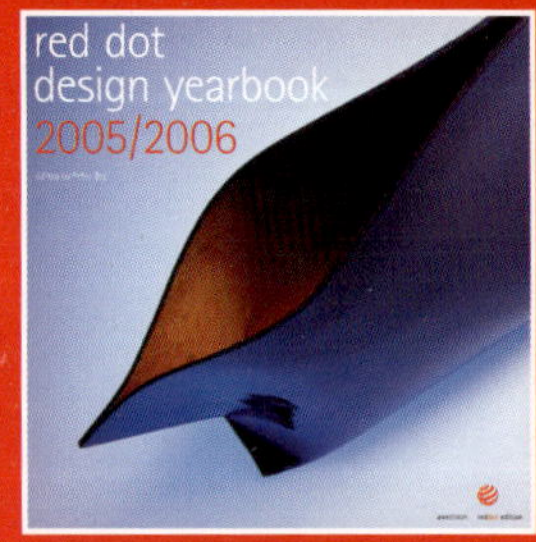

封面照片：由皮亚·明格斯拍摄的封面展现了伊塞尔哈根的博瑞公司的阿卡时包系列。由Kirsten Hoppert，SteffenKroll组成的Vertijet工作室设计。

*Cover Photo:
The photo by Pia Mingels shows an Akashi bag of the BREE Collection GmbH & Co. KG, Isernhagen, designed by Studio Vertijet (Kirsten Hoppert, Steffen Kroll) in Halle, Germany.*

Akashi 女士提包, 2004

BREE Collection GmbH & Co. KG,
Isernhagen
Design: Studio Vertijet
(Kirsten Hoppert, Steffen Kroll), Halle
www.bree.com
www.vertijet.de

必备品——极限造型。对手提包外形设计技巧的理解总是与社会传统和传统技术背道而驰。譬如，如今我们所熟知的色彩缤纷，款式多样的高级女士手提包最初是在1800年法国第一帝国时期出现的，那时的女士衣着已经变得更加贴身而且设计更加大胆。在英国，尤其在贵族阶层，人们把手提包称之为"必备品"。手提包之所以必备是因为它装有社交生活必备的所有物品，如扇子、镜子和名片。与制鞋业中的皮革加工业的历史相比，手提包制造业还是相当年轻的。然而，各式各样手提包的普及速度却要迅速得多。如今，手提包和人们所穿的鞋一样，成为了一种表现个人品味的方式。阿卡时手提包将高雅奢华，耐人寻味的外观表现形式与皮革加工的技术创新融为一体。在这款手提包的设计中，从制鞋业借鉴而来的众所周知的皮革成型技术扮演了重要的角色。皮革在拉紧状态下最后成型，然后进行粘合，这样，手提包的外观呈现出一种非同寻常的雕塑效果，而且几乎看不见任何接缝。之后，皮革经过打磨后表面色泽亮丽，并且富有质感的条纹对比色，使得这款手提包的外表尽显高贵气质，散发出独特魅力。这款手提包的设计，尤其是内置的提手设计，是制造商博瑞在造型语言上的大胆诠释。然而，对于阿卡时手提包来说，无论从造型、功能和美观效果上来说，它都在有意地挑战着极限，从而引领新的潮流。

The indispensables – shape to the limit. *The techniques of designing shape always have to be understood against the backdrop of traditions in society and craftsmanship. The classical female handbag as we know it today in its innumerable forms and colours, for instance, first appeared in the Premier Empire around 1800, when dresses became tighter and were designed less to conceal. In England it was called – particularly in noble circles – "The indispensable". Indispensable because the handbag contained all the things of so much importance for social life such as a fan, a mirror or name cards. Compared to the history of leather processing for shoe production, the history of the handbag is thus still quite young. Yet, its triumphant spread was much more rapid, and in the various forms, today handbags have become as much an important expression of individual taste as the shoes one wears. The Akashi bag merges a highly interesting and extravagant language of forms with innovation in leather processing. Well-known techniques of leather shaping that have been borrowed from shoe production played an important role in its design. The leather is brought into its final shape under tension and is then glued. The handbag, thus, receives an unusual shape of sculptural appearance with hardly any seams. The leather is then brushed to a bright lustre and lined with material of contrasting colour: this lends the bag an elegant finish and exclusive appeal. The design, in particular the inside-lying carrying handle, gives a daring interpretation of the language of forms by the manufacturer, BREE. Yet, the shape, function and aesthetics of the Akashi bag are consciously brought to the limit – in order to create something new.*

摩纳哥 V4 概念手表，2005

TAG Heuer, La Chaux de Fonds, Schweiz
Design: Ross Lovegrove, London, GB
www.tagheuer.com

机械运动的化身——一款精心设计的时间机器。这款曾经被演员史蒂夫·麦柯奎恩戴过的表看起来像七十年代的产品，大的方型外壳与神秘的名字——摩纳哥使这款表分外引人注目。这与七十年代因史蒂夫·麦柯奎恩而声名鹊起的一种风格类似——不落俗套、诚实可靠。但并不为大多数的崇拜者所知的是：这是世界上第一款的防水机械记时器，并配有小型旋转装置。摩纳哥V4这款概念手表继续本着不落俗套的真理，再一次以革命者自居，打破了传统的以齿轮为转动装置制表业的审美观。在传统制表业中，转动装置是齿轮，然而摩纳哥V4却从汽车世界里的传动带传送中找到了灵感来源。摩纳哥 V4的整个技术和体系都是受到了汽车引擎的启发，这款设计是制表业革新的一个代表。机械上的创新使摩纳哥 V4的所有设计部件可以被放置进它特有的表壳里面。最能引起人们兴趣的设计部分为人工三维制造的斜面切割的蓝宝石晶体，沿着一定的弧度镶嵌在外壳边缘。小小的秒针就停留在四时和五时中间。发条盒中的电桥放置在蓝宝石里面，这样在后面也可以看到手表里面的运转情况。整个摩纳哥V4的设计灵感来源于1969年制造的摩纳哥标志的启发，代表了一种独一无二的创新精神。在设计和技术上都表现出了对传统手表制造的彻底改变，标志着不受传统束缚的设计新纪元即将开始。

A personification of the mechanical movement – a designed timepiece.
Worn by the actor Steve McQueen it shaped the look of the 1970s. The chronograph with the big squared-off case and the mystic name "Monaco" stood out. It was synonymous with a style, which was immortalised by Steve McQueen in the 1970s – unconventional and faithful. And what was unknown to most of its admirers: it was the world's first water-resistant automatic chronograph equipped with a micro-rotor mechanism. The concept watch MONACO V4 continues to act on a maxim of the unconventional and again acts as a guarantor for revolutionary innovations breaking the foundations of traditional watch making aesthetics. The traditional dynamics of the movement is transmitted by gears. The MONACO V4 though uses drive-belt transmission borrowed from the automotive world. The entire technology and architecture of the MONACO V4 has been inspired by car engines. The design is an expression of innovative watch making. The mechanical originality it houses shapes the entire design of the MONACO V4. The most intriguing design component is the bevelled sapphire crystal, manufactured in 3D, curving down to join the sides of the case. The small second hand is between four and five. The barrel bridges are in sapphire, allowing the movement to be visible from below. The overall design of the MONACO V4 is inspired by the iconic MONACO created in 1969 and represents a unique form of innovation. Design and technology signal a specific break with conventional watch making. Design without conventions for a new era.

MONACO V4
TAG HEUER
TAGHeuer

PORSCHE DESIGN

P'8404 保时捷镜架设计, 2005

Rodenstock GmbH, München
Design: Peter Kövari, München
www.rodenstock.de

审美观的转变。在奥黛丽·赫本和詹姆斯·迪恩之前的时代里，太阳镜就一直是时尚配饰的潮流引导者。然而，它们却不仅仅是具有装饰作用的时尚配饰；其主要作用是保护眼睛，防止阳光及紫外线和防风，正是这些才使眼镜成为真正的功能性产品。P'8404钛制太阳镜的设计理念完全符合时下的潮流转变。这就是说，时尚的太阳镜不仅要佩戴舒适，为眼睛提供良好的保护，更重要的是，它还须有美观时尚的外型。P'8404钛制太阳镜借助运动太阳镜的设计风格，眼镜的前部呈弯曲状，这样可以使眼镜具有足够的宽度来贴合脸形，使眼睛不受风沙及阳光的侵袭，从而提供最理想的保护。镜架由钛金属制成，这样会使太阳镜变得非常轻，并且耐腐蚀，同时还能够使那些对镍金属敏感的人不会再过敏。此外，特殊的钛合金具有极好的弹性，这一点使其成为眼镜设计领域的重要创新；镜片的安装采用了新的工艺：在一边不安装镜框的情况下，具有弹性的轮廓特性的太阳镜安装时仅仅需要考虑其整体的外部形状，P'8404太阳镜的美学表达完全符合这种功能上的创新；像丝带一样的安装部件的选取和接下来的其他步骤会根据耳朵和鼻梁的形状来设计，再与曲线的镜片相结合，使眼镜的外观给人以紧实感及简约感，从而完美地体现出保时捷设计品牌的高质量和精益求精。

Aesthetic crossover. *Before even Audrey Hepburn and James Dean, sunglasses had long been trendsetters in the accessory industry. However, they are not merely a decorative fashion article; their importance in eye protection against direct sunlight, UV radiation and wind makes them a true performance product. The P'8404 titanium sunglasses are designed to meet this current crossover trend. This means that modern sunglasses not only have to meet the highest requirements of comfort and protection, it is essential that they also look sporting and performance-oriented. The curvature of the front, borrowed from sports glasses design, makes it possible to keep the full width of the glasses close up to the face, giving optimal protection for the eyes against wind and sun. The use of titanium in the frames make the sunglasses extremely light, completely corrosion-resistant and antiallergenic for people who are nickel-sensitive. Moreover, the use of a special titanium alloy with excellent spring characteristics has made possible one of the most important innovations: the fixation of the glasses follows a new principle, with a one-side open, elastic profile fixing the glasses only on their exterior contours. The aesthetic expression of the P'8404 sunglasses is closely linked to this functional innovation: the ribbon-like character of the fixing elements is picked up and consistently followed in the design of the earpieces and nose bridge. This, in combination with the toric glass surfaces, produces a certain tightness and reduction of form that perfectly reflects the high-quality technical profile of the Porsche Design brand.*

Birkenstock Birki Pro / Birki 休闲鞋, 2004

Birkenstock, Novato, USA
Design: fuseproject (Yves Behar, Eskil Tomozy, Shawn Sinyork), San Francisco, USA
www.birkenstock.com
www.fuseproject.com

没有粗糙鞋边的"佩花嬉皮士"休闲鞋。
木屐是七十年代的产物。这种鞋是一种简单的，有一大块木头底的鞋，但它的外观却有数不清的变化：有花朵图案的，有牛仔布样式的还有用真正的鹿皮制成的。它们看起来非常酷，似乎完全来自老嬉皮士时代，那时的人穿着色彩鲜艳的，满是补丁的衣服。这种特别的鞋的形状很古老——想必肯定是受到了一些荷兰木屐的启发。Birkenstock Birki Pro是这种很有名的鞋子的一个有趣代表，鞋子采用了一体化设计，没有缝合的部分，没有多出来的鞋边，没有缝纫线和粘合面，而拥有这样精巧功能的木屐是为外科医生，护士或者厨师等需要长时间站立的人群而设计的。鞋里侧面的空隙可以保持脚的干爽，前足部分设计可以防止落下的物品砸到脚上，或是撞到桌子脚或其他障碍物上，由于这种鞋没有缝隙或是粘合表面，所以很容易清洗。此外，人体工程学也被考虑了进去，流线型鞋垫的设计可以很好地适应脚的形状。在鞋外面和底部有个特别的蜂巢结构可以适当地增大或缩小，就算是在光滑的表面上也可以找到一个稳定的支点。此外，有凹槽的鞋底可以把水排向两边——这个原理与汽车轮胎原理一致。Birkenstock Birki Pro与Birki休闲鞋重新诠释了当代制鞋业中著名同时又是古老的鞋子，它把设计新颖的外形，高度的实用性和人体工程学因素牢牢的结合在了一起，既是对古老样式的怀念，又是当代风格的体现。

Flower power without any rough edges
Clogs are a child of the 1970s. These shoes, simple slippers with a big wooden sole, have appeared in innumerable variations: with flower patterns, in jeans style or with genuine buckskin. They were cool and have always looked as if they came straight from the old hippies times when people wore colourful clothes and patchy overalls. And yet, the shape of this particular shoe is very old – the Dutch wooden clog certainly is only one of its many predecessors. The Birkenstock Birki Pro are an interesting interpretation of this well-known type of shoe. They are made out of just one piece – they have neither hinges, edges, seams nor bonding surfaces. The clogs with their sophisticated functionality are designed for the target groups of medical physicians, nurses or cooks, and they combine many features for people who are up on their feet all day long. Lateral air ducts keep the feet cool and dry – the reinforced forefoot section protects from falling objects, bumping into table legs or other obstacles. Due to their construction without seams or bonding surfaces, the shoes are easy to clean. Ergonomics also played a major role. Due to their design with a flowing foot cushion, the shoes smoothly adapt to the shape of the foot. A special honeycomb structure at the outer and bottom side of the shoe, alternately growing and waning, provides a firm grip even on slippery surfaces. Furthermore, the grooved tread profile clears water away to the sides – a principle similar to that of a proper car tyre. The Birkenstock Birki Pro and Birki Clogs reinterpret a well-known – and original – shoe form in contemporary style, giving it new interesting features and a high degree of well-designed functionality and ergonomics.

线状台灯, 2004

Artemide Group S.p.A.,
Pregnana Milanese, Italien
Design: Ora-Ïto
Vertrieb: Artemide GmbH, Fröndenberg
www.artemide.com

最简洁的线条。灯光决定了空间，如果设计的好的话，光源也会成为房间里的一道风景线。线形台灯就像一条自由穿梭的丝带，在房间里蜿蜒而过，最终落在了在桌面上。它最大限度地遵循一贯的简约风格，并凭借其丝带般的外形成为房间的一个生动要素。这种强烈而生动的效果由于桌灯自身的简约和有如数学般的理性之美而给人们留下了非同寻常的第一印象。一线式台灯结合了意大利阿特米德众多产品的优秀传统，其中包括米歇尔・德・卢基的著名设计Tolemeo和理查德・萨帕在七十年代的经典之作——低压卤灯。法国新锐设计师欧若依图设计的这款一线式台灯的一个创新之处在于它把光源定位在台灯的上臂上。这种新型灯光系统结构轻巧、高效低温，视觉冲击力很强，并可适应不同的光线环境。设计的另一个奇特之处体现在那从灯臂上微微突出一点的灯头设计，当点亮灯时，线条优美的边缘也会泛出红光。由于配有功能夹，一线式台灯甚至可以安装在非常狭小的空间内——非常节省书桌上的空间。

Lines of minimalism. *Light defines a space, and with a good design, the source of light becomes an important part of a room. The One Line table lamp appears like a ribbon, moving freely throughout the room, only to "settle down on the tabletop eventually, after several windings." It follows the design maxim of consistent minimalism and becomes a graphic element in the room due to its ribbon-like form. At first glance, this strong graphic image is quite unusual because it is entirely unpretentious and almost "mathematic" in its aesthetics. The One Line table lamp, thus, joins the tradition of many lamps by Artemide, which all create an unusual impression at first sight. Among these lamps are the well-known Tolomeo by Michele De Lucchi, and not to forget the low-voltage halogen lamp Tizio by Richard Sapper, another design classic since the 1970s. Another innovative element of the One Line table lamp by the designer Ora-Ïto is the positioning of the source of light in the upper arm of the lamp. A new Task Light System combines a compact construction with a good light efficiency and a low operating temperature. The system offers a strong visual effect and adapts itself to different light surroundings. Another aesthetically interesting component is the lamp head, designed with a fine edge lighting up in red and slightly extending beyond the edge of the arm. With a functional clamp, the One Line lamp can be mounted even in very tight spaces – saving a lot of space on the desk.*

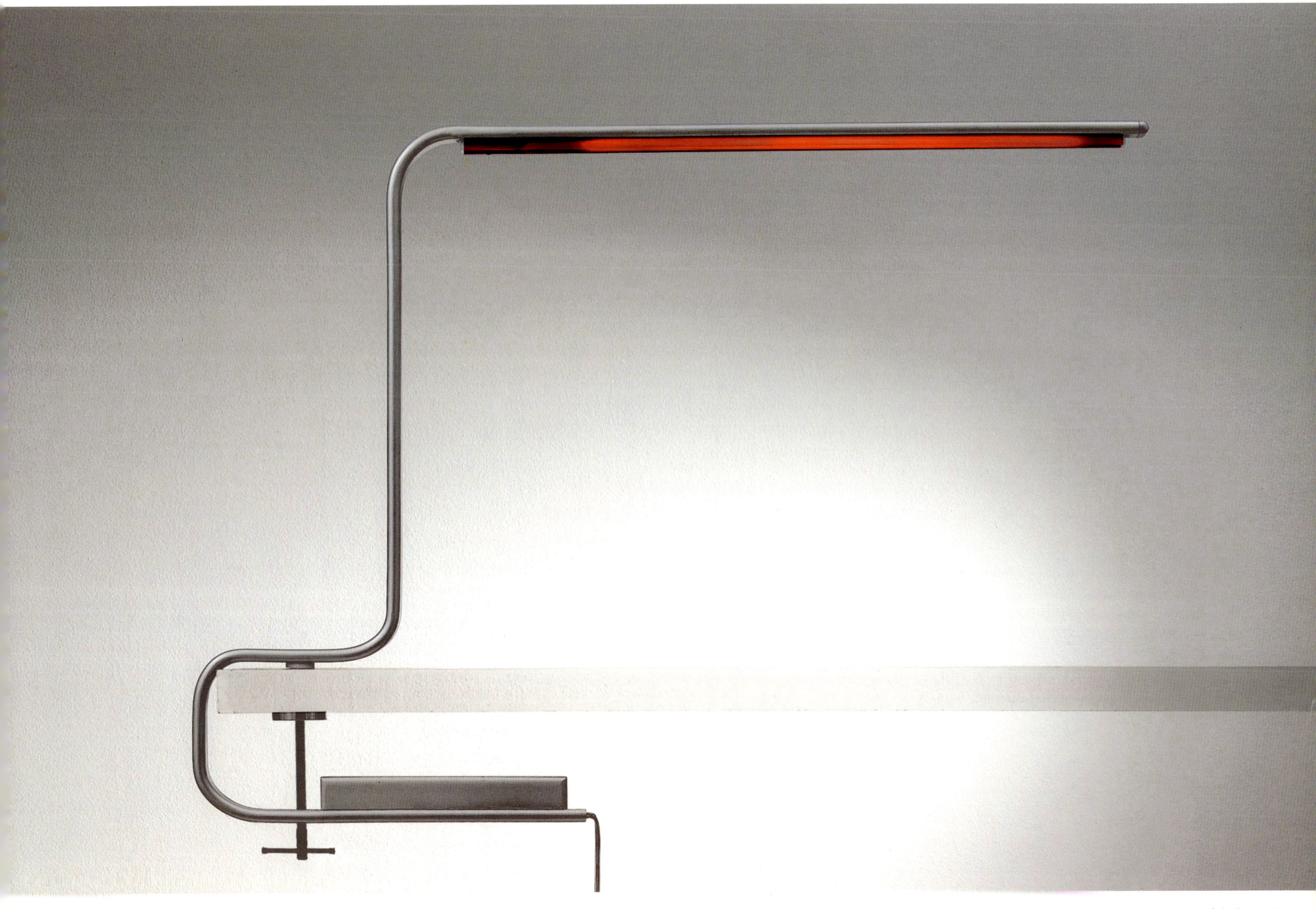

海鸥吊灯, 2004

Artemide Group S.p.A.,
Pregnana Milanese, Italien
Design: Jean-Michel Wilmotte
Vertrieb: Artemide GmbH, Fröndenberg
www.artemide.com

和谐之美。鸟类的翅膀充满了神秘的气息，这可能是因为它传达出一种想感受辽阔天空的愿望。在希腊神话“戴达勒斯与伊加勒斯”中，主人公利用蜡和羽毛制成翅膀，成功地逃出了克里特岛上的迷宫。这个故事强烈的表现了人想要与自然和谐相处的欲望。在设计家们看来，鸟翼的模型十分有趣，构造完美，比例和活动装置都无与伦比。海鸥吊灯的头部呈现鸟翼的形状，这种设计有利于光线传播，使光线可以均匀地分散在整个灯头表面而不会造成阴影。因此，它所投下的光线和谐而有动感。在灯的上部，自然地形成一个可以包含光源的开口，便于维修，同时也体现了产品把照明功能与整个空间融为一体的特点。可以说，哪里需要柔和流动的光线，哪里就有海鸥灯具。这款灯具的设计理念是以对称，同时又是不对称为特点的，并通过各种元件的搭配组合营造出多变的光线布局和情调。海鸥灯具通过借鉴鸟翼的模型而成功实现了创新，突出了照明的美学效果，和谐地照亮了整个空间。因此，这款灯毫无疑问地拓展了设计的创意空间。

Wings of harmony. *Birds' wings do have something mystical. A possible explanation for this could be the image they convey – the desire to experience the vastness of the horizon. The Greek myth of Daedalus and Icarus – the escaping like a bird out of the Cretan labyrinth with wings made of wax and feathers – is a highly potent image of this desire for harmony with the elements. For the design, the model of a bird's wing is also interesting, since it is perfectly well constructed; unsurpassed in its proportions and mechanisms of action. The head of the Mouette pendant lamp is designed in the shape of a bird's wing. It is made of one single piece of polypropylene, manufactured in a rotary die-cast process. This kind of design optimises light emission; it is dispersed evenly and without shadows over the entire surface of the lamp head. The lamp, thus, casts a harmonic and flowing light. In the upper part, the lamp is designed with an opening that contains the source of light. This allows easy and unproblematic maintenance, an important feature considering that the Mouette lamp was conceived for the illumination of work and communal spaces. The lamp is used in all those spaces where an even, flowing light is in demand. The concept of the Mouette lamp features a symmetric as well as an asymmetric version, and by combining a number of units the lamp can create various lighting compositions and moods. The Mouette lamp adapts the exemplary model of a bird's wing to realise new innovative and aesthetic results in lighting and to illuminate spaces in a harmonious way – thus, the lamp certainly does expand the horizon of design.*

红点奖：精品中的精品——获奖设计师
The best designers of the "red dot award: product design"

在“红点奖：产品设计”中，只有极少数具有卓越设计水平的产品能在评审团严格的评选标准中脱颖而出。每类产品中仅有三件会被提名，并通过民主投票的方式确定其最终结果。只有那些兼具独特个性与大胆创新的设计会最终赢得令人羡慕的“红点奖：精品中的精品”。以下是产品相关人员、设计者和设计团队的传记、自叙和照片。

In the "red dot award: product design" the jury reserves *the distinction of highest design quality for only a very few products. It can nominate three products from each product group for this award. The final selection is then made by democratic vote. Only design with excellent characteristics and maximum innovation receives the coveted "red dot: best of the best" award. The people behind these products, the designers and design teams complete with biographies, statements and photos, are presented in the following pages.*

设计师“红点：精品中的精品”

The designers of the “red dot: best of the best”

钻石桌子
Diamond tables

帕特丽夏・乌古拉
Patricia Urquiola

帕特丽夏・乌古拉出生于西班牙的奥维耶多，现在米兰居住和工作。她曾就读于马德里理工学院和米兰理工大学的建筑学院，并于1989年毕业。从1990年到1996年，她曾分别给米兰理工学院和巴黎国立高等工业设计学院的阿基利・卡斯蒂利奥尼和贝提内里当过助教；与此同时，她还和维科・马吉斯特提一起为帕多瓦的新产品开发办公室研究开发了"花"、"织布机沙发"、"轻便马车"以及"轻便马车长沙发"等新产品。从1996年到2000年，她一直在协助丽松尼事务所的设计小组工作。2001年，乌古拉在米兰创立了她自己的工作室，涉及产品设计、展位和展示厅陈列以及建筑等诸多领域。她的作品曾多次在设计展览和个人展览中被展示。2003年，她赢得了德国科隆"最佳体系奖"，获得了芝加哥雅典娜博物馆的优秀设计奖，并被爱乐装饰国际设计大奖赛评选为年度最佳设计者。此外，乌古拉还在众多院校和机构进行演讲，这些学校包括马德里理工学院建筑学院，芬兰的赫尔辛基阿尔瓦・阿尔托研究院，澳大利亚的设计博览会、悉尼家具展以及意大利米兰多莫斯设计学院等。2003年，她被任命为西班牙瓦伦西亚XIX CDIM设计大赛的评审团主席，并担任了2004年德国科隆国际家具展览会设计大赛的评委会成员。

乌古拉谈"美学与设计"

设计——指的是设计能够在实用的同时具有明确的一致性。我曾经尝试着给它一个广义的概念和一个纯粹的理解，不把一个设计作品看成是一个承载了一系列动作的容器，而是把它看成是包含了一定美学因素的社会价值的体现。我喜欢使用能定义空间的符号。设计使得不同概念间的交流变得顺畅、丰富，是通过视觉表现来达到的快乐的研究，并吸收了各种各样的色彩、形式以及人体工效学的理论。

Patricia Urquiola, *born in Oviedo, Spain, lives and works in Milan. She attended the Faculty of Architecture at the Madrid Polytechnic and at the Milan Polytechnic, where she graduated in 1989. From 1990 to 1996, she was assistant professor in the courses given by Achille Castiglioni and Eugenio Bettinelli both at the Milan Polytechnic and the ENSCI in Paris. Simultaneously she developed new products for De Padova and, together with Vico Magistretti, signed her name on the products "Flower," "Loom Sofa," "Chaise," and "Chaise Longue." From 1996 to 2000, she coordinated the design group at Lissoni Associates. In 2001, Patricia Urquiola opened her own studio in Milan in the fields of product design, booth and showroom display as well as architecture. Her works have been shown in several design and personal exhibitions. In 2003, she won the prize "Best System," Cologne, Germany, received the Good Design Award from Chicago Athenaeum, and was elected "Designer of the Year" by Elle Decoration International Design Award. Patricia Urquiola holds lectures at universities and academies, including the Faculty of Architecture at the Madrid Polytechnic, the Alvar Aalto Academy in Helsinki, Finland, as well as at the designEX COMFIA in Australia and the Domus Academy in Milan. In 2003, she was assigned Chair of the Jury of the XIX CDIM Design Award, Valencia, Spain, as well as Member of the Jury of the design award of "imm cologne," Germany in 2004.*

Patricia Urquiola on "Aesthetics and Design":

Design is design solutions that are functional but at the same time with a defined identity. I tried to create a multidimensional concept and a filtered perception. Reading the project as not being a container of actions, but rather as a social value with an aesthetic proportion. I like to use signs that could define the space. An idiomatic richness that enables communication between different concepts. A research for pleasure through visual perception. Absorbing colours, forms, ergonomics.

板式组合储物架
platten_bau shelving system

弗罗瑞恩·佩特里
Florian Petri

弗罗瑞恩·佩特里出生于1973年，曾学过木工，随后他来到德国达姆施塔特应用美术大学以及阿姆斯特丹的学院学习工业设计。自2002年取得文凭以后，弗罗瑞恩·佩特里就一直在一些设计工作室工作，像7.5工作室及Vogt+Weizenegger设计工作室。在这期间，他自己也完成了一些设计方案。他参与过的设计方案包括为赫门曼·米勒设计的“Mirra”办公室椅子，在7.5工作室进行的各种研究，以及在Vogt+Weizenegger设计室进行的“A计划”SINTER-CHAIR等等。从2003年起，弗罗瑞恩·佩特里开始在Kaether Weise家具公司从事设计工作。他的作品platten_bau储物架最早在2004年德国科隆国际家具展览会中展出。

弗罗瑞恩·佩特里谈“房间设计”

房间应满足在房间内居住和工作的人的需求。光这一点就已经很清楚的说明了房间必须呈多样化。

Florian Petri, *born in 1973, trained as a cabinetmaker and, subsequently, studied industrial design both at the University of Applied Arts in Darmstadt, Germany, and at the Gerrit Rietvald Academy in Amsterdam. After receiving his diploma in 2002, Florian Petri has been working, alongside personal projects, for design studios such as Studio 7.5 and Vogt + Weizenegger. He was involved in projects such as the office chair "Mirra" for Herman Miller as well as in various studies (Studio 7.5) and the "Plan-A" SINTERCHAIR (Vogt + Weizenegger). Since 2003, Florian Petri has been working for the furniture company Kaether & Weise. The shelf system "platten_bau" was first shown in 2004 at the "imm cologne," Germany.*

Florian Petri on "Designing Rooms":

Rooms should always meet the demands of the people who live and work in them. This alone makes it clear how varied rooms have to be.

多面体扶手椅
Facett upholstered furniture

罗南·蒲胡莱克与伊万·蒲胡莱克兄弟
Ronan und Erwan Bouroullec

罗南·蒲胡莱克与伊万·蒲胡莱克兄弟分别于1971年与1976年出生于法国的坎佩尔。在从国立装饰艺术学院毕业后，罗南就开始独立工作，并在弟弟伊万的协助下不断取得进展。那个时候的伊万还只是一个就读于赛尔齐－蓬多瓦兹艺术学院的学生。自1999年以来，他们两个兄弟就一直一起工作着。两兄弟互为一体，团结一致，为了共同的目标而奋斗，这种合作精神一直为人们所津津乐道。他们的作品曾经在很多的展览会上展示过，其中包括“2002年伦敦设计博物馆”和2004年6月的洛杉矶“当代艺术博物馆”。他们的作品还是一些博物馆永久性收藏品的组成部分，其中包括纽约现代艺术博物馆，巴黎的国立近代美术馆，　蓬皮杜中心以及葡萄牙里斯本设计博物馆。在以“Createur de l'Annee”命名的2002年法国巴黎巴黎家具展上，他们赢得了诸如the Grand Prix du Design de la Ville de Paris, 1998年的法国圣德田双年展的一等奖，以及1999年纽约国际家具博览会的设计新人奖等多种奖项。2003年，他们被日本爱乐装饰评选为年度最佳设计者。

罗南·蒲胡莱克与伊万·蒲胡莱克兄弟谈多面体系列

对于多面体系列概念的理解主要有两种方向：第一种关心的是结构和舒适感，这是一种有泡沫做成的材质，它没有任何可以看见的结构或根基，从而保证了座位的灵活性和柔软度，并使坐上的人感到很舒适。另一种方向的理解与泡沫体的覆盖有关，我们发明了一种垫罩，这种垫罩需要一定的缝纫，打摺以及样式设计的实际技能。而这种材质就是上述两种理解方向的论述结果。

Ronan and Erwan Bouroullec *were born in Quimper, France, respectively in 1971 and 1976. As soon as Ronan graduated from the École Nationale des Arts Décoratifs, he began working alone, progressively assisted by his brother Erwan, who at that time was still a student at the École des Beaux-Arts of Cergy Pontoise. The two brothers have been working together since 1999. Their collaboration is a constant dialogue, nourished by their single identities and striving towards a common goal. Their works have been on display in many exhibitions, including the London Design Museum in 2002 as well as the Museum of Contemporary Art in Los Angeles in June 2004. Their works are also part of some permanent museum collections, including the New York Museum of Modern Art, the Musée National d'Art Moderne, Centre Georges Pompidou in Paris, and the Lisbon Design Museum. Named "Créateur de l'Année" at the Salon du Meuble de Paris in 2002, they won multiple awards such as the Grand Prix du Design de la Ville de Paris and the First Prize of Saint-Etienne Biennale in 1998, as well as the "New Designer Award" of the International Furniture Fair in New York in 1999. In 2003, they were elected "Designer of the Year" by Elle Decoration in Japan.*

Ronan and Erwan Bouroullec on the Facett collection:

There have been two main directions for the concept of the Facett collection. The first one is concerned with structure and comfort. It is a collection made from foam, without any visible structure or feet. This gives great flexibility and softness to the seats and creates comfort. The second one is related to the covering of the foam body. We developed a padded cover that required some know-how in terms of sewing, pleat and pattern. The collection is the result of a discourse between these two directions.

Varino II 可变式厨具收纳组合
Varino II variable organisation system

托马斯·瑞特
Thomas Ritt
蒂诺·多普勒
Tino Töppler

托马斯·瑞特，1960年生。毕业于德国基尔艺术和设计高等专业学院工艺设计系。自1998年起，他就参加了一些志愿性质的图文和产品设计项目，其间与基尔的莱蒙设计公司一起获得了系统构建专利证书。1990年以后，托马斯·瑞特在艾贝克的开始了第一份工作，在那儿，他获得了些许奖励。1996他成为德国图林根的约若公司的开发部主管。1997年之后又到德国瓦伦多夫的Miele and Cie. KG，Die.Kuche公司当设计开发部的主管。他致力于设计语言系统化、产品品牌集中、产品政策协调方面的工作，而且已经获得了一些设计奖项。

蒂诺·多普勒，1972年生。于1989至1992年间学习机械艺术生产和修整，在接下来的一年里从事该专业的工作。1997至2000年，他在德国希尔德斯海姆的应用艺术学院学习工业设计，并且在2000年以工业设计师的身份参加了汉诺威Formfursorge的动手实践培训，凭借go-cart的设计理念，他的作品Muscle-Cart于2001年度在“ 幸运一击”设计师大赛中获得了特别奖，同年，他作为工业设计师进入布伦瑞克的厄尔根设计公司从事项目设计工作。2002年之后，他在德国瓦伦多夫的Miele and Cie.KG.Die.Kuche公司当工业设计师。

托马斯·瑞特和蒂诺·多普勒坚持直线型设计的成功原则：

成功源自于在充满竞争的市场中对自身明确的定位。米勒公司以直线型设计为公司宗旨，近百年来一直关注其产品的导向和市场对产品的要求。Vorino第二代产品仍然秉承这一宗旨，积极地减少了一些重复的部件，使其组合发挥出最大的功用来。这恰好明确地体现出直线的设计理念。

Thomas Ritt, *born in 1960, graduated in technical design at the Muthesius-Hochschule in Kiel, Germany. Since 1988, he had been working on free projects in graphic and product design, including a patent for a set-up system with Lemon Design in Kiel. From 1990 onwards, he made his first work experiences at Kubus Produktdesign in Einbeck, for which he received several awards. In 1996, he headed the Development Department at Zeuro GmbH in Thüringen. Since 1997, Thomas Ritt has been Head of the Design and Development Department at Miele & Cie. KG, Die Küche, in Warendorf, Germany, working on the systematisation of the design language, the focussing of the product brand and the coordination of the product policy, for which he received several design prizes.*

Tino Töppler, *born in 1972, trained in mechanical artwork production/retouching between 1989 and 1992, followed by a year of working in the profession. Between 1997 and 2001, he studied industrial design at the University of Applied Arts in Hildesheim, Germany, and during that time, in 2000, he also pursued a hands-on training as industrial designer at Formfürsorge in Hanover. For his go-cart design, the "Muscle-Cart," he received special approval at the Lucky Strike Junior Designer Award 2001. The same year saw his project-oriented work as an industrial designer at ergon.design in Braunschweig. Since 2002, Tino Töppler has been working as an industrial designer for Miele & Cie. KG, Die Küche, in Warendorf, Germany.*

Thomas Ritt and Tino Töppler on
"The Straight-line as Success Principle":
Success begins with a clear positioning within the competitive market. Miele with its straight-line Corporate Mission has been focussing for more than one hundred years on the direction of their products and their claim on the market. The Varino II also is designed to translate this mission. It is positively reduced to a few, recurrent elements, which in their combinability produce a maximum of use, constituting a clear straight-line product language.

Hansacanyon 单柄盥洗龙头洗手盆
Hansacanyon one hole basin mixer

莱茵哈德・亚茨克
Reinhard Zetsche
伯诺・萨阔博士
Dr. Bruno Sacco

莱茵哈德・亚茨克，1963年出生于德国的法兰克福，1999年创立了八爪鱼品牌。他生活在慕尼黑，服务于国际客户。八爪鱼品牌系列产品在同类产品中脱颖而出，曾获得“红点：精品中的精品”，“Design Plus”，“IF奖”，以及德国材料设计奖颁发的“最佳创意奖”。莱茵哈德・亚茨克是“transalpine”设计团队（三个设计工作室合作）的成员之一，这一团队多年以来一直凭借着其超凡脱俗的设计理念在家具设计领域中独领风骚。

伯诺・萨阔博士，1993年出生于意大利乌迪内。1956年他中断了在意大利都灵大学的学业，转而从事自己热爱的汽车设计行业，最初他在“Carrozzieri”Ghia和平尼・法瑞纳公司工作，1958年，他开始了在奔驰汽车公司作设计师的漫长职业生涯，1974年，他晋升为高级工程师，1975年至1999年春天，出任总设计师。伯诺・萨阔一直坚守着他的工作理念，那就是在尽可能鼓励员工创新的同时（他的员工曾获得1994年德国设计协会的设计团体奖），保持对品牌传统价值的尊重。

莱茵哈德・亚茨克和伯诺・萨阔谈“外观设计”

任何引用布克哈特的名言——“设计是看不见的”的人如果认为设计是隐藏的艺术，那他就是断章取义了。布克哈特在他1980年的发布会上想表达的其实是设计的任务就是使事物的隐藏部分再见天日，尽管这是二十世纪八十年代关于社会进程的观点；我们却不得不承认任何事物都有隐藏的一部分，尤其是日常生活中的灰色地带：比如说，与水的日常接触已转化成一种单调的例行公事；“洗手间”就是这种理解下产生的词汇。自由嬉水的无限美丽，与今日毫无动人之处的机械的用水之间已产生了巨大的差异。在这样的背景下，最近我们目睹了一种回归。洗浴场所重新考虑到洗浴礼节的敏感性。

Reinhard Zetsche *was born in 1963 in Frankfurt/Main, Germany, and founded Octopus Design in 1999. He lives in Munich, working for international clients. The products by Octopus Design have received, amongst others, the design prizes "red dot: best of the best," "Design Plus," "iF award," and the MATERIALICA prize "Best of Idea." Reinhard Zetsche is member of the design group "transalpin" (a project-oriented cooperation between three design studios), which over the past years has caused some stir by creating unconventional concepts in the field of furniture design.*

Dr. Bruno Sacco *was born in Udine, Italy, in 1933. In 1956, he interrupted his studies at the Turin Polytechnic to pursue his real passion as an automobile designer, gaining initial experience with the "Carrozzieri" Ghia and Pinin Farina. In 1958, he commenced his very long career as a designer of Mercedes-Benz vehicles. 1974 saw his promotion to Senior Engineer. Head of the Design Department from 1975 to spring 1999, Bruno Sacco remains true to his working philosophy which demands a maximum of innovation from his staff (Design Team of the Year 1994 at the Design Zentrum Nordrhein Westfalen) while retaining respect for the traditional values of the brand.*

Reinhard Zetsche and Bruno Sacco on "The Design of the Apparent":

Anyone who quotes Lucius Burckhardt's "Design is invisible" in the sense that design was the art of hiding, adopts a wrong interpretation. What Burckhardt rather intends to say in his 1980 publication is that the task of design is to bring to light that which lies hidden. (...) Admittedly the author is speaking, totally 1980s, primarily about social processes; but the hidden lies dormant within everything, in particular in the most grey areas of everyday life: The contact with the element of water in daily routine, for instance, has devolved into a dull ritual; the term "wet room" as such is an indication of this. The contrast between the infinite beauty of the free and natural play of water in both nature and culture and the mechanised unloveliness of today's use of water could not be any greater. Against this backdrop, we have recently witnessed a return. Baths again give room for the sensitivity of the bath ritual.

希洛·斯沃尔、西贝尔·弗莱肯斯坦、詹斯·普尔曼
Thilo Schwer, Sybille Fleckenstein, Jens Pohlmann

触摸！丝绒瓷器
touch! – porcelain with a textile surface

speziell produktgestaltung
芭芭拉·施密特
Barbara Schmidt

Speziell produktgestaltung是由西贝尔·弗莱肯斯坦（生于1973），希洛·斯沃尔（生于1973年）与詹斯·普尔曼（生于1971年）在2002年在奥分巴赫建立的。从1995年开始，他们三人便在奥分巴赫的设计学院学习，并于2001年毕业。西贝尔·弗莱肯斯坦最开始是学习金匠手艺的，后又师从设计学院退休的演说家、家具设计师斯蒂芬·黑利格教授，随后便以一个自由职业者的身份，从1998年开始在ID4工业设计工作室工作。希洛·斯沃尔在巴塞尔设计学院学习绘图。1998年，他又在德国士瓦本格明德的molldesign接受了专业培训，并在2002到2004期间作为家具产品开发设计者在Sedus Stoll公司工作。詹斯·普尔曼最初是一名家具设计师，从1996年开始，他成为奥分巴赫设计学院退休演说家，艺术家施道特教授的助手。2002年，这三个设计师成立了“Speziell produktgestaltung”设计工作室。

芭芭拉·施密特生于1967年，曾先后在德国的哈雷艺术和设计学院及芬兰的赫尔辛基设计学院学习。从1991年开始，她就成为了德国KAHLA公司的一名设计师，同时，她也偶尔在德国哈雷艺术和设计学院任教。她曾多次获奖，包括芝加哥和日本的最佳设计奖，以及“红点”设计大奖。

Speziell produktgestaltung的“丝绒瓷器”：

一种表层柔软且富有装饰性的陶瓷是非常新颖独特的。另外，这种表层也使其功能型增加：保温，易于取放。公司的设计者们因此也提到了这种三维涂层，即将一种产品与另一种产品配合起来。这种在陶瓷上使用织品的主意也被设计师们用在了KAHLA公司的不同系列的产品上，当然相关的体积和位置也进行了相应个性化地调整，以便更好的发挥其功用。可以说：新颖的外表激发了触碰的欲望；每次触碰都很有质感，都让使用者爱不释手。

speziell produktgestaltung *was founded by Sybille Fleckenstein (born in 1973), Thilo Schwer (born in 1973) and Jens Pohlmann (born in 1971) in Offenbach in 2002. Since 1995, all three studied at the Academy of Art and Design in Offenbach, finishing their studies as graduate designers in 2001. Sybille Fleckenstein had first trained as a goldsmith. After training with Prof. Stefan Heiliger, furniture designer and retired lecturer at the Academy of Art and Design in Offenbach, she had freelanced at ID4 Industriedesign since 1998. Thilo Schwer studied graphics at the Basel School of Design. In 1998, he trained at molldesign, Schwäbisch Gmünd, Germany, and worked as a furniture designer in product development at the Sedus Stoll AG between 2002 and 2004. Jens Pohlmann started working as a cabinetmaker. Since 1996, he has been an assistant to Prof. Klaus Staudt, artist and retired lecturer at the Academy of Art and Design in Offenbach. In 2002, the three designers founded the design studio "speziell produktgestaltung."*

Barbara Schmidt *(born 1967) studied at the Academy of Art and Design Burg Giebichenstein (HKD) in Halle, Germany, and at the Academy of Art and Design in Helsinki, Finland. Since 1991, she has been a designer at KAHLA/Thüringen Porzellan GmbH in Germany. She also holds teaching positions for instance at the HKD Halle. She has received many prizes, including the "Good Design Award" Chicago and Japan as well as the "red dot."*

speziell produktgestaltung on
"Porcelain with a Soft Surface":

A soft decorative coating for porcelain is new, surprising and extraordinary. Moreover, this surface extends the functional properties, serving as heat protection and an area to hold. Therefore, the designers of "speziell produktgestaltung" also speak of a three-dimensional coating, the imposition of a product onto a product. The idea to use a textile surface on porcelain was applied by the designers on various pieces in the KAHLA-Series. Dimension and position are individually adjusted for use. The innovative coating stimulates the sense of touch; each contact becomes a tactile experience and establishes a new connection with the user.

银鱼摄像机水下防护罩
SILVERFISH underwater housing for camcorders

克里斯汀·豪斯
Christian Hosse

克里斯汀·豪斯，1955年生于德国图林根州魏玛，并在那儿的VEB Weimar-Werk上了一所职业技术学校。随后在1977年到1981年间，他一直在德国茨维考的工程大学学习机器和设备组装。毕业时，他拿到了工厂设备改进方面的工程学位，还懂得一些水力学和气体学方面的知识。在1981到1989年间，他负责管理特殊用途机械。从1988年开始，他成为VEB Weimar-Werk合理化方式工程部的自动化和机械化组负责人。1990年，他加入了RWE机械电子部，担任构造工程师。从1993年起，克里斯汀·豪斯成为了德国Mechernich RWE公司电子机械设备和组件部的项目经理。

克里斯汀·豪斯关于“液氢形成和人类工程学”：
“银鱼”其实是在水下产生的：它获奖的造型是在液氢制造技术（内部高压铸模）过程中形成的，这又被 RWE 机械电子部继续改进用于批量生产，这种技术就是在高压下（大于1300百帕）水能扩大，钢管空隙对模具内部产生压力，使它们最后成形。这种方法的好处是：高度的可塑性使之较易成型，之后无需再处理。

Christian Hosse, *born 1955 in Weimar/Thüringen, Germany, attended the vocational school of the VEB Weimar-Werk in Weimar, Germany. Subsequently, between 1977 and 1981, he studied machine and installation assembly at the University for Engineers in Zwickau, Germany, where he graduated with an engineering diploma in the field of workshop facilities development as well as with additional knowledge in the field of hydraulics and pneumatics. Between 1981 and 1989, he worked as an engineer for special purpose machinery, and from 1988 as Group Leader of Automation and Mechanisation in the Engineering Department for Rationalisation Means at the VEB Weimar-Werk. In 1990, Christian Hosse joined RWE Mechatronics as a constructing engineer and, since 1993, has been Project Manager in the Department of Electromechanical Devices and Components at RWE Mechatronics in Mechernich, Germany.*

Christian Hosse on "Hydro-forming and Ergonomics":
SILVERFISH actually was born under water: It took its award-winning form in the process technology of hydro-forming (inner high-pressure moulding), which had been further developed by RWE Mechatronics for batch production, and in which water under high pressure (> 1,300 bar) distends steel tube blanks against the inside of a mould, forcing them into their final form. The advantages: high degree of mouldability into complex structures, hardly any necessary post-processing.

TOPEAK自行车帐篷
Bikamper tent

Topeak设计团队
Topeak-Designteam

Topeak设计团队的使命是渴望制造出自行车行业里经久耐用、使用方便、功能强大，却又在外形上不拘一格的自行车配件。“富于创意的理念是与对点滴细节的关注和对巧妙设计的独具慧眼，从而给生活带来无上的实用和便利。这一范例源于想要创造新产品，一种对提高和改良现有观念的长久的渴望，并且唤起与自行车相连的独特的情感。Topeak是一支由全球对工程、设计、销售和市场营销拥有极大热情的人紧密结合而成的团队，它始终探索着新方法，以期达到自行车行业里的独特要求。”

Topeak设计团队的“拓展自由”：

骑自行车意味着解脱与自由，当我们第一次学骑车的时候就发现了这种自由并且终生难忘。我们每次骑车的时候都能记起这种简单的解脱和单纯的自由。这种感觉不可遏制。Topeak提炼出了这种情感，从而创造出了自行车帐篷。

The **Topeak design team** *mission is the desire to build durable, functional, unique and user-friendly accessories for the bicycling industry: "Original concepts must come from care of details and an eye for intelligent design while bringing serious function and convenience to life. This paradigm is borne out of a constant desire to create new products, improve and refine existing ideas and thoughts, and evoke emotions that are uniquely associated with bicycles. Formed by a close-knit global team of engineering, design, sales and marketing enthusiasts, the Topeak team continually looks at new ways to approach bicycling and its special requirements."*

The Topeak design team on "Expanding Freedom":

Bicycling means escape and freedom. We discover this freedom the first time we learn to ride a bike and we never lose that feeling through our lives. We are constantly reminded of this simple escape and pure freedom every time we ride a bicycle. These feelings cannot be contained. Topeak's design team distilled these emotions to create Bikamper.

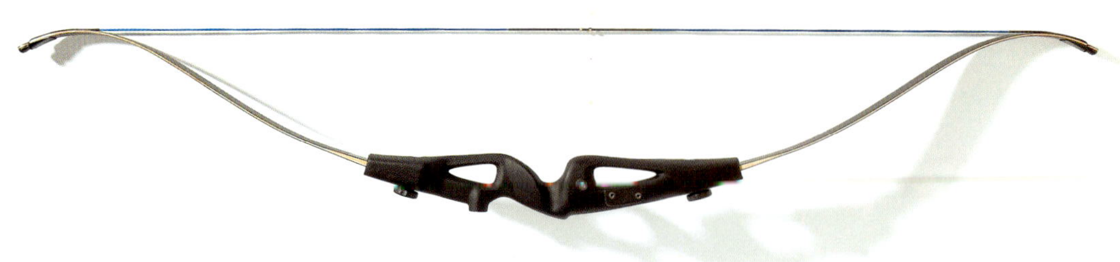

Initech Geologic 弓
Initech Geologic bow

爱恬·莱杜因
Etienne Redouin
尼古拉·哈摩依根
Nicolas Hamoignon

爱恬·莱杜因，1974年出生于法国的布卢瓦。1998年毕业于巴黎Creapole ESDI设计学院。在1996年到1997年期间，他既是Raison Pure国际设计公司的自由绘图设计者，又是MBD设计机构的产品设计者。他还参与了“路易·威登”公司的创新性设计。自1998年以来，他在法国里尔的迪卡侬集团（DECATHLON）担任产品设计。2002年，他是“Imaginew”核心队伍中的一员，“Imaginew”是迪卡侬集团的一项设计计划。2003年他被任命为巴黎迪卡侬国立高等装饰艺术学院（E.N.S.A.D）设计学院计划的领导人。1997年，在巴黎举行的“丰田RAV4”汽车装备设计比赛中，爱恬·莱杜因获得了第三名，此外，他还获得了2005年巴黎“Etoile du设计”比赛和2005年在德国的汉诺威举行的“iF大奖”奖项。

尼古拉·哈摩依根，1977年出生于巴黎。1995年到1998年就读于巴黎的Creapole ESDI设计学院，于1998年获得他的产品设计证书。同年，他在巴黎的Ad-Hoc设计公司和里尔的迪卡侬公司接受产品设计的培训。从1998年以来，他在迪卡侬公司工作，与Etienne Redouin携手共同设计溜冰鞋、旅行袋和塑料运动产品。2002年，他在“Etoile du design”设计比赛中获奖。第二次获奖是在2005年的“Etoile du design”和“iF 大奖”设计赛中。

迪卡侬的设计承诺：创造合适且经久耐用的解决办法：

我们的社会由重视外表进化到重视物质本身，这成为当今的主导思潮。我们认为迪卡侬设计对于顾客和产品使用者的承诺可以用使他们增进身心健康这一理念来体现。这一设计的社会职责也成为了迪卡侬的重点所在：迪卡侬渴望为广大群众提供积极的、更有意义、更具价值、更能激励人心的运动，但不会因此提高其产品价格。迪卡侬的设计很简洁，这种设计方法与运动相结合，从而向我们的顾客提供相关的解决方式。因为我们的设计者热爱运动，所以我们的一切努力都将集中在这一主要问题上。

Etienne Redouin, *born 1974 in Blois, France, graduated in 1998 from the Créapôle ESDI in Paris. Between 1996 and 1997, he had trained both as a freelance graphic designer at the agency Raison Pure and as a product designer at the agency MBD Design. He had also taken part in an innovation project at "Louis Vuitton." Since 1998, he has been working as a product designer at Decathlon in Lille, France. In 2002, he was a member of the "Imaginew" core team, a Decathlon design programme, and was appointed Design School Programme Leader in 2003 at Decathlon E.N.S.A.D., Paris. Etienne Redouin was awarded the third prize in the "Toyota RAV4" equipment contest in Paris in 1997, the "Etoile du Design" in Paris in 2005, and the "iF award" in Hanover, Germany, in 2005.*

Nicolas Hamoignon, *born 1977 in Paris, studied at the Créapôle ESDI in Paris from 1995 to 1998, and received his Product Design Certificate in 1998. The same year, he trained in product design at the Ad-Hoc design agency in Paris as well as at Decathlon in Lille, France. Since 1998, he has been working at Decathlon in Lille, together with Etienne Redouin, as a product designer for in-line skates, luggage, and plastic sport products. He was awarded the "Etoile du Design" in 2002, the second "Etoile du Design" in 2005, and the "iF award" in 2005.*

The Decathlon Design Commitment to create appropriate durable solutions:

Current thinking is that our society is evolving from the era of "appearance" to that of "substance." We like to think that Decathlon Design's commitment to the customer and the user of our products is expressed in this notion of increased well-being of body and soul. The social role of design takes on its full significance at Decathlon, where the desire is to offer the greatest number of people access to active sport and thus to give more meaning, more value and more emotion without translating this into higher prices. Decathlon Design aligns simplicity, valued by the design approach, to the practice of sports in order to offer the relevant solution to our customer. Because our designers are close to the practice of sport, the effort focuses on the essential.

LiTraCon™ 透光混凝土
LiTraCon™ light-transmitting concrete

艾伦·洛松齐
Áron Losonczi

艾伦·洛松齐，1977年出生于匈牙利的索尔诺克。1995年到2001年期间，他就读于布达佩斯技术大学的建筑系，于2001年获得了自然科学硕士学位。1999年到2000年，他就读于斯德哥尔摩的KTH建筑学校，2001年到2003年，就读于斯德哥尔摩的KKH建筑学校。LiTraCon™已经在米兰、东京、华盛顿、柏林、布达佩斯和斯德哥尔摩参展。2002年，“LiTraCon™透光混凝土”获得专利权。艾伦·洛松齐最重要的作品出现在《Domus》、《时代》、《建筑评论》和《细部》杂志上。自2004年以来，艾伦·洛松齐成为了匈牙利LiTraCon Bt.的所有者和代理总裁。

艾伦·洛松齐关于“为建筑业创造新的材料”：

当我受到了一件艺术品的启发后，我开始思考“透光混凝土”，那位艺术家将不同厚度的玻璃片镶嵌到大型的混凝土中，粗糙的混泥土材料变得柔和，通过过滤，同时改变透过它的光线，混泥土中还具有了一种新的质感。我立志要超越特定物体本身的界线，并努力把这一经验提升到建筑学的高度。

Áron Losonczi *was born in 1977 in Szolnok, Hungary. From 1995 to 2001, he studied at the Faculty of Architecture at the Technical University in Budapest, receiving his M.Sc. degree in 2001. He had also attended the KTH School of Architecture in Stockholm between 1999 and 2000, and later the KKH School of Architecture in Stockholm between 2001 and 2003. LiTraCon™ has already been on display in exhibitions in Milan, Tokyo, Washington D.C., Berlin, Budapest, and Stockholm. In 2002, the "LiTraCon™ - Light-Transmitting Concrete" was patented. Áron Losonczi's most important publications appeared in the magazines Domus, TIME, Architectural Review, and DETAIL. Since 2004, Áron Losonczi is owner and acting president of LiTraCon Bt., Hungary.*

Áron Losonczi on
"Creating New Materials for Architecture":

I started to think about light-transmitting concrete after having been inspired by an artwork. The artist embedded pieces of glasses of different thickness into a massive form of concrete. The rough material eased up and gained a new quality by filtered, spontaneously changing light coming through it. I made it to my objective to overstep the borders of a particular object and to lift this experience into architecture.

乔汉·莱恩内尔、玛丽亚·鲁特恩斯克、简·鲁特恩斯克
Johan Lionell, Maria Rutensköld, Jan Rutensköld

Pinc House 预制房
Pinc House prefabricated houses

Pinc–设计团队
Pinc–Designteam

Pinc–设计团队的成员包括了美术指导乔汉，他曾就读于斯德哥尔摩的Berghs媒体学校，创意指导及总监简·鲁特恩斯克，他拥有瑞典斯德哥尔摩的工商管理硕士学位，SAR/MSA设计师玛丽亚·鲁特恩斯克，曾就读于斯德哥尔摩皇家技术学院，特隆赫姆的挪威科技大学，和瑞典歌德堡的查尔摩斯技术大学，并且在皇家美术学院继续进修获得了建筑学学位。自2000年创办之际，Pinc–设计组已为瑞典，斯堪的纳维亚和国际上诸多的公司及组织设计过各种各样的作品。他们的设计包括展室和商品展览会设计、家具设计、室内装潢理念、和智能房屋领域的理念。在他们众多的客户中，惠普公司，宜家家居，爱立信，Hagstromer et Qviberg，JP摩根，Advokatbyran，Bird et bird，希尔顿酒店连锁管理集团，也同大量其他客户一样在Pinc这里设计过私人别墅。Pinc – 设计团队曾在瑞典全国NovaWood设计大赛中获得冠军，并在Sveriges Nalaremastare比赛中因出色的室内设计理念而获得2003“Basta Fargmiljo”设计奖。

The **Pinc design team** *are Johan Lionell (Art Director) who studied at Berghs School of Communication in Stockholm, Jan Rutensköld (Creative Director & President) who holds a MBA degree from the Stockholm University in Sweden, and Maria Rutensköld (Architect SAR/MSA) who studied at the Royal Institute of Technology in Stockholm, at the Norwegian University of Science and Technology in Trondheim, and at the Chalmers University of Technology in Gothenburg, Sweden. She also received a diploma for supplementary education in architecture at the Royal University College of Fine Arts. Since the start in 2000, the Pinc design team has worked on a variety of projects for Swedish, Scandinavian, and international companies and organisations. Their projects include showroom and trade fair design, furniture design, interior design concepts, and concept studies in the field of intelligent houses. Among their numerous clients are Hewlett-Packard, IKEA, Ericsson, Hagströmer & Qviberg, JM, Advokatbyrån Kaiding, Bird & Bird, Hilton Hotels as well as a number of private clients for whom the team has primarily designed private villas. The Pinc design team is winner of the national Swedish design competition Nova Wood and winner of the "Bästa färgmiljö 2003" design prize at the Sveriges Målaremästare competition for the best interior design concept.*

Pinc-设计团队在"Pinc 房子"设计中的设计理念:

一切都是从一件小小的私人项目开始的。几年前，我们去寻找一所新房子……但是最后，我们并没有秉承着大师的精神而涌现出任何想法。我们不得不自问，"未来斯堪的纳维亚的设计将会怎样？"（将来有一天回顾时），一些小东西（譬如弗兰克设计的Kartio玻璃制品）还不错，这些都是被全球公认的经典，大家都喜欢它们。不，我们在谈论的是一幅大的图画。一幅因积极、健康和愉快的生活方式而充满希望的美景：一个为普通的有心人而设计的完整的生活平台。或者换一种说法，我们的新房子在哪？当然我们有优秀的设计师，但他们并不是为所有人服务的。同那些精美新颖，并且大多数人负担的起的产品一并存在的问题是，为什么设计这一行业会完完全全忘记产品之中最重要的一项：私人房屋？ 我们是斯德哥尔摩的一家小设计公司，但我们接受了这一挑战：建造更好更美丽的家园，致力于更平衡的环境。超越家具能传达的东西。去斯堪那维亚的设计师们以前没有去过的地方。于是，在2003年的4月，我们步入了小型房屋这一领域。

The Pinc design team on "The Pinc House":

It all started as a small private project. A few years ago, we went looking for a new house. (...) But in the end, we didn't really come up with anything in the spirit of the old original masters...

We had to ask ourselves "whatever happened to the future of Scandinavian design (as it looked back then)?" The little things (like the Kartio by Franck) are OK. These are globally recognised classical icons, and everybody loves them. No, what we're talking about is the big picture. A hopeful vision for an active, healthy, and enjoyable lifestyle: the complete living platform for the attentive ordinary person. Or, in other words, where is our new house? Of course there are fantastic architects out there, but they're not for everyone. And the question remains, with good, innovative, affordable products for the masses, why has the industry totally forgotten the most important product of them all: the private house? We are a small design agency in Stockholm, and we took on the challenge: To build a better and more beautiful neighbourhood. To contribute to a more balanced environment. To go beyond furniture. To go where no Scandinavian design producer had ever gone before. In April 2003 we entered the small house sector...

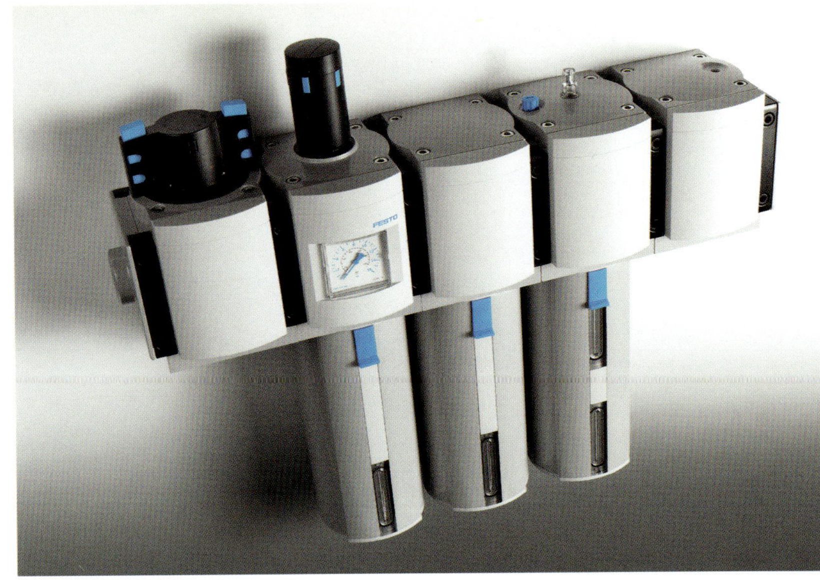

压缩空气气源处理单元MS12
MS12 air supply unit

简·克莱夫曼
Jan Kleffmann

简·克莱夫曼，生于1958年，最初，他是学习模形设计的学徒，1985年，他成功地完成了在德国霍尔茨明登的希尔德斯海姆的应用科技大学的工业设计专业课程。随后，分别在ALNO公司，Junghans Uhren GmbH和RotringGmbH公司研发部担任设计师。从1994年起，他开始负责位于德国埃斯林根的费斯托集团的产品设计。在他的指导下，费斯托集团的具有多样性功能的产品转变成为自始至终都秉承产品优秀设计的品牌化产品，同时还与设计上的高质量要求相结合。在很多国家以及国际上的设计大奖赛中都记述并采用了费斯托公司这种成功的设计理念。

简·克莱夫曼，“费斯托公司发展过程中的产品设计”：
我们的目标就是外部的产品质量要与内部的科技含量相结合，而成为“工程上的艺术”，要取得这样的成果不但要通过对生产上的高质量标准，更重要的是，在设计方面也要有同等的高质量要求。因此，在整个发展过程中，如何使设计，构造和生产都处于同等精良的高水平上就变得至关重要。设计的任务就是整合这些所有纳入其中的要求，并以一种合理的方式展现出来，只有这样，产品才可以在市场中保持其竞争力。

Jan Kleffmann, *born in 1958, started his professional education with an apprenticeship as a pattern maker. In 1985, he successfully completed his studies in industrial design at the University of Applied Sciences in Hildesheim/Holzminden, Germany. Subsequently, he worked as a designer in the research departments at ALNO AG, at the Junghans Uhren GmbH, and at the Rotring GmbH. Since 1994, he has been responsible for the product design at Festo AG & Co. KG in Esslingen, Germany. Under his guidance, the Festo products with their various functions have turned into consistently well-designed brand products, which incorporate the highest quality demands on design. Numerous national and international design prizes document the successful approach that the Festo Product Design has since adopted.*

Jan Kleffmann on "The Product Design in the Development Process at Festo":
The objective is to match the external quality of a product with the internal technical quality, the "Art of Engineering." This is achieved through high-quality standards in production and, importantly, through quality design of an equally high standard. It is, thus, essential to place design, construction, and production on an equally high level of sophistication during the entire development process. It is the task of design to communicate this in a convincing manner by integrating all disciplines involved. Products that are developed according to these requirements can remain competitive in the market.

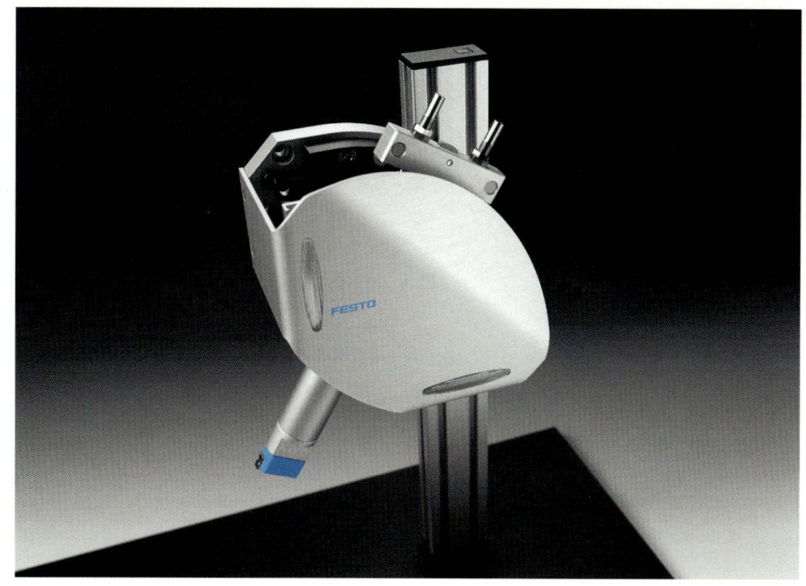

HSW操作模具
HSW handling module

卡罗琳・施密特
Karoline Schmidt
简・克莱夫曼
Jan Kleffmann

卡罗琳・施密特，从1997年至2001年在德国普福尔茨海姆应用科学大学和芬兰赫尔辛基艺术与设计大学学习工业设计。2003年她在费斯托公司参与了C-MBA项目，在这个过程中受到了更加专业的教育。2002年，她就已经成为了费斯托公司的初级设计师，并在德国埃斯林根的费斯托集团设计部从事产品设计工作。在她的技术型工业产品设计及研究中，28岁的她一直遵循着清晰的结构和简明的与语言表现形式的思路。她在费斯托公司的设计作品也获得了很多国内和国际上的设计大奖。

费斯托公司的产品设计：

费斯托一贯使用设计这一方式使产品变得更为美观，进而创造出品牌识别，正是这些，使产品得到了很高的认可度。这种认可度是通过特别的视觉传播来实现的，因为人类80%的信息来源于眼睛，而且这种方式比语言更能表达出产品的特质。设计使产品特性视觉化，展现了公司的形象，同时也显示出了与其竞争者的不同，这样就形成了品牌形象。费斯托产品的设计理念是在发展其新产品的过程中，有自己的一套完整设计工艺和固定组成要素。在一如既往地贯彻公司的设计理念时，产品设计不仅能使产品功能性趋于完美，使产品质量得到提升，同时还能够加强对其品牌的认知度和提高品牌价值。

Karoline Schmidt *studied industrial design from 1997 to 2001 both at the Pforzheim University of Applied Sciences in Germany and at the University of Art and Design in Helsinki, Finland. In 2003, she started to attend the C-MBA programme at Festo to receive further professional education. Since 2002, she has been Junior Designer at Festo, developing the product design in the Design Department at Festo AG & Co. KG in Esslingen, Germany. In her design of technical industry products and studies, the 28-old consistently follows a clear structure and concise language of form. Her work at Festo has been accompanied by many national and international design prizes.*

The Product Design at Festo:

Festo consistently uses design to generate an aesthetic appearance of the products and, thus, to create a brand identity, which has led to a high degree of recognition. It is the visual communication in particular that makes this possible, since humans perceive 80 per cent of all information through the eye. This makes it necessary to communicate values beyond words. Design makes quality visible, creates a company profile, differentiates from competitors, and shapes the brand image. The Festo Product Design incorporates an integrated process and a fixed constituent in the development process of new products. In consistently implementing Corporate Design, the product design does not only improve on the functional perfection of the products and their perceived quality value, it also heightens the brand recognition and raises the value of the brand.

斯蒂芬·斯达克、安东尼·海特、迈克尔·摩尔
Stefan Stark, Anthony Hatter, Michael Mauer

林德 T20 / T24 SP 型电动站式码垛车
Linde T20 / T24 SP electric stand-on pallet truck

迈克尔·摩尔
Michael Mauer
安东尼·海特
Anthony Hatter
斯蒂芬·斯达克
Stefan Stark

迈克尔·摩尔，1962年生于德国富尔达州罗腾堡，从1982年到1986年，他在德国普福尔茨海姆理工学院学习汽车设计，并在那里得到了德国辛德菲根的奔驰汽车公司设计部的工作，这也是他的第一份工作。1998年，他来到日本东京的奔驰高级设计工作室，担当总经理。一年以后，他被派回德国，主管MCC Smart公司的设计工作。2000年，迈克尔·摩尔来到瑞典Saab公司，出任设计执行总监。从2003年起，他在欧洲通用汽车公司担任最高设计师，后于2004年成为位于德国魏斯萨赫的保时捷公司设计部负责人。

安东尼·海特，1954年生于英国的纽卡索，他曾在科芬特里的兰彻斯特理工学院学习工业设计，并从1975年到1981年在伦敦皇家设计学院学习汽车设计。1981年毕业后，他来到位于德国吕塞尔斯海姆的Adam Opel公司的设计中心工作，后又于1986年到保时捷公司工作。三年中，他一直主管着保时捷公司的定制设计部门。

斯蒂芬·斯达克，1959年生于德国的沃尔夫斯堡，从1978年到1982年在柏林艺术专科学校学习工业设计，并在美国的帕萨迪纳设计艺术中心学院学习汽车设计。后来的几年中，他分别在奥迪公司和宝马公司担任设计师。从1989年至1992年，他在日本国际设计俱乐部负责工作室的设计工作。1992年，他转到德国魏斯萨赫的保时捷公司工作，负责汽车、运输及其它产品的设计。

林德设计组负责的林德 T20型号的电动码垛车：
林德 T20型号高性能电动码垛车的独特设计是在该产品中融合了创新的人体工效学原理，并集艺术性科技性于一身，它流畅及准确的操作性能表现出毋庸置疑的美学效果，更凸现出强劲动力与优雅外形的完美结合。T20型电动码垛车可以使操作者在操作中感到舒适、安全、灵活及准确，给予操作者一个展示自己卓越操作技巧及独自掌控的“平台”。

Michael Mauer, *born in 1962 in Rotenburg/Fulda, Germany, studied automobile design from 1982 to 1986 at the Polytechnic in Pforzheim, and from there secured his first job in the design area of Mercedes-Benz AG in Sindelfingen, Germany. He moved to the Mercedes-Benz Advanced Design Studio in Tokyo, Japan, as General Manager in 1998. A year later, he was put in charge of design at MCC Smart GmbH in Germany. In 2000, he moved to the Swedish Saab company as Executive Director Design and, since 2003, has also been responsible for Advanced Design at General Motors Europe. Since 2004, Michael Mauer is Head of the design area of Porsche AG in Weissach, Germany.*

Anthony Hatter, *born in 1954 in Newcastle, England, studied industrial design at the Lanchester Polytechnic in Coventry and automobile design at the Royal College of Art in London from 1975 to 1981. After his graduation, he joined the Design Centre at Adam Opel AG in Rüsselsheim, Germany, in 1981, and moved to the Porsche AG in 1986. For three years, he has been heading the Custom Design Department at Porsche AG.*

Stefan Stark, *born in 1959 in Wolfsburg, Germany, studied industrial design from 1978 to 1982 at the Berlin Academy of Arts and automobile design at the Art Center College of Design in Pasadena, USA. Subsequently, he worked as a designer both for several years at Audi AG and at BMW Technik GmbH, and then headed the Studio at the Design Club International in Japan from 1989 to 1992. In 1992, he moved to Porsche AG in Weissach, Germany, and has since been working as designer in the areas automobile, transportation, and product design.*

The Linde Design Team on the Linde T20 Lift Truck:
The unique design of the Linde T20 high-performance lift truck merges innovative ergonomics and state-of-the-art technology into a product, the dynamics and elegance of which meet the indisputable aesthetics of its smooth and precise manoeuvrability. The T20 provides the operator with sensible comfort, security, agility, and precision, giving operators a "platform" to demonstrate their virtuosity and sovereignty in handling the vehicle.

K 1200 S 摩托赛车
K 1200 S motorcycle

宝马集团设计团队
Designteam BMW Group

宝马集团设计团队的“摩托车的设计与美学”——“激情的个性”：

在现有的摩托车产品中，设计起着至关重要的作用。确切的说，当今摩托车作为一种运输手段已不再那么重要，而不管事实如何，还是有很多人渴望体验骑摩托车的那种快感，那种感觉是其它交通工具所不可比拟的。也许有人会认为，摩托车齐备的功能性应居于首位。如果真是这种情况，那么，由摩托车所带来的欲望与激情就不会那么显而易见。所以，具有个性化和感召力的设计和机器的整体外观在摩托车的设计理念中起着决定性的作用，目的就是让车主对摩托车有一种一见倾心的感觉，而这种感觉可激发他驾驶的欲望。摩托车设计师的任务就是立体地展现和激发出这种激情。

The BMW Group's Design Team on "Design and Aesthetics of a Motorcycle" or "The Personality of a Passion":

The design of a motorcycle plays an extraordinary role in the very existence of the product. Particularly, because today the motorcycle is largely unnecessary strictly as a means of transport. Despite this fact, many people do not want to miss the motorcycling experience. The feeling is incomparable to any other. One might assume that pure functionality has top priority in motorcycles. If this was really the case, however, the desirability and passion that motorcycles generate would not be as pronounced as they are. The design of the personality, the charisma and overall appearance of a machine are decisive for the design of a motorcycle. The objective is to make the relationship between the motorcycle and its owner conscious and to sustain it in order to heighten the experience of motorcycling. The task of the motorcycle designer is to represent and evoke passion.

罗伯特・G・艾伦、胡旭辉、斯科特・H・科蒂斯、威斯纳・克里帕
Robert Allan, Xuhui (Bill) Hu, Dwight Organ, Scott Curtis, Vesna Klipa

Z-Tech 气垫拖轮
Z-Tech tug

Z-Tech 设计团队
Z-Tech-Designteam
罗伯特・艾伦有限责任公司
Robert Allan Ltd.

罗伯特・G・艾伦是罗伯特・艾伦有限责任公司的总裁，同时主管**Z-Tech 设计团队**，他于1971年毕业于格拉斯哥大学造船专业并获得理科学士学位（优等生）。肯尼斯・D・哈佛德曾任温哥华机械电子工程公司总裁，他于1988年7月作为工程经理加入到罗伯特・艾伦有限责任公司中来。胡旭辉，毕业于中国武汉华中科技大学并获得造船及海洋工程专业的学位，在罗伯特・艾伦有限责任公司担任项目经理。海洋系统专家德怀特・D・奥根毕业于圣约翰斯的纽芬兰纪念大学，在1993年获得了船只系统设计专业的文凭，并于2003年取得了技术学士学位。斯科特・H・科蒂斯造船及海洋系统专家，在圣约翰斯的纪念大学学习，并在2002年及2003年分别获得了造船专业的文凭和海洋工程系统设计的文凭。威斯纳・克里帕负责项目造船部门，毕业于克罗地亚的Rijeka大学造船专业，并获得了理科学士学位。

罗伯特・G・艾伦的"设计操纵船舶的辅助拖轮的挑战性"项目：

这个项目的目的就是要创作出一个新颖的、有特色的设计来真正地突破现有的操纵船舶的辅助拖船技术，改进其性能，保证船员的安全。罗伯特・艾伦有限责任公司在新加坡会见了船员及操作部经理，以便更好地了解拖船的方方面面的操作情况和特殊拖船的需求等方面的事宜。通过这一次交谈，他对船员的操作喜好有了更清楚地了解，有些船员喜欢"拖拉机"式的拖船，而有些人喜欢"尾挂机"类型，但无论哪种类型都有其独特的操作优势。我们所要挑战的就是要创作出一个独特的设计，可以取其两者之精华而去其糟粕。

Robert G. Allan is President of Robert Allan Ltd. and Head of the Z-Tech Design Team. *He graduated with a B.Sc. degree (Honours) in naval architecture from the University of Glasgow in 1971. Kenneth D. Harford had been President of Mechtronic Engineering Corporation in Vancouver and joined Robert Allan Ltd. as Engineering Manager in July 1988. Xuhui (Bill) Hu is Project Manager at Robert Allan Ltd., with a degree in naval architecture and ocean engineering from Huazhong University of Science and Technology in Wuhan, China. Marine Systems Technologist Dwight D. Organ graduated from Memorial University of Newfoundland, St. John's, with a diploma of technology in marine systems design in 1993 and a bachelor degree in technology in 2003. Scott H. Curtis, Naval Architect and Marine Systems Technologist, studied at the Marine Institute of Memorial University, St. John's, receiving his naval architecture diploma in 2002 and his marine engineering systems design diploma in 2003. Vesna Klipa is Project Naval Architect, with a B.Sc. degree in naval architecture from the University of Rijeka in Croatia.*

Robert G. Allan on
"The Challenge of Ship-Handling Tug Design":
The objective was to create a new and distinctive design that would truly represent a breakthrough in ship-handling technology, and offer improvements in performance and crew safety. Robert Allan Ltd. met with tug crews and operations managers to gain a better understanding of the complete operation and specific tug requirements in Singapore. Emerging from that session was a clear understanding that some crews had a distinct preference for the "tractor" style of tugs, while others favoured the stern-drive type, each with unique operational advantages. Our challenge was to develop a single design that would incorporate the best features and eliminate the negative characteristics of both types.

保时捷 911 Carrera 跑车
Porsche 911 Carrera

迈克尔·摩尔
Michael Mauer

迈克尔·摩尔，1992年生于德国德国富尔达州罗腾堡，从1982年到1986年，他在德国普福尔茨海姆理工学院学习汽车设计，并在那里得到了德国辛德菲根的奔驰汽车公司设计部的工作，这也是他的第一份工作，同时，他还被委托为V-Class，the A-Class，SLK和SL型号作设计。1998年，他来到日本东京的奔驰高级设计工作室，担当总经理。一年以后，他被派回德国，主管MCC Smart公司的设计工作。2000年6月，迈克尔·摩尔来到瑞典Saab公司，出任设计执行总监。从2003年3月起，他在欧洲通用汽车公司担任高级设计师，后于2004年7月年成为位于德国魏斯萨赫的保时捷公司设计部门负责人。

保时捷公司：关于新型保时捷911Carrera的设计：
新型保时捷911的设计秉承了40年来911系列的一贯风格，外部造型新颖，包括轮子，车胎，并重点强调了汽车车身中部的设计。911系列的外观不仅使人觉得该跑车动力强大、简洁大方、优雅十足，更显著的改变还体现在分别在车头两侧配备的圆形大灯，辅助照明灯、更加突出的挡泥板、新型双侧车外后视镜、独特的焊接外观，以及汽车尾部体现完美空气动力学原理的扰流板。另外，通过更高级的私人部件设计，更体现出了新型911跑车的内饰的不同。

Michael Mauer, *born in 1962 in Rotenburg/Fulda, Germany, studied automobile design from 1982 to 1986 at the Polytechnic in Pforzheim, and from there secured his first job in the design area of Mercedes-Benz AG in Sindelfingen, Germany, where he was entrusted with design responsibility for the V-Class, the A-Class, SLK and SL models. In 1998, he moved to the Mercedes-Benz Advanced Design Studio in Tokyo, Japan, as General Manager and was intensively involved in advanced development work on various model lines. A year later, he was put in charge of Design at MCC Smart GmbH in Germany. In June 2000, he moved to the Swedish Saab company as Executive Director Design and, since March 2003, has also been responsible for Advanced Design at General Motors Europe. Since July 2004, Michael Mauer has been leading the Design area of Porsche AG in Weissach, Germany.*

The Porsche AG on the design of the new Porsche 911 Carrera:
The design of the new Porsche 911 is a consistent continuation of the 40 years of the 911 history. With the new design of the exterior – among other things wheels and tires as well as a stronger emphasis on the car's waist – the appearance of the 911 has simultaneously become more dynamic, clear, powerful, and elegant. Other marked changes are the new round headlights with separate auxiliary lights at the corners, more accentuated fenders, new double arm exterior mirrors, a changed appearance of the seams, and an aerodynamically optimised rear spoiler. The interior of the new 911 also distinguishes itself through the further advanced design quality of individual car parts.

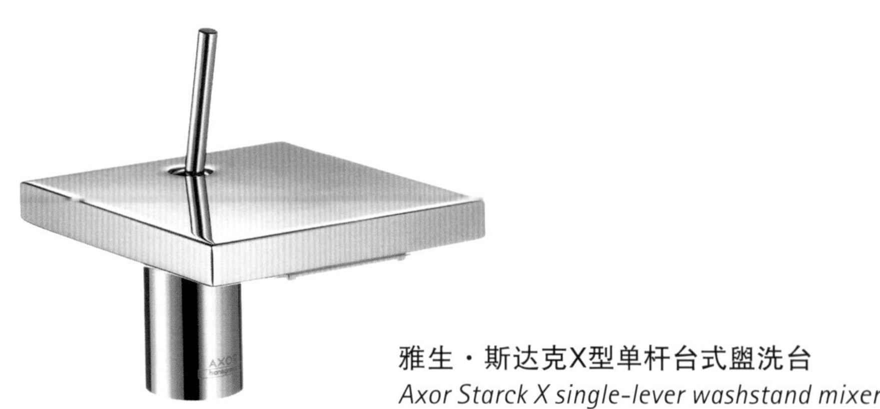

雅生・斯达克X型单杆台式盥洗台
Axor Starck X single-lever washstand mixer

菲利普・斯达克
Philippe Starck

菲利普・斯达克，1949年生于巴黎，他在产品及工业设计，建筑和内部建筑等领域从事多方面的工作。同时，负责多家旅馆，酒店，博物馆，个人住宅，及世界各地的建筑设计工作，足迹遍布东京、大阪、纽约、马德里、香港、墨西哥、伦敦、巴黎等。斯达克还是意大利米兰DA设计学院和法国巴黎装饰艺术学院等多家组织及机构的老师和顾问。他的作品在巴黎蓬皮杜艺术中心、京都现代美术博物馆和伦敦设计博物馆等各地展出。他的兴趣涉猎非常广泛，曾操刀设计包括Beneteau船只，德国杜拉维特、德国汉斯格雅公司的浴室套件、赫施公司、Axor，以及阿尔贝维尔奥运会的圣火，艾伦・米克力眼镜，美国“化石”公司的腕表，一个气象站和美国欧西亚时钟，彪马运动鞋等众多产品。菲利普・斯达克曾荣获多项大奖，其中包括：1980年的“奥斯卡灯光奖”；1987年的“芝加哥白金圈奖”，1997年的“哈佛优秀设计奖”；2001年的“金罗盘”奖，其中在1995年至2004年的多次获 “红点奖”以及2004年的“lucky Strike”设计师奖。

Philippe Starck *was born in Paris in 1949. He undertakes a wide variety of work in product and industrial design, in architecture and interior architecture. He was responsible for the design of many hotels, restaurants, museums, private houses and other buildings around the world, including in Tokyo, Osaka, New York, Madrid, Hong Kong, Mexico, London, and Paris. Philippe Starck is a teacher and consultant for various organisations and institutes, including the Domus Academy in Milan and the École des Arts Décoratifs in Paris. His work is on show in, amongst other places, the Centre Pompidou in Paris, the Museum of Modern Art in Kyoto, and the London Design Museum. Following his wide range of interest, Philippe Starck designed numerous different products, including boats for Bénéteau, bathroom suites for Duravit, Hansgrohe, Hoesch as well as for Axor, the Olympic Flame for the Olympic Games in Albertville, eye glasses for Alain Mikli, a wrist watch for Fossil in the USA, a weather forecast station and an alarm clock for Oregon Scientific, as well as shoes for Puma. Among the many awards Philippe Starck received are the "Oscar du luminaire" 1980, the "Platinum Circle Award of Chicago" 1987, the "Harvard Excellence in Design Award" 1997, the "Compasso d'Oro" 2001, several "red dot" awards between 1995 and 2004, as well as the "Lucky Strike Designer Award" 2004.*

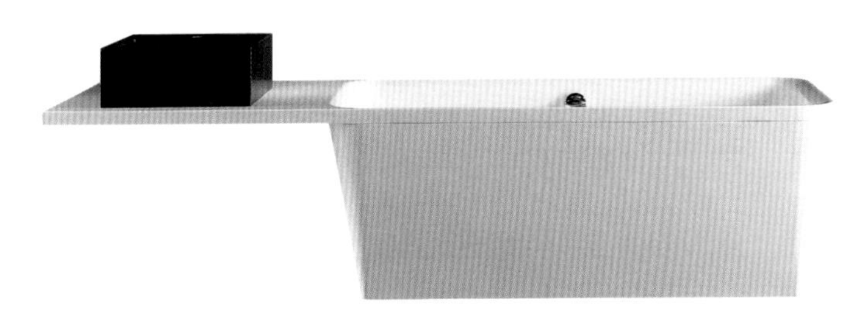

雅生·奇特里奥浴缸和盥洗台组合卫浴
Axor Citterio combination bathtub-washbasin

安东尼奥·奇特里奥
Antonio Citterio

安东尼奥·奇特里奥于1950年生于米兰附近的麦达。他曾在米兰理工学院学习建筑并在1972年成立了自己的工作室，其方向主要是针对工业设计领域。安东尼奥·奇特里奥负责意大利及多家国外公司的产品设计工作，其中包括Ansorg、Arclinea、Axor-Hansgrohe、B & B Italia、Flexform、Flos、Fusital、Guzzini、Littala、Inda、Kartell、Maxalto、Pozzi Ginori-SanitecGroup、Tre Piu、Vitra和Wall等公司或机构。1981年，他开始涉足于建筑及室内设计领域。安东尼奥·奇特里奥和帕德瑞夏·维也于1999年成立了涉及多项领域的"安东尼奥·奇特里奥及其合伙人"工作室，主要负责建筑设计、工业设计及图文设计。工作室的主要设计项目有：多住宅、交易中心、工业场地、重建的公用建筑、工作场所、办公室、展览室、和多家宾馆的规划。同时还处理公司沟通及公司形象工程，设备装置和图文方面的实施问题。从1999年至2002年，安东尼奥·奇特里奥分别在瑞士蒙得利索建筑学院和瑞士意大利大学任教。他获得过很多奖项，曾先后于1987年和1995年摘得了米兰每三年一次评选的"金罗盘"奖，2002年，作为室内设计师和建筑师的他摘得"名人殿堂大奖，并且被"建筑与住家"授予"2002年年度最佳设计师"称号。他为Kartell公司设计的"mobil"收纳柜系列等多项产品都在纽约现代艺术博物馆及巴黎蓬皮杜艺术中心进行了长期展出。2004年他因设计"Kelvin（Flos系列）"电灯和"Decanter（littala）"分别荣获了"红点奖"和法兰克福国际展览中心颁发的"设计奖"。

Antonio Citterio *was born in Meda (Milan) in 1950. He studied architecture at the Milan Polytechnic and opened his studio in 1972, mainly focusing on industrial design. Antonio Citterio works for Italian and foreign companies such as Ansorg, Arclinea, Axor-Hansgrohe, B&B Italia, Flexform, Flos, Fusital, Guzzini, Iittala, Inda, Kartell, Maxalto, Pozzi Ginori - Sanitec Group, Tre Più, Vitra, and Wall. In 1981, he started to work in the architectural and interior design business. "Antonio Citterio and Partners" was founded by Antonio Citterio and Patricia Viel in 1999 as a multidisciplinary studio for architectural design, industrial and graphic design. The studio develops projects for residential complexes and trade centres, industrial sites, the restructuring of public buildings as well as the planning of workspaces, offices, showrooms, and hotels. It is also operational in the field of corporate communications and the implementation of corporate image projects, fittings and graphics. From 1999 to 2002, Antonio Citterio taught at the Academy of Architecture of Mendrisio, University of Italian Switzerland. Among the many awards he has received are the Milan Triennial's "Compasso d'Oro" in 1987 and 1995. In 2002, he received the "Hall of Fame Award" as interior designer and architect, and was appointed "Designer of the year 2002" by Architektur & Wohnen. Several of his products, including the container unit "Mobil" for Kartell, are on permanent display at the Museum of Modern Art in New York and the Centre Pompidou in Paris. In 2004, Antonio Citterio received the "red dot" for the "Kelvin" lamp (Flos), and for the "Decanter" (Iittala) received the "Design Plus Prize" of Messe Frankfurt.*

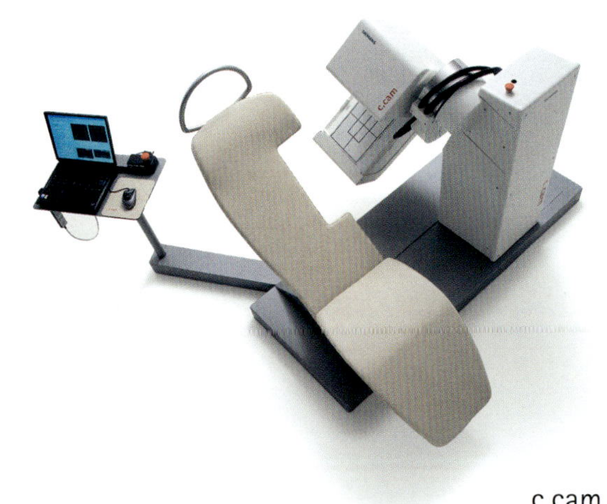

c.cam SPECT 扫描仪
c.cam SPECT scanner

安斯嘎· 格瑙
Ansgar Graw

安斯嘎·格瑙是美国西门子医疗器械解决方案公司的一名设计师。他在德国基尔的基尔艺术和设计专业学院获得了工业设计的学位，后分别为德国威斯巴登的Seiffert + Kahlcke，德国基尔的ma design，日本大阪的松下电工公司及巴西里约热内卢的NCS设计公司进行产品设计。他的作品荣获了很多国际设计大奖，其中包括：红点设计奖，iF设计奖及在IDEA，GOOD DESIGN和工业设计杂志竞赛中取得的奖项。

安斯嘎·格瑙，“设计要考虑患者的体会”：

西门子公司竭尽所能地想与医生和患者建立起长久而稳固的关系。因此，我们不仅要清楚地了解临床医生的需求，还了解病人的需求，只有这样，才能够研发出可行的产品解决方案。我们的目标就是要生产出让患者易于接受、使用方便，舒适的实用产品。只有这样，才能使顾客放松心情，从而不排斥医疗保健。

Ansgar Graw *is a designer with Siemens Medical Solutions in the USA. He holds a degree in industrial design from the Muthesius-Hochschule in Kiel, Germany. He has worked for Seiffert + Kahlcke in Wiesbaden, Germany, for ma design in Kiel, Germany, for Matsushita Electric Works in Osaka, Japan, as well as for NCS Design in Rio de Janeiro, Brazil. Ansgar Graw's work has received several awards in international design competitions, including the red dot design award, the iF design award as well as in the competitions IDEA, GOOD DESIGN, and iD Magazine.*

Ansgar Graw on "Designing the Patient Experience":

Siemens strives to create long-lasting partnerships with medical practitioners. Therefore, we have to clearly understand not only the needs and wants of clinicians but also those of their patients in order to be able to create sustainable solutions. Our goal is to make useful products that are emotionally approachable, comfortable and easy to use, because this is what eventually enables customers to make health care a positive experience.

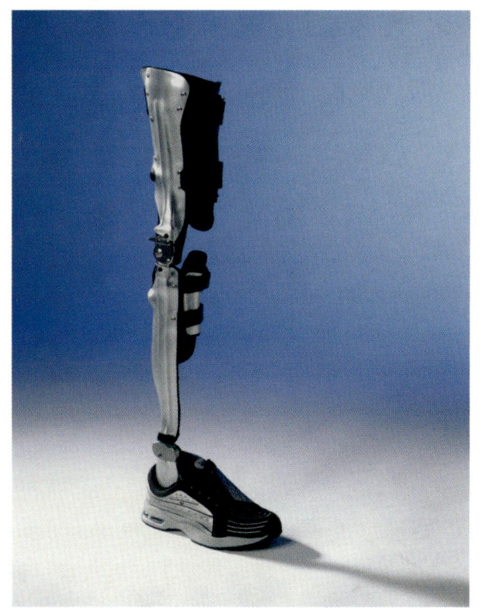

单侧关节系统
Unilateral joint system

亚历山大·万·阿瑟贝格
Alexander von Ascheberg
赫尔穆特·瓦格纳尔
Helmut Wagner

亚历山大·万·阿瑟贝格，1962年生于德国的曼海姆，通过三年的业内培训及学习，在1988年获得了人体修复及整形的结业证书。1988年至1993年期间，他曾在多家整形院当学徒，汲取了很多相关知识和经验。1993年至1994年，他就读于德国国立大学应用整形技术专业，并通过参加国立大学的考核，后于1994年2月在多特蒙德工艺商会获得了整形硕士文凭和欧洲文凭。从1994年4月起，他就一直在奥托·博克健康康复集团，从事开发与设计假肢的工作。

赫尔穆特·瓦格纳尔于1964年生于哈萨克斯坦，1972年来到德国。在1983年获得了科技大学证书之后，他来到帕德博恩科技大学学习机械工程并于1998年获得了学位。从那以后就一直在奥托·博克健康康复集团从事研发假肢与整形的工作。

亚历山大·万·阿瑟贝格与赫尔穆特·瓦格纳尔的关于“功能与设计”：

单侧关节系统的结构设计是建立在对生物力学的深刻理解和运用之上的。它独特的构造理念完美地凸现了假肢的三种主要任务，即：支撑性、保护性及矫形。所以，它不仅在功能上要仿效自然肢体，而且在外观上也须相当美观。

根据今天的质量标准及要求，为了更好地适应使用者生活习惯，假肢的功能性和设计就要并重了。既要让假肢的佩戴者感觉使用这个“支架”很舒服，同时还能够使他们穿“正常的”衣服，且无须隐藏这个支撑的东西。单侧关节系统能够使腿处于最佳的位置，形成一个纤细的支撑轮廓。患者的需要才是设计的唯一标准！因此设计对我们来说是非常至关重要的。

Alexander von Ascheberg, *born in 1962 in Mannheim, Germany, received his certificate as prosthetist/orthotist in 1988, after three years of training in the craft. As an apprentice between 1988 and 1993, he gathered experience in various workshops. Between 1993 and 1994, he attended the National School for Applied Orthopaedic Technology in Germany. Taking his examinations at the National School and at the Dortmund Chamber of Crafts, he received the Master Craftsman Diploma and the European Diploma in February 1994. Since April 1994, he has been working at Otto Bock HealthCare GmbH, developing and designing orthoses.*

Helmut Wagner, *born in Kazakhstan in 1964, moved to Germany in 1972. He received his Technical College Certificate in 1983 and, subsequently, studied Mechanical Engineering at the Technical University in Paderborn to receive his Diploma degree in 1998. Since then, he has been working in the development of prostheses and orthoses at the Otto Bock HealthCare GmbH.*

Alexander von Ascheberg and Helmut Wagner on "Functionality and Design":

The construction of the unilateral jointsystem is based on insights from biomechanics. Its unique construction method optimally performs the three main tasks of an orthosis: it supports, protects and corrects. Not only is it modelled on nature in terms of functionality, it also responds to aesthetic demands.

According to today's quality standards, function and design play an equally important role for the user's quality of life. The wearer of an orthosis wants to feel comfortable with the "brace." This includes being able to wear "normal" clothes and not having to hide the supporting technology. The unilateral jointsystem adapts to the leg in the best possible way, forming a slim supporting profile. It is the needs of the patient that set the standard – therefore design is highly important to us!

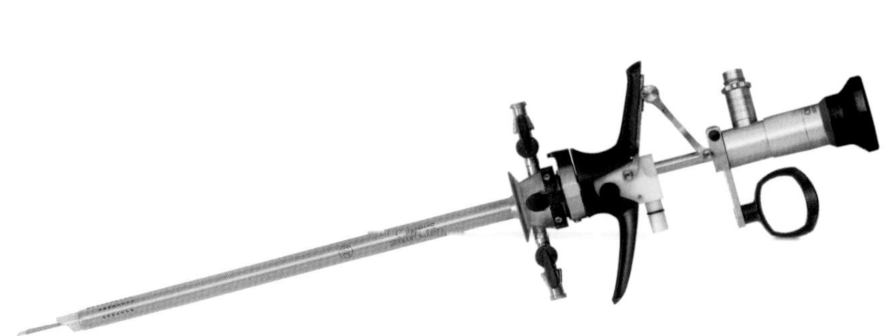

OES Pro-2 型前列腺切除仪
OES Pro-2 resectoscope

佛瑞德・海德
Fred Held
托马斯・马兹克
Thomas Märzke

佛瑞德・海德出生于1966年，1992年毕业于德国基尔的应用科学大学学习工业设计系。从1989年到1997年，他在汉堡的Windi Winderlich设计公司任职。1997年他开办了自己的公司——Held + Team。

托马斯・马兹克生于1971年。2003年毕业于德国埃森大学及埃森综合大学工业设计专业，毕业后来到Held+Team公司工作。

Held+Team关于“外科手术器械的设计”：
手术器械的基本技术要求是非常严格的。在卫生要求上，材料要经得起134摄氏度的高压消毒，无需外罩设计，没有自由发挥创意地空间，还要站在使用者的角度来设计，因为往往只有他们才是专家，设备要巧妙地结合生物工程学原理，并且需要在使用前后要能方便地安装和拆卸。设计不仅要使器械吻合上述要求，更重要的是，在适应了公司产品设计要求的一些具体特点后，还要确保在大量奥林帕斯器械的外形设计上，要体现出类似的结构。

Fred Held *was born in 1966. He studied at the Faculty of Industrial Design at the University of Applied Sciences in Kiel, Germany, and received his diploma degree in 1992. From 1989 to 1997, he was an employee at Windi Winderlich Design GmbH in Hamburg. Since 1997, Fred Held has been running his own company Held + Team.*

Thomas Märzke *was born in 1971. He studied industrial design at the University and Comprehensive University of Essen, Germany, and received his diploma degree in 2003. Since then, he has been an employee at Held + Team.*

Held + Team on "The Design of Surgical Instruments":
The basic technical requirements for surgical instruments are very strictly defined. The requirements on cleanability, on materials that have to withstand the autoclave sterilisation process at 134°C, and on a design without housing, leave little room for creative freedom. From the user's point of view – who is always an expert – the instrument has to offer perfect ergonomics of use as well as ease of assembly and disassembly before and after use. Design provides the link to integrate and meet these requirements but, above all, in being geared to the catalogue of features specified in the Corporate Product Design, it ensures a homogeneous structure in appearance for all of the hundreds of Olympus instruments.

Sqr 网络织毯
Sqr woven carpet

彼得·马力
Peter Maly
卡斯藤·戈尔尼克
Carsten Gollnick

彼得·马力于1936年出生，学习室内建筑专业，1960年取得学位，而后在“居家装潢”杂志编辑部工作。1970年他在汉堡创办了自己的工作室，其设计风格是将独特的几何外形与对简约，实用、持久的永恒追求相结合。

卡斯藤·戈尔尼克，1966年出生，从工业设计专业毕业。1990年，与人合伙创办了自己的第一个设计工作室，之后，在亚洲工作了相当长一段时间，1997年，他在柏林开设了自己的设计室。他的设计特点是融合了清晰的线条与漂亮的外形，使之搭配自然和谐。

彼得·马力和卡斯藤·戈尔尼克关于Sqr织毯：
在这款产品中，设计主要基于方块格子结构中多种形式的变换：使用多种不同的纱线，毛束不同，色彩却一致，结合了微微的浮雕式表面作为基本图案。纱线间的相互搭配，构成了明暗度的微妙变化，还显现出了相同底格上图形的生动变化。引用织布设计中的样式，在有金属色泽的接缝处使用特殊的纱线来体现各种各样的图案，使这种构图与整体图案相辅相成。

Peter Maly, *born in 1936, studied interior architecture, receiving his degree in 1960 and, subsequently, was a member of the editorial board of the "Schöner Wohnen" magazine. Since 1970, he has been running his own design studio in Hamburg. Geometrically shaped forms and the search for clarity, functionality and timelessness characterise his designs.*

Carsten Gollnick, *born in 1966, is a graduate industrial designer. After co-founding his first design studio in 1990, and spending considerable time in Asia, the graduate designer has been running his own design office in Berlin since 1997. The harmonious interplay of clear lines and sensuous shapes characterises his designs.*

Peter Maly and Carsten Gollnick on Sqr:
In its form, the design is based on a square – a grid in multiple variations: using different yarns, differing in tuft yet uniform in colour, generate basic patterns of a slight relief surface. The interplay with other yarns, graded in subtle shades of brightness, generate additional graphic pattern variations on the same basic grid. The collection is complemented by a range of patterns that use a special yarn for the metallic seam, quoting the motifs of textile design.

妙韵音乐设备
Wave Music System

塞斯·格林
Seth Green

塞斯·格林在Bose公司设计中心担任工业设计师。他生于1968年，成长在美国康涅狄格州西北角的一个乡村。1992年毕业于罗切斯特科技学院工业设计专业，并获得美术学士学位及学校最高荣誉奖。他的主要工作经历有：为纽约东奥罗拉的“费雪”公司设计儿童用品，为位于印第安纳州首府印第安纳波利斯的汤姆森电子公司设计电视和电话。他的多项产品都获得了“红点”奖，其中包括Bose妙韵音乐设备，Bose 3.2.1数字家庭影院系统和Bose轻柔舒适2号耳机。塞斯·格林现居住在美国麻萨诸塞州的牛顿市。

Bose公司设计组关于“Bose妙韵音乐设备的设计理念”：

Bose妙韵音乐设备是Bose妙韵收音机的第三代产品。这种新颖的设计旨在获得品牌视觉化效果。该设计的点睛之处在于把插放磁盘的驱动器托盘置于显示屏的下方，提供给使用者一个直观的视觉焦点。改进过的声音波导器使整体外形的高度可以设计地更低，其百叶窗排列的也更密集。这样，不仅外形简约，更提高了音质。另外，只有通过超薄遥控器才能操作Bose妙韵音乐设备，从而可以减少产品的分散控制。正是这些特点，结合了其它的重要而又巧妙的改动，才能使机器看起来美观简约，却又优雅十足。

Seth Green *works as an industrial designer at the Bose Design Center. He was born in 1968 and raised in the rural Northwest corner of Connecticut, USA. He graduated with a Bachelor of Fine Arts in industrial design from the Rochester Institute of Technology with Highest Honours in 1992. His work experience includes designing juvenile products at Fisher-Price in East Aurora, New York, and designing televisions and telephones at Thomson Consumer Electronics in Indianapolis, Indiana. In addition to the Bose Wave Music System, other "red dot" award recipients Seth Green has designed include the Bose 3.2.1 Digital Home Entertainment System and the Bose Quiet Comfort 2 headphones. Seth Green currently lives in Newton, Massachusetts.*

The Bose Corp. design team on
"The Design Philosophy of the Bose Wave Music System":
The Bose Wave Music System is the third generation of the Bose Wave Radio. The new design builds upon the acquired visual brand equity. Instrumental in the new design is the slot loading optical disc drive located below the display. This provides a single focal point for users. The redesigned acoustic wave-guide allows for a lower profile design with more closely spaced louvers. The result is a refined proportion, with improved acoustic performance. Operation of the Bose Wave Music System solely from the thin remote control allowed the elimination of distracting controls from the product. These key points, along with other important but subtle changes, culminate in a dramatic statement of elegance and simplicity.

汤姆・逊合尔、安德雷亚斯・迪米特利亚迪斯、安德雷亚斯・浩克
Tom Schönherr, Andreas Dimitriadis, Andreas Haug

Spheros R 37 经典型液晶电视
Spheros R 37 Masterpiece LCD TV

埃德蒙德・恩格力克
Edmund Englich
凤凰设计事务所
Phoenix Design

埃德蒙德・恩格力克生于德国的波霍特，1985年在德国汉诺威应用科学大学学习工业设计。1988年至1989年，因获国外交换生奖学金，他前往英国的布鲁内尔大学学习。1990年他来到荷兰的CID飞利浦公司工作，并于1991年获得了文凭。而后，恩格力克进入在德国士瓦本格明德的“molldeign”公司工作。从1998年起恩格力克在位于德国克龙那赫的Loewe公司工作，担任设计与设计管理部门的总设计师。他获得过很多奖项，其中包括1991年作为“molldeign”设计组成员而得到的“红点”年度最佳设计小组奖，因设计Loewe Spheros电视而与Loewe公司共同获得了2000年及2001年德国最高设计奖 “Bundespreis Produktdesign”。

安德雷亚斯・浩克和汤姆・逊合尔于1987年成立了**凤凰设计事务所**，慢慢地，该事务所逐渐发展成为了享誉国内外的大公司。在这期间，凤凰设计事务所受到了很多著名公司的青睐，后来都成为他们的长期客户，其中包括：汉斯格雅、雅生、夏普、西门子和LG。凤凰设计工作室的许多设计项目都获得了很多的重量级奖项，其中包括欧洲设计界梦寐以求的设计奖项——“Lucky Strike”设计师大奖。凤凰设计还曾连续三次蝉联设计排行榜榜首。今天的凤凰共有员工18人（包括设计师，插图制作人，专业模型制作人，和CAID专家），同时，凤凰设计还可以制作一流的室内平面模型并按客户要求时间进行轧制加工。其东京分公司主要负责亚洲客户，会现场参与项目设计，直到产品投入生产。2003年1月，安德雷亚斯・迪米特利亚迪斯加盟凤凰设计事务所，成为他们的管理合作伙伴。

埃德蒙德・恩格力克：“为消费者利益而设计”

高品质的设计能够从视觉上展现出产品整体的品牌价值，能够提升品牌形象，从而让消费者体会到产品确实是实实在在，其品质是坚若磐石的。

Edmund Englich, *born in Bocholt, Germany, started studying industrial design at the University of Applied Sciences in Hanover in 1985. Being awarded a foreign exchange scholarship, he studied at the Brunel University in England from 1988 to 1989. In 1990, he went to CID Philips Eindhoven in the Netherlands to work on his diploma, which he received in 1991. Subsequently, he worked at "molldesign" in Schwäbisch Gmünd, Germany. Since 1998, Edmund Englich has been Head of the Design and Design Management department at Loewe in Kronach, Germany. He received numerous awards, including the "red dot: design team of the year" award in 1991 as a member of the "molldesign" design team, and together with Loewe he received the German "Bundespreis Produktdesign 2000/2001" for the Loewe Spheros television.*

The design studio Phoenix Design *was founded by Andreas Haug and Tom Schönherr in 1987. It has since developed into a nationally and internationally renowned company. During this time, Phoenix Design attracted many renowned regular clients such as Hansgrohe, Axor, Sharp, Siemens, and LG. The Phoenix Design studio was honoured with the most important design prizes for its projects, such as Europe's most coveted design prize, the Lucky Strike Designer Award. Phoenix Design has reached first position in the "ranking:design" for three times in a row. Today, with a staff of 18 employees (designers, illustrators, trained model builders, and CAID experts), Phoenix Design is able to create class A surface models in-house and to deliver milling jobs just in time. The branch office in Tokyo conducts business with clients from Asia, attending projects on-site until they are ready to go into serial production. Since January 2003, Andreas Dimitriadis has been managing partner of Phoenix Design.*

Edmund Englich on
"Design as a Benefit for the Customer":
The high quality of a design visualises the overall value of the product, enhances the image of the brand, and thus creates a decisive and permanent benefit for the customer.

苹果影院电脑
Apple Cinema displays

苹果设计团队
Apple Design Team
苹果电脑有限公司
Apple Computer, Inc.

由乔纳森·依维带领的苹果设计团队，位于加利福尼亚的库比提诺，其成员都是从世界各地选拔上来的精英人士。乔纳森和他的设计团队被列入全球最有影响力的设计师之中，他们于2002年荣获了“红点年度最佳团队奖”。

The **Apple Design Team**, *led by Jonathan Ive, is based in Cupertino, California, and features hand-picked talent from around the world. Jonathan and his design team rank among the world's most influential designers. In 2002, they received the honorary award "red dot: design team of the year."*

HDR-FX1 HDV1080i 型便携式摄像机
HDR-FX1 HDV1080i camcorder

宫下伸
Shin Miyashita

宫下伸于1955年生于日本东京，他从东京高崎科技大学工业设计专业毕业后，于1975年来到索尼公司工作。他参与了电视摄像机等一系列产品的设计工作，其作品中不乏精品：BVW-200专业摄像机，BVP-700专业摄像机及HB-101 Hit-Bit电脑，以及SL-F1 Betamax便携式录像机。宫下伸日前在索尼创意中心担任艺术总监。

宫下伸关于“把使用者的需求放在第一位的设计工艺”

如果一个产品使用了新科技，那么它一定会有创新的功能。设计者的任务就是如何把这些新功能清晰地传达给使用者，使使用者容易理解并操作舒适；同时设计者还须着眼于产品的每一个方面，包括它的功能位置安排，外形，颜色和其它特性，至少也要尽可能地展现其设计的新功能，使产品更具吸引力，或者使用简单的，不加其它修饰的手法设计并展现这些新功能——这就是当我要开发或创作一样东西时所要遵循的基本原则。那种只在产品的“款式”上寻求突破的设计想法是并不足以吸引人们的。

设计HDR-FX1高清晰数码摄像录像机的关键环节就在于它的“过于高清晰”。站在摄像机后面的人不想以模糊的画面结束拍摄，那究竟什么样的设计布局才能让放在手中拍摄的画面达到稳定，高清晰？把控制面板放在什么位置才最方便？同时，即使布局很好，整体的重量能达到平衡吗？只有通过综合考虑这些问题，考虑到各种各样的情况和功能性，才有了今天这款摄像机。

Shin Miyashita *was born in Tokyo in 1955. After majoring in industrial design at the Ikuei Technical College in Japan, he joined the Sony Corporation in 1975. Subsequently, he was involved in a range of design projects, including for instance video cameras for broadcasting. Highlights of his works include the BVW-200 professional video camera, the BVP-700 professional studio camera, the HB-101 Hit-Bit computer, and the SL-F1 Betamax portable video deck. Shin Miyashita currently serves as Art Director at the Sony Creative Center.*

Shin Miyashita on
"Designing Technology with the User in Mind":

If an item uses new technology, it always has original functions. The designer gives thought to how to lay out these functions clearly for the user so the user can understand them easily and use them comfortably, and works on it from every perspective of position, shape, colour and other attributes. The bottom line is to maximise the presence of the desired functions, presenting them attractively, and to lay them out or design them using a simple approach that avoids unnecessary frills. This is my basic philosophy when creating or making something. Pursuing only "style" will not result in a product that appeals to people's emotions.

The key phrase for the design of the HDR-FX 1 Digital High Definition Video Camcorder was "ultra high definition." The person behind the camera does not want to end up with a blurry image. What kind of layout is best for obtaining stable, high-definition video in handheld shooting? What positioning of the panel makes it easiest to see? And even if the layout is good, what about the overall weight balance? ... This camera is the result of a thorough review of issues like these, of all kinds of conditions and functions.

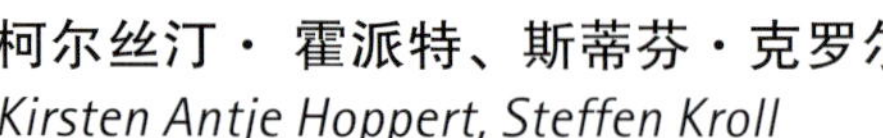

柯尔丝汀· 霍派特、斯蒂芬·克罗尔
Kirsten Antje Hoppert, Steffen Kroll

Akashi 女士提包
Akashi handbags

垂直喷射工作室
Studio Vertijet

2000年，柯尔丝汀·霍派特和斯蒂芬·克罗尔在德国哈雷的萨勒成立了**垂直喷射工作室**。柯尔丝汀·霍派特1973年生于德国的普劳恩，1992年到1998年期间，她在哈雷的艺术与设计学院学习室内建筑。随后，她与斯蒂芬·克罗尔合作，共同完成了她的研究生毕业作品——未来主义预制房屋。斯蒂芬·克罗尔1968年生于德国的哈次格罗德，曾是一名木工。在1992年至1997年之间，他在哈雷艺术与设计学院学习产品设计。1998年，他的毕业作品（女鞋及皮靴），荣获了德国巴伐利亚州的年轻设计师大奖。垂直喷射工作室为很多公司提供产品设计，其中包括COR、BREE、JAB ANSTOETZ、SKIA、AUTHENTICS、ELMARFLOTOTTO以及很多零散项目。2002年，由垂直喷射工作室设计“Scroll”座椅作为“新千年建筑”在台北的现代艺术博物馆作展出。同时，“Scroll”座椅还荣获了2002年“红点奖”，并分别于2003年，2004年设计的“Hob”家居休闲沙发椅及“Campo6”地毯也摘得“红点奖”。其设计的“Akashi”手提包系列还获得了2005年的“iF award”奖。

柯尔丝汀·霍派特和斯蒂芬·克罗尔关于“美与形式”：

如果能通过产品的外形，就能传达出其内在的品质，那一定是很完美的设计吧！如果设计师有强烈的想要创造出完美的外形和雕塑般的效果的欲望（那是一种不可言喻的抽象的外在的美的表现），并通过艺术的途径表达出来，那就更完美了！我们所有的设计都基于这样的理念，甚至是私人用品，比如为BREE公司设计的这款“Akashi”手提包系列，它曾是需要重新被塑造的无生命的东西，但只要通过精心的设计，它就会变的活色生香。对了，更重要的是，它还可以装东西呢！

The Studio Vertijet *was founded by Kirsten Antje Hoppert and Steffen Kroll in Halle/Saale, Germany, in 2000. Kirsten Antje Hoppert, born in 1973 in Plauen, Germany, studied interior architecture at the School of Art and Design in Halle from 1992 to 1998. Subsequently, she developed a futuristic pre-fabricated house together with Steffen Kroll on a post-graduate program. Steffen Kroll, born in 1968 in Harzgerode, Germany, trained as a cabinetmaker and, subsequently, studied product design at the School of Art and Design in Halle from 1992 to 1997. For his diploma work (lady's shoes and boots), he received the Bavarian State Award for Young Designers in 1998. The Studio Vertijet works for companies such as COR, BREE, JAB ANSTOETZ, SKIA, AUTHENTICS and ELMARFLÖTOTTO as well as on numerous freelance projects. The seat furniture "Scroll," designed by the Studio Vertijet, was shown in the Museum of Contemporary Art in Taipei, Taiwan, as part of the exhibition "Architecture for the New Millennium" in 2002. The Studio Vertijet has received the "red dot" for the seat furniture "Scroll" in 2002, for the lounge chair "Hob" in 2003, and for the carpet "Campo 6" in 2004. The handbag collection "Akashi" has also been awarded the "iF award" in 2005.*

Kirsten Antje Hoppert and Steffen Kroll on "Beauty and Form":

It is wonderful to look at surfaces that communicate depth. However, sensing the desire to recreate such an exciting surface or sculpture – an abstract representation of ineffable physical beauty – by oneself and thus in an artistic approach, is an even greater experience. All our objects are based on this idea. Even the individual elements for the handbag series "Akashi" for BREE were at one time lifeless material and had to be shaped. Only when folded in sophisticated ways, the material is transformed into sensual objects, that can be used for carrying things as well.

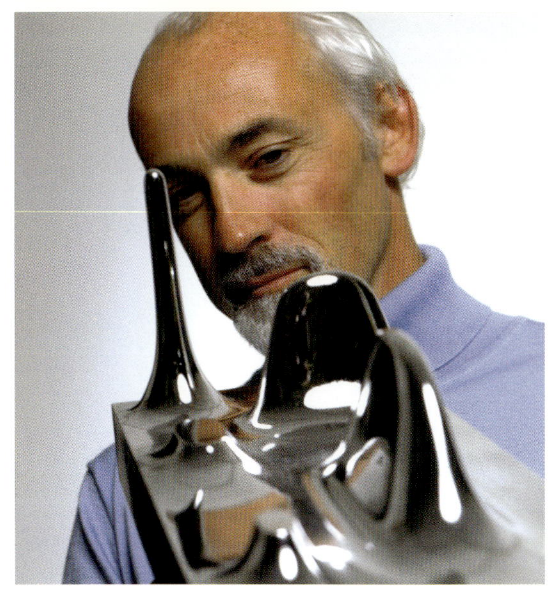

摩纳哥 V4 概念手表
MONACO V4 Concept Watch

洛斯・拉古路夫
Ross Lovegrove

洛斯・拉古路夫，于1958年生于英国威尔士的卡地夫，1980年毕业于曼彻斯特综合技术大学工业设计专业，并荣获一等优等学士学位荣誉。1983年，他在伦敦皇家美术学院获得了设计硕士学位。在二十世纪八十年代初期，他在西德的“青蛙设计”公司担任设计师，并参与设计了索尼公司随身听及苹果电脑等项目，之后又来到巴黎的Knoll国际公司担任顾问，获邀加盟Atelier de Nimes，同让・努维尔和菲利普・斯达克一道，为Cacharel、路易威登、爱马仕及杜邦等多家公司担任顾问。1986年，他回到伦敦成立了自己工作室，为多家客户提供设计服务，其中包括：空中客车、Kartell、Idee、标志汽车、三宅一生、瑞士豪雅手表及日本的伊东丰雄建筑事务所。他的设计作品在纽约现代博物馆及伦敦设计博物馆等世界各地多家设计博物馆进行长期的展出。洛斯・拉古路夫获得过多次的国际大奖，其中包括：1999年的“iF award”奖，2000年的“工业设计杂志最佳设计奖”，及2004年的皇家艺术学会颁发的“皇家工业设计师奖”。

洛斯・拉古路夫关于摩纳哥 V4 设计理念：

V4手表由里及外都体现了当代手表技术的一次革新，这款手表在结构上非常坚固，外形不乏活力。表盘主要由玻璃构成，无论从哪个角度都可以清晰的看到整个表内部奇妙的运动。V4的设计理念是，通过二十一世纪严格的几何原理的运用，使设计简洁大方，凸现出层次的美感。

Ross Lovegrove, *born 1958 in Cardiff, Wales, graduated from the Manchester Polytechnic with 1st Class BA Hons Industrial Design in 1980, and received his Master of Design from the Royal College of Art in London in 1983. In the early 1980s, he worked as a designer for "frog design" in West Germany, engaged in projects such as walkmans for Sony and computers for Apple Computers. He later moved to Paris as a consultant to Knoll International. He also joined the Atelier de Nimes along with Jean Nouvel and Philippe Starck to work as a consultant for, amongst others, Cacharel, Louis Vuitton, Hermes, and Dupont. In 1986, he returned to London and established his own studio. Ross Lovegrove has conducted projects for numerous clients, including Airbus Industries, Kartell, Idee, Peugeot, Issey Miyake, TAG Heuer, and Toyo Ito Architects in Japan. His works are on display in the permanent collections of various design museums around the world, including the Museum of Modern Art in New York (MoMA) and the Design Museum in London. Ross Lovegrove received many international awards. Among them are the "iF award" in 1999, the "ID magazine Good Design award" in 2000, and the "Royal Designer for Industry" by The Royal Society of Arts in 2004.*

Ross Lovegrove on the design of the MONACO V4:

The V4 is a revolution in contemporary watch design both from the inside and out. (...) The case is strong and powerful in its architecture, which is dominated by the inclusion of glass panels, which have been designed to provide a full insight into the wonders of the movement within from both sides and even the edges. (...) With the V4 I looked to simply tune the parts with disciplined 21st century geometries and finishes that combine to reveal the layered beauty of the invention.

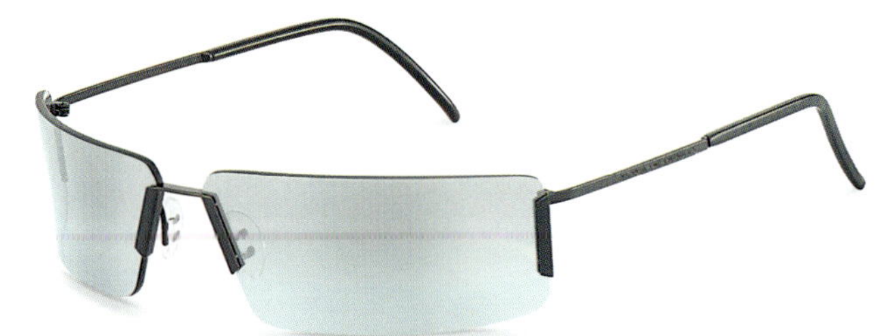

P'8404 保时捷镜架
P'8404 Porsche Design frame for eyeglasses

彼得·科瓦里
Peter Kövari

彼得·科瓦里于1936年生于匈牙利的布达佩斯，从1956年起，一直生活在德国。他曾在斯图加特科技大学学习机械工程专业并在乌尔姆造型学院学习设计。毕业后，他成为自由职业者，在各个领域从事设计工作。在这段时间里，他逐渐对眼镜设计领域慢慢精通起来。彼得·科瓦里荣获过多个大奖，其中包括“红点”奖及“Bundespreis Produktdesign”奖项。

彼得·科瓦里：“作为设计师我如何看待自己”：
我的作品拒绝光鲜的外表，而是从产品本身体现出我与时尚的这种关系。为了不完全脱离这种准则，在我的设计中我总是力求表现出这一点。伴随着时尚同时存在的是，每个时代都有其自己的审美观和语言表现形式。秉承着艾契尔的“简单即好”的原则，我觉得我有义务提供出最佳的可行性解决方案，而不是通过产品外观上的华丽来给顾客装点门面。恰恰相反的是，我努力从内容上、外观美感上及最佳的使用效果等方面来进行设计上有意义的创新。我追求从眼镜本身来透出的时尚感，并能让佩戴者对眼镜建立起一种持久的认同感。

Peter Kövari, *born in 1936 in Budapest, Hungary, has been living in Germany since 1956. He studied mechanical engineering at the Stuttgart Technical University and design at the Hochschule für Gestaltung in Ulm. After receiving his diploma, he first worked as a freelance designer in various fields. In the course of time, he gradually specialised in the main field of spectacle design. Peter Kövari was awarded several design prizes, including the "red dot" and the "Bundespreis Produktdesign."*

Peter Kövari on "How I See Myself as a Designer":
Rejecting the spectacular in my work is, in itself, a sign of my relationship to fashion. In order not to be utterly off the mark, I am looking for timeliness in my designs. Alongside the overtly fashionable, each era also has its own aesthetics and its own language of form. Following Otl Aicher's maxim that "reduction is a benefit," (...) I feel obliged to offer the best possible solutions because I do not want to affect a face with formal extravaganzas. Instead, striving for meaningful innovation in content, formal aesthetics and an optimum in usability, I aim to make spectacles that are fascinating in themselves, and which help establish a lasting identification between the wearer and the object.

埃斯基耳·特莫尼、维斯·贝哈、肖恩·森约克
Eskil Tomozy, Yves Béhar, Shawn Sinyork

Birki休闲鞋
Birkenstock Birki Pro / Birki Clogs

维斯·贝哈
Yves Béhar
埃斯基耳·特莫尼
Eskil Tomozy
肖恩·森约克
Shawn Sinyork

维斯·贝哈是美国旧金山"fuseproject"设计工作室的创建者。他曾在美国及欧洲学习工业设计，并从加利福尼亚州帕萨迪那的艺术中心设计学院获得了理工学士学位。在1999年建立fuseproject设计工作室之前，他曾担任硅谷frog设计工作室及Lunar设计工作室的首席设计帅。作为综合性的设计工作室，它从事着不同领域的设计项目工作，项目涉及科技、运动、生活方式和时尚等。

埃斯基耳·特莫尼是"fuseproject"设计工作室的设计工艺主管。他领导所有3D发展和模型创作的工作。他的作品在SIGGRAPH动画展，Alias/Waver-front的广告和网站上都颇有影响。

肖恩·森约克是fuseproject设计工作室的设计主管，确保着工作室能够运营正常，同时他也领导着最重要的项目，包括德国勃肯鞋，MINI，东芝，惠普的业务。他的设计也为fuseproject设计工作室赢得了很多荣誉。

维斯·贝哈关于"fuseproject工作室的设计理念"

人人都在谈论并逐渐认识到设计是任何建筑行业中最关键的部分。人们逐渐摒弃了那种认为只靠投放大量广告和一个所谓的"品牌"就能增加销量的想法，转而把目光投到产品精美优良的设计上去。这就是为什么在"fuseproject"工作室，我们把这种理念视为每次设计挑战的中心任务，并捕捉任何机会与使用者之间建立起感情上的交流。"fuseproject"工作室的设计宗旨就是建立品牌与消费者之间的联系，给顾客以美好的体验，传达出精彩的理念。最重要的是，我们认为好的设计会给人带来美好的享受。

Yves Béhar *is the founder of the design studio "fuseproject" in San Francisco, USA. He studied industrial design in Europe and in the USA, and holds a BS degree from the Art Center College of Design in Pasadena, California. Prior to founding fuseproject in 1999, he had been design leader at frog design and Lunar Design in Silicon Valley. As an integrated design firm, fuseproject is working on many projects in areas as diverse as technology, sports, lifestyle and fashion.*

Eskil Tomozy *is Technical Design Manager at fuseproject. He is leading all 3D development and prototyping efforts. His work has been featured in places like SIGGRAPH as well as in Alias/Wavefront's ads and website.*

Shawn Sinyork *is fuseproject's Design Manager who keeps things running smoothly and who leads the most important programs, including Birkenstock, MINI, Toshiba, and HP. His design contributions have earned many of the awards granted to fuseproject.*

Yves Béhar on "The fuseproject Design Philosophy":

Everyone talks about how design is finally becoming recognised as an important part of building businesses of any kind. People have gone from thinking that good advertising and the right "branding" are what sell products to understanding that well-designed products sell themselves. That's why at fuseproject we put experience at the centre of every design challenge and make emotional connections with the user at every opportunity. At the heart of all fuseproject design is the narrative, connecting brand and consumer, creating memorable experiences and engaging messages. After all, we believe that good design treats people well.

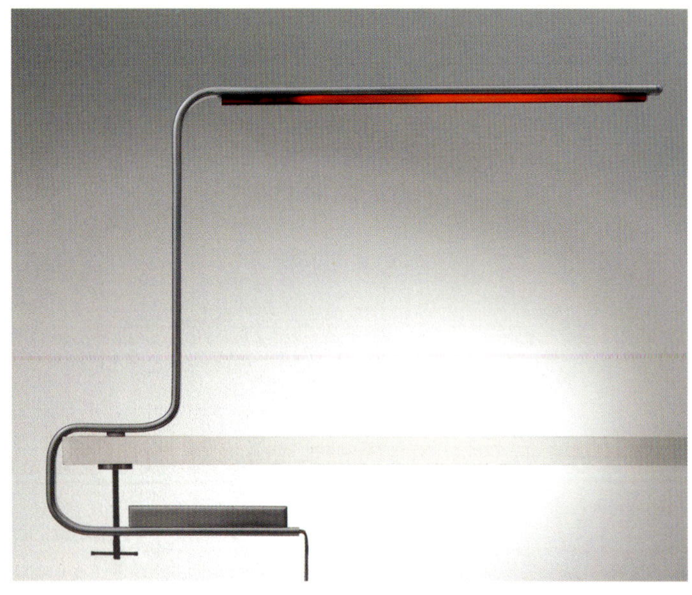

线状台灯
One Line table lamp

欧若・依图
ORA-ÏTO

欧若・依图是以法国年轻设计师Ito的名字命名的品牌，他与在建筑、图文及媒体传播领域内的专家团队一同工作。因此，欧若・依图还是一个代表着涉猎多个领域设计的工作室的品牌，其中包括：建筑设计、多媒体及媒体传播。欧若・依图从事多家公司的不同项目的设计工作，包括欧莱雅、喜力、阿迪亚斯、Kenzo、AIRband、本田、娇兰、Swatch和耐克公司。ORE-ITO设计的作品，于2000年在巴黎的卢浮宫展出，2001年在大阪的E&Y美术馆展出，2002年在莫斯科的俄罗斯国家历史博物馆展出，并于2004年在伦敦皇家音乐厅的海沃德美术馆展出。

ORA-ÏTO *is the brand name of a young French designer called Ito, who works with a team of experts in architecture, graphics and communication. In this way, ORA-ÏTO also functions as the name of a multi-disciplinary design studio in the fields of design, architectural design, multimedia, and communication. ORA-ÏTO is working on highly varied projects for companies such as L'Oréal, Heineken, Adidas, Kenzo, AIR band, Honda, Guerlain, Swatch, and Nike. The works by ORA-ÏTO have been exhibited in the Palais du Louvre in Paris in 2000, the E&Y Gallery in Osaka in 2001, the Russian National History Museum in Moscow in 2002, and the Royal Festival Hall at the Hayward Gallery in London in 2004.*

海鸥吊灯
Mouette suspension lamp

让・米歇尔・维尔莫特
Jean-Michel Wilmotte

让・ 米歇尔・ 维尔莫特，1948年生于皮卡第大区的苏瓦松的法国城，他既是一名建筑师，又是一个城市规划师和设计师。在1975年后，他成立了自己的工作室。现今，他的设计团队有来自不同国家的99名设计师，他完成的100多个设计项目遍布国际国内，如：黎巴嫩、欧洲、摩洛哥、韩国、日本、俄罗斯及美国等地。他的设计作品跨越工业设计和室内建筑，同样，他在不同的建筑项目上从事设计工作，如博物馆、建筑物的重新选址及当代改造等。作为城市规划师，他所倡导的理念是“城市景观的室内建筑”，是对“设计城市空间也要关注个人空间”的新诠释。

Jean-Michel Wilmotte, *born in 1948 in the French town of Soissons (Picardie), is an architect, town-planner, and designer. He founded his studio back in 1975. As of today, with his team of ninety-nine people of various nationalities, he has realised more than one hundred projects in France and abroad, including in Lebanon, Europe, Morocco, Korea, Japan, Russia, and the USA. His works range from industrial design to interior architecture. He is also working on various architectural projects for museums as well as on the relocation and contemporary remodelling of buildings. As a town planner, he has developed the concept of an "interior architecture of the urban landscape," a new approach to "designing urban spaces with as much care as private spaces."*

造型——新市场，新形式
Cutting the shapes – new markets, new forms

充满热情地尝试和大胆追求新颖形式是“客厅和卧室”系列产品设计的核心环节，重点强调的是“家具那捕捉眼球的影响力和显著的个性只有通过设计才能传达出来”，评审毕勇·达尔斯特姆，路易吉·发拉拉和马汀·克莱森更进一步证实了这种外形设计上的勇气——创作不是牺牲所有的代价去“满足你的眼睛”，当全世界的消费者的眼光越来越不再雷同的时候，取而代之的是要寻求新路线和新市场。这个过程就是去生产具有新象征主义的家具。沙发和椅子有如水晶般清晰的轮廓，诱使观看者想去触碰，他们想要看看它能否发出清脆的响声。家居设计从二十世纪六十年代的桶型椅子就着重强调功能上的改进要与现代的需求相一致。令人感兴趣的是有些地毯的设计重新诠释了包豪斯的主旨，有些地毯的图案是由电脑设计而成，这也正展示了设计界将怎样在这个紧密联系的世界里激发出新的创作手法。通过对产品的深思熟虑，评审们得出的普遍印象是令人惊叹的“任何事都可以”的设计理念。多样化的设手法以前总是存在于设计师的心中，但现在变成了事实。模糊平淡无奇的外观、丰富的色彩、保守的花呢布料，每一处的设计都在情理之中，却真实地再现了产品。正如评审们所说的那样：通过极高标准的设计，使完美的多样化表现形式相互和谐统一。因为设计出符合人体工效学的椅子或是沙发已经不再稀奇，那么最终要做到的就是设计要充满真情实感。

Zestful experimentation and daring new forms are important themes *in the "living rooms and bedrooms" category. Stressing that the furniture possessed the "expressive power and character only design can produce," the jurors Björn Dahlström, Luigi Ferrara and Mårten Claesson found further evidence of courage in forms which were not created to be "polite to the eye" at all costs, but instead pursue new routes and markets in a time when the universal customer no longer serves as model. And this process is producing new typologies of furniture. The crystal-clear forms – the contours of the sofas and armchairs, for instance, seem almost clipped – occasionally challenge the beholder. Familiar designs from the past such as the 1960s bucket armchair have undergone functional revision in line with contemporary requirements. While some carpets interestingly re-interpret familiar Bauhaus motifs, others have patterns that might have been computer-generated – showing how the mediatised world is inspiring new forms in this area, too. A resounding "anything goes" was the general impression made on the jurors by the products considered. The diversity of forms previously only existent inside designers' minds had now become reality. Surfaces with dull or mirror finishes, rich colours, staid tweeds – everything is legitimate. And this sovereign variety of styles is matched, as the jurors note, by an extremely high standard of design. Now that ergonomically designed chairs and sofas were "hardly unusual," the rest was "pure emotion."*

路易吉・发拉拉
Luigi Ferrara
加拿大
Kanada

毕勇・达尔斯特姆
Björn Dahlström
瑞典
Schweden

马汀・克莱森
Mårten Claesson
瑞典
Schweden

客厅与卧室
Living rooms and bedrooms

6900 沙发, 2004

Rolf Benz AG & Co. KG, Nagold
Design: Christian Werner, Hollenstedt/Appel
www.rolf-benz.de

6900沙发的设计是源于装饰艺术的基本准则，相比之下，它们极富个性并展现出丰富的视觉语言，反映了高品质的质量要求。在这种潮流的带动下，6900沙发体现了均匀的外形与精良材质的结合，是精致与粗犷、柔软与结实、细腻的织布与坚实的皮革的完美融合，体现出了一种阴柔和阳刚之美。以最基本的几何结构为构架，结合略为圆形质感骨架的靠背及扶手，极具纤细与优雅，设计结构宽松。“厚实”的坐垫与靠垫，与沙发的整体结构融合为一体。沙发的外部是优质的皮革，内部是精致的织布——体现出了一种巧妙并完美的“结合与融合”。通过这样的设计，这款沙发提供给使用者无与伦比的高质量以及完美的工艺制作。6900沙发以现代的“生活平台”作为基本构思，体现出了现代人的轻松与惬意。在沙发的后部边缘设有较矮的不易察觉的支撑腿，使沙发呈现出一种在空中浮动的感觉。

The design of the 6900 sofa model is oriented to the basic maxims of Art déco. These were characterised by a specific visual language rich in contrast, reflecting a high degree of quality awareness. Along the lines of this trend, the 6900 sofa model "plays" with proportions and materials; it combines both the filigree and the massive, the soft and the hard, soft fabric and firm leather as well as the feminine principle with the masculine. In the basic shape of a cube, a slightly rounded shell for back and armrests, extremely slim and delicate, creates the framework for voluminous, "thick" seat cushions and back pillows, integrated into the shape of the sofa. The frame is finest leather on the outside, fabric on the inside – a masterly and exciting "mix and match". In this way, the sofa is a piece of furniture for a resident setting a high value on the special, as well as an object of finest craftsmanship. The 6900 sofa model is conceived as a modern "life platform" allowing relaxing and lingering. The sofa rests on short legs, set back from the edge of the body, making them invisible to the observer and giving the sofa the impression of floating in thin air.

沙发, 2005

elmarflötotto GmbH, Gütersloh
Design: Stefan Diez, München
www.elmarfloetotto.de

这套沙发系列由于其创造性的添充物使得它的外型看上去很舒服平和。外部的帆布面结合内部的织布结构，并在其中添加了Ergofill和橡胶泡沫碎片。除了长沙发自身的稳固性，外观明显的缓冲性设计重新诠释了古典长沙发的设计理念。这套长沙发系列包括有：两座沙发、沙发椅、沙发凳和长沙发凳。可提供的产品颜色有：桔红、葡萄紫、午夜蓝及灰蓝色。

The Couch series owes its comfort and calm shape to an innovative padding. The outer canvas lining contains a textile interior structure attached to the lining and in itself filled with Ergofill and rubber foam flakes. Aside from giving Couch its stability, this cushioning results in an unmistakable shape – the reinterpretation of the classic Chesterfield. The couch series consists of a two-seater, a chair, a stool and a bench. It is available in red-orange, bordeaux, midnight blue and blue-grey.

绳绑系列沙发, 2004

Leolux Meubelfabriek BV, Venlo, NL
Werksdesign: Leolux Produktentwicklungsabteilung
Design: People on the Move, Venlo, NL
Vertrieb: Leolux Möbelfabrik GmbH, Krefeld
www.the-silly-side.com
www.leolux.com

Silly-Side的绳绑系列沙发是由被绳子捆绑的两大块橡胶泡沫组成的。这是其基本的设计理念——整体设计风格就是要刺激你的视觉感官。该系列的独特匠心之处在于突破传统的家居材料，取而代之的是Silly 座椅设计理念——极具弹性的结实“皮肤”结合使用荣获专利的新技术，最终设计成有三种不同颜色的款式类型。

The String chair of the Silly-Side collection consists of two rubber foam elements connected to one other with several strings. This is the basic idea – the design is supposed to deliberately provoke the eye. A characteristic of this collection is the lack of traditional upholstery. Instead, the Silly seating concepts have an extremely elastic, strong "skin", applied using a patented application technique. Three versions are available for the final finish, each in different colours.

Magnum 桌子, 2005

Team 7 Natürlich Wohnen GmbH, Ried, Österreich
Design: Martin Ballendat, Simbach
www.team7.at/kontakt/vertriebspartner
www.ballendat.de

通过减少视觉语言及复杂的工艺，Magnum桌子展现出来令人震撼的强烈对比。采用樱桃树，胡桃树等优质木材让该款桌子呈现出一种清晰的优雅性。同时还提供由山毛榉、桤木、橡树、枫树等木材制作的桌子。另外，桌上配有白色玻璃板，给人以明亮的视觉效果。结构上采用手拉抽取式设计，可折叠的桌面，使桌子的长度可以从50厘米到100厘米，总长度可达到350厘米。

The Magnum table lives on the exciting contrasts resulting from a reduced visual language and a sophisticated technique. High-quality wood like cherry or walnut create a clear elegance of the table, which is also available in beech, core beech, alder, oak and maple. With a white colour glass top, the table yields a light impression. Functional is a one-hand extraction mechanism. An integrated fold-out top allows an extension of the table by 50cm or 100cm up to 350cm in total length.

Relounge mit 凳子, 2004

Dietiker Switzerland, Stein am Rhein, Schweiz
Design: greutmann bolzern Designstudio, Zürich, Schweiz
www.dietiker.com

Relounge椅子可以在客厅、休息室和接待室使用。12毫米粗的钢管从椅子的前端边缘到后部分托起整个底座，并把椅背设计成适合靠坐的弓形。在先前出品的椅子是在胶合板为骨架的上面放上皮革或是织布等家具装饰材料。椅子有镀铬表层和涂有粉末表层的两种款式可供选择。

Relounge is a chair used in the living-, waiting- and reception areas. A 12mm steelrod runs from the chair front edge into the vats and up to the back, creating a bow that supports the back of the seat shell. The pre-press plywood shell is covered with leather or fabric, the upholstery likewise. The frame is available in a chrome-plated or powder-coated version.

FK 碗状沙发椅, 2004

Walter Knoll AG & Co.KG, Herrenberg
Design: Preben Fabricius,
Jørgen Kastholm
www.walterknoll.de

二十世纪九十年代末，KF设计的桶形座椅被视为“现代设计”的最佳典范。今天，在全世界内被誉为古典中的经典。FK 沙发椅正是这种潮流的诠释，是FK家族系列中的代表之作。其特殊的轮廓注定要成为“简约派艺术风格的代表”。

At the end of the 1960s, the FK bucket seat advanced to become the model par excellence of "modern design". Today, it represents the classic valid design throughout the world. The FK lounge chair is a interpretation of this trend and a member of the FK family. With its significant contours, it is predestined to become an "icon of minimalism".

CLOU 装饰织布, 2005

nya nordiska textiles gmbh,
Dannenberg
Werksdesign: Design-Team nya nordiska
www.nya.com

Scherli的圆点型织布，就像用线串起来的小珠子一般散落在织布的表面。虽然该产品采用较多的粗质毛线来加工成图案，但以做工精美并闪亮的聚酯纤维为底面，能透过圆点型的表面闪出光芒。高低错落有致的结构，粗质感与光泽感的相互掩映，体现出该产品的三维视觉效果。根据季节的变换，有四种颜色可供选择：黄色（春）；粉绿色（夏）；紫罗兰金棕色（秋）；白色（冬），每一款都是公司产品的经典颜色。

Scherli dots, strung together like beads and placed all over the surface, dominate this fabric. A delicate, brilliantly glossy polyester base is shining through the dots whilst the pattern is formed by the use of voluminous matt yarns. The optical appearance of three-dimensionality is created by the low-and-raised-structure and the interplay of matt-and-shine-effects. Four shades, based on the seasons, each show their typical colour, varying from yellow (spring), green-pink (summer), gold-violet-brown (autumn) to white (winter).

LIA-PALACE 装饰刺绣, 2005

nya nordiska textiles gmbh,
Dannenberg
Werksdesign: Design-Team nya nordiska
www.nya.com

如纸一般的Lia，设计上极具远东色彩，为刺绣提供了完美的底面。通过使用朴实加高科技的刺绣工艺，达到了令人赏心悦目的织布效果。使用卢勒克斯细线绣出准确生动的菱形图案，更加突出了黑，白，灰三种颜色的布局。

The paper-like, almost Far Eastern appearance of Lia makes it a perfect base for embroidery. The desired excitement of the fabric is achieved by using stark contrasts – embroidery on a high-tech base. Strict and graphical lozenge shapes, embroidered with iridescent Lurex threads, accentuate the colour range consistent in black-white-grey.

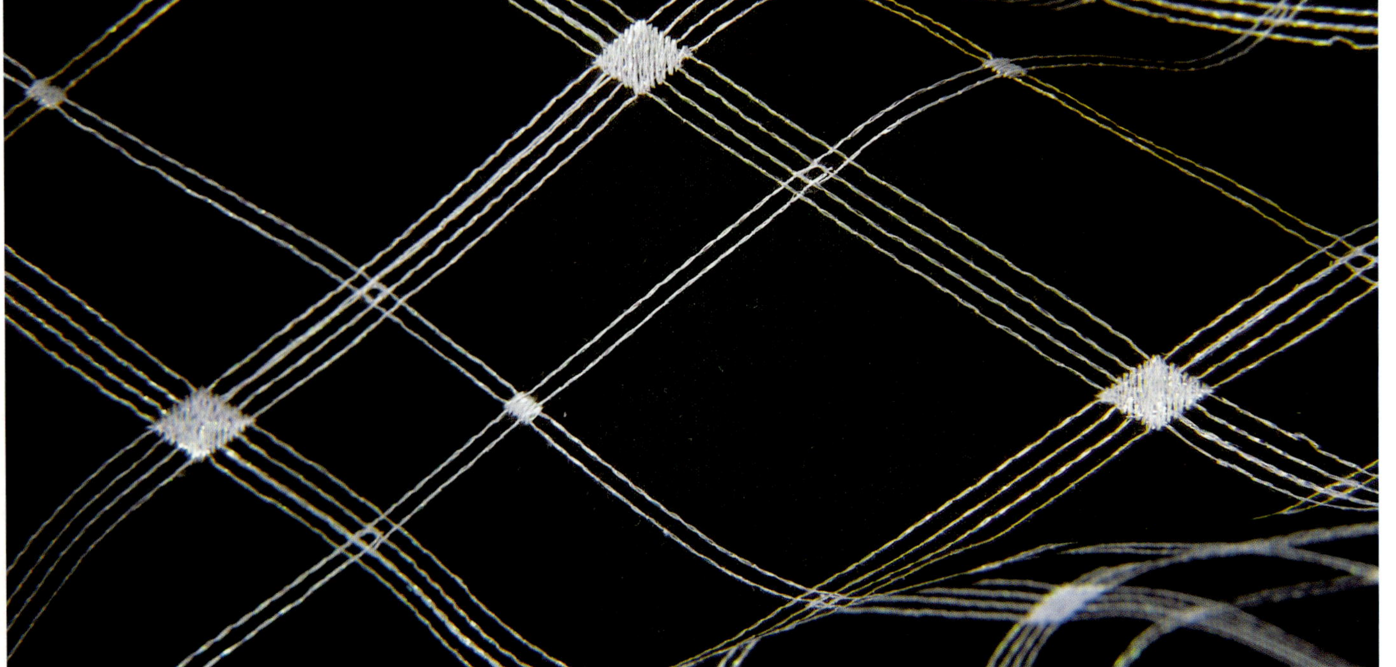

ANDORRA 装饰纺织品, 2005

nya nordiska textiles gmbh,
Dannenberg
Werksdesign: Design-Team nya nordiska
www.nya.com

仿佛是施了魔法，水平的棱形块仿似在半透明的织布间滑动。更重要的是，不同的设计手法而织绘成了稍显不规则的织物表面，并在产品的工艺中使用了不同质地的线，其中包括纯丝，聚酯纤维，乙酸酯，这些都突出了材料的特性。其颜色分布从冷色调（黑，白，灰）到暖色调（红，金黄），使用这样的织布让朴实无华的底面（panel）充满了舒适的家一般的感觉。

As though applied by magic, horizontal cording stripes slide across a semi-transparent fabric. Significant is the slightly irregular surface of the fabric which results from the different behaviour during the finishing process of the different yarn qualities such as pure silk, polyester and acetate and accentuates the different brilliances of the individual materials used. The colour range starts from Cool (black-white-grey) and ends in Hot (red-golden). Simple, straight panels obtain a homely touch by using this fabric.

Black Jack 室内装饰沙发, 2004

Machalke Polsterwerkstätten GmbH & Co. KG, Hochstadt
Design: Steven Schilte, Naarden, NL
www.machalke.com

Black Jack这款沙发体现了传统的立体感，并采用纤细的镀铬金属杆作为支架，给人以飘逸的感觉。即使把它作为较大的组合沙发摆在角落里，竟也显轻盈，在不经意间迎合了现代客厅的整体氛围并传达出自己的独特个性。它的独特功能主要体现在附带备用靠垫，可根据地点的不同摆放在靠背上或扶手旁，这样就可以把它变成一个舒适的沙发床。这种可调整性的功能不需要复杂的工艺，只需要有一个智能的磁铁系统就可以改变沙发的形状和结构。其最基本的设计理念就是要制作一个沙发，而在支撑功能上没有具体的要求。

Black Jack is a sofa programme in the tradition of cubic shapes, yielding an impression of floating lightness due to the slim chrome-plated metal rod. Even as a larger corner combination, the sofa appears light, adapting itself to modern living room ambiences unobtrusively, yet with a clear message. Its functionality is expressed in variable back elements attachable at different places on the back or armrest, thus turning the sofa into a comfortable couch bed. The adjustment function doesn't require involved mechanics; an intelligently packed magnet system takes care altering shape and form. The basic design idea was to create a sofa, which doesn't require concessions as to line management supporting functionality.

水晶椅子, 2005

Walter Knoll AG & Co.KG, Herrenberg
Design: EOOS, Wien, Österreich
www.walterknoll.de

水晶椅子的设计源于传统的座椅设计理念，其目的就是去重新诠释“椅子的高贵”。它功能强大，外形紧凑：椅子的主体结实地摆放在地板上，像是从地面里生长出来，以欢迎的姿态展示着自己。外部结构紧实而内部却柔软舒适，温和的斜坡形扶手极好地结合了人体功效学原理。不管作为餐椅、休闲椅或是会议用椅，水晶椅子使坐着都成为一种特别的享受。

The Crystal chair is designed as a reminder of the origins of seating, with the objective to reinterpret the "dignity of a chair". Crystal is a structure with a high degree of functionality and formal strictness. Resting solid on the floor, the corpus seems to grow out of the base, opening itself in a welcoming manner. Strict on the outside, soft on the inside, gently sloping armrests provide support in the ergonomically well though-out upholstery. As a dinner, lounge or conference chair, it quite simply makes sitting a special experience.

凹面火焰盘, 2004

mono-Metallwarenfabrik Seibel GmbH, Mettmann
Design: Franz Maurer, Wien, Österreich
www.mono.com

由灯油发出的明亮光线，浮动在拉过绒的不锈钢碗型凹面体里。反射出的光芒使整个房间沉浸在柔和的灯光下，这件艺术品是由mono公司精工制作出来的。

A flame – generated by lamp oil – hovers over a brushed stainless steel bowl. The reflection immerses the entire room in a soft light. This art object is meticulously crafted at mono.

LOU 5874/094 地毯, 2004

JAB Teppiche Heinz Anstoetz KG, Herford
Werksdesign: Elke Klar
www.jab.de

LOU地毯特殊的视觉及触觉效果是由新颖的织线加工设计而成。高水平的精工制作使地毯的精良做工包括两个不同的层面，由frise线织成条形编织样式的密实底部和开阔的表层。毛线是由高品质的新西兰羊毛加工而成，卷曲造型的地毯表面显得格外抢眼。该款极具吸引力的地毯以温暖，亲切的外观使客厅变得更为舒适。

The special optics and haptics of the LOU carpet are achieved by using an innovative yarn. With a high degree of craftsmanship, this carpet is a sophisticated construction of two different levels, a tight base and an open top surface made of long-woven frisé yarn. This yarn consists of high-grade New Zealand wool and dominates the optics of the carpet with its curling structure. The result is an inspiring carpet surface, setting a cosy accent in the living room with its warm inviting appearance.

ZIP 5947/999 地毯, 2005

JAB Teppiche Heinz Anstoetz KG, Herford
Design: Christian Werner, Hollenstedt/Appel
www.jab.de

ZIP地毯从一系列的地毯设计中脱颖而出，主要体现了韵律感、整体感、活力感的主题。不对称的断裂表层像是处于线性光谱图案里，这种视觉元素很容易迷惑你的眼睛，使地毯看起来更为纵深。前一层图案像是织在另一层图案的上面或前面。从不同的角度，地毯呈现出三维效果，那是从“快速” 到“冷静”的转变。

The ZIP carpet is from a series of carpet designs dealing with the themes of rhythm, structure and dynamism. The asymmetric fracture within the line raster pattern creates a visual element to confuse the eye, giving this carpet an unusual depth. One level seems to lie above or in front of the other. Depending on the angle of vision, this carpet has a three-dimensional effect, changing from "fast" to "calm".

手工海洋毛束地毯, 2004

Tai Ping Carpets, Düsseldorf
Werksdesign: Michaela Schleypen
www.taipingcarpets.de

海洋系列地毯使人联想到宽广无垠的南方海岸。该款地毯采用纯手工制作的毛束，使混合的颜色呈现出波浪的造型，有如映照下的阳光或星辰闪烁的天空，让人目不暇接。新的毛束加工工艺使颜色呈现出极其精美的融合，在毫米间竟能显出颜色的多种变化。立体浮雕式的结构栩栩如生地模仿了波浪的流动，从而加强了颜色布局的生动性。纯手工制作工艺使其从结构上将朴实的线条变成了外观的三维效果。起初，不同层面使用单色调设计的立体结构使地毯给人一种真实的感受。而外观对我们的吸引力不仅体现在视觉上，还有触感上。该款地毯由新西兰羊毛制成，有多种颜色、款式和大小可供选择。

The infinite space of the South Seas served as inspiration for the Ocean carpet. The hand-tufted carpet bedazzles the eye with colour melanges in the shape of waves seemingly reflecting the sunlight and turning the ocean into a starry sky. The colour melanges appear extremely delicate and, due to a new tufting process, allow the display of colour variations in the range of millimetres. The playful colour arrangement is highlighted by a relief structure imitating the flow of waves in a lifelike way. This kind of hand-crafted structure expands the plain line pattern to a three-dimensional appearance. For the first time, the result was a monochrome design in different layers with a relief structure reflecting a realistic impression. The surface appeals to the observer not only visually, but haptically as well. The carpet is made of New Zealand wool and is available in many colours, shapes and sizes.

长体花瓶, 2004

Design: SANI
Sani Saksuwan
Bangkok, Thailand
sani@sani.co.th

Pink Punk长体花瓶是由手工制作而成，把半透明的亚克力材料包在铝制框架里，外部由真皮包裹制成。其半透明的特点，使插在花瓶里花的根茎活灵活现地展现在大家的眼前。该款花瓶是限量发售，仅售500只并在每个花瓶上都有其序列号。

The Pink Punk tall vase is a hand-made vase made of translucent acrylic in an aluminium frame wrapped with real leather. With its translucent character, the vase displays the stems of flowers in an interesting way. It is a limited edition, only 500 pieces, with each one having a serial number.

Flakes 椅子, 2004

Arkitekterne maa Schmidt, Hammer & Lassen K/S, Aarhus, Dänemark
Werksdesign: SHL Design
Vertrieb: Van Laar Agentur, Düsseldorf
www.shl.dk

Flakes椅子的最初设计理念是要把它设计成粗犷并具有新美学特色的椅子。它是由玻璃纤维和钢材制作加工而成、可分层叠放的椅子。该款椅子重新诠释了玻璃纤维这种材料——它可制作成各种各样款式的椅子，比如可以在纤维玻璃的内部浇铸成不同的图案或标志，还可以把织品牢牢的固定在其中，使它们通过这种半透明的材质在外部清晰可见。这是一种新的设计手段，可以使织品应用在椅子的设计上，也使得建筑师和设计师在装潢设计中有更多的选择。Flakes椅子是由经久耐用的材料加工而成，因此受到很多喜好耐用型家具的消费者的青睐。即使椅子不能再继续使用，其玻璃纤维和金属也可以回收再利用。

The background to the construction of the Flakes chair was to design a robust chair with fresh aesthetic qualities. It is a modern stacking chair made of fibre glass and steel. The reinterpretation of fibre glass allows a diversity of chair versions, for instance, casting it with logos or fabric embedded and visible through the translucent material. This new way of utilising fabric on a chair gives architects and designers plenty of options to decorate a space. Flakes is made of durable and long-lasting materials for people who appreciate sturdy furniture. At the end of its life cycle, both fibre glass and metal can be recycled.

Lagoa 系列, 2003

Accademia srl, Manzano, Italien
Design: Arch. Enrico Franzolini, Udine, Italien
www.accademiaitaly.com

Lagoa系列组合沙发的设计理念是给人以轻巧的感觉。这套组合沙发包括一个普通的座椅、一个扶手椅、有两种高度可选择的凳子。压铸而成的铝架使这套沙发具有灵活的多样性。椅座和椅背是由木质材料加工而成（着色的橡木）。可供选择的还有由聚丙烯制成的或外部贴有织布或皮革而制成的椅子。由橡木制成的款式有自然色、漂白色、铅灰色。由聚丙烯制成的款式有白色，烟灰色和橙色。也可以选择在光泽度高的铝架上喷上灰色清漆或涂上单色（白色，烟灰色，桔色）粉末，结合镀有颜色的金属，不锈钢或者铝。Lagoa系列沙发由里及外都体现出了经久耐用的品质。这款系列产品在航海或驾船中也非常适用。

The Lagoa collection is designed to yield an impression of lightness. It consists of a regular chair, an armchair and a stool with two different heights. A die-cast aluminium frame gives the collection a high degree of versatility. The seat and the back are made of wood (stained oak); alternatively, they are also available in polypropylene or cushioned with fabric or leather. The wood version is available in oak with the colours nature, bleached, lead grey or wengè. The polypropylene version is available in white, anthracite grey or orange. The frame is alternatively made of high-gloss aluminium, varnished grey and powder-coated monochrome (white, anthracite grey or orange); combinations with chrome-plated metals, stainless steel and aluminium are possible as well. Lagoa is durable and conceived for both inside and outside use. The collection is also suitable for use in marine or boating ambiences.

outlook 4 窗帘杆, 2004

interstil Diedrichsen GmbH & Co. KG, Steinhagen
Design: Design AG (Frank Greiser), Rheda-Wiedenbrück
www.interstil.de
www.design-ag.de

outlook 4是黑色碳质管与刨光铬质环的完美结合，而且突出了黑色碳管上织品结构与金属表层的强烈对比。尽管铬环与碳管在同一水平线上，但是铬环与织品的末端融合在一起，能够特别突出碳管的两端。铬环可以调整到管的两侧，这样可以在整个系统安装更为精确。整套装置不需要任何中间的支架就可以支撑稳固，这种构造是建立在工程学的原理之上的，运用远离中心的布局在碳管的里面加入一个坚硬的绳子，使其具有张力。这种张力通过隐藏在铬环内的螺丝钉旋转体现出来，使支撑杆可以承受不同重量的窗帘。在每个圆环的内部插入了透明的塑料，这样移动窗帘就没有声音。

outlook 4 is a symbiosis of black carbon tubes and brackets in a polished chromium finish, yielding an interesting contrast between the textile structure of the carbon tube and the metallic surface. Bracket and end pieces have merged into one, setting a strong accent to each side of the tube, although being in line with the tube. The brackets are adjustable sideways, allowing a precise installation of the system. The integral mechanism allows extreme wide spans without intermediate brackets. The mechanism is based on an engineering principle in which a hardened string running inside the tube in an off-centre arrangement is put under tension. The tension is applied by turning a screw hidden inside the brackets, allowing the pole to be adjusted for any curtain weight until perfectly straight. Movement of the curtain is silent due to the application of transparent plastic inserts into each individual ring.

Graduate 书架, 2004

Molteni & C, Giussano, Italien
Design: Jean Nouvel, Paris, Frankreich
www.molteni.it
www.jeannouvel.fr

Graduate是一个书架，外观朴实，结构却复杂。结实的木质书架隔板固定在墙上，几根金属的直柱挂在标准的凹槽内形成不同的高度。木质或铝质的隔板用不易看见的钩子挂在凹槽中被固定在不同的高度上。这种设计与正常结构次序相反，隔板不是支撑在地面上，而是挂在一个高高的书架上，这不仅让人感觉书架很轻盈，而且使用上极为灵活。在隔板的上部有个复杂的转向拉杆系统，可以使实际为25公斤的重量，平均地分散在一米长的隔板上。

Graduate is a shelving system with an essential appearance but complex structure. A strong wooden shelf is fixed to the wall at the top; a number of metal uprights with regular notches are hooked to this at different heights. Wooden and aluminium shelves held by invisible hooks are positioned level with the notches. The reversal of the structural sequence, with shelving that hangs from a high shelf instead of resting on the floor, brings extreme versatility combined with a different sense of lightness. A complex system of tie-rods contained in the upper shelf allows an actual weight load of 25kg, evenly distributed on a shelf one metre long.

感官享受与高科技
Sensuality and new technologies

厨房正在成为充满尖端科技的地方吗？越来越多的媒体宣传证明了事实却是如此。配带有电视的冰箱和由点击鼠标就能迅速控制的炉具再也不是未来的幻想。这些有趣的发展似乎已经激起了未来的潮流。同样，三位评审阿部真代，金哲昊和斯坦梵·伦吉尔都被这些特别产品所带来的感官享受所深深吸引。例如，瓷器与其它材料出人意料的完美结合不仅使人体会到新的触觉感受，而且还给产品带来了优美外观和全新的功能。这种“新的感官享受性”进一步体现在那些厨房用具上——它们的设计重点就是强调触觉感。新产品结合新科技带来的那种“人类触感”令评委们深深地折服，这些新产品的背后好似都藏满了故事，它们正在吸引着你去对那种全新生活方式场景探个究竟。评审们总结说，“厨房用具”领域内的设计水平非常的高，那些倍受人们青睐的功能再一次证明了年度的技术革新。一切都是高质量与功能性的完美结合，才给厨房带来了诸多益处。

Is the kitchen becoming a site of sophisticated technologies? *The increasing level of media integration suggests this might be the case. A refrigerator with integrated television set or a cooker rapidly adjusted by the click of a mouse are no longer futuristic visions. These interesting developments seem set to inspire future trends. All the same, the jurors Masayo Ave, Chul-ho Kim and Stefan Lengyel were equally struck by the sensual quality that distinguished no small number of products. For example, the unexpected combination of porcelain with other materials made for new tactile experiences and lent products new grace and functionality. This "new sensuality" was further expressed in fittings whose design empathises with the sense of touch. These methods of combining specifically "human" sensations with new technologies impressed the jurors, who were particularly taken by products which "tell a story" and hint at new lifestyle scenarios. As a general conclusion the jurors state that the standard of design in the "households and kitchens" group was extraordinarily high, with this year's innovations again being defined by highly considered functionality. In conjunction with special qualities, it is a functionality that brings any number of advantages to the kitchen.*

金哲昊
Chul-ho Kim
韩国
Korea

阿部真代
Masayo Ave
意大利
Italien

斯坦梵·伦吉尔
Stefan Lengyel
德国
Deutschland

家居用品和厨房用具
Households and kitchens

+INTEGRATION® 厨房, 2004

Poggenpohl Möbelwerke GmbH, Herford
Werksdesign: Manfred Junker
www.poggenpohl.de

+Integration厨房设备的内涵呈现出新颖的外观设计，并结合了全新的设计元素。独特的比例和高品质的材料以个性的方式诠释了现代的奢华生活。宽广的外观有着和谐统一的颜色：亮黑，亮灰和亮白，这与令人感觉特别的瑞士梨木、胡桃树和zebrano的木质台面装饰形成了鲜明的对比。从地板到天花板的这些组成部分是联系支撑建筑和整个房间设计的纽带，从审美的角度看，它们既与厨房的整体规划相统一，又独立于整个结构环境。此外，+Integration厨房设备把目前单一功能的厨房空间设计成为房屋的通讯中心。每个独立的部分都强调了多媒体元素的加入，使家居功能延伸至厨房。优雅的厨房高柜上装有完善的家庭影音系统，创造了一个全新的视觉空间。另一创新之处是智能家居技术的应用，提供给厨房智能的互联网络。整个房间的设备都通过+Integration系统进行控制。同时，这个系统包括有电话通讯设备和互联网。通过做工考究的接触板就可以进行简单而又清晰地操作。

The +Integration kitchen concept shows an innovative front design and integrates new design features. Unusual proportions and high-grade materials define contemporary luxury in a new individual way. Massive fronts, homogeneous in colour, made of Parapan in brilliant black, brilliant grey or brilliant white, contrast with expressive exotic wood veneers such as Swiss pear, walnut or zebrano. Floor-to-ceiling components as tie between the supporting architecture and the room design allow an aesthetically aligned planning of the kitchen, independent of constructional circumstances. +Integration turns the so far mono-functional earmarked kitchen space into a communication centre of the house. Solitary pieces of furniture, aesthetically highlighting the multimedia elements, represent an expanded living room function. Elegant highboards, each integrating a complete home entertainment concept in itself, create new visual spaces. Another innovation is the Smart Home technology, offering new possibilities to network the kitchen intelligently. The entire home equipment can be centrally controlled with the +Integration system. At the same time, this system includes telephone communication and an Internet access. The operation via a discreetly designed touch panel is simple and self-explanatory.

Actyes 厨房, 2004

Sunwave Corporation, Tokio, Japan
Werksdesign: Satoshi Taguchi, Hiroyuki Kikuchi, Hideyuki Takaku, Yoichi Ito
www.sunwave.co.jp

Actyes是一种新型的厨房系统。它只提供了厨房的内部设施和整体设计框架。特别之处在于，这种新型的系统呈现了一种属于个人风格的厨房。使用者们可以通过调整厨房的结构使其适应自己的生活方式。厨房的各种设施的布置也可以随时、随意地轻而易举地变换。将水槽、燃气灶、料理台等厨房的基本设备置于一个类似于门框型的简约的结构中，这样，在其下面就产生了一个很大的可用于储藏的空间，里面还可选择性地放进储藏柜、组合柜和/或诸如洗碗机之类的厨房里的一些其它设施。Actyes是一个可以不断变化的并且可以提供交流场地的厨房。创新的设计——"魔法抽屉"能从料理台两侧同时抽出。水龙头的横向设计也使得水槽两边能同时使用。通过这种设计，使用者们可以在厨房面对面地操作，从而创造了一个自然的交流空间。

Actyes is a frame and module system especially developed to present a kitchen with an individual profile. The system allows users to adjust the kitchen to one's own personal lifestyle. There is always the possibility of easily changing the arrangement of all kitchen elements. The concentration of all basic functions (sink, stove, water connections, etc.) in the gate created a large storage space just below. It can be filled alternatively with receptacles, cubes and/or other kitchen components such as a dishwasher. Actyes is a dynamic and communicative kitchen. Innovative "magic drawers" can be accessed from two sides. A lateral positioning of the faucet allows to use the sink from both sides as well. In this way, users can work in the kitchen face to face, creating a natural communication atmosphere.

滑道系统, 2005

Leicht Küchen AG, Waldstetten
Werksdesign: Manfred Deffner
Design: Hawa AG, Mettmenstetten, Schweiz
www.leicht.de
www.hawa.ch

滑道系统创造性地将滑动玻璃板应用于橱柜设备中。通过玻璃板的滑动，可以关闭厨房空间或者重新安排厨房空间，从而使厨房面貌焕然一新。这一系列包括滑动玻璃板和壁龛设备两个部分。其中，滑动玻璃板可以完全滑到一边，而背面和侧面都镀层的壁龛成为了厨房的一部分。在其覆层的表面或者是内部能安装诸如厨具、架子、照明设备等不同的厨房设施。玻璃墙可以是完全透明的、半透明的或者完全不透明的。滑道式系列优于其他同类产品的一个最大特点就是玻璃墙可以上锁，因此，孩子在厨房里是绝对安全的。滑动玻璃门可以全部或者部分打开厨房空间。

The Slide system is an innovative combination of glass sliding panels and cabinet elements. It gives the kitchen a new appearance by offering the possibility to close spaces of the kitchen or rearrange it with glass sliding panels. The system consists of glass sliding panels, which can be slid aside, and a niche wall system for the full surface cladding of back and side panels of a part of the kitchen. On and in this wall panel cladding, different functional elements can be fitted, like cabinet elements, shelves or lighting. The glass walls can be fully, partly or non-transparent. This system also increases among other things child safety in the kitchen as the walls are available with a locking function. The glass sliding doors can open the kitchen partly or completely.

可抽出式拐角橱柜, 2005

Kesseböhmer GmbH, Bad Essen
Werksdesign
www.kesseboehmer.de

LeMans创造性地设计出可置于拐角处的拉出式碗柜。使用者能很容易地拿到碗柜里的任何东西。两个“圆形剧场”式的托盘可以全体抽出，这样，使用者就能很容易地利用整个碗柜的空间。托盘的外形设计精美，这不仅提供了最大的贮存空间而且使得托盘能被毫不费力地移动。圆形的不对称式的设计使人联想到LeMans赛车道的曲线，设备名称的灵感也来源于这一著名的竞赛轨迹。打开碗柜的步骤是确定的。碗柜有两种移动方式——旋转和拉出，它们相互补充，使得碗柜使用起来更加方便，打开或者关闭碗柜设备也更加容易。

The innovative design of the LeMans corner unit pull-out allows access to the entire content of the cupboard. The two "arena" trays can be pulled out completely, making the full space easily accessible for the user. The shape of the trays was optimised in such a way that they can be moved effortlessly, but still offering maximum storage space. The rounded asymmetric design is reminiscent of the Le Mans race track curve progression; the famous race track was the inspiration for the name of the unit. The sequence of motions is exactly defined; two directions of movement – turning and pulling out – are combined for easy access. The LeMans unit can thus be handled with ease and comfort all the way in and out.

Jumbo 地板碗柜, 2004

Holzprojekte Härtenberger HKH GmbH, Hunderdorf
Werksdesign: Stephan Härtenberger
Design: Alno AG, Pfullendorf
Vertrieb: Alno AG, Pfullendorf
www.haertenberger.de
www.alno.de

Jumbo地板碗柜的设计既实用又美观。它既可以与小厨房完美地搭配，也可以是大面积厨房里的用具。其内部体积很大，而且事先安排好了瓶子等用具的摆放位置，这样就增加了它的储存容量。具有高光泽度的外表面可以采用白色、深蓝色、香草色和红宝石色，也可以采用不锈钢材料。

The functionally and aesthetically designed Jumbo floor cupboards are integrated into the kitchenette or added to the array upon completion of construction. With generous dimensions and a clearly arranged storage space for bottles, they provide additional storage capacities. The high-gloss front components are available in white, lapis blue, vanilla, ruby red or in stainless steel.

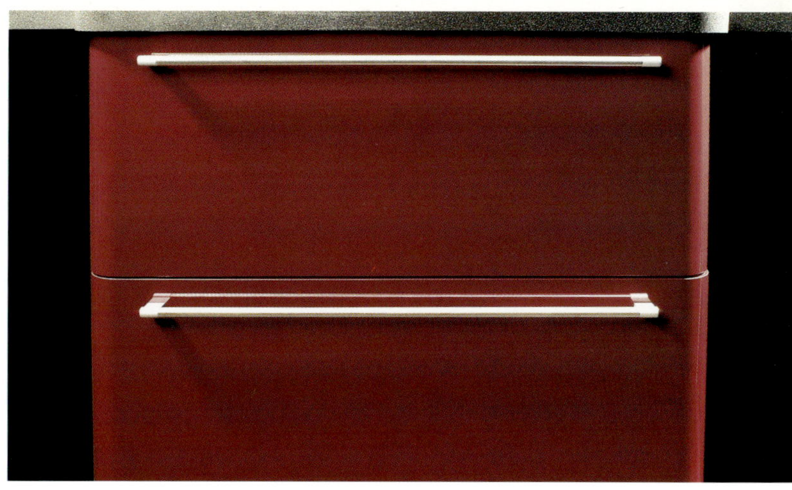

Cora 餐桌及工作台, 2004

Becherer Möbel + Innenausbau GmbH, Elzach
Werksdesign: Rochus Becherer
www.becherer.com

由于其简单大方、回归质朴的设计，无论是在私人场所还是在工作场所，这种装有对角形桌腿的桌子都有很多种用途。这种桌子的传统的做法是利用双榫把正方形的桌腿和桌子的顶部连接在一起，这种设计实际上也具有美学元素。餐桌可以采用樱桃木、枫木、胡桃木等材料，也可以根据个人的需要制作出体现个人风格的餐桌。

Due to its plain design reduced to bare essentials, the table with diagonally attached legs is suitable for many purposes, in private as well as work spaces. The classic way of joining – double tenons connecting square-shaped legs with the top – is an aesthetic design element at the same time. The dining room table is available in cherry, maple or walnut and can be manufactured according to individual needs.

Edition Rosenblatt 厨房家具, 2005

Weitz-Möbelmanufaktur GmbH, Seifhennersdorf
Werksdesign
www.manufaktur-weitz.de

Edition Rosenblatt不仅完美结合了人体工效学原理，还具有个性化的外观设计。这一系列具有三个基本特色：一是拥有自成一体的结构，二是表面的一层呈倾斜状，三是可以随意地摆放厨房中的各种设备。安装这个装置时遵循的基本框架源于一个机械工程的自给自足的系统。工作空间的不同高度是为了适应烹饪的不同需求而设计的，它反映了以人为本的设计理念。

The Edition Rosenblatt combines a high degree of ergonomics with a very characteristic impression. Basic features of the series are a stand-alone construction, a sloping front of the floor units and the option to freely place the components anywhere in the kitchen space. The basic structure for mounting the units is a self-sustaining girder system derived from mechanical engineering. The different heights of the work spaces are an expression of a user-friendly design geared to the needs and wants of the cook.

Orga-Box / Top Volume²
烤箱抽屉和厨房收纳柜，2004

Fennel GmbH & Co. KG, Bad Oeynhausen
Elco Kunststoffe GmbH, Gütersloh
Werksdesign
www.fennel.de
www.elcokunststoffe.de

由于有两个储存转换器，炊具抽屉系统能提供一个大的储存空间。170毫升的抽屉容量为烘烤盘和其它烘烤、煎炸设备提供了存放空间，此外，它也可容纳其它炊具柜中不超过100毫米高的设备。烘烤盘和烘烤架放在上面的抽屉中，而其他烹饪器具放在下面的抽屉中，这样一来，下面的空间就变得整洁有序了。超过150毫米的基座高度，使得再高出50毫米——即使220 毫米的抽屉也能插进去。被抬起的面板装置阻碍了滑动系统的下降，从而阻止了面板接触到地面。

The cooker drawer system creates a large storage space thanks to two volume variants. With its 170ml drawer, it offers space for baking dishes and other baking and frying accessories for all cooker cabinets from a plinth height of 100mm. This results in a clear order underneath the cooker with the baking trays and gridirons in the top drawer, and all the other cooking utensils underneath in the bottom drawer. With a plinth height of more than 150mm, the 50mm higher drawer with a height of 220mm can be inserted. A panel lifting mechanism counteracts a lowering of the sliding system, preventing the panel from touching the ground.

储物柜，2005

Leicht Küchen AG, Waldstetten
Werksdesign: Manfred Deffner
www.leicht.de

清洁、明确的面板的外观形状和轻型厨房体系很好地结合在了一起。通过制成透明的玻璃材料，它独立成型并且中性。因此，与其它任何材料搭配都不会产生问题。它的厚度已被减少到目前同类产品中的最低水平，大约是4到7毫米。超薄的外部形状虽注重产品的灵活性，但是仍然不会影响本身的其它性能。在背面再粘上铝等其它相似的支撑材料后，4毫米厚的玻璃板就可以单独地作为面板使用了。由于其视觉中立、易于搭配、环保且耐用，玻璃材料成为厨房设备的最理想的材料。

The clean and unmistakable front form blends well into the Leicht kitchen system and, by reducing it to the transparent material glass, it is self-contained and neutral, thus allowing combination with other materials without any problem. The front thickness has been reduced to the absolute minimum of approx. 4-7mm. The ultra thin fronts emphasise the lightness of the product, but are nevertheless sufficiently robust for all normal uses in this area of the kitchen. The 4mm thick glass is a single pane safety glass, which is glued to an aluminium or similar support that is slightly rounded at the back. Glass is an ideal material for use in the kitchen because of its visual neutrality, ecological harmlessness and durability.

量子速度 HF 86 Q 560 型光波微波炉
Lichtwellenofen, 2005

Siemens Electrogeräte GmbH, München
Werksdesign: Frank Rieser,
Gerd E. Wilsdorf
www.siemens.de/hausgeraete

量子速度HF 86 Q 560型光波微波炉能在几分钟内就给深度冷冻的食物加热完毕。加热一个完全冷冻的皮萨饼只需5分钟，而在一般的微波炉中则需要加热25分钟。这个设备的特征是具有不锈钢外壳及安装在外壳上的功能强大的操作组件和清晰的电子显示屏。

The quantum speed HF 86 Q 560 lightwave oven can heat up deep-frozen food within minutes. A deep-frozen pizza just takes 5 minutes instead of the usual 25 minutes in a conventional oven. The unit features a stainless steel housing with high-grade function elements and a clear electronic display.

s-line HB 330 580 整体烤箱和加热抽屉, 2004

Siemens Electrogeräte GmbH, München
Werksdesign: Gerd E. Wilsdorf,
Peter Hamm, Andreas Hackbarth
www.siemens.de/hausgeraete

在S流线型烤箱的设计中，两条狭长的直角型铁巧妙地避免了操纵盘和下开门的分离，制造出一种平和的光学印象，这种印象在该设备被安置在墙角的情况下尤为明显。S流线型烤箱的机身上涂有半镜面漆，而且被涂成点状格子图案，这些设计使机身的玻璃前端给人以舒服的视觉享受。同时，高质量的坚固金属把手上注有公司标识，这更突显出了S流线型烤箱的标准规范化设计。为了搭配S流线型机身，加热抽屉只有29厘米高，并且兼具预热餐盘、食物保温等多项功能。两者恰好可以嵌入88厘米高的标准机身当中。烤箱的控温范围在40至80度之间。

In the design of the s-line oven, two vertical metal-profiled strips avoid any separation between the operating panel and the drop-down door. This creates a calm optical impression, particularly in the case of a corner installation. With its semi-mirrored finish and a discreetly dotted grid pattern, the glass front yields a restful visual impression. The high-quality solid metal handle with inscribed brand logo underlines the exacting standards of the unit. With a height of 29cm, the warming drawer, styled to match the s-line oven, allows many functions, from pre-warming plates to keeping food warm. The temperature range is selectable from 40 to 80 degrees. Both units together fit into the standardised 88cm high niche format.

SE20T 593 EU 立式洗碗机, 2005

Siemens Electrogeräte GmbH, München
Werksdesign: Wolfgang Kaczmarek
www.siemens.de/hausgeraete

西门子SE20T 593 EU是一款设计典雅的不锈钢质地的洗碗机。操作可通过触摸传感器的方式进行，既方便用户，又具有很强的实用性。用户可以在机身上部进行项目选择。在洗碗机工作时，前门的显示屏上以文本形式显示出所选择的功能、剩余时间和其它特殊功能。洗碗机的上层金属篮子可以通过调整高度来调节承重量。该款独立式洗碗机工作时噪音低，只有44分贝，因此适用于开放式厨房。同时，该洗碗机配有伺服锁，可以使机门自动关闭，并易于打开。

The Siemens SE20T 593 EU free-standing dishwasher has an aesthetic stainless steel design. The operation via touch sensors is user-friendly as well as functional. It allows an easy selection of programmes from above. While the dishwasher is operating, the display at the front of the door shows the chosen programme, the remaining time and special functions in plain text. The height-adjustable upper basket (rackmatic) increases the variability in terms of load. The free-standing dishwasher is very quiet with its 44dB and is therefore suitable for open plan kitchens. Thanks to the servo-lock the door closes by itself and can be opened easily.

KG 36 U 198 / U 199
型冰箱, 2004

Siemens Electrogeräte GmbH, München
Werksdesign: Christoph Becke
www.siemens.de/hausgeraete

这些单独的不锈钢设备既可以独立放置，也可以共同组合成为一个新的设备。这种设计低调、大气，与厨房环境相映生辉。组合型设备的产生是为了追赶大容量的冷却工具的潮流。四个冷却区的温度可以各自单独调节。不仅外形设计具有较高品位，内部设计也是如此，如带嵌入功能的托盘，瓶架、可延伸的抽屉等。内部采用冷色调及混合材料；外壳则采用不锈钢材质。这中冰箱是百分之百的无氟利昂（FCKW/FKW）机器。

These solitary stainless steel devices can be set up as single units or as side-by-side combination. The design is timeless and low-key so that the units adapt themselves harmoniously to the kitchen environment. As side-by-side combination, the design consequently follows the trend toward high-volume cooling devices. The temperature of the four cooling zones can be adjusted individually. The high-grade exterior is continued inside, with telescope-supported trays, bottle racks and extendable drawers. The interior is designed in cool colours. The material mix points toward the exterior stainless steel finish. The unit is 100 per cent FCKW/FKW-free.

3 TS 750 型洗衣机

Balay BSH Electrodomésticos
España, S.A., Montañana (Zaragoza)
Werksdesign: Ralph Pietruska,
Robert Sachon
www.balay.es

3 TS 750型洗衣机是对Balay系列产品的一种创造性的应用。这一系列产品都具有不锈钢的外观。它的特点是具有一种特殊的隔音设备和多种其它功能，这些功能都被清晰有序地排列并展示出来。中心镶嵌的面板采用了特别的设计，它不仅强调了控制性设备的重要地位还定义了整个产品系列的外观设计。而且，其旋钮是可回转的。

The washing machine 3 TS 750 is an innovative appliance of the Balay product range in stainless steel look. It features among a special acoustic isolation an over-dosage control and extensive programme functions, shown in a clearly arranged display. An expressive design of the panel with a central inlay element accentuates the control elements and defines the appearance of the overall product range. The knob is retractable.

3VS 551ID 洗碗机

Balay BSH Electrodomésticos
España, S.A., Montañana (Zaragoza)
Werksdesign: Ralph Pietruska,
Robert Sachon
www.balay.es

3VS 551ID洗碗机是对Balay系列产品的一种创造性的应用，这一系列产品的外观都是不锈钢的。洗碗机在工作时非常安静，它拥有计时器和显示屏等设置，主要通过一个可回转的旋钮来控制。通过镶嵌在洗碗机内部的透明装置的变化可以区分出不同类别的产品。洗碗机的可调节的篮子和精心设计的其它组件进一步完善了对其产品的优质印象，同时也映衬出了Balay系列中其它产品的优点。

The 3VS 551ID is an innovative dishwasher of the Balay product range in stainless steel look. It is very quiet and possesses among an extensive timer function with the according display a retractable knob to set the main functions. By variations of the transparent inlay element, different product classes can be generated. Variable baskets and well-elaborated accessories complete the high-quality impression, which reflects to the other products of the Balay product range.

3 XM 205 H 型空调

Balay BSH Electrodomésticos
España, S.A., Montañana (Zaragoza)
Werksdesign: Tim Müller, Robert Sachon
www.balay.es

这种设备提供了一个灵活的，应个人需要而进行调节的气候控制系统。由于它具有制冷、供暖、净化空气和湿度控制这四种特性，一年四季都非常有用。它也很容易搬运，不需要组装并且可以与任何一种居住环境相融合。带有大型显示屏的电子操控系统能够很容易地凭感觉控制，使用者既可以随时设置温度和性能选项也可以设定长期使用模式。这一产品也符合Balay系列产品的视觉语言的设计理念。

The appliance offers a flexible and individually adjustable climate control. Due to the four features – cooling, heating, air cleaning and moisture control – it is useful throughout the year. It is easy to transport, doesn't require installation and integrates harmoniously in any living environment. An electronic control with a large display is intuitive to handle: temperature and feature selection can be regulated directly, or can be programmed for long-term use. The design corresponds to the visual language of the Balay product range.

PAM 21011 移动式空调, 2004

Robert Bosch Hausgeräte GmbH, München
Werksdesign: Yvonne Weisbarth
www.bosch-hausgeraete.com

PAM 21011移动式空调设备设计得很有吸引力，最主要的原因是其外观设计很艺术，操作过程舒适而且简单。这种空调最初研发时是为了它能灵活地在家庭或工作场所中使用。亮色和暗色的结合运用，使这个设备总体看起变小了。另一方面，大型的液晶显示屏与周围形成强烈的对比且易于观看，所有的功能、参数和信息都可在这里显示出来。同时，符合逻辑的操作引导能够轻易地被使用者所理解。为更好、更有效地进行空气交换，通过一个按钮就能操控另一个发动机来驱动侧面的空气出口，同时镶嵌在内部的固定的负离子发生器可以净化空气，提高空气质量。空气过滤器安装在设备的前部而且更换起来很方便，用来装冷凝水的大水箱的集成手柄（integrated handle）可以很容易地处理抽水过程。为了安全起见，当水箱装满水的时候，空调会自动关闭。舒适地手柄处理系统和设备底部的四个小滑轮确保了机器非常灵活，易于搬运。

The PAM 21011 mobile air-conditioning unit owes its strong appeal, above all, to its aesthetic design, comfortable technique and ease of operation. The air-conditioner has been developed primarily for flexible use in living and working areas. Due to the combination of light and dark colours, the overall size of the housing has been reduced optically. The large LCD display is strong in contrast and easy to read. All functions, parameters and messages are displayed, and the logical navigation concept is easy to understand. For a better and more efficient air exchange, additional motor-driven lateral air outlets can be activated by the push of a button, while the built-in negative ion generator improves air quality. The air filter is located in front of the housing and can be replaced easily. The large tank for condensed water has an integrated handle for easy extraction. For additional safety, the air-conditioner shuts off automatically when the tank is full. Comfortable handles and four castors at the bottom of the unit guarantee a high degree of mobility.

WA65205 AL 洗衣机, 2004

Gorenje d.d., Velenje, Slowenien
Werksdesign: Rok Jenko, Lidija Pritržnik
Vertrieb: Gorenje Vertriebs GmbH, München

D65225 AL 滚筒式干衣机, 2004

Gorenje d.d., Velenje, Slowenien
Werksdesign: Rok Jenko
Vertrieb: Gorenje Vertriebs GmbH, München

超级触摸式系列洗衣机和滚筒式干衣机采用了现代极具美感的技术，外观设计漂亮大方。透过正面面板上的纵向卷曲结构和对其组件设计理念的抽象解释，人们对该设备的优质的性能和漂亮的外观有了一个大体的了解。洗衣机的外部结构大体上是固定的，这就促使整体的设计更容易达到和谐统一。改良后使用者可以更容易且高效地洗衣服并甩干。33厘米宽的门可以开至少180度，这样，拿取衣物就非常容易了。整个洗衣过程都是依照智能化的"巫师洗涤系统"（Wash Wizard System）的自动提示而进行的。这一软件安装在电子控制面板上，给使用者提供了关于洗衣和干衣过程中的所有必要的信息。

The washing machine and tumble drier of the Premium Touch line has state-of-the-art technology and an attractive look. Vertical convolutions on the front panel and a minimalist interpretation of the design elements give the appliance its characteristic and attractive appearance. The outer form of the washing machine is identical, which enables integration in terms of design. Its improved functionality enables the user to wash and dry clothes more easily and effectively. A large 33cm wide door with an opening angle of more than 180 degrees makes it easy to fill and empty the washing machine. The intelligent Wash Wizard system leads the user through all washing programmes. The software on the electronic control panel provides the user with all the necessary information about the washing and drying process.

VSR 8000 传感式巡洋舰清洁机器人
Reinigungsroboter, 2004

Siemens Electrogeräte GmbH, München
Werksdesign: Jörg Schröter
www.siemens.de/hausgeraete

传感式巡洋舰（Sensor Cruiser）清洁机器人在设计中特别注重使用者使用的舒适度和产品的易操作性。机器人真空吸尘器由一个移动装置和一个基本固定装置两部分组成。通过综合运用它的视觉和触觉传感器，真空吸尘器记录下了各种障碍物，如楼梯或是桌腿，然后绕过它们安全地行走。另外，还有一个灰尘传感器能分析出将要被清除的灰尘和尘土的种类，并且自动地选择合适的清洁程序。圆型的外观、较低的高度和在顶端装有一个保护器确保了它具有较大的灵活性，也防止了吸尘器卡在或是夹在家具下面。如果灰尘收集器已满或者是可充电电池快用完时，移动装置就自动地返回到其基本固定装置的位置，这时仍然可以自动地进行真空吸尘。

The designers of the Sensor Cruiser cleaning robot put particular emphasis on a high degree of user comfort and easy operation. The robot vacuum cleaner consists of a mobile unit and a base station. With its integrated tactile and optical sensors, the cleaner registers any barriers like stairs or table-legs, safely driving around them. An additional dust sensor analyses the degree of dust and dirt to be picked up and automatically selects the suitable cleaning programme. A rounded shape and a low construction height with additional protectors on the top surface allow good mobility and prevent sticking or jamming of the unit under furniture. If the dust collector is full or the rechargeable battery nearly flat, the mobile unit automatically returns to the base station where dust is vacuumed off automatically as well.

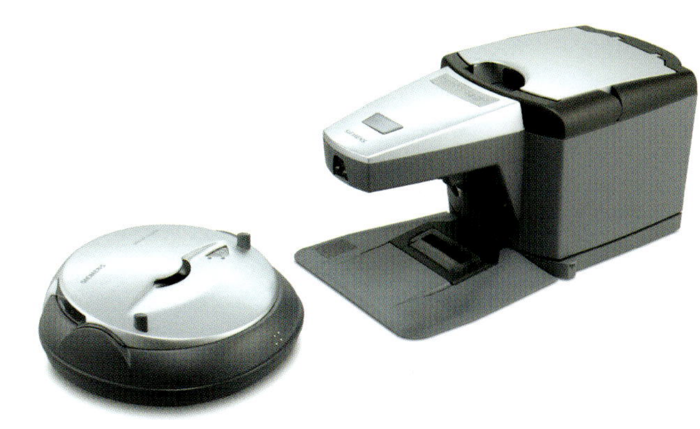

s-line LC 58 950 抽油烟机, 2004

Siemens Electrogeräte GmbH, München
Werksdesign: Gerd E. Wilsdorf,
Peter Hamm, Andreas Hackbarth
www.siemens.de/hausgeraete

S型产品系列中的LC 58 950烟机是一台90厘米宽的不锈钢设备，在它的边框处还镶有雕刻玻璃，这一设计蕴含着整个系列的高标准设计理念。优雅的前部线条设计，包括浮雕一样的品牌名称，也同样应用到了S系列的灶具的把手中去。机身上装有一个金属过滤器和一个实用的电子显示屏，该金属过滤器还可以在洗碗机中很容易地清洗。

The LC 58 950 hood of the s-line series consists of a 90cm wide stainless steel corpus and etched glass. The design underlines the high claims of this series. The elegant front profile is repeated in the door handle of the s-line oven including the relief-like integrated brand name. The unit is equipped with a metal fat filter, which can easily be cleaned in the dishwasher, as well as a functional electronic display.

EKEW 957.0 F 玻璃陶瓷炉灶, 2005

Küppersbusch Hausgeräte AG,
Gelsenkirchen
Werksdesign: Klaus Keichel
www.kueppersbusch.de

考虑到现代饮食健康的需要，此款产品由内置玻璃陶瓷架和拥有四个加热炉灶区的中央烹调区组成。这些实用性的设备拥有漂亮的外观，操作方便。各种菜式的烹饪（尤其是亚洲清淡菜式的烹饪）,在专用的炒锅烹饪区内，可以直接放在玻璃陶瓷凹槽处或是专门的炒锅上进行。五个加热区域均配备了快速加热反应装置， 在短短几秒钟之内便可使温度达到最高点，这样有利于节省宝贵的能源。三回路或双回路区能完美配合不同尺寸的锅形， 避免不必要的能源消耗。电子触摸传感器控制着烹饪区的加热和所有其他功能。清晰方便的图例控制面板能随时提醒用户设备所处的操作状态，方便操控。其它设计更保证了使用的安全性，如余热提示功能、假日关机功能（缩短操作时间）、防止儿童接触的安全锁以及中央关闭功能。面板边缘的独特设计更为您的厨房设计锦上添花，几乎适合各种厨房风格。

The built-in glass ceramic hob with a central wok cooking zone, surrounded by four ökospeed plus cooking zones satisfies modern requirements for a light and healthy cuisine and, at the same time, fulfils the highest demands with regard to design and functionality. A variety of dishes, particularly those following the trend for a light Asian cuisine, can be prepared in the wok cooking zone, either directly in the glass ceramic recess or by using the wok pan. All five cooking zones are fitted with fast-response ökospeed plus heating elements, which heat up in just a few seconds, thus saving precious energy. The triple- and dual-circuit zones adapt ideally to different pan sizes and avoid unnecessary energy consumption. The sensor touch electronic controls regulate the cooking zones and all further functions. The clear, user-friendly hob control graphics ensure that the user is always informed and in control. A safe operation is assured by residual heat indicators, a holiday shut-down feature (limiting operation duration time), a child lock and a central switch-off function. The facet edge design is an eye-catcher in every kitchen, harmonising with almost any style of kitchen.

DIE 995 F Inselesse / PKY 875 P02 玻璃陶瓷抽油烟机

Robert Bosch Hausgeräte GmbH, München
Werksdesign: Roland Vetter
Design (Inselesse): Eisele Kuberg Design (Frank Eisele), Neu-Ulm
www.bosch-hausgeraete.com

DIE 995 F烟罩为不锈钢质地，两边都装有成角度的玻璃，其独特的设计能满足个人或专业的不同要求，使之成为家用厨房装饰的焦点。此产品专为吊棚式炉具而搭配设计，并配有快速反应按钮和数字显示屏。三个速度控制器、一个强度设置、一个过滤器饱和指示装置以及预设十分钟操作功能等显示出了该产品优越的性能。另配有的三个20瓦卤素灯，其独有的调整光线功能使烹饪过程别有一番情趣。

90厘米宽的PKY875 P02玻璃陶瓷架专为方便用户而设计，用户可在两端同时使用。平滑雅致的磨砂玻璃遍布四周，前后不锈钢板设计绝对是任何厨房的装饰焦点。与DIE 995 F烟罩相搭配，它被设计成独特的蝴蝶形状。触摸控制板使两侧的四个快速加热炉盘区的使用更加便捷。此外它还拥有17个加热级别，完全电子控制，独立的电子感应按钮，加热电子元件等设备，随时为烹饪好每一道佳肴做着准备。

The DIE 995 F chimney hood is made of stainless steel and an angled glass screen on both sides, thus forming the centre of an individually designed kitchen. Its aesthetic design meets all professional demands. The hood is designed for ceiling mounting over stand-alone ovens and is equipped with short-stroke buttons and a digital display. Three control speeds plus an intensity setting as well as a saturation indicator for filters and a ten-minute post-operation function are an expression of a high degree of functionality. The joy of cooking is additionally enhanced by the equipment with three 20-watt halogen lamps as well as a dimming function for the work space.
The 90cm wide PKY 875 P02 glass ceramics cooking hob is user-friendly and can be operated from two sides. An elegant design with smoothly grounded glass facets at the sides and stainless steel panels at the front and back result in the unit being an absolute highlight in any kitchen. Suitable to the DIE 995 F chimney hood, it is designed in butterfly shape. TouchControl facilitates the use of the four high-speed cooking zones on both sides. With a fully electronic control featuring 17 power levels, a zone expansion via a separate sensor button and parboil electronics, every hobby cook is equipped with the means for the successful preparation of any dish.

PKC 887T01 玻璃陶瓷炉灶

Robert Bosch Hausgeräte GmbH, München
Werksdesign: Roland Vetter
www.bosch-hausgeraete.com

PKC 887T01玻璃陶瓷烹饪炉灶的显著的特点在于第一次创新地将Piezo触摸控制操作技术应用于炉盘设计中。控制面板由铝制成，上面设有集成的传感器按钮，轻轻地一按就可以选择所需要的功能。凹进去的控制面板在加热时只能达到很低的温度，因此是特别安全的。除了Piezo触摸控制设备外，炉灶还包括了配备17个加热级别的电子控件。四个快速区域和两个环形的烹饪区域以及装在每一个烹饪区域上的有切断电源功能的计时器，都使得这个专业的炉灶设备更加完善。

The PKC 887T01 glass ceramics cooking hob features an innovative Piezo TouchControl Operation new to cooking hobs. The control panel consists of aluminium with integrated sensor buttons. A gentle push is all that is needed to select the function desired. The recessed control panel heats up to a lesser degree and is therefore especially safe. Aside from the Piezo TouchControl Operation, the cooking hob includes a fully electronic control with 17 power levels. Four high-speed and two dual-circuit cooking zones as well as a timer with switch-off function for each cooking zone complement this professional hob.

PCL 985 FEU 天然气炉灶

Robert Bosch Hausgeräte GmbH, München
Werksdesign: Roland Vetter
Design: Eisele Kuberg Design (Frank Eisele), Neu-Ulm
www.bosch-hausgeraete.com

天然气很方便快捷，通过调控，又能很精确地控制温度，这就实现了快速到达沸点温度、可以精确地调控温度而且在关闭后不会产生余热。PCL985 FEU燃气灶装有新的点火设备，保证了安全便利地使用天然气。点火、监控火苗和必要时熄火的操作都是由电子设备完成的。铸铁平底锅支架可以置于大火力灶头、火力较小的灶头或者跟炒勺一起放在二台标准火力灶头上使用。灶具一只手就可以点燃，同时适用于天然气和液化气。

Gas is very fast and allows heat to be controlled very precisely. This results in extremely fast boiling, finest temperature adjustment and switching off without after-heat. The PCL 985 FEU gas hob is equipped with the innovative FlameTronic feature, guaranteeing maximum safety and convenience in the handling of gas. The flame is electronically ignited, monitored and extinguished if required. The cast iron pan supports are positioned above a high-speed burner, an economy burner, a wok- and two standard burners. The burners are ignited with one hand and are suitable for use with both natural and liquid gas.

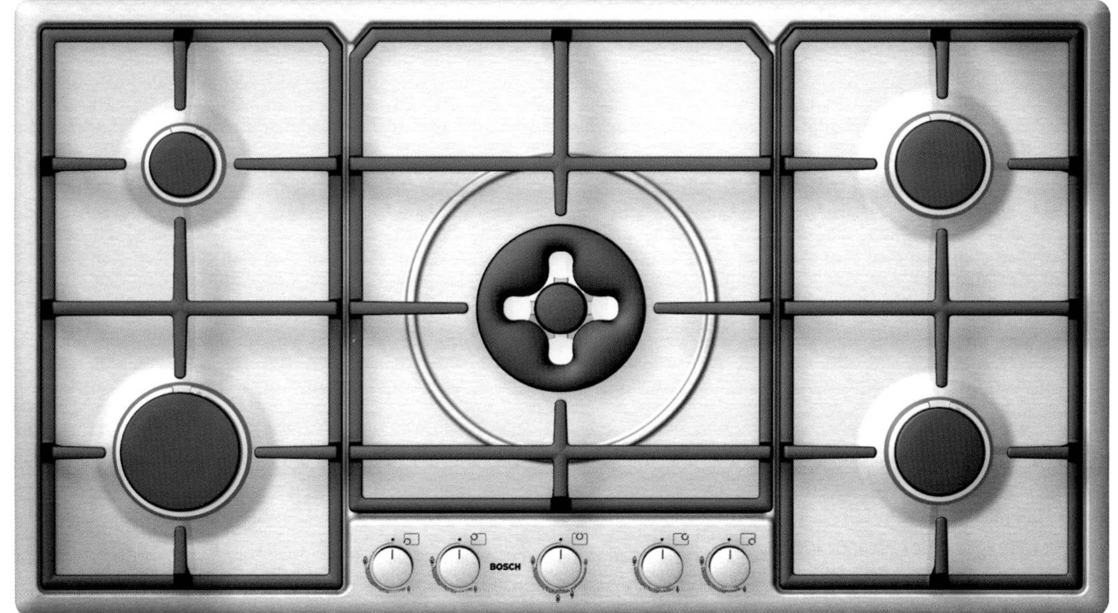

KSW 38920 冷藏式酒柜

Robert Bosch Hausgeräte GmbH,
München
Werksdesign: Hans-Reinhart Janssen
www.bosch-hausgeraete.com

高贵典雅的设使得KSW 38920冷藏式酒柜可以与任何一个厨房相匹配。圆拱形的玻璃门和高品质材料的应用给人留下个性化的独特印象。具有铝制外框的双层绝缘门与防紫外线的玻璃结合在一起创造了理想的存储环境。该设备包括七个木制架子，其中有六个可以移动并可调整高度。其内部设有两个数码温度计，随时可以准确显示温度。温度控件能把温度控制在6摄氏度到14摄氏度以内。

Due to its elegant design, the KSW 38920 wine refrigerator adapts itself to virtually every kitchen. The arched glass door and the high-grade materials used give the unit an individual and characteristic impression. A double-insulated door with aluminium frame in combination with UV filter glass creates optimum storage conditions. The device contains seven wood shelves, six of which are removable and height-adjustable. Two digital thermometers inside display the precise temperature. A stepless temperature control allows settings between +6 and +14 degrees centigrade.

WFM C6400 全自动洗衣机

Robert Bosch Hausgeräte GmbH,
München
Werksdesign: Roland Vetter,
Ralph Stand
www.bosch-hausgeraete.com

WFM C6400是专门为美国市场设计的新一代洗衣机，在使用时衣物可从前部放入。高93厘米，宽68厘米的设计改变了洗衣机在家庭中所占的面积。控制板安装在正面的顶部，从而消费者不需弯腰就可以很容易地选择所需程序。大开口和滚筒使得取拿衣物更加容易，不仅如此，洗衣时也更加轻柔，不易磨损衣物。

The WFM C6400 front-loading washing machine is an innovative washer generation conceived for the US market. With a width of 68cm and a height of 93cm, its design creates new washing machine proportions for the household. The control panel at the front top allows easy selection of programmes without having to bend over. The extremely large opening and barrel make loading and unloading easy and help to wash clothes gently.

HBN 78R770 型烤箱

Robert Bosch Hausgeräte GmbH,
München
Werksdesign: Roland Vetter
www.bosch-hausgeraete.com

HBN 78R770型烤箱的旋转门能打开180度角，从而提供了一个安全舒适的通向烤箱内的通道。作为一个特大型号的烤箱，它为超大型的烘烤器皿提供了足够的空间，同时也能一起烘烤多份食物。全玻璃面板和玻璃门上的防止儿童开启锁为用户提供了最大限度的安全保障。烤箱的特点是具有可显示文本的电子对话屏及光亮的可回转旋钮。内部优质的GranitEmail瓷釉涂层不仅非常漂亮，而且还有高度的抗震性、耐磨性和抗酸性。由于采用了高分解技术，烤箱的另一个特点是其具有一个高效率的自我清洁系统，因而无需再使用其它的化学洗涤剂。

The swing door of the HBN 78R770 fitted oven with an opening angle of 180 degrees provides a comfortable and safe access to the interior. As a particularly large-dimensioned oven, it provides sufficient space for extra large roast dishes or several serving portions simultaneously. With its large-surface full-glass door, the unit offers a high degree of security, as does a child lock with door latch. The oven features dialogue electronics with a text display as well as a retractable knob with a lighted ring. The design with the high-grade enamel coating GranitEmail on the interior yields an aesthetic impression and renders the oven highly shock- and scratch-resistant as well as acid-proof. With its pyrolysis technology, the oven features an efficient self-cleaning system without having to resort to chemical detergents.

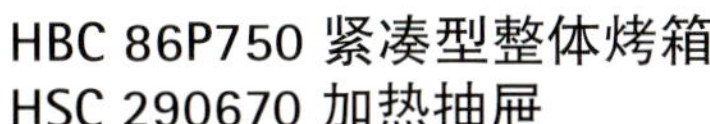

HBC 86P750 紧凑型整体烤箱
HSC 290670 加热抽屉

Robert Bosch Hausgeräte GmbH,
München
Werksdesign: Roland Vetter
www.bosch-hausgeraete.com

因结构简洁紧凑，HBC 86P750“美食家”烤箱与微波技术结合在一起使紧凑的内部空间变得更加舒适。烤箱有六个主要的部件，包括微波、计时器、防水的旋转开关和保证儿童安全的保险锁等，这些特色部件提高了烤箱的舒适性和安全性。所有的加热组件、自动程序以及重量指示器都是经久耐用的。42升超大容量的烤箱是由GranitEmail瓷釉涂层制成的，它还有一个自动的热解自我清洁系统。用于预热的铝制抽屉大小合适，它是烤箱系列产品的重要辅助设备。烤箱高29厘米，非常适合给菜保温。在没有干扰的情况下，和了酵母的生面团在烤炉中能很快地发酵，餐具也能很快地预热。烤炉的内部采用不锈钢材料，装有强化玻璃制成的加热板。能完全展开的伸缩式抽屉负荷重量达25千克。烤箱可以在40摄氏度和80摄氏度之间进行控温调节。

Due to its compact construction, the HBC 86P750 fitted gourmet oven with integrated microwave offers a high level of comfort in tight spaces. Featuring six heating modes including microwave, a timer, an immersible rotary switch and a child safety lock, the oven provides superior convenience and safety. Functional as well as reliable is the plain display for the different heating modes and the automatic programmes as well as a weight indicator. The large oven with a volume of 42 litres is made of the enamel coating GranitEmail and includes an automatic pyrolytic self-cleaning system. The fitted preheating drawer is made of aluminium and serves as a functional supplement to the fitted compact ovens of this series. With a height of 29cm, it is very suitable for keeping dishes warm. Yeast dough can rise without disturbances, and tableware can be preheated. The interior, made of stainless steel, is equipped with a heating plate made of hardened glass. The drawer features a fully extending telescopic drawer suitable for loads of up to 25kg weight. The temperature can be adjusted steplessly in a range from 40 to 80 degrees centigrade.

RC 型冰箱

Neff, München
Werksdesign: Gerhard Nüssler
www.neff.de

RC组合式冰箱设计独特，侧面均采用坚硬的材料制成，其外部也使用了大量的不锈钢材料。该产品的显著特点是外部采用了不锈钢覆层，尤其是背面的覆层使得冰箱可以放在不靠墙的地方。冰箱的容量高达261升，其中有四星级的冷冻舱74升。本产品有许多创新，包括拥有超级冷冻选项的电子温度调节器，自动制冷功能和自动冷冻控制的功能。冰箱的内部不仅光滑、容易清洗，而且还配有Silver-Clean功能。RC冰箱的内部装有高亮度低噪音的照明设备。具有记忆功能的警报系统非常灵敏，冷冻仓的温度稍有升高就能立即发出警报。

The RC fridge-freezer combination has a distinctive design with strong lateral parts and massive stainless steel profiles. As the unit features a stainless steel panelling, which includes the rear as well, it can be placed away from the wall. The fridge-freezer has a volume of 261 litres, 74 litres of which belong to a 4-star freezer compartment. The appliance contains a number of innovative features: it has an electronic temperature regulation with a super-freeze option and an automatic freezing function as well as an automatic freezing control. The inside is smooth and easy to clean and equipped with the SilverClean function. The RC fridge-freezer has a particularly bright interior lighting and is very low-noise. An active warning system with memory function signals a temperature increase in the freezer compartment.

ERC 3711 WS 伊莱克斯酒柜, 2004

Electrolux Home Products S.A.,
Zaventem, Belgien
Werksdesign: Electrolux Home Products,
Electrolux Industrial Design Centre
Europe (Per Börjesson,
Lennart Johansson, Calum Armstrong,
Ollie Moore, Martin Beeh),
Porcia, Italien
Vertrieb: AEG Hausgeräte GmbH,
Nürnberg
www.electrolux.com

冷藏式酒柜采用了最新的制冷技术和多种优质材料，如光亮的铝材料、防紫外线的玻璃材料和精选的桦木材料等。只要调节到适合的温度，无论是红酒，白酒还是香槟都可以存放在这个既实用又美观的储藏柜中。此外，巧克力和香烟还可以存放一个独立的抽屉中，可以保持其原有风味。透过明亮雅致的玻璃门和集成的照明系统，使用者可以很容易地看到里面的东西。通过自主运作的操作面板和数码温度显示屏，使用者能很容易地设置内部的温度和湿度。传感器控制着内部和外部的温度，而且当储藏柜的门忘记关闭或被无意打开时，它还能发出信号音。冷藏式酒柜可以单独使用也可以和其他设备结合使用。

The Wine Keeper combines high-quality materials such as metallic aluminium, UV-filtered insulating glass and polished birch with state-of-the-art cooling technology. In the functional and aesthetic Wine Keeper red, rosé and white wine as well as champagne can be stored at the right temperature. Furthermore, chocolate and cigars can be stored in a taste-preserving way in a separate drawer. An elegant glass door and integrated lighting allow the user to check or look at the content. A self-explanatory operating panel and a digital temperature display make it easy to set the temperature and the internal humidity. Sensors monitor the inside and outside temperature and a tone signals when the door has accidentally been left open. The Wine Keeper can be used as a free-standing or integrated appliance.

Miele G 1000 洗碗机, 2004

Miele & Cie. KG, Gütersloh
Werksdesign
www.miele.de

G 1000代米勒牌洗碗机把漂亮的外观设计，简单的操作理念和现代尖端技术结合在一起，应用于同一个设备中。所有的操作控件和指示器都集中在外部面板上，这样就能很容易地选择符合逻辑顺序的程序。这一系列包括两种型号，一种型号可以垂直或倾斜的插入内置的洗碗筐，另一种型号则在机顶上设置了综合操控系统。G 1000系列产品的开发是为了满足当今新的市场的需求，它在很多方面都创立了新的标准，特别是在洗碗筐的灵活性、两种不同的高度选择、显示屏的操作及其10升的容量非常经济等方面。一种新颖的内部装盐的容器使得再次补充盐变得既简单又容易。

The G 1000 generation of Miele dishwashers combines good looks, a simple operating philosophy and innovative technology in one and the same unit. All operating controls and indicators are centred on the fascia panel to allow simple, logical programme selection. The range comprises models with upright and inclined inset fascias as well as fully integrated models with top-edge controls. It has been developed to meet current market requirements and sets new standards particularly with the high flexibility of its baskets, its two different heights, the display operation and its economicalness (10-litre programme). An innovative in-door salt container allows simple and easy refilling.

米勒 S 4 小型吸尘器, 2004

Miele & Cie. KG, Gütersloh
Werksdesign
www.miele.de

米勒S4系列小型真空吸尘器在清洁性能、卫生标准和使用的便利性等方面丝毫不亚于大型的真空吸尘器。这一系列有三个操作控件：一个旋转的选择器开关、底部的+/–开关和射频处理控制器。这款小型真空吸尘器采用了优质材料，持久耐用，对环境无污染，它操作简单，小巧便利。S4系列微型地板真空吸尘器还装有可伸缩性的不锈钢吸尘管，可以通过三种方式进行调整。总之，该款产品操作灵活，可清理范围十分广泛。

The Miele S 4 is a compact vacuum cleaner with the cleaning performance, the hygienic standard and the convenience of use of a large vacuum cleaner. The concept has three operating elements: a rotary selector switch, +/- foot switches and RF handle controls. The vacuum cleaners have been designed with high-quality materials and surfaces. They are durable and have improved ergonomic characteristics. This results in their simple and self-explanatory use as well as their low weight. The floor vacuum cleaners of the S 4 line have a stainless steel telescopic tube that can be adjusted in three ways. They have a high degree of flexibility and provide a large range of movement.

GSN 1580 x 洗碗机, 2004

Arcelik A.S., Ankara, Türkei
Design: frog design europe GmbH, Herrenberg
Vertrieb: Blomberg Vertriebsgesellschaft mbH, Ahlen
www.arcelik.com
www.frogdesign.com
www.blomberg.de

不锈钢的表面和类似于无烟煤颜色的面板的设计让GSN 1580 x型洗碗机看起来非常地明快大方。该产品的一个创新是第一次将不带直流电刷的发电机应用在洗碗机上，它能够持续地调节水压和喷雾器的喷雾速度。因此，该设备下层篮子中的碗、碟在高水压高温度的环境下集中地高强度地清洗，而上层篮子中的玻璃器皿则可以在一个低水压低温度的环境下清洗。

The GSN 1580 x dishwasher with its stainless steel front and anthracite-coloured panel has a clear design. An innovative feature is the brushless DC motor, which has for the first time been used in a dishwasher. This allows to continuously regulate the water pressure and the speed in the spray arm. Thus, in the mixed programme pots and pans in the lower basket can be cleaned intensively with full water pressure and high temperatures, while the glasses in the upper basket are cleaned with a low water pressure and low temperatures.

集尘袋式真空吸尘器, 2005

LG Electronics Inc., Corporate Design Center, Seoul, Korea
Werksdesign: Kyu Kwan Choi
Vertrieb: LG Electronics Deutschland GmbH, Willich
www.lge.com

集尘袋式真空吸尘器不再采用千篇一律的圆形外观设计，而是采用几何形的设计，但它同时又能与现存的圆形设计精巧地融合在一起。这一设计着重于实用性，外形简单大方。它的理念主要来自于一个活跃的、动态的、新型的和时尚的真空吸尘器形象。符合人体工程学的把手设计也突显出了动态设计的理念。电源开关和电线卷轴按钮安装在醒目的位置上，能很容易地找到并操作（手和脚可以同时开启）。

The design of the canister vacuum cleaner is an escape from the existing round type vacuum cleaners; even its geometrical design is well blended with the existing ones. Functional and simple form of the design is based on the main concept of an active and dynamic, new and modern vacuum cleaner image. An ergonomic carrying handle emphasises the dynamic design; the power and cord reel button can both be easily found and operated (with both hand and foot).

洗衣机 & 烘干机, 2004

LG Electronics Inc., Corporate Design Center, Seoul, Korea
Werksdesign: Ho il Jeon, Soon Uk Kwon
Vertrieb: LG Electronics Deutschland GmbH, Willich
www.lge.com

拥有简单欧式外观设计的洗衣机和配套设计的烘干机有着自身的外形优点。方形的稳重形象让人们觉得使用一定会便捷、可靠。由于妥善布局了机器上的控件，任何使用者都能很容易地凭感觉使用这款机器。透过衡量洗衣重量的传感器和每分钟1600转的直接驱动变极器马达的应用，使本品更显出其超低噪音、低振动的优良性能。

The simple European look of the washing machine and a drier in matching design has its own premium image. They present a convenient and reliable user interface through the solid image of a square. A well-organised control layout allows easy and intuitive use of the machine for any users. A super-low noise and an impressive low vibration is made possible through the perception of a sensor of laundry weight and a 1,600rpm direct drive inverter motor application.

法国 Dios 冰箱, 2005

LG Electronics Inc., Corporate Design Center, Seoul, Korea
Werksdesign: Seon-Kyu Kim, Kun-Jun Seok, Kyeong-Chul Cho, Je-Seung Choi
Vertrieb: LG Electronics Deutschland GmbH, Willich
www.lge.com

性能优良的法国Dios冰箱在其冰箱门的设计上显示出了传统的欧式风格。冰箱上装有复杂的彩色发光二极管显示屏设备。这款与眼睛齐高的对开门冰箱扩大了原本狭小的内部空间，提供了存放大型食品的广大空间，增强了其实用性。三抽屉式的冷冻室可以倾斜抽出，这样，在取拿食物时就可以减少冷空气的流失，从而增强了冰箱的实用性。

The premium French Dios refrigerator shows a traditional European contour style door design. It is equipped with a sophisticated colour LED display. The dual door is applied to grow out from the narrow chamber of an existing side-by-side type refrigerator. It has an extensive space to store large-sized food as well as enhancing the usability by a user-friendly eye-levelled fridge. The triple drawer style of the cool chamber can be tilted – this enhances the usability by minimising the outflow of cool air when taking out food.

LG “酒窖”酒柜, 2005

LG Electronics Inc., Corporate Design Center, Seoul, Korea
Werksdesign: Seon-Kyu Kim, Woon-Kyu Seo, Yong-Hun Chang
Vertrieb: LG Electronics Deutschland GmbH, Willich
www.lge.com

LG“酒窖”酒柜继承了传统储藏特点，即对光线、温度和震动的变化非常敏感。它还代表了用眼、口、鼻品酒的传统。简单的结构设计意味着较高的经济效率和生产力。高性能的电子调温系统能提示使用者找到储存红酒和白酒的适宜温度。

The LG Wine Cellar represents the tradition of storing wine, which is sensitive to light, temperature and vibration, and also the tradition of tasting wine with the eyes, nose and mouth. The puristic design structure spells economical efficiency and productivity. A functional electronic thermostat lets the user find the temperature that is right for red and white wines.

Dios 电视冰箱, 2005

LG Electronics Inc., Corporate Design Center, Seoul, Korea
Werksdesign: Seon-Kyu Kim, Kyung Soo Park, Han Young Doh, Tae-Hong Kim
Vertrieb: LG Electronics Deutschland GmbH, Willich
www.lge.com

Dios电视冰箱创造性地在冰箱门外侧安装了一个高分辨率的13寸TFT液晶显示屏。这一设备主要是为了花很多时间在厨房的用户而设计的。液晶显示屏两边的切面扩大了它的可视范围，其整体的设计也给人以韵律感。

The Dios TV refrigerator innovatively attached a 13-inch TFT LCD TV in a high resolution. It is designed for the user who spends much time in the kitchen. The chamfer placed on the left and right side of the LCD Screen allows a wider look and the overall design gives a rhythmic effect.

SC7830 真空吸尘器, 2004

Samsung Electronics Co., Ltd.,
Seoul, Korea
Werksdesign: Byung-Kook Baek,
Gwan-Woo Shin
www.samsung.com

SC7830型智能真空吸尘器在设计时运用了黑蓝色与银色，两种颜色的对比更显其外观简洁大方。“聪明翼”自动工作系统能吸进空气中最微小的灰尘，因此通过出口处的就是完全干净的无污染的空气。智能电子显示屏和照明指示器结合在一起，共同监控过滤器的运作，当过滤器需要更换时，还会播放一段音乐来提醒使用者。

In the design of the SC7830 intelligent vacuum cleaner, the colours dark-blue and silver create a sharp contrast to the accentuation of its plain shape. An automatically working Smart Wing system absorbs even the finest dust in contaminated air, leaving completely clean and pollutant-free air through the outlets. An intelligent digital display integrates a light indicator for monitoring filter life and plays a little melody when the filter has to be replaced.

AS-09HPA 型空调, 2004

Samsung Electronics Co., Ltd.,
Seoul, Korea
Werksdesign: Hyun-Joo Sim,
Joo-Hee Ryu
www.samsung.com

AS–09HPA型壁挂式空调着眼于其纤细的流线型外观设计，其侧面呈L形。移开前面的过滤网后，从面板到叶片的连续的弧面曲线型设计让整台机器呈现出一个明快的外形。用户面板上的可更换式机械装置可换成多种颜色及材料，交互式面板加快了显示照明速度，而其原本是取决于空气流动速度的。AS–09HPA型空调允许静音操作，属于A级节能产品。它的特点是具有自动清洁功能、自动关机除湿模式和制冷、供暖模式的自动转换。

With its L-shape from the side view, the AS-09HPA wall-mounted air-conditioner puts particular emphasis on a slim design. When removing the front grill, the continuous curvature from the panel to the blade creates a clean image. The changeable mechanism of the user panel allows for a wide variety of colours and materials. The interactive panel accelerates the display lighting speed depending on the ventilation speed. The AS-09HPA allows silent operation and ranges in the Grade A energy efficiency class. It features an auto-cleaning function and a power-off mode for dehumidification, as well as an automatic cooling/heating change mode.

智能条码微波炉, 2005

Samsung Electronics Co., Ltd.,
Seoul, Korea
Werksdesign: Sei-Ill Jeon, Ji-Ho Kim
www.samsung.com

智能微波炉装有条码扫描器，可以阅读速食食品的条码信息，并且在触摸屏（液晶显示屏或发光二极管）上显示出烹制它的下一个步骤。因此，只要把菜的条码扫描到微波炉上，然后跟着屏幕上的指示步骤去做，即使再难做的菜也能很快做好。因为使用了如纯铝等的纯金属材料，智能微波炉给人以高贵典雅的印象。暗黑色玻璃和银白色的铝制把手的反差对比更加强了这一印象。

The Smart Oven Bar-Code MWO is equipped with a scanner reading the bar-code information of the instant meal and showing the relevant next preparation step for it on the touchscreen (LED, LCD). Thus, even hard-to-prepare dishes turn out successful by just scanning the bar-code of the meal and following the instructions on the screen. The oven yields an elegant high-grade impression due to the use of genuine materials such as aluminium. This impression is intensified by the contrast between black-tinted glass and a handle made of silver-coloured aluminium.

UPS 05 对开门式冰箱, 2004

Samsung Electronics Co., Ltd.,
Seoul, Korea
Werksdesign: Jeong-Min Kim,
Hea-Me Lee
www.samsung.com

UPS 05是既美观又实用的一款冰箱。离开冰箱越远，它的外观形态就变得越模糊，而当你渐渐靠近，它又才慢慢地重新变得明朗起来。其外观设计可以改变，以适应消费者对于颜色和材料的不同喜好。另外，冰箱灵活可变的储存空间和适宜各类食物储存的最佳温度，也是个人生活方式的体现。用户面板容易理解和操作，其中包含了一个易于查看的宽屏显示器，还有一些设计简单、易于操作的轻触式按键。通过对大量使用者的储存行为和习惯的调查，设计出了创新的内部结构。为正常尺寸的一半大小的冷冻仓，可以用来存放较小的需要完全冷冻产品。

The UPS 05 is an aesthetic and functionally designed refrigerator. With increasing distance from the unit, the pattern of the exterior fades out, only to softly reappear again when approaching it. The exterior design can be altered and individually adapted to customer preferences with regard to colour and material. With a flexible and convertible storage space and an optimised storage temperature for all foods, the unit is an expression of an individual lifestyle. The user panel is easy to follow and includes a wide display for better visibility and soft-touch keys with a plain design. The innovative interior design is the result of an extensive research among users as to their storage behaviour and habits. Thus, there is a freezing compartment half the usual size for storage of smaller deep-frozen products.

AEG-厘米伊莱克斯嵌入式洗碗机，2004

AEG Hausgeräte GmbH, Nürnberg
Werksdesign: Roberto Pezzetta
www.aeg-hausgeraete.de

AGE–90厘米伊莱克斯嵌入式洗碗机特别适合于以下几种厨房：没有柱基的厨房；厨房中的地柜没有固定在墙上或是厨房中有个单独摆放东西的架子。根据人体工程学设置的高度和洗碗机宽大的门可以使用户轻而易举地够到洗碗机里的篮子。功能按钮和显示装置都被安置在门的边缘处。洗碗机篮里设计了不同大小的架子，这使得无论什么样的盘子都能很容易地放进洗碗机中，同时也保证了其最佳的洗涤效果。“传感器控制”功能可以根据盘子上的污渍量，通过电子监控而整个清洗过程。该设备的各种技术指标，如能源和水的消耗、清洗程序和噪音级别等都位列同类产品中的最高水平。

The innovative AEG-Electrolux 90cm built-in dishwasher is particularly suitable for kitchens without a plinth, or for kitchens, the floor cupboards of which are mounted "floating" to the wall, or for kitchens with the components placed on single stands. An ergonomically favourable high position of the unit in the kitchen cabinet and a wide door facilitate the access to the dishwasher basket significantly. The function buttons and -displays are integrated into the edge of the door. With a functional and variable dishwasher basket design, any kind of dish can easily be placed into the unit, guaranteeing best cleaning results. With the "sensorcontrol" feature, the cleaning programmes are monitored electronically, according to load and degree of dish stain. The technical specifications such as energy- and water consumption, dish washing programmes and noise level of the unit range at the highest level in the industry.

Cafamosa CF220
全自动蒸馏咖啡机, 2004

AEG Hausgeräte GmbH, Nürnberg
Werksdesign: Rainer Mendler
www.aeg-hausgeraete.de

Cafamosa CF220型全自动蒸馏咖啡机的外形明快，设计简洁时尚，这与AEG Neue Klasse产品系列的设计理念相吻合，这一理念赋予了该产品明确的设计风格，与该品牌特点保持了一致。各种功能操作都可以通过面板上的按键和显示屏来实现，机器的本身高性能更是加快了整个设备的运转速度。研磨装置和蒸汽喷气嘴的结合使用提供了专业的全自动准备及提供了适合的温度控制。由于咖啡和水的量可以根据个人口味加以调整，所以无论是煮浓咖啡、普通咖啡还是卡布其诺咖啡，它都能带给你香醇浓郁的专业品质。

The clear, compact and modern visual language of the Cafamosa CF220 espresso machine is geared to the design of the product line "AEG Neue Klasse", giving the unit an unmistakable design- and brand identity. A logical and functional assignment of function- and display elements on the front side and a professional technology facilitate the operation of the device. An integrated grinding gear and the steam nozzle provide professional comfort for optimum and fully automatic preparation. With the option of individual adjustment of the amounts for coffee and water, espresso, coffees or cappuccinos can be prepared with professional and excellent aroma quality.

Nespresso C+D 90 Essenza
蒸馏咖啡机，2004

Nestlé Nespresso SA, Paudex, Schweiz
Design: Les Ateliers du Nord
(Antoine Cahen, Philippe Cahen),
Lausanne, Schweiz
www.nespresso.com
www.adn-design.ch

Nespresso C+D 90 Essenza蒸馏咖啡机的设计体现了一种高度自由化的特征，它的整体创新理念集中于功能和工效两个方面。整个机器的核心装置是由杠杆提供动力的CBU——压缩酿造单元——装置，它的运用可以替换内胆固定装置，区别于其他的Nespresso机型。CBU使内胆可以从机器上部轻松装入，只需简单的一步——关闭杠杆——就可以实现替换，在重力的作用下内胆便会自动落入内部容器中。简约风格的设计理念使该款机型不仅操作简单方便，使用时还饶有趣味。

The Nespresso C+D 90 Essenza has been designed with a high degree of liberty. It has an innovative overall concept in regards to the general concept, the functionality and the ergonomics. The machine's central design element is a Compact Brewing Unit (CBU) powered by a lever. This replaces the capsule holder common to other Nespresso machines. The CBU allows the capsules to be filled conveniently from above, to replace them in a single simple step (closing the lever) and automatic disposal into an internal container via gravity, when opening the lever. Due to a consistent minimalist design the use of the machine is easy, intuitive and almost playful.

NESPRESSO

MyCup 咖啡机, 2004

Melitta Haushaltsprodukte GmbH & Co. KG, Minden
Design: OCO-Design, Münster
www.mycup.de

MyCup咖啡机的外观设计的独特之处在于其不仅外形朴素、方便实用，使用时还饶有趣味。该款咖啡机由四部分组成，其独特的设计明确地划分了四个不同的功能区域。MyCup咖啡机是第一款配备了驻香润湿系统的机型，可以做出口味更加香醇的咖啡，此外，这款咖啡机还配备了高级MyCup咖啡垫。其所有设计都是把MyCup咖啡机的精妙的技术理念和给用户带来最大方便的信念完美结合的印证。

The factual elegance of the MyCup coffee maker is based on the interplay of its plain, functionally oriented basic form with its playfully shaped elements. The design follows a four-part basic construction, clearly defining the individual function areas. The MyCup is the first single-serve unit working with a pre-brew aroma system for a more intensive taste. The elaborate technical concept behind the MyCup coffee maker, especially developed MyCup coffee pads and a high level of user-friendliness are convincingly united in the design.

Mahlkönig K 30ES 咖啡豆研磨机, 2004

stawert Mühlenbau GmbH & Co. KG, Hamburg
Design: Carsten Gollnick product design & interior design (Carsten Gollnick, Maja Finke, Felix Ballerstedt), Berlin
Vertrieb: Mahlkönig Vertriebsgesellschaft mbH, Hamburg
www.mahlkönig.de
www.gollnick-design.com

Mahlkonig K30ES是一款针对专业市场而设计的高级咖啡豆研磨机。它集创造性的咖啡研磨技术和精妙的烹饪美食理念于一身。该研磨机可以将咖啡豆在最短时间内磨成最精细的咖啡粉末。Mahlkonig K30ES并不像市场上现有的咖啡豆研磨机那样，将咖啡豆先贮存在储存杯中再进行计量，而是可以随时根据咖啡吧台师傅所需下料，进行精确计量而后研磨，这样就保证了磨出的咖啡粉末的新鲜度。更重要的是，在整个制作过程中也不会使咖啡豆的香气丧失掉。高层次的美食需求，再加上精确设计的三维立体外观构成了该款磨具的设计理念核心。

The Mahlkönig K 30ES is a single espresso grinder for the professional market. It combines an innovative technical concept of espresso grinding with an upscale gastronomic design concept. The idea of the development was to realise the shortest way from the whole bean through the finest grinder into the cup. The coffee beans are not, as with the existing grinders, ground into a storage and dosing chamber, but are freshly and directly ground on demand, as desired by the barista, with very accurate dosing and, most importantly, without any loss of aroma into the portafilter. This high gourmet demand in combination with the three-dimensional visualisation of the technical precision is the heart of the grinder concept.

Impressa Z5 Espresso-/ 全自动咖啡机, 2004

Jura Elektroapparate AG, Niederbuchsiten, Schweiz
Design: Zemp + Partner Design, Zürich, Schweiz
Vertrieb: Jura Elektrogeräte Vertriebs-GmbH, Nürnberg
www.jura.com
www.zemp-objects.ch

IImpressa Z5正面外观设计高贵典雅。所有的操作设备都自然地向使用者倾斜。它的背面和侧面设计虽不张扬却各具特点，它们也是为煮咖啡而专门设计的。Impressa Z5的创新之处在于其“一触即发”式单键卡布基诺咖啡制作装置。牛奶泡沫和咖啡通过两个单独的管道直接流入杯中并在杯中混合。旋转开关技术装置更使你只需简单地按下或者旋转一个按钮，所有的操作和运行步骤就会自动完成。

The Impressa Z5 has an elegantly designed front. The operating elements are curved towards the user. The side and back with their unobtrusive as well as striking elements are part of a basic shape that has been inspired by coffee. One innovation of the Impressa Z5 is the One Touch Cappuccino jet: The frothed milk and the coffee run through two separate tubes directly into the glass or cup. Thanks to the Rotary Switch navigation, all operating and programming steps can be easily set just by pressing and turning the switch.

Café 2 全自动咖啡机, 2004

Severin Elektrogeräte GmbH, Sundern
Werksdesign: Frank Fulgoni
Design: Feder Design, Münster
www.severin.de

Café 2的“傻瓜型”按键设计几乎满足了所有喜欢喝咖啡的人的需要。当准备咖啡时，每一个使用者都可以根据自身的需要来冲调咖啡。Café 2外观典雅高贵，内部采用了先进的技术。这种外形设计的咖啡机是非常独特的，它包括两个咖啡隔间和一个过滤器，这样一来，也可以采用传统的方法煮咖啡。同样，这种新型的冲泡方式也缩短了咖啡和水接触的时间，咖啡变得不那么苦了而且易于被身体所消化吸收。

The design of the Café 2 is user-friendly and self-explanatory, geared to the needs of nearly all coffee drinkers. When preparing coffee, every user can individually determine how his or her coffee shall be brewed. The Café 2 yields an elegant impression and is equipped with sophisticated technology. As the only machine of its kind, it includes two coffee compartments with a permanent filter so that the coffee can be prepared the conventional way as well. With an innovative brewing system, it is also possible to reduce the time of contact between coffee and water. The result: the coffee is less bitter and better digestible.

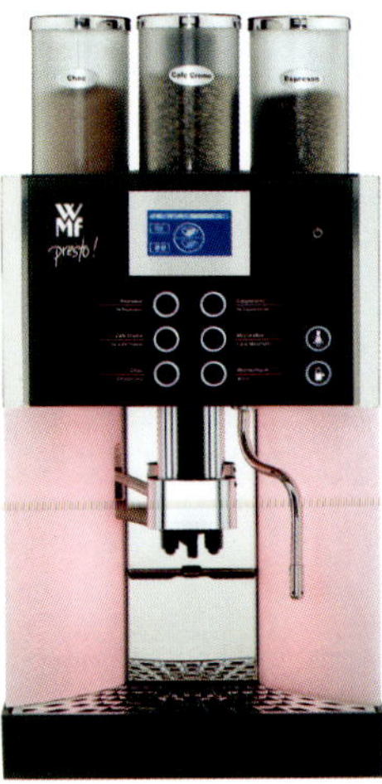

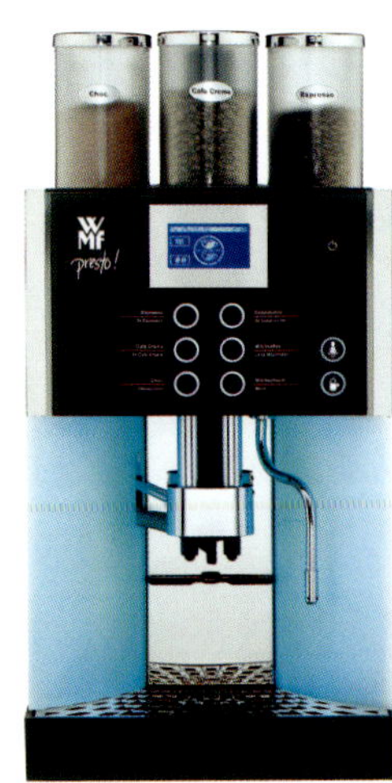

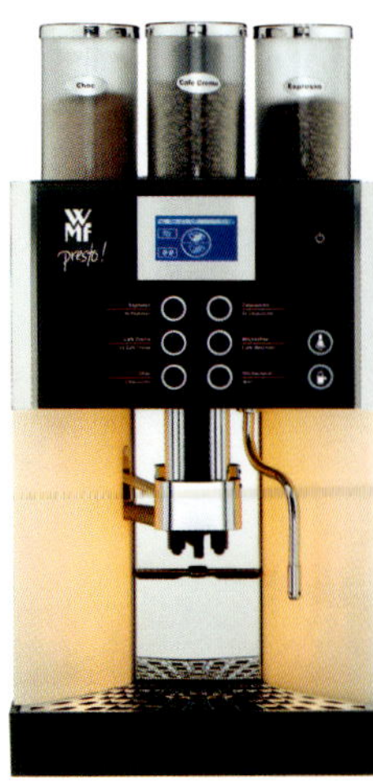

WMF Presto 咖啡机, 2005

WMF Württembergische
Metallwarenfabrik AG,
Geislingen/Steige
Werksdesign: Reinhard Boos
www.wmf.de

WMF Presto是一款适宜于多种场所的专业咖啡机。它的创新之处在于可以制作出具有专业水平的咖啡饮品，如高品质的热巧克力、Choc等饮品。WMF Presto咖啡机备有一个咖啡杯，一个大的水罐和一个可以长期使用的水管结合配件，它不仅可以与一到三个磨具相连，还具有许多其它的功能。尽管这款机器采用了先进的技术，但其机身只比DIN A4 宽一点，只有32.5厘米，非常节省空间。半透明的材料所展现出来的轻盈设计理念使WMF Presto适用于任何场合。除此之外，设计者还在机器的操作台的灯光设计上别出心裁，使操作台看起来就好像是专门为冲调咖啡而打造的灯光迷离的舞台，别具一番情趣。只需按一个按钮，自我演示系统就会启动，向顾客进行操作演示。

The WMF Presto coffee machine is a professional percolator for the most diverse spaces. Innovative is the option that the Presto can prepare all coffee specialties and, by request, hot chocolate such as Choc and Chococcino with premium quality. The WMF Presto is equipped with a barista cup, a large water tank and a permanent water connection. The coffee machine can be fit (according to preferences) with one to three grinders. Despite this technical diversity, the machine measures only 32.5cm in width, thus being only slightly wider than a DIN A4 sheet, saving space. The atmospheric light concept of the WMF Presto adds a special mark to any ambience. An emotional module is the illumination of the worktop as stage for brewing one's own hot drink. The self-explanatory display is operated with touch buttons, allowing an intuitive user guidance.

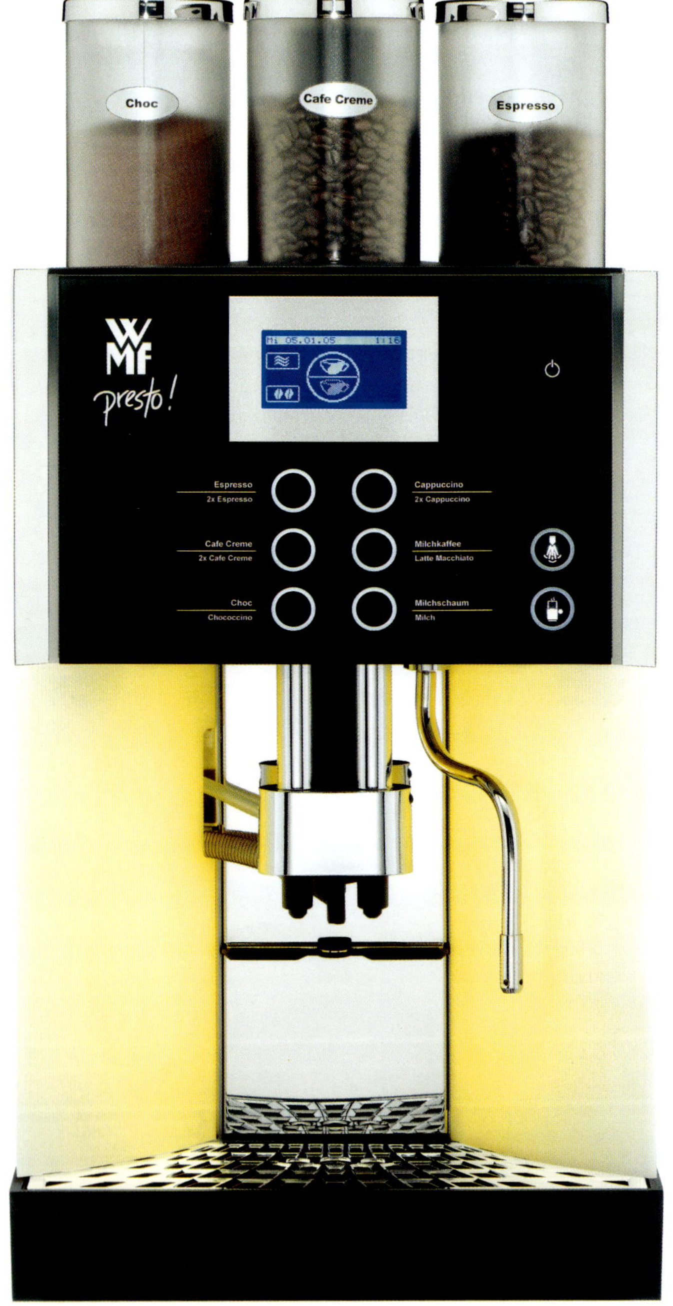

BeerTender 生啤制作机, 2004

Heineken, Amsterdam, NL
Krups, Paris, Frankreich
Design: NPK Industrial Design, Leiden, NL
www.beertender.com
www.npk.nl

BeerTender生啤制作机为顾客提供了一种在家里就可以享用新鲜生啤的方法。该款机器由一个中心设备和一个容量为四升，可反复使用的小啤酒桶组成，可以随时提供新鲜爽口的生啤。BeerTender可以将啤酒冷却至适当温度，产生一定量的泡沫，并保证整整一杯的生啤在一定压强下仍能保持新鲜。该装置不仅外观精巧，使用更是极其方便。

BeerTender offers a new way of drinking draught beer at home. The system consists of an appliance and a four-litre returnable beer keg and provides the best quality draught beer experience ready to be used at any time. The BeerTender appliance cools the beer at the right temperature and keeps the beer at the correct pressure ensuring a perfect glass of fresh draught beer with the right amount of foam. Although the appliance has been designed with focus on convenience and ease of use, its appearance won't go unnoticed.

旅行用多次开启盖（Solo Traveler Plus™ Re-Closable Lid）

Solo Cup Company, Highland Park, USA
Design: Metaphase Design Group, Inc., St. Louis, USA
www.solocup.com
www.metaphase.com

这款多次开启盖的设计是独一无二，它专为旅行者在旅行途中饮用咖啡而设计。它的设计符合人体工程学原理，附带一根滑动条，易于开关。凸起的旋钮可左右转动。其外形酷似传统的热饮专用杯的拱形盖儿，可从上方合上盖子。不同的地方在于此款设备在内部还有另外一个可沿内部沟槽旋转的装置，可在凸起的滑动条内滑过，使杯盖在不被损害的情况下开启或关闭。用户也可利用此滑片自行调节每次从杯中流出的热饮量。此杯盖由聚苯乙烯制作而成，清洁环保。

The Solo Traveler Plus™ Re-Closable Lid is conceived for coffee-drinking en route. It is designed with an ergonomically well thought-out lid and a slider to easily open and close the spout with one finger of either the right or left hand. The exterior part is similar to a traditional dome-shaped lid for hot drinks with a punched opening in the upper part. However, there is a second rotating disk running around the inside of the exterior lid in a round track. This disk can be turned with the slider across from the spout so that the lid can be opened and closed repetitively without damaging the lid. The user can also individually adjust the flow quantity of the hot drink with the slider. Both lid parts are made of environmentally friendly, thermoformed polystyrene.

Kellogg's Drink 'n Crunch™
便携式杯装麦片

Kellogg Company, Battle Creek, USA
Design: Metaphase Design Group, Inc., St. Louis, USA
www.metaphase.com

Kellogg's Drink'n Crunch™便携式杯装麦片是一款新颖的杯型包装设计，为旅途中的人们提供了方便的麦片饮品。此款设计基于"杯中杯"概念，当足够量的牛奶加入到外层杯中后，内部杯中的麦片便被吸入到大杯中，与牛奶混合。外层杯边的小窗口便于用户随时了解所加牛奶量是否足够。揭开包装锡纸后用户就可像从杯中饮水那样吸用自己冲制的麦片饮品了。当从边上的小口吸出牛奶时，麦片就可从内部纸杯中随之流入口中。

Kellogg's Drink 'n Crunch™ Eat-on-the-Run Cereal is an innovative nested cup design – the first to offer true single-handed cereal consumption in the car or on the run. The design is based on a "cup-within-a-cup" concept whereby a pre-packaged cereal inner cup is snapped into an outer cup once the appropriate amount of milk has been added to the latter. A see-through window on the side of the outer cup allows users to easily measure the amount of milk needed. After a foil seal is pulled off, one simply tips the cup as if one were drinking water from a glass. Cereal then flows into the mouth from the inner cup while milk simultaneously flows from a small rim slot in the outer cup.

Normann 漏斗, 2004

Normann Copenhagen, Kopenhagen, Dänemark
Werksdesign: Poul Madsen, Jan Andersen
Design: Boje Estermann, Paris, Frankreich
www.normann-copenhagen.com

漏斗是日常生活中的重要用品，但它占用了很大的厨房空间。这种新型漏斗的创新之处在于它的外形可以灵活多变，其设计采用了旧式的反射式相机的运作原理，即当日光强烈照射时，涂有防晒油的部件就折叠成手风琴一般了。经开发工程师的通力合作，最终开发出了一种特殊的柔软的材料。这种材料制成的设备能非常灵活地折叠起来，而且它足够坚硬，不易变形，同时又非常地耐用，可以抗寒耐热，并可多次反复折叠。这种新型的漏斗很是实用且节省空间、易于清洗而且外形十分漂亮。

The design of the funnel is a solution for the problem that a funnel is an important part of the daily household, but it needs a lot of space in the kitchen. The innovation with the funnel is that it is flexibly designed. Its form adopts the functionality of an old reflex camera, which had a soft sunscreen folding out like an accordion when the sun got too strong. In cooperation with engineers, all parties developed a special soft material – flexible enough to fold it together, hard enough to keep its shape and durable enough to take the cold and even hot as well as the repetition of folding the funnel. The end product is a functional, space-saving, easy-to-clean and aesthetically designed funnel.

Assam / Pavina / Canteen 双壁玻璃杯, 2004

Bodum AG, Triengen, Schweiz
Werksdesign: Bodum Design Group (Masato Yamamoto)
Vertrieb: Peter Bodum GmbH, Kaltenkirchen
www.bodum.com

Assam / Pavina / Canteen 双壁玻璃杯，由光纤硅酸盐玻璃制成，营造出一种饮品漂流在杯子里的感觉。这种特殊玻璃不受温度剧变的影响，其杯壁也比陶瓷壁薄得多，这些特性使这种材料极其适合制造双壁玻璃。你可以长时间拿着一杯滚烫的热饮而手指却毫发无伤。和普通的单壁玻璃杯相比，这种杯子能更持久地保持热饮的温度或是冷饮的凉爽。阿萨姆系列玻璃杯底端设计得更窄，而在顶端更宽，这样即使手较小，拿杯也很容易。派维纳系列玻璃杯的边缘更窄，令杯子呈现出圆形。这种设计只能用于双壁玻璃杯，而几乎不可能应用于单壁杯中。卡迪恩系列玻璃杯则是典型的纸杯形状，但也是由双壁玻璃制成。

The double-wall tumblers Assam, Pavina and Canteen are made of borosilicate glass, creating the impression of "floating" beverages inside. This particular sort of glass is resistant to temperature shocks, and the glass walls are much thinner than ceramics. These characteristics make the material very suitable for double-wall glasses; a hot drink can be held in one's hand for a long time without burning one's fingers. Hot drinks stay hot longer, cold drinks stay cold longer than with regular single-wall glasses. The Assam line is designed narrower at the bottom and wider at the top, making it easier for small hands to hold the glass. The Pavina line features a narrower edge, giving the glass a round shape. This design is only possible with the double-wall; it would hardly be possible to drink out of a single-wall glass of the same design. The Canteen line has the typical paper cup shape, also made of double-wall glass.

mono-giro 苹果刀

mono-Metallwarenfabrik Seibel GmbH, Mettmann
Design: Jessica Battram, Reekenfeld; Christina Schäfer, Witten
www.mono.com

mono–giro单向苹果刀是一款可绕着苹果核切割苹果的工具。如将grio留在所切割完的苹果上还可以保持苹果的新鲜，使切完的苹果不变色。

The mono-giro apple cutter is a functional tool for cutting spirally around the apple's core. If you leave giro on the freshly cut apple, then the apple will not turn brown nor dry out.

唇膏型保温杯, 2005

Bodum AG, Triengen, Schweiz
Werksdesign: Bodum Design Group (Carsten Joergensen)
Vertrieb: Peter Bodum GmbH, Kaltenkirchen
www.bodum.com

这款唇膏型真空保温杯是1983年成功设计的周年纪念版系列产品。刚刚问世时，它是一款非常时尚而且实用的设计。极富特色的唇膏形状设计使得倒饮料变得非常容易。这个保温杯最初被设计成两个隔热的玻璃层，这样就能使咖啡即使在调制后的六小时内温度仍旧保持在75摄氏度。它最初的设计容量是0.5升，而现在的双壁不锈钢质地的周年纪念版容量改为了一升。

The Lipstick vacuum flask is the anniversary edition of the successful 1983 design. Back then, this was a very trendy and functionally designed vacuum flask. The characteristic lipstick shape made it easy to pour beverages out of the bottle. The original version of the Lipstick was built with two layers of insulation glass and was capable of keeping coffee at a temperature of 75 degrees centigrade after six hours had already passed. The original held 0.5 litre. The anniversary edition is now made of double-wall stainless steel with a volume of 1 litre.

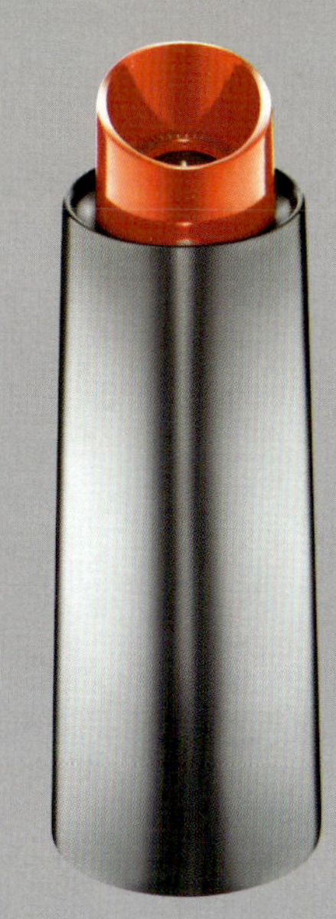

Intensa 多功能加热锅, 2005

Fissler GmbH, Idar-Oberstein
Design: milani d&c (Britta Pukall), Ertenbach/Zürich, Schweiz
www.fissler.de
www.milani.ch

Intensa多功能加热锅功能强大，质量过关。其构思巧妙的烹调系统支持各种功能，让每天在厨房的时光变得简单美妙。流线型设计带来明亮的视觉效果，外形设计大方亲切。此外，该款机器把个性化的的设计和极具创意的ThermoStar温度显示器等额外的智能化功能结合在了一起。当加热完毕时，它还会发出信号，提醒使用者要调低温度。ThermoStar温度显示器还可以根据温度而改变颜色，低温时为蓝色，高温时则变为红色，例如在水沸腾时，显示器就变为红色。锅盖还可以存放在侧面把手旁边的储存专用仓的位置上。其锥形设计使得同样直径的锅都可以与之匹配。

Intensa has a high degree of functionality and quality. The cleverly thought-out cooking system supports the user with a variety of functions, thus making daily kitchen work easier. Flowing lines create a visual lightness and the language of forms has a friendly look. The independent design integrates intelligent additional functions such as an innovative ThermoStar temperature display. This function signalises the user when the cooker can be turned down after heating up. The ThermoStar changes its colour from blue when it is cold to red when for example water is on the brink of boiling. The lid can be stored safely in the functional storage spaces close to the side handles. Due to their conic shape, even pots with the same diameter can be stacked inside one another perfectly.

TM 31 多功能搅拌机, 2004

Vorwerk Elektrowerke GmbH & Co. KG, Wuppertal
Werksdesign: Uwe Kemker, Rolf Strohmeyer
Vertrieb: Vorwerk & Co. Thermomix GmbH, Wuppertal
www.vorwerk.de

TM31是一种用途广泛的厨房设备。它集搅拌、绞肉、研磨、揉捏、称重、烹饪和蒸汽烹调等多种功能于一身。该设计理念以简洁结构为基础，但也融入了现代时尚元素。操作显示屏和搅拌容器是连接机器和使用者的桥梁，也理所应当地成为了整个设计的核心。这个多功能设备既符合人体工程学的要求，同时还极为实用。各种操作组件井然有序地排列在一起，因此各种功能和操作都变得一目了然。由于它结构精巧，材质精良，因此清洗和保养也相应也变得很容易。

The Thermomix TM 31 is a universal kitchen appliance. It combines mixing, mincing, grinding, kneading, weighing, cooking and steam cooking functions in one device. The design concept is based on a compact, closed structure and has a modern language of forms. The operating display and the mixing container are the user interfaces and as such central to the design. The design of the different functions is ergonomic as well as practical. Thanks to the efficient arrangement of the operating elements the numerous functions and the use of the appliance are largely self-explanatory. Due to its form and the choice of materials the appliance is low-maintenance and easy to clean.

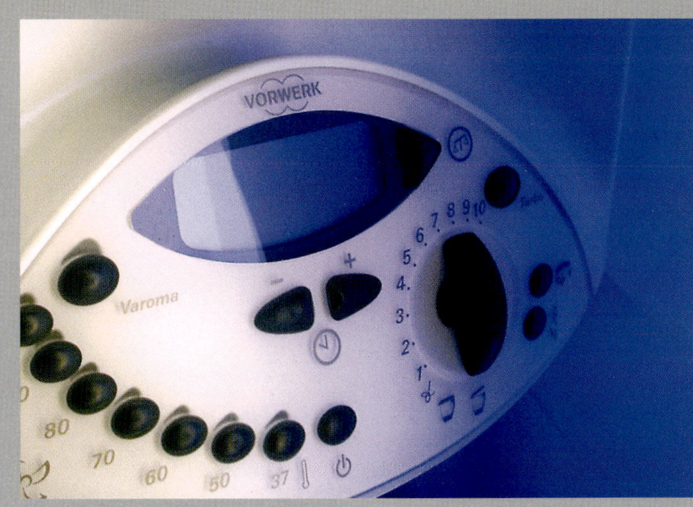

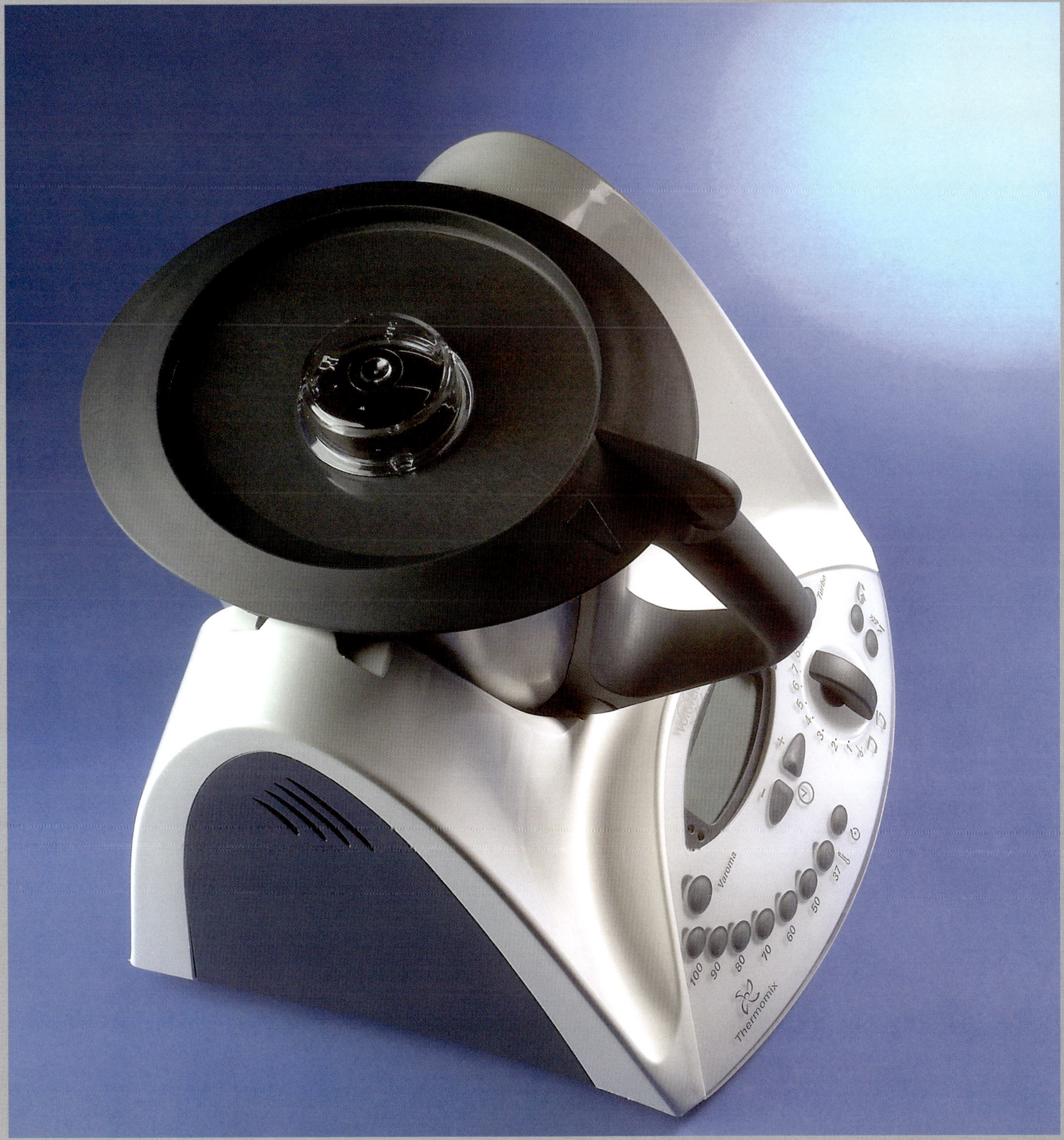

Ercolino 食盐/胡椒粉调味瓶, 2005

Silit-Werke GmbH & Co. KG, Riedlingen
Werksdesign
www.silit.de

新型Ercolino调味瓶(可装多种调味品,例如盐或者胡椒粉)十分实用, 当你把它置于桌子上的时候，它会前后摇摆。但是由于Ercolino调味瓶的制作技术精湛，瓶子里的盐或者胡椒粉并不会从瓶中洒落出来。此外,它的底座还特别厚实，在任何情况下都可以保持直立。因此，往瓶中添加调味品就变得十分简单易行。

The inventive and functionally designed Ercolino salt/pepper shaker swings back and forth when placing it on the table. Due to a sophisticated technique, spilling of salt or pepper is prevented. With its extra heavy base, the Ercolino shaker stands upright in any situation. It is conceived in such a way that filling the shakers is made easy.

Veria 不粘锅, 2005

Silit-Werke GmbH & Co. KG, Riedlingen
Design: Teams Design, Esslingen
www.silit.de

Veria平底不粘锅可在各种类型的煤气灶和电磁炉上使用。不粘平底锅由韧性铝压铸而成，表面镀有希拉钢，能够有效的防止食物粘黏。它还使用了防划痕、耐用的钛合金表面,可以在大火下提供防糊保护；采用符合人体工程学而设计的防滑握柄，保证了使用的安全。

The Veria anti-stick pan is suitable for all stove types, including induction stoves. It is manufactured in robust aluminium die-cast quality. The Silitan anti-stick coating prevents sticking of food effectively; the pan features a scratch-resistant, long-life titanium surface. A wide flame protection prevents burns. The ergonomically designed anti-slip handle allows a safe use.

Elements 烹饪组合, 2004

Silit-Werke GmbH & Co. KG, Riedlingen
Design: de Gast deSign, Mailand, Italien
www.silit.de

Elements烹调组合是包含炊具、餐桌和冰箱在内的一种新型的烹调系统，是烹饪、上菜和存储的一条龙式设计。不同的锅具、碗具、焙盘等厨房用品可以自由组合，发挥其功能的最大化。各个部分相互兼容，可叠起堆放，十分节省空间。此外，该系统还适用于各种炊具，可提供多种健康的烹调方式。

The Elements cooking system is an innovative system for cooker, table and fridge. It is well thought out and designed for cooking, serving and storing food. Many combinations are possible with the different pots, bowls, casseroles and inserts, which have multi-functional seals. All elements are compatible with each other and stackable to save space. The system is suitable for all kinds of cookers and offers many healthy ways to prepare food.

Avalon 火锅套件, 2004

A. & J. Stöckli AG, Netstal, Schweiz
Werksdesign: Herbert Forrer
Design: André Gilli, Arth, Schweiz
www.stockliproducts.com

此款电火锅套件将Avalon小型电炉具和与之匹配的大型火锅完美结合在了一起。Avalon小型电炉具由铬钢制成，其简洁协调的设计和实用的功能使生活变得简单起来，使烹饪也成为一种乐趣。持续的温度调节保证了食物在一个适宜的温度里，同时也适用于电磁炉。

The electric fondue set is an innovative combination of the Avalon electric rechaud with a matching, large fondue pot. The Avalon electric rechaud made of chromium steel makes everyday life simpler and more attractive due to its simple and organic design and its functionality. The continuous temperature adjustment ensures that the food does not get too hot. The fondue pot is suitable for induction.

Alpine 奶酪火锅套件, 2003

A. & J. Stöckli AG, Netstal, Schweiz
Design: André Gilli, Arth, Schweiz
www.stockliproducts.com

Alpine奶酪火锅套件设计非常经典，它吸取了内层的各种优点，营造出一种火锅氛围。此套件中央是一个小型电炉具，其外形设计非常优美简洁。此小型电炉配有一个可供烘焙的炉具和一个将热量通过较厚的平底盘均匀传递的加热盘，以供电磁炉使用。

Due to its timeless design the Alpine cheese fondue set integrates into any interior and creates the ambience suitable for a fondue. The centre is a rechaud with an impressive design due to its form, which has been reduced to the essentials. The rechaud has a safety burner for paste and a warming plate suitable for induction, which distributes the heat evenly through a caquelon base.

Genesis Pizza- 电烤炉, 2004

A. & J. Stöckli AG, Netstal, Schweiz
Design: Fredy Dubach, Bäretswil, Schweiz
www.stockliproducts.com

Genesis Pizza电烤炉功能强大，可以在烤出自制的比萨。实用的面团切割器毫不费力就可以切割出制作比萨面饼所需的块料。该电烤炉有大小两种火力可供选择，能够烘焙出颜色均匀的松脆比萨面饼。不粘平底锅可以防止比萨饼粘黏锅底。如果关掉低火，此器具还可用作电烤炉。

Genesis is a multi-functional raclette and grill appliance, with which even home-made pizzas can be baked. With the functional dough cutter mini pizza bases can be prepared easily. The appliance has upper and lower heating, which provide even browning and a crunchy pizza base. Pans with non-stick coating prevent the pizzas from sticking. By switching off the lower heat, the appliance becomes a raclette grill.

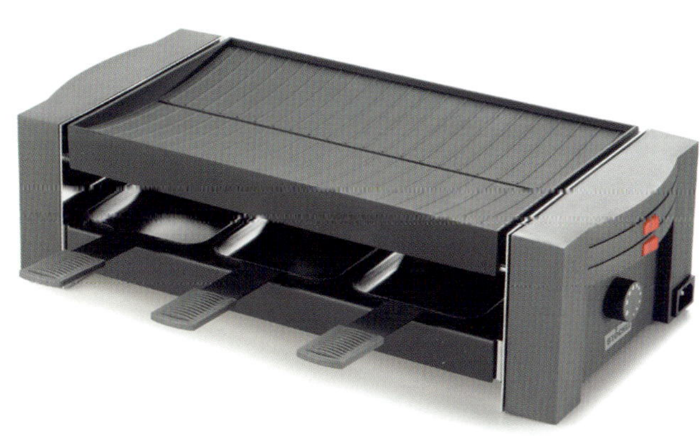

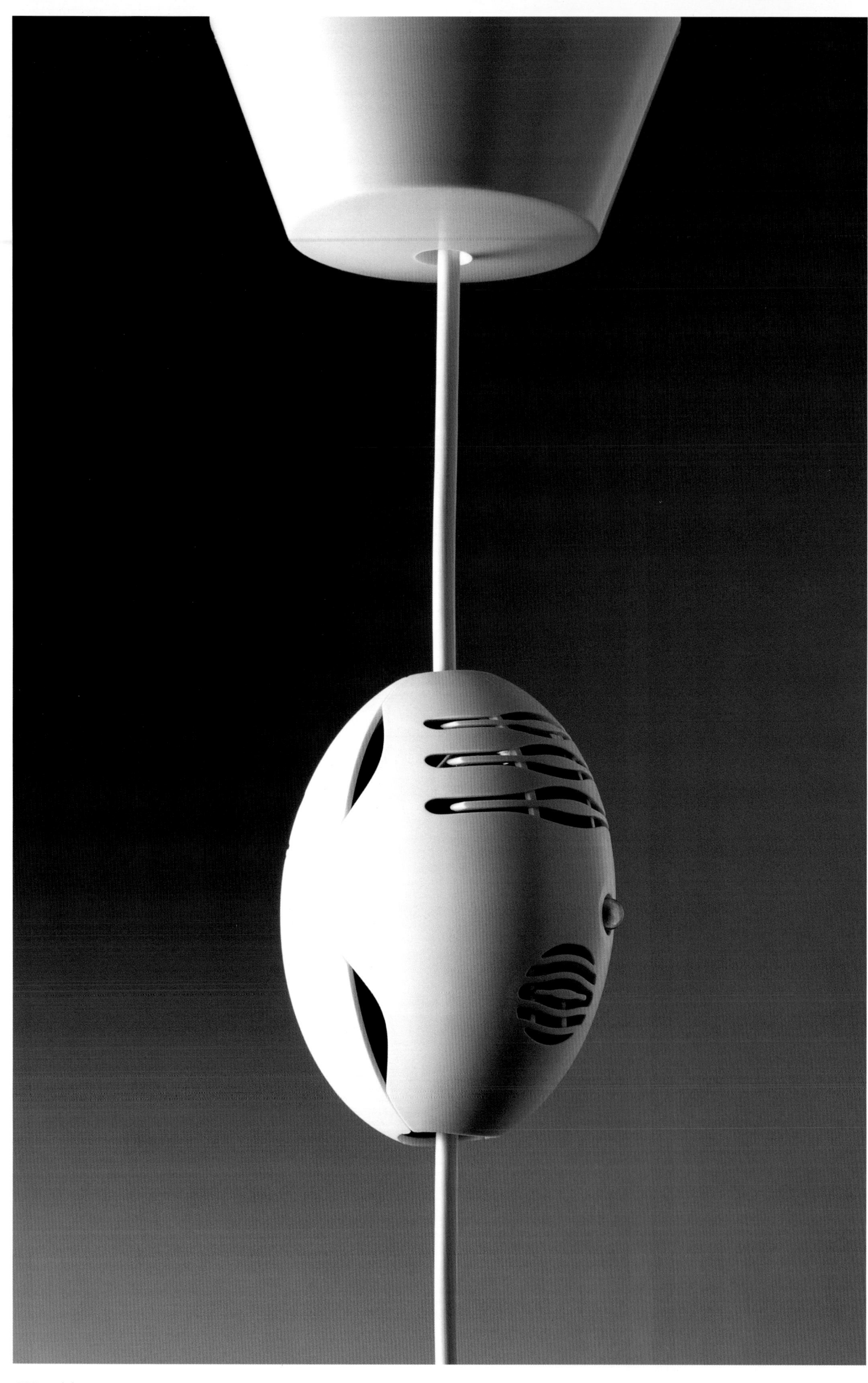

火灾报警器, 2004

OG Invent, Stockholm, Schweden
Werksdesign: Michael Olsson,
Rickard Grönstedt
Design: Ergonomidesign AB
(Marcus Gabrielsson, Pelle Reinius),
Bromma, Schweden
www.snapalarm.com
www.ergonomidesign.com

此火灾报警器是一款独具创新、广受欢迎的烟雾探测器。它利用光学技术，外形新颖别致。它安装简易，便于安放。此火灾报警器的一个显著特点就是拥有专利安装技术——只需将报警器置于灯绳之上，轻轻合拢即可，无需使用其它工具。此火灾报警器可以在任何一种不粗于2厘米的灯绳和链条上使用。

The Snapalarm is an innovative and appealingly designed smoke detector. It works with optical technology and has been given an original shape. The Snapalarm is easy to install and easy to put in the right place. A unique feature of the Snapalarm is a patented installation technique. One simply places the alarm on the cord of a pending lamp with a click, no tools needed. The Snapalarm is suitable for all cords and chains up to 2cm in thickness.

Elixyr 餐具系列, 2004

KAHLA/Thüringen Porzellan GmbH, Kahla
Werksdesign: Barbara Schmidt
www.kahlaporzellan.com

Elixyr产品系列将碗与汤匙的形状结合起来。此系列包括大量的碟子、主菜盘、菜盘、碗以及一些有手柄的餐具。这些握柄的设计自然流畅，宛如汤匙一般。因此，无论是拿取或是使用这些餐具都变得简单易行。Elixyr产品设计旨在可以让使用者牢固地握紧手柄，因此，手柄的上部被设计为螺旋状，目的是让大拇指接触时感觉更为舒适。Elixyr产品外形平滑，侧面整齐，能够排成一列，可在自助餐中使用。瓷器的质感下，那种不甚对称的外表给餐桌营造出出一种崭新的感觉。

The Elixyr design combines the forms of bowl and spoon. The range consists of a large number of plates, platters, dishes, bowls, and containers with a kind of handle that seems to grow out of them – just like a spoon. Thus, they can be held, carried and used easily. Elixyr wants to be grasped. The upper surface of the handle is rotated so that the thumb comes to rest on it more comfortably. Elixyr has flowing forms with straight sides, due to which they can be arranged in a line such as for example for a buffet. They go partly beyond the symmetry otherwise typical of ceramics and chinaware, thus creating new orders on the table.

自由精神收藏品, 2004

Rosenthal AG, Selb
Design: Robin Platt, London, GB
www.rosenthal.de

原本仅是附属品的设计——碗，以它那富有活力的设计，被列入了自由精神周年收集品之中。它的基本元素是方形——不同大小、不同深浅的有棱角或长方形碟子或盘子，其有机的视觉语言通过超薄瓷器而显得更加突出。多样化和创新性的产品及其相应的玻璃碗具和碟子也被包含了进来。这样一来，长方形的玻璃托盘与餐盘就形成了鲜明的对比，小玻璃碗与高汤和美食融为一体。原来，自由精神是一个提倡创新、现代以及展示令人拍案惊奇佳肴的平台。

The dynamic design of the rolling Spirit bowl – originally created as an accessory – was incorporated into the Free Spirit anniversary collection. The basic elements are the square-shaped and rectangular plates and platters of different sizes and depths; their organic visual language is emphasised by a particularly thin porcelain. Diversity and creativity are added with matching glass bowls and -plates; in this way, the rectangular glass underplate stands in an interesting contrast with the matching dinner plate, and small glass bowls fit into the deep soup- and gourmet plates. Free Spirit is a platform for a creative, modern and surprising presentation of food.

Tema餐具系列, 2004

Thomas Trend Factory, Selb
(Rosenthal Group)
Design: Stefan Diez, München
www.rosenthal.de

Tema银器系列把目光转向了大众时尚餐具设计。在大份的意大利面和精美的菜肴旁边，传统的银器显得毫不起眼；设计师设计出一种更大的餐具系列。Tema餐具吸取了传统的铲形银制餐具的特点，并独具趣味性的区别：有时铲形餐具及各种小汤匙像是回归了传统，而有时它又走在了时代的最前端。为了与托马斯时尚工厂的亚洲收藏品相匹配，设计师还专为亚洲设计出了一系列产品，其中包括有楞角的瓷质汤匙和一双木质筷子。

The development of the tema silverware series oriented itself to the larger proportions of up-to-date dinnerware design. As conventional silverware creations usually appear quite inconspicuous next to oversized pasta- and gourmet plates, a slightly larger collection was designed. tema is reminiscent of the classic shape of spade silver. This results in playful differences: sometimes the spade is attached in the traditional way, as with various small spoons; at other times, the spade moves up to the front. Matching the Asia Collections of the Thomas Trend Factory, the Asia Set was the result, consisting of a shapely and functional porcelain spoon and a pair of chopsticks made of wood.

简单生活方式收藏品, 2003/2004

Hutschenreuther, Selb
(Rosenthal Group)
Werksdesign
www.rosenthal.de

简单系列是本年度中最具创意的收藏品，它包含了柔滑的有机外形的瓷制以及看起来非常和谐的附属品。简单系列迎合了“感观外形”的设计思路，给人以柔滑、细腻、轻巧的印象。当它被用来盛装和展示食品时，它会让人情不自禁地去抚摸其身上的浮雕和那些低调的装饰；当用它就餐时，也不会有任何的光反射。此外，该系列灵活多样的产品系列可以有多样的就餐安排：单一组件提供了多种组合的可能，它们可以被组合成不同的小套件使用。两种规格的圆形碗既可用作托盘，又可在餐桌中央作为饰品而使用，极具艺术气息。

Easy is an innovative collection for the entire duration of the year, consisting of a porcelain line with soft organic shapes and complementary accessories. Easy is designed with sensuous forms, yielding a soft, delicate and handy impression. Reliefs appealing to the touch and low-key decorations are the basis for a pleasing presentation of food, without superimposing the natural optics of dining. The diverse product line meets demands for a flexible set-up: the single component parts offer various possibilities of combination and are available in small individual sets. Ring-shaped bowls in two sizes can be used as underplate or as decorative table centrepiece.

genio 桌上的炉子, 2004

Thomas Trend Factory, Selb
(Rosenthal Group)
Design: Stefan Diez, München
www.rosenthal.de

genio桌上的炉子引领了日常烹调和就餐习惯的新方式。制造锅所使用的多层材料使锅受热均匀；用最少量的水和文火烹调，可以做出健康的不含脂肪的食品。此外，使用genio系列可以把刚烹调出锅的食品直接拿上餐桌。使用这个餐具还需配套使用“仪诺万”制造的瓷器组合，这些组件由新型瓷器合成物制成，经久耐用，可以经受温差变化，热存储能力高。此组件易于保温，因此不需要把食品置于其他的餐具中就可达到保温的效果。

The genio oven-to-table programme explores a new access to everyday cooking and dining habits. The multi-layer material used for the pots provides a uniform even heat distribution, allowing a gentle and healthy preparation of foods without fat and with a minimal amount of water. With the genio programme, the meals can be picked up from the kitchen and placed directly onto the dining table. The programme includes matching porcelain components made of Inovan, an innovative porcelain compound featuring a high degree of durability, resistance to temperature changes and a high heat storage capability. Food doesn't have to be filled into extra bowls and is kept warm more easily.

WMF 儿童餐具系列, 2004

WMF Württembergische
Metallwarenfabrik AG,
Geislingen/Steige
Design: Mocca Design
(Claudia Köhler, Irmy Wilms), Berlin
www.wmf.de

这些钢制餐具达到了美学和技术上的双重创新，制造出了个性化的儿童专用刀具。这些看上去非常小巧可爱的餐具，也可作为标准刀具来使用。此外，它还运用了激光技术，通过印在餐具手柄上可爱的造型，丰富并发展了个性化的激光装饰理念。该产品外形比列协调、圆润丰满，规格大小符合了儿童的人体工程学原理。

The First Lyric children's cutlery range is an aesthetically and technologically innovative interpretation of personalised cutlery for children. On the basis of the Lyric tableware cutlery, which is available as a standard regular design-oriented cutlery and additionally in different individualisable laser-decorated versions a decoration concept was developed, employing the same laser technology. The proportions are more rounded and soft in shape; the size was adapted to child ergonomics.

最佳收藏版餐具, 2005

WMF Württembergische
Metallwarenfabrik AG,
Geislingen/Steige
Design: Peter Bäurle, Geislingen-Eybach
www.wmf.de

此套刀具收藏品设计柔滑而圆润，精致凸出的浮雕表面让这一系列更加出彩。该设计比例与当今刀具的流行趋势保持一致，更凸显出了它那长长的刀柄、紧密的设计以及带给人美好感观享受的前端刀体。视觉收藏品中另一个重要的因素就是尽管材料厚度达5毫米，但刀具外形却很纤细，毫无笨重和夸张之感。与高厚度材料制作的高端产品带给人们的那种笨重的印象相比，此刀具的设计精巧且极具平衡感。这一系列专为对设计和产品价值有高需求的目标群体而设计。

The Vision cutlery collection is designed in a soft and fully rounded style combined with finely accentuated relief surface details. The proportions correspond to current trends in cutlery design with emphasis on long handles and compact, sensually designed front parts. An essential element of the Vision collection is the high material thickness of 5mm; however due to the slim contours it never appears unwieldy or exaggerated. The impression of a high-end product related to the material thickness is delicately balanced against the well-adjusted overall proportions. Vision is designed for target groups with highest demands in regards to design and product value.

Ikea Intakt 厨具, 2004

Ikea of Sweden AB, Älmhult, Schweden
Design: Ergonomidesign AB
(Ulrika Vejbrink, David Crafoord),
Bromma, Schweden
www.ikea.com
www.ergonomidesign.com

Intakt是为了提高烹调质量而设计的厨具，同时也使烹饪更加简单便捷。此系列中的每一个产品都具有与众不同的功能：产品的握柄被压制成一对塑料组件，手感舒适。产品外观上有各种凹凸面，不仅看起来动感十足，还让人觉得格外亲切。这组炊具握柄厚实，且与手型恰好吻合。厨具上还有一个功能孔，方便悬挂。总之，这套产品彰显了该系列的特征，体现出设计的一致性。

Intakt is a series of kitchen tools made to improve and simplify cooking. Every tool of the series has its own functionality. The handles of the tools are moulded in two plastic components, which result in a good comfortable grip and a contrasting accent. The shapes consist of varied convex and concave surfaces, yielding a friendly and dynamic expression. The handles are filled to gain thickness and fit nicely in the hand. They also have a functional hole to hang the tools up with. The consistent design features a product family.

Helix, 艺术8139餐具, 2005

Auerhahn Bestecke GmbH, Altensteig
Design: Cairn Young, London, GB
www.auerhahn-bestecke.de

Helix银质餐具外观优美，设计十分具有亲和力。该设计中最引人注目的是握柄的上端进行了塑性扭转。这种形态设计象征着动态和运动，通过延展使产品比例变得更加和谐，强调了一种"纯粹主义"的现代化的外形。螺旋状扭转的灵感来源于双螺旋的启示，使餐具扁平的外形顿时变得俏皮起来。此外，它并不是仅仅从表面上增加了餐具的实用性，还结合了餐具本身的浑然天成般地一体化雕刻，打破了其中规中矩的印象，带给使用者一种流动的感觉。这种最新的设计特征与动感、自然外形的结合使Helix银质餐具在很大范围内满足了正规的餐桌陈列和布局的要求。

The Helix silverware is sensual and designed with an emotional appeal. The most noticeable design feature is the plastical twist of the upper part of the handle. This formal design element symbolises dynamics and motion, accentuating puristic modern contours with stretched proportions. The spiral-like twist, derived from the image of a double helix, resolves the flat appearance of the silver in a playful way. This element is not an added surface application but acts as an integral sculptural component of the silverware itself, resulting in the expression of motion and the resolution of static impressions. The synthesis of up-to-date design features with dynamic, natural shapes allows the Helix silverware to be suitable for a wide range of formal tabletop set-ups and compositions.

TWIN 餐具系列, 2005

Zwilling J.A. Henckels AG, Solingen
Werksdesign
www.zwilling.com

Twin Cuisine餐具采用了可旋转的手柄设计。其手柄的特殊构造提供了理想化的受力分配，顿显刀具良好的平衡感。旋转式全尺寸刀舌的设计可以有多种形式的使用方式，这对于烹调刀具可以说是一种创新。刀柄由防滑塑料制成，弧度优雅，动感十足；刀舌由亚光不锈钢制成，也略带弧度。

TWIN Cuisine is a knife series with a rotated tang. The special construction of the handle provides an optimal distribution of weight and thus a noticeably better balance of the knife. The rotated full tang allows a language of forms, which is innovative for a cooking knife. The handle is made of non-slip plastic with an elegant curve – a dynamic, which is supported by the tang made of matt stainless steel, which is also slightly curved.

让・诺维尔餐具, 2004

Georg Jensen, Frederiksberg, Dänemark
Design: Jean Nouvel, Paris, Frankreich
www.georgjensen.com
www.jeannouvel.com

让・诺维尔不锈钢制餐具系列线条流畅，极具美感，给人一种纯净简单的感觉。弧状外形在清晰锋利的刀刃的衬托下而显得尤为明显。每件刀具都经过仔细度量，以保证受力平衡。正如法国设计大师让・诺维尔所评价那样："一把刀仅使用一块金属制成，外观毫无瑕疵，设计极为巧妙。叉子的两边都经过定型，让惯用左手和惯用右手的人都适宜使用。"

The Jean Nouvel stainless steel cutlery series has clean and aesthetic lines, which create a pure and simple look. The curved form is emphasised by clear as well as sharp cuts. Each and every piece of cutlery is carefully measured to ensure perfect distribution of weight and balanced gravity: "The knife is formed out of one piece of metal, resulting in a look that is both pure and architectural. The fork is sharpened on both sides and thus suitable for left- and right-handers." (Jean Nouvel)

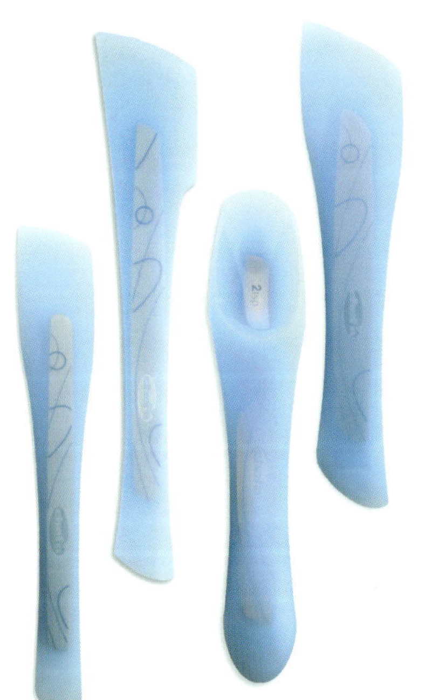

Switchit 硅树脂刮刀, 2003

Chef'n Corp, Seattle, USA
Werksdesign: Jason Germany
Vertrieb: Lurch AG, Hildesheim
www.chefn.com
www.lurch.de

Switchit牌刮刀与祖母们曾经使用过的刮刀很相似。它由硅树脂制成，握感舒适，是卫生且理想的烹调器皿。这款设计解决了使用传统刮刀时，食物易卡在握柄和刮刀之间的缝隙中这一问题。Switchit牌双刃刮刀外表坚固。如将双刃合在一起，就会看到它是无痕结构，且没有角度和弯度偏差，不易滋生细菌。

Switchit is a rubber scraper, similar to those used by our grandmothers. Made of silicone, it is a sanitary and optimised cooking utensil, which sits well in the hand. The design solves the problem of conventional scrapers, in which food gets caught in the gaps between the handle and the scraper. The Switchit Dual Ended scraper is based on the principle of form consolidation. Putting both ends together results in a seamless construction without angles or corners where bacteria could thrive.

Schärfbank磨刀器, 2004

mayer und thiele gbr, Wuppertal
Design: vitamin d, Wuppertal
www.mayerundthiele.de
www.vitamin-d.de

这款采用优质材料而作成的磨刀器操作简便、容易，宛若一件极具创意的厨具。它由优质的硬瓷制成，在无釉处磨刀相当于3000个结晶粒度。这种材料比钢铁还坚硬，特别适用于打磨厨具。由于减少了手腕的动作，刀具打磨变得更加容易，刀具便随时都可以保持坚韧锋利了。

With easy handling and high functionality as well as high material quality, the sharpening bench resembles an innovative kitchen tool. It is made of fine and robust hard porcelain. Sharpening knives on the unglazed surface is commensurate with a 3,000 grain size. As this material is harder than steel, it is particularly suitable for whetting kitchen tools. With a few motions of the wrist, the knife can be sharpened easily. The basic cut of the knife is preserved at all times.

西曼蒂克挂墙式设计, 2005

SieMatic Möbelwerke GmbH & Co. KG, Löhne
Werksdesign
www.siematic.com

西曼蒂克挂墙式设计包括了栏杆、壁龛、可伸展的照明设备以及自由定位支点。整个设计体现出了柔滑的像地平线一样弧度的构思，其表面进行了阳极氧化亚光处理，使整体显得高贵而优雅。这一设计在规格和设计等方面蕴含了高度的个性化选择。这个系列的托盘多达20多种颜色，另外还有多功能厨具可供选择。

The SieMatic onWall system consists of a railing, niche elements, a length-variable lighting profile as well as freely positionable spots. The underlying formal idea is a soft, convex flowing horizontal line. The matt anodised surface creates an elegant appearance. The system offers highly individual options in terms of both size and design. The carrier plates are available in more than 20 different colours. Several function-oriented kitchen elements are also available.

陶花瓶系列, 2005

Porzellanmanufaktur Fürstenberg, Fürstenberg/Weser
Design: Kap Sun Hwang, Kellinghusen
www.fuerstenberg-porzellan.com

在这个系列陶花瓶的生产过程中，对陶瓷的处理方式是与众不同的：三种不同规格不同直径的蓝白相间的花瓶烧制出炉后，风干直至与皮革的硬度相当。随后，根据特定的形状而把它们切割成大小不同的圆环。花瓶又按照不同的颜色被重新组合起来。这种工艺制造出来的花瓶触感极佳，拥有丝绸般的表面以及清晰流畅的外形，其优雅色调也平添了无限情趣。

In the production of the Tao vase series, porcelain is processed in an unusual way: Three identical blue and white vases are produced in three sizes and diameters and are left to dry until they get as hard as leather. Afterwards they can be cut into rings of different sizes according to a given pattern. The vases can then be put together again with different colours. This results in interesting haptic qualities with a silky surface as well as clear forms and a fine and dramatic colouring.

TAT 8SL1 Solitaire 压缩式面包机, 2004

Robert Bosch Hausgeräte GmbH, München
Werksdesign: Helmut Kaiser
Design: Porsche Design GmbH (Christian Schwamkrug, Jörg Tragatschnig), Zell am See, Österreich
www.bosch-hausgeraete.com

TAT 8SL1 Solitaire压缩式面包机外形美观，选材考究，力求使用户操作达到简易快捷。此系列由不锈钢和藏蓝色塑料制品制成，附带小型面包加热支架以及方便实用的操作显示屏，能够显示面包的烘焙成色。大的面包切片使用分开的面包架盛装。这个设计采用高纯度的石英加热器和可调节的电烘焙控制，这些都保证了出品优质的烤面包。烘焙之后，使用所谓的“抬头式”技术可以将面包切片轻轻抬起。盛装面包屑的托盘可自由取下，方便清洗。

The aesthetically designed TAT 8SL1 Solitaire compact toaster is made of high-grade materials, integrating user-friendly technology. The cool-touch housing consists of stainless steel and dark-blue plastics. Comfortable is an integrated bun warming rack as well as a functional optical progress display indicating the current degree of browning. Large toast slices are held in place with a divided bread lift. Good toasting results are attained due to the high-grade quartz heating and a variable electronic browning control. After toasting, the slices are gently lifted with the so-called soft lift-up technique. An integrated crumb tray can be removed and cleaned easily.

胡桃夹子, 2003

EMS-GRIVORY, Domat/Ems, Schweiz
Werksdesign: Thomas Jeltsch, Christian Kruse
www.emsgrivory.com

胡桃夹子的设计在功能和形式上可以说是直奔主题。本着"集中一体化"的设计原则，全部功能与组件都集中在一个几乎是一步到位而制作出的元件上。此设计集复位功能、两片颚式结构以及传力杠杆于一身。单层夹板的加工过程允许将不同的材料集中于一个元件上。此设计反映了不同组件间的承重关系，而受力和人体人体工程学原理则决定了支杆的交叉位置。单层夹板结构中不同的材料运用给使用者带来了一种新鲜的视觉效果，它把材料塑造出来的外形上的阳刚之美自然而然地转化成了一种轻柔弹性的感觉。

The nutcracker design reduces form and function to the essentials. The design principle is "total integration"; all functions and mechanisms are integrated in a one-piece component, which is produced in a one-step manufacturing process. The design consists of a joint with a reset function, two jaws as well as the leverage for the transmission of force. The mono-sandwich manufacturing process allows the combination of different materials in one component. The design reflects the load-bearing of the components, while aspects of support and ergonomics determine the levers' cross sections. The three material layers of the mono-sandwich structure are particularly attractive visually. Materials and shape form a flowing transition from the rigid joints to the elastic spring.

菜板, 2005

RoyalVKB, Zoetermeer, NL
Werksdesign: Jan Hoekstra
Design: Nikolaï Carels, Overveen, NL
www.royalvkb.com

这款菜板的设计极为实用方便：在切割食物之后，可使食物顺利倒入锅中而不发生任何洒落。它易于端起，颜色多样，适用于不同食物。此菜板在设计过程中考虑到了在小型菜板上切割食物后，入锅的过程中可能会发生洒落，因此，这款聚丙烯制成的菜板在两个边缘处微微弯曲，并且能够轻易端起；另外，其个性化的双色设计提醒使用者在切割不同的食物时要使用不同的面板：一面用于切割肉类，另一面用于切割蔬菜，防止交叉污染，滋生细菌。

The functionally designed cutting board allows to cut food and let it slide into the pan without spilling anything. It is easy to lift and designed with different colours for different foods. The cutting board takes into consideration that, with smaller cutting boards, the food will fall off sideways when trying to slide it into the pan. This polypropylene cutting board however is curved on both sides to prevent this from happening, making it easier to lift as well. The two colours can be used to remind the user what sort of food was cut on which side: poultry on one side, vegetables on the other. In this way, cross-contamination with salmonella is prevented.

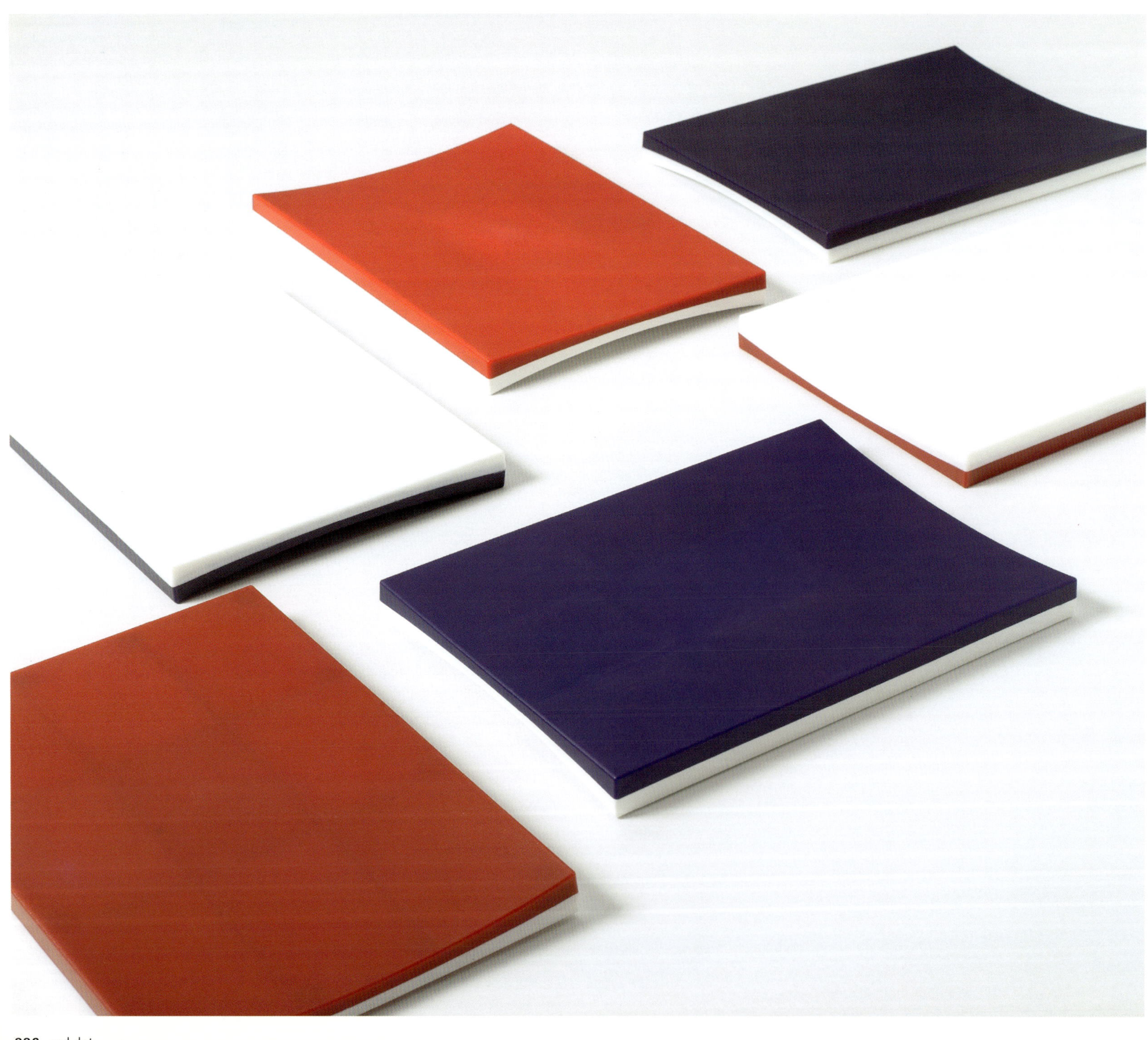

剥蒜器, 2005

RoyalVKB, Zoetermeer, NL
Werksdesign: Jan Hoekstra
Design: Ineke Hans, Arnheim, NL
www.royalvkb.com

使用这款剥蒜器可以使人们在剥蒜后，双手不会粘染蒜味。另外，不锈钢剥皮器还可以做“肥皂”使用。首先，只需轻轻转动，蒜皮就可以被剥去，这也有利于完好保存大蒜的味道。然后，当在流水下清洗剥蒜器时，手上残留的蒜味也会随之洗掉，其实，这全归功于一种特殊的不锈钢设计。

The functionally designed garlic crusher facilitates easy crushing of garlic cloves without smelly hands. The stainless steel crusher additionally acts as "soap". First, the cloves are crushed with a simple rolling motion. This has the advantage that the garlic intensifies in taste even more. Later, when rinsing the crusher under running water, the garlic smell is removed from the hands at the same time. This is possible due to a design with a special kind of stainless steel.

“对话”玻璃杯, 2004

Rösle GmbH & Co. KG, Marktoberdorf
Design: Heinrich Stukenkemper, Castrop-Rauxel
www.roesle.de

“对话”系列设计应了高贵典雅的正餐文化之所需。该餐饮用品系列集美观实用于一身。玻璃制品由高纯度的铅晶制玻璃制成，一种高雅的感受呼之欲出。与之相配的不锈钢餐盘则呈现出另一种优雅的样子，其宽边的衬托更增添了魅力。两三个玻璃杯以及一个不锈钢餐盘组成了这套餐具。

Dialogue is a design line for a sophisticated dining culture. The product line for the segments eating and drinking combines innovative functionality with timeless aesthetics. The glasses of the line are made of high-grade lead crystal, stirring up an appetite for classiness. A matching stainless steel tablet creates an elegant framework, underlining its charm with a wide rim. Two or three glasses with matching stainless steel tablets are combined to one ensemble.

“对话”上菜系列, 2004

Rösle GmbH & Co. KG, Marktoberdorf
Design: Heinrich Stukenkemper, Castrop-Rauxel
www.roesle.de

相信“对话”的上菜系列产品一定会成为使专业人士、审美学家以及鉴赏家们都感到满意的新产品：方形的设计中加入了制冷设备，可以长期保持鲑鱼或者奶酪的新鲜。三种不同形状的外盖构成三种基本的设计，其他瓷制或木质的产品更为这一系列提供了多样化的选择。

The serving system of the Dialogue design line is an innovation for practitioners, aesthetes and connoisseurs. A cooling element integrated into the square-shaped system keeps salmon or cheese fresh for a long time. Three different cover shapes govern the design of the basic versions. The serving system offers many expandabilities with different components made of porcelain and wood.

“对话”家庭料理, 2004

Rösle GmbH & Co. KG, Marktoberdorf
Design: Heinrich Stukenkemper, Castrop-Rauxel
www.roesle.de

“对话”系列的调味瓶套装设计的一定会令人心动，它还结合了美观与功能性，可以根据个人不同口味及喜好，加入佐料做出佳肴。调味瓶套装可以盛装醋、油、盐和胡椒，或是只用来盛装盐和胡椒。一个方便的手柄更是让它变得魅力十足起来。

The cruet stand of the Dialogue design line is expressive and combines aesthetics with functionality. It turns the meal into a dish exclusively according to one's own preferences. It is available as cruet stand with vinegar, oil, salt and pepper or as smaller ensemble with salt and pepper. The design includes a functional carrying handle.

Zyliss 番茄去皮器

Zyliss AG, Zürich, Schweiz
Design: IDEO, Palo Alto, USA
www.zyliss.com

Zyliss番茄去皮器采用了不锈钢小锯齿刀片制作，特别适用于柔软水果和蔬菜，可轻易剔除它们的外皮。位于番茄去皮器顶端的锋利的小刀片可以除掉水果和蔬菜上的伤痕。

The Zyliss Tomato Peeler is fitted with a stainless steel, micro-serrated blade especially developed for peeling soft fruits and vegetables. It makes the removal of tomato skin from the fruit flesh easy. An ultra-sharp mini blade on the tip of the tomato peeler helps to remove small blemishes such as bruising on fruits and vegetables.

Duo摩擦器

Zyliss AG, Zürich, Schweiz
Design: IDEO, Palo Alto, USA
www.zyliss.com

Duo摩擦器的外形符合人体工程学原理，轻巧灵便。高质量的不锈钢摩擦器保证了好的摩擦效果，防滑橡胶托能够紧紧吸附在滑腻的厨房操作台上。无论是帕尔马奶酪、巧克力、酸橙还是胡萝卜，Duo摩擦器都能够快又好的摩擦食物，保证了食物右边规整细腻而左边线条粗犷。它设计先进，外形纤美，存放简易，可以放置于任何一个抽屉中，使这个厨房帮手更加实用。

本系列中的旋转奶酪摩擦器采用了大型的研磨组件，保证了使用效率，手摇柄和摩擦器之间垂直连接，使得整件器械就仅仅包含两个组件。

With its ergonomic shape, the Duo Grater is very handy. The high-quality, stainless steel grater surface ensures perfect results, while non-skid rubber feet provide a secure grip on slippery kitchen worktops. Whether Parmesan cheese, chocolate, limes or carrots – the Duo Grater speeds up the work of grating foods significantly, providing a fine side on the right and a coarse side on the left. Its advanced design results in a slim shape. It is easily stored away in any drawer, which makes this innovative kitchen aid extremely useful.
The rotary cheese grater of this series is efficient due to a large grater element. The hand crank and the grater are directly connected to one another so that the entire unit consists of just two components.

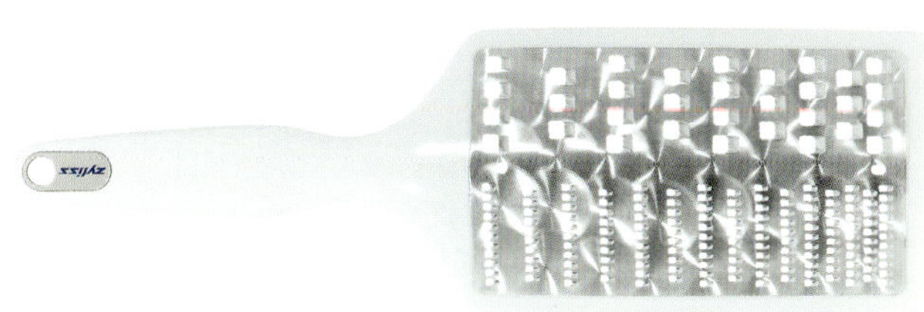

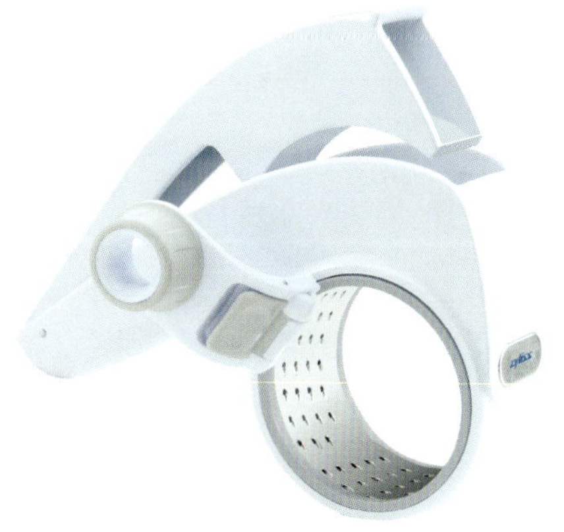

SafetyCan² 开瓶器, 2004/2005

William Levene Ltd, Farnborough, GB
Werksdesign: Andrew Thornton, Bruno Herren
www.williamlevene.com

SafetyCan²开启器可用于罐头和拉环开启，且开启之后的容器上不会留下尖锐的边缘。它的外形生动美观，符合人体工程学原理，特别是螺旋钮能够最大的发挥效率，降低了开启所需的旋转圈数。获得过专利的设计组件保证了轻易地开启盖子而不会产生锋利的开口。拉环开启器设置在了SafetyCan²的握柄上。

SafetyCan² is a functional can and ring-pull opener, which leaves no sharp edges on the lid or rim of opened cans. It has an aesthetic as well as interesting shape. Its ergonomic design, especially of the winder knob, maximises the efficiency in reducing the amount of turns necessary to open the can. It is equipped with a patented high quality mechanism for a durable efficient removal of the can's lid time after time without creating leaving sharp edges. The body of the SafetyCan² has got a ring-pull opener incorporated into the handle.

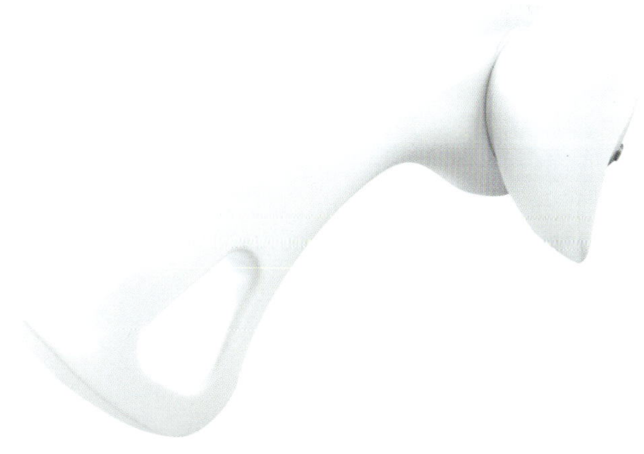

Ellipsis BL 745 立式搅拌器, 2004

Kenwood Ltd., Havant, GB
Werksdesign
Vertrieb: De'Longhi Deutschland GmbH, Seligenstadt
www.kenwoodworld.com
www.delonghi.com

Elipsis BL 745搅拌器采用金属底座，外观奢华。亚光的不锈钢和玻璃结合，呈现出一种冷峻的外观，更彰显底座和高脚杯之间搭配的和谐。闪亮的指示灯按钮构成了视觉上的亮点。Elipsis搅拌器配备了五种速度设定和一个脉冲/清除按钮。新型Kenlock式密封系统以及可以从各个方向放入的高脚杯，都使操作这个搅拌器变得更加地舒适简便。

The Ellipsis BL 745 blender with full metal base has an extravagant appearance. Matt finished stainless steel in combination with glass create a cool look and underline the harmony between base and goblet. The illuminated buttons are an optical highlight. The Ellipsis features five speed settings plus a pulse-/clean button. The innovative Kenlock seal system and a goblet that can be easily placed from all sides make the handling of this stylish blender very comfortable.

多伦多平底无脚酒杯, 2005

Sahm GmbH + Co. KG, Höhr-Grenzhausen
Werksdesign: Prof. Michael Boehm
www.sahm.de

在设计多伦多平底无脚酒杯时，设计者的目标是制造出一种真正意义上的多功能玻璃杯，适于盛装任何种类的饮品。此平底无脚酒杯可以用于盛装任何一种无酒精的饮料，轻度酒精饮品，鸡尾酒以及啤酒，包括大麦酿造的啤酒等饮品。因此，美食家们不再需要为不同种类的饮品去购买不同类型的杯子。此杯中央部分较细，易于把握；其微弧型酒杯的外观使多伦多平底无脚酒杯的外观酷似高脚杯。

When designing the Toronto tumbler, the aim was to create a glass that is a real multi-purpose glass and as such suitable for any kind of drink. The tumbler can be used for all non-alcoholic drinks, long drinks, cocktails and beers including wheat beer. The gastronome does no longer have to buy individual glasses for each brand or kind. Thanks to its waist, which makes it easy to hold, and a slightly curved chalice, the Toronto tumbler has the look of a goblet.

Classico 保温壶, 2005

alfi GmbH, Wertheim
Design: Tassilo von Grolman, Oberursel
www.alfi.de
www.tassilo-von-grolman.de

Classico是真空保温壶外形美观，款式不易淘汰。它采用了多种材料，这些材料之间构成了有趣的对比。该真空保温壶采用镀铝内胆（或者镀铬铜内胆）和镀铬金属握柄。更重要的是：你只需用一只手就可以提起保温壶。Classico保温壶容量规格是一升，制作过程中还添加了alfi-Dur耐用硬玻璃。

Classico is an aesthetic and timeless vacuum flask with materials generating an interesting contrast. The corpus consists of an aluminium satin finish (or chrome-plated brass alternatively) while the handle is made of chrome-plated metal. An essential functional aspect is the possibility to handle the flask with just one hand. Classico has a volume of one litre and features an alfiDur hard glass insert.

Stelton 迷你咖啡机, 2005

Stelton A/S, Kopenhagen, Dänemark
Werksdesign: Mads Surel
Design: Someones Design
(Frederik Gundelach),
Kopenhagen, Dänemark
Vertrieb: Stelton Verkaufsbüro
Deutschland, Meinerzhagen
www.stelton.com
www.someonesdesign.dk

Stelton迷你咖啡壶使你很容易就能变成一个离不开咖啡的人。它基于人们常常独立饮用咖啡的这种现代生活方式而设计。这款咖啡壶包含一个新型的过滤系统，以方便将个人喜爱的咖啡豆碾磨后，将咖啡直接倒入杯中。此咖啡壶设计精妙，兼具功能性和经济性。

The Stelton minibrewer makes it easy to be a real coffee drinker. It is designed for a modern everyday lifestyle where people often drink coffee alone. It includes an innovative filter system designed to prepare the coffee directly in the cup, using exactly those coffee beans one prefers. The design is well thought out, functional and economic.

Eva Solo 牛奶和糖套件

Eva Denmark A/S, Maaloev, Dänemark
Design: Tools Design (Claus Jensen,
Henrik Holbæk), Kopenhagen, Dänemark
Vertrieb: Eva Deutschland, Moorrege
www.evadenmark.com

方便的糖罐外形优美流畅，还附带了一个实用型茶匙，它可以在将容器倒置时，自动送出满满一茶匙的糖。而当使用完毕之后，防漏牛奶罐可以用橡胶塞子盖紧。此套件使用了玻璃，不锈钢，硅氧烷橡胶以及塑料制成。

The functional and aesthetically designed sugar container includes a practical insert, which automatically delivers an exact teaspoon full of sugar when turned upside down. After use, the milk dispenser with drip-free lip can be closed with a snug-fitting rubber lid. The set consists of glass, stainless steel, silicone rubber and plastics.

Eva Solo 泡茶罐

Eva Denmark A/S, Maaloev, Dänemark
Design: Tools Design (Claus Jensen,
Henrik Holbæk), Kopenhagen, Dänemark
Vertrieb: Eva Deutschland, Moorrege
www.evadenmark.com

这款泡茶罐可以有两种泡茶方式。一是可以让茶叶自由地在水面上漂浮，倒茶时用过滤器将茶叶隔离；或者将茶叶放在过滤器中，泡制时间足够长之后，用力挤压柱塞。这款泡茶罐在功能上大大地做了一番创新，除了具备专利的过滤系统之外，它的顶端还配备了一个自动滑盖，可以在倒茶时自动开启；此外还有一个专门的防漏茶嘴，氯丁橡胶制作的外罩也兼备了美观和功能性，能够保持茶的温度。

With this tea maker, tea can be brewed in two different ways. One can let the tealeaves float freely in the water, holding them back with the filter when pouring a cup, or one can put the tealeaves in the filter and once the tea has brewed for long enough, fully depress the plunger. Functional innovations of the tea brewer are, besides the patented filter system, a flip-top lid automatically opening up when pouring a cup, as well as a patented, drop-free spout. An aesthetic as well as functional innovation is a neoprene cover to keep the tea warm.

Modulares 竹制菜板, 2004

Lignum arts GmbH, Fürstenfeldbruck
Werksdesign: Thorsten Huth,
Tobias Jung
Vertrieb: Brucker Loft, Fürstenfeldbruck
www.lignum-arts.de

外形美观的厨房用竹制菜板包含多个30 × 15厘米的组件，可以做菜板、上菜板，甚至可以接连起来形成一个更大的操作台面。由于竹质材料坚硬密实的表面及其生长迅速的特性，不同组件之间可以通过压磨侧面而相互连接。菜板已经上过食用油，其嵌入式橡胶垫的运用在使用时就更不易打滑。

The aesthetically designed kitchen cutting board consists of 30 x 15cm modules which can be used as small cutting or serving boards or be joint together to form larger cutting surfaces. The modules are connected via a milled profile. The bamboo material is well suited for this purpose, since it has a hard and dense surface and offers ecological advantages due to its fast growth. The cutting board has been oiled with food-safe oil. Drilled-in rubber feet provide good grip.

Hansamotion
水龙头, 2005

Hansa Metallwerke AG, Stuttgart
Design: NOA, Aachen
www.hansa.de
www.noa.de

Hansamotion是一款像雕塑一般的开放式水流导管浴室龙头，给人带来感官上的美好享受。其创新的开放式设计外形，水流就好似山泉涌出，展现了水流的灵动轻柔的自然美。Hansamotion新型出水口还能使水流形成独特的形状，其开放性设计使水流量显得尤为丰富，但实际情况却是水流量减少了33%。

Hansamotion is a sensual and sculptural bath tap with an open water duct. It presents the water in an innovative open design, thus stylising the naturalness and fascination of water in a mountain stream. This creates a multi-faceted soft, flowing image of the water. The newly developed Hansastream water outlet lets the water flow in a special shape, and due to the open presentation, the amount of water appears to be significantly larger and more voluminous. This impression is created although the flow of water is reduced by 33 per cent.

Navis N1 切割机，2004

Gebr. Graef GmbH & Co. KG, Arnsberg
Design: Delta Form Industriedesign (Detlef Belter), Melle
www.graef.de
www.deltaform.de

Navis N1切割机配备了悬臂发动机，可以垂直切割位于切刀下的物体，并可随心所欲地放置它们。此切割机的另一优点体现在清洗过程中：其封闭性的结构可以防止设备底部碎裂，避免残留物。不用的时候，切刀可以轻松地放置在保险座上。彩色的操作部件，彩色的暂停开光和总开关更平添了Navis N1的魅力。看得出，Navis N1在装备设计上也是经过深思熟虑的，它那150瓦的大功率发动机以及镀钛特殊切刀保证了理想的切割效果。

The patented Navis N1 cutting machine has a cantilevered motor, which makes it possible to catch the cut objects directly under the knife and to put them down as required. Another advantage of the construction is the cleaning process: The closed construction prevents crumbs or remains from getting underneath the device. Thanks to the safety-catch the knife can be easily replaced. The colourful design of the operating elements as well as the switches for momentary and permanent use characterise the look of the Navis N1. The equipment of the Navis N1 is well thought out, too: the strong driver motor with 150 watts, along with a titanium-coated special cutter, guarantees an optimised cutting result.

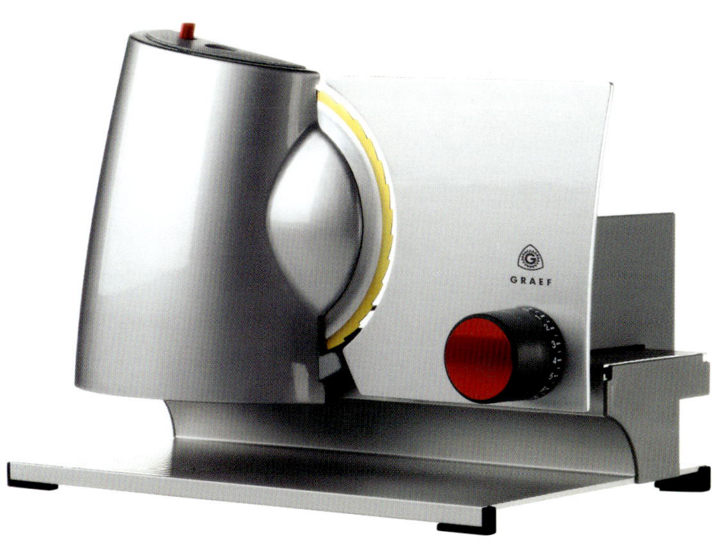

KWC Eve 厨用水龙头，2005

KWC AG, Unterkulm, Schweiz
Design: NOA, Aachen
Vertrieb: KWC Deutschland GmbH, Herrenberg
www.kwc.com
www.noa.de

Eve是一款设计精妙、实用的厨房用水龙头。它的外观柔滑，纤细，在集束光的照射下显现出细小的光圈。纽珀的射流曝气机加入了光圈，使水槽更像一个工作间。光圈还照亮了喷嘴，仿佛深绿色的琼浆。Eve将魅力与功能性相结合，制造出优美的厨房用品。

Eve represents an innovative design and function-oriented kitchen faucet with integrated light. Characteristic soft and slim shapes create a gracile aura. The hidden Neoperl pull-out aerator incorporates a ring of lights, which lights the sink as a workplace. The ring of lights also illuminates the water jet and makes it look like a plasma stream. Eve combines fascination and function in a gracile kitchen sculpture.

Mini-Max 保鲜盒, 2004

Tupperware France S.A., Joue-les-Tours, Frankreich
Werksdesign: Tupperware Global Design Group
Vertrieb: Tupperware Deutschland GmbH, Frankfurt/Main
www.tupperware.com

Mini–max（最小–最大）保鲜盒系列可以折叠，延展，或“三和一”组装起来。此系列可以相继打开每一个放置层，延展成所需的大小，当确立所需大小后，就可以放入食品，用安全封封紧并储存起来。Mini–max系列的可堆放性大大节省了冰箱的空间。即使是处于完全延展的状态下，保险盒也可放入冰箱之内。Mini–max系列折叠之后仅有2厘米高，节省了洗碗机和冰箱中的空间。这个系列有700ml和950ml两种规格可供选择。

Mini-Max are collapsible, expandable, stackable three-in-one bowls. They can be expanded to the required size by popping out the layers one by one. Once the right size has been reached, the food is filled in, sealed with a safety seal and stored. Due to the stackable design, the Mini-Max series is highly space-saving for use in the fridge. Even when completely unfolded, the bowls fit into the fridge. In their collapsed form they are only 2cm high, thus requiring little space in the dishwasher or fridge. Mini-Max is available in two sizes: 700ml and 950ml.

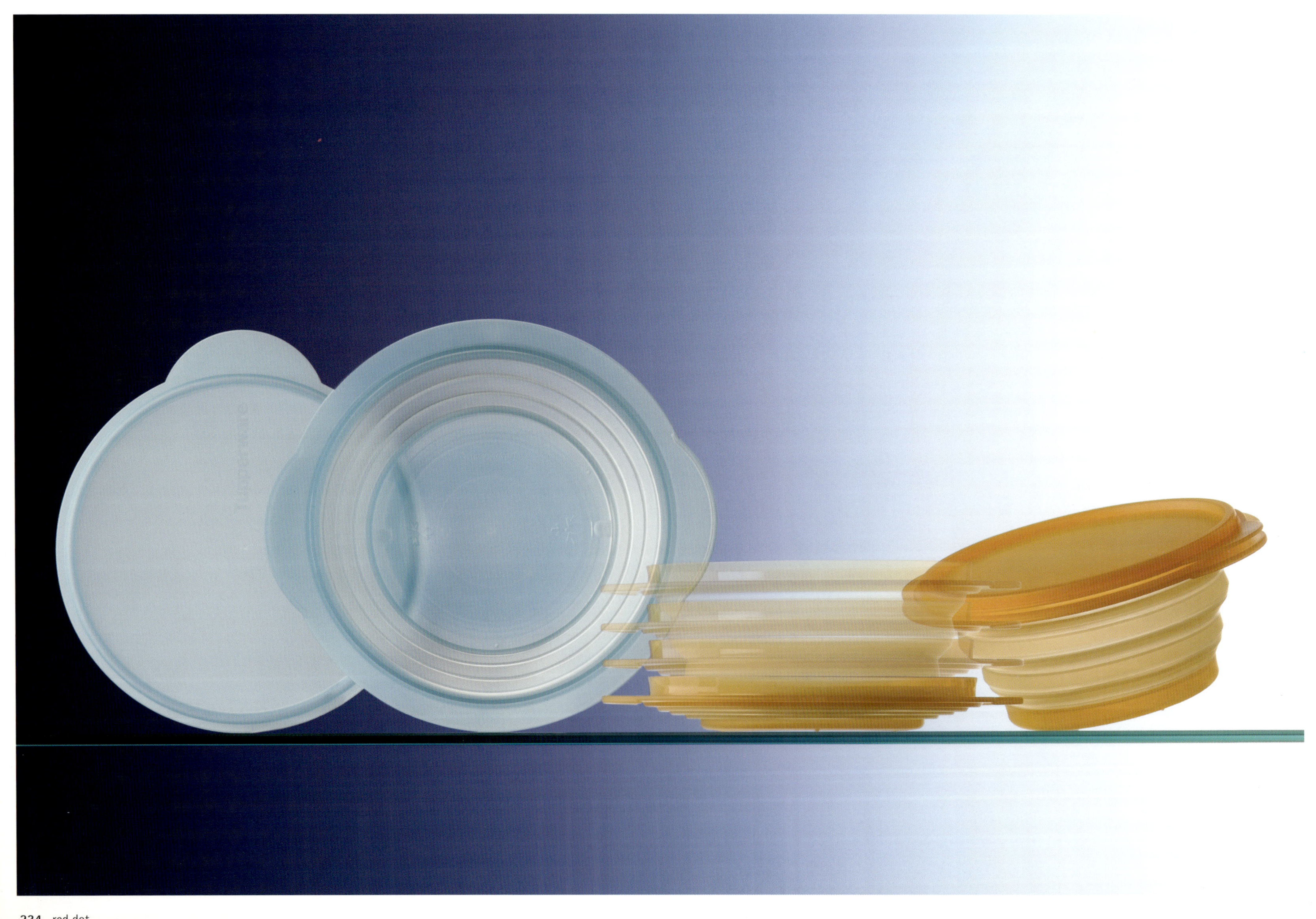

Fit + Fresh 沙拉碗, 2005

Emsa Werke Wulf GmbH & Co. KG, Emsdetten
Design: RazorBite Design Studio, Porthcawl, GB
www.emsa.com
www.razorbite.com

Fit + Fresh将沙拉去水器与外形美观的沙拉碗结合起来。它可以使备餐到上菜过程衔接的天衣无缝，同时使用时还不占空间。沙拉碗在备餐和上菜时都可以使用，去水篮亦可做筛子使用。Fit + Fresh可以用于沙拉、蔬菜、水果的清洗和上菜，不需另使用洗碗机就能做到干净清洗。

Fit + Fresh combines a salad spinner with an aesthetic and high-quality salad bowl in a functional design. Next to its functional advantages due to the seamless transition from preparation to serving, Fit + Fresh also saves space. The salad bowl can be used for preparation and serving; the spinning basket can also be used as a sieve. Fit + Fresh is suitable for washing and serving salads, vegetables, and fruit, and is also dishwasher-proof.

磁力锅垫, 2004

Ikea of Sweden AB, Älmhult, Schweden
Design: Sweedish Designstudio (Henrik Kjellberg, Mattias Lindqvist), Stockholm, Schweden
www.ikea.com
www.sweedish.se

这是一款内含五块磁铁的锅垫，可用于支撑任何一种锅底为磁性材料的锅具，亦可在电磁炉上使用。在往餐桌上放置热勺或热的平底锅时，它可以保护桌面，并提供了稳固的支点。强大的磁力使锅垫更容易吸附于锅底，因此，当把锅从炉具上端起时，锅垫已经吸附在锅底上了。由耐热硅氧烷制成，其材质耐磨，清洁卫生，很容易清洗，还可以使用洗碗机进行清洗。更为神奇的是，由于加入了钕磁，使它还能够吸附在冰箱门上。

Magnifik is a pot stand designed with five embedded magnets so as to be suitable for all pots with a base made of magnetic material, i.e. suitable for use on an induction stove. It protects the tabletop when placing hot pots and pans on it, giving them a secure foothold. As Magnifik sticks easily to the base of the pot due to the strong magnets, the pot can be carried from the worktop to the table with the pot stand already attached to the base of the pot. Magnifik is made of heat-resistant silicone, which is hygienic, easy to clean and dishwasher-safe. The material is very durable and non-breakable. Due to the construction with neodymium magnets, Magnifik sticks to the refrigerator door as well.

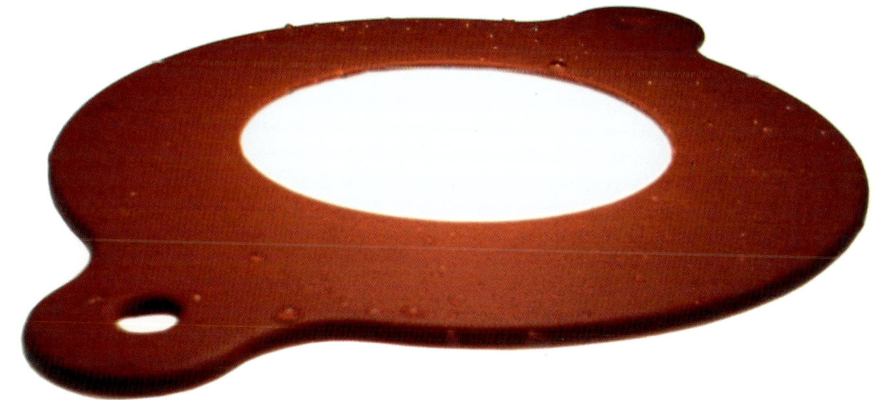

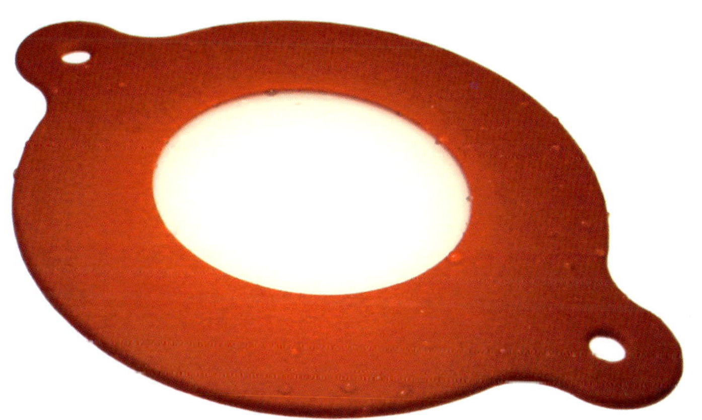

ErgoRapido 二合一式无线吸尘器，
2004

AB Electrolux, Stockholm, Schweden
Werksdesign: Christian Ågren, Esbjörn Svantesson, Kim Lim, Oskar Fjellman, Elisabeth Piper-Mäkitalo
www.electrolux.com

一般说来，消费者是不愿意用大的吸尘器吸取小碎屑的，ErgoRapido二合一式无线吸尘器便应运而生了。这款轻巧的吸尘器吸尘效果好，使用方便，能够快速吸起灰尘和脏物，过滤器易于清理。它的外观设计得更是恒久优雅，清晰简约。暗红的金属色给人一种优雅的印象，完美地与家庭环境完美的融合到一起。

The ErgoRapido 2 in 1 cordless vacuum cleaner is designed with the knowledge that consumers don't want to use a large vacuum cleaner to pick up small spills. The lightweight unit delivers excellent cleaning results and has been designed for ease of use, including an easy-to-clean filter. The unit is designed with a timeless elegance and a visual language of clarity and simplicity. It easily handles and quickly takes care of dust and dirt. The cayenne metallic colour lends an elegant impression and integrates seamlessly into the home environment so the unit can always be at hand.

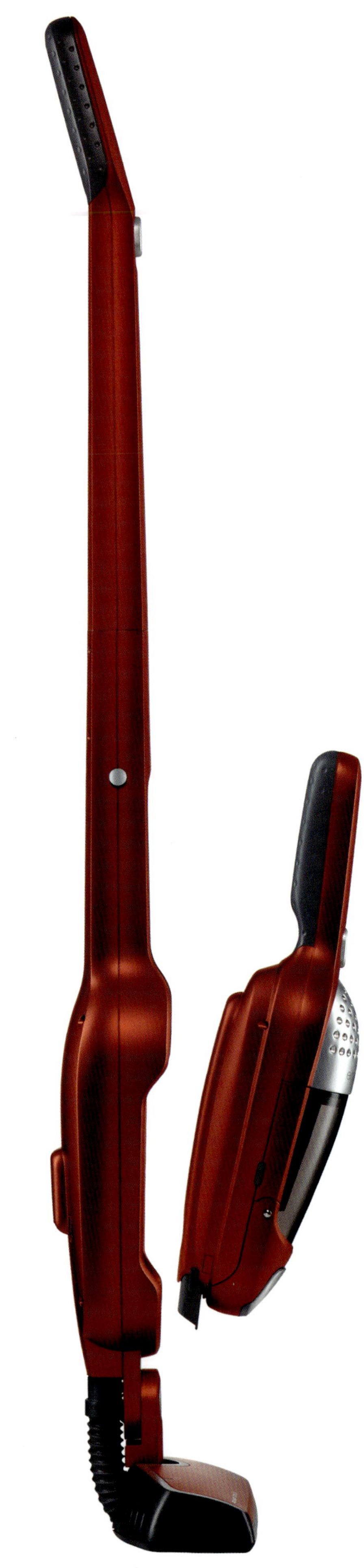

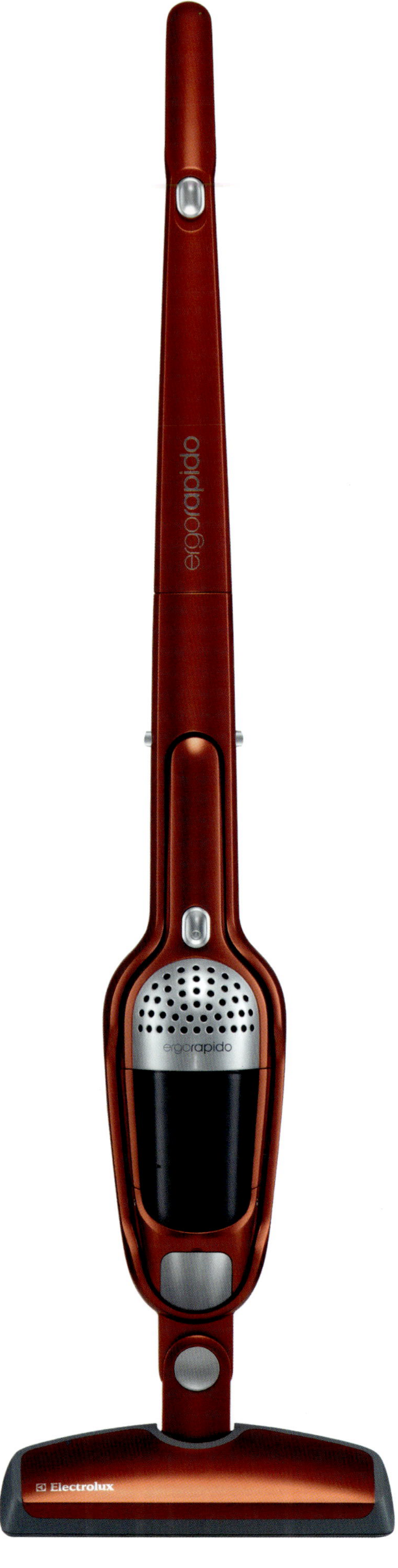

XL 1062 E 吸尘器, 2004

De'Longhi S.p.A., Treviso, Italien
Werksdesign:
De'Longhi Industrial Design Center
Vertrieb: De'Longhi Deutschland GmbH, Seligenstadt
www.delonghi.de

设计奢华的XL 1062 E型“ta ba ta”款吸尘器是一款新型功能强大的吸尘器。它设计灵活，能够在各种生活环境中使用。根据不用的需要，此款吸尘器经过旋转（De' Longhi旋转系统）可有多种变化，其中包括：地板吸尘器，用来清理死角的望远镜状吸尘器，用来清理沙发和汽车内部灰尘的便携式吸尘器等。五层过滤器采用Explora吸嘴，旁翼可折叠，压缩的方形灰尘袋不会黏附着任何灰尘和脏物。

The extravagant design of the XL 1062 E "ta ba ta" vacuum cleaner presents a high level of innovative functionality. As a flexible vacuum cleaner and "all-rounder", it adapts smoothly to any living environment. According to demands, the cleaner can be turned into a floor unit, a telescope cleaner for inaccessible spaces, or a hand unit for the cleaning of sofas or car interiors, with just a few turns (De'Longhi Nautilus System). A five-fold filter system, the innovative Explora suction nozzle with fold-away side wings, and the compact square dust bag remove any kind of dirt and dust.

ECL-SB5 吸尘器, 2004

Toshiba Corporation, Tokio, Japan
Werksdesign: Toshiba Design Center
(Toshiyuki Yamanouchi)
www.toshiba.co.jp

几乎人人都会喜欢使用样式美观且雅致的吸尘器来清扫房间，正是基于此种理念，ECL-SB5吸尘器应运而生。此款吸尘器外形美观，功能强大，设计目的在于创造出一个理想的清扫氛围，寻找一种广受欢迎的吸尘器外形。此款吸尘器可以说是一室、两室住宅或小型住宅的得力助手。吸尘器的刷子可以旋转，双重吸力发动机和离子刷能够彻底吸附灰尘。吸头轻轻拧一下就可以卸下，轻轻按动操作开关之后，此款吸尘器便可以变成垂直的便携式吸尘器。坚固的弧形握柄以及短距离可伸长型吸头吸引了很多人的目光，受到了无论是成年人还是儿童的普遍青睐。

The ECL-SB5 vacuum cleaner is based on the concept that people would like to clean their home with style but elegance as well. The functional and aesthetic design attempts to define the ideal scene for a vacuum cleaner and to find a universal shape for this appliance. Conceived as a second vacuum cleaner in the house, for one- to two-bedroom apartments or small compact homes, the rotating brush, the double suction motor and an ion brush guarantee a thorough dust absorption. By removing the stick with one turn and by operating a simple switch mechanism, the unit can be changed into an upright hand vacuum cleaner. A robust curved handle and a steplessly extendable stick appeal to a large target group from children to adults.

Oxy 3 真空吸尘器, 2004

AB Electrolux, Stockholm, Schweden
Werksdesign: Kim Lim, Christian Ågren, Oskar Fjellman, Esbjörn Svantesson
www.electrolux.com

Oxy 3吸尘器的设计旨在为使用者提供最大的方便。为了使吸尘性能达到最优，它采用了一体化设计。这款吸尘器符合人们的环保意识，可以创造出健康的生活环境。它采用了软性散播系统，使用HEPA H13过滤器，这样就可以最大限度地将清洁空气排出。Oxy 3系统配有密封箱，其余的附件可以通过联锁系统添加到吸尘器上。液晶屏上蓝色的控制灯亮起则表示清洁过程正在进行。操作灯的布局方便使用者，吸尘管不仅易于操作而且半径较大，有利于保证空气较好地流通，确保了较大的吸力。总之，此款吸尘器将优美的外观，强大的功能，方便用户的设计完美地集于一身。

The Oxy 3 vacuum cleaner has a user-friendly design and is equipped with a holistic system for maximised cleaning performance. The appliance meets high demands of ecological awareness and creates a healthy living environment. Thanks to a soft diffusion system with a HEPA H13 filter, the maximally cleaned air is softly blown out. The Oxy 3 system is integrated in an air-tight casing and the accessories are equipped with an air-tight interlocking system. A blue control light on the display signals the efficient cleaning process. The buttons for operating the performance are located user-friendly at the handle of the suction hose. The larger hose diameter facilitates an optimised air flow and a high suction performance. The result is a symbiosis of aesthetics, function and user-friendliness.

Gioel G401 / G402 / G403
吸尘器

Gioel, Trento, Italien
Design: MM Design, Brixen, Italien
www.gioel.it
www.mmdesign.org

此款清洁系统的创新在于它包含了两个部分：配备了水过滤器的吸尘器和蒸气炉，手柄部位采用了复杂的技术使这两部分分离。它操作起来简单，插座电源线卷起来放在机器内部。设计此款吸尘器的主要出发点是要能方便实用和操作简单，因此，这款机器体积小，移动方便，即使在人的背后也能够绕过去；因此，它毫不费力地就能够清洁楼梯和书架等难于清理的区域。此款机器还考虑到了外形和材质。它外形亲切，犹如宠物一般；符合人体工程学原理的设计使其更易于使用。

The innovation of this cleaning system is that it consists of two parts: the first is a vacuum cleaner with water filter while the second is a boiler for producing steam. The separation of these parts is achieved by a sophisticated mechanism fitted into the handle; it is simple to use and also acts as a wind-up mechanism for the power cord. One of the main aspects when designing this system was the practical and easy way the cleaning appliance should be handled, creating a machine that would be compact and easy to move around, even on one's back, to make cleaning stairs or shelves an effortless job. The design played with shapes and materials as well. The resulting appearance yields a friendly impression, almost reminding one of a pet. Ergonomically designed details build a bridge to the user.

Opair 袜子夹, 2004

monopezzo, Klein + Gärtner GbR, Ladenburg
Werksdesign: Frank Gärtner, Armin Klein
www.monopezzo.com

Opair设计可以保持短袜在洗涤后晾干或存储时成对而不会丢失。同时它也能够保证短袜在晾干时成对地被夹在晾衣架上，而不是随意搭在晾衣绳上。三维设计以及哑光表面给人一种高品质的印象，同时它们的触感极佳。Opair采用塑料领域中最新的技术，配备真正可回收、可清洁的凹槽，用防紫外线的可热塑材料制成。

The Opair keeps pairs of socks reliably together when washing, drying or storing them. For drying socks, the pairs are hooked up to the holders, which in turn are simply hung up on the clothesline. The three-dimensional design, in combination with a matted surface, yields a high-value impression and a comfortable feel to the touch. Implementing up-to-date realisations in the field of plastics technology, Opair consists of genuine, recyclable, detergent-, tumbler- and UV-proof thermoplastic.

TA-FVX2 熨斗, 2005

Toshiba Corporation, Tokio, Japan
Werksdesign: Toshiba Design Center (Yukie Chiba)
www.toshiba.co.jp

TA-FVX2型无线蒸汽熨斗设计轻便小巧，设计上极大地结合了用户的使用习惯。此款熨斗迎合了日本市场消费者对小型熨斗的喜爱这一主要潮流。TA-FVX2熨斗是一款家用豪华型无线蒸汽熨斗，其设计的重点集中在熨斗的金属表面上，而其它部位的设计也让使用者觉得安全可靠。此款熨斗在颜色选择上选用了黑白两色，以创造出一种整洁和高品质的氛围。开放式的手握柄是东芝蒸气熨斗的一大特色，同时也为用户提供了更大的便利。

The design of the TA-FVX2 cordless steam iron focuses on an impression of lightness, emphasising the high degree of user-friendliness as well. The design meets the demand for small-sized steam irons as the primary market trend in Japan. The TA-FVX2 was developed as a luxury model of a cordless steam iron for household use. The design thus focused in particular on the task to give the metal surface for ironing as well as the other parts a reliable impression. The colours chosen for the unit are black and white exclusively so as to yield a clean impression and to emphasise its high value. The open handle bar, characteristic design element of the Toshiba steam irons, additionally facilitates the handling of the iron.

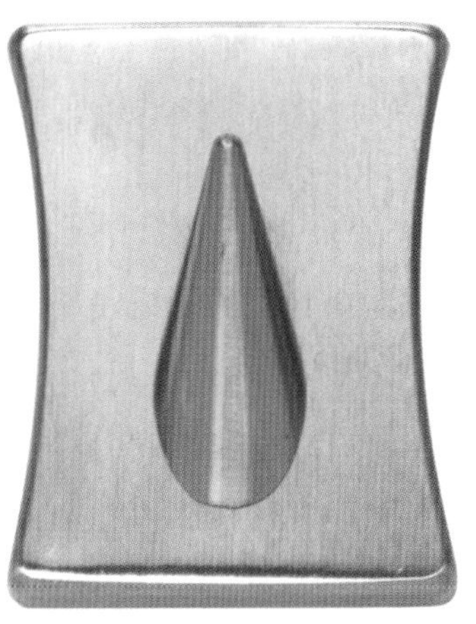

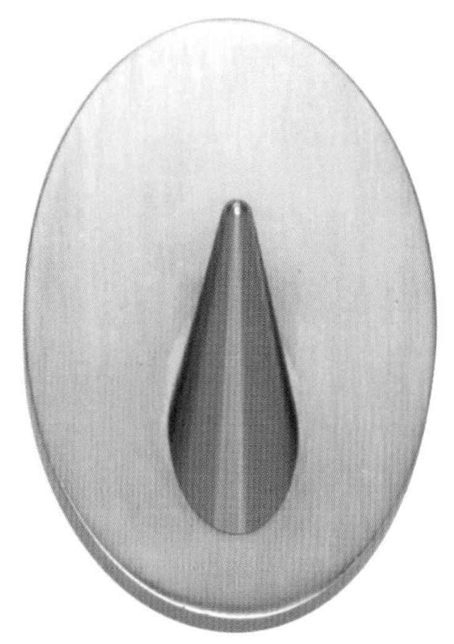

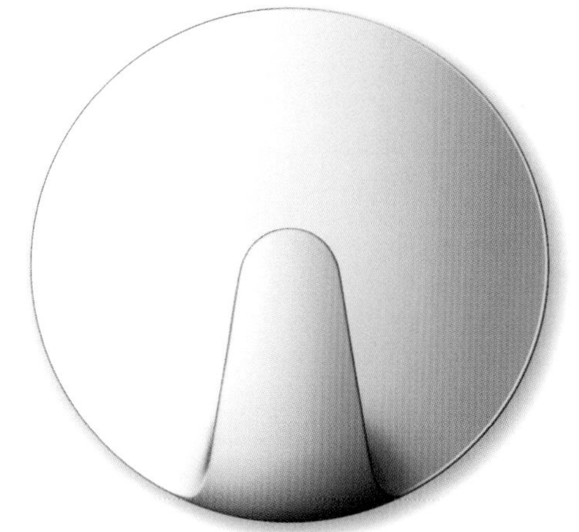

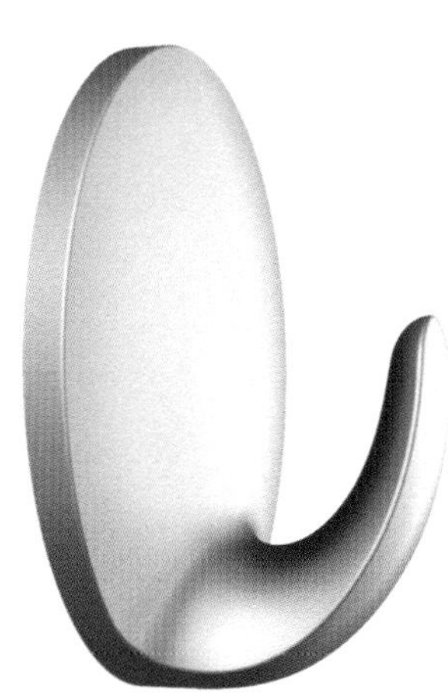

tesa Powerstrips® 金属钩, 2005

tesa AG, Hamburg
Design: Designkontor (Jens Plewa), Hamburg
www.tesa.com
www.designkontor.com

tesa Powerstrip®金属钩系列采用了新技术，设计符合人体工程学原理，其独特的造型也独具魅力。新型Powerstrip®系统首次在金属钩系列中出现，它吃力大，拆下时也不会留下任何痕迹。在瓦片和墙壁上使用时，它具有安装省力，钻孔灰尘小的特点。此项技术可以在任何材质的表面上使用，其符合人体工程学原理的设计特别能满足在各种底座上使用的需要。它基本的形状（手柄状）易于抓握或拆除。金属钩的设计凸现出一种几何的美感，简洁大方，持久耐用。

The tesa Powerstrips® metal hooks form a synthesis of innovative technology, ergonomic use and attractive sustainable design. The innovative Powerstrips® system, maintaining a firm hold and removable without any traces, is used with this family of metal hooks for the first time. It avoids laborious and dust-producing drilling and holes in tiles and walls. The technology can be used on almost any surface. The hooks' ergonomics has been designed especially for all aspects of mounting and use. The basic shape (handle shape) can be easily gripped for mounting or removal. The hooks' design has been reduced to an aesthetic combination of a few basic geometrical forms, thus focusing on the durability.

tesa Powerstrips® 塑料钩, 2005

tesa AG, Hamburg
Design: Design 3 (Sabine Schober, Wolfgang Wagner), Hamburg
www.tesa.com
www.design3.com

单个或者三个一组的塑料钩的造型时尚，不易过时。它们作为耐用的大众型消费品，在全球范围都有售。塑料钩吸取了tesa Powerstrip®系统的优点，黏附安全，拆下时亦不会在物体表面留下任何痕迹或者破坏物体表面。塑料钩设计独特，可以在多种场所和地点使用。

The plastic hooks, single and in strips of three, have a modern yet timeless design. They are intended as durable mass products for international distribution. Thanks to the tesa Powerstrips® system, the hooks provide safe adhesion and can be removed without leaving marks on or damaging the surface. Due to their special design, the hooks are suitable for diverse applications and locations.

PHD 5560 吹风机, 2004

Robert Bosch Hausgeräte GmbH,
München
Werksdesign: Helmut Kaiser
Design: Silke Wendt Product Design,
Hohne
www.bosch-hausgeraete.com

博世离子吹风机是一款创新性产品，其外形大方简洁。符合人体工程学原理的手柄以及均衡的重量分布使操作起来特别舒适，不易产生疲劳感。操作控制布局简洁，同时方便左右手控制。吹风机内的负离子发生器能够降低静电，增加风量，使秀发有光泽而柔顺。新增的指示灯和空气压缩器保证了头发容易成型，骤转冷风功能可以更好地固定发型。进风口处的隔栏可以防止头发被卷入吹风机内，还可以随意拆下清洗。为了避免吹风机损坏，还增加了一个橡胶圈。手握柄处还设计有一个便于悬挂的圆环。

The design of the Bosch beautixx comfort ion hair drier is characterised by its clear shape and innovative functionality. The ergonomic handle and the weight balancing allow excellent handling, making styling easy, not tiring. All operating controls are easy to reach and placed for left- as well as for right-hand use. The built-in negative ion generator reduces static electricity and adds volume and body, resulting in shiny and smooth hair. An additional diffusor and an air flow concentrator attachment guarantee perfect styling results, while the cold shot function helps setting the hair. The inlet grill prevents hair from getting sucked into the appliance and can be easily removed for cleaning. To protect the drier from damages, a rubber ring has been integrated into the design. A practical loop for hanging the drier is integrated in the handle.

PHD 3305 吹风机, 2004

Robert Bosch Hausgeräte GmbH, München
Werksdesign: Helmut Kaiser
Design: Silke Wendt Product Design, Hohne
www.bosch-hausgeraete.com

博世“回音”吹风机外形设计简单明了，使用方便，体现了一种创新。其手柄设计充分结合了人体工程学原理而设计，其机身重量分布均匀，使用舒适且操作容易，方便左右手控制使用。橡胶圈的加入不仅与整体设计完美地融合在一起，而且还能够在平滑表面上安全的放置吹风机。骤转冷风功能可以在降低温度的同时，保持吹风机的风速不变，可迅速使头发定型。PHD 3305配有空气压缩器和一个方便操作的指示灯，特别适用于长卷发造型。

The design of the Bosch beautixx eco hair drier is clear and innovative in functionality. An ergonomic handle and the weight balancing allow easy, comfortable use. All operating controls are easy to reach and placed for left- as well as for right-hand use. A rubber ring was integrated into the housing as coherent design element, allowing safe placement of the unit on slippery surfaces. The cold shot function serves to reduce the temperature while the blow intensity remains unchanged. Thus, single portions of hair can be cooled off and settled easily. The PHD 3305 is equipped with an air flow concentrator attachment as well as a functional diffusor, particularly suitable for longer, curly hair.

决不妥协——纯粹主义的重新诠释

Uncompromising – purism re-interpreted

过去，评委们偶尔会把不断发展的“休闲、运动、健康和休闲游”类产品看做是“短期”的产品；而在今年，我们却看到了材料简化、突出实用功能性这样一个清晰的趋势。特别是在设计简洁、功能一目了然的运动系列和休闲装备中，评委温纳·艾司令格（德国）、安妮特·朗（德国）和克瑞丝汀娜·拉萨斯（意大利）赞扬它们是拒绝“任何一种妥协”。体育装备的设计在功能性考虑上做到了细致入微，同时外观设计得简洁明了，为用户提供了极大的方便，在这一点上，很多产品亦无需赘言：例如，某产品被设计成射手的弓箭，其功能便不言自喻；骑车度假所使用的帐篷运输简易，且安放简单。尽管可以这样下结论说：运动装备这种功能性更强、更便于使用的趋势将持续下去，但是评委们却注意到被很多人所忽视的一点，那便是：“50岁以上”的目标群体仍然没有引起人们足够的重视。我们应该注意到，在未来的设计中，还要考虑到目标群体的年龄会慢慢升高这一点。评委没有对日后可能的发展方向提出建议，例如设计是否应该从某一年龄段出发，是否应该先满足这一年龄段人的需求。但是关于设计的未来这一问题，终究是不容忽视的。

While past jurors occasionally described the products *in the constantly developing “leisure, sports, wellness and caravaning” category as “short-lived,” this year sees the emergence of a clear trend in favour of reduced materials and function. Particularly the clearly designed and self-explanatory sporting and leisure equipment demonstrated a refusal to make “compromises of any kind,” as the jurors Werner Aisslinger, Annette Lang and Kristiina Lassus approvingly remark. Combined with functionality defined down to the last detail, the reduced form makes the sporting equipment more accessible to the user. Many products need no further explanation: an archer's bow, for instance, is designed so that its mode of function is self-evident, or a tent devised for cycling holidays is easy to transport and erect. Although it seems safe to assume that the trend towards more easily handled sports equipment will be enduring, the jurors noted that an important aspect continues to be neglected: the “50+” target group is largely invisible still. Remarking that in future design would have to take into consideration the fact that target groups are progressively getting older, the jury left open the questions of the possible direction such design might take or whether specific age-orientation was justifiable in the first place. But the importance of the issue to the future of design is undeniable.*

克瑞丝汀娜·拉萨斯
Kristiina Lassus
意大利
Italien

华纳·艾司令格
Werner Aisslinger
德国
Deutschland

安妮特·朗
Annette Lang
德国
Deutschland

休闲、运动、健康、外出度假
Leisure, sports, wellness and caravaning

adidas 1 跑鞋, 2004

adidas-Salomon AG, Herzogenaurach
Werksdesign
www.adidas.de

阿迪达斯1是一款新型跑鞋，它自身带有减震垫，能够不断地进行自我调节并自动有效地进行减震。它之所以能具备这样的功能是因为它能够通过传感器和磁铁来感应减震带，然后借助微型电脑了解到减震带是松弛亦或是紧绷。它适用于电池控制的线缆系统，从而在跑步的过程中进行有效的减震。其工作原理就好比人的反射神经。神经就是个磁性感应系统，传感器就装在跑鞋后跟的位置，磁铁就放在鞋的中底夹层。

adidas 1 is a running shoe that provides intelligent cushioning by automatically and continuously adjusting itself. It does so by sensing the cushioning level, using a sensor and a magnet. It then understands whether the cushioning level is too soft or too firm via a small computer. It adapts with a battery-operated cable system to provide the correct cushioning throughout the run. It works like a human reflex nerve. The nerve is a magnetic sensing system, where the sensor sits just below the runner's heel and the magnet is placed at the bottom of the midsole.

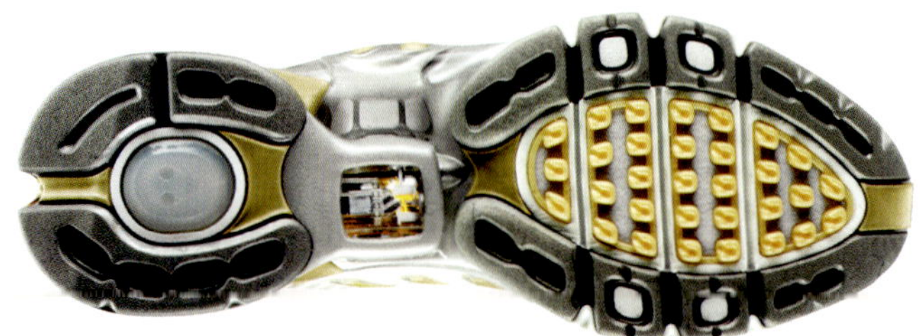

ClimaCool Feather II 网球鞋, 2004

adidas-Salomon AG, Herzogenaurach
Werksdesign
www.adidas.de

ClimaCool Feather II的设计创新可以说是阿迪达斯历史上的革命性创举。简洁的鞋身完全由鞋底架支撑着，它能够固定住鞋跟，保护脚心部位并且保证了理想且灵活的弯曲或扭转。鞋面的设计是把底架扭转到前面，形成拱形，嵌在外底和放有减震垫的鞋底夹层里。这样的设计能够确保脚的前部在向侧面运动的过程中不会扭伤。整体说来，这些装置保证了即使在快速奔跑的过程中，使用者也能保持极好的灵活性。ClimaCool Feather II是为巴黎的法国网球公开赛而专门设计的。

The innovation of the ClimaCool Feather II is its holistic construction. The minimalist upper is completely surrounded by a supportive chassis. It stabilises the heel, supports the midfoot area and secures optimal torsion characteristics. On the outer side, the chassis swings to the front in an arch and is embedded between outsole and cushioning midsole. This construction serves to counteract the extreme strain on the forefoot during lateral movements. The supportive elements are placed in a way that at the same time permits optimal flexibility during quick sprints. The ClimaCool Feather II was created especially for the French Open in Paris.

T-Mac Hug 篮球鞋, 2004

adidas-Salomon AG, Herzogenaurach
Werksdesign
www.adidas.de

T-Mac Hug这款篮球鞋是根据Hug独有的“三维环抱”技术而设计的。“Hug”是创新性的无鞋带闭锁系统，运用可调节杠杆，把脚固定到最舒服、安全的位置。它的灵感来自于先进的下坡滑雪靴技术。Hug装置安装在鞋的顶端，它被牵引线连接到鞋的后部，使整个装置处于张力之中，在鞋的后跟处由滚动杠杆系统控制的闭锁装置调节。扭转调节枢纽可使滚动物沿着线上下移动，给运动员以最完美、最舒适的感觉。

T-Mac Hug is a basketball shoe designed with Hug System technology. Hug is an innovative laceless compression closure system that, with the flip of a lever, locks the foot into a position of high comfort, security and control. The inspiration behind Hug comes from high-tech downhill ski boots. The Hug element fits over the top area of the foot. It is attached to the rear of the shoe by cables, which put the element under tension, which is maintained by a closure device on the heel counter. The closure device, a slider/lever system is used to control the fit. Turning the adjustment wheel moves the slider up and down on the thread, giving the athlete the most precise fit possible.

X-下部齿轮内衣, 2005

X-Technology Swiss GmbH,
Freienbach, Schweiz
Werksdesign: Prof. Bodo W. Lambertz
Produktion und Vertrieb: Trere s.r.l.,
Asola, Italien
www.x-technology.com
www.trereinnovation.it
www.x-undergear.com

X-下部齿轮内衣的设计目的是为了让身体在滑雪、奔跑以及攀岩等剧烈运动中还能够保持37摄氏度的恒温。这项设计是医生、科学家和职业运动员集体智慧的结晶。该功能内衣把三种关键性的功能结合起来而产生能量。37度CCR技术使这款内衣具有使身体的不同部位具有不同的冷热效应的功能。震动系统通过减震的方式改变存储能力。因为内衣紧贴身体，所以能够有效的进行减震。由于在紧张的状态下，身体不同部分会受到不同的力，而这款内衣正好可以保证身体的营养供给和血液循环，从而为运动员的绝佳表现创造了良好的条件。

The X-UnderGear® functional underwear has been designed to keep the body at a constant temperature of 37 degrees centigrade when engaging in extreme sports such as skiing, running or rock-climbing. The design was created in cooperation with medical doctors, scientists and professional athletes. X-UnderGear® combines three essential functions to accumulate energy. Thanks to 37°CCR-Technology, the underwear has a warming or cooling effect in specific areas of the body. The Vibratronic system mobilises reserve capacities by reducing the vibration. The underwear fits close to the body, thus absorbing vibrations effectively. This supports the nutrient supply and blood circulation due to the compression, which has effects of different strengths on the body. This creates ideal conditions for top performances in sports.

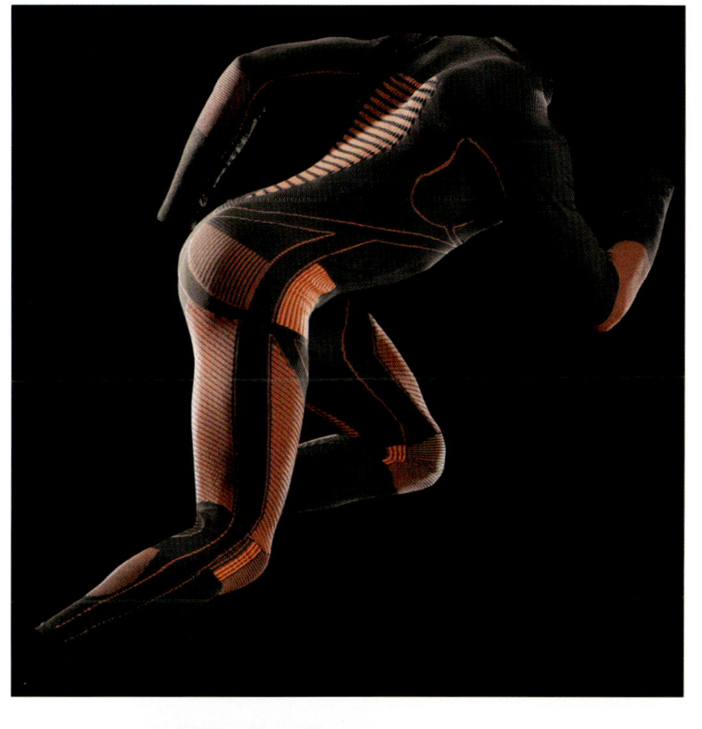

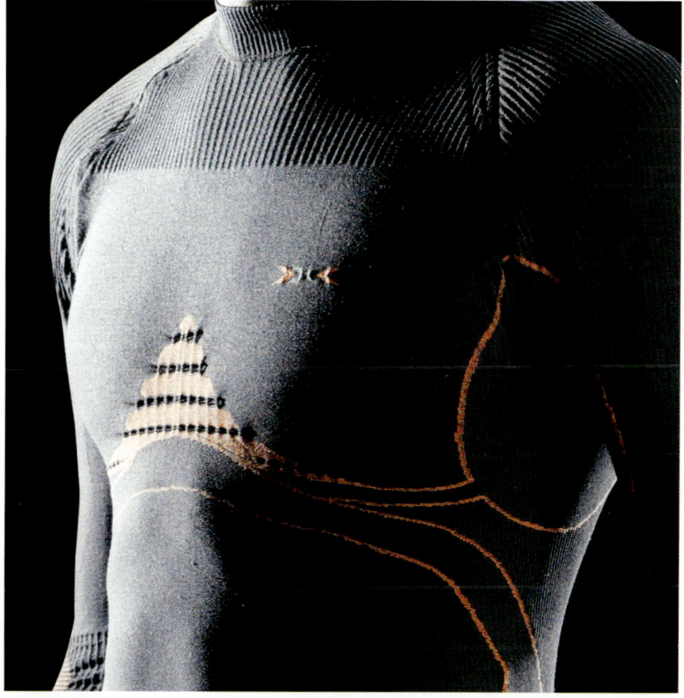

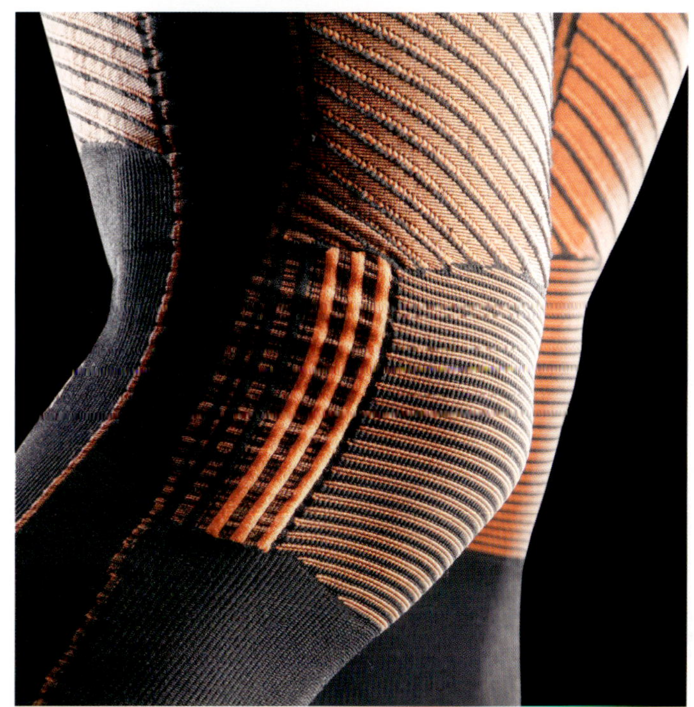

GoBike 折叠自行车, 2003

Le Groupe GO inc., Quebec, Kanada
Werksdesign: Philip Brook
Vertrieb: ECC Efficient Cycle Concepts GmbH, Nürnberg
www.gobikeonline.com

GoBike折叠自行车对现代的都市生活来说是具有革新意义的交通工具。这款自行车折叠和打开仅仅需要15秒钟，像玩具一般，但它可是一款真正的自行车。它为人类快节奏的生活方式而提供了极大方便，其最吸引人的地方是做到了运动和科技之间的完美平衡。由于受到生物形态的启发，设计时结合了诸多高科技的特点，诸如均一大小紧凑型几何学框架、质量很轻的铝制框架的车身和叉架结构等。

The GoBike is an innovative mobility solution for the modern urbanite. Although it does fold/unfold in a mere 15 seconds making it a marvel of convenience for our fast-pace lifestyle, it is a serious bicycle. Its appeal lies in its harmonious balance between aesthetics and technology. Inspired by biomorphic lines, the design blends in high-tech features like a one-size-fits-all compact frame geometry, lightweight aluminium frame and fork construction.

Pride Dura Ace 20 赛车, 2005

Simplon Fahrrad GmbH, Hard, Österreich
Werksdesign
www.simplon.com

The Pride Dura Ace 20的诞生是十年来建造高质量的MTB和公路赛车车架的经验的积累。由于它创新的单体结构构造，其车架十分轻巧，并且具有很好的稳定性。Pride Dura Ace 20型号的Simplon S8叉架是百分之百的单体构造，选材完全采用高单元碳纤维。这种新型的叉架的最大的优点便是叉架部分具有很强的不易弯曲性，而且这款自行车骑起来特别舒服。

The Pride Dura Ace 20 is the result of ten years experience in constructing high-quality MTB and racing cycle frames. Due to its innovative monocoque construction the frame is very light and it has better series stability. The Simplon S8 fork of the Pride Dura Ace 20 model is a 100 per cent monocoque construction and is made completely of high module carbon fibre. Essential advantages of this new fork are a high rigidity of the fork blades and superior driving comfort.

Canyon F10 碳钢极限赛车
Rennrahmen, 2005

Canyon Bicycles GmbH, Koblenz
Werksdesign: Lutz Scheffer, Hans-Christian Smolik
Design: Institut für Verbundwerkstoffe GmbH (Michael Kaiser), Kaiserslautern
www.canyon.com

The Canyon F10 carbon Ultimate是在车体超轻框架上的一种具有革新意义上的进步。它的外形和构造上的设计都别具一格，最引人注目的要算是获得专利的下垂叉架，它有喇叭形的方向杆和圆锥形的舵管。这种设计的目的是要在车轴托架底部和车头前管部打造出极强的竖固性，从而在任何情况下都能保证最大量的动力传输和安全。很窄的车座和叉行的踏板，让这种构架变的十分轻巧。虽然看起来有些“硬”，但是这种“硬”对冲刺和下坡都是极其重要的，更能彰显出驾驶的乐趣。正因为每种车架都必须和车手进行完美地配合，所以这个系列一共有七种车型。精心设计的结构和车座还有车前管的角度都可以根据需要而调节到最佳状态，便于使不同的车架高度，从而带给人以更多的享受。

The Canyon F10 Carbon Ultimate is an innovative advancement of the ultra-light racing frame. The design is independent in terms of appearance as well as construction. A striking feature is the patent pending fork with its trumpet-shaped steering shaft and its conical steerer tube. The aim of this design was to create high stiffness in the bottom bracket axle and head tube area for maximum power transmission and safety in any situation. The slim seat stays and fork legs contribute to the low weight of this frame and demonstrate that, despite its extreme stiffness, which is very important for sprints and downhill rides, it offers more riding comfort. Since every frame has to fit its rider perfectly, it is available in seven different sizes. Carefully thought-out geometries and seat and head tube angles adjusted to the respective frame height optimise the riding qualities.

导航稳定的发光二极管, 2004

Basta France S.A.S., Clamecy, Frankreich
Werksdesign: Bernard Mosset
Design: rosenthal design
(Christian Marx), Essen
Vertrieb: Basta Deutschland GmbH, Schwerte
www.basta-deutschland.de

带有指示灯的自行车前灯靠动力发光二极管技术所散发出来的光覆盖面更广，而且寿命更长，因此更能保证安全。在骑车的过程中，电容器在一直给内部的灯进行稳定充电。即使自行车停下来了，发光二极管却依然在工作。指示灯的设计包括一个白色的反射器。它的整体性设计使自行车组装起来比较容易，更适合个人的不同需要。该设计最具创新之处在于可以长期使用的不锈钢托架。

The Power-LED technology of Pilot bicycle front lights provides a higher light output and a longer life cycle, thus offering more safety. During the ride, an integrated steady light is charged up by capacitors. When the bike stops the LED will still work. The design of the Pilot includes a white reflector. Due to an integrative design, the assembly effort is lesser when tailoring the bike to individual needs. Innovative is a new long-lived stainless steel bracket.

Trelock LS 610 自行车尾灯, 2004

Trelock GmbH, Münster
Werksdesign
www.trelock.de

LS 610型号的尾灯外观华丽，其内部装有四个大马力的发光二极管。因此，即使是220度的照明角度，也同样能提供足够的照明电力。设计中因为有可调节的支架，从而使后灯在直径17厘米到32厘米的范围内都可以使用。此外，其侧压式车锁只需一只手就可以操纵，使安装变得容易。另一个功能性特征就是电池的调节指示器。

The LS 610 rear light has an elegant look and is equipped with four high power LEDs, which provide full luminous power in a lighting angle of 220 degrees. The design with its adjustable holder makes the rear light suitable for diameters from 17mm to 32mm. The snap lock that can be operated with one hand ensures easy mounting. Another functional feature is the battery change indicator.

Cole 车轮系列, 2004

Amor Manufacturing Corporation, Taipei, Taiwan
Werksdesign

Cole车轮在辐条方面解决了以往的常规辐条所面临的问题，他们采用新颖的悬挂式DSA辐条和油嘴似的设计，包括双线辐条，标准的轮辋加油嘴，还有在Cole SS和DS集线器凸缘上6毫米的圆柱型的可移动的黄铜加油嘴等。双线的黄铜加油嘴，被嵌入CNC-碾的凹处，这样一来，辐条就可以在集线器凸缘上开槽。这种设计能够让Cole车轮较普通的车轮更具优点。

Cole wheels approach the spoke in an innovative way that overcomes the issues associated with standard spokes. They use a patent pending DSA spoke and nipple design, which involves a double threaded spoke, standard rim nipple, and a 6mm cylindrical movable brass nipple in the Cole SS and DS hub flanges. The threaded brass nipple, inserted into the hub in CNC-milled recesses, allows the spoke to fit through a slotted hub flange. This design allows Cole wheels to achieve a number of advantages over standard spoke wheels.

啮合式LED头灯, 2004

Zweibrüder Optoelectronics GmbH,
Solingen
Werksdesign: Rainer Opolka
www.zweibrueder.com

啮合式LED头灯体积小、重量轻、亮度强，使用方便，这主要归功于PPT(能量转换技术)。它仅仅需要一节电池，价格相当便宜。一个小型的变压器就可以把1.5伏电压转变成LED所要求的电压。这种灯对于驾驶安全来说是个巨大的贡献。它的内部包含了三个集成电路：一个白色的在前面，两个蓝色的在后面。这种啮合式LED头灯是前后灯一体化的。

The Joggled LED head light is very small, light, easy to wear and extremely bright. Thanks to PTT (Power Transformation Technology) it only requires one inexpensive battery. A micro-transformer converts the voltage of 1.5V to the operating voltage required for the LED. The lamp is an active contribution to safety and is equipped with three chips: a white chip at the front and two blue chips at the back. The LED-Lenser Joggled lamp is a front and rear light in one.

LED-蛙人潜水灯
LED-Taucherlampe, 2004

Zweibrüder Optoelectronics GmbH,
Solingen
Werksdesign: Harald Opolka
www.zweibrueder.com

光的折射能缩小水下光线的照射范围。只需用一个轴向的瞄准仪，LED蛙人潜水灯就能到达难以想象的60米深的海底。灯头是由高质量的不锈钢制成的，灯体部分采用的是抗震安全的合成材料。符合人体工程学的设计更平添了它的魅力。四款小巧的电池能确保连续使用50多个小时，电力集成电路的使用寿命是10万个小时；如果一周用三次的话，两极真空管能持续使用600年。灯体颜色一般是黑色或是红橙色。

Light refraction rules out longer illumination ranges under water. With an axial collimator, the Frogman LED divers lamp reaches an unforeseen focussing depth of up to 60 metres. The head part of the lamp consists of high-quality stainless steel, the body of shock-resistant and fail-safe synthetic materials. Its ergonomic design is exceptional and convincing. Four mignon batteries guarantee more than 50 hours of continuous light. The Power-Lightchip has a service life of 100,000 operating hours; when operating the lamp three hours per week, the diode will last 600 years. The lamp is available with a black or neon-coloured body.

戈尔 Airvantage 保温服，2004

W.L. Gore & Associates GmbH,
Feldkirchen-Westerham
Werksdesign
Design: fpm factor product münchen
www.wlgore.com
www.factor-product.com

戈尔Airvantage是一种新型的，可以根据个人需要而调节的保温服。作为一种透气防风、可调节的隔热体，它可以夹在马甲或者夹克里面。这样，这种保温服装不管冬夏都可以穿。由于天气变化或运动而引起的增减衣服非常的不方便且浪费时间，但是有了这种产品，这种担心就成为多余。另外，这种设计也很轻便，通过人体工程学而设计的戈尔Airvantage特殊的空气袋，可以把里面充满气体，或者也可把空气抽出来。隔热的程度还可依使用者按照自己的意愿进行调节。

Gore Airvantage is an innovative, individually adjustable insulation. As a breathable, wind-proof and adjustable insulation it can be integrated in vests or jackets. Thus, the functional wear can be used in summer as well as winter. An inconvenient and time-consuming changing of layers due to differences in temperature caused by weather changes or physical activity is no longer necessary. This design concept also saves weight. Via an ergonomically designed Gore Airvantage operating unit specific air chambers are inflated by breath or deflated. The desired degree of insulation can thus be adjusted by the wearer.

Mantis HE 高尔夫两轮推车, 2005

Thermoplastik Erich Müller GmbH, Dieburg
Design: Wolf Udo Wagner, Frankfurt/Main
Vertrieb: CarbonFunctions Vertriebs GmbH, Pforzheim
www.carbonfunctions.de

Mantis HE高尔夫两轮推车的设计融生活方式和功能性特征为一体。由于它可旋转的特性，所以双手很容易操纵。操作平台是以人体工程学为基础而设计成的圆形把手，通过手里的几个按扭就可以实现所有的操作。和传统的推车不一样的是其高尔夫袋能够很容易地就位。这些材料（碳、铝）和形状已经按照高尔夫运动员的要求而做了调整。这款推车很容易携带，折叠后甚至可以放进保时捷911跑车的后备箱里。可充电式锂离子电池保证了它可以在长时间、长距离下使用。控制发动机的信息通过感应无线技术来传送。不论是上坡还是下破，Mantis HE都能开得稳稳当当。

The design of the Mantis HE golf caddy combines lifestyle and functionality. Due to its swivel function, the steering can be easily operated with both hands. The user interface is an ergonomically designed circular handle, which incorporates all user functions in a few buttons. The golf bag easily clicks into place as opposed to conventional caddies. The materials (carbon, aluminium) and form have been adapted to suit the requirements of the sporting golfer. The product is easy to transport and compact enough to even fit into the boot of a 911. The lithium-ion rechargeable batteries last the distance. The information to control both motors is sent via induction wireless technology. At ascents and descents the Mantis HE continues to drive steadily.

KLAFS

Proteo 桑拿房, 2004

Klafs Saunabau GmbH & Co. KG,
Schwäbisch Hall
Design: Henssler und Schultheiss
Productdesign, Schwäbisch Gmünd
www.klafs.de
www.henssler-schultheiss.de

Proteo桑拿房的设计简洁大方，一目了然。它使用了上等材料，采用了最好的工艺。这些优秀的设计元素都是按标准尺寸组成的，当然也可自由组合。侧墙交替使用了有条纹的镶板、白杨板、铁衫板和暖色调的铜镜，凸现出它的雅致和过硬的质量。Proteo桑拿房的内部也是精心设计而成的，宽大的软边长椅提供了一个可以惬意蒸桑拿的场所。

The Proteo Sauna is designed with a clear, reduced visual language. It is made from high-grade materials, with workmanship at its best. The modular combination options of these premium design elements allow "games without frontiers". The sidewalls, alternatively made of Zebrano veneer, aspen, hemlock or warm-toned brass mirrors, underline the impression of classiness and top quality. The interior of the Proteo Sauna is carefully designed as well: wide, soft-edged benches provide superior sauna comfort.

VAM-6101 小提琴干燥箱, 2005

Concise Living Co., Ltd.,
Taichung, Taiwan
Design: Duck Hsieh, Peggy Tsai,
Taichung, Taiwan
www.concise-living.com

这款小提琴干燥箱是为防止小提琴受潮或其预防其它的不利因素而专门设计的。这个箱子的主要结构是由透明的多碳酸脂原料制成，然后用碳合成物加固。这种原料可以加固箱子本身的结构，并且让箱子的外观更具有美感。此外，压缩空气由真空装置来完成的。自动的电子指示器监控着温度、湿度、及内部压力。它还利用了玻意耳马里奥特定律来获取双重的安全保障：首先通过挤压将空气排出，同时给内部的TPU垫原料充气，然后气垫就可以把整个小提琴环绕住，从而提供最稳妥的保护。

The Violin Dry Box has been designed particularly to protect violins from humidity and other harmful factors. The main structure of the container is made of transparent polycarbonate material, which is reinforced by a carbon composite. This choice of material re-enforces the structure of the container and gives it an aesthetic appearance. The vacuum storing conditions are created by pumping out air. An automatic electronic indicator monitors the temperature, humidity, and internal pressure. Incorporating Boyle-Mariotte's law provides double safety: The air is pumped out via extraction while the internal TPU cushioning material is inflated to embrace the violin.

VAM-5101 Vam 抗潮干燥箱, 2005

Concise Living Co., Ltd.,
Taichung, Taiwan
Design: Duck Hsieh, Peggy Tsai,
Taichung, Taiwan
www.concise-living.com

Vam抗潮干燥箱集功能性和美学于一体，可以用来防止电子设备受潮或者遭受其它破坏。有了这种箱子的保护，设备的寿命就能更长，质量也能够更持久。抽出空气能够使环境保持干燥，更适合3C产品的保养。储藏条件是由内部的湿度器控制的，当箱子不在真空状态下，或者是湿度太高时，内部的真空装置就能显示出来。极其柔软的TPR塑料制作的把手是按照人体工程学设计的。箱体部分是采用透明的多碳酸脂制作而成，其结构是典型的“凹槽”形设计，目的是为了能抗重压。

The Vam Anti-Moisture Dry Box is a functional and aesthetic container, which protects electronic devices from humidity and other harmful elements. Protected by this container, devices have a longer life and retain their quality. Pumping out air creates dry conditions, which are also suitable for preserving 3C products. A built-in hygrometer monitors the storing conditions and a built-in vacuum display indicates when the container is no longer in the vacuum mode or is too humid. The handle made of soft TPR has an ergonomic design. The main body is made of transparent polycarbonate and the structure is reinforced by a "fillister" design in order to resist the strong pressure.

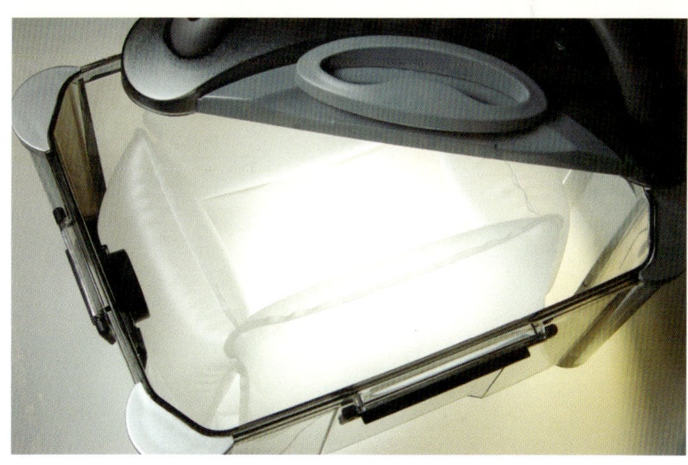

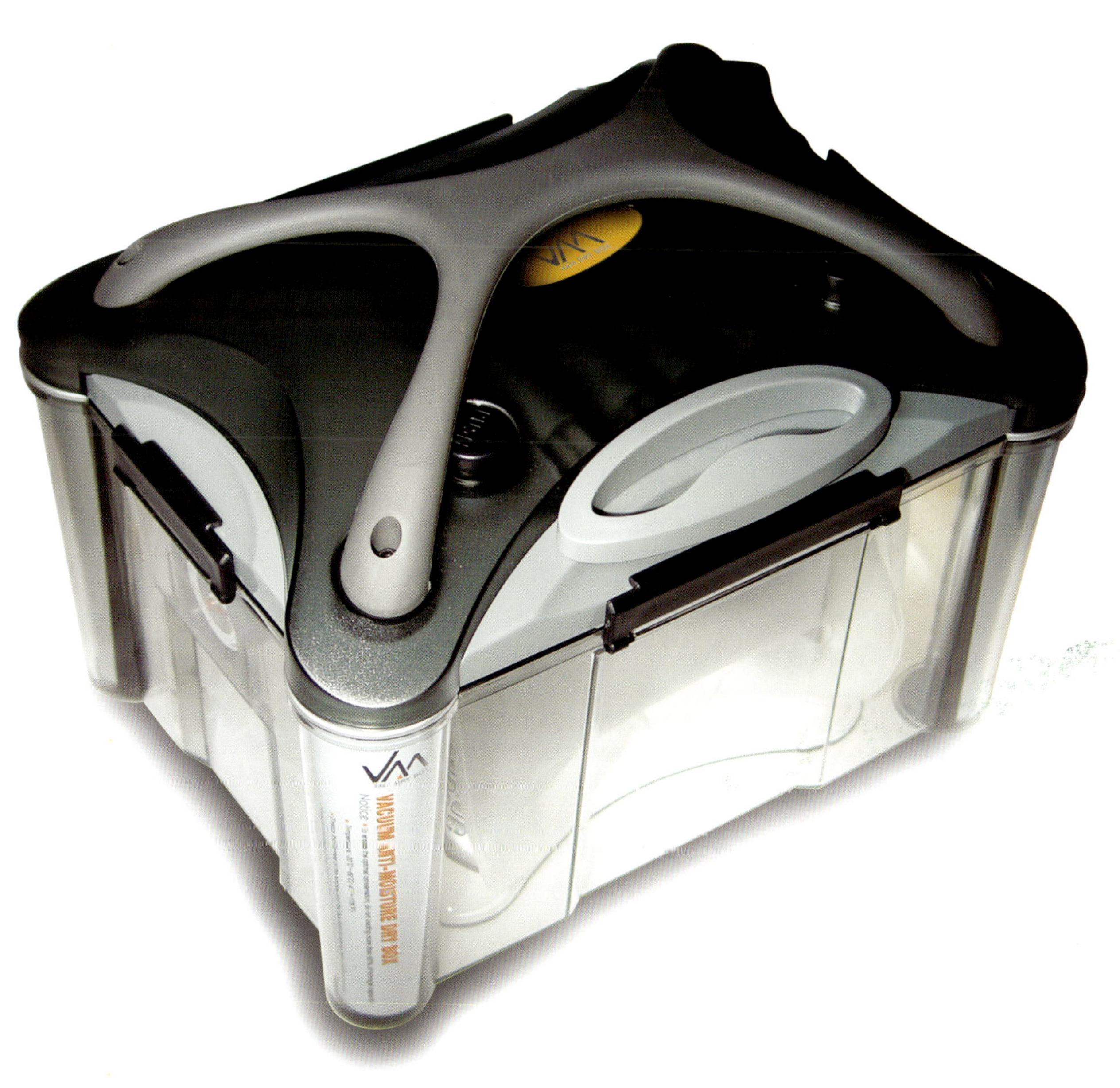

12x36 IS II 双筒望远镜, 2004

Canon Deutschland GmbH, Krefeld
Werksdesign
www.canon.com

12 × 36 1S II双筒望远镜在设计上采用了更为先进的技术，创造出更为理想的结构。体积上，它们比普通的双筒镜小10%左右，而在重量上却减轻了26%左右。12倍的放大功能能够清晰的观察到远处的物体。由于外瞳孔处的直径达36毫米，双筒望远镜在逆光的条件下也可以使用。其高质量的光学图象稳定装置可以完全消除震动，即使是在冬天带着厚厚的手套，大型的调焦按扭也能保证您使用轻松自如。橡胶外壳的表面手感较好，大大提高了在户外使用时的耐用性。大的橡胶眼杯让您使用起来更舒坧。这款双筒望远镜是为那些热爱大自然的人们以及运动员们而精心准备的。

The prism binoculars 12x36 IS II have an improved optical construction. They are around ten per cent smaller and approximately 26 per cent lighter. A twelvefold magnification creates a high presence also of very distant objects and thanks to the 36mm diameter of the exit pupil the binoculars can also be used in adverse lighting conditions. A high-performance optical image stabiliser cancels shake and vibration almost completely. The larger focusing button allows easy focusing for example when using the binoculars with gloves in winter. Rubber-armoured surfaces provide good grip and higher durability for outdoor use. Large rubber eyecups support comfortable use. The prism binoculars have been developed particularly for nature lovers and water sports athletes.

Silhuett 睡袋

Fjällräven, München
Werksdesign: Åke Nordin
www.fjallraven.com

Silhuett睡袋能够根据个人身体比例的不同进行调节，从而能在最大程度上保证了热量不散失。睡袋的各个部分只需拉绳就可以很容易的折叠。封闭的睡袋顶部区域要确保能裹住身体并可在脸部周围套个拉绳。头部位置提供了足够的空间来放置枕头。睡袋的拉链上还配有封条，可在恶劣天气下提供良好的保护。

The Silhuett sleeping bag adjusts to the individual body proportions, thus providing the highest degree of heat retention. Individual areas can be closed easily and functionally with tightening cords. The closed head area of the sleeping bag is created by closing the body area and tightening a cord around the face. The head area offers sufficient space for a pillow. The sleeping bag's zipper is equipped with a weather seal.

Amphib 旅行背包, 2004

Boblbee AB, Malmö, Schweden
Werksdesign: Jonas Blanking
www.boblbee.com

Amphib旅行背包利用人体工程学原理设计，是专门适用于划船或者是探索大峡谷之类运动的背包。它具有百分之百的防水性、既轻巧又防震。真空泡沫装置制成的外层能够很好的适应身体并支撑身体，这样也可以承受更多的货物重量。此外，Amphib也已经把在运动鞋领域里的成果应用到背包的设计中，人们已经研究出专门的机器用来制造像大号运动鞋那样的Amphib背包。

Amphib is an ergonomically designed backpack for sports such as kayaking or canyoning. It is 100 per cent waterproof, very light and shockproof. Shells made of vacuum expanded foam adjust to the body, support it and allow carrying heavier loads. Findings from the field of sport shoes have been transferred to backpack design. One innovation is the development of special machines to manufacture the Amphib backpack like a large sport shoe.

Victory FL 32 蔡司双筒望远镜, 2004

Hensoldt AG Carl Zeiss Gruppe, Wetzlar
Design: zed AG (Thomas Steuri), Zürich, Schweiz
www.zeiss.de/sportsoptics

Victory FL 32新型双筒望远镜具有很好的成像效果。用氟化物玻璃制作的特殊镜头，保证了最低的色彩边缘效果和高度的边缘清晰度。而且，它还拥有前所未有的高分辨率、对比度、真实色彩以及图象明亮度。胜利FL 32双筒望远镜小巧而实用，它不仅采用了新的计算光学技术，而且其设计构思也极富科技含量。由于使用了高质量的尼龙和60%的玻璃纤维，它既轻巧又结实。

Victory FL 32 are innovative binoculars with a high image quality. Special lenses with fluoride glasses provide lowest colour fringing and high edge sharpness, which results in extremely high resolution, contrast, as well as colour-true and bright images never seen before. Victory FL 32 are compact due to newly calculated optics and a high-tech construction. Thanks to the use of high-performance polyamide with 60 per cent glass fibre, the casing is very light and robust.

comforto Laola 休闲躺椅, 2004

Haworth GmbH, Ahlen
Design: Simon Desanta,
Borgholzhausen
www.haworth.de

Comforto Laola是一种既美观又实用的休闲躺椅。它既可放在客厅等休闲场所，也可以放在家里。不论在任何环境里，它都能让人进入十分放松的状态。一个管状钢制圆环把各个接口连接起来。椅架本身有一层保护地板的覆盖物。椅架可以有如下的几种选择：黑色粉末涂层、银色金属、还有镀铬的。这种躺椅表面上还有一个能提供支撑的网状结构,同时附带一个额外的布垫或皮垫子。

comforto Laola is an aesthetic as well as functional recliner for waiting areas, relaxation zones, and homes. It initiates creative relaxation phases in any environment. It has a tubular steel ring construction with connecting knots and the frame has a floor-protecting cover. The frame is available in the following versions: powder-coated black, silver-metallic and chrome. Further variants are a self-supportive mesh construction or an additional fabric- or leather-covered padding.

长把修枝剪,园艺工具, 2004

Fiskars Brands Finland Oy Ab,
Billnäs, Finnland
Werksdesign: Olavi Lindén,
Markus Paloheimo
Vertrieb: Fiskars Brands Germany
GmbH, Herford
www.fiskars.com

这种长把修枝剪设计符合人体工程学原理，可用来对苹果树或者是红醋灌木进行深度修剪。此剪刀可以用双手进行操作，简单方便，即使在那些不易够着的地方，修剪起来也同样容易。事实上，这款剪刀的可双手操作功能本身就是一大优点，尤其是在修剪那些粗大的树枝时，它能防止肌肉受伤，所以也很适用于连续作业。虽然使用十分简单，但这种长把修枝剪却是一种新型的修剪工具。这一产品还有两种规格可供选择。

The Long Reach Pruner has an ergonomic design for pruning for example apple trees or currant bushes, where you have to cut deeply into the dense growth. It is easy to operate with both hands and allows comfortable cutting in places which are difficult to access. Using both hands is a great advantage, particularly when cutting thicker branches. It is also sensible in continuous light work, since it prevents muscle injuries. Even though very simple, the Long Reach Pruner is a new kind of cutting tool. It is available in two sizes.

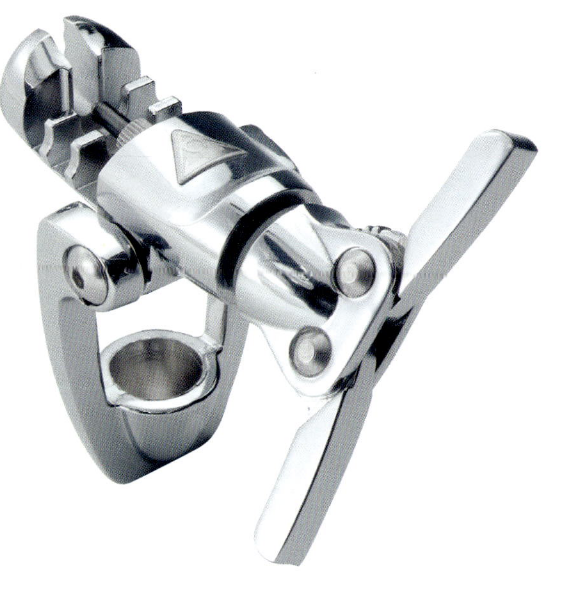

Droid 链条修理工具, 2005

Topeak, Inc., Taichung, Taiwan
Werksdesign: Louis Chuang, Byron Tsai, Dennis Chiang
Vertrieb: RTI Sports GmbH, Urmitz
www.topeak.com

Droid链条修理工具的功能性美学是基于这样的理念，即：好的设计是美和情感的流露。当你打开它后，Droid的外形轻巧，就好象一个忠诚的伙伴。这款工具是由不锈钢铸造而成。当伸开它的铝制“耳朵”时，他们就变成控制杠杆，成为修理和维护自行车链条的专业工具。该工具只有135克重，轻巧灵活，正好可以放到自行车车座上的挂包里。

The functional aesthetics of the Droid Chain Tool follows the idea that good design always implies beauty and emotion. When folded, the Droid's compact shape resembles a faithful canine companion. Its robust body is made of cast stainless steel. When extending its aluminium "ears", these become levers and Droid turns into a professional tool for repairing and maintaining bicycle chains. With its light weight of only 135 grammes, it fits into the bicycle's saddle bag.

Calais 201-5 投饵增效器, 2004

Shimano, Inc., Osaka, Japan
Werksdesign: Kenichi Kwasaki, Masakazu Iwabuchi
Vertrieb: Shimano Germany Fishing GmbH, Krefeld
www.shimano.com

Calais是一款外观简单的投饵增效器。一整块铝制框架外加上Dartanium拖网打捞垫圈，确保了Calais投饵增效器即使在条件十分恶劣的情况下也可以进行有效的工作。这款增效器的技术特征正好符合禧玛诺对产品的高质量要求。

The Calais is a low profile baitcasting multiplier. The one-piece aluminium frame and Dartanium drag washers enable the Calais to work effectively under the most extreme conditions. The technical features of this multiplier correspond to the high quality standard requirements of Shimano products.

Pizzoni “生活方式”烤架, 2005

LoeweVonAppen GmbH, Hamburg
Werksdesign: Moritz Böttcher, Sören Henssler, Peter Jaritz, Dorothee Krause, Ragnar Sturm in Zusammenarbeit mit dem Fachbereich Design und Medien der Fachhochschule Hannover
www.loewevonappen.de

Pizzoni烤架采用了高科技材料，集创新的设计和功能性于一体，使用起来灵活自如，充分考虑到了工效学因素。这款产品给烧烤架带来了一种全新的产品设计理念——即Pizzoni“生活方式”烤架。Pizzoni烤架携带方便轻巧，节省空间，干净便于存放。此外，Pizzoni烤架安装简单安全，不需要任何工具辅助，只需简单几步就可以完成整个安装。

Pizzoni combines technically advanced materials with an innovative design and innovative functionality, which focuses especially on flexible and spontaneous use while being highly ergonomic. The Pizzoni thus presents a unique product concept for a barbeque grill – the Pizzoni Lifestyle Grill. Pizzoni can be conveniently carried when in its compact transport state and it is space-saving as well as completely clean when stored. Pizzoni can be simply and safely assembled in just a few simple steps without the use of any tools.

iLife 空气净化器, 2004

OSIM International Ltd, Singapur
Werksdesign
www.osim.com

OSIM iLife空气净化器为现代的居家生活提供了清新的空气。它使用了“Multi-Action Tru-Air”净化程序。其布局合理、造型美观的外形可谓是在外观设计方面提出了一种新的理念。它是生活品质的象征，洁白精致的清新外形使人耳目一新。小型“GEON”外形与其基本功能融为一体，透出一种纯净的精髓。机器前部持续发出的淡蓝色的光，从心理上暗示了净化过程还在进行，同时也可以暗示滤光器是否需要更新。光滑的外形再加上柔软的材料，从整体上营造出了一种舒服的感觉。如果把这个设计分为两部分，从不同的侧面来看这个设计的话，那么在视觉上就会给人以更纤细、更华丽的美感，OSIM的品牌价值正是通过如此精湛的设计以及健康的理念而得以完美展现。同时，ilife产品也恰恰通过它的洁净、优美、实用、整体化地设计等优点，而把公司的健康生活理念一一展现出来。总之，OSIMilife产品的简洁却不失高贵雅致，使它不论是与家居生活，还是与办公环境都能完美结合。

Providing clean air for contemporary living, the OSIM iLife is an air purifier that creates harmony in the home. Utilising a "Multi-Action Tru-Air" purification process, the external design offers a new concept by introducing a logical and attractive look. Symbolic of well-being, the white form exudes refreshing cleanliness, whilst the fusion of the minimal GEON form and the primary function, exemplifies the essence of purity. The design centres on the soft indigo glow emanating from the front, which psychologically provides a constant reassurance of the purification process, whilst indicating when filter renewal is required. Sleek contours have been unified with subtle use of materials. Sectioning the form into two parts creates a visually slimmer and more elegant shape. The OSIM brand value is reflected through good design and the concept of well-being. The iLife instils the company's philosophy of healthy living through its clean aesthetics, a reflection of its function and an overall holistic design solution. The simplicity and elegance of this OSIM iLife enables it to fit seamlessly into any home or office environment.

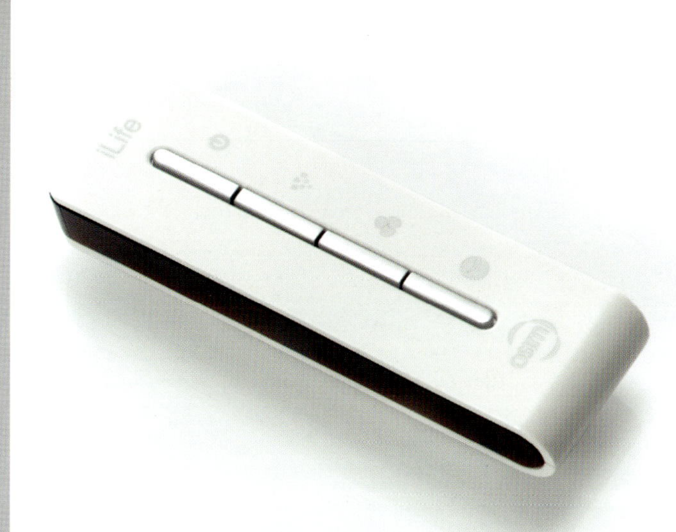

Dino 玩具系列, 2005

Plan Creations Co., Ltd., Bangkok, Thailand
Werksdesign: Warunee Piyawannawong
www.plantoys.com

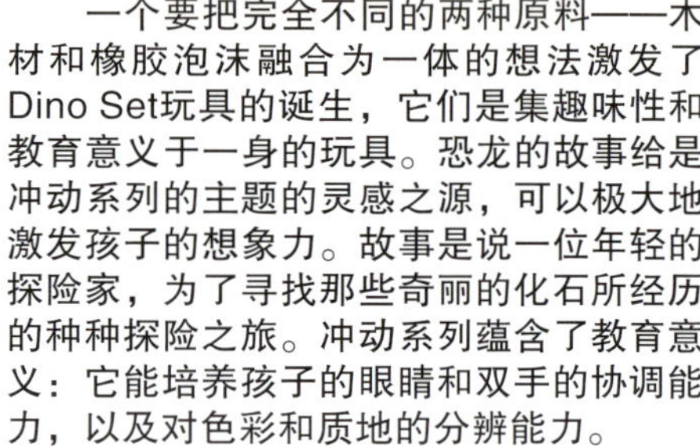

一个要把完全不同的两种原料——木材和橡胶泡沫融合为一体的想法激发了Dino Set玩具的诞生，它们是集趣味性和教育意义于一身的玩具。恐龙的故事给是冲动系列的主题的灵感之源，可以极大地激发孩子的想象力。故事是说一位年轻的探险家，为了寻找那些奇丽的化石所经历的种种探险之旅。冲动系列蕴含了教育意义：它能培养孩子的眼睛和双手的协调能力，以及对色彩和质地的分辨能力。

The Dino Set is based on the idea to explore and integrate two distinctively different materials, wood and rubber foam, to create a toy that is fun and educational. As fuel to a child's imagination, the story of the dinosaurs inspired the theme of the Impulse Set. The story begins as a young explorer sets out on an expedition to discover the amazing fossils. The Impulse Set also has many educational benefits; for it helps foster the development skills such as eye-hand coordination, colour and texture differentiation.

亲近色彩颜料盒, 2004

Pelikan Vertriebsgesellschaft mbH & Co. KG, Hannover
Design: yellow design | yellow circle, Köln
www.pelikan.de

亲近色彩颜料盒既可以用于教学，也可以满足个人爱好之所需。在外形它做到了稳定性和功能性的完美结合，精心考虑了使用者的需要。盒子丝丝合扣。这样能防止无意识中盒子滑开。滑盒可以叠放也可以套放，也可用来盛水，还配有一个刷子架。

The ProColor paintbox can be used for school or hobby. The aspects of stability and functionality are positively integrated in the form, which is oriented towards the user. The slipcases click into place, closing up the paintbox. This prevents inadvertent opening, such as in a school satchel. Stacked or placed one inside the other, the slipcases also serve as a stable water box with an integrated brush stand.

Pineo 矿泉水瓶, 2005

Naturquell S.A., Estamariu, Spanien
Design: Designstudio Lippe, Köln
Vertrieb: Naturquell Mineralwasser Vertriebs GmbH, Köln
www.pineo.com

这款矿泉水瓶重量很轻、不会碎裂。该设计本身是为了传达一种产品的美学理念：即使是塑料瓶子，也能完美地体现饮用水的价值所在。产品本身符合国际国内标准。瓶子呈锥形，与上部相连的瓶颈越往下越细。从上部到瓶身直到瓶底部分的弧度平坦而光滑。乍眼一看，这个瓶子就是个简单、光滑、塔状的容器且顶部和上部匀称分布。由于它符合了人体工程学设计，即使瓶子重量很轻，瓶子中部的大小合适的尺寸也能让人们的双手很容易就握住。

The mineral water bottle is a lightweight and break-proof container, which has been designed to convey a product aesthetics that meets the value of drinking water adequately despite its plastic shell. National and international legal functional requirements had to be incorporated. The bottle's conical, downward tapered neck sits on its distinct shoulder. The angular transition from the shoulder to the chest area is followed by a smooth, even contour down to the base. At first glance, the bottle is a simple, smooth and towering container; symmetrically round, with a distinctly shaped head and shoulder area. Thanks to its ergonomic design, the diameters in the chest area and the good grip allow the bottle to be easily grasped with a medium-sized hand despite its net weight.

Ladegast-Orgel 风琴控制台, 莱比锡, 2004

Hermann Eule Orgelbau GmbH, Bautzen
Design: Dr. Ing. h.c. F. Porsche AG, Stuttgart
www.euleorgelbau.de
www.porsche-design.com

保时捷公司通过对具有历史意义的Ladegast风琴的整修，以此来纪念座落于莱比锡的具有文化与历史意义的尼古拉大教堂。从1723年到1750年，这个神圣的建筑便是德国作曲家约翰・塞巴斯提安・巴赫的主要活动场所。在这里，他完成了他的大部分的风琴作品。1862年，德国北部管风琴建筑家Friedrich Ladegast在尼古拉大教堂完成了他的乐器制作，这推动了巴赫在十九世纪下半叶的风琴作曲中对浪漫主义的诠释。保时捷公司的参与还有另外一个因素，那便是没有任何一种乐器可以像古典管风琴那样，用如此震撼的声音，完美的表达了保时捷公司所注重的东西：力量、活力与美感。但是，保时捷公司不仅仅是充当一个赞助商的角色。因为风琴制造家Friedrich Ladegast时代的风琴控制台早已不复存在了，所以保时捷的设计师采用了黑檀木来制作表层，用闪亮的不锈钢做键盘和音栓，还为合唱团设计了管风琴的脚踏键和椅子。就像室内设计师Franz-Josef Siegert在谈到其设计意图时说道：“设计师特意将管风琴的控制台设计成与教堂环境截然不同的风格，但却仍然保留在古典主义的背景下，让人情不自禁地想到了汽车。”

By supporting the restoration of the historic Ladegast organ, Porsche wants to honour the cultural as well as historical significance of the Nikolai Church in Leipzig. Between 1723 and 1750, this sacred building was Johann Sebastian Bach's main place of activity; here he performed a major part of his organ work. In 1862, Friedrich Ladegast completed an instrument in the Nikolai Church, which had a formative influence on the romantic interpretation of Bach's organ compositions in the second half of the 19th century. Another factor for the involvement of Porsche is that no other musical instrument embodies the Porsche values such as power, dynamics and aesthetics as exemplary as the classical pipe organ with its voluminous sound. However, Porsche's role is not limited to that of a sponsor. Since the original console of the organ builder Friedrich Ladegast no longer existed, Porsche designers created new surfaces made of ebony and brushed stainless steel for keyboard and stops and also designed the pedals and the seat for the choirmaster. "The console has been intentionally designed in contrast to the church environment, but remains in the classical context and refers to the automobile production", thus Franz-Josef Siegert, Head of Interior Design, explains the designers' intention.

新背景下的品牌，令人鼓舞的建筑材料

Brands in new settings, and inspiring architectural materials

“室内设计”类中对品牌的展示可以说是中心主题。人们怎样才能把一个独特的品牌所包含的信息以一种直白的却毫不失掉其本质方式传递出去？这甚至涉及到会展上展位的布置。对这个难题的巧妙解决获得了评委马丁·伯格曼、丹尼·维勒特、约阿希姆·浮士德的一致好评。他们认为感官上所体现出来的品质和产品的整体性对于室内设计类的创新尤为重要，那些设计观念方面成功的案例得到了人们的肯定，同时也用一定的情感价值传递着该品牌信息。品牌在建筑空间里得到形式上的证明，甚至取暖装置也向人们展示出令人赞许的品质。例如：极具美学设计的炉子的发明，在取暖的同时，人们也好像是在房间里欣赏优美的雕刻作品。与设计和外形结构可以相提并论的是，创新——也成为了建筑的重要组成部分，漂亮的墙砖和富有新意的门口台阶的设计就可以证明这一点。另一个重要趋势便是利用自然原料比如木材之类，却在同时展现出了和原材料完全不同的特征，这本身就是对新的建筑材料大胆尝试。正如评委们所说的那样：这些原材料给我们的建筑和室内设计的想象力提供了丰富的灵感源泉，创造了无限的可能性。评委们一致认为：这种新的、像田园诗般优美的原料质地，将会为未来建筑的发展而确定基调。

The staging of brands is a central theme in the “interior design” category. *How can the message of a particular brand be transported in such a way that it loses nothing of its substance and immediacy even in the architecture of, say, a trade-fair stand? Skilful handling of this difficult task received all the more credit from the jurors Martin Bergmann, Joachim Faust and Danny Venlet. Accordingly, they viewed “sensual qualities” and the manner of “product integration” as being particularly important to the innovations in the “interior design” category. In the case of successfully implemented concepts, a surplus emotional value was palpably created alongside the brand message – the brand became physically manifest within the architectural space. The heat sources, too, demonstrated impressive formal qualities: the inventive aesthetics of stoves, for instance, lends them the appearance of sculptures within a room. In regard to design and physical structure, equally creative use was made of important architectural components such as aesthetically designed wall tiles and innovative mountings on doors. Another important trend is the exploration of new building materials based on natural models like wood but at the same time displaying wholly new attributes. As the jurors see it, these materials are ideal sources of inspiration to the imaginations of architects and interior designers, opening up countless possibilities for use. This new, even “lyrical” material quality is one, the jurors feel sure, which will set the tone of future developments.*

马丁·伯格曼
Martin Bergmann
奥地利
Österreich

丹尼·维勒特
Danny Venlet
比利时
Belgien

约阿希姆·浮士德
Joachim Faust
德国
Deutschland

建筑和室内设计

Architecture and interior design

柏林保时捷设计商店, 2005

Porsche Lizenz- und Handelsgesellschaft mbH & Co. KG, Bietigheim-Bissingen
Design: KMS Team GmbH (Michael Keller, Dirk Koy, Sven Sonnendorfer, Andreas Niessner), München; Studio Matteo Thun (Matteo Thun, Claudia Blum), Mailand, Italien
www.porsche-design.de
www.kms-team.de
www.matteothun.com

唯美、互动以及高科技的参与让消费者更真切地体会到保时捷设计的核心命题："奢华品工程师"。这个概念上兴起于理性原则和情感因素的融合，把自然原料与工业原料做以恰如其分的结合——一面是黑橡木地板外加石材，另一面是半反射的有色玻璃墙和钛色亮漆，整体就好比是静态的直角线和动态的数字动画并存。

商场的中心是"未来之门"，它的设计是基于一种被称为"扫描桌面"的新奇性互动的应用。在房间的中心有一个黑色的立方体。如果在这个立方体的上面放上保时捷设计的产品的话，就可以在三面（左、中、右面）的墙壁上产生虚拟矩阵，这样参观者可以顺势很容易的找到所选择的产品的位置。一旦确认，产品就会"浮出水面"，相应地，可以从墙的前面，左面和右面给观看者做放大的演示。与此同时，相关的产品信息可以在"扫描桌面"的表面被看到。

另一个特点是它具有"晚间购物"的功能，这一功能表明了不论在外部空间还是内部空间，都能打破白天与夜晚的区别：所有的在展示窗口的产品都可以使用触摸控制（手势确认），用交互箭头就可以进行选择。所选择的物体就会单独被光亮笼罩着，"扫描桌面"自动激活，相应的图像就会接二连三出现在墙壁上。

The blend of aesthetics, interaction and high technology allows customers to experience the core statement of Porsche Design's "engineers of luxury". The conceptual starting point is the connection of the principles of rationality and emotion. The combination of natural and industrial materials – dark oak flooring and elements made of slate on one hand, and half-mirrored tinted glass walls and titanium-coloured lacquer on the other – expresses this principle, as does the juxtaposition of calm orthogonal lines and dynamic digital animation.
The heart of the store is the "Gate to the Future" which is based on a novel interactive application called "scantable". At the centre of the room there is a black cube. Placing a product onto the cube produces a virtual matrix of all of Porsche Design's products on three walls – on the left, in the centre, and on the right. The viewer makes a rapid descent down to the point at which the chosen product has been located. Once identified, the product is "brought up" to the surface and finally displayed on the three walls in oversized views from the front, the left and the right. At the same time, the corresponding product information becomes readable on the surface of the "scantable".
Another new feature is the "night shopping" function which represents a break in the nocturnal separation of exterior and interior spaces: all of the products in the display window may be chosen via interactive arrows using touch control (gesture recognition). The selected object is individually illuminated and the "scantable" is automatically activated with the corresponding image sequence.

PORSCHE DESIGN
SMOKING TOOLS
P'3633
PD3 Feuerzeug. Außergewöhnliches Design durch
markante TwinBody-Form. Patentierte Circular Flame-
Düsenöffnung mit 30 microfeinen Öffnungen.
Sturmsichere Anwendung. Piezo-Zündung, Sichtfenster
für Füllstandskontrolle, Tank aus Trogamid®. In fünf

Terra LED 地砖, 2004

Royal Mosa, Maastricht, NL
Werksdesign: Design Team Mosa
www.mosa.nl

Terra LED是一个LED照明系统，它有两种型号和两种颜色，成为Terra Maestricht系列地砖的重要组成部分。这种发光二极管地砖给普通的地板砖引进了令人惊异的新元素，凸现出它与众不同的特征。这种照明技术允许插入发光二极管，所以这些特殊的地砖可以同时和普通的地砖放在一起。所有的地砖都是同一尺寸、同一厚度、同一质量，既适用于地板，也适用于公共建筑的墙壁，且铺设和安装都很简单方便。

Terra LED is an LED lighting system in two sizes and colours which can be incorporated into the tiles of the Terra Maestricht collection. These LED floor tiles introduce surprising elements in tiled floors, resulting in strikingly conspicuous marks. The lighting technique allows the insertion of LED's so that these specially equipped tiles can be laid simultaneously with regular tiles. The tiles are all of the same size, thickness and quality, suitable for floors and walls of public premises. They are easily laid and handled.

Linea LED 地面及墙砖, 2004

Royal Mosa, Maastricht, NL
Werksdesign: Design Team Mosa
www.mosa.nl

Linea LED系列墙砖在制作的时候加入了发光二极管。该墙砖外观典雅大方且极富有个性化色彩。发光二极管照明技术的使用寿命长，尤其适合用在那种长期潮湿的地方。获得专利的Mosa LED设备所需要的安装表面积非常小。在大小和厚度方面，这种LED墙砖可以同普通的墙砖结合的天衣无缝。这种创新的设计具有平滑的外形并且有许多种组合选择。最常用的是白色的亮砖和色彩偏暗的墙砖，规格有两种，分别是30厘米 x 45厘米或是15厘米 x 45厘米。

The tiles of the Linea LED collection are manufactured with an integrated LED lighting. They are aesthetically designed and have a very characteristic appearance. The lighting technique allows for a very long life cycle and is suited optimally for use in spaces exposed to continuous moisture. The installation surface of a patented Mosa LED fitting is very small. With regard to size and thickness, the LED tiles can be seamlessly combined with regular tiles. This innovative design has an even shape and many combination options. The basis are the white shining and matt wall tiles measuring 30 x 45cm and the special size of 15 x 45cm. Both versions have even-grounded edges.

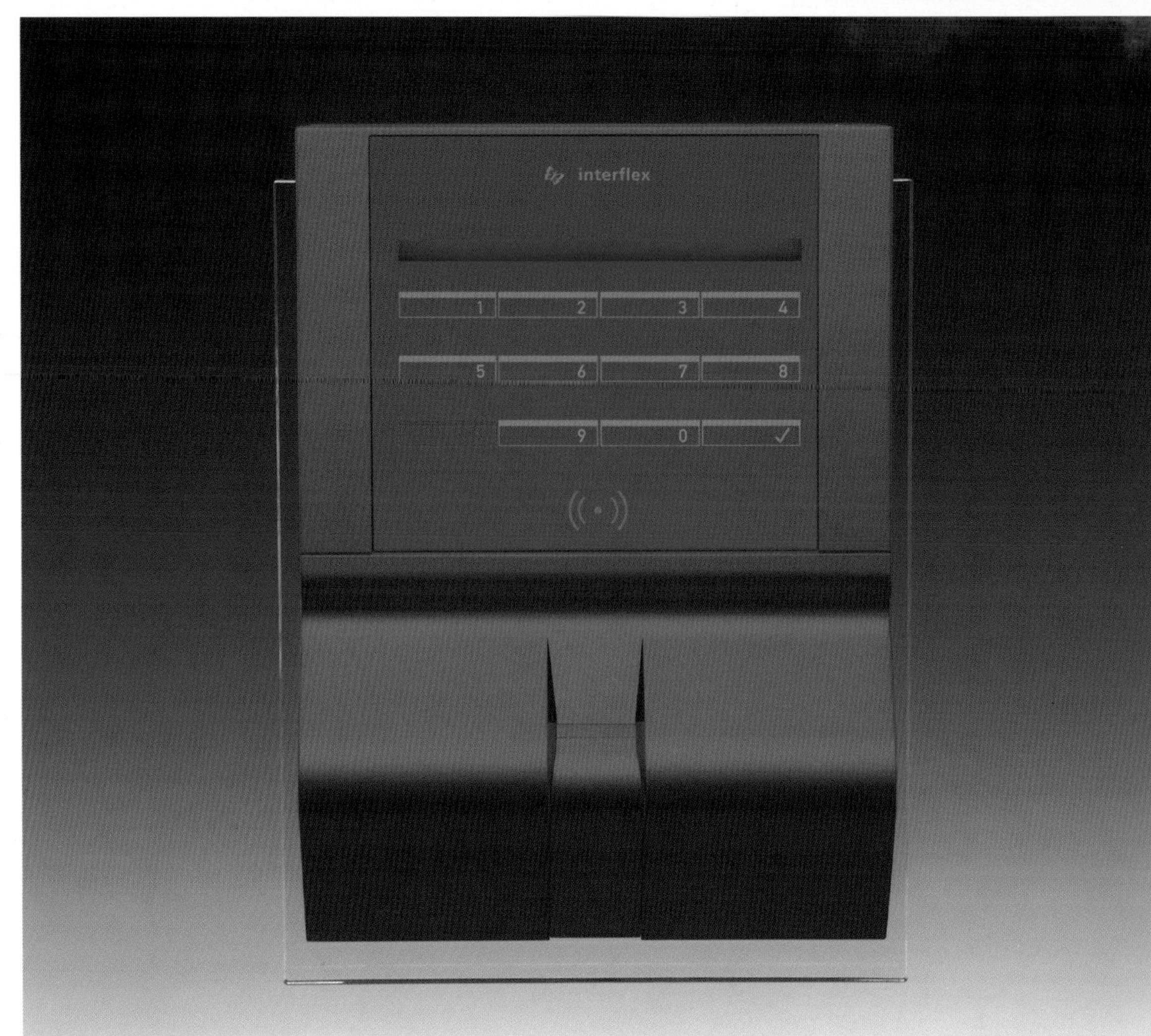

IF-P 600 FP 指纹终端

Interflex Datensysteme GmbH & Co. KG, Stuttgart
Design: Neumeister + Partner (Christiane Frank), München
www.interflex.de
www.neumeister-partner.de

这款生物信息识别读写器是通过感应卡和指纹确认而使用的，可在户内户外方便地使用。它还可以通过非接触式感应卡，结合了指纹确认的电子钥匙链和个人身份识别号码（PIN码）而识别用户。这种纤细的壁装式装置与任何环境都可以自然地融合，既适用于个人，也可以用于商业和工业建筑。它小巧的外罩和简约的外形，无论是在户内还是在户外都可以很容易地安装在墙壁上。这款设备融合了精美的设计和高科技的电子学，凸现出其过硬的品质和巧妙的结构，带给人们最大化的便利。

The biometric access control reader for proximity cards and fingerprint recognition for indoor and outdoor application combines the recognition of users by contactless proximity cards, key fobs or PIN with verification by fingerprint. The slim wall-mounted device blends in naturally with any environment and can be used in private life as well as in conjunction with commercial and industrial buildings. The slim housing with its concise appearance, available for indoor and outdoor use, allows for easy installation on walls. The IF-P 600 FP combines a sturdy construction, high-tech electronics, maximum user convenience and an aesthetic design reduced to the essential.

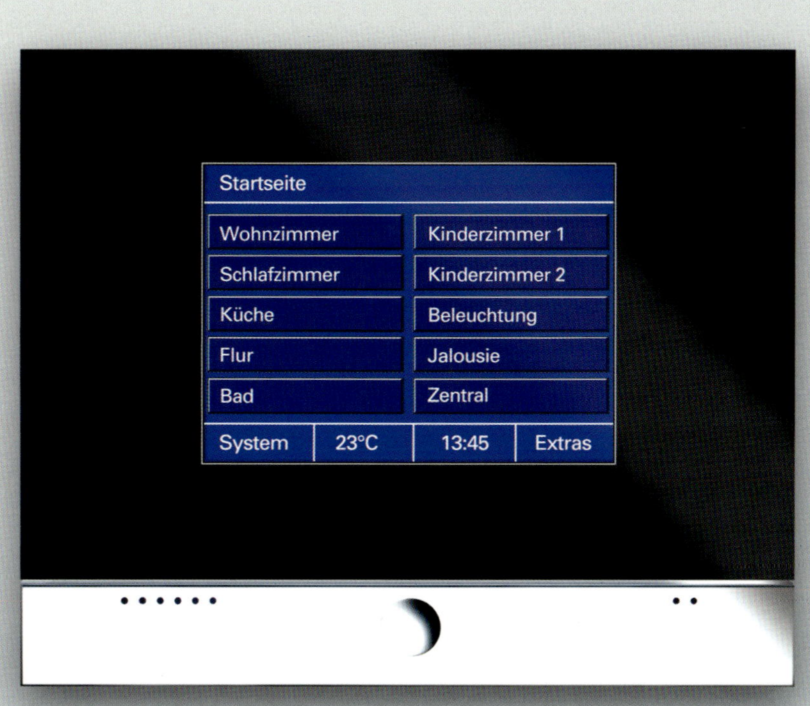

房间控制面板, 2004/2005

Busch-Jaeger Elektro GmbH, Lüdenscheid
Design: Prodesign (Bernd Brüssing), Neu-Ulm
www.busch-jaeger.de
www.prodesign-ulm.de

房间控制面板为EIB系统提供了直觉的、个性化的控制。它不仅仅可以应用在家庭中，在许多其它的工业领域甚至是商业设备中也可广泛应用。单色的或彩色显示器被设计成可以通过笔尖或者指尖来控制的触摸屏幕。除了常规的功能之外，用户也可以编制功能来控制整个系统。展示按扭的功能可以进行个性化处理，经存储后可供个人使用。在彩色显示器下面，我们可以看见一个狭槽，可以用来存放控制触摸屏幕的笔和内存条。信息功能可以保证手写的信息显示在屏幕上。

The room and control panels provide intuitive and individual control of EIB systems in homes as well as in many fields of industry and business facilities. A monochromatic or colour display is designed as a touchscreen operated via a pen or fingertip. The room and control panels allow up to 100 functions to be carried out. Besides the standard functions the user can also programme additional functions for controlling and monitoring systems. The function of display buttons can be personalised and stored for individual use. A slot for a memory card and a pen for operating the touchscreen can be found behind a cover located beneath the display. An information function allows handwritten messages to be left on the screen.

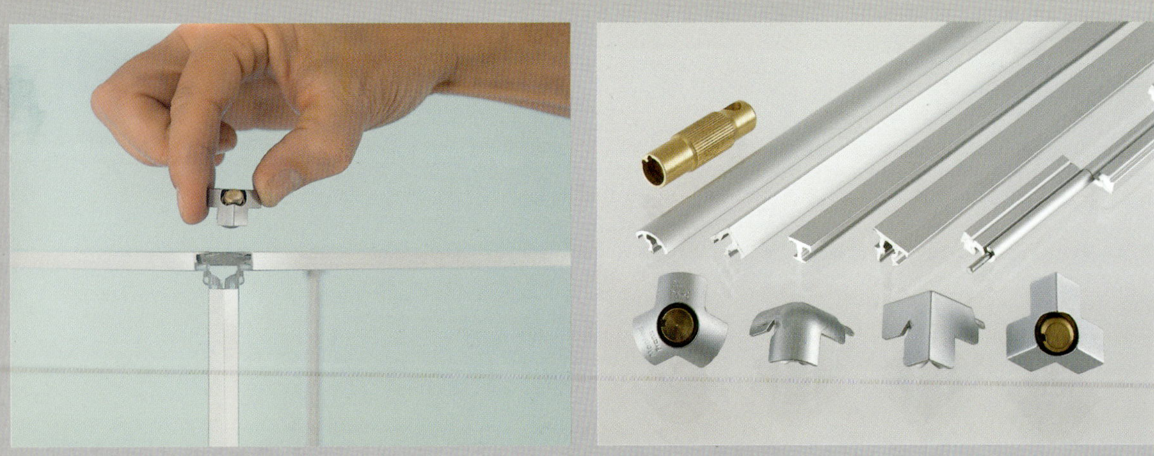

PCS 面板连接系统

Frank Europe GmbH, Bad Kreuznach
Design: Manfred Frank Systems Ltd.
(Manfred Frank), Auckland, Neuseeland
www.frankeurope.de
www.manfredfrank.com

获得专利的PCS（面板连接系统）是一种可满足多种要求的多功能玻璃陈列柜系统。它在博物馆使用，被用来展示专业产品，也可作为一种家居高品质的设计组成部分。该连接系统安装简单、功能强大，既不需要用螺钉，也不需要用胶水，只需通过结合丙烯酸面板和铝条饰品，就可以制造这种高度结实的立方体。

The patented PCS (Panel Connecting System) is a multi-functional showcase system for a variety of requirements. It is used in museums, as a display for professional product presentations, and as a high-quality design element at home. Thanks to the simple and functional connecting system no screws or glue are needed. The highly robust cube is created by joining acrylic panels with filigree aluminium profile strips.

平衡壁炉, 2005

Conmoto GmbH & Co. KG,
Herzebrock-Clarholz
Design: Peter Maly, Hamburg
www.conmoto.com
www.peter-maly.com

这款“平衡式”组合壁炉的设计本身代表了一种室内设计理念。这套炉子可以由三种不同大小的木制储存柜和一把水平方向的长椅组合在一起，当然也可以有很多种摆放方式，其中最具美感的是悬浮式：它既可把所有的部分牢牢的固定在墙上，也可选用不锈钢脚来提供支撑。另外，还有一个完整的不锈钢火炉支架和一个用来支撑炉门的不锈钢横杆可供选择。

The "balance" modular stove is an interior design concept in itself. The stove unit can be horizontally combined with three different sizes of log storage cabinets and a bench element, allowing for a variety of settings. Particularly aesthetic is the "floating" version with all elements mounted firmly to the wall; alternatively, a stand-alone option with stainless steel feet will be available. Optional extras include: an integrated stainless steel fire iron holder and a stainless steel bracing rail to open the front door upwards.

Plaza 无烟囱式壁炉, 2005

Conmoto GmbH & Co. KG,
Herzebrock-Clarholz
Design: Sieger Design GmbH & Co. KG
(Michael Sieger), Sassenberg
www.conmoto.com
www.sieger-design.com

Plaza是完全不需要烟囱就可以放在屋子里任何地方的壁炉，非常灵活。古典的设计能适合不同的室内风格。燃烧的胶产生火焰，火苗大小可以用另外的燃烧盒来逐步地进行调节。由各种颜色，各种材质制成的多样化的嵌入式框架营造出一种特别的氛围。Plaza壁炉一共有三种类型：地板式的、台式的，还有壁挂式的。

Plaza is a flexible fireplace which can be placed anywhere in the house without need for a chimney. The classic design adapts to different ambiences. The open flame is produced by a burning gel. The intensity of the red and yellow flames can be steplessly adjusted with an additional burning box. Changeable clip-on frames with various colours and types of material can create additional accents. Plaza is available as a floor version, a pedestal version with base as well as a wall-mounted version.

DoNuts 组合式桌椅, 2004

Extremis NV, Gijverinkhove, Belgien
Werksdesign: Dirk Wynants
www.extremis.be

DoNuts是一款神奇的组合式桌椅。膨胀的座位部分是由优质尼龙制作而成的，形状就好像是油炸圈饼。到桌子前面一看，您就能发现至少能容下六个人的位子。靠背和桌面采用了符合人体工程学的设计，所以人们可以坐得很舒适。和平常的那些花园里桌子的相比，这种桌子为花园注入了活力。无论是草地里、露台上还是太阳下、树阴中，这种桌子都可以方便地在任何地方使用。

DoNuts is a surprising table-seating combination. The inflatable seating part is made from superior quality nylon in a round donut-like shape. Upon joining the table you will notice there is plenty of space for six people. The backrest, as well as the ergonomic tabletop, are designed for optimum comfort. Compared to other garden tables, the light DoNuts table introduces mobility into the garden. The table can be used wherever required: on the lawn, on the patio, in the sun or in the shadow.

“纯粹”门把手系列，2005

Jado, Rödermark
Design: Artefakt Industriekultur, Darmstadt
www.jado.com
www.artefakt.de

作为生活必须品——门把手，“纯粹”系列一直秉承把门把手当作是“整体中不可缺少的那一部分”的设计理念。作为我们生活的内部世界和外部世界的分界点，门把手担当了重要的任务，至少可以算是整个建筑结构的重要组成部分之一。“纯粹”门把手朴实大方的设计，巧妙地提高了现代建筑的吸引力，在设计与功能之间追寻着平衡。这种把手很容易固定，故这一系列产品都具有新型的、新颖的迅速固定系统。这种系统可以使把手在没有任何辅助设施下，更加容易地进行安装。再加上相对应的球形把手和橄榄式窗把手，可以说，“纯粹”系列产品几乎能与所有的建筑元件完美地结合在一起。

As a handle series for living areas, Pure is always "a part of the whole concept" as well. As an interface between the world we live in and the outside world, the door handle is a key product and part of the structural make-up of the building. Pure deliberately avoids grabbing the limelight and subtly enhances the modern architecture, seeking a balance between design and function. Being especially easy to mount, the series has a completely new developed and patented rapid attachment system which facilitates the assembly of the handle without any visible attachment elements. Complemented by the corresponding door knob and window olive/ handle, Pure allows uniform fitting for all opening construction elements in the living area.

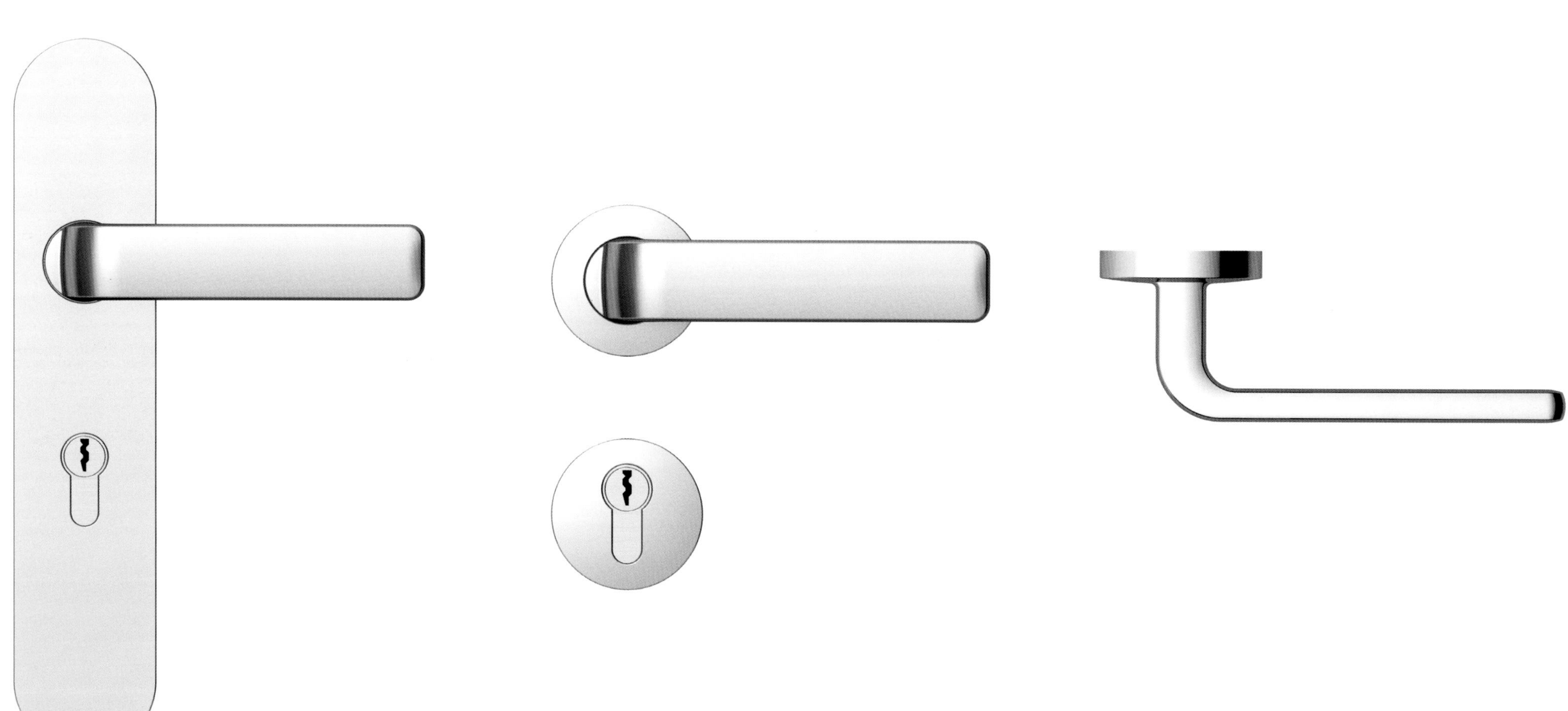

Celsius 自动滑动门系统, 2005

Dorma GmbH + Co. KG, Ennepetal
Werksdesign: Michael Glanz
Design: designafairs GmbH
(Christoph Böninger), München
Georg Kaluza, Velbert
www.dorma.de
www.designafairs.com
www.kaluza-design.de

自动滑动门系统由于其工艺复杂，迄今为止还仅仅应用于商业上的工程方面。而现在，Celsius已经打开了通向新世界的通道，它可以提供一种专门的解决方案，给无障碍建筑提供了完美的解决方案。它体积小、操作稳定，安装和运行都十分容易。小型的卡西尼可以提供各种辅助功能，即使是重达80公斤的滑动门，也能迅速地被开启。强劲的组件格外引人注目，不仅仅是因为它的质量好、设计新颖，还因为它价格适中。

Owing to their complexity, until now automatic sliding door systems have only been found on the project side of the business. Now the Celsius has opened the way to a brave new world, offering tailored application solutions plus the perfect answer for barrier-free building. It is compact, quiet in operation and easy to install and commission. As with the smaller Cassini, it offers a wide range of auxiliary functions – as well as a fast opening action for sliding doors up to 80kg. The powerful drive unit is impressive not only for its high quality and advanced design but also its particularly attractive price.

维京大西洋航空公司
JFK 机场贵宾候机室, 2004

Design: Virgin Atlantic Airways
(Hilary Clark, Chris Sharples),
Crawley, GB
www.virgin-atlantic.com

维京大西洋航空公司的贵宾候机室是JFK机场一个引人注目的地方，它联系着检票与离港两个不同的世界。根据机场的要求，贵宾休息室透明度不能超过25%，可以通过它概略地展现出喷气飞机的外观。这一要求也是设计11英尺高建筑物的最基本要求。内部空间由6个有珍珠光彩的隔板隔开，构建出塔状的波浪起伏的外观，从而构成吧台和许多体现亲密感的座位布局，同时充分考虑到了营造属于自我的舒适感和私密感。这种令人印象深刻的构造展现出柔和的、有着微妙颜色变换的照明效果，那种景色真是美不胜收：一面映衬着闪烁无垠的天空，而另一面则是生机勃勃的大地。走出贵宾休息室，走入机场大厅最达40英尺的空间，乘客可以一览无余地看见机场候机楼和跑道——那便是每一个乘客展开自己精彩的旅途故事的舞台！

The Virgin Atlantic Clubhouse maintains a visual presence within the terminal, combining the two worlds of check-in and departure. It was required by the terminal that no more than 25 per cent of the transparency of the Clubhouse would be permitted to block views out to the jet liners. This requirement was the primary origin for the 11-foot high structures. The space is defined by six of these pearlescent screens rising in undulating towers, forming the bar and more intimate seating areas that combine both comfort and privacy with a privileged view. These impressive structures are illuminated with soft, subtle colour-shifting patterns – on one side the shimmering skyline, the glowing earth on the other. Open to the 40-foot ceiling of the main structure, with sweeping views of the terminal and runway, the lounge becomes a stage set for the unfolding story of each passenger's journey.

耐克足球固定系统 – 欧洲锦标赛 2004

P2 Group, Heemstede, NL
Design: Jump Studios
(Shaun Fernandes), London, GB
www.p2group.nl
www.jump-studios.com

耐克足球固定系统的理念来自于人体中皮肤、肌肉和骨骼之间的相互作用。在运动方面的运用还受到了克力斯・坎宁安为歌手比约克所拍摄的录影带的理念所启发——“一切都是充满爱的”。一个固定的系统好似光滑干净的皮肤，但同时，还添加了带有技术功能的框架。这种体系类似多米诺骨牌，它可以在墙上进行展示，形成以点、破折号、直线所组成的坐标方格，从而使产品井然有序且清洁干净的展示于零售店的墙面上。

The concept for the Nike Football Fixturing System was born from the idea of the interplay between skin, muscle and bone. With regard to the athlete, and inspired by Chris Cunningham's Björk video, "All is full of love", the fixturing system superimposes the sensuality of a pure glossy white skin over that of a technologically functional frame. The system plays out across the wall like dominoes, forming a grid of points, dashes and lines, giving the product a sophisticated order and cleanliness across the retail wall.

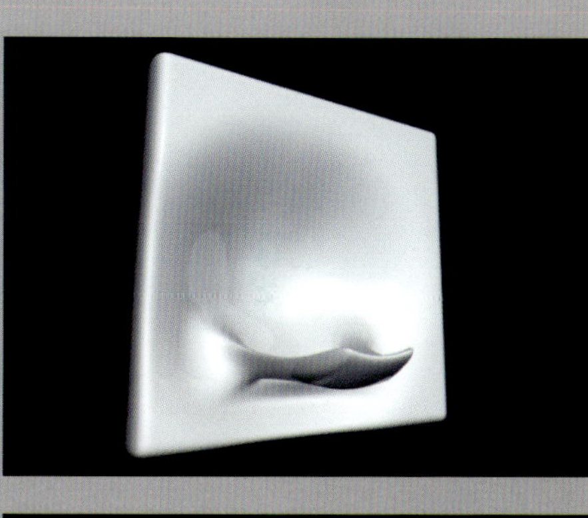

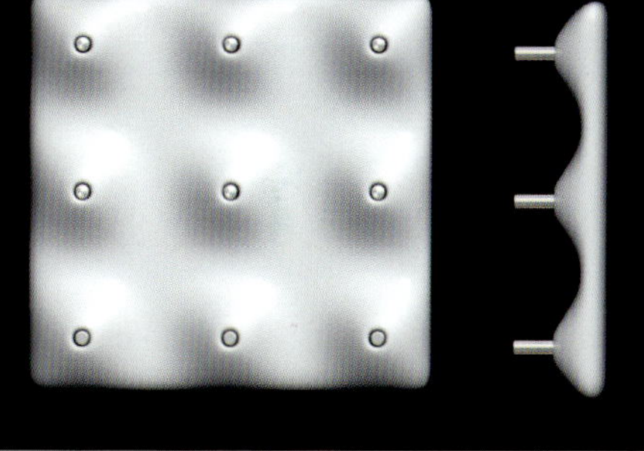

机器的新美学

The new aesthetic of machines

设计的重要性在“工业和手工艺”领域里的剧增清楚地显示出了这个领域里的流行趋势——评委肯尼斯·盖瑞治、克洛斯和裘连诺·莫利那瑞一致认为这一发展是积极的、正面的。许多年来，他们一直在告诉我们，在家庭生活中，设计是处于中心地位的；但是在工作的地方，人们却忽视了去创造一个和谐的氛围，而这种情况现在看起来正在改变。大型的机械工厂被设计得极具吸引力，这不论是从理念上还是外观上，都会给我们的工作环境带来一种全新的美感。与此同时，在声音和工效方面，人们也已经有了绝妙的解决办法。在评委看来，这些工厂和机器的创新的工作流程理念将引导工作场所里的建筑向更新、更富有魅力的方向发展。这种探索的一个很重要的任务就是寻求新的方法，并且从美学上提高设计作品的层次。我们要在自然世界里寻找创作原形，在此基础上研究新的技术和策略。评委们尤其欣赏在这种基础上设计的特殊的机器造型，它们成功地与整个产品的理念融合为一体。

The trend in "industry and crafts" is clearly defined by *the growing importance of design – a development viewed as entirely positive by the jurors Kenneth Grange, Odo Klose and Giuliano Molineri. For many years, they remind us, people left homes in which design was central and went to places of work where little thought had gone into creating a coherent atmosphere. This situation now seems to be changing. Huge mechanical plants are being impressively designed in regard both to conception and appearance, and introducing to the work environment a new, attractive aesthetic. At the same time, excellent solutions have been found for acoustic and ergonomic problems. In the view of the jurors, the highly innovative workflow concepts underlying these plants and machine parts are leading to a new, and interesting, "architecture" of the workplace. A major part in the search for fresh approaches and the progression towards an aesthetically enhanced world of work is likewise played by research into new technologies and strategies based on models such as the natural world. The jurors were fascinated by the very specific and contemporary appearance of machine parts designed on such foundations then successfully integrated into coherent product-family concepts.*

裘连诺·莫利那瑞
Giuliano Molineri
意大利
Italien

奥杜·克洛斯
Odo Klose
德国
Deutschland

肯尼斯·格兰奇
Kenneth Grange
英国
Großbritannien

工业与工艺
Industry and crafts

VHER 1/8 手控阀门, 2004

Festo AG & Co. KG, Esslingen
Werksdesign: Karoline Schmidt, Jan Kleffmann
www.festo.com

手柄阀属于坚固的手工操作阀产品系列，这种产品能够在恶劣的环境中使用。不仅适用于铸造车间和焊接车间等的金属设计，同样也适用于食品加工行业。在设计过程中，阀门的人性化设计得到了高度的重视。只需用三个手指就能很容易地进行操作，也能很容易地克服巨大的压力。手柄阀用做主气动开关时可以锁定。蓝色的旋钮使整个设计颜色鲜明。当被按下去后，开关就被锁定了，而且可以用市场上常见的锁来为它加上一层保护。开关上可能会装有一个附有单独说明的标牌。通过使用不同的联接板，手柄阀和新装置的接口方向是可以改变的。安装传感器的集成槽使手柄阀能够根据现行要求进行测量，这个小小的串联尤其适合安装在控制面板上，这样开关就成为唯一可见的部件，而它的简洁设计也使其外表显得大方而高雅。

Hand lever valves belong to the product family of robust, manually operated valves used in harsh environments, for metal design in foundries, welding shops, etc., but also in the food processing industry. Great emphasis was placed on the ergonomic design of the switch, so that it can be easily operated with three fingers. Greater forces can be easily overcome. When used as a main pneumatic switch, the hand lever valve can be locked. The blue knob is integrated into the design and has a contrasting colour. When pressed down, the switch is locked and can be secured with a commercially available lock. A plate with an individual description may be placed on the switch. By using different connecting plates, the connection direction with new devices is variable. Integrated slots for mounting sensors make the hand lever valves capable of sensing in accordance with current requirements. This small series is especially suited to mounting on a control panel: the switch then becomes the only visible component and its design gives it a simple and elegant appearance.

电磁阀 VUVB, 2005

Festo AG & Co. KG, Esslingen
Werksdesign: Jan Kleffmann
www.festo.com

这种新型磁阀是使用聚合技术构建的阀系列的一种，它具有坚固、经济、标准化的特点。这个系统设计中有作为单个阀的，也有作为阀组或阀岛的，使其能够应用于自动化的任何一个领域。这种阀仅用一个螺栓就能很简便、快速、安全地安装在稳定的用途条上或者单独的附属基础上。在设计中很重视模块化特征。能进行电子控制的模块部件的结构很清晰并且形成一个单元。正如所有费斯托公司的产品一样，蓝色被用作控制组件。

This new solenoid valve is part of a robust, economic and modular line of valves constructed using polymer technology. Designed as an individual valve, valve manifold or valve terminal, the system can be used in any area of automation. The valves can be easily, quickly and securely mounted with just one screw on a stable manifold strip or individual sub-base. The design emphasises the modular nature. The electrically controllable modules are clearly structured and form a unit. As with all Festo products, the colour "blue" is used for control elements.

SFC-DC 马达控制器, 2005

Festo AG & Co. KG, Esslingen
Werksdesign: Karoline Schmidt, Simone Mangold, Jan Kleffmann
www.festo.com

SFC-DC是一种新的DC马达控制器，它为使用直流电马达的单个驱动单元承担了全部的定位控制功能。所有的功能都是通过一根电缆来传输的。进行定位和判断的装置可以有两种方式： 通过PC上的序列界面或者直接通过装置上的人机界面。宽大的显示器和四个选择按钮使用起来舒适自如，并且和费斯托公司的其他装置一样，都不需要为了使用它而对操作者进行专门的培训。同时SFC-DC能够防水。它可以用螺丝钳直接安装在机器上，也可以用H导轨安装在控制盒里。新的马达控制器的外壳和费斯托公司的设计风格非常地协调，并且是为了电子领域其它产品的开发而设计的。一块被模具挤压成型的铝块被切割成要求的长度，界面区域的弯曲表面面向用户，上面还安装有键盘、显示器和LED信号系统；水平表面则是所有接口和插头的平台。

The SFC-DC is a new DC motor controller that assumes complete position control functions for a single separate drive unit with direct-current motor. All functions are transmitted through a single cable. The settings for commissioning and diagnosis can be made in two ways: By serial interface on a PC or directly on the device through HMI (Human-Machine Interface). The large display and the four selection buttons provide for comfortable use and are identical to other Festo devices, which means that no retraining is necessary for use. The SFC-DC is protected against splashed water. It can be mounted either directly on the machine with mounting clamps or in the control cabinet using an H-rail. The new motor controller housing is coordinated with Festo Corporate Design and is designed for additional product developments in the electronics area: An extruded aluminium profile is cut to the required length. The curved surface of the interface area, on which the keyboard, display and LEDs are located, faces the user. The level surfaces are platforms for all types of connections and plugs.

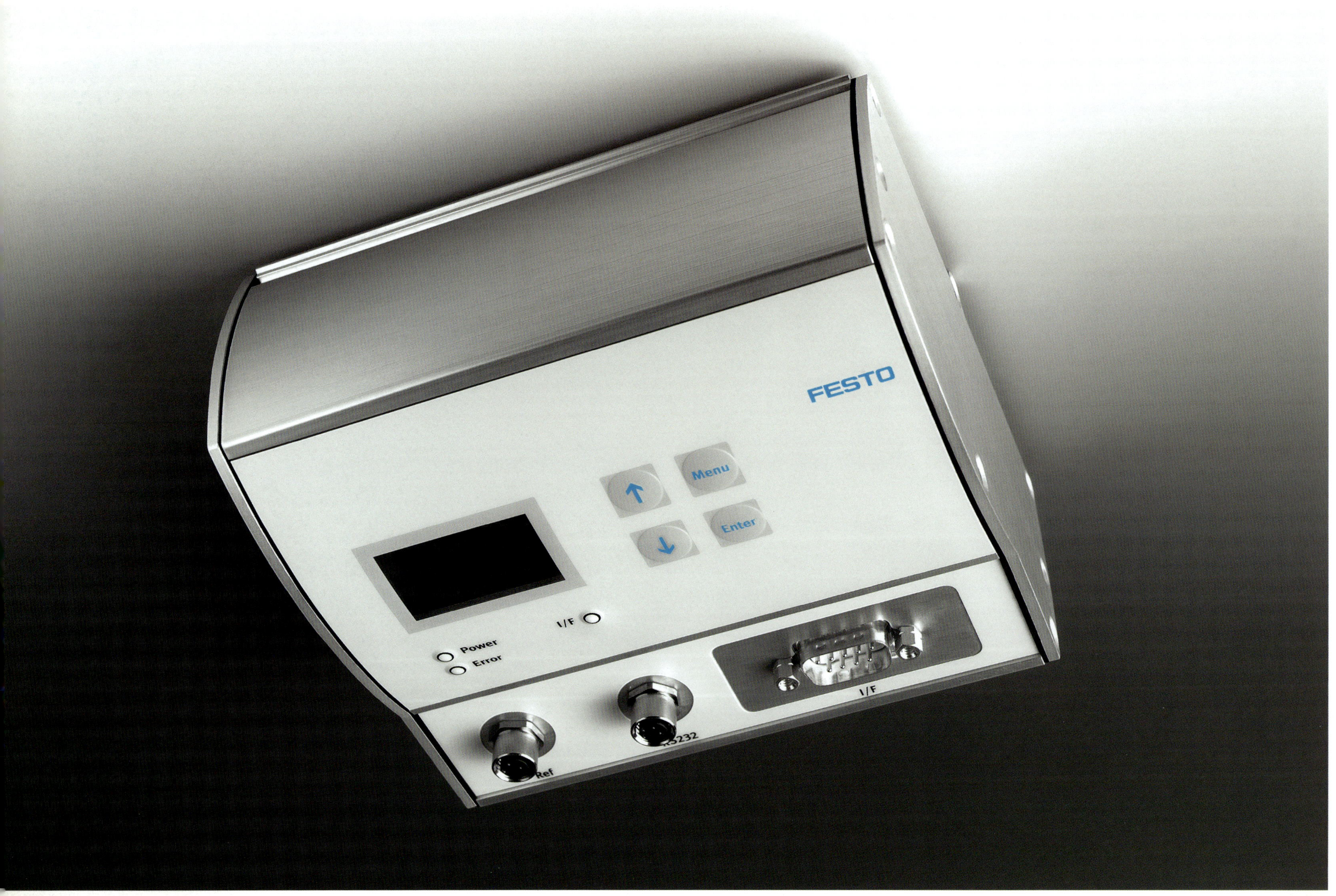

SFC-LAC 马达控制器, 2005

Festo AG & Co. KG, Esslingen
Werksdesign: Karoline Schmidt, Simone Mangold, Jan Kleffmann
www.festo.com

SFC-LAC是一种新的AC马达控制器，它为使用交流电马达的单个驱动单元承担了全部的定位控制功能。所有的功能都是通过一根电缆来传输的。进行定位和判断的装置可以有两种方式： 通过PC上的序列界面或者直接通过装置上的人机界面。宽大的显示器和四个选择按钮使用起来舒适自如，并且和费斯托公司的其他装置一样，都不需要为了使用它而对操作者进行专门的培训。同时SFC-LAC能够防水。它可以用螺丝钳直接安装在机器上，也可以用H导轨安装在控制盒里。新的马达控制器的外壳和费斯托公司的设计风格非常地协调，并且是为了电子领域其它产品的开发而设计的。一块被模具挤压成型的铝块被切割成要求的长度，界面区域的弯曲表面面向用户，上面还安装有键盘、显示器和LED信号系统；水平表面则是所有接口和插头的平台。

The SFC-LAC is a new AC motor controller that assumes complete position control functions for a single separate linear drive unit. All functions are transmitted through a single cable. The settings for commissioning and diagnosis can be made in two ways: By serial interface on a PC or directly on the device through HMI (Human-Machine Interface). The large display and the four selection buttons provide for comfortable use and are identical to other Festo devices, which means that no retraining is necessary for use. The SFC-LAC is protected against splashed water. It can be mounted either directly on the machine with mounting clamps or in the control cabinet using an H-rail. The new motor controller housing is coordinated with Festo Corporate Design and is designed for additional product developments in the electronics area: An extruded aluminium profile is cut to the required length. The curved surface of the interface area, on which the keyboard, display and LEDs are located, faces the user. The level surfaces are platforms for all types of connections and plugs.

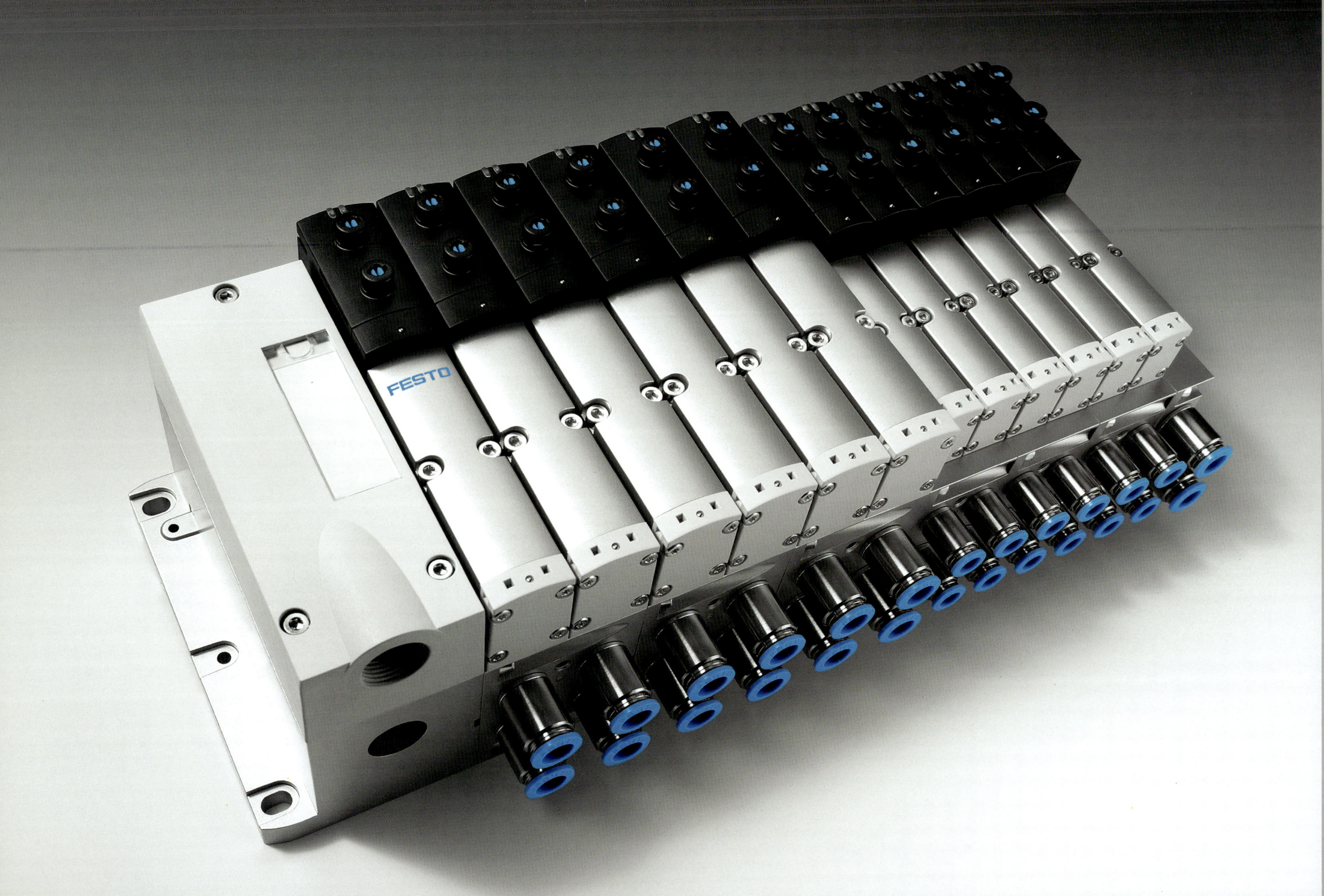

标准化阀岛, 2005

Festo AG & Co. KG, Esslingen
Werksdesign: Karoline Schmidt, Jan Kleffmann
www.festo.com

这种坚固的阀岛有效地实现了模块化设计，并且是由阀门和采用了精密电子技术和气动界面的连接板组成的。该阀岛可用于较小的系统中，由于它的附件设计得巧妙，使其能够安装一系列气动开关，这样它能够配合多阀系统进行扩展。标准阀控制着单气动气缸、旋转模块和夹具的空气供应。该阀岛可以用在一些行业的自动化生产中，如机动车生产、家具工业、轮胎和家用玻璃的生产、医药工程、印刷和造纸工业等行业中。该设计重视气动、电子和手动操作模块的标准化。该阀安装和拆卸非常简单（即插即用），标记板可单独进行书写。这样，很大的模块就构成了紧凑简明的单元。

This robust valve terminal has an effective modular design and consists of valves and connecting plates with sophisticated electrical and pneumatic interfaces. It is used in small systems and thanks to its cleverly designed accessory system, which enables the mounting of a wide range of pneumatic switches, it can be expanded for systems with a very high number of valves. Standard valves control the air supply for individually pneumatically driven cylinders, swivel modules and grippers. The valve terminal can be used in the automation of vehicle production, the furniture industry, in the production of tyres and consumer glass, in general mechanical engineering and in the printing and paper industries. The design emphasises the modular nature of the pneumatic, electrical and manually operated modules. Assembly and disassembly of the valves is very simple (plug in), the marking plates are individual writable. Very large modules thus form a visually compact unit.

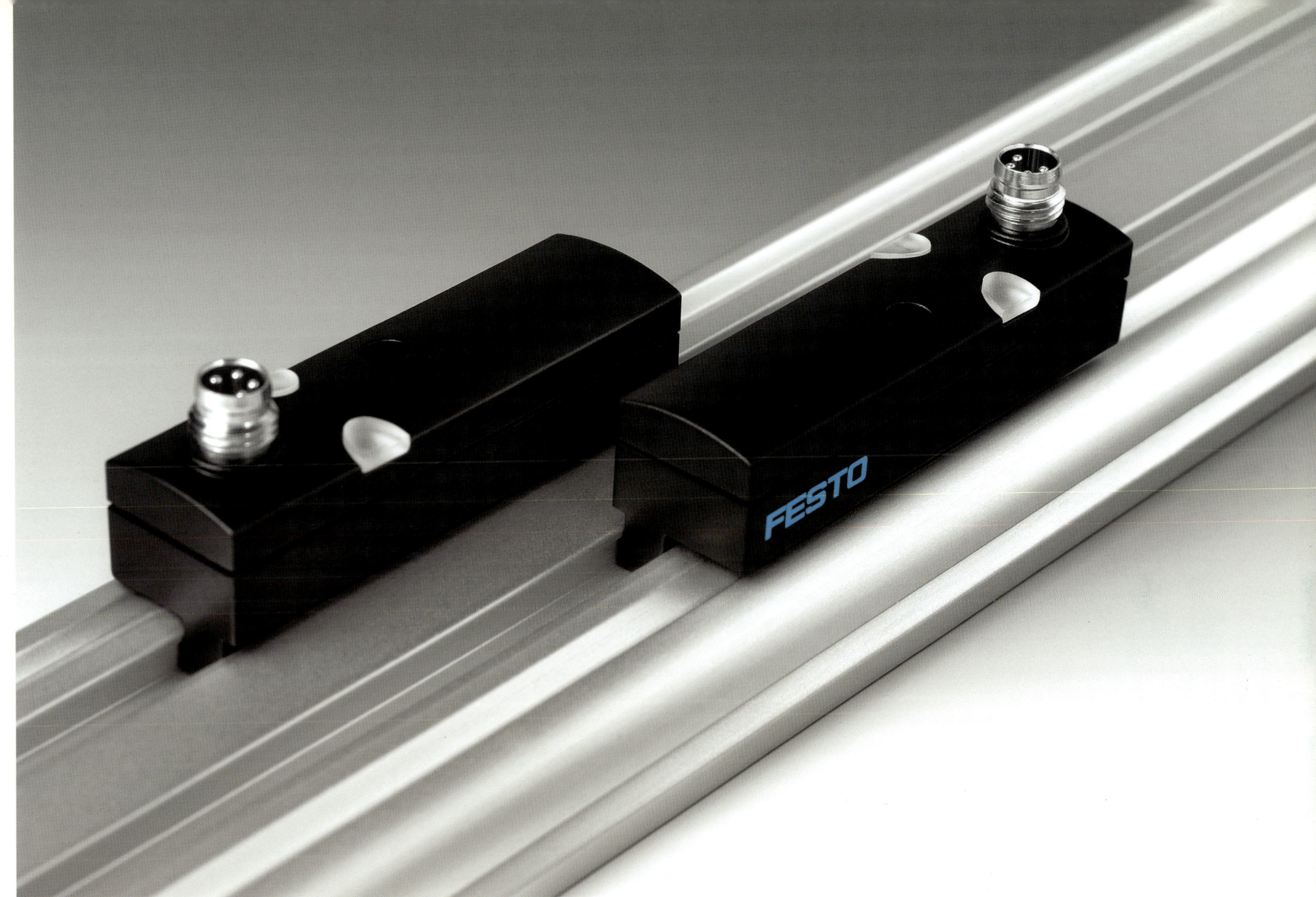

SMAT-8E 位移传感器, 2005

Festo AG & Co. KG, Esslingen
Werksdesign: Karoline Schmidt, Jan Kleffmann
www.festo.com

SMAT-8E是一种用于路径检测的位移传感器，安装在有T型槽的气动驱动器中。在大量的应用中，例如夹持、挤压、物体检测、质量分类、磨损检测等环节里，关于冲程的局部的模拟报告就足够了。SMAT-8E涵盖了整个测量范围，它的测量范围是50毫米，且设计得非常坚固。其测量范围是独立于所使用的驱动装置的。在任何一个带有T型槽的汽缸内都能安装该传感器，并且配有主动的模拟量输出模块，因此用户必须而且只需要和PLC建立连接即可。两个集成的LED可以显示操作状态以及是否超出测量范围。该产品的外形能支持各种应用中的线性特征。两个LED上有一个放大了的发光表面区域，这样就能够很容易地从距离上确定其操作状态。

The SMAT-8E is a position transmitter for path detection on pneumatic drives with T-slot. For a number of applications, such as clamping, pressing, detecting objects, quality sorting and wear detection, analogue reporting on one part of the stroke is sufficient. The SMAT-8E covers the measuring range. It has a working range of 50mm and a very robust design. The working range is independent of the drive used. Mounted in any T-slot cylinder and equipped with an active analogue output module, the customer must only establish the connection with the PLC. Two integrated LEDs indicate the operating status and an out-of-range position. The shape supports the linear nature of the applications. The LEDs have an enlarged lighting surface area so that the operating status can be easily determined from the distance.

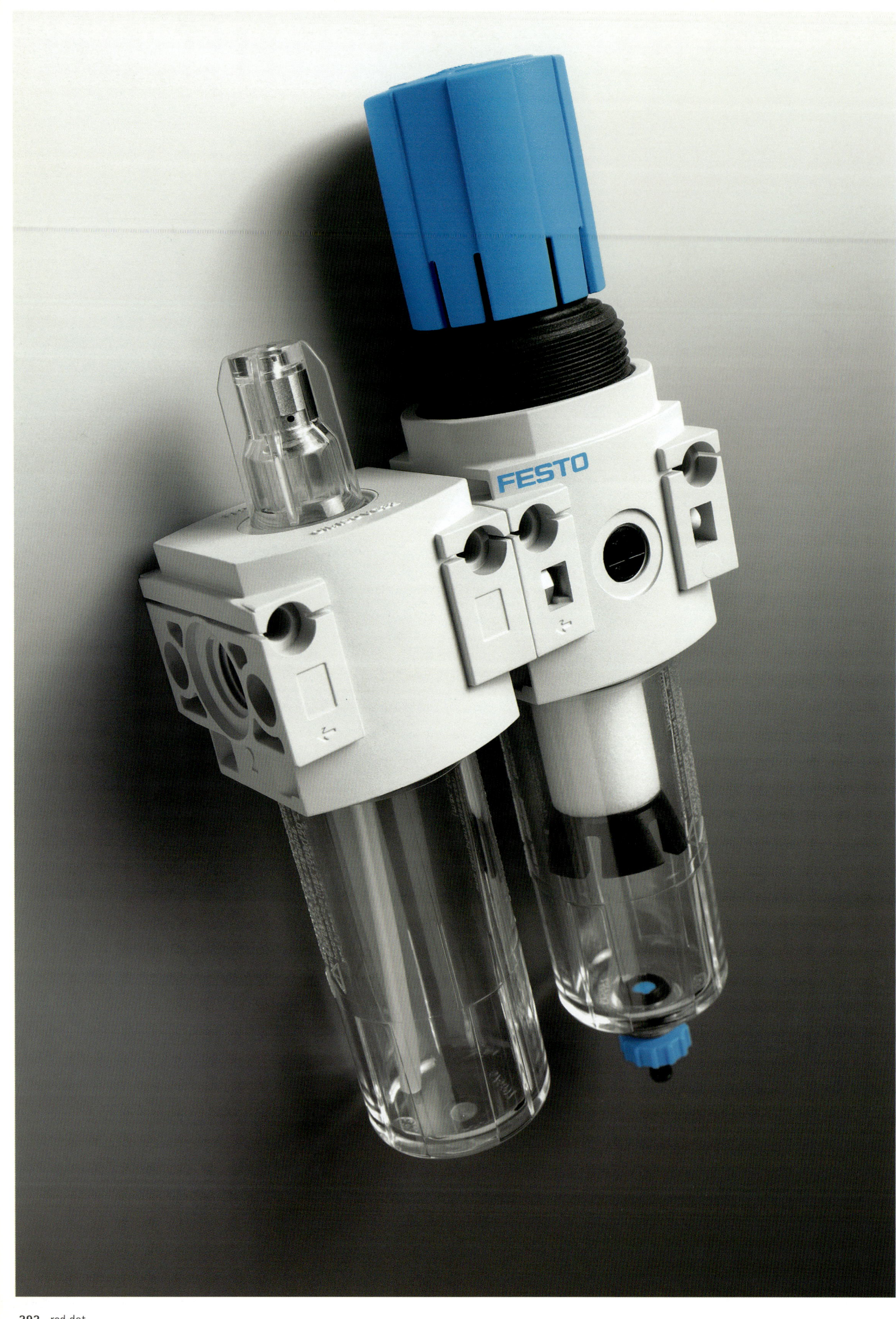

压缩空气联件

Festo AG & Co. KG, Esslingen
Werksdesign: Karoline Schmidt,
Jan Kleffmann
www.festo.com

这个系列的产品拓展后几乎可以应用于所有的行业。这个服务单元完全关注于核心功能，同时也能为压缩气源的供应承担一切基本功能，例如过滤、控制和空气润滑等。高（空气）流速的微型模件是为潜在的大容积的用户而设计的。这也完全可以与现有的产品系列联系起来。压缩气联件也能非常容易地安装，用户自己就可以进行安装和转换或者补充，而不需要将其拆开。DB系列的另外一个独特卖点就是它是第一个以较低价格来完全重新设计的气源处理单元。不难理解，结构清晰的组件经有机地组合而成的紧凑单元，能轻松融入到现代生产系统中。模块化的特征通过弯曲的正面得以体现，并且与费斯托公司的设计风格相一致，蓝色同样被用作控制组件。

This expansion of the product line can be used in almost all industries. The service unit is absolutely focussed on core functionality and offers all common basic functions for compressed air supply, such as filtration, control and air lubrication. The miniature modules that nevertheless have high (air) flow rates are designed for customers with high potential volumes. It is completely connectible to the existing line of products. The compressed air preparation unit is also extremely easy to assemble: assembly and conversion or supplements can be done by the customer himself without having to disassemble the unit. An additional unique selling point is that the DB Series is the first completely redesigned air preparation unit in the lower price segment. Easy-to-understand, clearly structured components are visually integrated in modern systems manufacturing as very compact units. The modular nature is emphasised through the curved fronts and is coordinated with Festo Corporate Design. The colour "blue" is used for control elements.

Siplace X系列, 2004

Siemens AG, München
Design: designafairs GmbH
(Andreas Preussner), München
www.siemens.com
www.designafairs.com

Siplace X系列表面贴装设备是富有艺术感的机器，它使用了新技术，设计非常人性化。该产品是表面贴装机中第一个采用新数字生产平台的系统，并且采用了创新性的视觉技术。视觉上较低的高度以及透明度使其能进行很好的纵览，并且可能在入口处的侧面进行操作，方便快捷。另外，智能供料器模块的应用使其更具人性化。与上一代产品相比较，该设备通过对先进技术的积累和运用，使该产品在贴装工作和精密程度上都得到了快速的提高。贴装系统是用可回收的原料生产的。该产品系列的设计也提升了希普利斯公司的形象。

The Siplace X series surface mounting equipment is a state-of-the-art placement machine with innovative technology, designed user-friendly. It is the first system with a new digital production platform of placement machines, equipped with the innovative Vision technology. A low construction height and transparency in the field of vision provide a good overview and enable portal side operation. The use of intelligent feeder modules additionally enhances user-friendliness. Compared to the predecessor generation, the placement performance and precision was increased by new collect & place head technologies VHS (Very High Speed). The placement system was manufactured using recyclable materials. Its design supports the corporate image of the Siplace product family.

彩色一次性用品, 2005

Hermann G. Schütte & Co GmbH, Achim
Design: PPS International, Hamburg
Vertrieb: Hans Schwarzkopf & Henkel GmbH & Co KG, Hamburg
www.schwarzkopf-professional.com

专门的自动售货机所出售的一次性工具能够在劳动中起到不同的保护作用，并且证明了一些小的琐碎的物品也确实能在给头发染色和造型时派上用场。对于专业的施华蔻美发用品而言，这种设计就是基于以上的指导思想，即收集那些尽管在车间里是零星、琐碎或平常的东西，然后在基本工作中进行完全地改变，从而实现功能上的革新。例如普通的乳胶手套——那是当美发师不得不使用化学产品的时候所必需的物品。

The disposable tools in a functional dispenser box provide protection and demonstrate that "odds and ends" can indeed also celebrate the experience of hair colouring and forming. For Schwarzkopf Professional, the background to this design is the guiding idea to pick up even casual, trivial or banal things in the shop and thus to break new ground with detailed changes in the basic work space. Exemplary for this are the common latex gloves – a must for hairdressers when they have to work with chemical products.

染碗, 2005

Inotech Medizintechnik GmbH, Nabburg
Design: Robert Kipry, Braunschweig; Jens Bingenheimer, Bad Harzburg
Vertrieb: Hans Schwarzkopf & Henkel GmbH & Co KG, Hamburg
www.schwarzkopf-professional.com

染碗是美发工具中新一代产品的使者。在东方传统的启发下，符合人机工程学原理的实用工具便产生了。任何一只手都可以轻易地拿起它的把手。这样，染碗就能够很容易地传递给助手。这款产品真正的创新是备忘夹，可以把染发剂外部包装的插图颜色与染碗内的颜色联系起来，使美发师能够很容易地区分出不同碗中颜色的细微差异。

The colour bowl is a ambassador of a new generation by Salon Tools. Inspired by oriental traditions, a functionally ergonomic form language ensued. Twin hand grips are suited to be hold with either hand. In this way, the colour bowl can be easily passed on to assisting associates. One real innovation is the memo clip. For the first time, the lids of the outer packaging of hair colours can be attached to the bowl, allowing for an easy differentiation of colour nuances in different bowls.

美发推车, 2005

Design: Sonia Zvirbulis, Wolfsburg; Jessica Nebel, Braunschweig
Vertrieb: Hans Schwarzkopf & Henkel GmbH & Co KG, Hamburg
www.schwarzkopf-professional.com

施华蔻专业生产的外表高雅小巧的可移动式手推车是为了帮助美发师应对这个动态的世界而设计的。它结合了高档手提箱和美发工具箱的特点，无论在功能和外形上都非常适合于美发行业。这个手推车包括整齐地装在一个抽屉里的两个基本层面，一旦它被打开，上面的抽屉就会自动向上翻动，这样就会使原先隐藏起来的抽屉立刻显现出来。一些比较重要的工具，例如镜子、发刷、梳子以及发卷，马上变得触手可及。

The elegant and compact-looking portable trolley from Schwarzkopf Professional is designed to be the answer to the increasingly mobile world of the hairdresser. It combines the features of a high-quality suitcase with a classic service station and is geared, in function and appearance, to the hairdressing world. The trolley consists of two basic units, which fit neatly inside one another. Once it is unlocked, the upper drawer unit moves up automatically. This reveals the drawers that were previously protected. The most important tools such as mirrors, brushes, combs and rods are instantly to hand.

软管挤压器, 2005

aha Kunststofftechnik GmbH,
Fränkisch-Crumbach/Odenwald
Design: Kathrin Westkämper,
Braunschweig
Vertrieb: Hans Schwarzkopf & Henkel
GmbH & Co KG, Hamburg
www.schwarzkopf-professional.com

软管挤压器采用了一种原理使它首次可能完全清空软管，还能挤压出少量的东西。它也是第一个把美发沙龙的美学需求考虑进来的产品。在原理上，软管挤压器的外形就像一面鼓，绕着周围外表柱体的压力边缘旋转。当把软管的尾部折叠起来，并将其安全地固定在一个槽里时，即使是糊状的染发剂也能用很小的力量就可把它挤出来。

This tube squeezer employs a principle, which makes it possible, for the first time, to completely empty the tube and extract only small amounts of it as well. It is also the first which takes into consideration the aesthetic demands of a hair salon. In principle, the tube squeezer is shaped like a drum rotating against the contact pressure lip of the surrounding exterior cylinder. As the tube is securely fixed with its bottom fold in a slot, even pasty colours can be extracted with only little effort.

专业工具包, 2005

Bodenschatz Lederwaren GmbH &
Co. KG, Presseck
Design: Maria Sofia Karanthaki,
Braunschweig;
Nils Göbel, Braunschweig
Vertrieb: Hans Schwarzkopf & Henkel
GmbH & Co KG, Hamburg
www.schwarzkopf-professional.com

工具包的使用让日用品变得更加方便实用了。在美发沙龙里它模糊了功能和时尚之间的界限。工具包给那些随时使用的工具穿上了一件安全和漂亮时尚的外衣。它可以用来存放剪刀、发刷、梳子和发夹等美发工具。它的基本构造就是一个含有两块重叠嵌板的饰带，在嵌板的中心放置比较重要的工具；而可以把剪刀等工具放在另一面的套子里加以保护，因为只有在剪发的时候才会用到它。

The tool holster is a practical interpretation of an everyday product, blurring the line between function and fashion in the salon. It provides a safe and attractive housing for valuable tools that need to be kept ready for use at all times. The result is a functional and aesthetic tool holster for the storage of scissors, brushes, combs, and clips. The basic underlying thought is the sash consisting of two overlapping panels holding the valuable tools in its centre. The valuable scissors are protected by a cover flap as they are only needed for the actual step of cutting.

染发刷, 2005

Geka Brush GmbH,
Bechhofen/Königshofen
Design: Klaudia Bartsch, Braunschweig;
Agnes Zuber, Wolfsburg;
Anke Eigenbrodt, Braunschweig;
Michael Grasshoff, Braunschweig
Vertrieb: Hans Schwarzkopf & Henkel
GmbH & Co KG, Hamburg
www.schwarzkopf-professional.com

施华蔻专业所生产的新染发刷系列使发型设计师在他们富有创造性的染发工作中能够像艺术家一样表现自己。这个系列的外形遵循了统一的设计风格，其中包括传统的染发刷、可更换刷头的染发刷以及带梳子的染发刷。该产品最具有新意的是其圆形的手柄在尾部逐渐变细，变成一个柔软的带有弹性的尖端，便于美发师的操作。

The new colour brush range from Schwarzkopf Professional enables stylists to express themselves as artists in their creative colouring activities. They constitute a product family pursuing a uniform design language in the shaping of handles and shafts. It consists of a classic brush, an interchangeable brush and a brush with comb. The most innovative and striking feature is the rounded handle which elegantly tapers into a soft, flexible point.

Aviana 推车脚轮，2005

Tente-Rollen GmbH, Wermelskirchen
Design: Squareone GmbH
(Prof. Martin Topel), Düsseldorf
www.tente.com
www.squareonedesign.de

Aviana推车脚轮遵循了腾德公司的传统，有着自己清晰、独立的视觉表达方式。在总体形状和几何构造上，它的滚轮柱体部分、圆形表面和外形在过渡清晰平滑。同时，该产品也与推车实用的外形相协调起来，从而成为整个推车合理的组成部分。其设计最主要的是对其环形拱和参考面的严格选择，即只在纵横轴线上安装悬挂部分。与传统的钢脚轮相比较，该产品重量大大减轻，并且因其较高的机械稳定性而在要求的标准范围内的性能表现很突出。由于轮子侧面的导航系统，当把推车拉出工作间时，脚轮不会被卡住。独立且外表平滑的轮盖很容易清洗，锌板制的零部件则能提供长期防护，避免腐蚀。

With its clear and self-contained visual language, the trolley castor Aviana follows the tradition of Tente. It interprets the interplay of cylindrical parts, circular surfaces and shapes in transition as to their geometry and overall size. In this regard, it also picks up the functionalistic-technoid shape of trolleys, thus becoming a logical part of the system. Formally dominant are the circular arches and the strict selection of referral levels, only looking for their pendants in the vertical-horizontal axis. Aviana offers the advantage of considerably reduced weight in comparison to conventional steel castors and excels with higher mechanical stability within the demanded norms. Due to the lateral wheel leads, there is no wedging of the castors when pulling the trolley out of galley compartments. The self-contained and smooth-shaped housing allows easier cleaning; zinc-plated components offer a long-lasting protection against corrosion.

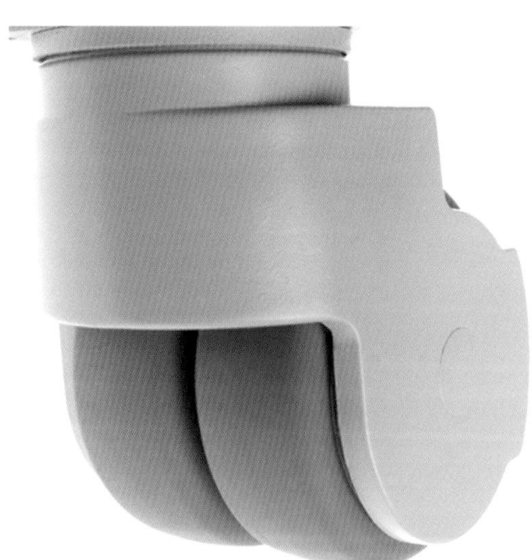

Type 2250 手持分析仪, 2004

Brüel & Kjær Sound & Vibration Measurement A/S, Naerum, Dänemark
Design: Steve McGugan Industrial Design, Lyngby, Dänemark; John Boye, Struer, Dänemark
www.bksv.com

2250型分析仪是一种在专业领域使用的声音与振动分析仪。通常，在狭长的检测杆或高高的烟囱顶端，声音与振动的测量是很难进行的。因此，在开发和设计过程中，就必须把用户的需求和想法置于核心地位。一个由70名用户组成的国际小组承担起了设计工作，这样一个全新的设计新鲜出炉了。这个设计考虑周到，即使在最恶劣的条件下，它也能轻松可靠地被使用。眼下，2250型分析仪正在试图超越用户的要求，开发出更新的功能，使其更具特点。

Type 2250 is a sound and vibration analyzer for field use. Conditions are often difficult – measuring in narrow inspection shafts or on the tops of tall chimneys. Therefore, the needs, requirements and ideas of users were central in development and design. An international panel of 70 users contributed and the result is a completely new design with well thought-out functions, making it easy and reliable to use, even under extreme conditions. Type 2250 attempts to go beyond user requirements and incorporate new design features.

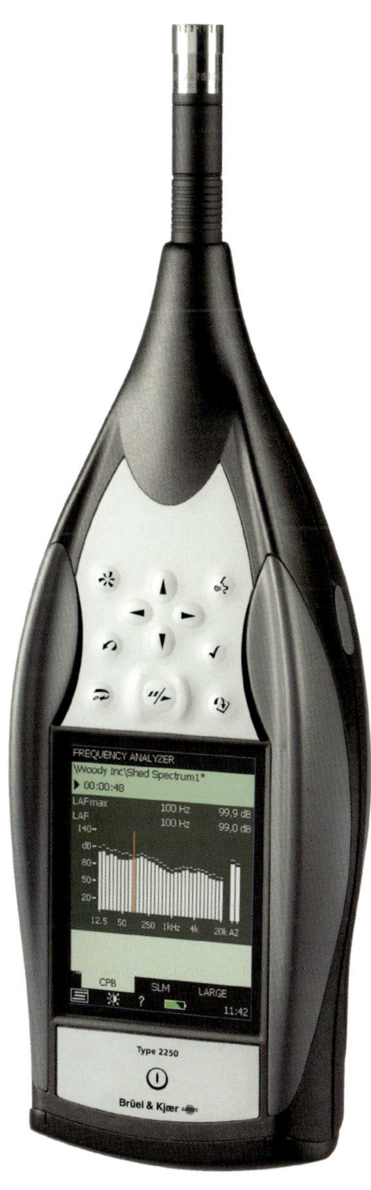

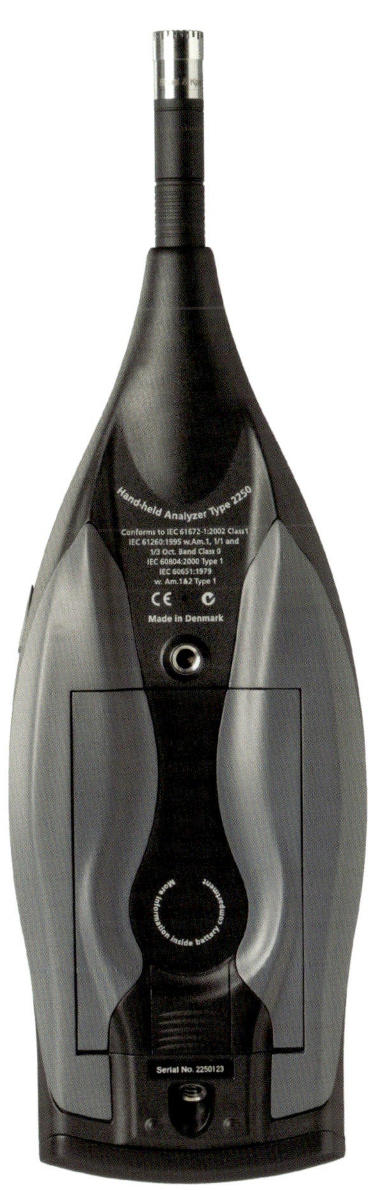

可调式弹性夹，2004

Bessey & Sohn GmbH & Co.,
Bietigheim-Bissingen
Design: Weinberg & Ruf, Filderstadt
www.bessey.de
www.weinberg-ruf.de

这种弹性夹采用活动臂设计，其开口宽度可以无限制地调整。这个特点能够确保即使在很宽的跨度下，夹子仍能握住它并产生恒定的夹力。两个柔性的防滑手柄和垫块使得夹具能够免受损坏，同时这些设计也使它显得更与众不同。柔性的零部件和漂亮的颜色按照清晰的结构设计而呈现出有趣的分布，这使得夹子的使用简便而舒适。

With the movable clamping arm the opening width of the VarioClippix spring clamps is infinitely adjustable. This guarantees good handling even with wide span lengths. A constant clamping force can be obtained with any span length. Soft anti-slip two-component handles and soft pads allow damage-free clamping. The design was intended to create a high recognition factor. Due to the soft components, the result is an interesting colour distribution with a clearly designed structure – the clamps are handled easily and comfortably.

斯蒂尔 TS 700 两用切割机，2005

Andreas Stihl AG & Co. KG, Waiblingen
Design: busse design ulm GmbH
(Michael Tinius), Elchingen
Vertrieb: Stihl Vertriebszentrale
AG & Co. KG, Dieburg
www.stihl.de

斯蒂尔TS 700是一种专门的手控和车载两用切割机。它性能稳定持久，设计建立在人性化服务之上，以用户为导向而设计。斯蒂尔TS 700的外观像锥形一样向前指向切割片。一个大的拱形外壳构成了整个设计的主体，使机器有看起来强劲有力，并且还能从理想的角度监控切割片的工作。

The Stihl TS 700 is a cut-off machine for professional manual and cart use. It is founded on the features performance, durability and service-friendliness, setting standards in user-oriented design. The overall shape of the Stihl TS 700 is conically directed forward toward the wheel. The design is dominated by the large arched cover. This gives the unit a powerful, dynamic feeling and permits an optimised view of the wheel.

斯蒂尔 BR 500 / BR 550 / BR 600 送风机，2005

Andreas Stihl AG & Co. KG, Waiblingen
Design: busse design ulm GmbH
(Sven Schaarschmidt, Michael Tinius),
Elchingen
Vertrieb: Stihl Vertriebszentrale
AG & Co. KG, Dieburg
www.stihl.de

这一送风机系列满足了部分用户日益增长的多方面需求，这些需求主要包括性能、效率、振动、噪音、燃料消耗以及废气排放等。该产品的动力单元外形紧凑，表面凸起的形状使其构成了一个防尘，安全，且在很大程度上独立的单元，使机器运行时的声音洪亮而饱满。送风机的零部件使整体结构看起来清晰而整齐，同时还不失其强大的功能性。

The blower family is designed against the background of increased demands on the part of users with regard to performance, ergonomics, vibrations, noise emission, fuel consumption, and exhaust emissions. The power unit has a compact shape consisting of convex surfaces. Thus it constitutes a largely self-contained unit resistant to dirt and damage, underscoring the pleasantly quiet and sonorous sound of the machine. The appearance is clearly structured due to its components and indicates their functions.

deSIGN 42 信号塔, 2005

WERMA Signaltechnik GmbH + Co. KG, Rietheim-Weilheim
Werksdesign
www.werma.de

高档的机器设计常常需要配备顶级的信号设备。在这个设计紧凑的发光二极管（LED）信号塔的帮助下，两或三种事先确定的状况仅用一个信号装置就可以显示了。当没有主动信号的时候，由于半透明的灯罩没有颜色，信号塔外表显得很“冷”。只有在激活之后，信号灯的颜色才会充满了整个信号塔。该信号灯塔还非常地经济实惠，它的寿命可长达50000个小时，且电力消耗较低，维护容易。由于它远远低于500毫安的开关电流速度，使得信号灯塔可以通过PLC来触发信号装置。

High-class machine designs nowadays demand top-grade signalling equipment. With the aid of this compact-designed LED signal tower two/three predefined conditions can be displayed with just one signal device. When there is no active signal the tower has a "cool" appearance due to the colourless translucent dome. Only upon activation the signal colour appears to be breathed into the tower. Due to its long life cycle of up to 50,000 hours and a low power consumption the signal tower is economically advantageous and maintenance-free. The low switch-on current rate of far below 500mA offers the opportunity of triggering the device via PLC.

WM 海空周转箱, 2004

WM-Logistik GmbH & Co. KG, Bocholt
Werksdesign
Vertrieb: WM-Logistik GmbH & Co. KG, Bocholt
www.wm-group.com

物流领域内的这种设计必须遵循它自身的规则，每一设计步骤都需要考虑到实用性。WM海空周转箱把胶合板、波纹状的硬纸板和新型的金属封装系统结合起来，非常新颖且耐用。节省了大量空间，减轻重量达40%，使其性能达到最优。与此同时，胶合板箱的稳定性和负重能力得到了保证，搬运和处理货物的效率也有所提高。而且该产品造价不高，可循环使用。

The design for the use within logistic services follows its own rules. It deals with functionality of an art in respect of its inevitable processes. With a high level of functionality the WM Sea-Air-Box combines the materials plywood and corrugated cardboard with an innovative metal closure system. While stability and load capacity in relation to plywood boxes are retained, and the efficiency of handling and disposal is increased, economy of space and a weight reduction up to 40 per cent provide an imputed optimisation. The WM Sea-Air-Box is lightweight, low-priced and recyclable.

WSR 1400-PE 手锯

Hilti AG, Schaan, Liechtenstein
Design: Rino Kappler, Lichtensteig, Schweiz
www.hilti.com

WSR 1400-PE是一种用来进行拆迁、建筑和石材贸易的往复式锯。它是根据人体工程学原理进行设计的，把手使用起来轻松方便。该产品采用了崭新的“智能力量（Smart Power）”技术，它包括一个可变动力控制的发动机和一套智能感应系统。当在大负荷下进行快速切割的话，可以将其加大动力达三倍以上，从而保证了对材料能有一个最佳的切割速度；当在较小的负荷下运转时，这种技术也可减小功率，以一个理想的速度进行切割。这样便降低了关键部件的热量，减轻了机器磨损，使其非常结实耐用。

The WSR 1400-PE is a reciprocating saw for demolition, general construction and masonry trades. It is ergonomically designed and allows a good handling. The saw is equipped with the technique Smart Power™ which is an innovation incorporating a motor with variable power control and an intelligent sensing system. When cutting under heavy loads, the WSR 1400-PE maintains the optimum cutting speed for fastest cutting in every material by boosting power to more than 300 per cent when required. Under lighter loads, Smart Power™ keeps the saw running at the same optimum cutting speed requiring less power. This reduces heat and wear on critical parts, creating a very durable system.

WSJ 850-EB, WSJ 850-ET 竖锯, 2004

Hilti AG, Schaan, Liechtenstein
Design: Proform Design
(Stephan Niehaus), Winnenden
www.hilti.com

符合人体工程学原理而设计的手柄，小巧的外形以及合理的开关位置，使得这种竖锯能让工作变得更加舒适。一种新型的夹紧和引导系统使得竖锯能沿着切割线进行精确而垂直的切割。另外，即使连续使用，它也可以顺利地运转，不会产生强烈的震动，令操作者感觉舒适的同时又不耗费体力。一种新型的，可直接附着的灰尘清除模具DRS确保了该竖锯也可以在无尘环境中进行操作，且还能够很好地观察锯刃和切割线的工作情况。这种工具有把手持型（ET）和桶型（EB）两种形式可供选择。

The jigsaws offer a high level of work comfort due to an ergonomic handle, a compact design and optimised switch positions. An innovative clamping and guiding system allows precise and rectangular cutting along the cutting line. The tools are running smoothly without heavier vibrations and are comfortable as well as unexhausting, even in continuous use. An innovative, directly attachable dust removal module DRS allows operation even in dust-sensitive environments and offers a good view of the saw blade and the cutting line. The tools are alternatively available as handle (ET) and as barrel (EB) versions.

TE 16, TE 16-M, TE 16-C
电锤, 2004

Hilti AG, Schaan, Liechtenstein
Design: busse design ulm GmbH (Michael Tinius), Elchingen
www.hilti.com

TE 16、TE 16–M、TE 16–C这一系列产品是根据人体工程学原理设计的小巧的多功能电锤钻。该产品采用先进技术，选材精良，为高水平的工程基础提供了保障。其本身性能稳定可靠，使用持久。对于在中度直径范围内进行一系列的钻锚栓孔而言，TE 16是一种强有力的、能轻松使用的电锤钻。不仅如此，TE 16–M还是一个多功能工具，可以用来锤钻、旋钻、混合、起螺丝以及进行凿破。TE 16–C还可在石材上进行轻型凿破，在混凝土上进行抛光或清理的附加功能。该产品的运用简化了作业流程，可在多种行业工程里作业。

The family TE 16, TE 16-M, TE 16-C are compactly and ergonomically designed multi-functional rotary hammers. They are equipped with advanced technology, high-grade materials and offer a high-level engineering. They allow high performance, reliability and durability. The TE 16 is a powerful yet comfortable rotary hammer for the serial anchor hole drilling in the medium diameter range. The TE 16-M is a multi-functional tool for hammer drilling, rotary drilling, mixing, screwdriving and chiselling. The TE 16-C is equipped with an additional chiselling function for light jobs on masonry and finishing or cleaning up on concrete. The family simplifies the working process and offers a wider range of applications to the tradesman.

TE 706-AVR 錾锤, 2005

Hilti AG, Schaan, Liechtenstein
Design: busse design ulm GmbH (Michael Tinius), Elchingen
www.hilti.com

从机器设计的对称性出发，再加上符合人体工程学原理的设计，TE706–AVR錾锤去除了多余的倾斜力，使其物理震动大大减少。这样，几乎在把手的任何位置进行操作都不会感到太累；减少了原先2/3的震动性能使得机器能够进行长时间的操作，以及（或者）达到机器比较高的日常性能。它的表面温度较低，操作起来很舒适。另外，该凿切锤革新的技术观念就是把无刷电动机和主动充气冷却系统融合到一起，再加上其坚固的构造，共同确保了该机器能够长久使用。

Due to its symmetrical and ergonomic design, additional tilting forces are eliminated with the chiselling hammer TE 706-AVR, resulting in less physical vibrations. Thus, operation in nearly all holding positions is less exhausting; up to 2/3 less vibrations allow a longer operation time and/or significantly higher daily performance. A low surface temperature facilitates comfortable handling. The innovative technical concept of the chiselling hammer TE 706-AVR integrates a brushless motor and a holistic, active pneumatic cooling of the motor. This and a robust construction guarantee a long life cycle.

EVO 角磨机, 2004

C. & E. Fein GmbH, Stuttgart
Design: Henssler und Schultheiss Productdesign, Schwäbisch Gmünd
www.fein.de
www.henssler-schultheiss.de

EVO是一种专业的、带有引导潮流的操作理念的角磨机。它的四个感应触垫使用户在任何工作位置都可以简便毫不费力地开关，再加上符合人体工程学的外形设计，使整台机器操作起来更为舒适。

EVO is an angle grinder for professional use with a trendsetting operational concept. Four sensor touchpads allow for an easy and energy-saving switch-on in all working positions. In combination with a new, ergonomically designed shape of the casing, the operation of the unit has been improved markedly.

Shur-Line Premium Ergonomic 颜料刷, 2004

Shur-Line, St. Francis, USA
Design: Metaphase Design Group, Inc. (Brian Bone, Heath Doty, Bryce Rutter), St. Louis, USA
www.metaphase.com

Shur-Line颜料刷是为专业画家和那些执着于“自己动手”人士而设计的产品系列。这个系列包括三种不同的刷子，处处设计都尽量做到使其性能达到最优化，分别适用于三种不同类型的工作。圆边和手柄处柔性的材料代替了传统颜料刷上那尖锐的拐角和坚硬的金属箍，非常符合人体工程学原理。为了使握着更舒适安全，以及控制更稳定，每个颜料刷上的主要的紧握区都将形状彻底改变并更换了表面材质。塑料箍代替了原来有褶的金属箍，安装并锁定在手柄的中心部位。原来在传统颜料刷的金属箍上是用来将刷毛固定在手柄上的，而现在的新技术使得手柄和刷毛之间进行过渡更加自然平滑，并且使其效果更加立体，还保证了使用者的握刷姿势更加舒适而自然。

Shur-Line paint brushes are a line of premium brushes for the professional painter as well as the serious do-it-yourselfer. The product line includes three different brushes specifically designed to optimise user performance in three different types of painting tasks. Ergonomically round edges and soft materials in the handle replace the sharp corners and hard metal ferrules found on traditional paint brushes. Primary grip zones on each of the brushes are anatomically shaped and textured for superior grip comfort, grip security and brush control. The crimped metal ferrule binding the bristles to the handle on traditional paint brushes was replaced by a plastic ferrule that fits and locks into the core of the handle. This innovation allows for a much smoother transition between handle and bristles and creates a more three-dimensional handle that ensures greater comfort and natural grip postures.

Kärcher KM 70/20 C
手推式清扫车, 2004

Alfred Kärcher GmbH & Co. KG, Winnenden
Werksdesign: Denis Dammköhler
Design: Pearl Creative, Ludwigsburg
www.kaercher.com

KM 70/20 C是一种手推式清扫车，其设计极具实用性和吸引力。它的创新之处在于可以通过方便地调节主滚刷来适应要打扫的表面。手推柄可以根据用户的身高和用户能够伸到的距离来进行调节，另外还有一种双面刷可供选用。通过两个轮子来驱动的结实的金属主滚刷使这款手推式清扫车的操作变得非常容易。动力车由坚固的金属（合成）传动装置来控制，这样在拐角处也能进行很好的直线控制并可继续进行清扫。为了能明确地定位，所有的操纵装置都做成了黄色。除此之外，KM 70/20 C手动式清扫车可以防震并且设有自动保险装置，塑料外壳可回收。

The Kärcher KM 70/20 C is a functionally and attractively designed push sweeper. It is innovative due to the easy adjustment of the main roller brush to suit the surface being swept. The push handle is adjustable to suit the user's height and reach. It is also available in a version with two side brushes. The push sweeper Kärcher KM 70/20 C is easy to operate as the rugged metal main roller brush is driven via the two wheels. The power train is managed with a robust metal/synthetics transmission. This produces good straight-line control and constantly good sweeping results in bends. For easy orientation all controls are yellow. The Kärcher KM 70/20 C is shock-resistant, fail-safe and designed with an one-piece plastic frame which is recyclable.

Parcel Depot 邮递系统, 2005

Siemens AG, L&A PA, Konstanz
Design: designafairs GmbH
(Andreas Preussner), München
www.siemens.com
www.designafairs.com

Parcel Depot是一个占地面积很小的包裹站，它是一个为敦豪全球速递（DHL）提供“第一或最后一英里解决方案”提供24小时服务的系统。每个包裹站被中央系统控制和监管着。对于包裹的安全储存和领取而言，Parcel Depot是一种新的解决方案，因为它简化了用户界面，变得高度的人性化。相信凭借着它那独立的外形、醒目的颜色，能够很容易地被诸如联合包裹公司、法国邮政等欧洲客户所采纳。

The Parcel Depot is a pack station for the Deutsche Post (DHL) and a 24-hour system for the "First/Last Mile Solution" with minimum floor space requirements. Each pack station is centrally controlled and supervised. The Parcel Depot is an innovative solution for safe storage and pickup of packages and parcels, offering a high degree of customer-friendliness due to a simplified user interface. The self-contained and individual colour design can easily be adapted to other European clients (e.g. UPS, French Post).

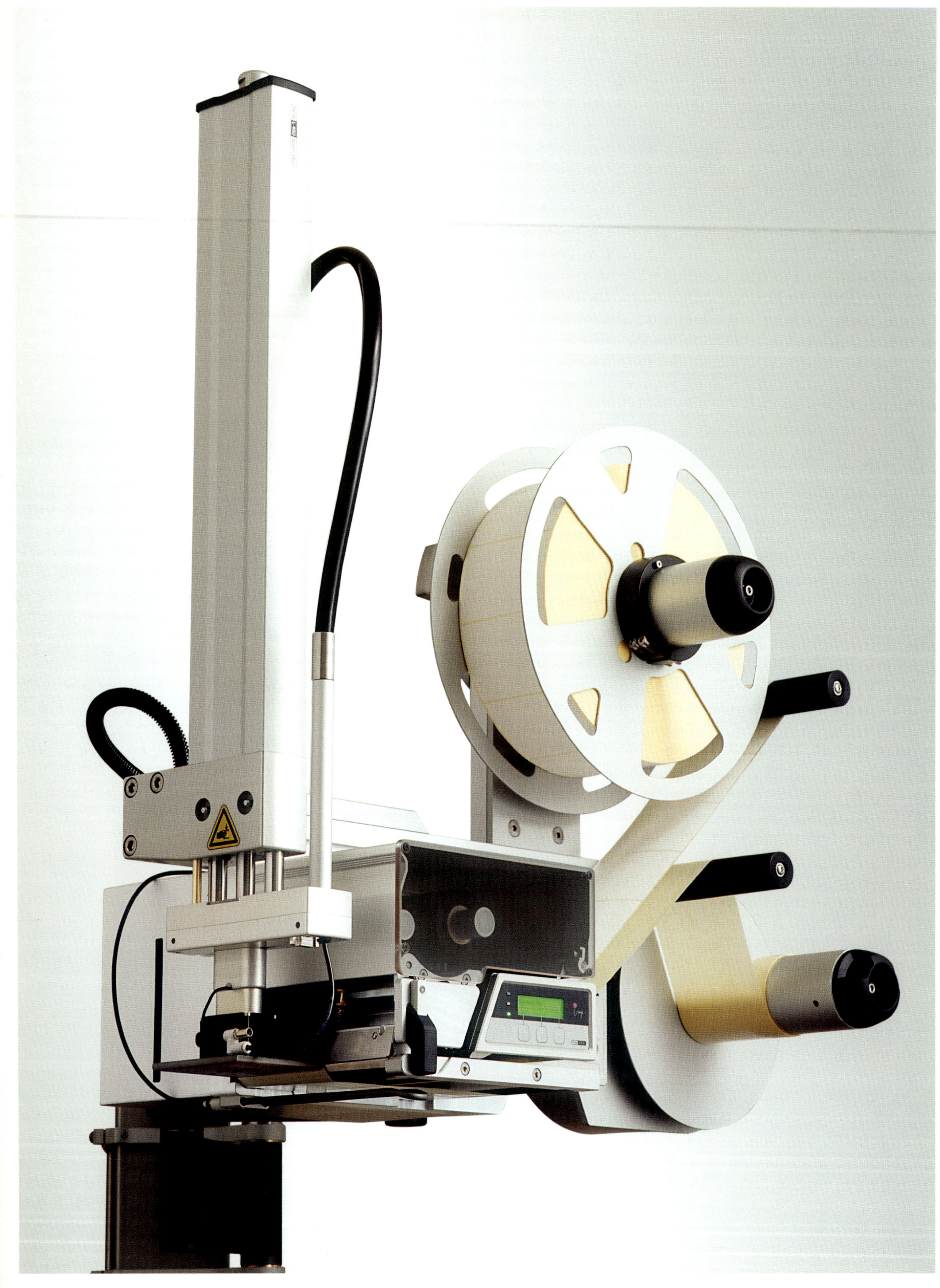

Imaje 2000 系列工业印刷应用系统, 2004

Imaje AB, Göteborg, Schweden
Werksdesign: Jörn Schmoldt
Vertrieb: Imaje GmbH, Stuttgart
www.imaje.com

Imaje 2000系列的设计富有人性化，其主要特点体现在其安装、操作和维护简易，操作成本低。Imaje 2000系列的模块化结构使其能满足各种个性化生产要求，即使竖直安装也能如同水平安装一样稳定运行。不同的模块可根据不同的需要进行简易组合，这一设计加上所采用的高质量材质，确保了2000系列能够在工业环境下进行长时间的稳定运转。由于其灵活紧凑的设计，2000系列能够方便地集成在任何生产线上。此外，该系统的软件所提供的网络服务也使安装和升级可以随时随地轻松完成。

The Imaje 2000 labelling system is designed user-friendly. Key features of the unit are easy installation, operation and maintenance, resulting in low operational costs. The modular construction of the system allows an adaptation and installation of the unit to the respective production requirements in a vertical as well as horizontal arrangement. The different modules can easily be exchanged or supplemented. This and the use of high-quality materials guarantee a long life cycle and an environmentally sound operation. Due to its compact design, the unit can be integrated into any production line without any problems. The system software provided and an integrated web server allow an easy installation and system update in any location.

WSE 激光雕刻系统, 2004

Tampoprint AG, Korntal-Münchingen
Design: bgp design Stuttgart
(Stefan Grobe, Knut Braake)
www.tampoprint.de
www.bgp-design.com

WSE是一种模块化激光系统，用于进行铭刻和对各种各样的塑料、金属、玻璃以及陶器零件进行精加工。这种激光系统也可以给手机、汽车驾驶舱、工具或医疗器械进行表面抛光处理。作为同类产品中，也是同性能的产品中体积最小的一款，它可为多样化的焦距和结构型号提供高度集成的模块化系统理念。通过中心支持结构，它的三个小工作舱、防护罩和控制单元能够以不同的组合方式连接起来。WSE系统配备有发动机驱动的防护罩，使工作室的操作安全而舒适。打开该产品，其外壳就会沿着环形路径向后退。该产品创新性的技术特征反映在其动感的外形上，这表明了当代人们在对产品的设计方面，提出了越来越高的要求。

The WSE is a modular laser system for applying inscriptions and for refinement of the most diverse plastic, metal, glass or ceramic parts. Cell phones, automobile cockpits, tools or medicine devices are surface-finished with the help of this laser system. Being the smallest laser system of its kind and performance level, the WSE workstation offers a highly integrated modular system concept for the most diverse focal distances and construction unit sizes. The three components work chamber, protection hood and control unit can be connected in different combinations via the central support structure. With its motor-driven protection hood, the work chamber allows secure and comfortable operation. When opening the unit, the cover retreats backwards on a circular path. The innovative technical character of the unit is reflected in the dynamic outer appearance, pointing out the higher demands, with regard to design, for investment goods.

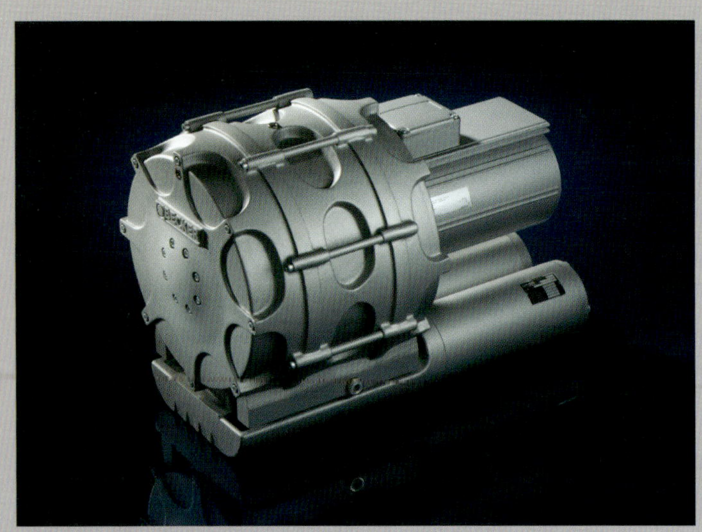

SVw 190/380 鼓风机模块, 2004

Gebr. Becker GmbH & Co. KG, Wuppertal
Werksdesign: Martin Becker, Ulrich Wilkesmann, Carldieter Hollmann, Dirk Schäfer
Design: André Kunzendorf, Wuppertal
www.becker-international.com

SVw 190/380鼓风机模块的创新之处就是所有零件的集成水制冷工作。这样，鼓风机就不用再依赖于直接的冷却空气，而是即使在温暖或有灰尘的环境下，也能够融入到专用机床中的任何位置。该产品几乎恒温的压缩过程使冷空气能够进入或排出，显著地提高了工作效率。可以说，这种模块化设计极大满足并适应了对机器在性能方面的要求。

The innovative aspect of the blower module SVw 190/380 is an integrated water cooling of all components. Thus, the blower does not depend on direct cooling air anymore and can be integrated anywhere in production machines, even in a warm and/or dusty environment. Its near isothermal compression provides a cool air inlet/outlet and increases the efficiency markedly. The modular construction can adapt to and meet additional demands with regard to performance.

CX1000 模块化工业电脑

Beckhoff Industrie Elektronik, Verl
Design: Design AG (Frank Greiser), Rheda-Wiedenbrück
www.beckhoff.de
www.design-ag.de

CX1000是一种紧凑的工业电脑，是为在标准轨道控制柜中使用而设计的。由于其为标准化结构，所有零件根据所需功能而聚合在一起。电源模块能够通过不同的处理器、各种接口模块与CPU模块连接起来，例如对于显示器而言，有多种不同的现场总线系统、DVI、USB、RS232等等。接口模块设计得较低，由于所有接口线相连接，就算是最小的控制柜也能使用。

The CX1000 is an Industrial PC in a very compact housing, designed for use in the control cabinet on a standard rail. Due to its modular construction, the components are plugged together depending on the required function. The power supply module can be combined with CPU modules with different processors, and various interface modules, e.g. for displays, such as various fieldbus systems, DVI, USB, RS232, etc. The interface modules are built with a lower height. With all connected interface cables the smallest control cabinets can be used.

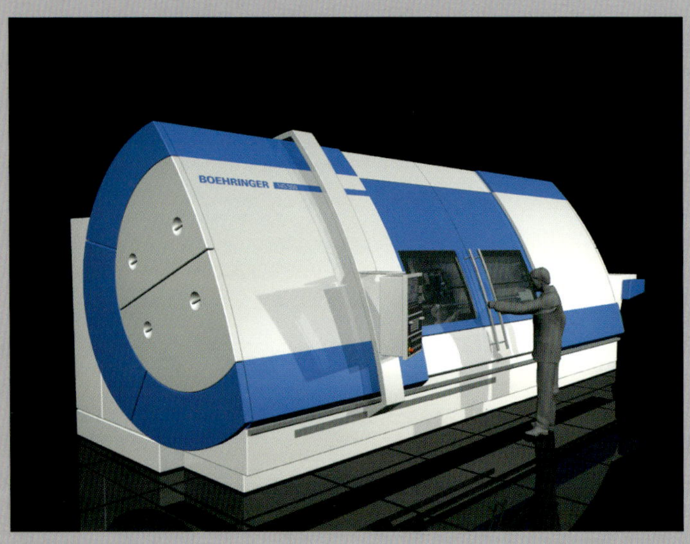

NG 400 CNC-车床, 2004

Boehringer Werkzeugmaschinen Vertriebsgesellschaft mbH, Göppingen
Design: Hartmann + Hartmann GmbH, Augsburg
www.boehringer-werkzeugmaschinen.de
www.hartmannundhartmann.com

CNC NG400车床是一个由三部分组成的系列中的一个产品。在统一的视觉表现方面，该系列被看作是统一的模块化设计系统。NG400车床的设计体现了人性化的设计特点，且外形也非常美观大方，被用来生产特殊用途的机器以及造船。在它的整体性设计中，前部的设计突出了创新机器的概念；向后的斜面和拱形表面令NG400车床看起来更小巧，也方便了起重机从顶部就可以装卸。

The CNC lathe NG 400 is part of a three-part product line conceived in a unified visual language as modular construction system. Fields of application of the user-friendly and aesthetically designed NG 400 are the manufacturing of special-purpose machines as well as shipbuilding. Due to an integrated functionality, the front design underscores the innovative machine concept. The backward-sloped and arched surface makes the NG 400 appear smaller, allowing for crane loading from the top.

SmartTest 多功能检漏仪, 2005

Pfeiffer Vacuum Technology AG, Asslar
Design: Tesign (Christian Bunse, Prof. Georg Teodorescu), Lohmar
www.pfeiffer-vacuum.net

SmartTest多功能测漏仪设计美观，是一种性能优秀的多功能测漏仪。它可以快速而可靠地达到入口压力最高为25毫巴，最小可检测率为5×10^{-12}毫巴，同时还还具有很短的恢复时间。接口的广泛选择性使其能很容易与其它机器进行集成化处理。测漏仪设计坚固，维护简单，从而降低了用户的成本。

The aesthetically designed SmartTest is a high-performance and heavy-duty tool for leak detection. It offers quick and reliable results at a maximum intake pressure of 25mbar and a minimum detectable leak rate of 5×10^{-12}mbar l/s as well as a short recovery time. A broad selection of interfaces allows easy integration. A sturdy construction and minimal service efforts result in reduced costs for the user.

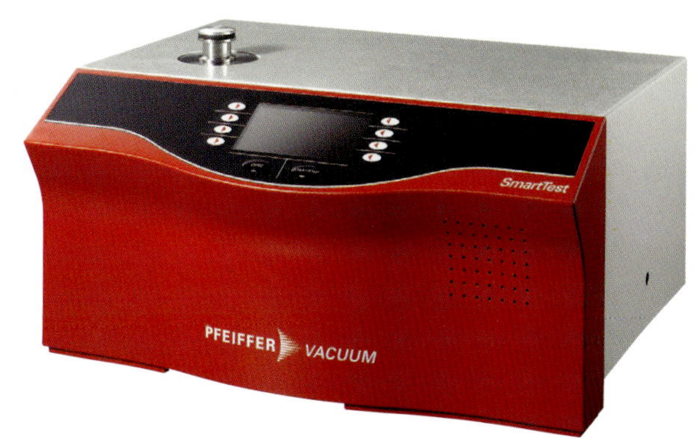

WoodEye 木材扫描器, 2003

Innovativ Vision AB, Linköping, Schweden
Design: Björn-Åke Sköld, Norrköping, Schweden
Vertrieb: WoodEye Scannersysteme GmbH, Siegen
www.woodeye.se

WoodEye是一个先进的成像系统，能在最快的生产速度下测量、检查和改进已刨好的木材。其设计力求融简单化、灵活性以及人体工程学原理于一体。这种设计简化了构造、操作、清洗和维护工作程序，其轻便的外壳很容易进行拆卸及调节，使其能很好地为人们提供服务。

WoodEye is an advanced imaging system for measuring, inspecting and optimising sawn and planed timber – at full production speed. Simplicity, flexibility and ergonomics are the main objectives of the design concept. The WoodEye design simplifies configuration, operation, cleaning and maintenance. The lightweight casings are easy to detach, providing good access for service or readjustment.

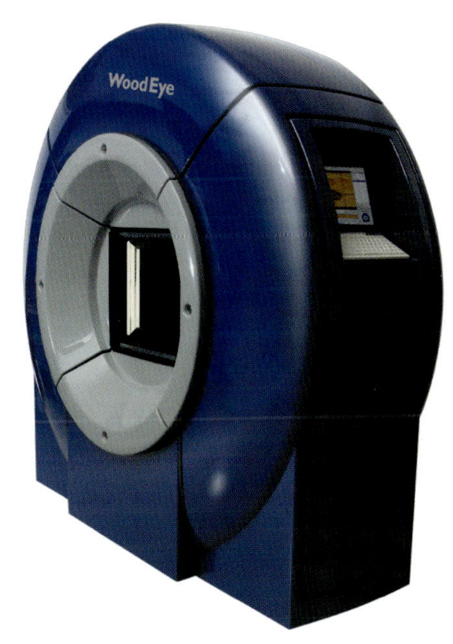

DeltaSol A 太阳能装置电子控制装置, 2005

Resol GmbH, Hattingen
Design: rosenthal design (Christian Marx), Essen
www.resol.de
rdesign91@aol.com

DeltaSol A是一种电子控制装置，是为在非洲或拉丁美洲使用简单太阳能加热设备而设计的。有时，这些加热设备没有遮盖或者是应对恶劣环境的防护装置，这也正是该产品应该设计得简单而坚固的原因。从该产品的圆形机身就能表现出上述特征。

DeltaSol A is an electronic control device for simple solar heating equipment used in Africa or Latin America. Sometimes those installations have no roof or protection against the environment. That is the reason why the product should be kept simple and robust. The round housing of this device should illustrate the product features.

Thermoformer B 1880
密封包装机, 2005

Uhlmann Pac-Systeme GmbH & Co. KG,
Laupheim
Design: Starczewski Design Team, Ulm
www.uhlmann.de
www.starczewski-design.de

B1880热成型机是一种用于塑型、加料和密封泡罩的高速系统（高速生产：1300个/分钟）。这种机器在设计时考虑到了用户的高质量要求，并且把外形设计、人体工程学、安全性能与经济性等要素结合在了一起。创新地利用覆面理念可彻底防止噪音，设计得很人性化。防护门是由着色的锻压玻璃制成的，这种玻璃既可防刮伤，也不易震碎。仪表盘上的滑动和关闭装置能保证方便地得到所有的聚合体。机器框架中装有不锈钢衬条和媒体装置，这种设计符合药品制造的要求，并便于对机器进行清洗，也保证了空气的清洁。

The thermoformer B 1880 is the fastest system for forming, filling and sealing of blisters (high-speed production: 1,300 blisters/min). The machine design visualises the high quality demands of the company and combines form, ergonomics, safety at work and economical viewpoints. The innovative cladding concept results in complete noise protection and user-friendliness. The protective doors are made of tinted laminated glass that is scratch-resistant and splinter-proof. The sliding and closing mechanism of the panels guarantees optimum and easy access to all aggregates. The pharmaceutical-compliant design with stainless steel lining and media installations in the machine frame facilitates easy cleaning and guarantees a clean room atmosphere.

Temo 舵柄头, 2004

Gebrüder Frei GmbH & Co., Albstadt
Design: reform design
(Mathias Wagner), Stuttgart
www.frei.de
www.reform-design.de

Temo舵柄头能够与另外的控制装置组装在一起，例如按钮、摇臂式开关和模拟开关等，而较低部位可以与显示器、键盘和主开关安装在一起。这样，用于电力驱动车的Temo转向装置就使用户在使用时感到非常舒适，并有可能投入大规模生产。Temo舵柄头以其独特的设计，可与不同厂商不同品牌的产品的视觉语言相呼应。

The Temo tiller head can be fitted with additional control elements such as buttons, rocker switches and analogue actuators. The lower section can be fitted with a display, keypad and key switch. As a result, the Temo steering unit for electrically driven vehicles provides high user comfort and considerable possibilities for mass production. Temo can be easily integrated with the visual language of different manufacturers and brands.

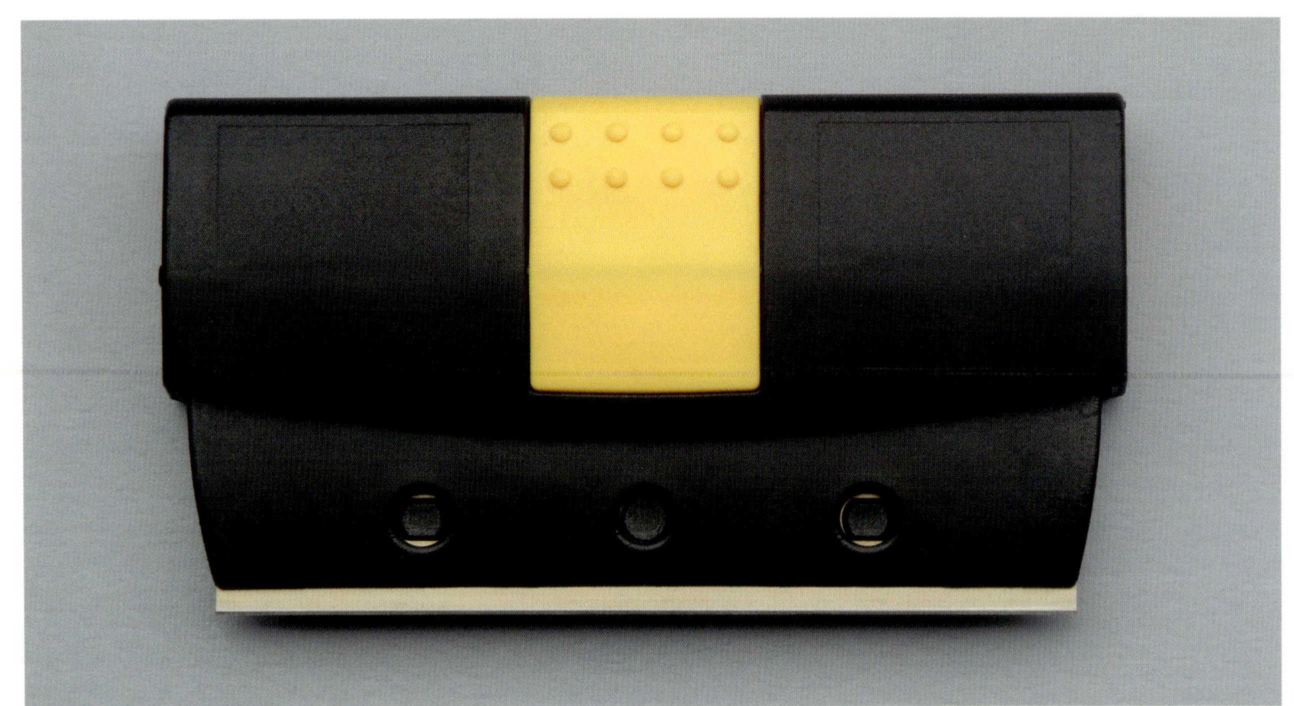

VERMOP®

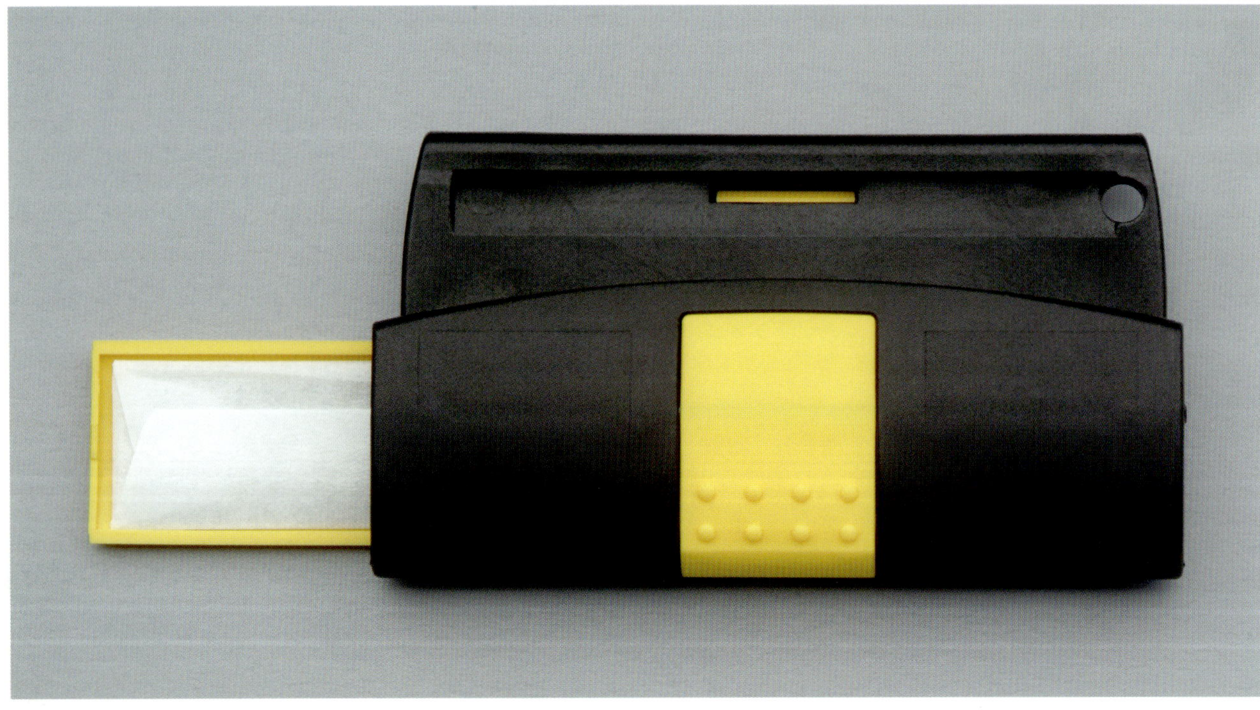

Glassman专业窗户清洁器, 2004

Vermop Salmon GmbH, Wertheim
Design: Ottenwälder und Ottenwälder, Schwäbisch Gmünd
www.vermop.de
www.ottenwaelder.de

Glassman专业窗户清洁器是专业擦窗工具系列中的一个不可缺少的部分，即使在很高的地方也能快速、安全、有效地使用。该产品操作简单，无论是清洁建筑物的内部还是外部，Glassman窗户清洁器都能够快速、方便地打开，当清洁完成后轻易地闭合。再加上一个伸长的手握接合器（同样也是伸缩杆），使得清洁工作能在特殊条件下继续进行，如在很高的建筑物上作业，或是在需要跨过不能承受一个人重量的区域里作业时，它都能派上大用场。

The Glassman window scraper is an inherent part of the working equipment of professional window cleaning teams and allows a fast, secure and efficient handling even in high places. It is designed in a quite self-explanatory manner. When cleaning interior and exterior façades, the scraper can be opened, applied, cleaned and closed swiftly and easily. A functional, extended grip adapter, also being used as attachment for the telescope bar, allows protracted work even at great heights or across areas that will not bear a person's weight.

技术变革和移动性的令人兴奋的路径
Technological innovations and exciting paths of mobility

现代交通都采取什么样的形式呢？对于评委，肯尼斯·格兰奇，奥杜·克洛斯和裘连诺·莫利那瑞而言，红点设计奖，即产品设计是一个几近完美的有力的平台，因为在这里既可以提出问题，并且可以从产品中找到答案。评委会发现汽车的设计标准尤其高。对于新技术和实用性等的问题已经找到了创新性的答案，而且为了寻找这些技术的新的应用领域的试验已经开始了。汽车的范围是多样化的：一些车型是现代的，没有过多地宣扬传统，或者可以说是在每个认为合适的界定范围里和深入调查的目标群体中是清晰的，其它的则仍在寻找清晰的形式来表现。评委们发现其它机动车的设计类型也同样很吸引人，他们尤其对于公共汽车和摩托车感兴趣，它们是集美观与功能性于一身，让人印象深刻。用一个同样高的标准就能将另外一种交通方式区别出来；例如，在设计的卓越性上，轮船就是一个重要例子。这些都让评委会推测到：在未来的交通运输领域的发展趋势中，对设计的追求也将迅速兴起。

What forms does contemporary mobility take? *For the jurors Kenneth Grange, Odo Klose and Giuliano Molineri the red dot award: product design is a well-nigh perfect vantage point from which both to pose such questions and to find the answers stated in the products. The jury found the design standard of the automobiles especially to be extremely high. Innovative answers were being offered to questions of new technologies and functionality, and experimentation was being stimulated by the search for new areas of application for these technologies. The spectrum of automobiles is diverse: while some models are clear, no-frills avowals of tradition or in every regard "suitable" for a clearly defined and well-researched target group, others still seek a clear language of forms. The jurors found the design of other vehicle types to be equally interesting, and were particularly taken by the shapes of the buses and motorbikes, for instance, whose aesthetic couples the appropriate with the impressive. A similarly high standard distinguished the other transport means; a ship, for example, offered a prime example of design excellence. These impressions led the jury to speculate that these areas of human mobility may well usher in future trends for design in general.*

奥杜・克洛斯
Odo Klose
德国
Deutschland

肯尼斯・格兰奇
Kenneth Grange
英国
Großbritannien

裘连诺・莫利那瑞
Giuliano Molineri
意大利
Italien

交通
Transports

欧宝 Astra GTC, 2005

Adam Opel AG, Rüsselsheim
Werksdesign
www.opel.com

和其他的欧宝Astra车型一样，欧宝Astra GTC的设计是强劲动力和情感的和谐结合，这种风格也以非常一致的方式在这款车型上得到了延续。除了车篷和前面的保险杠之外，整个车身都是重新设计的，特别值得强调的是前面玻璃延伸超出了现在的位置，一直延伸到了车顶的前部，这种设计就算是一个新特色了，这样使得驾车的感觉就像坐在飞机驾驶舱里一样。欧宝Astra GTC并不仅仅是这个小巧车型系列中的另一款三门式车型，相反，它是一款单独的功能齐备的车型，体现出了 种极大地创新。

Like the other Opel Astra models, the design of the Opel Astra GTC is a harmonious blend of powerful dynamics and strong emotions. This potency has been adapted and continued with this model in a most consistent manner. Apart from the hood and front fenders, all body parts have been newly designed; a special highlight is the realisation of a front windscreen extending beyond the actual screen position far into the front portion of the roof. This design feature is offered as an additional option. The result is a driving sensation like being in an aircraft cockpit. The Opel Astra GTC is not just another three-door version of a compact car series; rather it is an independent, self-contained and innovative model version.

GG TC 980

梅塞德斯 – 奔驰 B-Klasse, 2005

DaimlerChrysler AG, Stuttgart
Werksdesign: DaimlerChrysler AG, Bereich Design, Sindelfingen
Vertrieb: DaimlerChrysler Vertriebsorganisation Deutschland, Berlin
www.mercedes.com

小型运动旅行车是为满足用户对杰出的设计质量和具有代表性的外观及性能的要求而专门设计的，这款汽车同时适用于工作、家庭、休闲娱乐等场合。由于它的发动机和传动装置是按照“三明治理念”进行安装的：部分在前面，部分在乘坐厢的下面，因此尽管其外形设计紧凑，该新式旅行轿车还是提供了像大型的豪华旅行车一样的内部空间。外观紧凑的“Vision B”和“Vision R”(大型)在视觉语言上表现是一致的：车前脸处三条横穿过的散热隔栅上镶嵌了奔驰的星形标志，它们一起构成了奔驰跑车系列视觉外观上的主体。镀铬的车体前身水平延伸上去，使其看起来非常宽敞而且坚固。这种设计也恰恰象征了该车的一些特性，彰显出力量、统治、动力等因素。前身有一个设计得很精细但又很明显的箭形刷子，加上保险杠里的大型输气管更加深了它的视觉印象。力量感十足的车身两翼线条设计显示出向前的强劲动力；与此同时，车的后部也设计得宽阔而又平坦。

The Sports Tourer is the answer to requests for an automobile with outstanding design qualities and representative character, suitable for family, leisure time and occupation likewise. Due to an arrangement of engine and transmission according to the "sandwich concept", partially in front of, partially under the passenger compartment, the modern touring car offers the space of larger limousines and estates cars despite compact exterior dimensions. The Compact Sports Tourer "Vision B" shares its visual language with the "Vision R" model: a front grill with three cross fins and the integrated Mercedes star. The sportive Mercedes-Benz front grill with central star dominates the overall appearance. Horizontally stretched profiles, decorated with high-quality chrome applications, give the front section a wide and very strong appearance. The design thus symbolises attributes such as strength, sovereignty and motivation. A discreet but highly visible arrow-shaped sweep of the front section and large air ducts in the bumper lining enhance this optical impression even further. The line management of the side section with powerful shoulders shows a strong forward urge. The rear is characterised by broad and flat proportions.

R 1200 GS 摩托车

BMW Group, München
Werksdesign: Designteam der BMW Group / Designteam Motorrad
www.bmw.com

R 1200 GS遵循了所有宝马摩托车的传统，即通过设计和自身所展现出来的视觉特征，来展示它创新的设计以及其机器的独到之处。该车型的外形特别，能让你即使在远处，也能一眼分辨出来。宝马GS的前保护杠与车身设计、不规则前灯及后座下面的行李架相和谐地融合在一起。与上一代更轻便、马力更大的车型相比，紧凑的表面，小巧的燃料罐以及轻便的外壳，都突出了它更是一款运动性能突出的摩托车。后架和后轮胎之间的透明处理，以及转向杆后面壳上的小孔设计都使整个车身重量大大减轻。

The R 1200 GS follows the tradition of all BMW motorcycles, displaying its unique and innovative engineering as well as the special features of the machine by way of design and its own individual visual character. This model has an unmistakable silhouette, visible even from a distance, and immediately recognisable as a BMW GS with the front fender "beak" integrated into the bodywork, the asymmetric headlight unit and the luggage rack under the pillion seat. The sportier character of this motorcycle, compared to its predecessor less weight, more horsepower –, is accentuated by its tauter surfaces, a narrower fuel tank and a visually accentuated lightness. The transparency between rear frame and rear tyre, as well as the hole in the rear housing of the swing arm, visually support the considerable weight reduction.

宝马 5er 旅行车

BMW Group, München
Werksdesign:
Designteam der BMW Group
www.bmw.com

宝马5系列旅行车使新的宝马5系列作为一个整体变得更加完美，它将运动性能、舒适度、宽敞的空间及实用性功能这些特征最大程度地结合在了一起。智能轻便技术采用铝或钢制造车身，可使汽车空间更大而重量却更轻。这样，这种新的豪华轿车就成了商务、家庭和休闲的最佳伙伴。不管作为标准装备还是作为选择之一，这一旅行车系列的出现都使技术和安全特征得到了足够的重视。同时，这一车型还具备一下这些功能，如自动操控、动力驱动、向上倾的显示器以及可调节的前灯等。与上一代车型相比，它的后背箱盖是全自动的，这使这款新车型的行李箱操作更容易，也提供了更大的存储空间。

The BMW 5 Series Touring is rounding off the new BMW 5 Series as a whole, providing a supreme blend of sporting performance, refined comfort, spacious dimensions and practical function all in one. Intelligent lightweight technology with an aluminium/steel bodyshell means more space and lower weight. This elegant new car is therefore an ideal partner for business, family, and leisure time. Either as standard equipment or as an option, the Touring comes with all the highlights in technology and safety features boasted by the new innovative BMW 5 Series Sedan, such as Active Steering, Dynamic Drive, Head-up Display as well as Adaptive Headlights. And in comparison with its predecessor, the new model offers a much larger and even more variable luggage compartment with convenient access thanks to automatic operation of the tailgate.

大众高尔夫 Plus, 2005

Volkswagen AG, Wolfsburg
Werksdesign
www.volkswagen.com

“高尔夫Plus”填补了经典高尔夫和途安之间的空白。该车秉承了高尔夫系列一贯的风格，拥有倾斜的发动机盖，狭长的车顶及垂直下降的尾部，都使这一车型变得与众不同。由于其挡风玻璃的位置较高，而使其发动机盖、挡风玻璃和车顶之间的连接更加变得平滑起来。车顶曲线微微下降，一直延伸到了尾部，勾勒出了整车的线条。它的内部设计也遵循了高尔夫系列的哲学，即在现有的外形和设计下，做到最大化的实用。和谐的理念以及构造中极富情感性的因素，使高尔夫Plus用它特有的设计创造出了一种独立的形象，它也是对经典高尔夫理念独特的诠释。

The Golf Plus fills the gap between the classic Golf and the Touran. The characteristic silhouette shows that it belongs to the Golf family with its sloping bonnet, the long roof and the very steep rear, except that the transition between bonnet, windscreen and roof is even smoother due to the higher windscreen position. These contours are continued with a bold roof curving gently to the rear. The interior design also follows the Golf philosophy of achieving a high level of functionality in a contemporary shape and design. Harmonious in concept and with considerably emotive components in its structure, the Golf Plus creates a self-contained image with all of its design features and is therefore a completely unique interpretation of the timeless Golf idea.

奥迪 A6, 2003

Audi AG, Ingolstadt
Werksdesign: Audi Design Team
www.audi.com

Audi A6的外观设计非常流畅。关键因素就在于奥迪车常用的装有侧输气管的单幅格栅。从侧面看，三条线很自然地勾勒了车身的线条。与车窗齐平的动力线很自然地延伸到车尾，这样使人们觉得A6即使是在静止的时候都有一种向前的动力。双人小汽车式车顶弧线与突出的肩线相结合，为全车打造了一种动力感十足的形象。肩线反过来在突出的扰流器边缘结束，这样即使汽车在高速运行的时候也能达到最大的稳定性。同样，A6的内部设计也给人一种加速的印象，所有的细节都带给人一种动感，更加突出了A6新的动力品质。正如奥迪新的外观代表了A6的产品创新一样，以驾驶者为导向的驾驶室内设计也代表着其内部的创新。

The exterior of the Audi A6 yields the impression of flowing elegance. An essential element is the single-frame grill with lateral air ducts. In the side view, three lines clearly define the car body. The dynamic line at sill level, gently rising to the rear, creates the impression of a forward urge of the A6 even when the car is stationary. The coupé-like roof line provides additional thrust, creating an extremely dynamic profile in conjunction with the prominent shoulder line. The shoulder line in turn ends in a prominent spoiler edge contributing to maximum stability even at high speed. The interior of the Audi A6 creates an impression of acceleration. All details have acquired a sense of motion, accentuated with a quality of dynamism new for Audi. Just as the new external face symbolises the product innovation of the new A6, so does the driver-oriented cockpit symbolise the interior.

BV2S 滑雪头盔, 2004

Bombardier Recreational Products Inc., Valcourt, Kanada
Werksdesign: BRP Design Team
www.brp.com

BV2S是一种为在极端的情况下使用而设计的滑雪头盔。它可以说是代表了迄今为止对于一个长期的设计难题的最好的解决方法：那便是在一个滑雪者可能遇到的最坏的天气状况情况下，怎样在高速滑行时既要呼吸，同时又能保持完全清晰的视野。

The BV2S is a snowmobile helmet designed for particularly extreme conditions. It is innovative in that it represents the best approach so far at tackling the double problem of breathing out and, at the same time, maintaining a crystal clear visual field while travelling at speed under the worst possible weather conditions a snowmobiler can encounter.

Sea-Doo RXP 私人游艇, 2004

Bombardier Recreational Products Inc., Valcourt, Kanada
Bombardier Recreational Products Inc., Cogan Lake, USA
Werksdesign: BRP Design Team
www.brp.com

Sea-Doo RXP私人游艇的设计背景经历了一个大的转变，着眼于开辟一个水上的新乐园。著名的Sea-Doo RXP游艇的外形在经过一段时间的构思后进行了改良。Sea-Doo RXP游艇配备有动力强劲、低噪音的四缸发动机，从而确保了驾驶者能拥有纯粹的水上驾驶乐趣。

The background to the design of the Sea-Doo RXP is a paradigm shift breaking new ground for fun on the water with this personal watercraft. The shape of the well-known Sea-Doo has been refined and conceived in a new unit of time. The Sea-Doo RXP watercraft is equipped with a powerful and environmentally sound four-cycle engine guaranteeing pure driving fun.

WF3000 系列可升降式码垛推车，2004

Crown Equipment Corporation,
New Bremen, USA
Werksdesign: Mike Gallagher
Vertrieb: Crown Gabelstapler GmbH & Co. KG, München
www.crown.com

WF3000是一种用途广泛的多功能可升降码垛推车，它的应用范围很广泛，例如用于小而拥挤的货仓、零售地点和生产地点等。该设计的目的就是要生产出一种非常坚固、紧凑、可移动的推车，便于使用，并且富有人性化和吸引力。液体形成的拱状的动力装置顶盖是圆形的，与流线型设计的较低装置相结合，传达了一种有力量和友好的感觉。新型的X 10™手柄保证了仅仅用一只手就可以很舒适地控制一切主要功能（如抬升，驱动，示警信号等），提高了操作的舒适度和效率，更易控制。这样一来，操作杆能够快速地执行所有的工作顺序，而不被打断或者进行令人厌烦的启动及停止之间的转换。另外，将示警信号开关集中到了手柄上也十分具有新意。

The WF3000 is a versatile stacker lift truck for a wide range of applications such as small-crowded warehouses, retail and manufacturing facilities. The design objective was to create a very robust, compact and manoeuvrable truck that is easy to use, friendly and inviting as well. The rounded design of the hydro-formed and arched power unit cover, combined with the flowing lines of the lower unit, communicates a sense of strength as well as friendliness. An innovative X10™ handle allows control of all primary functions (lifting, driving, signal horn) comfortably with one single hand, enhancing comfort, control and efficiency. Thus, the operator can swiftly perform all task sequences without interruptive and annoying start/stop transitions. Innovative as well are the signal horn switches integrated into the handles.

尼奥普兰星际线超级长途客车，2004

NEOMAN Bus GmbH, Stuttgart
Werksdesign: Andrea Lipp,
Michael Streicher, Achim Burmeister
www.neoplan.de

星际线是一种高级大型客车，在技术、设计以及安全性方面在可谓是长途客车中的顶级。立体的外形设计以外科医生手中的手术刀一般地精细方式，仔细地去除了一切多余的棱角，形成了一种独特的像雕塑一般的车体，这样的车身流露出勃勃生机，自然而然地传达出一种自信。车体外部视觉表现向前一直延伸到车厢内，传达出一种与众不同的空间体验。

The Starliner is a premium-class coach ranging at the top of the travel coach segment in terms of technology, design and safety. In "surgeon-like manner" the exterior cubic shape has been carefully reduced of any unnecessary or excess angular corners. Simply everything not needed in the usual cube shape has been cut away. The result is a sculpture-like body with quite unique proportions. The punchy and expressive front exudes self-confidence. The basic visual language of the exterior is carried forward into the passenger compartment, conveying an outstanding spatial experience.

尼奥普兰 Trendliner 客车，2004

NEOMAN Bus GmbH, Stuttgart
Werksdesign: Andrea Lipp,
Michael Streicher, Achim Burmeister,
Stephan Schönherr, Sven Gaedtke
www.neoplan.de

Trendliner客车既可以用来进行长途旅游，也可做短途游，同时也可用做通勤的班车。车头的设计使其给人一种大胆而自信的印象，流线形设计传达出一种强劲的动力感。另外，它的精密的底盘架上还配备了EBS电气刹车系统，也可选配ESP电子稳定装置。

The Trendliner travel coach is conceived as an overland bus with universal features for tours and excursions as well as for meeting the demands of commuter traffic. The design of the front gives the coach a bold self-confident impression; the line management conveys powerful dynamism. The Trendliner features a sophisticated chassis frame equipped with EBS (Electro-Pneumatic Braking System) and optionally with ESP (Electronic Stability Programme).

MAN Lion's Regio 客车，2004

NEOMAN Bus GmbH, Salzgitter
Werksdesign: Stephan Schönherr,
Sven Gaedtke, Britta Hachenberg,
Kenan Erdinc, Firat Arnt, Thoralf Keipert,
Andrea Lipp, Michael Streicher,
Achim Burmeister
www.man-mn.com

Lion's Regio客车系列的理念就是进行模块化设计，为乘客提供更大的空间舒适度。现今及上一代的汽车都以新的方式适应或是诠释了它的风格，并且使之成为设计中的实质性部分。在MAN combi和旅行客车系列中，传统和连续性结合在了一起。整个设计都显现出一种整体的视觉表现力，赋予该高科技产品一种友好而协调的印象。

The concept of the Lion's Regio combi bus family is structured modularly, offering more spatial comfort. Style elements of both the current and the previous bus generation have been adapted or interpreted newly and become part of the design basics. They combine tradition and continuity in the MAN combi and travel coach family. The holistic visual language consistently permeates the entire design, giving the high-tech product a friendly harmonious impression.

Nacos XX-5 船用驾驶台, 2004

Sam-Electronics GmbH, Hamburg
Design: müller/romca Industrial Design (Martin Jahnke), Hamburg
www.sam-electronics.de
www.muellerromca.de

Nacos系列的重新设计涵盖了13个模块，包括不同型号、键盘、插口、和基座的监测器。另外，还设计了各种各样的附件，例如太阳罩、控制球、旋转安装的监测器等。模块化的设计减少了储存和生产成本，并且形成了Nacos产品的统一的外形。在所有前控制面板上都有不显眼的、平滑而宽敞的部分。这样，用户的焦点就集中在了设备的界面上了。将金属片零件的大半径和塑料机身连接起来就形成了一个舒适且非常实用的界面。这种机身满足了在船上因海浪颠簸而所需的高操作要求，同时也满足了ISO8468关于船用驾驶台的结构和设备的专业要求。

The redesign of the Nacos product line covers 13 modules including monitors of different sizes, keyboards, socket and base. In addition, various accessories have been designed such as sun visor, trackball and swivel-mounted monitor. The modularity reduces storage- and production costs and gives Nacos devices their overall appearance. All front panels have unobtrusive, smooth and generous proportions. Thus, the focus of the user is concentrated on the equipment interface. The connection of large radii of the sheet metal components and plastic housing elements results in a comfortable high-value interface. The housings meet the high operational demands on board of a ship, caused by swell, and also meet the specific requirements of ISO 8468 about the structuring and equipment of ship bridges.

为感官而设计——卫生间里的新品质及舒适系列产品

Design for the senses – new qualities in the bathroom and wellness range

在“卫生间、供暖、卫生清洁设备和空调”系列中，**应用了新型材料的新产品触感良好**，尤其是体现在了浴缸的设计上。这一切都正在对卫浴产品重新进行一种有趣的诠释。同样，这种趋势也迎合了用户的要求，因为在浴室里，人们可以尽情地放松自己并恢复体力。评委弗朗塞斯科·米拉尼，沃弗岗·K·梅尔–哈兹和朗·纳巴罗强调说，卫生间的设计，对于人体的七种感官而言，都是非常具有吸引力和令人愉悦的，所以这对于设计者来说，也是一项永不停止的任务。这些新产品在设计上如此地追寻简约，朴素地几乎与外表粗糙的材料一样，而在感官上，却是令人愉悦的。但这种大方的设计也扩展了卫生间的空间。简约的外形，实用的性能与整体风格达成了一致，因此它们能够以一种和谐的比例，毫不费力地适应新的空间。另外，创新性还体现在了特殊的遥控设备当中。多亏了互联网，使整个卫生间和卫浴产品都可以和使用者进行沟通，人们甚至在回家的路上就可以通过手机来向浴缸发出信号，而当他们到家时，就会发现，热水已经准备好了。

Soft forms and new materials are important aspects *in the "bathrooms, heatings, sanitary installations and air-conditioning" category. New lines in combination with innovative materials which also possess attractive tactile qualities are producing interesting re-interpretations of the bathtub in particular. This trend also caters to the needs of the user, too, since the bath is somewhere people can relax and recuperate. The creation of bathrooms that are "attractive and pleasant" to all seven senses is an important on-going task for designers, stressed the jurors Francesco Milani, Wolfgang Meyer-Hayoz and Ron Nabarro. And while these new lines so reduced as to be almost archaic were pleasing to the senses, as were likewise the rather matt-looking materials, at the same time their generous design expanded the dimensions of the bathroom. Because the reduced and highly functional fittings followed a similar trend, they were able to effortlessly adapt to the new proportions. Innovative, too, were the signs of emergent mediatisation. Thanks to internetworking concepts, integral bathroom and wellness products have begun to communicate. People on their way home can already signal the bathtub from their mobile phones, and find a hot bath waiting when they get there.*

弗朗塞斯科·米拉尼
Francesco Milani
瑞士
Schweiz

朗·纳巴罗
Ron Nabarro
以色列
Israel

沃弗岗·K·梅尔–亥兹
Wolfgang Meyer-Hayoz
瑞士
Schweiz

浴室、取暖、卫生清洁设备和空调
Bathrooms, heatings, sanitary installations and air-conditioning

“聪明水疗馆”浴缸，2005

I-House Incorporadora LTDA.,
São Paulo, Brasilien
Design: Indio da Costa Design
(Indio da Costa, Camila Fix,
Augusto Seibel, Felippe Bicudo,
Eduardo Azevedo),
Rio de Janeiro, Brasilien
www.ihouse.com.br
www.indiodacosta.com

“聪明水疗馆”浴缸让洗浴变得更加舒适。它的水温、水量、洗浴用品配置、不同的水按摩方式、光线明暗以及其它参数都可以单独地进行调整，而且调整后的所有参数都可在整个洗浴期间保持一致。用户可以通过移动电话或固定电话、互联网或掌上电脑在远处就可以开始进行洗浴的遥控准备工作。在其功能性方面，其考虑周全的设计使该浴缸变得易于操作而实用。可以说，“聪明水疗馆”浴缸在不经意间，便传达出它那集清晰简约而人性化的外形与高技术和高档材料的完美结合，体现出了一种现代技术下的创新。

The Smarthydro bathtub provides bathing comfort, because water temperature, water level, bathing additives, different hydromassage programmes, light intensity and other parameters can be adjusted individually; all settings are retained for the entire duration of the bath. The bath preparation can be activated remotely per mobile or fixed-line phone, the Internet or via Pocket PC. Once the bath is prepared the user is notified by phone or the voice system of the tub. Operating the tub is well thought out as to functionality, thus simple and practical. The Smarthydro bathtub was conceived primarily to convey precisely this kind of modern technology: a clear, minimalist friendly shape as well as a harmonious combination of technology, finesse and premium-grade materials.

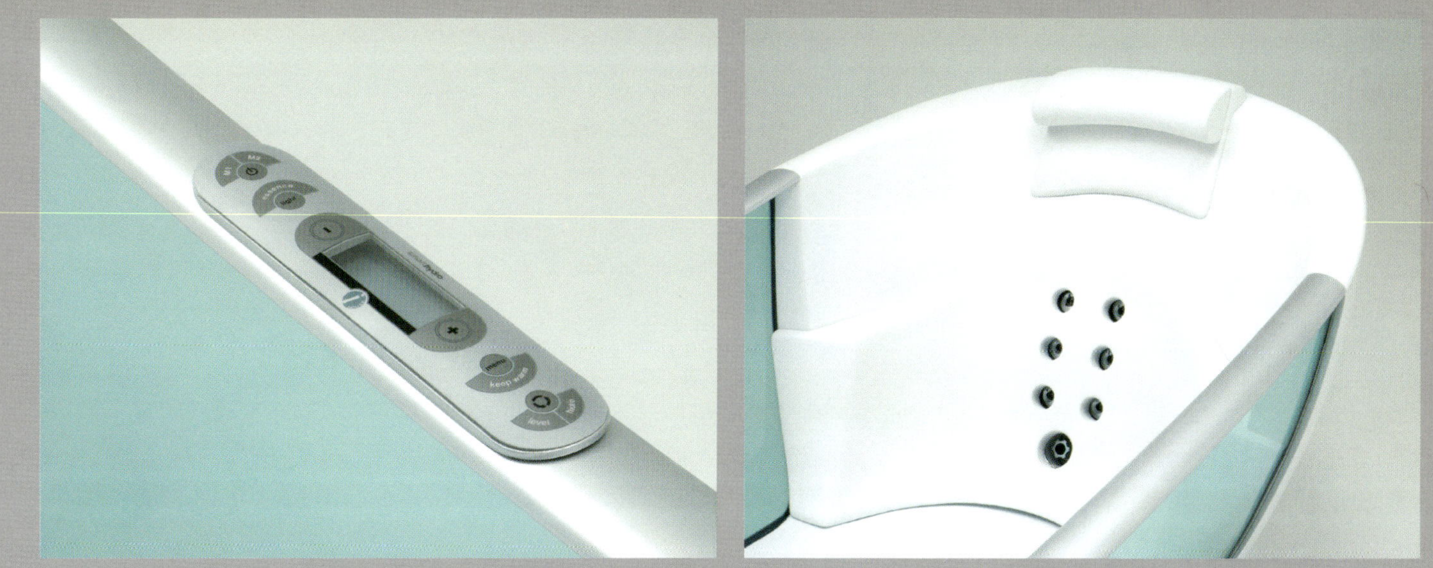

Conoplan淋浴房/Conoduo浴缸，2005

Franz Kaldewei GmbH & Co. KG, Ahlen
Design: Sottsass Associati, Mailand, Italien
www.kaldewei.com
www.sottsass.it

当今，休闲洗浴逐渐变成了人们生活中的主角。Conoplan淋浴房和Conoduo浴缸的设计灵感来源于力求简约的卫生间设计。Conoplan和Conoduo不仅代表了一种独立的建筑和几何外形，还符合人体工程学要求，给人以舒适的感觉。该产品有很多不同的款式和容积可供选择，几乎能适应所有类型的卫生间的内部结构。喷头和浴缸配有新型下水管道，设计师还将其设计成为一个独立设计的组成部分。下水管道与整体的外形轮廓相符合，因此，它就自然而然地成为了该产品的一部分，符合人体工程学的设计也让人们在使用时感到格外舒适。

The idea for the design of the Conoplan shower tray and the Conoduo bathtub was inspired by the need for a simplification of the bathroom. The act of bathing and relaxing is becoming the protagonist. Conoplan and Conoduo represent a self-contained architectural and geometric form, ergonomic and comfortable. They are available in a variety of versions and dimensions, adapting to all types of bathroom interiors. Shower tray and bathtub are designed with an innovative drain, developed as part of the self-contained architectural shape. The drain follows the overall contours. It is thus becoming part of the product and contributes to comfortable and ergonomic design.

G Type V3.0® 系列淋浴喷头，2005

Damixa a/s, Odense, Dänemark
Design: gneiss group, Kopenhagen, Dänemark
Vertrieb: Damixa Armaturen GmbH, Iserlohn
www.damixa.com

G Type V3.0®系列在功能上体现了一种创新。这种双手柄龙头是卫生间和厨房两用的，它的水流和冷热水的混合是通过侧面指向喷水口的方形操作装置来控制的，与对混合控制台的控制很相似，这样就保证能进行连续的手动转换，产生独特的控制上的舒适触感。

The G Type V3.0® series is designed with an innovative functionality. The water flow and the mixing of cold and warm water of this two-handle faucet for bathroom and kitchen are controlled via laterally to the body/spout placed square operating elements. Similar to the controls of a mixing console, this ensures a steplessly manually shifting, offering a unique haptic control comfort.

地中海帆船之星椭圆形舒适浴缸，2005

Bette GmbH & Co. KG, Delbrück
Werksdesign
www.bette.de

这款浴缸的特别之处在于其无缝镶板。立式的浴缸和镶板首次作为一个整体而成功地制作出来。浴缸和镶板一起组成了一个由高品质的钢或瓷釉制成的独立单元。这种创新的镶板技术免除了既昂贵又耗时的贴瓷砖的步骤。浴缸和镶板之间没有连接点，使其表面卫生并且容易进行清洁。

The special feature of the BetteStarlet Oval Comfort bathtub lies in the panelling formed without seams. For the first time, a stand-alone bathtub, including panelling, has been successfully produced as one piece. Bathtub and panelling form a single unit made of high-quality steel/enamel. This innovative panelling technology renders expensive and time-consuming tiling work superfluous. The jointless connection between bathtub and panels provide a hygienic easy-to-clean surface.

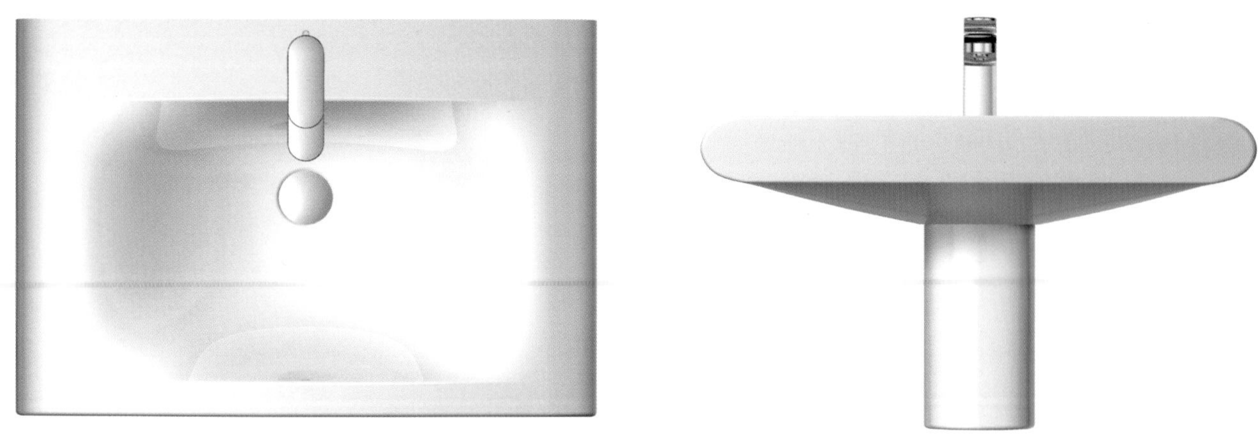

Elements 陶瓷系列, 2005

American Standard Europe BVBA,
Brüssel, Belgien
Design: Artefakt Industriekultur,
Darmstadt
Vertrieb: Ideal Standard Deutschland,
Bonn
www.idealstandard.de
www.artefakt.de

Elements陶瓷系列产品采用了合适的材料，使它看起来柔软而富有几何美感，与众不同。该系列中的水盆中设有一个镶嵌在陶瓷盆中的下水通道，这就使你看不见普通的下水孔。Elements系列包括多种型号和技术规格的水盆、马桶和坐浴盆，满足了多样化国际化的市场需求。

The Elements ceramic series is distinguished by suitable materials and a soft but geometrically conform shape. The sink units of this series have a water overflow channel integrated into the ceramics, which means there is no ordinary overflow hole. The Elements series includes sinks, water closets, bidets in a variety of sizes and technical versions to meet the demands of the international market.

Tonic 客卫设施, 2004

American Standard Europe BVBA,
Brüssel, Belgien
Design: Artefakt Industriekultur,
Darmstadt
Vertrieb: Ideal Standard Deutschland,
Bonn
www.idealstandard.de
www.artefakt.de

也许正是在房间里最小的地方才能最好地展现主人好客的精神。Tonic客卫系列洗漱间就在关注这个主题，提供了多种对客卫的解决方案，从建筑角度来看，这一问题通常是被忽视的。“功能完善而不拒人千里”是Tonic客卫设施的基本设计理念。这个系统的独立的解决方案为在处理或大或小的空间条件里（主要是有限空间）时提供了极大的灵活性。调节好的零件组装起来很简便，从与现有环境相匹配的设计简单的盥洗盆，到整套客卫完整的解决方案，Tonic客卫系列都能提供所有的部件。显露在外的设备取代了新的上下水的装置，一切都表明了Tonic客卫的主旨是定位于革新。

It is just the "smallest area in the house" that represents the hospitality of the host most clearly. The Tonic Guest wash place system focuses on this topic, offering various solutions for the guest toilet, which is usually neglected architecturally. "To be system but not to show system" is the design basis of Tonic Guest. The individual planning possibilities of the system offer flexibility in responding to strengths and weaknesses of the, mostly limited, space situation. The well-adjusted components can be arranged easily. The Tonic Guest system offers all components, from the simple washstand, which can be neutrally integrated in the existing ambience, up to a complete guest toilet solution. The exposed installation supersedes a new installation of the water connections, and it predestines Tonic Guest for use in spaces subject to renovations.

Glance “欢迎”客卫设施，2005

Jado, Rödermark
Design: Artefakt Industriekultur, Darmstadt
www.jado.com
www.artefakt.de

Glance“欢迎”客用盥洗台是迎客文化中的一个必要的组成部分。它和谐地结合了水流元素和现有的建筑中的几何元素，是一个将各种各样的功能性元素组合在一起的设计，其设计重点放在了洗漱和清洁这些实际的活动上。一种精密技术使设计变得简单但同时却并未影响质量。所有电枢线圈位置独立，为洗漱提供了一个较为宽敞的空间，并且使得即使在复杂而狭小的空间中也能够安装面盆。一种新型门的机械装置维持了整体的封闭性特征，下面的大容积的储藏柜也能开启。一个隐藏式镜子悬挂系统使得使用者可以自由选择镜子的安装，镜子可以安装在可附着的、可移动的照明系统上。

The Glance Wellcome guest sink is intended to be part of the culture of welcoming guests. It combines smoothly flowing elements with contemporary architectural geometry. The various functional elements are combined to a unified design, focusing on the actual activities of washing and cleaning. A sophisticated technology allows simplicity in design without compromising quality.
A self-contained positioning of all armature elements creates a generously spaced area for washing and allows mounting of the sink even in complex and tight spaces. An innovative door mechanism maintains the overall closed character and allows access to a generously dimensioned storage space underneath.
A concealed mirror mounting system provides for individual combination of freely selectable mirror elements, which can be universally fitted with an attachable and relocatable lighting system.

Components 盥洗台系列, 2003

Alape, Goslar
Design: Sieger Design GmbH & Co. KG, Sassenberg
www.alape.com
www.sieger-design.com

Components盥洗台系列体现了这样一种设计任务，即将标准化的一系列面盆类型和形式与较低的工具成本，所用材料的独特美感结合在一起。Components系列包括的一些设计上非常漂亮的立方体的、圆柱形的面盆，它们都可以有多种不同的使用方式，还可以不用拼接地做出柱式盥洗台。

The design of the Components basin system is an expression of the design task of combining a broad range of basin versions and forms of a standard programme with low tool costs and specific aesthetics of materials used. The Components series includes formally interesting objects like cubes, cylinders or columns which can be put to use in most different ways; a washstand in column shape can be realised without irritating splices.

Escale 盥洗台, 2003

Jacob Delafon Paris (Kohler France), Paris, Frankreich
Werksdesign: François Kergoet, Hubert Maître
Vertrieb: Kohler GmbH, Oer-Erkenschwick
www.jacobdelafon.com
www.kohler.com

宽敞的Escale柱式盥洗台的形状灵感来源于迎风远航的船只，并结合了日本餐饮服务中器具的传统形状。清晰的几何形状创造出了时尚的氛围。坚固的水平台面与面盆连在一起，面盆超过了台面，但看起来也是一个独立的单元。可放置物品的台面设计得很宽敞，可以很好地收纳一些卫浴用品。

The generously designed Escale washstand owes its shape to an inspiration: the idea was to resemble an inflated sail in the wind, combined with the customary shape of Japanese dinner services. Clear geometric forms create a light modern ambience. A solid horizontal tabletop is combined with a wash bowl that seems to grow out of the tabletop, yet appearing to form one single unit after all. The placement surface is generously designed, offering sufficient space for accessories and bathroom utensils.

Serie F1, 盥洗台, 2004

Keramag AG, Ratingen
Design: Porsche Design GmbH, Zell am See, Österreich
www.keramag.com
www.porsche-design.com

F1系列的线条设计得平滑而自然，并且由于其部分平面是倾斜的而产生了美妙的视觉效果。F1面盆"像高脚杯一样的"特征清晰地显现出了水是如何流出的，它向前倾斜着，倾向使用者的一端。陶瓷和高品质的实木组合在一起，构成一个不同寻常的整体。这种立式的盥洗台能够安置在屋内的任何一个角落，从任何方向都可方便使用。

The F1 series is designed with a smooth natural line management, displaying a high degree of optical presence due to slanting section plains. The goblet-like character of the F1 washbasins symbolises the "presentation" of water: the washbasins invitingly lean forward towards the user. The combination of ceramic with high-quality real wood creates an exciting and unusual unity. The awarded, free-standing washbasin can be placed within the room so that it is reachable from all sides.

劳芬 Palomba 系列盥洗台, 2005

Laufen Ceramconsult AG, Laufen, Schweiz
Design: Palomba Serafini Associati, Vigasio, Italien
Vertrieb: Laufen GmbH, Staudt
www.laufen.com

Palomba系列的设计灵感来源于池塘的形状，它是一套组合了家具的设计简单大方的盥洗台。平滑的陶瓷表面覆盖着器官形状的面盆，让固定和流动的元素平滑地过渡了起来。面盆嵌入到盥洗台表面清晰的边缘中，没有任何缝隙。边缘平滑的台面和一个有机的凹面组合在一起，这种不寻常的组合创造出了一种视觉和触觉上的悬念。盥洗台的基座包括一个直角的几何形状的盥洗台面板，并设计成一个悬空的桌面。面板清晰界定的边缘与陶瓷的质感形成鲜明的对比，面盆像流动的湖水一样,和谐地与盥洗台面板完美融合在一起。可以说,Palomba系列面盆是多种几何形状互相作用的结果，即形成了一个没有了边缘的立方体。面盆侧面的厚度延续了下来，这就产生了一种几何艺术外形，并能够以多种方式进行组合。即使技术性地将其拆卸，也不会产生任何破坏性的空洞。

The Palomba Collection is based on the idea of lagoons and is a simple washstand set with furniture. A smooth ceramic surface covers an organically shaped sink, thus creating smooth transitions between fixed and flowing elements: the sink merges seamlessly into the defined edges of the washstand surface. An optical and haptic suspense is created from a highly exceptional – for ceramics – combination of edges, smooth surfaces and organic hollows. The base consists of a geometric washstand panel, designed with right angles and intended to act as a kind of suspended tabletop. The sharply defined edges of the panel contrast with the impression of the ceramic. The sink is integrated in the washstand panel with the harmony of a lagoon. The washbasin bowl in the Palomba Collection is an interaction of geometric shapes. The result is a cube that has lost its edges. The thickness of the sides of the basin is constant. This results in a geometric art form that can be combined in a variety of ways – technically detached from the mounting, which does not contain any tap holes.

Happy D 盥洗台, 2004

Duravit AG, Hornberg
Design: Sieger Design GmbH & Co. KG, Sassenberg
www.duravit.de
www.sieger-design.com

Happy D系列外形的设计融经典和古朴于一体。这一系列产品的视觉焦点是一个40厘米宽的方形盆和一个曲面的前门与底座。底座可以采用不同的表面处理方式，如美国樱桃木、美国胡桃木，光泽度极佳的白色西莫克木、枫木或者斑马木条，还可以使用深棕色的檀木薄片等材料。陶瓷和底座间通过一条很窄的环形铬合金轨道把它们恰当地连接了起来，这种过渡既实用，也非常具有美学价值。根据65厘米、80厘米和100厘米宽的不同的家具类型，盥洗台可以有多种选择，加上带曲面门的底座，整个设计看起来非常完整。或者，底座也可以作为一个小型的储藏柜，设计成可抽拉式，装上抽屉或是隔板，再加上式样简单的铬合金手柄，就成为了一个实用的储物空间。

The Happy D series is designed with classic and archaic shapes. Highlight of the new series is a square-shaped bowl, 40cm in width, combined with a base with curved front doors. The base is available with different front finishes: American cherry tree, American walnut, high-gloss white, sycamore maple or zebrano genuine wood stripe look, as well as dark-brown macassar genuine wood veneer. The transition from ceramic to base is functional as well as aesthetic. A narrow circumferential chrome rail creates a felicitous interconnection. The choice of washstand options is extended by furniture versions of 65, 80 and 100cm in width, supplemented by fitting bases with curved doors. Alternatively, the base is also available as simple console with extractable bases and floor units with doors or drawers and a plain chrome rail handle.

斯达克 X 卫浴系列, 2005

Duravit AG, Hornberg
Design: Philippe Starck, Paris, Frankreich
www.duravit.de
www.philippe-starck.com

斯达克X卫浴系列体现了水作为一切生命之源的主题。立体的马桶和高40厘米的坐浴盆，构成了这个系列的基本框架。高89厘米的有着陶瓷台面的锥形或圆柱形的盥洗台也出现在了卫浴产品的竞技场上，但却并未打破整体理念中卫浴产品那种平滑的外形。57厘米宽的盥洗台安装置在金属的控制台上，另外还有110厘米宽白色、黄色或铂金色的盆可供选择，构成了另外一种独特的美感。光泽感极好的白色更加烘托出这一卫浴系列的设计美学和其结构特性。该系列总体上由16个陶瓷产品，五件家居产品和三种不同的浴缸造型组成。体现出一种卫生间里的新文化。

The Starck X bathroom series expounds the topic of water as life elixir for all living beings. Cubic WCs and bidets, 40cm in height, comprise the basic outline of the series. In conical or cylindrical shape, the 89cm high washstands enter the bathroom arena on a ceramic platform without interrupting the smooth contours of the overall concept. The washstands, 57cm in width, are placed on metal consoles; an enlarged version with 110cm width offers an additional tray in white, yellow or platinum. The bathroom series is designed with aesthetic and constructive particularities, manufactured in high-gloss white. The Starck X series is overall comprised of 16 ceramic units, five pieces of furniture and three bathtub versions. The design is intended to be the harbinger of a new culture in the bathroom.

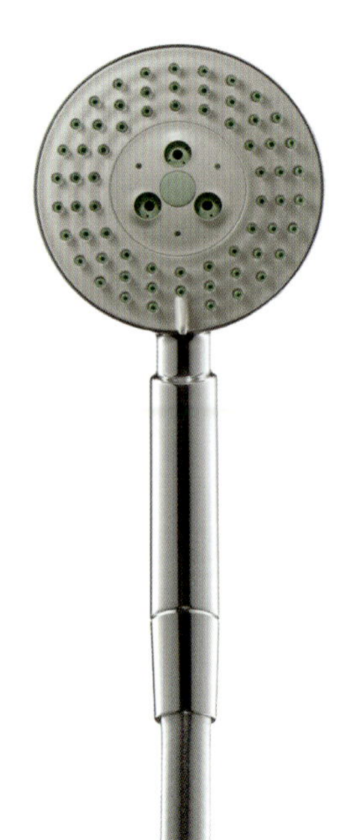

Raindance 皇家空气花洒, 2004

Hansgrohe AG, Schiltach
Design: Phoenix Design, Stuttgart
www.hansgrohe.com

Raindance皇家空气花洒宽大的花洒直径为350毫米，是该类产品中最大的一款。它简约的设计和超薄的喷头给人一种纤细但很强烈的印象。高质量的表面和生产的高精密度显现出其虽雅致但却毫不张扬的设计。Raindance皇家空气花洒可以从225个喷嘴里喷洒出柔和的水流，让你产生一种全新的淋浴体验。

With a head diameter of 350mm, the Raindance Royale AIR plate shower head is the largest of its kind. Its minimalist design and the ultra-flat shower head yield a slim but straightforward impression. The rather elegant and unobtrusive design is enhanced by the superior quality of all surfaces and excellent manufacturing precision. The Raindance Royal AIR pours soft drops out of 225 nozzles, allowing a whole new shower experience.

Raindance S 100 空气 3 喷射式手持花洒, 2005

Hansgrohe AG, Schiltach
Design: Phoenix Design, Stuttgart
www.hansgrohe.com

Rindance S 100空气3喷射式手持花洒是Raindance产品系列中设计最紧凑的一款。它设计得非常轻薄，面积也有所缩小，直径为100毫米，特别适用于在浴缸和较小的淋浴间里使用。由于AIR技术采取了一种专利的空气与水流混合技术，所以该花洒具备了三个不同的能单独调整的喷管装置，从而使得淋浴变得异常舒适。

The Raindance S 100 AIR 3 Jet hand shower head is the most compact model of the Raindance family. With its flat design, reduced size and a diameter of 100mm, it is particularly suitable for bathtubs and smaller shower cubicles. Three different individually adjustable water jet settings offer a high degree of comfort in the shower due to the patented, advanced AIR technology for combined air/water swirl flow, employed for the first time.

雅生・斯达克水龙头, 2004

Hansgrohe AG, Schiltach
Design: Philippe Starck, Paris, Frankreich
www.hansgrohe.com

雅生・斯达克所设计的单杆面盆龙头的功能明晰，整体显现出一种纤细的感觉。该产品的设计旨在关注核心部位。作为此设计宗旨的视觉表现，精致的柱形手柄和纤细的外形以及管状的出水口共同构成了一个统一的几何体。极简设计的外形要归功于一个直径仅为35毫米的筒状操纵杆J27。

The design of the single-lever washstand mixer by Axor Starck is slim and clear in function as well as effect. As visual expression of a design maxim focusing on the essentials, the delicate cylindrical handle together with the slim shape and the tubular outlet, constitute a geometric unity. The minimalistic design is possible with the innovative joystick cartridge J27 with a diameter of only 35mm.

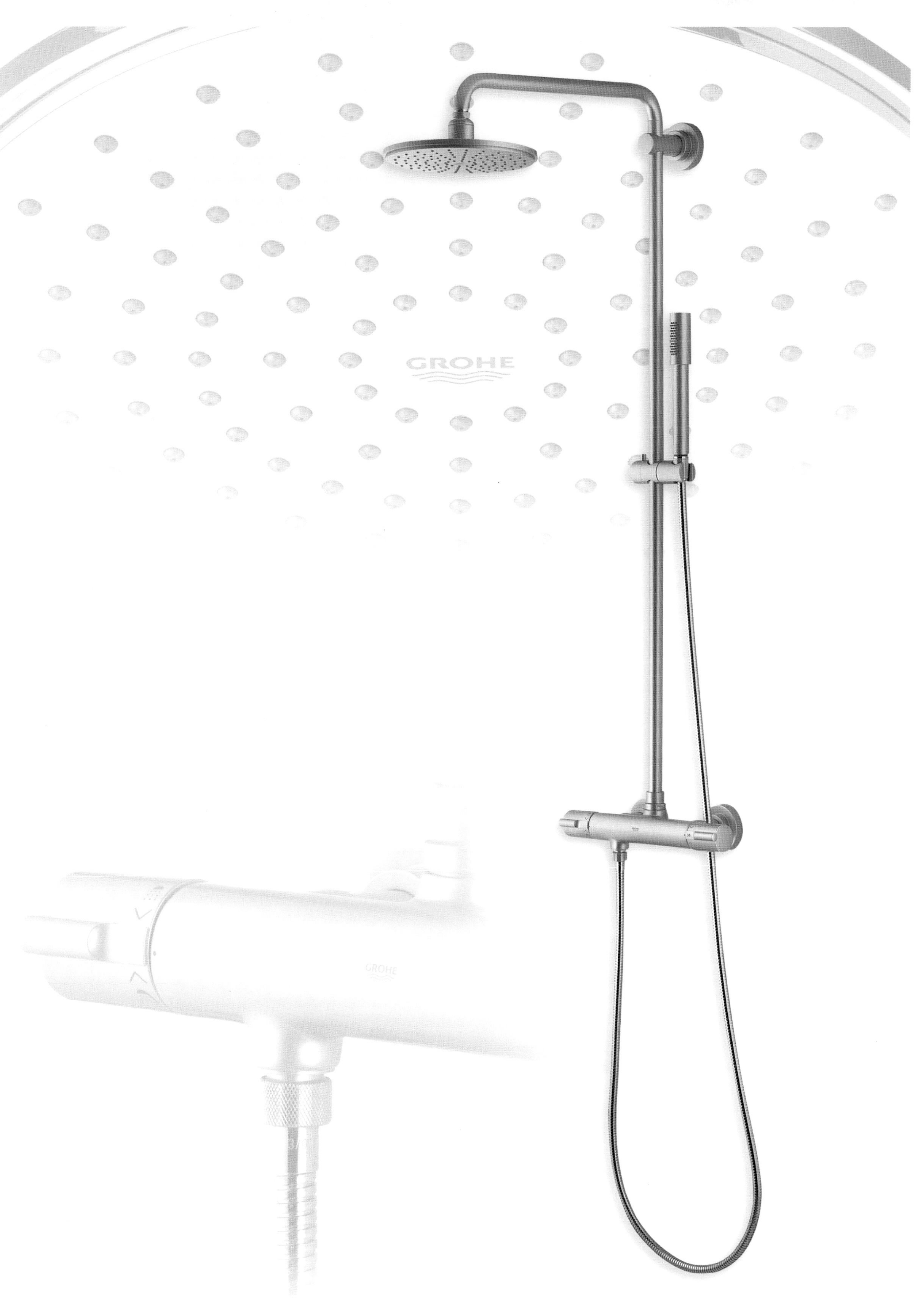

高仪“阵雨”花洒，2005

Grohe Water Technology AG & Co. KG, Hemer
Werksdesign: Jochen Allard
www.grohe.de

“阵雨”花洒系列的设计着眼于极简主义的原始外形和乐趣。这种戏水的哲学是受了远东思想的影响。极简的外形设计使其功能简单，非常实用。有柱形开口且对称的设计结构凸现出其工艺的坚固，精密的材料表面清晰且高雅，并且每个细节的比例都设计得很均衡。直径达210毫米的超宽喷头上有120个闪烁着金属绿光的硅铜喷嘴，它们产生的丰富水流能够覆盖整个身体，令使用者在其中能得到充分的放松甚至还可寻求到刺激。另外，水流既可以从宽大的固定花洒中流出，也可以从杆状的手持花洒中涌现。

With the Rainshower shower system the focal point is on the archetypal shape and the enjoyment of minimalism. The philosophy of water rendition is influenced by Far East concepts. The reduction to the simple familiar results in a clearly recognisable functionality: symmetric design structures with cylindrical openings, solidity in craftsmanship, and sophisticated material surfaces – clear, elegant and finely proportioned in every detail. 120 silicone spray nozzles, shimmering in metallic emerald green, in a particularly wide oversized shower head with a diameter of 210mm, produce an opulent rainshower capable of enveloping the entire body – for relaxation or for stimulation. The water can be set to flow either through the large-surface shower head or through the hand shower in wand-shape.

Toca 和 Toca XP 淋浴房, 2004

Kermi GmbH, Plattling
Werksdesign
www.kermi.de

Toca和Toca XP系列淋浴房的基本设计特征就是为了追求一致的视觉效果。这种理念关注于基本的几何形状，例如方形和圆形。合适的长方形结构、坚固的扶手以及毛巾架的宽度是相同的，并形成了一个统一体。方形的装置和外形高雅的支脚也彼此协调。附件装置和毛巾架也非常实用，它们都可从里面冲水，这样就很容易进行清洗。门的开关都很平滑且容易，即使在淋浴设施和地面安装在同一条水平线上。Toca淋浴间是由无框的玻璃定制的。这一系列生产的Toca XP淋浴间，采用墙作为背后的连接体，因而其宽度很舒适，而且倾斜角度可以进行调节。

An essential design feature of the Toca and Toca XP shower cubicle series is the consistent visual language. The concept focuses on the basic geometric forms square and circle. With identical width, the fitting cylinders and the solid hand- and towel rails form a unity. The square-shaped fittings and the elegant appearing stabilisers are mutually harmonised as well. Fittings and towel rails are functional; they are flush on the inside, allowing easy cleaning. An integrated lift-drop mechanism allows smooth opening and closing of doors, even when installing the unit flush with the ground. The Toca cubicles are custom-made with a frameless all-glass construction. With a wall connection profile, the Toca XP cubicles, produced in series, allow a comfortable width- and slant adjustment.

新型 Der Credo 暖气片, 2005

Kermi GmbH, Plattling
Design: Artefakt Industriekultur, Darmstadt
www.kermi.de
www.artefakt.de

新型Der Credo暖气片的设计基础是对关键之处的关注和力求简单化的努力而得来的。这种貌似简单的卫生间暖气片却引领了时尚的卫生间风格。在设计方面，所有功能性元素的融合都反映在了固定装置和对连接技术方面的高要求上。独特的垂直侧面与精致的水平交叉管道形成鲜明的对比。最突出的设计特征是两个墙面安装拱柄，它在把暖气和墙壁整合为一个整体上发挥了重要作用。下面在肉眼看不到的地方放置着一个可调整的三维安装系统，明显便利于安装。另有两种类型的墙面连接拱柄可供选择，分别为“边缘”或“软边缘”，并且可根据不同的卫生间设计而进行单独调整。

Focusing on essentials and a commitment to simplicity – this is the basis for the design of the new Credo radiator. The result is the pure form of a bathroom radiator picking up and reflecting trendsetting bathroom style worlds. The high claims as to design are mirrored in the formally harmonious integration of all functional elements – with regard to both the fixtures and the connection technology. The distinctive plane vertical profiles create an exciting contrast to the delicate horizontal cross pipes. The most prominent design features are the two wall-mount arches. They are instrumental in merging radiator and wall into one single unit. Below it, invisible to the eye, a three-dimensional adjustable mounting system is located, facilitating installation considerably. Two versions of wall connection arches are available, "edge" or "softedge", and allow an individual adjustment to the bathroom design.

Bagnotherm II 暖气片，2005

AFG Arbonia-Forster-Riesa GmbH, Riesa
Design: Andreas Struppler, München
www.arbonia.de

Bagnotherm II的所有设计特征都协调地自然而和谐。然而，由于其明显伸出的横管以及它们之间变化的空间，使其总体印象更加鲜明。由于使用了隐秘的人性化安装技术，清晰的视觉印象没有被任何障碍物所破坏。针对Bagnotherm类型中整齐的面板而设计出了一种实用的解决方案，即有一个弹阀和一个50毫米的中心装置。Bagnotherm II包含了一些实用且富有美感的附件，例如折叠起来的毛巾杆，毛巾环，还有毛巾柜和毛巾钩。所有的部件都是高质量的铬合金面制成的，并且与暖气的整体设计搭配和谐。Bagnotherm II有很多种不同的类型，几乎适合于任何一种类型的卫生间设计，其长度范围从40到90厘米，高度范围从75到180厘米不等。

All design features of the Bagnotherm II have been harmonised. However, the overall impression is more distinct, due to noticeable projecting transverse tubes and their changed spacing. With a concealed and mounting-friendly fixing technique, the clear optical impression is not disturbed by any obstacles. A functional solution was found for the design of the trim panel of the Bagnotherm version with a cartridge valve and a 50mm centre fitting. The Bagnotherm II includes functional and aesthetic accessories such as a fold-out towel bar, a towel ring as well as repositories and hooks. All parts are high-quality chrome-plated and interact harmoniously with the design of the radiator. The Bagnotherm II is available in a multitude of versions and dimensions for nearly every bathroom situation, ranging in lengths from 40 to 90cm and in heights from 75 to 180cm.

lion 家庭动力中枢, 2005

OTAG Vertriebs GmbH & Co. KG, Olsberg
Design: WILDDESIGN (Marc Ruta, Markus Wild), Gelsenkirchen
www.otag.de
www.wilddesign.de

lion家庭动力中枢是一种用来保留热量和动力的设备，它体现了一种创新且设计得很美观。其外形给人一种价值不菲的印象，并且传达出该设备的实用性特征。由于有了动力和热量的连接器，用户在自己家里就可以使用该产品获得光源和热量，而在此之前这些只可能出现在较大型的建筑物里。这是一种有效的、环保的动力供应方式，该产品不仅提供了家里所需要的100%的热量，而且也能发出占到家用大概80%的电力。

The lion Powerblock is an innovative and aesthetically designed block heat and power plant. The casing yields a high-value impression and conveys the functionality of the unit. With a power-heat coupling, heretofore possible only in larger buildings, the lion allows generation of light and heat in one's own home. In an efficient and environmentally friendly power supply manner, the block heat and power plant generates not only 100 per cent of the heat needed for the house, but up to 80 per cent of its electrical power as well.

attika GEO 蓄热炉, 2004

Attika Feuer AG, Cham, Schweiz
Werksdesign: Erwin Hauenstein, Matthias Zäh
www.attika.ch

远远看去，460公斤的GEO蓄热炉像一尊朴素的石雕一样优雅地立在房间里。它前部的灰白色的石头衬托出它的光滑，而陶瓷玻璃又把人们的注意力转移到了火上面。光滑的地面皂石构成了右面和后面部分，这就使得GEO能够安放在房间中央。左面部分则与整体形成了鲜明的对比，上面安装着负重门和气流调节器。燃烧的空气通过转动一个圆形操作装置来进行控制，通过这个装置，能显示出旋转的全过程。GEO是特别为热量不足的房屋设计的。炉子的前部和钢制的部分能够按照房屋布局进行移动，这就使得蓄热炉能够根据需要而安置在一个理想位置。

The 460kg GEO storage stove still elegantly stands in a room like a simple stone sculpture. The grey stone on the front side frames the sleek, high ceramic glass drawing the attention to the fire. The smoothly ground soapstone dominates the right and rear side which allows GEO to be placed in the centre of the room. The left side offers a contrast of steel upon which the loading door and the air regulator are located. The combustion air is controlled by turning a round operating element displaying the rotation. GEO has been especially designed for low-energy and passive housing. Depending on the room layout, the front and steel side can be exchanged which enables the storage stove to be ideally positioned.

Bella Vista 化妆镜, 2004

Keuco GmbH & Co. KG, Hemer
Design: .molldesign – reiner moll & partner, Schwäbisch Gmünd
www.keuco.de

Bella Vista化妆镜设计有一个非常薄的化妆柜。只要将它放置在化妆台上，相信凭借它那高雅的设计，它都是一件令人愉悦的物品。一种创新的灯光传导技术能为使用者的脸部提供均匀而直接的照明。其灯光不仅使用寿命长，且耗电量很低。Bella Vista化妆镜有两种款式可供选择：墙上安装型和一种站立型。由于有了实用的活动臂，该化妆镜可以向任何方向移动，并可进行单独调整。

The cosmetics mirror Bella Vista is designed with a very flat cabinet. Due to its sensual-elegant impression, it is a piece of delight on any dressing table. An innovative light conducting technology provides an even and direct illumination of the viewer's face. The light source used is maintenance-free and has a low power consumption. The Bella Vista cosmetics mirror is available in two wall-mounted versions and a stand-alone version. With a functional flex arm the mirror can be moved in all directions, allowing individual adjustment.

Twin 指甲工具套装, 2005

Zwilling J.A. Henckels AG, Solingen
Werksdesign: Dieter Thomas
www.zwilling.com

也许是对某种全新事物的追求，才导致了Twin Innovent指甲锉的发明，它是由最好的白色骨瓷制成的，其锉面可以防止磨损。即使斜放在指甲下面，其薄薄的边缘也可以将指甲锉的很干净且很舒适。其独特的交叉部分使有着透明光亮手柄的指甲锉非常地结实。必要时该产品也可在流水下进行清洗。由“白金”制成的Twin Innovent是一个特别的指甲保护器。

The quest for something totally new led to the development of the Twin Innovent nail file made from the finest white bone china. The fine filing surface is resistant to wear and tear. The thin edges file cleanly and comfortably, even aslant under the nails. Due to a specific cross-section, the file with its ~~glazed handle~~ is extremely strong. If necessary, the file can be cleaned under running water. Made of "white gold", the Twin Innovent is nail care of a very special kind.

Twin 盒子, 2005

Zwilling J.A. Henckels AG, Solingen
Design: André Kunzendorf, Wuppertal
www.zwilling.com

Twin盒子是一套外观设计高雅而耐用的修剪指甲工具，它由银白色氧化铝制成。该工具包括了两个抽屉和一个内盒，其中内盒是由黑色玻璃纤维加固的合成金属制成的。用来放置工具的镶嵌盒由固体泡沫橡胶制成，其中两个镶嵌盒是可互换的，且内部设计各有千秋。修剪指甲的工具是用Twinox不锈钢制成的。

Twin Case is an elegant and durable manicure set made from silver-metallic anodised aluminium. The set contains two drawers and an interior made from black fibreglass-reinforced synthetic material. The inlays for picking up instruments, made from solid rubber foam, are exchangeable and allow for versions with different contents. The manicure instruments are made from satin-finished Twinox stainless steel.

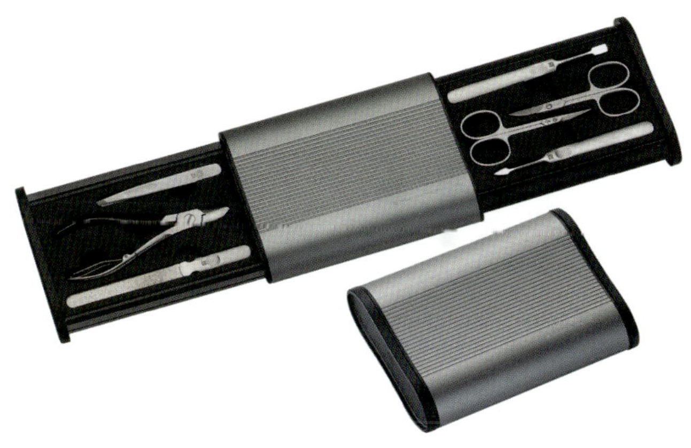

Twin Scope 指甲钳, 2005

Zwilling J.A. Henckels AG, Solingen
Design: Suwada (Tomoyuki Kobayashi), Niigata, Japan
www.zwilling.com

Twin Scope指甲钳的特色主要在于其设计、触觉和锋利程度之间的和谐搭配。创新主要体现在了其触觉良好的指甲钳的功能性上。一种微型望远镜弹簧代替了恼人的摇摆、转动或缓冲的弹簧。一种新设置的削剪范围使得削剪质量得到提高；符合人体工程学原理的手柄使得当它放在一个平坦的表面上时，指甲钳的末端好像是“飘浮”在桌子上端的，这样就避免了对指甲钳末端的损害。

The Twin Scope nail nipper features a homogeneous interplay of design, haptics and sharpness. Innovative is the functionality of the nipper, haptics have been optimised. A miniature telescope spring replaces the irritating flap-, turn- or buffer spring. The cutting quality is enhanced by way of a newly arranged cutting range; due to the ergonomic handle the nipper tip is "floating" above the tabletop when placing it on an even surface. Thus, damage of the fine tip is prevented.

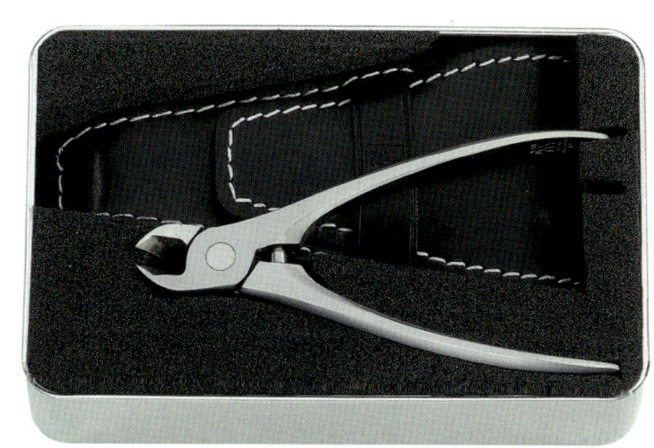

iCON 电扇, 2004/2005

Airflow Developments Ltd.,
High Wycombe, GB
Werksdesign: Airflow Design Team
(John Kelly)
Vertrieb: Airflow Lufttechnik GmbH,
Rheinbach
www.airflow.com

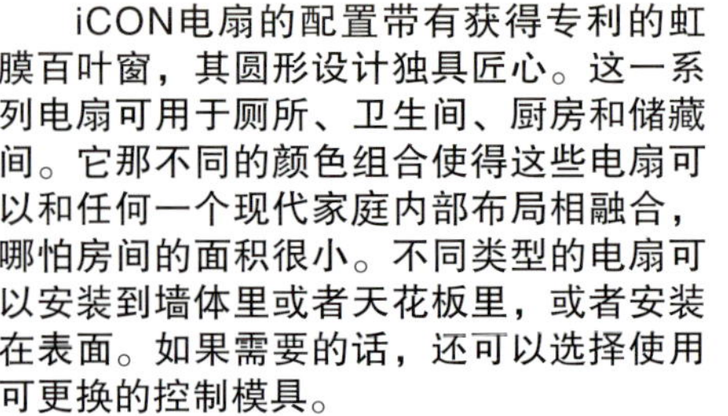

iCON电扇的配置带有获得专利的虹膜百叶窗，其圆形设计独具匠心。这一系列电扇可用于厕所、卫生间、厨房和储藏间。它那不同的颜色组合使得这些电扇可以和任何一个现代家庭内部布局相融合，哪怕房间的面积很小。不同类型的电扇可以安装到墙体里或者天花板里，或者安装在表面。如果需要的话，还可以选择使用可更换的控制模具。

iCON is a series of fans for toilets, bathrooms, kitchens and utility rooms in an innovative round design with patented iris shutter. With different colour combinations, these fans can be integrated into any modern day home interior, even in the smallest room. Depending on the version, they can be installed recessed into the wall or ceiling, or surface-mounted. A selection of interchangeable control modules is available upon request.

CAF-D3 空气净化器, 2004

Toshiba Corporation, Tokio, Japan
Werksdesign: Toshiba Design Center
(Keiji Chikuma, Tomiaki Ishihara)
www.toshiba.co.jp

CAF-D3是一种空气净化器，主要适用于家中有婴儿或者有健康状况不好的人用。该设计关注的主要因素是空气的清洁度和与室内装饰很好的协调与适应性。该装置通过其平滑的表面设计，简化了其形象上的复杂性。它的控制灯并不明显，而且灯光很暗。这样一来，整体外观就给人一种舒适的、富含人性化的印象。由于采用了实用的旋转开关装置，以及便利于清洁的外形，更进一步地提升了产品的人性化程度，这对于视觉有障碍的人更为实用。

The CAF-D3 is an air purifier for households with infants or health-conscious people. The design focused on the key term purity and a good adaptability to the interior decoration. The impression of complexity has been reduced with this unit by using a flat surface design. The control lights of the unit are unobtrusive and dimly luminous. In this way, the materials used create a luxurious and user-friendly impression. The user-friendliness is enhanced by functional rotary switches and contours facilitating operation of the purifier even for visually handicapped persons.

Malong 马桶盖, 2005

Hamberger Sanitary, Rosenheim
Werksdesign/Designmanagement:
Wolfgang Schüller
Design: Brodbeck Design, München
www.haro-san.de
www.brodbeckdesign.de

Malong马桶盖的波浪形线条和简单的边缘处线条的灵感来源于东亚的寺庙。清晰的视觉表现形式和座盖的边缘在形象具有创新性。在座盖和按照人体工程学设计的座位之间的几何边缘设计为V形，给人一种高雅的印象。加上圆形的、抛光的边缘，使得清洁工作也简单易行，同时使Malong具备了一种舒适的触觉感受。

The rolling line as well as a concise edge lining of the Malong toilet seat are inspired by the harmonics of an East Asian temple. Innovative are the clear visual language and the edge profile of the lid. The V-shaped arrangement of the edge geometry between lid and ergonomic seat creates an elegant impression. In combination with rounded and polished edges, the arrangement allows for easy hygienic caretaking, giving the Malong comfortable haptics as well.

乔丹 Step by Step 儿童牙刷, 2004/2005

Jordan AS, Oslo, Norwegen
Design: Fido industridesign as
(Morten Kildahl, Merete Nes,
Øyvar Svendsen), Oslo, Norwegen
www.jordan.no
www.fido.no

乔丹Step by Step是一个儿童牙刷系列。该系列包括三种不同的牙刷。这一系列产品的创新之处在于每一支牙刷都是专门为相应年龄段的儿童而设计的。乔丹Step by Step遵循了儿童不同的发育水平，牙科因素，人体工程学和不同的购买动机。该牙刷遵循了儿童的成长规律，旨在帮助儿童建立良好的生活习惯。乔丹Step by Step系列的一贯的视觉表现方式涵盖了从可爱而幼稚的几何外形到更秀气、更成熟的形式。这种表现方式再加上漂亮的包装，使得儿童选择一支合适的牙刷变得更加简便。此外，所有的牙刷都是依据了人体工程学原理，专为父母和孩子而设计。

Jordan Step by Step is a series of children's toothbrushes. The concept consists of three different toothbrushes. The innovation with this series is that each brush is specially designed to its group of age. Step by Step follows the evolution of the child on different levels: dental aspects, ergonomics and motivation. The toothbrushes are to establish good habits for the rest of life, and to follow the development of the child. The consistent shape language of the Step by Step series ranges from the childish geometrical forms to a slimmer and more mature child expression. This language of forms, together with the packaging makes it easier to choose the right toothbrushes. All the brushes are ergonomically formed for parents and children.

auroMATIC 560,
控制面板, 2004

Vaillant GmbH, Remscheid
Design: Vistapark GmbH,
Wuppertal
www.vaillant.com
www.vistapark.de

auroMATIC 560的控制面板和操作理念是建立在auroMATIC 330温控器的基础上的。为了控制更加复杂的太阳能系统，auroMATIC 560的外壳更新了技术，并且还加上了Vaillant温控器系列的设计特点。由于在外形和控制装置上采用了同样的设计，它使得安装者能够更加容易地操作和安装控制器，并且解决了采用传统取暖技术的温控器和使用太阳能技术的温控器之间的差别。这使得太阳能技术得到了广泛的认可和应用。

The control panel and operational concept of the auroMATIC 560 are based on the calorMATIC 330 control unit. The larger housing of the auroMATIC 560 uses additional technology for controlling more complex solar systems and incorporates the design of the Vaillant control unit series. With the same design of shape and controls, it is easier for the installer to handle and configure the control unit, and it resolves differences between units with conventional heating technology and those with solar technology. This leads to an increased acceptance and use of solar technology in general.

Weishaupt 燃烧器系列

Max Weishaupt GmbH, Schwendi
Design: Teams Design, Esslingen
www.weishaupt.de

这五种燃烧器的功率范围从12到500千瓦不等，还设计了供燃汽和燃油使用的统一的平台。数字化的控制方式使得该燃烧器安装简便，操作精确，并且非常有可能将其安装到复杂的汽车系统中。燃烧器的设计经过了仔细的协调，整体设计稳重低调，而且在外形和颜色上与市场上所能买到的供暖锅炉相适应。所有的零件都安装在一个稳定的合金底座上，并且用一个合成金属所制成的顶帽加以保护。各种合适材料的组合使其表面容易清洁，延长了它的生命周期。此外，不同型号燃烧器的操作和安装是以标准化的合理操作模式为基础的。

The five burners in the power range of 12 to 500kW are designed with a uniform platform strategy for gas and oil burners. A digital furnace management allows easy setting, exact operation and many possibilities of integration into complex bus systems. The burner designs were carefully coordinated. They are unobtrusive, adapting themselves in shape and colour to the commercially available heating boilers. All components of the burners are placed on a stable die-cast base. They are securely protected with a cover cap made from synthetic material. The long life cycle of the burners is expressed in a finish appropriate for the materials involved, with easy-to-clean surfaces. Handling and mounting of the different burner sizes is based on a standardised logical operation mode.

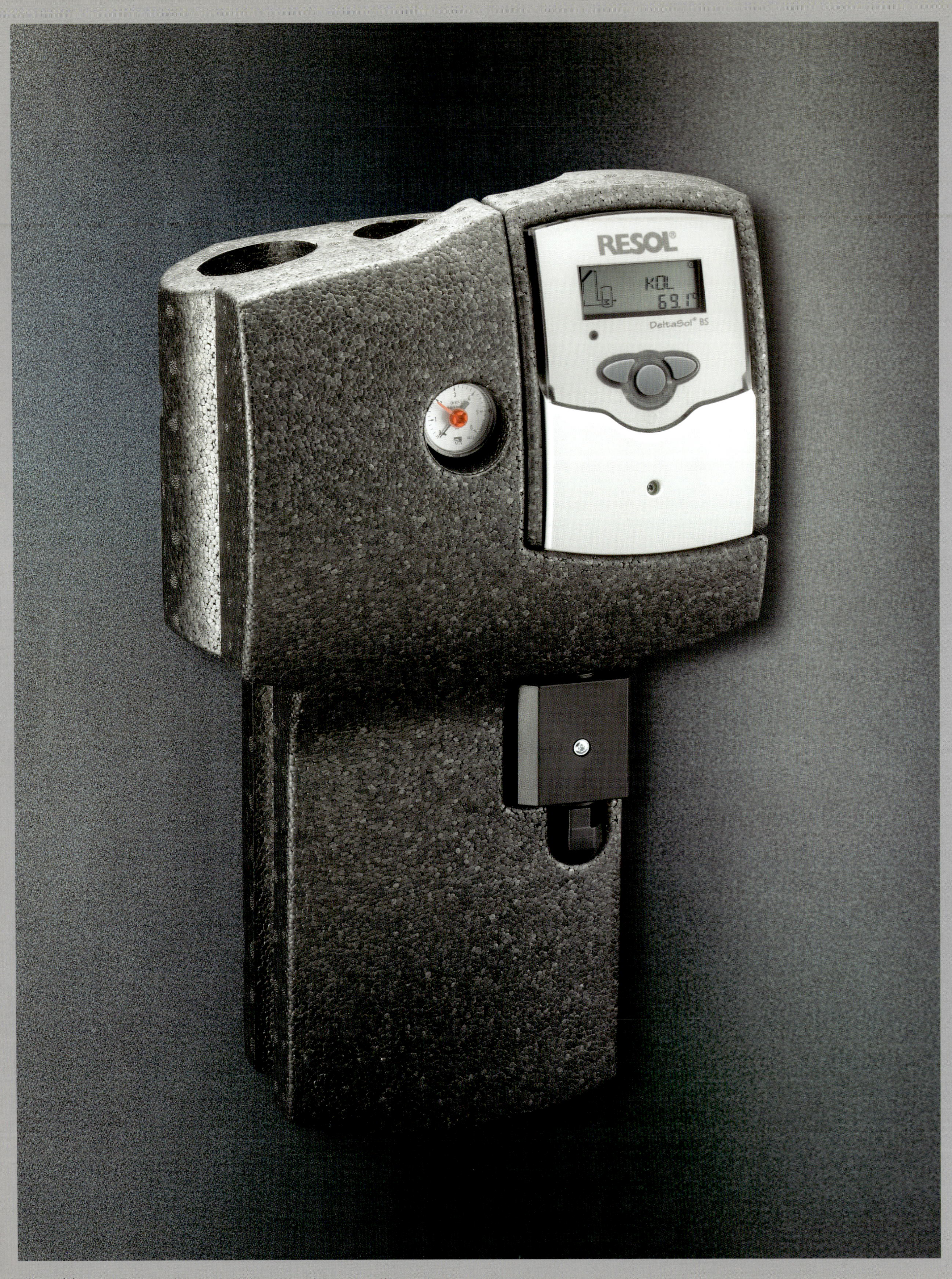

EcoFlow 太阳能蓄电池, 2004

Pommerening Armaturenwerk GmbH & Co. KG, Hameln
Resol GmbH, Hattingen
Design: rosenthal design
(Christian Marx), Essen
www.paw-armaturen.de
www.resol.de
rdesign91@aol.com

EcoFlow太阳能蓄电池主要是用于在太阳能热量加工装置中对太阳能的提取，它把安装在屋顶的太阳能收集器和加热系统连接了起来。将隔热材料所必需的聚乙烯成分进行一定地加工设计，这个新产品就诞生了。不仅如此，改设计还融入了所有连接中的电子控制装置和水力驱动设备。可以看到该产品设计得非常紧凑，能够简便地就地安装，操作或维护简单，仅仅需要拿掉表盖就可以了。

The EcoFlow solar station controls the heat extraction in a solar heat processing unit. It is the link between the collectors located on the roof and the heating system. The polyethylene parts necessary for insulation were designed in such a way that the result was a new product. Electronic control device and hydraulic equipment of all connections have been integrated into the design. The solar station is built in a compact way, allowing simple on-site installation. For operation or maintenance of the unit, all one has to do is to pull off the cover.

DHE-SL 电热水器, 2005

Stiebel Eltron GmbH & Co. KG,
Holzminden
Design: Dirk Schumann, Büro für industrielle Formentwicklung, Münster
www.stiebel-eltron.com

新一代DHE即热式电热水器的特征不仅仅在于它那极具吸引力的外形设计、蕴含高科技的技术零部件的使用，还结合了Stiebel Eltron产品本身不断地创新、设计上的人性化和整体的高质量，带给使用者安全上的保障，让人倍感舒心。该热水器的设计目的是要“以其最美丽的形式”给用户带来热水。因为经常进行不断变化的温度选择，过去的DHE偶尔会出现冷热不均的现象。现在，除了两种设定好的温度外，你也根据个人喜好，从四种新的淋浴项目中选择一种有利于健康的方式。虽然它的功率很大，但仍非常节约能源，让人更加称心如意。与同类的其他产品平常的外观相区别，新一代DHE即热式电热水器展现了完全重新诠释产品设计的一种方法。新的设计让人产生了深刻的视觉印象，在整体设计上与公司产品达到和谐统一。

The combination of attractive design, the use of high-tech components, constant product innovation, safety, wellness and user-friendliness, as well as the high Stiebel Eltron quality, are characteristic of the new generation of DHE instantaneous water heaters, bringing the user hot water "in its most beautiful form". Cold shocks are a thing of the past with the DHE, because the infinitely variable temperature selection is always maintained – accurately. Aside from the two original programmable temperatures, you can now also select from one of four new wellness shower programmes for good health. The heaters are powerful, yet energy- and water-saving, providing a high degree of comfort. Different from the usual appearance of other products in this segment, they point the way to a complete reinterpretation of object design. Without losing the corporate product identity, the new design creates impressive visual highlights.

面向患者的无障碍造型和更优秀的设计

Handicap-free forms and enhanced design for the patients

在"生命科学和医药"领域，**体贴入微的设计的重要性正在提高**，这可能是评委沃弗岗·K·梅尔–哈兹，弗朗塞斯科·米拉尼和朗·纳巴罗所认定的今年的主要趋势之一。他们告诉我们，更多的考虑将要针对"当面对超大型的医药器械时患者的感受是什么样的"，令这些设备看起来不那么恐怖已经成为设计师重点考虑的因素。更进一步地说，在患者和医生之间创造一种和谐的气氛是最重要的。对评委来讲，最有吸引力的莫过于能为身体有缺陷的人设计辅助设施的一些创新方法。例如，假肢和矫行器，能够不再像现在这样，让人一眼便识别出来；相反，它们甚至可以创造出一种运动的氛围，表现出一种对身体残疾的积极正面的态度。正如评委们所强调的那样，当今关注的焦点主要在于"简约的设计和新材料的有效使用"。评委们都从这样一个方面来积极做出评价，那就是即便是最简单医疗设备的设计也要满足医疗生活中每天的需求。一个好的医疗器械设计中的简单易懂的操作界面非常重要，也许在为数不多的病例中，它就能大大降低医护人员出错的可能性。

今年，"生命科学和医药"国际评委会第一次对送往"红点设计奖：生命科学设计"的产品做出评价。作为红点设计奖的一个部分，这一独立奖项也许是对这样一种需求所做的回应，那便是人们对医疗技术、微观和生物工艺学上领域内产品设计的不断进步。

The growing importance of considered design *in the "life science and medicine" category was perhaps one of the major trends discerned this year by the jurors Wolfgang Meyer-Hayoz, Francesco Milani and Ron Nabarro. Much thought, they tell us, is going into "how the patient feels when confronted with oversized medical apparatus." Making such equipment look less intimidating has become a focal design consideration. Moreover, the creation of a harmonious atmosphere for patient and physician is foremost. Highly interesting for the jury were the innovative approaches to designing auxiliary devices for the physically handicapped. Foot and arm prostheses, for instance, or walking aids, are no longer instantly recognisable as such, and instead radiate a sporting aura conveying a positive attitude towards physical disability. The focus lies, as the jurors stress, on "extremely reduced design and the deployment of new materials." The jurors rate very positively a further aspect: the fact that the design even of "simple" medical instruments addresses the day-to-day demands of medical life. Supported by easily understood user interfaces, a considered design may in individual cases actively eliminate the risk of error on the part of doctors or nursing staff.*

This year for the first time, the international jury in the category "life science and medicine" assessed the products that had been submitted to the current "red dot award: life science design." As part of the red dot design award, this independent award responds to the special demands on design both in medical technology and in the micro and biotechnology industry.

朗·纳巴罗
Ron Nabarro
以色列
Israel

沃弗岗·K·梅尔–亥兹
Wolfgang Meyer-Hayoz
瑞士
Schweiz

弗朗塞斯科·米拉尼
Francesco Milani
瑞士
Schweiz

生命科学与医药
Life science and medicine

reddot design award
life science design

Symbia SPECT·CT-扫描仪，2004

Siemens Medical Solutions USA,
Hoffman Estates, USA
Werksdesign
www.medical.siemens.com

Symbia是第一种通过单光子发射计算机断层成像技术，从而把CT诊断技术和SPECT成像功能结合在一起的扫描仪。临床医生仅仅只需一个步骤的剖析，就能在前后影像上判断出器官的运转情况。此外，它还具备了一些新型特点，例如有一个集成的患者信息娱乐系统，配有15英寸的TFT平板显示器，立体扩音器和DVD播放器，这些使得患者能够知道自己的检查情况，还可以听听音乐或者看看电影。这些解决方案提高了患者的舒适度，尤其是患者在做长达30分种SPECT检查的时候，因为这时患者必须保持一动不动。按照人体工程学原理为患者设计的辅助设施（例如头垫，胳膊垫，膝盖垫等等），为所有年龄群的患者提供了正确而舒适的位置。Symbia通过一个简单的、直观控制的界面来操作，产品的整体外形传达出先进的技术，没有让患者或者操作人员感到丝毫不适。

Symbia is the first scanner to combine diagnostic CT and SPECT studies with TruePoint SPECT·CT technology. Physicians can evaluate organ functions in context with the anatomy in one single step. Innovative features such as an integrated patient infotainment system with a 15-inch TFT flat panel, stereo speakers and a DVD player allow patients to inform themselves about the examination, listen to music or watch a movie. These design solutions enhance patient comfort particularly during SPECT examinations, in which the patient has to remain still for up to 30 minutes. Ergonomically designed patient accessories (headrest, armrest, knee bolsters, etc.) provide for correct and comfortable positioning of patients in all age brackets. Symbia is operated by a simple, intuitive control interface and the overall appearance of the product conveys state-of-the-art technology without intimidating either patient or operator.

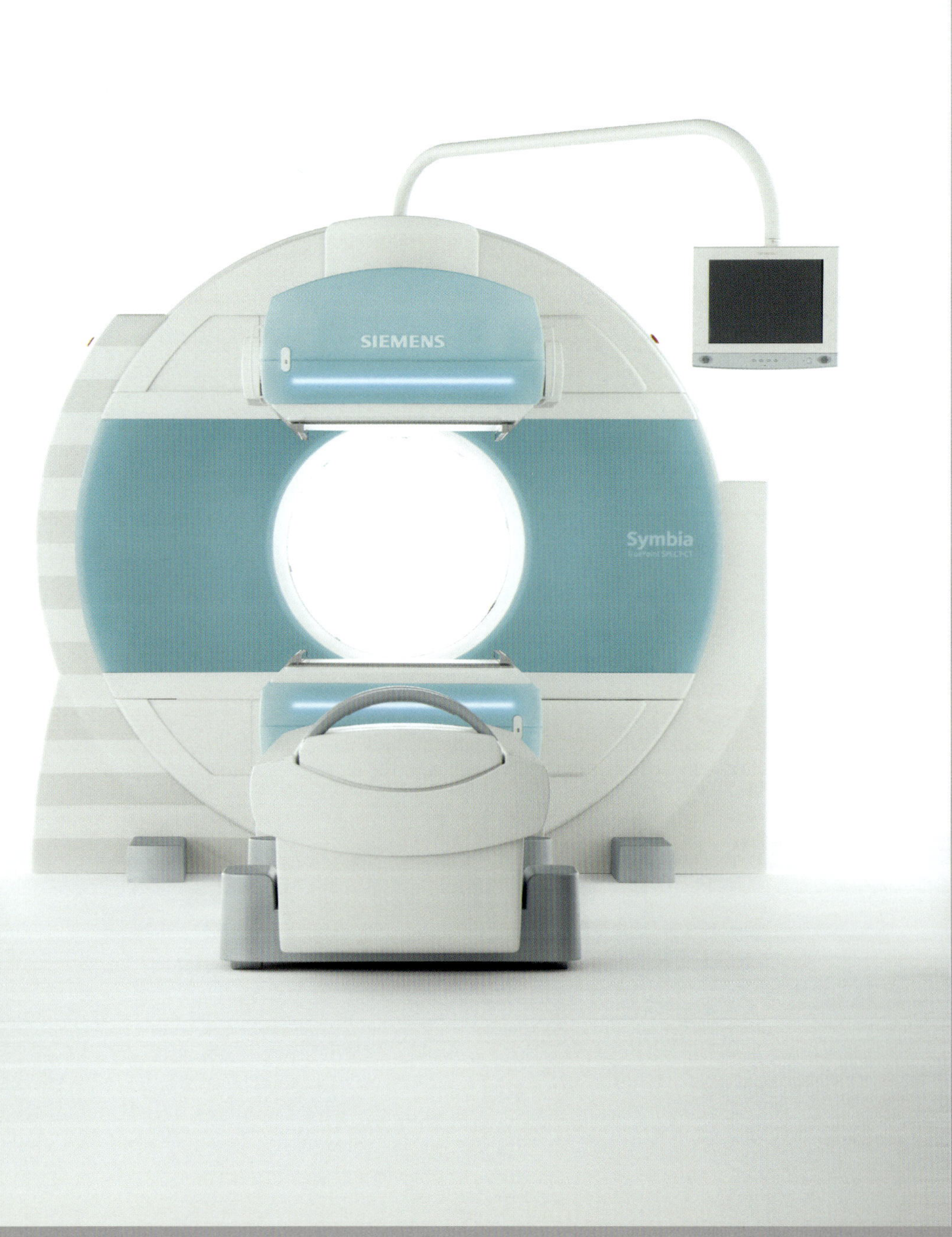

Somatom Spirit 双层CT系统, 2005

Siemens AG, Medical Solutions, Forchheim
Design: designafairs GmbH (Klaus Thormann), Erlangen
www.siemens.com
www.designafairs.com

多层螺旋CT Somatom Spirit的设计富有人性化，外形时尚美观，并且符合人体工程学原理。简洁直观的操作界面可以引导操作者进行整个检查过程。创新的多层螺旋CT以亚秒级转速运转，在实际应用中可以显示出一种卓越的成像质量。该CT机主要特点在于其标准化和扩展的3D成像编辑选择。一天可以对多达50个病人进行检查。Somatom Spirit安装步骤简单，也不占用空间，是一种性价比很高的设备，可广泛地应用于各种医疗机构中进行临床诊断。

The patient- and user-friendly multislice computer tomograph Somatom Spirit is trendsetting, appealing and designed ergonomically. An intuitive and simplified user interface leads the operator through the entire examination process. The innovative multislice CT works with sub-second rotational speed and displays an excellent image quality during all kinds of routine applications. The CT features a standard and an extended 3D image editing option. Up to 50 patients can be examined on one single day. The Somatom Spirit requires only some few installation steps and little space. It is an inexpensive and cost-effective device for any facility and clinical routine.

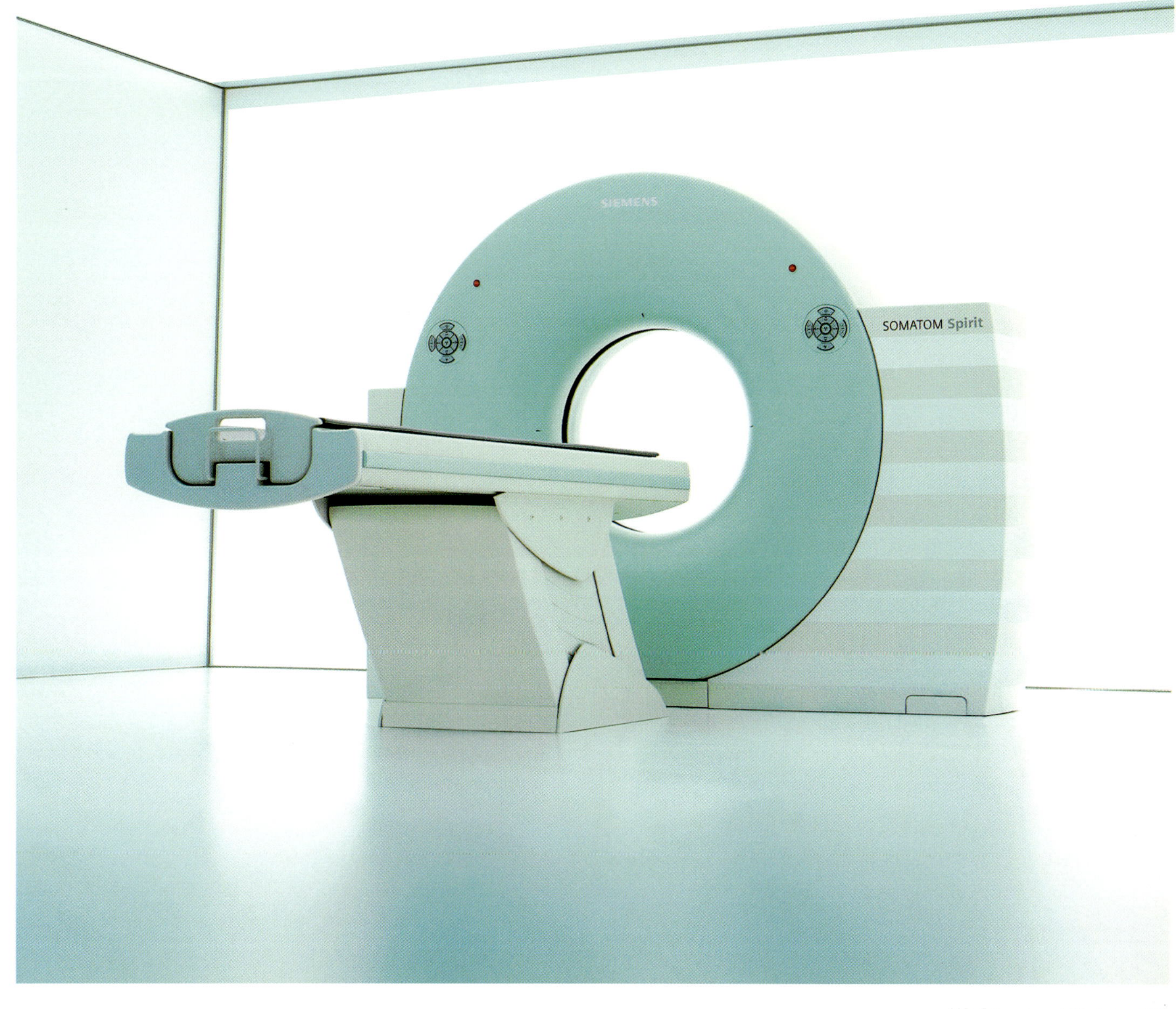

Magnetom Espree
核磁共振成像系统, 2004

Siemens AG, Erlangen
Werksdesign: Cornelius Becker, Cecile Mohr, Bernd Montag, Wolfgang Gößwein
Design: designafairs GmbH (Gerd Helmreich, Sebastian Maier, Alexander Müller), Erlangen
www.siemens.com
www.designafairs.com

Magnetom Espree 是世界上第一个1.5 – tesla开放式核磁共振成像系统，其腔体直径达到70厘米。该系统结构紧凑，长度仅为125厘米，可以保证在由高位系统提供成像质量和最佳诊断的同时，考虑到开放系统下的病人舒适度。与所有传统的开放系统相比，这种创新的磁体设计可以为病人提供更多的自由。在超过60%的检查中，病人的头部都可以保持在扫描仪的外面。

The Magnetom Espree magnetic resonance system is the first 1.5-tesla magnetic resonance tomograph in the world with a tunnel diameter of 70cm. A compact length of only 1.25 metres combines the patient comfort provided by an open system with the imaging quality and best possible diagnosis offered by a high-field system. An innovative magnet design offers more freedom for patients than all conventional open systems; in over 60 per cent of examinations the patient's head remains outside the system.

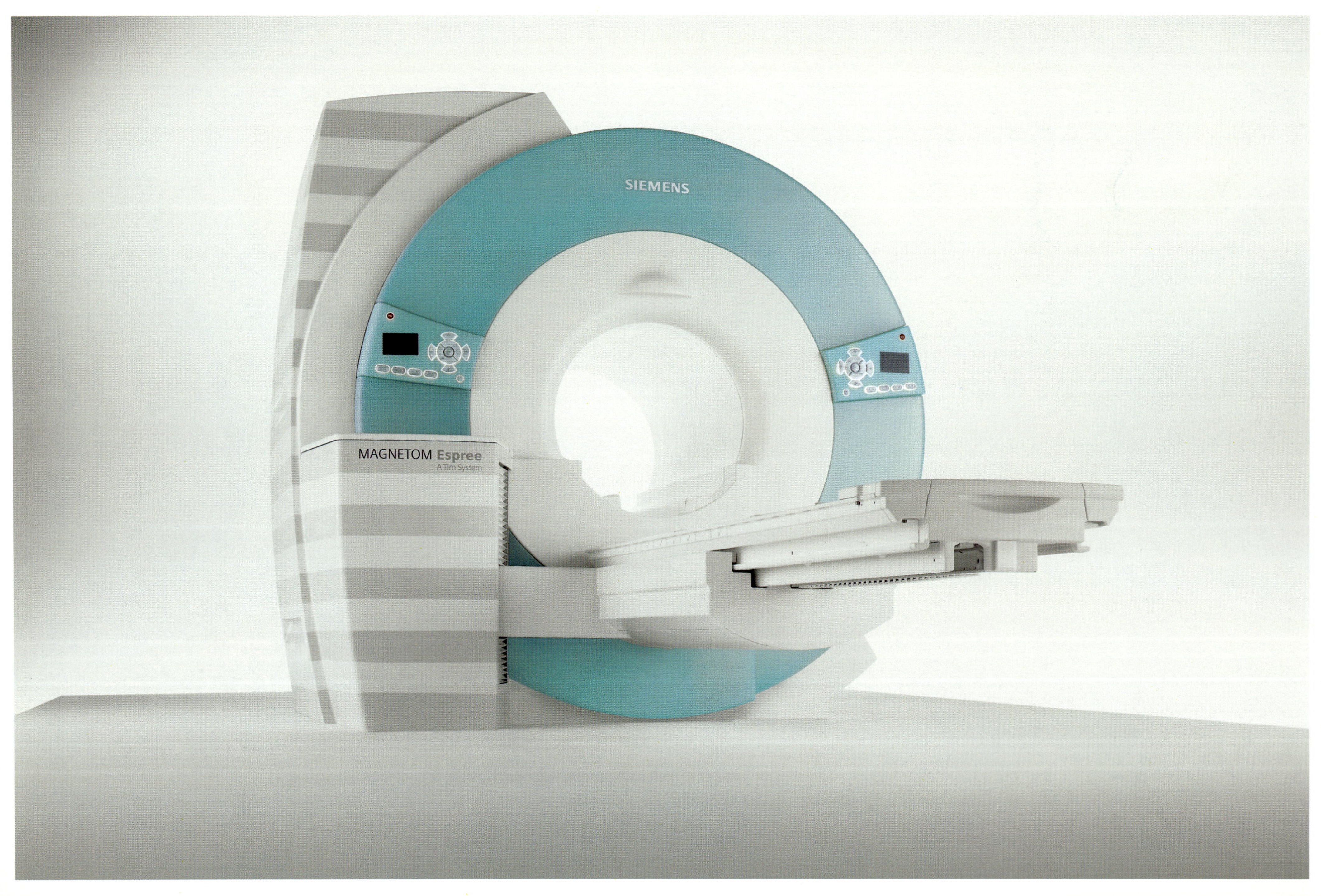

Magnetom C!
核磁共振成像系统, 2004

Siemens AG, Erlangen
Werksdesign: Peter Distler,
Stefan Domalski, Deert Gellner,
Karsten Großhauser
Design: designafairs GmbH
(Gerd Helmreich, Alexander Müller),
Erlangen
www.siemens.com
www.designafairs.com

Magnetom C!核磁共振成像系统是一种用于进行放射诊断的永久磁体。它是同类中非常紧凑的一种磁体，磁极直径为132厘米。该系统由于能从侧面滑入而特别富有人性化。C形设计、270度的全面开放，以及在磁体上方和下方之间很大的距离，使病人感觉很宽敞，也为操作人员留下了足够的空间。在极板和新的卷缆装置系统之间的大的空隙是为体态比较臃肿的病人而设计的。与其他系统相比较，由于它的空间宽敞且运行速度较快，加上其独特的100厘米的成像长度，能够提供卓越的成像质量和一种更为经济的工作流程，而且不需要使用昂贵的氦技术。由于其外形设计新颖活泼，颜色宜人，自然而然地营造出了一种愉快和友好的气氛，使得该系统几乎能够融入到任何风格的设计中去。

The Magnetom C! magnetic resonance system is a permanent magnet used for diagnosis in radiology. With a diameter of 132cm, it is a very compact magnet of its category. The system is particularly patient-friendly due to the sideway slide-in access. The C-shape, the very large 270-degree panoramic opening and the large distance between the upper and lower parts of the magnet give the patient a feeling of free space, leaving enough room for operating personnel. A large gap between the pole plates and a new spool system were designed with overweight patients in mind. A more economical workflow, in comparison to other systems, is possible due to the high spatial and high speed resolution, as well as the unique image length of 100cm. The system delivers excellent image quality, achievable without the use of expensive helium technology. The shape and colour accentuate the pleasant und humane ambience created by the system which integrates into any interior design.

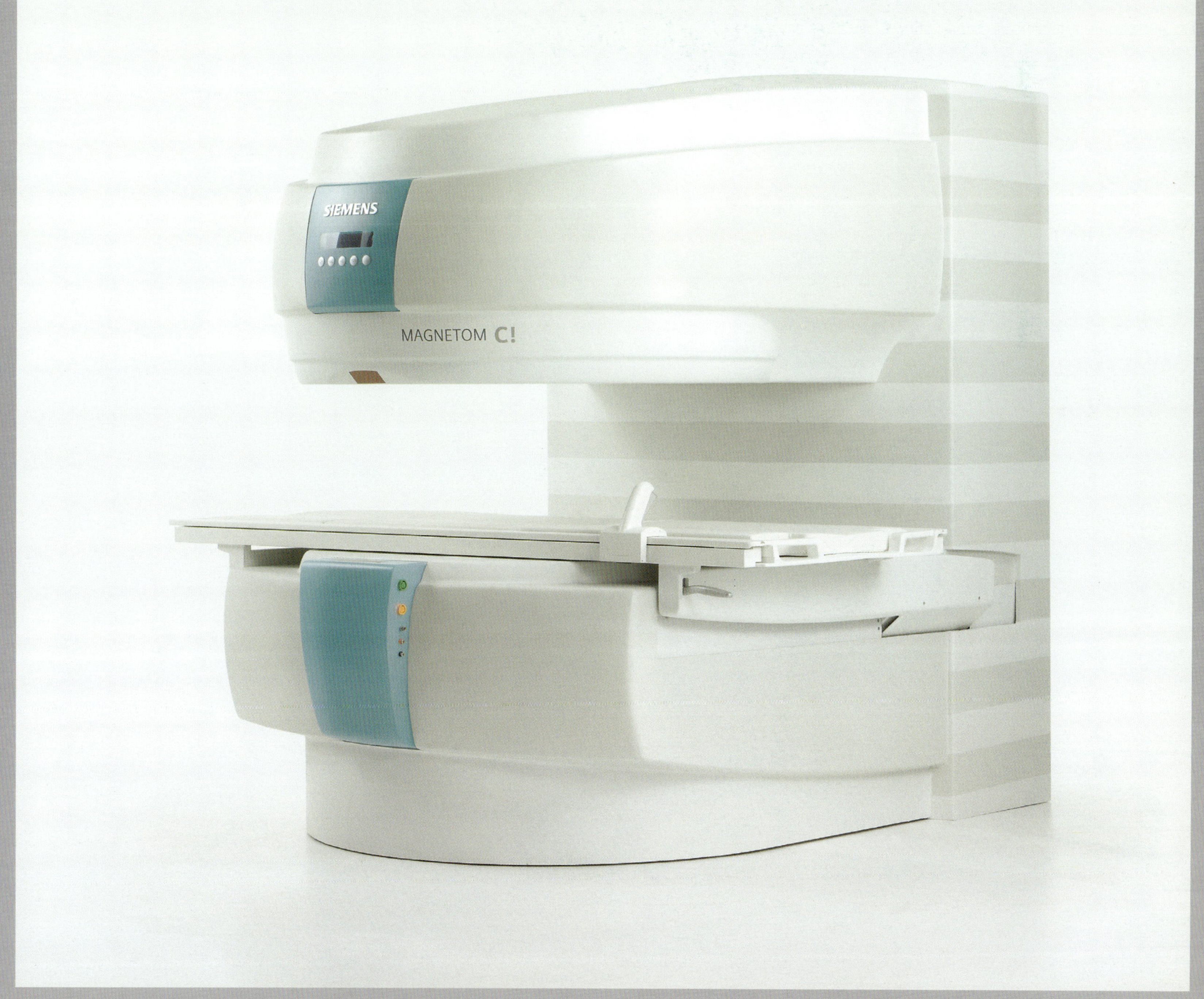

DynamicArm 假肢, 2004

Otto Bock HealthCare GmbH,
Duderstadt
Werksdesign: Otto Bock HealthCare
Products GmbH, Wien, Österreich
Design: vertical pre-production
management GmbH, Wien, Österreich
www.ottobock.com
www.vertical.at

DynamicArm的开发是基于临位仿生原理，即观察和分析自然的机械装置和过程以及其向实际技术解决方案的转化过程。DynamicArm是第一种使用微处理器控制，并且具有连续传动装置的电子肘关节。这种多变的传动装置使得该产品非常接近自然而真实的胳膊活动，甚至在拿着很重的物体时，也能够快速、准确地找准位置。单臂或者双臂有缺陷的人们现在可以充分利用DynamicArm的强大的性能，每天享受到更多的自主性。这些技术上的创新都融入到了这款外形很自然的肘关节中，通过硅酮元素的添加，也使得噪音大大降低。

The development of the DynamicArm was based on Orthobionic® principles – the observation and analysis of natural mechanisms and processes as well as their translation into practical technical solutions. The DynamicArm is the first microprocessor-controlled electronic elbow with stepless gears. This Vario-transmission provides a close approximation to natural arm movements and allows for a quick, exact positioning of the hand – even with heavy objects. People with unilateral or bilateral upper extremity limb deficiencies can now take advantage of the high functionality of the DynamicArm and enjoy greater independence every day. These technological innovations have been incorporated into a natural-appearing elbow with unobtrusive, noise-dampening silicone elements of a different shade.

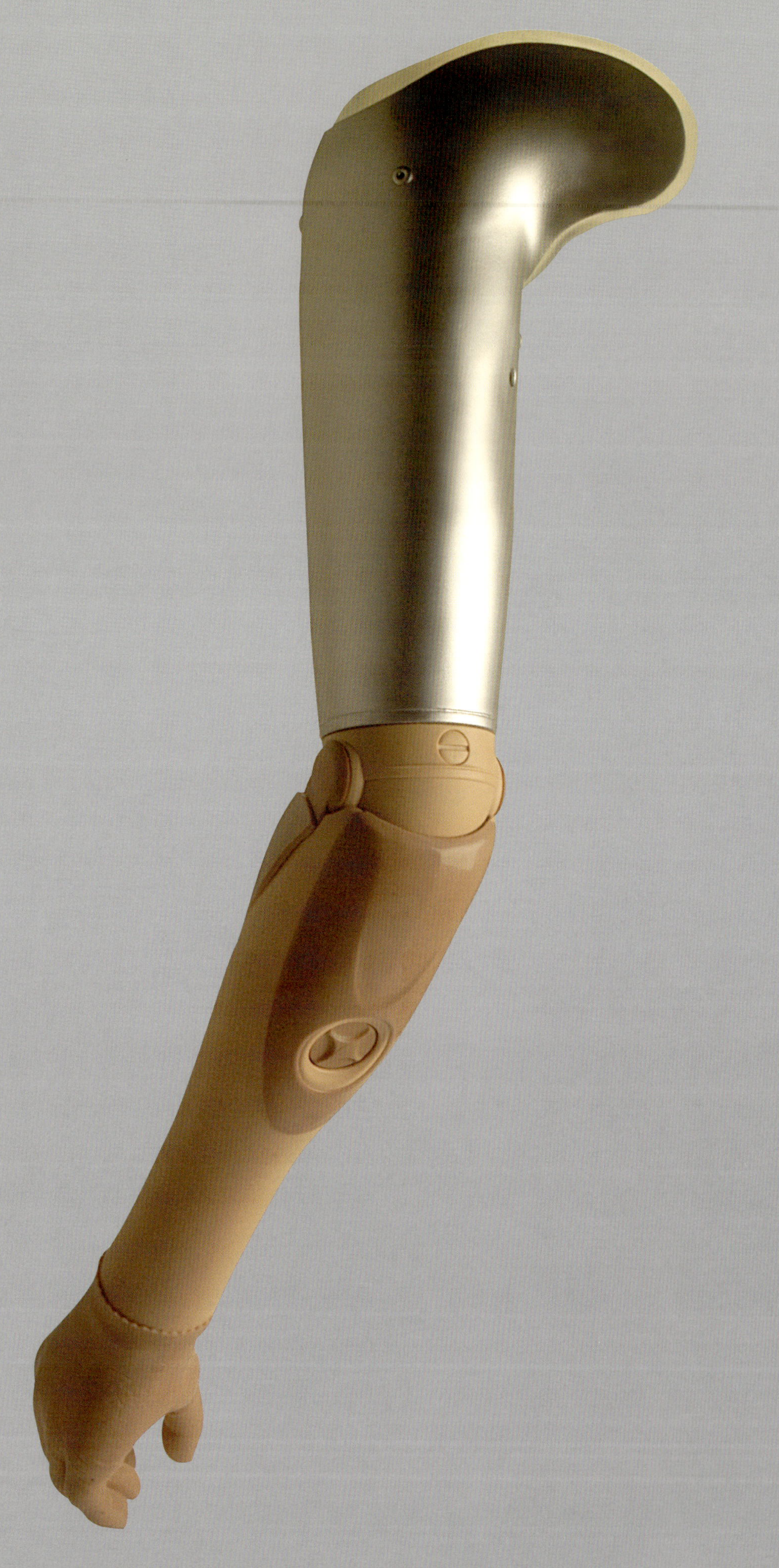

Hansaton Leonardo VC
数字化助听器，2004

Hansaton Akustik GmbH, Hamburg
Design: Pilotfish GmbH, München
www.hansaton.de
www.pilotfishproducts.com

Hansaton Leonardo VC是一款非常袖珍的一流的数字化助听器。由于其设计充满活力，且有两种颜色可供选择，使得Leonardo VC不再被认为是一个助听器，而更像是一个高科技的助手。另外，双重外壳的设计也使得只需简单更换外壳就可以选择不同的颜色。

The Hansaton Leonardo VC is a first-class digital hearing aid system of extremely small size. With its dynamic, two-coloured design, the Leonardo VC is no longer perceived as a hearing aid, but rather as a high-tech helper. In addition, the dual-shell design allows for an individual colour choice, simply by exchanging the housing shell.

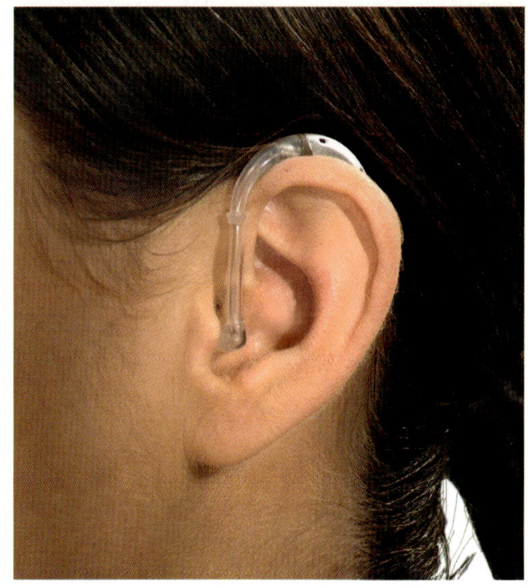

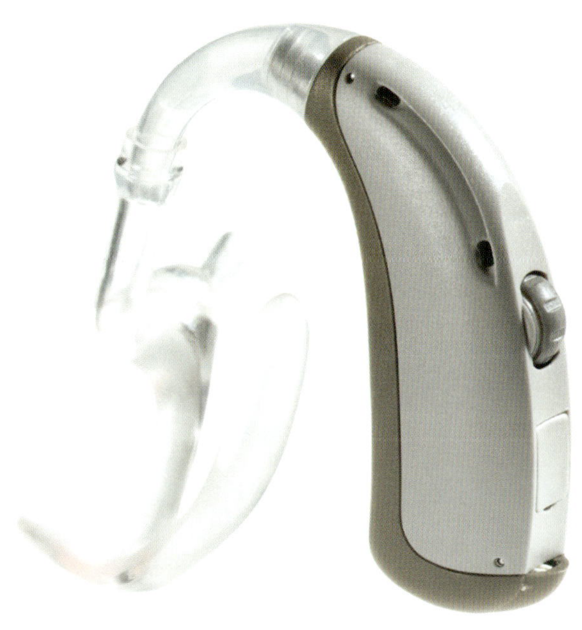

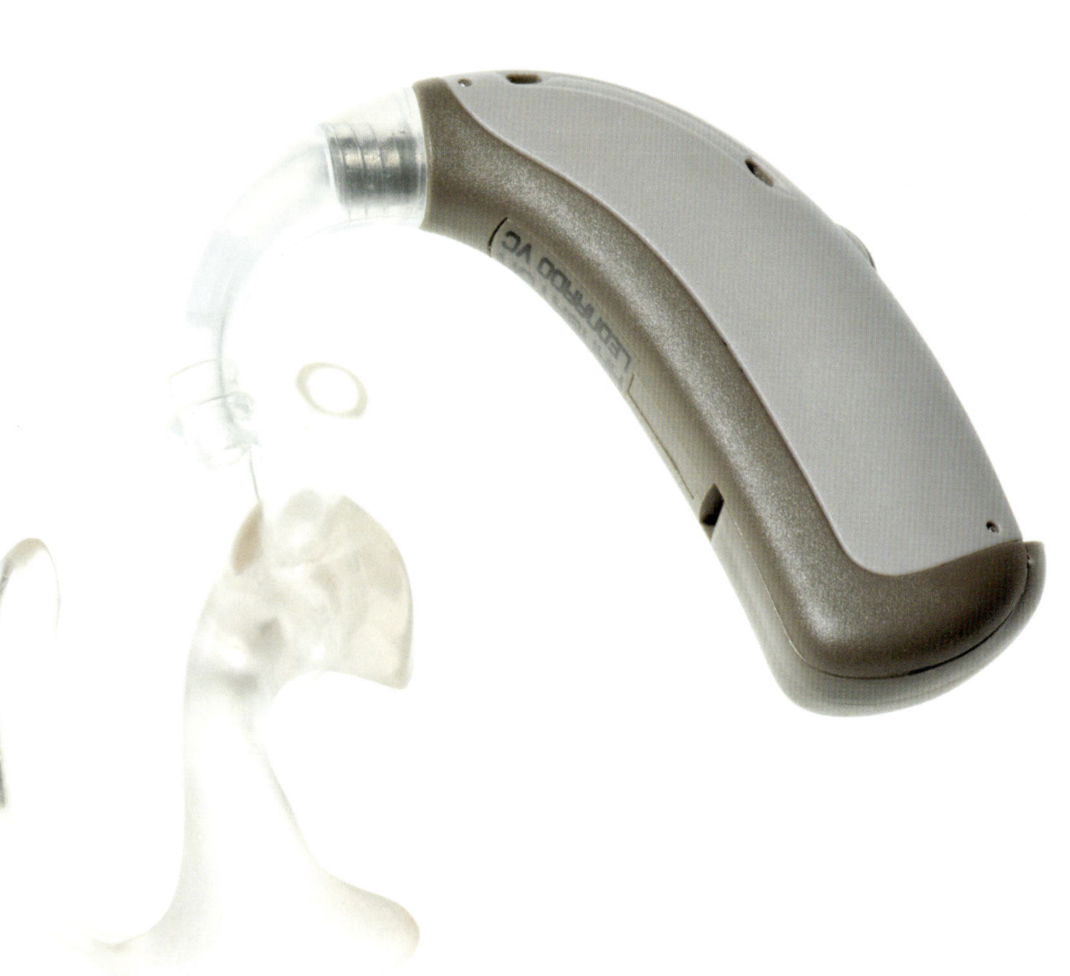

culta 阅读照明灯, 2004

Derungs Licht AG, Gossau, Schweiz
Werksdesign: Samuel Furrer
Design: Zeug Designgroup
(Erwin Weitgasser, Detlev Magerer),
Salzburg, Österreich
Vertrieb: Herbert Waldmann GmbH &
Co. KG, Villingen-Schwenningen
www.derungslicht.com

culta阅读照明灯外形精致纤细，性能稳定。它将不变的经典设计和创新的功能结合起来，能够与任何一个房间的风格相融合，可以创造令人愉悦的氛围，打造一种品质生活。将灯的头部倾斜就能够很容易地进行开或关，代替了找开关的过程。在其顶部的LED定位灯便于人们在黑暗中找到灯的位置。有冷灯反射器的卤素灯让人们的使用更加舒适。此外，由于它配备了两层灯罩，灯散发出来的热量非常低，不会有被灼伤的隐患。culta共有三种款式可供选用，分别可以安装在墙上，桌子或地板上进行使用。

The culta reading lamp is delicate, slender, but stable after all. It combines a timeless design with innovative functionality and can be integrated into any room where it creates a high degree of quality of living and a pleasant atmosphere. By tilting the head of the lamp, it can be easily turned on and off – no cumbersome search for a switch. An LED orientation light in the head of the lamp facilitates locating the lamp in the dark. A halogen lamp with cold light reflector offers a high degree of comfort; due to the double wall casing the heat emission of the lamp is quite low; there is no hazard of burns or other injuries. culta is available in three versions: as wall, table or floor lamp.

Lehnen Evolution 卫浴设施, 2005

Lehnen edel:stahl GmbH, Wittlich
Werksdesign: Alois Lehnen
Design: Brodbeck Design, München
www.lehnen-edelstahl.de

Evolution系列卫浴设施外形雅致，能够适应不断变化的生活状况。由于其表层的牢靠质量和过硬的工艺，再加上美观的外形，使它能够协调地与繁杂的卫生间设计融合在一起。高雅的外表下融合了它的稳定而可靠的构造，这使得使用者能够在公共系统中也能根据在私人环境下的DIN18024和18025进行操作。该设备将明亮的元素与不锈钢拉丝结合起来。有涂层的不锈钢管的表面设计得没有接缝，方便清洗。着色的零件第一次能够直接投入使用，而无需根据完全由不锈钢生产的零件的优点来进行分配。在卫生间，淋浴，浴缸和面盆旁都可以使用它们。

Evolution is an elegant-appearing bathroom equipment series capable of adapting to changing life situations. Due to the high surface quality, the reliable workmanship and the aesthetic shaping, it blends harmoniously into the sophisticated bathroom design. The elegant outer appearance holds in itself a stable and reliable construction allowing for an operation in public systems according to DIN 18024 and 18025 in private surroundings. The system combines colourful elements with brushed stainless steel. The powder-coated stainless steel tubes are designed with a seamless, easy-to-clean hygienic surface. For the first time, coloured component parts can be put to use without having to dispense with the advantages of an element entirely made out of stainless steel. Evolution ist an extensive programme for rest room, shower, tub and sink.

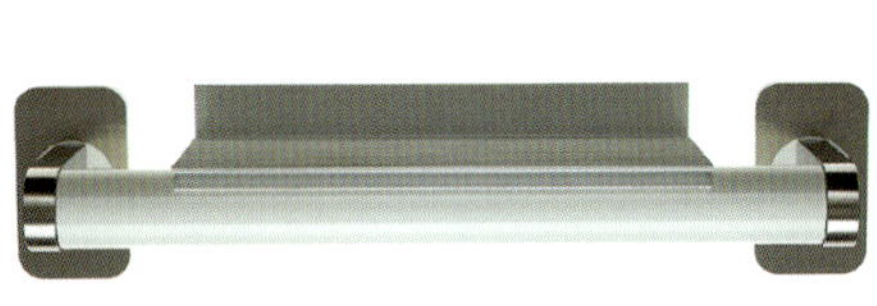

inEos 牙齿扫描仪, 2005

Sirona Dental Systems GmbH, Bensheim
Werksdesign: Peter Fornoff,
Wolfgang Eiff
Design: designafairs GmbH
(Thomas Blümel), Erlangen; DTC
(Nadjaf Mougoni), Bensheim
www.sirona.com

inEos牙齿扫描仪是inLab系统的附加部件，它使得牙科医生能够在不到一秒钟的时间之内把牙齿划伤的情况复制下来并且用数字进行记录，还可记录齿桥的状况、整个颌牙具和修补颌的状况。用这种方法就可更快更好地进行CAD/CAM修复。inEos并没有从视觉上利用单光子激光扫描仪来分析牙齿的状况，而是使用荧光灯投影系统把检查时间从5分钟减少到大约20秒。当用inEos测量齿桥的时候仅仅需要10到35秒，时间上的缩减更加地给人们带来方便。另外，整个颌模型也可以用该设备进行扫描。当扫描完时，一个三维的形象就会出现在电脑屏幕上，而此时牙科医生也做好开始工作的准备了。

The dental scanner inEos is an additional component to the inLab system and enables the dental technician to copy and digitally record the image of single snags, bridge situations, whole jaw models and complementary jaw situations within fractions of a second. In this way, CAD/CAM restorations can be done faster and more efficiently. inEos does not analyse the dental situation optically with a single-point laser scanner, but employs a striplight projection system reducing the time for measurement from about five minutes down to approx. 20 seconds. This reduction in time is even more noticeable when gauging a bridge situation with inEos which only takes anywhere from 10 to 35 seconds. In addition, whole jaw models can be scanned with the device. Right after having taken the shot a three-dimensional image appears on the computer screen, and the dental technician is ready to begin work.

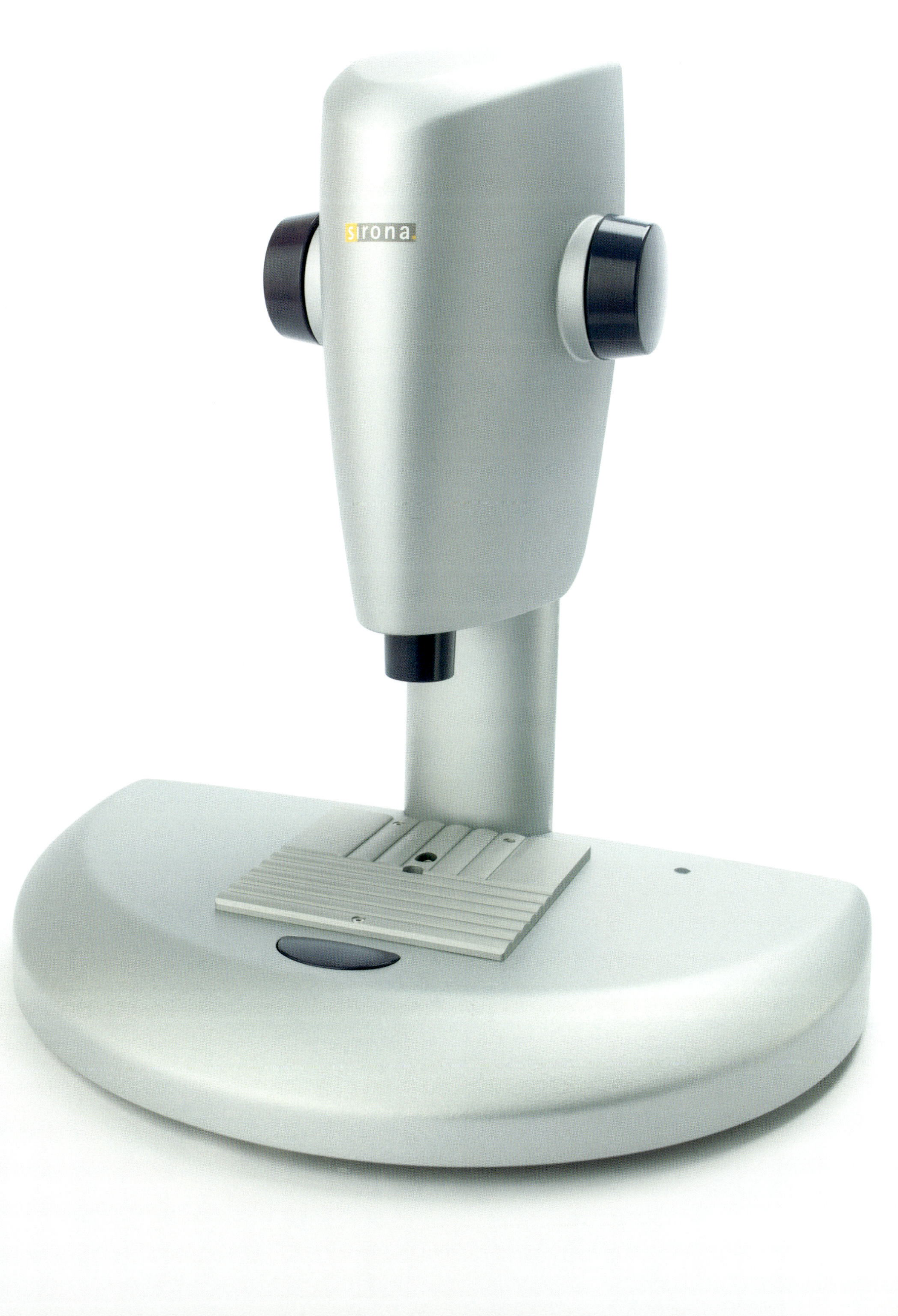

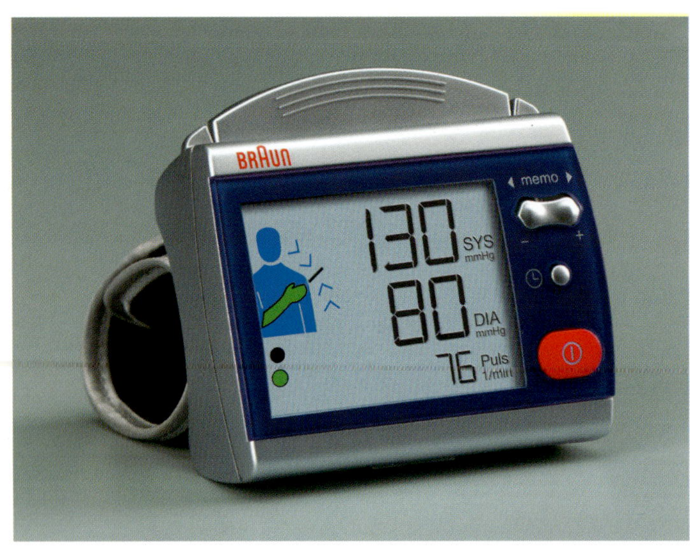

SensorControl BP 3000
血压仪, 2005

Braun GmbH, Kronberg
Werksdesign: Peter Hartwein
www.braun.com

SensorControl BP 3000血压仪使人们在家中就可以测量到精确的血压。血压仪具备进行自我调节的EasyClick技术，防止不正确的调节，并保证正确的临床阅读。由于它采用了扩张技术，使得检查过程是很轻柔温和的。EasyClick不是在减压阶段检查血压，而是在扩张阶段进行检查，这就意味着要求的最高压比较低。

The SensorControl BP 3000 blood pressure monitor optimises exact measurement of blood pressure at home. The blood pressure cuff is equipped with an innovative self-adjusting EasyClick technology, helping to safeguard against incorrect adjustment and ensuring clinically accurate reading. With its soft inflating technology, the measurement process is gentle. Instead of measuring the blood pressure in the decompression phase, EasyClick measures it in the inflation phase. This means that the maximum pressure required is lower.

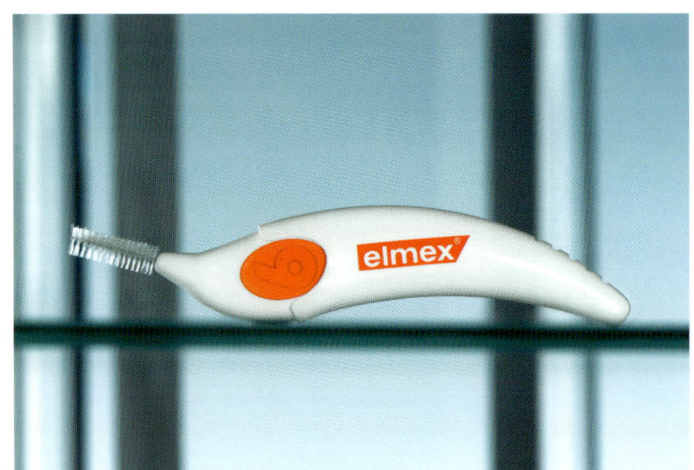

elmex Interdental 牙刷, 2004

Gaba International AG, Münchenstein, Schweiz
Design: OCO-Design O.K. Nüsse (Brigitta Podobrin), Münster
www.gaba.com
www.oco-design.de

Interdental牙刷在设计中考虑到了清洁齿缝的重要性。这套工具包括了带有把手的一个小牙刷，牙刷上还有一个保护帽。根据人体工程学而设计的把手是在瑞士联邦苏黎世高等工业大学的科学家们的合作下开发出来的，该把手有一个用着色的软塑料制成的容易握住的凹处，这样也为分辨不同型号的牙刷提供了帮助。

The Interdental Brush has been designed taking into account that cleaning the interdental spaces is becoming increasingly important. The set consists of a handle with a little brush combined with a protective cap. It is easy to use, in the dental practice as well as at home. The ergonomically designed handle, developed in cooperation with scientists at the ETH Zurich, has a special easy-grip indentation in coloured TPE (soft plastic); this also serves as an aid to identifying the different brush sizes.

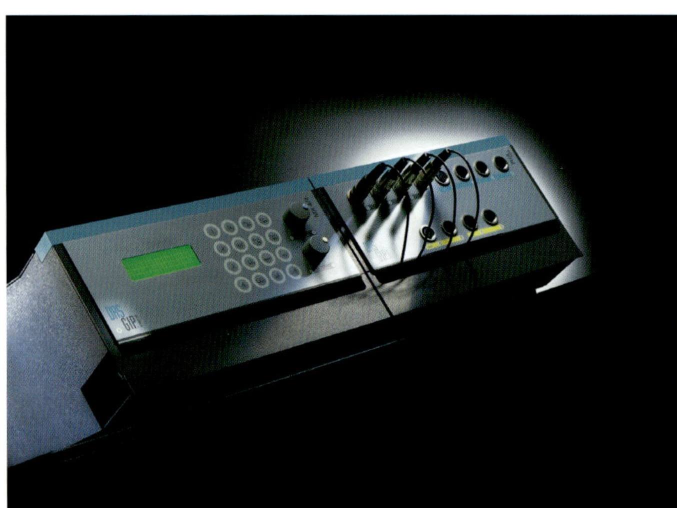

DASGIP cellferm-pro
细胞培养系统, 2003

DASGIP AG, Jülich
Werksdesign: Matthias Arnold, Werner Carl
Design: WILDDESIGN (Marc Ruta, Markus Wild), Gelsenkirchen
www.dasgip.de
www.wilddesign.de

DASGIP cellferm-pro是一组进行人类、动物和植物细胞培养的并联系统。模块化的设计有利于在实验中和工业范围内的不同的应用中实现高度灵活性。DASGIP cellferm-pro可在单独的模块进行下列工作，例如定剂量、排气体、搅动等，这些都能够融入复杂的培养系统中。该设计外形井然有序，让人觉得非常整洁。培养系统中的不同模块进行了统一设计并有相同的外形特征，能够一个挨一个地码放起来。

DASGIP cellferm-pro is a parallel system for the cultivation of human, animal and plant cells. The modular design facilitates highest flexibility for different applications on an experimental and industrial scale as well. DASGIP cellferm-pro offers single modules for e.g. dosing, gassing and agitation, which can be combined to complex cultivation systems. The design displays a high degree of tidiness. The different modules of the cultivation system are designed uniformly and have an identical overall size. They can both be stacked and set side by side.

EndoEye 摄像式关节内窥镜, 2005

Olympus Deutschland GmbH, Hamburg
Design: Held + Team (Fred Held), Hamburg
www.olympus.de
www.heldundteam.de

EndoEye摄像式关节内窥镜是一种用来对膝关节进行外科手术的新产品。它创造性地第一次将符合人体工程学的并具有强大功能性的光学设备、冲洗设备和摄像工具都融入到一种工具中。通过调整主轮子，将监控器上的影像旋转过程像旋转的光缆一样融合得很好。从操作者的角度来看，三种工具整合成为一个紧凑的单独设备。只需要用一根电缆来连接该工具和设备，并引导它以符合人体工程学的恰当角度降下来。

The EndoEye videoarthroscope is technically a completely new product for surgical operations at the knee joint. For the first time, the ergonomic and functional unit of optics, rinsing unit and camera are combined into one device. An image rotation on the monitor by adjusting the thumb wheel is integrated as well as the rotatable light fibre cable. From the operator's point of view, three instruments have merged into one single compact instrument. Only one cable has to be used to connect the instrument to the equipment, leading the instrument downwards at an ergonomically reasonable angle.

HiQ+ 手持腹腔镜, 2004

Olympus Deutschland GmbH, Hamburg
Design: Held + Team (Fred Held, Burkhard Peters), Hamburg
www.olympus.de
www.heldundteam.de

这种扩散性很小的手持腹腔镜把看起来好像将对立的几个方面都结合在了一起：缝合时甚至可以在工具转动轴上方进行灵敏的活动，可变的压力转换可以调节，直到将针稳定地固定住，应力针可进行直觉上的移动。该设计传达出的那种牢固的感觉一览无余，同时传达了这样一种想法：用自己的手握住这个简单而可靠的工具吧！柔软的线条设计也符合人体工程学的要求。

The design of this minimally invasive laparoscopic hand-held instrument combines seemingly contradictory aspects: a sensitive movement over the roll-axis of the instrument while sewing, the variable force transmission up to a very strong clamping of the needle and the intuitive releasing of the stressed needle. The design visualises the grip possibilities and simultaneously conveys the idea of holding a simple and reliable instrument in one's hands. The soft line management shows the ergonomic claims.

pipetus 移液器, 2004

Hirschmann Laborgeräte GmbH & Co. KG, Eberstadt
Design: heitlinger form und technik (Karl-Leo Heitlinger), Schwäbisch Gmünd
www.hirschmann-laborgeraete.de

该移液器在技术部件做了补充，使其移液功能做到了最大化。该产品优先考虑的是实验室的形象塑造和功能上的精确性，以及在其手动装置上的简便操作。该系列以平滑的、流线型的线条和过渡与极具对比性的硬的水平线条为特征。设计重点集中于位置上正确的交叉，以及调整参数和角度。因为它是一个手动装置，并且90%的用户都是女性。一旦移液器插入到手柄中，移液器轴、手柄轴以及两轴的轴距就形成了一个理想的操作几何体。更有新意的是有一个具有不受限制的铰链功能的墙体托架，这使得实验室里的助手能够在他或她认为舒适的任何位置悬挂该手动装置。

The pipetus has been functionally optimised and supplemented in its technical components and pipette functions. Priority was given to the visualisation of laboratory know-how itself, functional precision and ease of operation where manual devices are involved. Smooth, flowing lines and transitions and a contrasting, hard horizontal line characterise the product range. Maximum attention was paid to anthropometrically correct cross sections, adjusting parameters and angles, as it is a manual device, and 90 per cent users are women. Once the pipette is inserted in the pipette hand, the pipette axis, the handle axis of the device and the distance between both axes form the ideal operating geometry. A further innovation is a wall bracket with an unlimited hinge function. This allows the laboratory assistant to suspend the manual device in any position which he or she finds comfortable.

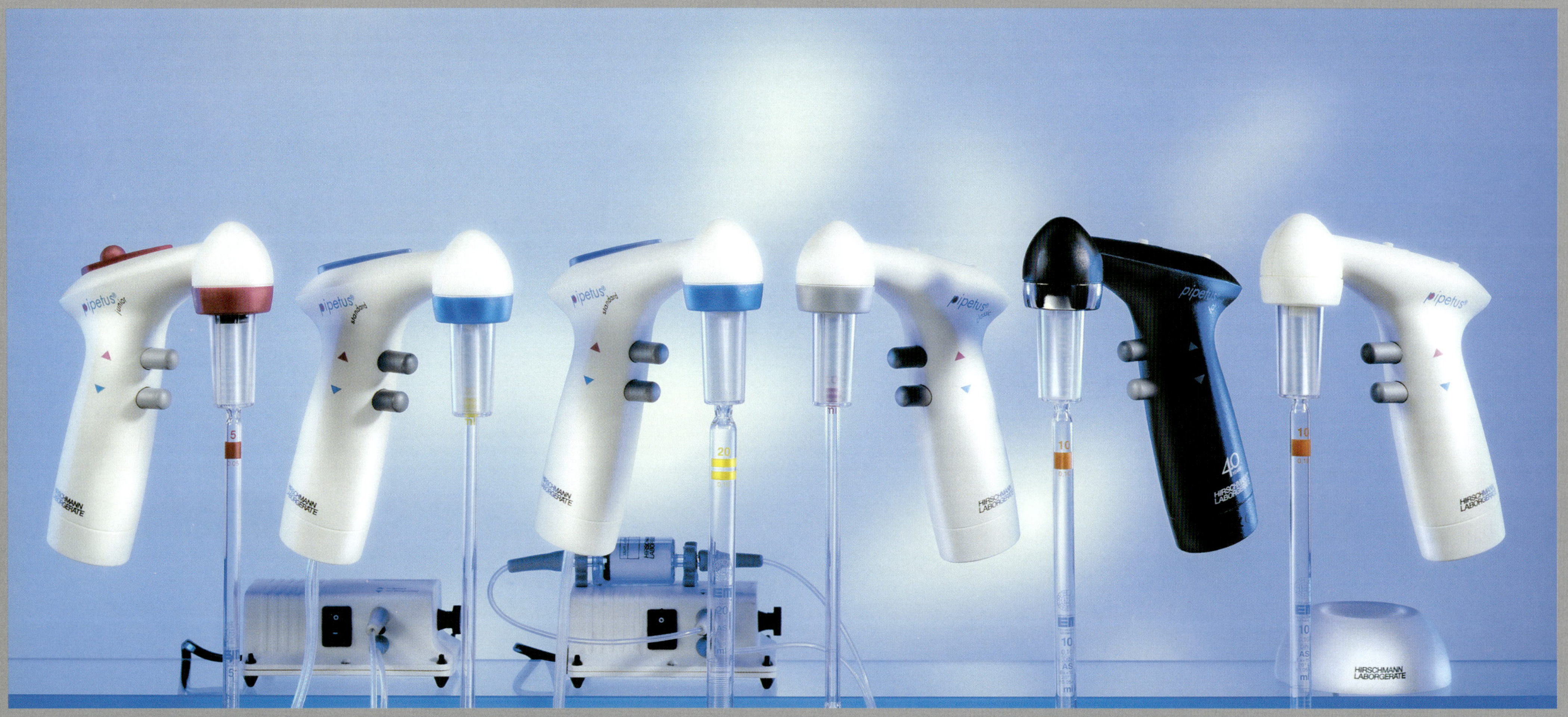

OLA 2500 S3i 奥林巴斯实验室自动化仪器，2003

Olympus Diagnostica Lab Automation GmbH, Freiburg
Design: Ottenwälder und Ottenwälder, Schwäbisch Gmünd
Vertrieb: Olympus Diagnostica GmbH, Hamburg
www.olympus.de
www.ottenwaelder.de

OLA 2500是一种用于实验前分析的实验室自动化仪器，它可以缩短实验室的处理过程。该仪器的开发意图是要在最大程度上避免处理过程中出现的错误率和延迟现象。由于OLA 2500在实验室中要发挥主导作用，因此在它的可靠性、精确度和人性化方面就需要有较高的要求。这些要求是通过把尖端技术、先进的软件和线条清晰、牢固的工业设计相结合来实现的。由于每一个实验室配备有不同厂家生产的不同分析仪，所以OLA 2500的设计中就采用了一种使所有不同种类的试验管都能进行处理的方法。该仪器是一个中央分配站，它能够在几分钟之内完成开帽，放射及对样本进行正确分类的自动操作等一系列处理。

The OLA 2500 is a laboratory instrument automating pre-analytical steps, thus reducing processing periods in the laboratory. The device was developed with the intent of avoiding the highest error rates and delays arising in the process. As the OLA 2500 takes on the leading part in the laboratory, high requirements as to reliability, precision and user-friendliness were demanded. This was accomplished by combining robust technologies, a superior software and a clear, strong industrial design. As each laboratory is equipped with different analysis devices from different manufacturers, the OLA 2500 is designed in such a way that all sorts of test tubes can be processed. The device is the central distribution station which automates decapping, aliquoting and the correct sorting of samples in a matter of minutes.

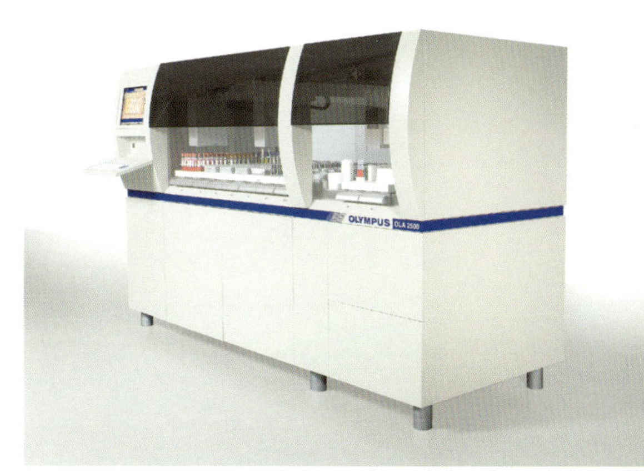

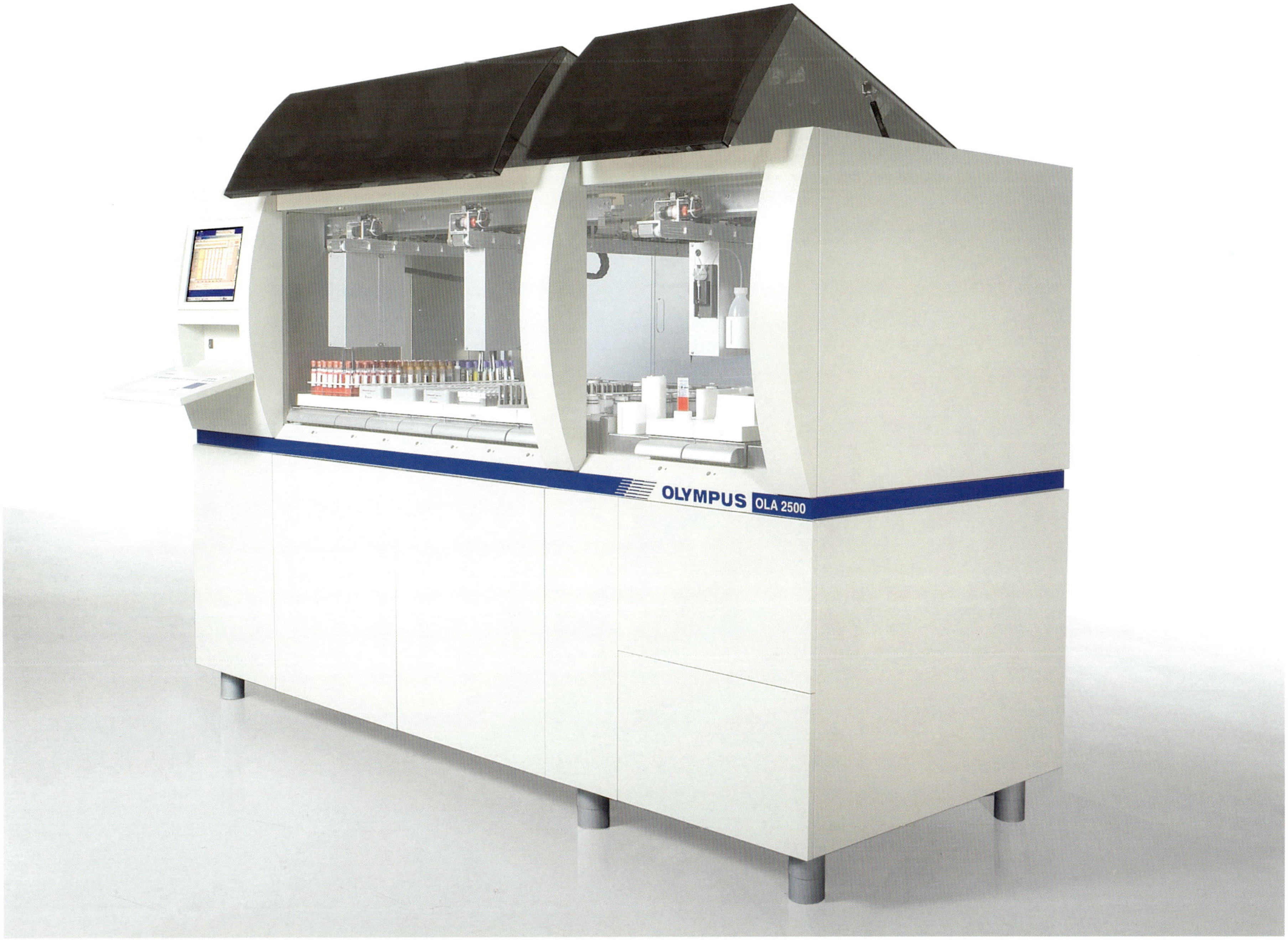

A 200 电动轮椅, 2004

Otto Bock HealthCare GmbH,
Duderstadt
Werksdesign
www.ottobock.com

结构紧凑的A 200电动轮椅是为那些生性活泼的残疾人而设计的，他们常常希望自己能在室内室外都独立行动。该产品镀银的金属骨架更加突出了它高雅而时尚的外形。由于总宽度仅为57厘米，重量仅为69千克，因此它是一种非常轻便的电动轮椅，能够轻松地通过狭窄的通道。28Ah的胶体电池可以为更加宽广的活动范围提供动力，其最大负重为100千克。A 200的移动速度最高可达6千米/小时，活动范围约为20千米。它能爬上12度的坡度，这样就可以让使用者自己做决定是否去旅行或者赴宴。为了在旅行期间也能方便使用，A 200能够很迅速而简便地进行拆卸还，可将它放置于汽车内当成一个特殊的座位。

The compact A 200 electric wheelchair has been designed for active people who want to move independently in- and outdoors. The elegant, modern look is further emphasised by its silver-metallic frame. With its overall width of 57cm and a weight of only 66kg, it is one of the extremely light electric wheelchairs and also fits through narrow doors. 28Ah gel batteries provide a large radius of mobility with a maximum load of 100kg. The A 200 has a maximum speed of 6km/h and has a range of approx. 20km. It is suitable for gradients of twelve per cent. Thus it allows its user to make spontaneous decisions such as trips or visits to restaurants. To optimise the logistics when travelling, the A 200 can be disassembled quickly and easily. Its use as a seat in a special vehicle has been certified.

先锋 Ti Ultra 轮椅, 2005

Otto Bock HealthCare GmbH,
Duderstadt
Werksdesign
www.ottobock.com

先锋系列中的Ti Ultra轮椅以其漂亮的设计可谓是在轮椅世界里将一些至今都不相共存的特征融合在了一起，开创了可折叠轮椅系列中新的轻薄重量等级。驱动轮调节器，是活动轮椅所特有的，并且可以保护驱动轮位置的可调节性，但现在却被牢固焊接的骨架部分所取代了。该骨架部分完全是组装而成的，并且牢固地焊接到骨架管和运动型的短推手中，给人一种坚如磐石的感觉。这些反过来又减少了零件的数量和总体重量。根据具体的坐姿以及附加的部件，算上Ti Ultra的脚踏和扶手侧板也仅重7.9千克。该产品最好是被那些对使用轮椅比较有经验的人所使用，因为他们知道自己最佳的坐姿而不需要再进行调节。在确定顺序的时候，驱动轮位置以一种格栅形式显示出来，随后再进行焊接。这种创新使得在使用时的稳定性与固定轮椅不相上下。

The aesthetic design of the Ti Ultra from the Avantgarde series represents a fusion of features for a wheelchair which seemed incompatible so far, thus opening up new weight classes in the segment of foldable wheelchairs. The drive wheel adapter, typical for active wheelchairs and securing the adjustability of the drive wheel position, has been replaced by a solid-welded back frame part. This frame part is a complete assembly group firmly integrating the back frame tube as well as sportive short push handles, giving the impression of a monolithic system. This in turn reduces the number of component parts as well as the overall weight. According to the individual sitting position and depending upon extra fittings, the Ti Ultra only weighs 7.9kg including footrest and side parts. It is thus conceived for experienced wheelchair drivers who have found their personal optimum sitting position which they don't need to readjust. When placing the order, the wheel position is indicated in a grid pattern and then welded accordingly. This innovation results in a driving stability of the Ti Ultra closely resembling that of a fixed wheelchair.

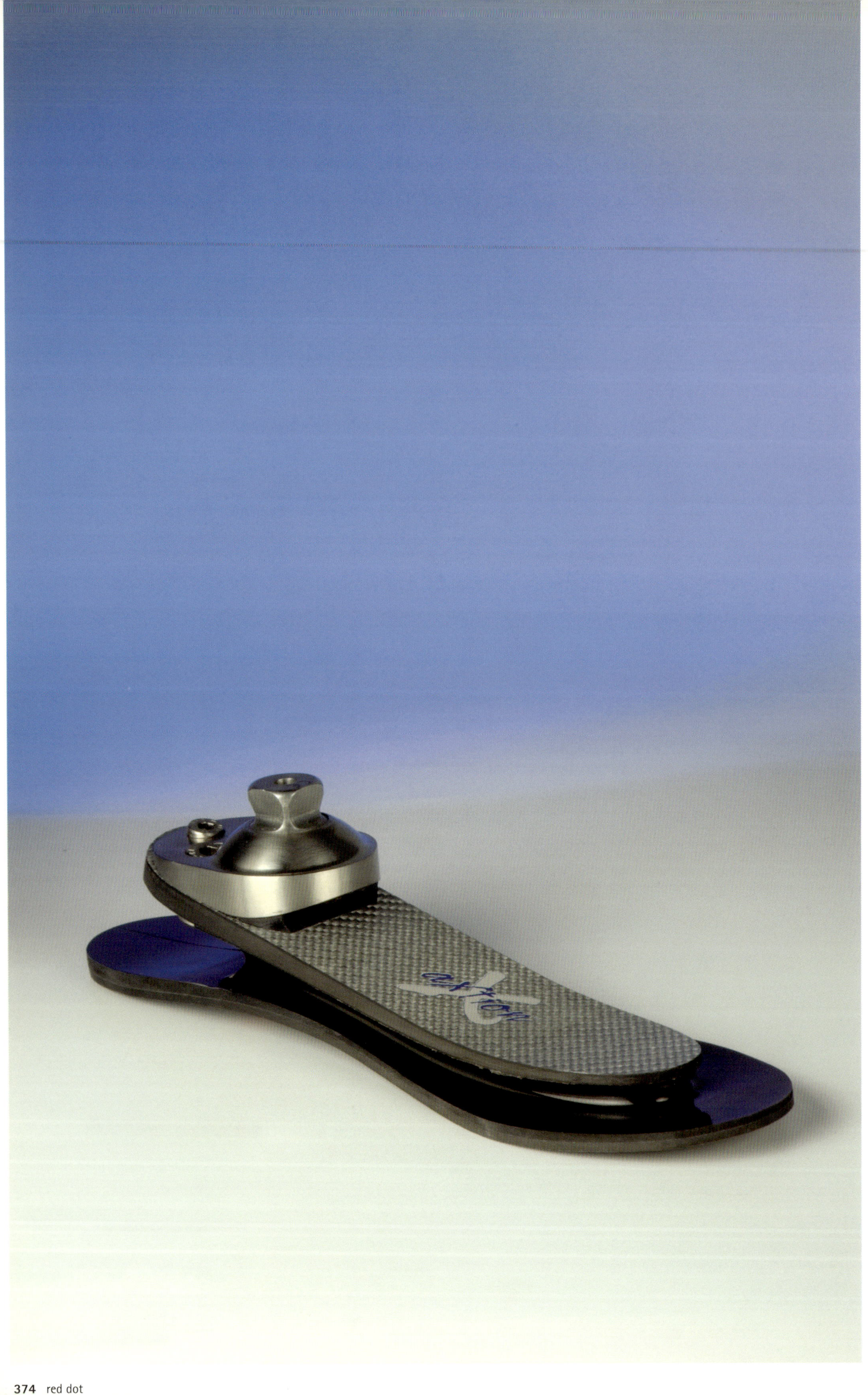

1E56 Axtion 脚板, 2004

Otto Bock HealthCare,
Utah Design and Manufacturing Center,
Salt Lake City, USA
Werksdesign: Sarah McCarvill
www.ottobock.com

1E56 Axtion是供那些生性活泼的截肢者使用一种假脚板，它的高度很低。合成材料的运用和独特的设计创造出有着三维表面的外观，令人感觉很新颖。这款假脚板很是轻便，但却有着突出的功能性。在足跟提供强大动力的支持下，碳和聚氨酯的混合结构可以使脚部得到缓冲，将足跟到脚掌之间进行平滑过渡，使走路时更加舒适。当前脚给了使用者更多的力量和移动趋向时，动力碳纤素脚趾盘能够提供很好的支撑和能量的回转。该假脚板同样适用于运动员，因为进行训练时他们的脚会承受强烈的震动。

The 1E56 Axtion is a prosthetic foot for active amputees with a low fitting height. Ingenious use of composite materials and design create an appealing look with a three-dimensional surface. The foot provides light weight and high function. Supported by the dynamic heel element, the hybrid construction of carbon and polyurethane features shock absorption and enables a smooth transition from heel strike to foot flat – for more comfort while walking. The dynamic carbon fibre toe plate provides excellent support and energy return at the forefoot giving the user added confidence and mobility. The prosthetic foot is also well-suited for athletes exposing their foot to stronger shocks while exercising.

3R60 EBS-膝关节, 2004

Otto Bock HealthCare GmbH,
Duderstadt
Werksdesign: Andreas Mühlenberendt,
Steffen Sawatzki
www.ottobock.com

3R60是一种用管状骨架构造方式植入的五个轴的假膝关节。它的主要特点在于拥有一个能够在走路时减震及缓冲的单元，提高了使用者走路时的舒适性。通常，假肢是隐藏起来的，以防那些或嘲弄、或同情的人们看到，但3R60的设计却使用了相反的策略，即优雅地将其表现出来。假肢的那些零件并不需要掩饰在一些泡沫装饰物下面，而且，与其他假肢因其尖锐的边缘经常使泡沫装饰物遭到损坏相反的是，3R60有一个柔软的前端帽来保护其泡沫表面。人们更多的关注来自于其操作上的简便性，使得假肢医生能够容易地将假肢安到患者体内。而且在侧面就能很容易地进行水力学上的调整。此外，一个封闭的且牢固的前部经过了强化处理，被喻为“残疾人的保护神”，它为腿部提供了稳固的前端保护。

The 3R60 is a five-axis prosthetic knee joint implanted by means of a tube skeleton construction method. It features a shock absorption unit dampening hard steps, thus enabling comfortable walking for the user. Usually, prostheses are concealed from the looks of intrusive, sympathetic or nosy people, but the design of the 3R60 supports the opposite tactics of deliberately "showing". The component parts of the prosthesis do not have to disappear under some foam cosmetics, and – contrary to other prostheses often damaging the foam cosmesis due to hard-cutting edges – the 3R60 has a soft front cap conserving the foam cover. Particular attention has been devoted to ease of operation for the prosthetist fitting the prosthesis to the patient. Adjustment of the hydraulics is easily accomplished from a lateral position. In order to offer front protection as well, thus "protecting" the amputee in the figurative sense, the 3R60 features a closed and well-fortified front reinforcement.

人们和他们的习惯——新办公室的空间

People and their rituals – space for the new office

对于办公室的设计，哪些趋势和潮流能表现出社会是处在不断变化中的？根据评委马丁·博格曼，约阿希姆·浮士德和丹尼·文莱特的观点，在这个问题上最重要的不是那些静止的家具，而是一切内在因素之间的清晰的相互联系的关系。一些习惯性的约束已经悄悄地潜入到了办公室的家具里了：你再也找不到肾形的桌子；与此同时功能性方面的因素，例如可调节性和组合家具作为了今年的主题而出现。办公室的椅子也显示出很多有趣的变化，包括新的解决“办公室紧张”的方法。这些评委们对几乎所有产品都拥有极高的设计标准而印象深刻。圆珠笔和其他重要的办公室工具在功能上都是一致的，而且非常醒目且具有创造性。此外，评委会还进一步认识到了新的照明条件的出现必将改善办公室的工作氛围；同时，新型的地板在塑造新的美感方面有一定潜力。当问到办事处的外观时，这些评委们一致陈述了这样的观点，即尽管存在一些不确定性，但现在仍然是在设计和创新上进行投入的正确时刻，它事关勾勒未来工作领域的草图，以及在可预见的发展上发挥作用。每一件东西都有着令人兴奋的前景——桌子、储物柜、屏幕监控器——将继续变小并且变得可移动。相信未来将属于更加简约的形式，这些形式一定能适应不同的工作个体以及他们的习惯。

In what ways are trends in the office and administration sector *addressing the increasing mobility of society? Crucial in this regard, according to the jurors Martin Bergmann, Joachim Faust and Danny Venlet, is not so much the static furniture than the coherent interconnection of all the intrinsic elements. Restraint has crept into the forms of office furniture: the kidney shape has vanished, while functional aspects such as adjustability and combination emerged as this year's key themes. The office chairs revealed a number of interesting developments, including new approaches to the principle of tension. The jurors were impressed by the "extremely high" design standard of virtually all the products. Ballpoint pens and other important office tools were functionally coherent and strikingly inventive. The jury further discerned the emergence of new "lighting situations" that would potentially enhance the work atmosphere in offices, while innovative floor coverings were providing new aesthetic potential. Asked about the outlook for the branch, the jurors unanimously voice the opinion that the present, despite its uncertainties, is the "right time" to make major investments in design and innovation. It is a matter of drafting scenarios for the working world of the future, and acting on the foreseeable developments. With the exciting prospect that everything – desks, cabinets, flatscreen monitors – will continue to shrink in size and become more portable, the future belongs to the more simple forms potentially adaptable to working individuals and their rituals.*

丹尼・维勒特
Danny Venlet
比利时
Belgien

约阿希姆・H.浮士德
Joachim Faust
德国
Deutschland

马丁・伯格曼
Martin Bergmann
奥地利
Österreich

商业与行政办公设备
Offices and administration

Ahrend 1200 会议桌, 2004

Koninklijke Ahrend NV, Amsterdam, NL
Design: Meyer en Van Schooten Architecten, Amsterdam, NL
Vertrieb: Ahrend GmbH & Co. KG, Dreieich
www.ahrend.com
www.meyer-vanschooten.nl

无论是在工作中或是会议上，Ahrend 1200会议桌都折射出令人着迷的灯光。集成照明和玻璃或压克力制桌面的结合使其外表格外引人注目。Ahrend 1200的框架是铝或是铬制成的，表面还有粉末涂层。桌子的模块化构造使得它能用于各种不同的布局。在设计Ahrend 1200的时候，设计师们作出了以下评价：我们对灯管和半透明材料的喜爱是设计Ahrend 1200的灵感来源，相信它是一件无论放在哪里都能吸引眼球的家具。

The new table system Ahrend 1200 throws an inspiring new light on work and conferencing. The combination of integrated lighting and the glass or acrylic tabletop gives it a very striking appearance. The frame of the Ahrend 1200 is made of aluminium with a powder coating or chrome. The modular construction of the table allows it to be used in various different configurations. The architects had the following comment about the background of their design work for Ahrend: "Our fascination with light and translucent materials was the keynote for the design of the Ahrend 1200, a piece of furniture that will catch the eye wherever it is placed."

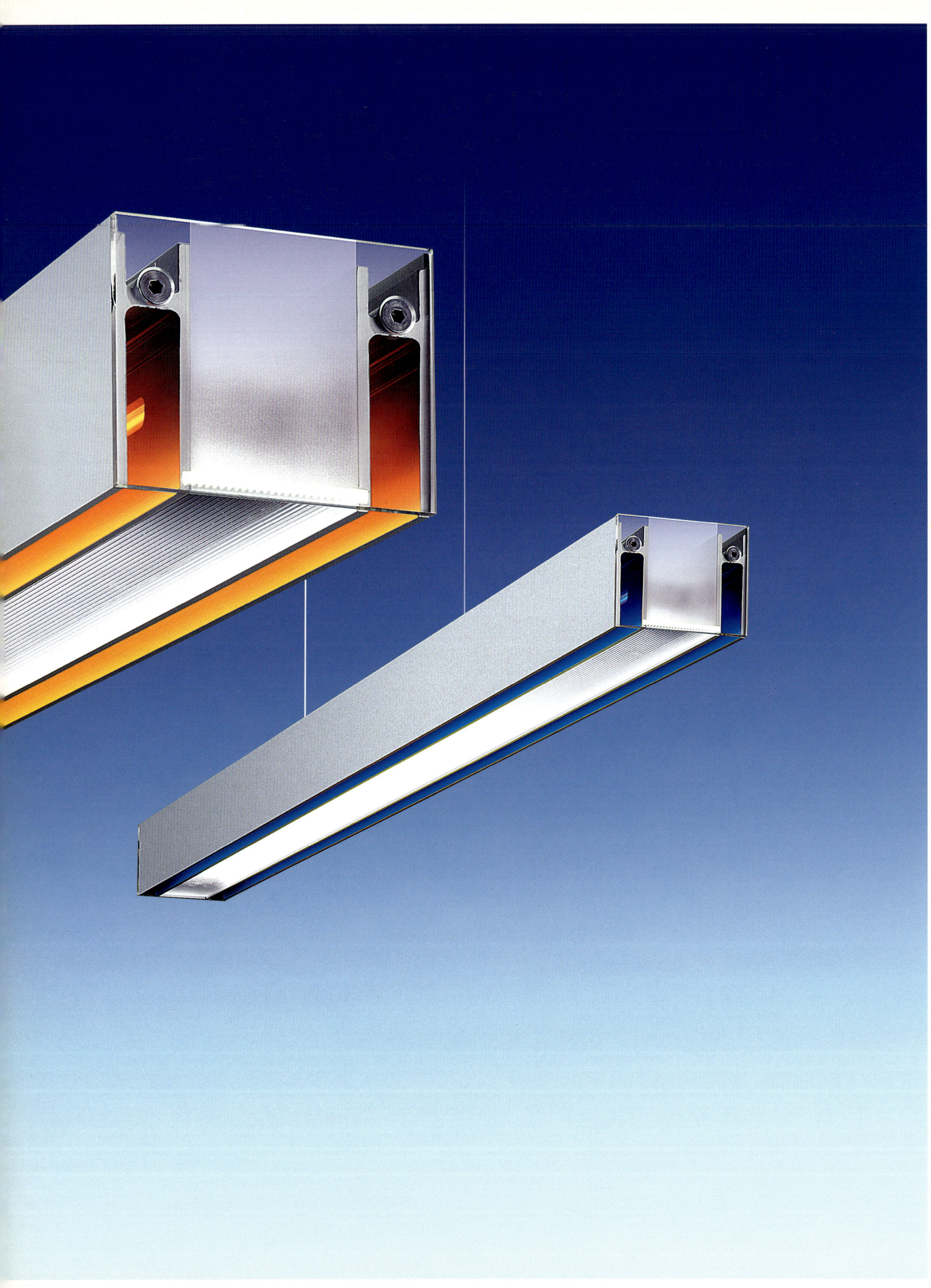

iMexx 挂灯，2004

Grimmeisen Vertriebs GmbH,
Wasserburg a. Inn
Design: Grimmeisen Licht
(Gerhard Grimmeisen),
Wasserburg a. Inn
www.grimmeisen-licht.de

iMexx挂灯是一款外形设计紧凑的多功能光源，它融合了各种理念，可用于在办公室和多个建筑领域。两个垂直H型的独立设计与一个兼具透明的和半透明的压克力玻璃前面板相结合，能够让使用者观察到灯的内部构造。这款灯是以T5灯光技术和不同的光学应用成果为基础，监控器也明亮地闪烁着，该监控器由多个亚克力玻璃制成并有着微小棱镜结构，采用该结构是为了使光产生折射效果和减弱强光。H型的外观、反射性表面，以及内部颜色过滤器的一种特殊光学系统形成了灯罩的中空的内腔，多彩的灯光恰好填充了进来。iMexx可以用作吸顶灯或者用作直接或间接照射的吊灯，壁灯，绳灯或是落地灯。有1 × 54W，2 × 54W，3 × 54W 这三种不同的规格，可满足多样化的要求。

The iMexx suspended lamp is a compact multi-functional source of light for office and architectural spaces and combines various concepts. A self-contained design and the construction with two upright H profiles in combination with a transparent, partially translucent front panel made from acrylic glass provide an insight into the lamp. Based upon the T5 lamp technology and the use of different optics made from acrylic glass with micro-prism structures for light refraction and glare reduction, the monitor workstations are illuminated precisely. A special optical system with a light window in H profile, reflective surfaces, and interior colour filters cause the hollow chambers of the lamp casing to be filled with coloured light. The iMexx is available as direct ceiling light or as directly/indirectly irradiating suspended lamp, wall lamp, cord and floor lamp. The 1 x 54W, 2 x 54W and 3 x 54W power settings allow a professional use.

Mod 地毯, 2004

Carpet Concept Objekt-Teppichboden GmbH, Bielefeld
Design: Carsten Gollnick, Berlin
www.carpet-concept.de

Mod以其大胆的创新使人们为之惊奇。该设计不同寻常的独特个性来源于一种新的纱线。专门开发的外层人工合成纱线构成了地毯的表面，这种编织结构起源于传统的编织。这款地毯设计的精妙之处在于将漂亮的颜色和精致的设计巧妙地结合在了一起，是一种极富想像力的创新。

Mod surprises with daring innovation. The extraordinary individual character of the programme stems from a new yarn. Specially developed, synthetically coated threads form the surface. The woven structure has its origin in traditional weaving. The effective feature of this invention of creative lateral thinkers is the combination of fine colours and delicate design.

Think 办公椅, 2004

Steelcase Werndl AG, Rosenheim
Design: Prof. Glen O. Löw, Hamburg
www.steelcase.de

Think是一种能自然地适应使用者的身体及其活动的座椅。它采用了Your Power™技术，即由体重来激发的坐姿变换机制，使得座位的调节方式与人体活动相似。Think座椅能够根据使用者各自的体重而为他们调节出最佳的坐姿，这样使用者就能够全身心地关注于工作。Your Profile™座位和椅子的感应背遵循了人体脊骨和盆骨的自然构造。感应背与身体的外型相吻合，这样就给予了使用者一种与身体相适应的动态而舒适的支撑。另外，Your Preference™技术使得轻轻调节椅子就可以实现四种舒适的选择。可调的手臂（高度，深度和斜度）可以自动向后推与工作面相接触，当然也能够很容易地推回到原来的位置。

Think is a chair that intuitively adapts to the user's body and body movements. Your Power™ – the weight-activated posture mechanism allows for flowing movements similar to those of the human body. It offers optimum posture for the user's respective body weight, thereby enabling complete focus on at work. Your Profile™ – seat and back flexors follow the natural movements of spine and pelvis. Back flexors mould themselves to the body shape, thus providing a dynamic comfort cocoon that adapts to the body. Your Preference™ – four comfort settings can be achieved with a single turn. Adjustable arms (height, depth and incline) are automatically pushed back upon contact with the work surface. They can be easily pushed back to their original position.

FlexBox, 模块化办公家具, 2004

Steelcase Werndl AG, Rosenheim
Design: Stefan Brodbeck, München
www.steelcase.de

FlexBox是一种模块化的办公家具，它能够简便地进行调整和延伸，创造出更大的办公灵活性。这套家具包括一个单独的框架，有两种结构型号（40 × 40和40 × 80）可供选择。获得专利的快速连接装置使该产品能够不用任何工具就可以进行装配，只需旋转90度或180度就可以把那些盒子安放进去，这也是一个设计中的一个亮点。FlexBox能够应用的地方几乎是无限的，从“脚轮上的储存凳”到略显成熟的FlexBox面板，每一款都很实用。此外，FlexBox打开后使用方式也是多种多样的：架子、拉门、抽屉、悬挂的文件夹，而且其前部的设计使得它的用途更广泛了。它可以安装在柱基上，框架的底座上或者是脚轮上。一枚硬币就能方便地进行拆卸，可以说FlexBox是一款用途广泛的移动的办公家具。

FlexBox is a modular storage space system that can be modified and extended easily, thus creating greater office flexibility. It consists of a single carcass in two frame sizes (40 x 40 and 40 x 80cm). It can be configured without the need for tools, thanks to a patented quick connector. Mounted boxes can thus be installed by turning them 90 or 180 degrees, and it also serves as a design element. The number of ways in which FlexBox can be used is almost limitless – from "storage space stools" on castors to full-fledged FlexBox panels. FlexBox can be opened and used in a variety of ways: shelves, sliding flaps, drawers, suspended file frames and a selection of fronts make FlexBox universally usable. Boxes are mounted on plinth bases, frame bases or castors. A simple coin suffices for dismantling and the box can be used as a moving container.

Lamy pickup 圆珠笔, 2004

C. Josef Lamy GmbH, Heidelberg
Design: Wolfgang Fabian, Mannheim
www.lamy.de

Pickup圆珠笔将两种方便的书写用具结合在了一起：它既是一种圆珠笔，同样也是一个简单的记号笔。对于那些经常外出的商务人士或经常需要书写的人士，以及在书写的同时还要做标记的学生而言，它真可谓是一个不错的伙伴。它的外壳和别针是由同一块不锈钢制成的。外壳前面部分来打开记号笔的功能性按钮，同时也充当了具有防滑功能的握笔部位，它由手感舒适的黑色塑料制成。精密的旋转装置、可动的伸缩端，以及可拆卸的黄色文本记号笔的设计都是很实用的。这种多功能笔同时配有黑色的Lamy圆珠笔芯M22和黄色的记号笔芯M51可供替换。

The pickup combines two fully-fledged writing utensils: it is the first ballpoint pen, which is also a marker with a simple classy design. As such, it is an excellent companion for business people on the move, for people writing a lot and for students who need to write and mark things at the same time. Housing and clip are made from one piece of stainless steel. A functional pushbutton in the front section of the housing to unlock the marker, as well as the non-slip grip section, consists of haptically convenient black plastic. Functional is a sophisticated turning mechanism and a movable telescopic point, as well as the removable yellow text marker. The multi-system pen is equipped with a Lamy ballpoint refill M 22 black and a marker refill M 51 yellow.

Textmarker 记号笔 490, 2005

Pelikan Vertriebsgesellschaft mbH
& Co. KG, Hannover
Design: yellow design | yellow circle, Köln
www.pelikan.de

每一条由Pelikan记号笔划出的线条就像是在书写者和记号笔之间架起了一座美丽的桥梁，为他们创造出一种感情上的联系。由于着色比其它记号更柔软、更优美，Pelikan让人感受到一种上佳的质量，五颜六色的笔身更加强化了这种印象。符合人体工程学的外形使这种笔握起来感觉舒适。每一种笔身的颜色实际都代表了记号笔各自的颜色，这就便于在购买时进行选择。黑色的中心部分是记号笔的关键部位，对于使用者而言，它的手柄很容易被辨认出来。这款记号笔的每一个侧面都有条纹凸显出来，这使得握笔更加稳定，还帮助使用者为握笔提供了一个单独的位置。

The sweeping lines accomplished with Pelikan markers create something of an emotional bond between writer and pen. With a softer, more elegant effect than other markers, the Pelikan suggests high quality: an impression reinforced by the subdivision into coloured functional areas, and the ergonomic form making the pen pleasant to hold. The container colours each represent the respective colour of the marker – this facilitates the choice at the point of sale. The black centre part is the focal point of the marker and is recognisable for the user as the handle. Ribbed elements to either side offer additional hold and allow an individual hand position.

Pritt 修正带, 2004

Henkel KGaA, Düsseldorf
Werksdesign: Henkel Design Team
www.prittworld.com

Pritt修正带很适合在纸或传真上进行快速、干净、精确的修改，而不会在影印本上留下痕迹或污渍。这种修正带用完就能干，也就意味着修改过的地方就能够马上进行书写或者进行打印。修正带的宽度仅为4.2毫米，使得它成为修改打印文本上单独一行字的理想工具。除了单纯的功能方面，该设计还关注了美感、人体工程学以及舒适的手握方式。与以往的传统产品不同的是，该产品可以在纸张上方平滑而非竖直地移动。不同颜色可以根据修正带的各种功能性区域进行调整，同时不同的颜色也反映出它在Pritt修正带产品中的不同产品系列。

Pritt's Correction Roller Comfort is suitable for quick, clean and accurate corrections on paper and facsimiles, without leaving marks or stains on photocopies. The roller applies dry, which means that the corrected area can be written or typed over instantly. The band width of 4.2mm makes the roller ideal for correcting single lines of typed or printed text. In addition to purely functional aspects, the design focuses on aesthetics, ergonomics and a self-explanatory way of holding the roller. Unlike its conventional predecessors, the roller is moved flat – as opposed to upright – over the paper. The colour scheme is geared towards the various functional areas of the correction roller and reflects the membership in the Pritt correction roller product family.

Klöber Ciello 办公椅, 2005

Klöber GmbH, Überlingen
Design: Klöber Design-Team
www.kloeber.com

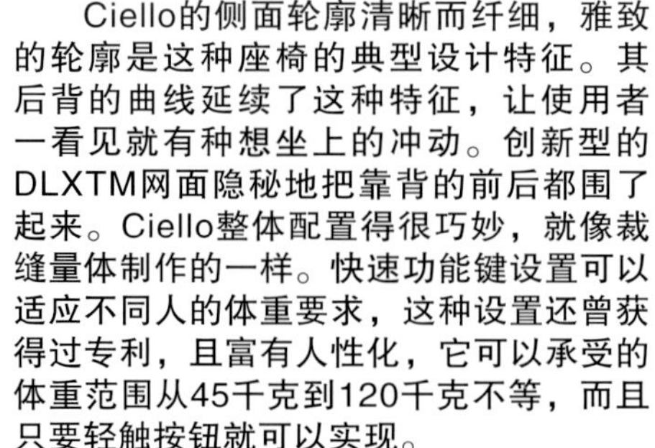

Ciello的侧面轮廓清晰而纤细，雅致的轮廓是这种座椅的典型设计特征。其后背的曲线延续了这种特征，让使用者一看见就有种想坐上的冲动。创新型的DLXTM网面隐秘地把靠背的前后都围了起来。Ciello整体配置得很巧妙，就像裁缝量体制作的一样。快速功能键设置可以适应不同人的体重要求，这种设置还曾获得过专利，且富有人性化，它可以承受的体重范围从45千克到120千克不等，而且只要轻触按钮就可以实现。

Ciello has a clear and slim profile. The elegant silhouette is a characteristic design feature of the chair. It is continued in the curved line of the backrest and invites you to recline. Due to the innovative DLX™ (Duo-Latex) mesh cover, it encloses the front and back of the backrest unobtrusively. Fitting perfectly like a tailor-made suit, Ciello can be adjusted with a patented, user-friendly quick set function to the individual bodyweight ranging from 45 to 120kg – all at the touch of a button

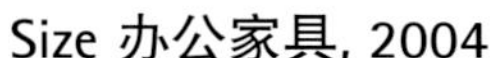

Size 办公家具, 2004

Renz GmbH, Böblingen
Design: Jehs + Laub, Stuttgart
www.renz.de

简约是Size书桌系列的设计特征。虽然这一系列有各种不同的型号，但它们无一例外都拥有纤细的表面和骨架，并支撑着60毫米厚的桌面。可以说，这种桌子的形式迎合了忙碌的工作环境对安静和清晰的线条的需求。高质量的材料的运用（例如金属漆和名贵木材），为人们提供了多种选择，同时可以悄无声息地传达出自己的个性。

Minimalism is the hallmark of the Size desk programme. Variously sized but consistently slim cheeks and frames casually support a 60mm-thick desktop whose archaic form caters to the need for tranquillity and clear lines in a hectic workplace environment. High-quality materials such as metallic lacquers and elegant woods provide various options of introducing a personal note to the executive floor.

X 射线高级多功能地毯, 2004

Toucan-T Carpet Manufacture GmbH, Krefeld
Werksdesign
www.toucan-t.de

X射线地毯是一种有着清晰线形结构的高级多功能地毯。在传统的毛束生产过程中，基础布料用来当做起固定作用的线，然后掩藏在表层绒面之下。而X射线的基础布料却恰恰与此相反，它成为了地毯设计中一个显而易见的部分。为了生产这种产品，人们还专门研制出了特殊的聚酯纤维基础布料。

Ray X is an exclusive, heavy-duty carpet with a clear linear-shaped structure. In the conventional tufting manufacturing process, the primary cloth serves exclusively as thread fixation and disappears under the surface pile (visible fibre). In contrast to this principle, the primary cloth of the quality Ray X is visible and becomes a visual component of the carpet design. A particular polyester primary cloth was developed especially for this product.

PC-可写和可重写索引登记本，2004

Esselte Leitz GmbH & Co KG, Stuttgart
Design: Hauer & Ege GmbH, Stuttgart
www.esselte.com

这款PC可写和可重写索引为记录的持续更新提供了高度的灵活性。由于PC可写索引的封皮是透明的，标准的A4打印纸能够按照要求插入或进行交换。可重写索引的封皮为薄薄的层状，这样就能方便地用塑料橡皮擦掉文档。

Allowing inscriptions to be continuously updated, the PC-writable and rewritable indexes offer high flexibility. Thanks to the transparent front cover of the PC-writable index, printed standard A4 sheets of paper can be inserted and swapped around as required. The rewritable index has a laminated front cover, thus the text can easily be erased with a plastic rubber.

Maxi 可扩展式文件袋，2005

Esselte Leitz GmbH & Co KG, Stuttgart
Werksdesign
www.esselte.com

可扩展式文件袋的一个功能性设计很好地解决了堆积如山的文件页数的问题。该产品的所有类型都有一个20毫米的侧面折痕，它为不断增加的文件页数及小册子提供了一个足够的存储空间。Maxi的封皮不仅坚固耐磨，它还有一个理想的防撕裂的保护措施。金属封边和活动盖的使用更使这款文件袋更加结实而实用。

The expandable pockets have a functional design which is ideal for increasing "mountains of paper". All versions have a 20mm side fold, which creates enough space for numerous pages and also for brochures. The Maxi covers have several innovative features: they are robust and have an optimised anti-tear protection. Furthermore, they are also available with metal-reinforced filing margins and flap lids.

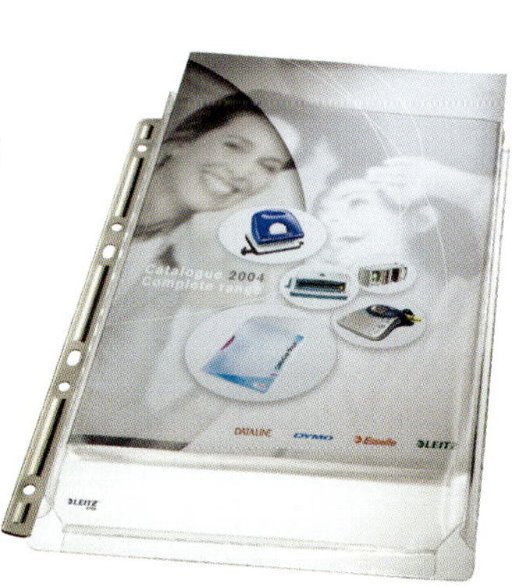

Divide it up 活动文件夹，2004

Esselte Leitz GmbH & Co KG, Stuttgart
Werksdesign
www.esselte.com

Divide it up文件夹带有可伸缩式钩子，使得它不仅成为办公室里理想的可悬挂文件夹，甚至可以当做外出办事时理想的皮夹。一个滑入式悬塞与封闭的橡胶制成的边角，再加上其耐用的透明封皮和一个CD包的配置，使将重要的文档简便而安全地从办公室带出来成为可能。同时，不同颜色的六个分界索引便于对文件进行分类管理。

Divide it up comes with retractable hooks making it ideal both as a suspension file in the workplace and as a wallet for mobile use. Thanks to slide-in suspension taps, rubber corner closure and a durable transparent cover as well as a CD pocket, important documents can be simply and safely transported from the office, while a multicoloured six-part divider supports the organisation of contents.

在简约和复杂之间——通讯产品世界的新造型

Between reduction and complexity – new forms for the world of communication

组合性功能是“多媒体和家用电器”系列产品中非常明显的发展趋势，在这个领域中，以前互不相干的设备正在迅速地融合为一体。评委深泽直人、安德丽亚·芬克–安劳夫和塔帕尼·海万恩认为，在未来的设计中，需要更加清晰界定的只是到底是把电话和相机结合在一起，还是把相机和电话结合在一起。一个产品中组合的设备种类越多，它就必须做到越来越清晰和简明，因此，实用性和操作的人性化在该设备的设计中就成为了最重要的因素。其中一种非常有吸引力的产品就是MP3播放器，它是一种相对发展比较晚的产品，但评委们认为它可以给人们带来无穷的乐趣。一些MP3播放器看起来像贵重的珠宝，而其他的播放器则将设计集中在技术层面上。正如评委们所说，高设计标准总会伴随着多样化的创新。集成显示器是令人惊叹的，你不得不叹服它们显现出来的那种纯粹的美学，完美的声质等，评委们更加强调，未来，就在于影像处理的发展过程上，即使是拍照手机也能提供非常高的照片分辨率。而且，由于这些技术逐渐变得在普通大众的消费能力之内，我们相信，更加有吸引力的趋势必将出现。

Combination is clearly the trend in the area of *"media and home electronics," where previously discrete devices are rapidly fusing. The jurors Naoto Fukasawa, Andrea Finke-Anlauff und Tapani Hyvönen remark that design will in future need to more sharply define whether a "telephone has been combined with a camera, or a camera combined with a telephone." The more device genres combined in one display, the more clear and self-explanatory it had to be: appropriate functionality and user friendliness were therefore important aspects in the design of such equipment. One of the most interesting products is the MP3 player, a relatively young device type for which the jurors discern "any number of exciting conceptions." Some MP3 players looked like precious jewellery, while the design of others concentrated on the technical aspect. The "very high overall standard of design," as the jurors put it, was accompanied by a diverse spectrum of innovation. The integratively designed displays were persuasive due to their purist aesthetic, and new forms of sound quality were emerging likewise. The development of imaging processes is where the future lies: even cameras integrated into mobile phones offered extraordinarily high resolution quality, stress the jurors. And since such technologies were becoming increasingly affordable, further interesting trends could be expected for sure.*

深泽直人
Naoto Fukasawa
日本
Japan

塔帕尼·海万恩
Tapani Hyvönen
芬兰
Finnland

安德里亚·芬克–安劳夫
Andrea Finke-Anlauff
德国
Deutschland

多媒体与家用电器
Media and home electronics

苹果迷你电脑, 2005

Apple, Cupertino, USA
Werksdesign: Apple Design Team
www.apple.com

苹果迷你电脑是苹果的一款台式机，它是为任何一位希望使用苹果OS X来启动电脑，并且希望享受iLife'05乐趣的人士而设计的。iLife'05是苹果公司的一套最新软件，主要用来处理数码照片和音乐，剪辑电影以及制作音乐。电脑尺寸为5 × 16厘米，重量仅为1.32千克。该电脑配置齐全，采用了PowerPC G4处理器，，并且配有可观看DVD影碟和进行CD刻录的托盘式康宝光驱，此外还配备了硬盘，扬声器，还能够装配Airport Extreme进行无线网络连接并支持蓝牙技术。它建立在一种BYOKDM系统（携带你自己的键盘和鼠标）上，这样你就既可以使用已有的外围设备，或是选择新的设备组合。苹果迷你电脑拥有一个圆滑的镀铝外壳，表面为聚碳酸酯制成，下面还有三层的基座。基座的其中一层是橡胶底，这样就能为桌子提供保护，并且避免了苹果迷你电脑向周围滑动。

The Mac mini is a desktop computer for anyone looking to get started with Mac OS X and features iLife '05, the latest version of Apple's innovative suite of software for managing digital photo and music collections, editing movies and creating music. Its size is only 5 x 16cm, its weight 1.32kg. The computer comes complete with a PowerPC G4 processor, slot-load combo drive for watching DVD movies and burning CDs, hard drive, speakers, and can be configured with Airport Extreme and Bluetooth wireless communications. It's a BYOKDM system (Bring Your Own Keyboard and Mouse) so you can use the peripherals you already have, or choose a combination of new devices. The Mac mini is enclosed in an anodised aluminium extrudate housing with a polycarbonate top surface and a triple-layer bottom case. One of the three layers of the bottom case is the rubber foot, which protects your desk and keeps your Mac mini from sliding around.

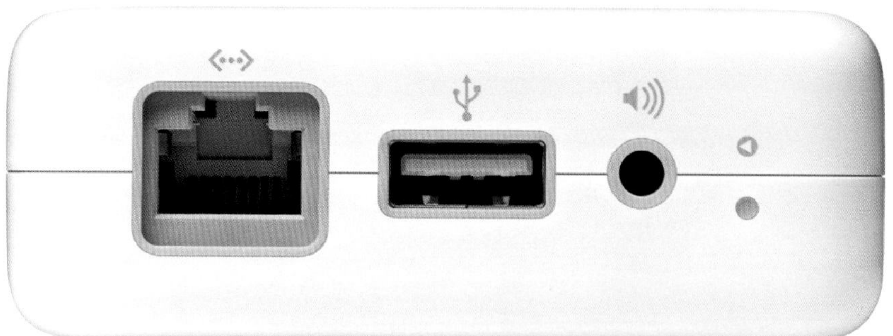

AirPort Express 无线基站, 2004

Apple, Cupertino, USA
Werksdesign: Apple Design Team
www.apple.com

AirPort Express是一款只有手掌大小，且有AirTunes功能的无线基站。它可以提供与网络及打印机的无线连接，并且能够把iTunes音乐带到家庭的任何一个地方。在Mac和PC上它能以每秒54兆的速率来传输数据。这种多功能的装置使得用户能够拥有一个不需要线缆而连接的宽带互联网接口和一台无线USB打印机。这种装置小巧、轻便而紧凑，使得顾客能够扩展当前的无线网络，或者在外出时创建一个即时无线网络。AirPort Express的主要特点就是AirTunes能够在家用立体声音响或一套动力驱动扬声器上播放你的iTunes音乐，因此它可以把音乐带到家中你喜欢的任何地方进行欣赏。内置独特的AC调制解调器使得您能够把AirPort Express直接插入墙壁插座，不需要多余的线缆和动力支持。由于它的模块化设计，您也可以方便地给它添加一条电源线，或者是更换插头，便可使其具有更大的兼容性。

AirPort Express is a palm-sized wireless base station with AirTunes, providing a wireless connection to the Internet, a printer and the ability to stream iTunes music to any room in the house. It works with Macs and PCs to deliver wireless data rates up to 54 megabits per second. The multi-function device lets users share a single broadband Internet connection and USB printer without cables. The small, lightweight and compact device enables customers to extend the range of their current wireless network or create an instant wireless network on the go. Featuring AirTunes for playing your iTunes music wireless on your home stereo or powered speakers, AirPort Express brings your music to wherever in your home you like enjoy it the most. An internal universal AC adapter allows you to plug the AirPort Express directly into a wall socket without extra cables or a power supply. You can also quickly add a power cord or change the plug for worldwide compatibility due to its modular design.

iMac G5 电脑, 2004

Apple, Cupertino, USA
Werksdesign: Apple Design Team
www.apple.com

iMac G5是一款非常节约空间的“一体化”电脑。iMac配有以G5为基座的宽屏平面显示器，带有插槽的吸入式光驱，硬盘和立体声扬声器，所有这些配置都浓缩在5厘米厚的机盖内。iMac G5有两种款式：17英寸和20英寸，后者的显示器上甚至能够并排显示两页多纸。双层塑料壳悬在镀铝支架上方，将重心保持在了中间位置。支脚是用一块镀铝板制成的，并一直延伸到的机盖后面，其间并没有明显的连接装置。只需用一个手指轻触就可以调节iMac显示器的观看角度。iMac G5的调节范围很宽，可以平缓地从后倾25度延伸到前倾5度。此外，它的风扇工作时也异常安静，可以通过扬声器栏栅将冷空气吸入该系统。先进的热量控制软件能使风扇按照所需要的快慢来进行旋转，整个运转过程也非常安静。盒子背面的一个缝隙可以使热量通过机顶而排放出去。沿着基座边缘，松开三个螺丝，就能够打开后盖，露出用来服务和升级的整个系统。

The iMac G5 is a space-saving all-in-one computer. The iMac has a G5-based logic board, a widescreen flat-panel display, a slot-load optical drive, a hard disk and stereo speakers, all within a 5 cm thin enclosure. The iMac G5 comes in two sizes: the 17-inch iMac and the 20-inch iMac which can show more than two full pages, side by side, on its display. The luminous twin-layer plastic enclosure hangs suspended from an anodised aluminium stand, attached at its centre of gravity. The foot is formed from a single sheet of anodised aluminium that rolls into the rear of the enclosure with no visible mechanism. Adjustments to the iMac's display viewing angle can be made with the touch of a finger. The iMac smoothly tilts from 25 degrees backward to 5 degrees forward. The ultra-quiet blowers draw cool air into the system through the speaker grill. Advanced thermal software spins the fan as fast or slow as needed, for a whisper-quiet operation. A slit in the back of the case allows heat to escape through the top. By unfastening three screws along the bottom edge, the rear cover can be removed, exposing the whole system for upgrades and service.

OFF
iPod

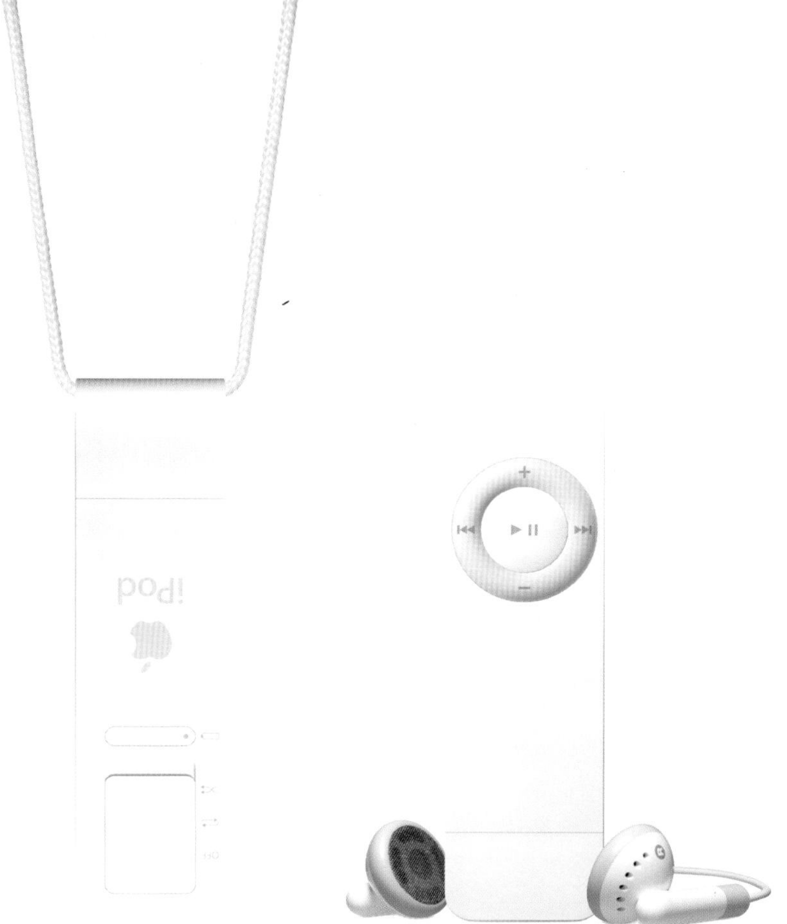

iPod Shuffle 数字音乐播放器, 2005

Apple, Cupertino, USA
Werksdesign: Apple Design Team
www.apple.com

iPod Shuffle是一款数字音乐播放器，它秉承了iPod机的创新的设计理念，设计中融入了新技术——iPod Shuffle。这款播放器能够从用户的曲库或播放列表里随机选择歌曲，iTunes以及AutoFill的同步运行能够自动从用户电脑完整的曲库中选择最佳的歌曲数量来自动填充iPod Shuffle。把iPod shuffle直接插入电脑的USB端口，用户就能便捷地从Mac或者PC上传输音乐。作为便携式USB闪存，iPod存储容量加倍增加，达到了1千兆，以支持个人文档和电脑间文件的互换。iPod Shuffle比一包口香糖的体积还小，非常轻便。PC/ABS外壳几乎是无缝的，其设计坚固，外形紧凑。iPod Shuffle有自己的挂绳，可以随心所欲地佩带在身上。此外它的控制键像任何一款iPod机型一样容易使用，诸如播放、暂停、跳转、重复、组合、锁定等操作都是用大拇指触摸一下即可控制。圆形的、符合人体工程学的控制盘以及单键按压的滑动键都使你毋须观看便可轻松聆听曼妙的音乐。iPod Shuffle有两种款式：一款能储存120首歌曲，容量为512兆，另一款容量为1千兆，能储存240首歌曲。

The iPod Shuffle, a digital music player, is based on iPod's pioneering and widely used shuffle feature, which randomly selects songs from the user's music library or playlists. It works seamlessly with iTunes and its new AutoFill feature, which automatically selects the perfect number of songs to fill the iPod shuffle from a user's complete music library on their computer. Users can conveniently charge and transfer music from their Mac or PC by plugging the iPod shuffle directly into a USB port. The iPod shuffle doubles as a portable USB flash drive with up to 1GB of storage space to back up personal files and exchange them between computers. The iPod shuffle is smaller and lighter than a pack of gum. The almost seamless PC/ABS shell is robust and very compact. The iPod shuffle comes with its own lanyard so it's ready to wear right out of the box. The controls on the iPod shuffle feel as intuitive and easy to use as those on every iPod model: Play, Pause, Skip, Repeat, Shuffle and Hold are controllable at the touch of a thumb. The circular, ergonomic controls and the one-click slider make it simple to listen without looking. The iPod shuffle is available in two models: 512MB for storing up to 120 songs and 1GB for storing up to 240 songs.

明基 Joybook S72 电脑, 2004

BenQ Corporation, Taipei, Taiwan
Werksdesign: BenQ Lifestyle Design Center
Vertrieb: BenQ Deutschland GmbH, Hamburg
www.benq.com

明基Joybook S72是一款专为在电脑上进行专业性工作的人士而设计的高端笔记本电脑。同时，它也满足了几乎是私人用户所有的需求。电脑两侧设有方便接入的多媒体和DVD-ROM插口，标准配置中还包括了坚固的铝镁合金部件和能接收电视节目的内置电视插口，以及小型的视听无线遥控等。该笔记本电脑按照人体工程学设计，边缘为流线型，便于开关。14寸的TFT LCD宽屏显示器使你即便是长时间地使用，眼睛也不会感到疲劳。

The BenQ Joybook S72 high-end notebook was designed exclusively for professional work at the computer. At the same time, it meets all demands of a private user. Ports for multimedia and DVD-ROM are located to either side of the housing and are easily accessible. A robust aluminium-magnesium alloy, an internal TV port for receiving TV programmes en route, and the small wireless remote control for audio-visual functions complete the package. With its rounded edges, the notebook has an ergonomic shape and is easily opened and closed. The high-resolution 14-inch TFT LCD widescreen display allows longer work sessions without fatigue.

明基 7350C 扫描仪，2005

BenQ Corporation, Taipei, Taiwan
Werksdesign: BenQ Lifestyle Design Center
Vertrieb: BenQ Deutschland GmbH, Hamburg
www.benq.com

明基7350C扫描仪的设计宗旨在于要尽量节省空间。该扫描仪的下端被设计为一个稳固的可折叠的支腿。这样的话，它就可以对着书本或者文件竖直放置。设计中一个金属夹的运用使得该设备也可以挂在墙上，更有利于节省空间。这款扫描仪的上盖是可以拆卸的，这样在扫描比DIN A4格式大的书籍时就会格外方便。扫描仪的背面专门设计了一个空间用来存放驱动光盘。这样就解决了当扫描仪被几个人使用时，必须去找适当驱动器的问题。

The BenQ 7350C scanner is designed in a space-saving way. The lower part of the scanner is constructed as a stable, foldaway leg. In this way, the scanner can be placed upright against books or folders. With the integrated metal clamp, the unit can be hung on a wall as well. The detachable cover allows scanning of thick books in formats larger than DIN A4. An integrated compartment at the back side serves for storage of the driver CD. This solves the problem of having to find the right driver when the scanner is used by several people.

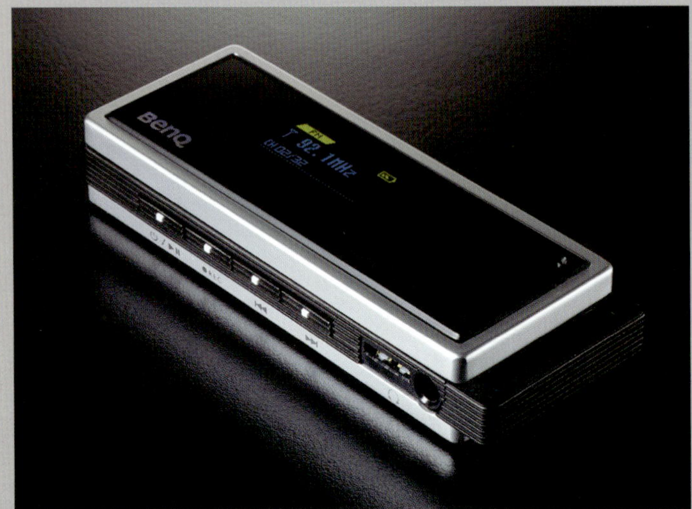

明基 Joybee 200 音频播放器，2004

BenQ Corporation, Taipei, Taiwan
Werksdesign: BenQ Lifestyle Design Center
Vertrieb: BenQ Deutschland GmbH, Hamburg
www.benq.com

明基Joybee 200是一款音频播放器，它的尺寸仅为76 x 29 x 16毫米。这种便携式MP3播放器配有FM/AM广播，还有内置的可录音话筒。闪亮的OLED 显示屏安装在一个镜面后，这样不仅方便了阅读，还能够让显示屏得到很好的保护。无线广播使其能在车载立体声系统上播放MP3文件。机器上还配备了对讲机，为短距离的交流提供了方便。BenQ Joybee 200在形式和颜色上都设计得大方稳重，为了避免损坏，还随机配备了一个黑色皮套提供保护。

The BenQ Joybee 200 is an audio player measuring just 76 x 29 x 16mm. Part of the equipment of this portable MP3 player is an FM/AM radio and a built-in microphone for voice and sound recording. The bright, easily readable OLED display is safely positioned behind a glass surface. The wireless frequency allows playing MP3 files over a car stereo system. An integrated walkie-talkie function for short-distance communication provides additional user comfort. To avoid damage, the Joybee 200, discreet in form and colour, can be carried in a black leather case when outdoors.

明基 P31 智能手机, 2005

BenQ Corporation, Taipei, Taiwan
Werksdesign: BenQ Lifestyle Design Center
Vertrieb: BenQ Deutschland GmbH, Hamburg
www.benq.com

考虑到个人和商务需求，明基P31集通讯，PDA和数字化摄像功能记录于一体。当把它握在手中时，垂直的设计会让人觉得手感不错。手机后面的功能键设计得很富有人性化，当水平使用时，它就能简便地进行摄像操作。手机天线隐藏在机身内，从而使其整体外形看起来非常坚固而独立。操作PDA时可依据个人要求打开触摸屏或是键盘。P31的外形尺寸为117 × 52 × 21毫米而重量仅为150克。小巧玲珑的机身非常方便，完全可以毫不费力地装入你的上衣口袋里。

Conceived for private and business demands, the P31 combines communication, PDA and digital image recording in one device. The vertical design supports the user comfort of a mobile phone and PDA unit when holding it in one's hand. The function buttons on the back side are arranged user-friendly and allow easy camera operation when using the device horizontally. The antenna is concealed within the housing, contributing to a solid and self-contained structural shape. For operating the PDA, a sensor screen or a keypad can be activated, according to requirements. With 117 x 52 x 21mm and its little weight of 150 grammes, the P31 is handy and can be tucked away in any pocket.

明基 Joybee 105 音频播放器, 2005

BenQ Corporation, Taipei, Taiwan
Werksdesign: BenQ Lifestyle Design Center
Vertrieb: BenQ Deutschland GmbH, Hamburg
www.benq.com

明基Joybee 105播放器的机身是硅制成的，小巧的机身却集合了多种功能。不用单独的线缆，它就能完成数据交换并且给电池充电，这使得这款播放器能够使用户在户外很方便地听自己最喜欢的音乐。整个机身设计地现代感十足，但却衔接得很自然。O形圈能够将Joybee 105挂在项链上，但是也能用一个磁铁挂钩将其挂在皮带或者衬衫上。小巧的闪存MP3播放器让移动变得随心所欲。USB隐藏在硅制机身的较低部分里，一把弹簧锁将其保护起来，这种锁既能使用户方便地接触USB界面，同时也预防丢失。

This versatile and compact player in a silicone housing allows exchange of data and recharging of batteries without an additional cable. In this way, it is possible to listen to one's favourite music outdoors without interruption. The modern design complements the outfit in a natural way. The O-ring allows carrying the Joybee 105 on a necklace, but it can also be attached to belt or shirt with a magnetic clip. The tiny flash-drive MP3 player allows maximum freedom of movement. The USB jack is concealed in the lower part of the silicone housing. It is secured by a latch which allows easy access to the USB interface, but which cannot get lost at the same time.

明基 M300 手机，2004

BenQ Corporation, Taipei, Taiwan
Werksdesign: BenQ Lifestyle Design Center
Vertrieb: BenQ Deutschland GmbH, Hamburg
www.benq.com

明基M300是一款有着金属外壳，外形小巧玲珑的手机，而且摸上去手感非常好。可以多角度转动的按键让使用最频繁的功能也可以很简便地进行操作；同时，也避免了无意地碰到其他按键。由于使用了TMT技术，显示屏的效果更加清晰，甚至可与TFT屏相媲美。这款电话的内置相机使拍照变得轻松随意；一个集成镜面可以方便地进行自拍。为了保护环境、降低成本，M300是用专门的可回收材料生产的。颜色设计上也没有使用气雾喷雾。

The BenQ M300 is a compact mobile phone with metallic housing and a good tactile feel. With its larger-dimensioned buttons, the functions used most are easily handled on the M300. At the same time, unintentional activation of other functions is avoided. Due to the use of TMT technology, the display delivers a sharp, bright high-grade picture, comparable with a TFT panel. With the built-in camera, photos can be shot easily; an integrated mirror facilitates the shooting of self-portraits. For purposes of environmental protection and cost reduction, the M300 is manufactured exclusively from recyclable materials. Aerosol spray colours are not used for colour design.

SIEMENS
SK 65

西门子 SK65 手机, 2004

Siemens AG, München
Design: Phoenix Design, Stuttgart
www.siemens.com/mobile
www.phoenixdesign.de

西门子SK65是一款针对时刻有通讯需要的商务人士而设计的高级移动电话。它是西门子的第一款与MS Outlook或Lotus Notes同步运行的，可以收发e-mail功能的手机，而这些是通过应用所谓的“黑莓植入”技术而实现的。这就意味着用户只要一按键就可以自动接收e-mail。因此，沟通就可以通过e-mail发送而轻松实现；而且，由于持续的数据同步传输，信箱内的邮件以及日程表总是更新的。这款手机还将精密的设计与其卓越的技术功能性和高度的使用舒适感结合在了一起。另一点值得强调的是该手机创新的交叉装置，将底盖旋转90度角就立刻呈现出有37个闪光按键的完整键盘。这样以来，写e-mail就像在家中写信一样简便，一旦信写好了也可以随时发送出去，而往回旋转90度键盘就能重新合上。

The Siemens SK65 is a high-grade tri-band mobile phone for business users depending on communication any place, any time. It is the first mobile phone of Siemens with a sophisticated e-mail synchronisation with MS Outlook or Lotus Notes, made possible by integrating the so-called BlackBerry Built-In Technology. This means: users receive their e-mails en route automatically, at the push of a button. Communication via the common e-mail programmes is thus possible, and, thanks to continuous data synchronisation, the mail in-box as well as the calendar are always up-to-date. A sophisticated design combines technical functionality with a high degree of user comfort. Highlight is the innovative cross-to-type mechanism unveiling a full-size keyboard with 37 illuminated keys at a quarter-turn of the bottom shell. Writing e-mails is as easy as from home. Once the mail is written and sent, the keyboard can be fold up again with one 90-degree turn back.

西门子 SF65 手机, 2004

Siemens AG, München
Design: designafairs GmbH
(Roger Münstermann), München
www.siemens-mobile.com
www.designafairs.com

西门子SF65手机不仅是一款功能齐全的手机，还是一个高级的数码照相机。该手机外形线条流畅清晰，亮丽的银白色机身更凸显出它的独特魅力。该照相机配备了130万像素的镜头和四倍连续数码变焦功能。18兆的内存能够储存300张普通VGA格式的照片；内置LED闪光灯让用户在照明条件很差的情况下也能捕捉到细致的影像。TFT的旋转式屏幕同时也是一个影像捕捉器，其分辨率达到了128 × 160像素，能显示多达 65,536种的颜色。独特的折叠旋转式装置使其屏幕可以旋转180度。该手机重量约为96克，待机时间为16天。它能够在900和1800兆赫的GSM网络中操作，并且支持GPRS Class 10。

The SF65 mobile phone by Siemens is a fully-fledged digital camera as well as a functional clamshell mobile phone. The design is clear with an elegant impression in high-gloss polar white. The camera features 1.3 megapixels and is equipped with a stepless fourfold digital zoom. The 18MB memory offers storage space for up to 300 pictures in the common VGA format; a built-in LED flashlight guarantees good pictures even when lighting conditions are poor. The swivel-mounted TFT display serves as viewfinder, displaying a maximum of 65,536 colours with a resolution of 128 x 160 pixels. The fold-swivel mechanism allows to turn the display by 180 degrees. The phone weighs approx. 96 grammes and is operational for 16 days in standby mode. It operates in the GSM networks 900 and 1,800MHz and supports GPRS Class 10.

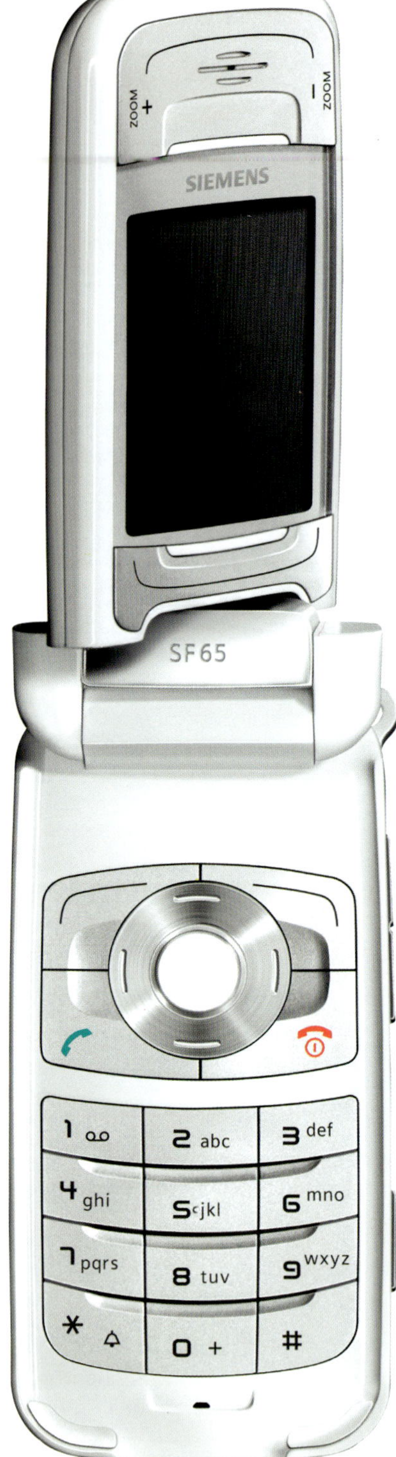

西门子 SK65 手机, 2004

Siemens AG, München
Design: Phoenix Design, Stuttgart
www.siemens.com/mobile
www.phoenixdesign.de

西门子SK65是一款针对时刻有通讯需要的商务人士而设计的高级移动电话。它是西门子的第一款与MS Outlook或Lotus Notes同步运行的，可以收发e-mail功能的手机，而这些是通过应用所谓的“黑莓植入”技术而实现的。这就意味着用户只要一按键就可以自动接收e-mail。因此，沟通就可以通过e-mail发送而轻松实现；而且，由于持续的数据同步传输，信箱内的邮件以及日程表总是更新的。这款手机还将精密的设计与其卓越的技术功能性和高度的使用舒适感结合在了一起。另一点值得强调的是该手机创新的交叉装置，将底盖旋转90度角就立刻呈现出有37个闪光按键的完整键盘。这样以来，写e-mail就像在家中写信一样简便，一旦信写好了也可以随时发送出去，而往回旋转90度键盘就能重新合上。

The Siemens SK65 is a high-grade tri-band mobile phone for business users depending on communication any place, any time. It is the first mobile phone of Siemens with a sophisticated e-mail synchronisation with MS Outlook or Lotus Notes, made possible by integrating the so-called BlackBerry Built-In Technology. This means: users receive their e-mails en route automatically, at the push of a button. Communication via the common e-mail programmes is thus possible, and, thanks to continuous data synchronisation, the mail in-box as well as the calendar are always up-to-date. A sophisticated design combines technical functionality with a high degree of user comfort. Highlight is the innovative cross-to-type mechanism unveiling a full-size keyboard with 37 illuminated keys at a quarter-turn of the bottom shell. Writing e-mails is as easy as from home. Once the mail is written and sent, the keyboard can be fold up again with one 90-degree turn back.

西门子 SF65 手机, 2004

Siemens AG, München
Design: designafairs GmbH
(Roger Münstermann), München
www.siemens-mobile.com
www.designafairs.com

西门子SF65手机不仅是一款功能齐全的手机，还是一个高级的数码照相机。该手机外形线条流畅清晰，亮丽的银白色机身更凸显出它的独特魅力。该照相机配备了130万像素的镜头和四倍连续数码变焦功能。18兆的内存能够储存300张普通VGA格式的照片；内置LED闪光灯让用户在照明条件很差的情况下也能捕捉到细致的影像。TFT的旋转式屏幕同时也是一个影像捕捉器，其分辨率达到了128 x 160像素，能显示多达 65,536种的颜色。独特的折叠旋转式装置使其屏幕可以旋转180度。该手机重量约为96克，待机时间为16天。它能够在900和1800兆赫的GSM网络中操作，并且支持GPRS Class 10。

The SF65 mobile phone by Siemens is a fully-fledged digital camera as well as a functional clamshell mobile phone. The design is clear with an elegant impression in high-gloss polar white. The camera features 1.3 megapixels and is equipped with a stepless fourfold digital zoom. The 18MB memory offers storage space for up to 300 pictures in the common VGA format; a built-in LED flashlight guarantees good pictures even when lighting conditions are poor. The swivel-mounted TFT display serves as viewfinder, displaying a maximum of 65,536 colours with a resolution of 128 x 160 pixels. The fold-swivel mechanism allows to turn the display by 180 degrees. The phone weighs approx. 96 grammes and is operational for 16 days in standby mode. It operates in the GSM networks 900 and 1,800MHz and supports GPRS Class 10.

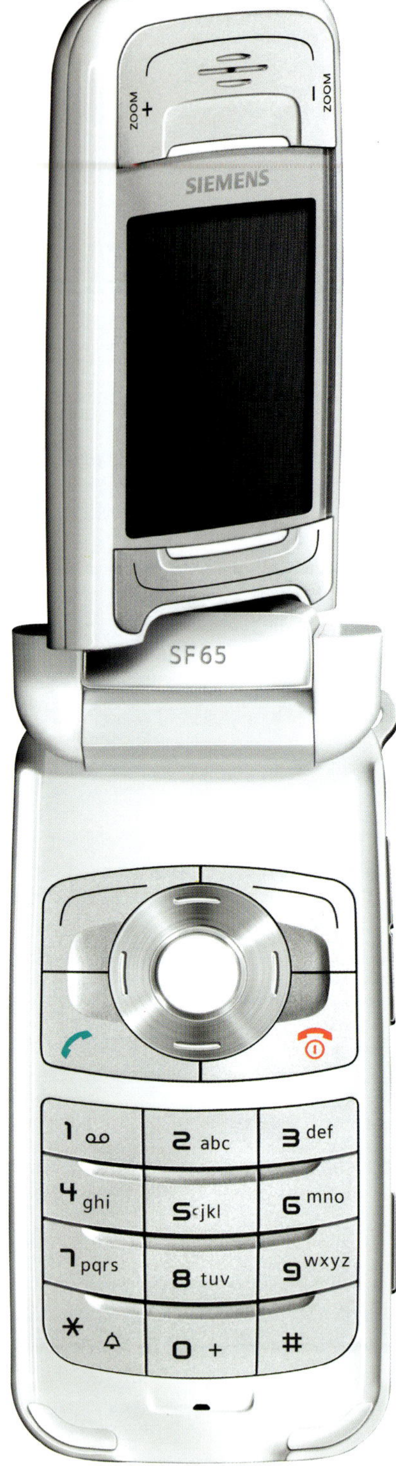

西门子SL65 手机, 2004

Siemens AG, München
Design: designafairs GmbH
(Bianca Fleischer, Nico Michler),
München
www.siemens-mobile.com
www.designafairs.com

与它上一代的机型一样，SL65三频支持手机的外形设计得很纤细。该手机的上部包括屏幕在内都是可以滑开的，滑开后键盘便露了出来，而将其合上时，SL65的外形却是非常小巧，机身尺寸仅为90 × 48 × 20毫米，轻便的机身仅重99克。SL65内置了具有录像功能的VGA摄像机，还拥有5倍变焦数码镜头和640 × 480像素。清晰而生动的65000色确保了清晰的图像质量，同时专门开发的动画制作技术和3D的应用也可以让你体验其与众不同的游戏和娱乐功能。

Like its predecessor, the SL65 tri-band mobile phone is designed with a slider housing. The complete upper part of the phone including display can be slid up, thus revealing the keypad. In this way, the SL65 has a compact format when closed, measuring just 90 x 48 x 21mm. With 99 grammes it is very light as well. The technical equipment features an integrated VGA camera with video function, fivefold digital zoom and 640 x 480 pixels. The clear and vivid 65K colour concept guarantees a good picture quality, and specially developed animations and 3D applications contribute to outstanding gaming and entertainment fun.

泛泰 P1 手机, 2004

Pantech & Curitel, Seoul, Korea
Werksdesign: Hwa Joon Roh
www.curitel.com

P1是一款有内置数码相机的超薄手机。它的宽大屏幕直接安装在不锈钢机身表面。P1设有210万像素的摄像头，并且配有自动对焦功能和LED闪光灯。另外，P1拍照时还分为特写模式或是全景拍摄，可以根据不同需求对拍摄方式进行选择。另一个功能方面的创新就是应用了文本-语言技术（TTS）。有了这种功能，SMS信息就可以转化为语言信息。同样地，日程和闹钟或者提醒信息也能发出声音来。内置的MP3播放器和电子词典使其功能更加完整。

The P1 is a very flat mobile phone with integrated camera. Its wide display is directly mounted onto the stainless steel housing surface. It is equipped with 2.1 megapixels, an autofocus function and a colour LED flash. In addition, the P1 offers options for close-up as well as panorama shots. With regard to the mobile phone functions, the innovative element is the integrated text-to-speech technology (TTS). With this function, SMS messages can be converted into spoken text. Similarly, appointments and alarm or reminder sounds can be announced by voice. The integrated MP3 player and an electronic dictionary complete the extensive package.

泛泰 PH-K1000V 手机, 2004

Pantech & Curitel, Seoul, Korea
Werksdesign: Se Min Jeon,
Sung Jae Kim
www.curitel.com

PH-K1000V是一款旋转式手机。为了使它那像数码相机一样的外形更加突出，手机的镜头设计得就像真正的数码相机镜头一样。整个机身都是用铝制成的，可循环使用，非常环保。相机的按键清楚地排列着，并且是按水平的使用方式来设计的，与传统相机的使用方式保持一致。该手机设有310万像素镜头，一个MP3播放器，LCD显示屏以及GPS。另外一个特色就是该手机上配有电视功能，它不仅可以用于观看电视，而且可以记录电视节目。这款相机手机的尺寸仅为94.5×48×25.5毫米，可以轻松地放置于衣袋里面。

The PH-K1000V is a swivel-type clamshell mobile phone. To emphasise the digital camera look, the lens was formed just like that of a genuine digital camera. The entire housing is made of aluminium and can be recycled environmentally friendly. The camera buttons are clearly arranged and designed for use in horizontal position, accommodating the conventional use of cameras. The unit is equipped with 3.1 megapixels, an MP3 player, an LCD display as well as GPS. An additional feature is a TV function, which doesn't only allow watching TV, but recording of programmes as well. With just 94.5 x 48 x 25.5mm, the camera mobile phone fits in any pocket.

泛泰 PH-L4000V 手机, 2005

Pantech & Curitel, Seoul, Korea
Werksdesign: Kyung Yun Kim,
Sung Jae Kim
www.curitel.com

一个大大的镜头使PH-L4000V给人的第一印象就像是一款微型摄像机。而近看才发现该手机就是一款多功能的摄像手机，机身尺寸仅为88.7×53.5×25.2毫米。这款手机的210万像素的镜头和2倍光学变焦确保了它能够提供十分清晰的录制图像。该机支持MPEG4格式的视频录制，并且配置了MMC存储卡。当录制视频的时候，用户只要像使用正常摄像机一样从侧面手持住它就可以了。摄像机和手机之间的转化也非常简单：只要将能旋转270度的屏幕旋转一下，手机键盘就露出来了。内置天线令人们取拿手机变得更方便。另外，该手机还兼容了MP3播放器和FM广播，其强大的功能不得不令人叹服。

With its large lens, the PH-L4000V looks like a miniature camcorder at first glance. On closer inspection, the unit presents itself as a versatile camcorder mobile phone measuring just 88.7 x 53.5 x 25.2mm. A resolution of 2.1 megapixels and a twofold optical zoom guarantee high-definition video recordings. The unit supports the MPEG4 video format and is equipped with an MMC memory card. When recording videos, the user holds the unit with a lateral grip just like a regular camcorder. The metamorphosis from camcorder to mobile phone is easy: once the swivel-mounted display, rotatable by 270 degrees, is flipped up, the phone keypad shows up. The antenna was placed within the housing to keep the phone handy. Additional features are an MP3 player and an FM radio.

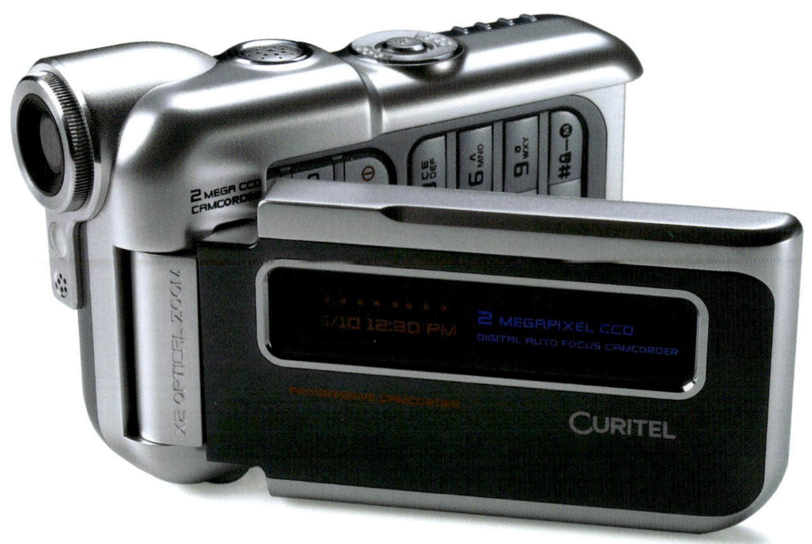

索爱 J200i 手机, 2005

Sony Ericsson Mobile Communications Int. AB, Düsseldorf
Design: Sony Ericsson Mobile Communications Int. AB, Lund, Schweden
www.sonyericsson.com

J220i手机设计朴素简约，堪称经典。独特的技术处理使得它使用简便，易于抓握。当那40和弦的优美铃音从机身背面单独的扬声器上发出时，一定会显出它的与众不同。J220i内还设有强大的图片库，都可用作待机墙纸。多个小游戏也可以为人们打发掉许多无聊的时光。

The J200i mobile phone is timeless and plain in design. Its technical equipment contributes to its user-friendliness and easy handling. 40 polyphonic ring tones provide a strong recognition factor and a good sound quality over a separate loudspeaker on the back side. The J200i features a large picture gallery for a fancy individual design of the display background. In addition, the unit includes many games.

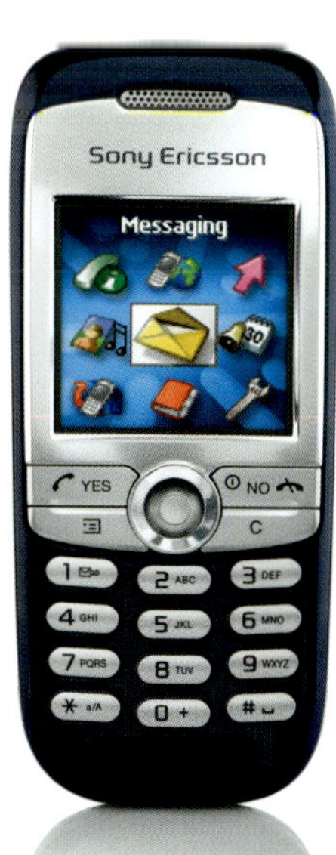

索爱 K700i 手机, 2004

Sony Ericsson Mobile Communications Int. AB, Düsseldorf
Design: Sony Ericsson Mobile Communications Int. AB, Lund, Schweden
www.sonyericsson.com

K700i手机将相机和手机结合在了一起。该手机有着毫不张扬的金属处理表面，但在不经意的外表下却突出了它的实用功能：从前面看，K700i看起来像一个传统手机；从背面看，它则更像一个便携式数码相机。机身集成了QuickShare™功能，可以能快速而简便地拍摄并发送照片。该手机也可以拍摄视频短片。四倍数码变焦能使你拍出的相片更具有创意，内置的FM广播还在闲暇时播放音乐，使人放松身心。

The K700i mobile phone combines camera and phone in one device. The unit presents itself in a matter-of-fact metallic finish and deliberately emphasises the relevant functions: from the front, the K700i looks like a conventional mobile phone; from the back, it looks like a handy digital camera. It is equipped with a so-called QuickShare™ function, allowing fast and easy taking and sending of photos. Video clips can be shot as well. The fourfold digital zoom offers creativity when taking images, and the integrated FM radio offers music for relaxation.

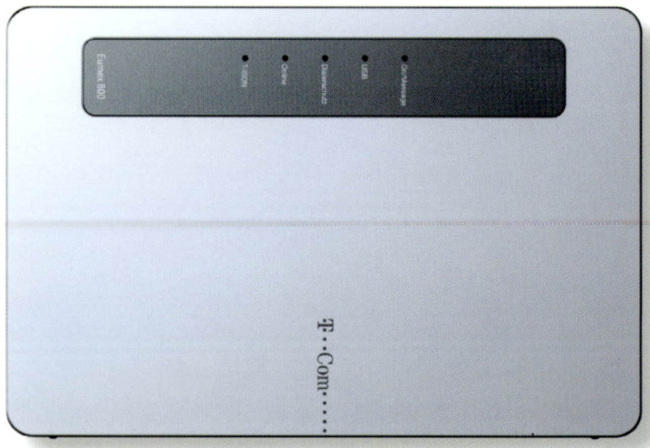

Teledat 301 DSL-调制解调器, 2005

Deutsche Telekom AG, T-Com, Bonn
Werksdesign: Klaus W. Kugler
Design: ma design, Kiel
www.telekom.de
www.ma-design.de

Teledat 301ADSL–调制解调器是T–Com最初生产的连接PC和ADSL网络的产品。该产品简明的设计令它使用起来非常简便。所有的部件质量都很不错，银色的顶盖设计更加突出了这一点。顶盖连同底部外壳的凹处进一步让人觉得这款设备的外形非常地玲珑纤细。

The Teledat 301 ADSL modem is T-Com's start-up product connecting the PC to the ADSL net. The clear design conveys the ease of use and the high quality of all connections. The silver top cover emphasises the high quality and, together with the recess in the bottom housing, helps to define the slim silhouette of the device.

Eumex 300 IP 电话系统, 2005

Deutsche Telekom AG, T-Com, Bonn
Werksdesign: Klaus W. Kugler
Design: ma design, Kiel
www.telekom.de
www.ma-design.de

Eumex 300 IP电话系统能使多达三种的同类电话形成一个网络，并且可以把PC和ISDN 网络连接起来。这就能进行正常的电话连接，并且可使用有标准电话的因特网协议（VoIP）。该系统主要的功能性特征就是大的TAE插头可被掩盖起来放置，形成的角度使其能安装在桌面和墙壁上。该产品低调中却有透露着高雅，这种设计几乎能与所有的家用设施相兼容，并且使先进的网络技术成为生活空间中的一种自然元素。

The Eumex 300 IP phone system can network up to three analogue phones and connect a PC to the ISDN network. This allows a normal telephone connection as well as usage of the Internet Protocol (VoIP) with standard telephones. Main functional feature is the covered placement of the bulky TAE plugs. The resulting angled shape allows tabletop use as well as wall-mounting. The unobtrusive elegance of the product makes it compatible with all home settings and helps state-of-the-art networking technology become a natural element of the living spaces.

Eumex 800 电话系统, 2005

Deutsche Telekom AG, T-Com, Bonn
Werksdesign: Klaus W. Kugler
Design: ma design, Kiel
www.telekom.de
www.ma-design.de

Eumex 800 IP电话系统能使多达八种同类电话形成一个网络，并且可以把PC和ISDN网络连接起来。该系统主要的功能性特征就是连接区域虽然被掩盖起来了，但仍可轻松被找到，这就使其能便捷地用电线把已经安装好的外壳连接起来。该系统清晰的设计令人觉得它的使用也会很简便，给用户以一种强烈的安全感。

The Eumex 800 phone system can network up to eight analogue phones and connect a PC to the ISDN network. Main functional feature is the covered, but still easy accessible connector field that allows comfortable wiring with the housing already mounted. The clear design communicates the idea of ease of use, thus reducing user insecurity.

Sinus 300i 无绳电话, 2005

Deutsche Telekom AG, T-Com, Bonn
Werksdesign: Klaus W. Kugler
Design: Design 3
(Jan-Michael von Lewinski,
Alexander Ksoll), Hamburg
www.telekom.de
www.design3.de

Sinus 300i代表着T–Com进入了新的ISDN无绳电话领域。简约、冷艳而高雅的外观主导着这一系列产品的美感。该设计避免了时尚元素，从而在视觉上延长了产品的生命周期。该产品总体设计上的重要部分就是电话中心部位的圆形键盘。这种键盘能支持所有的基本功能，并且仅用一个手指就能够操作。这种新颖、互动的设计使其能简便而直观的利用ISDN网络的所有特征。Sinus 300i无绳电话也能用于具备DECT（Sinus P/PA 622）基站的桌面。

The Sinus 300i represents T-Com's new entry-level segment of cordless ISDN phones. Plain, cool elegance dominates the aesthetics of this product line. The design avoids fashionable elements to optically enhance the long life cycle of the product. An important part of the overall key design is the central, circular keypad of the unit. This keypad supports all the basic functions and can be operated with a single finger. A new, interactive design allows easy and intuitive use of all ISDN network features. The cordless Sinus 300i can also be used in a table unit with integrated DECT base station (Sinus P/PA 622).

三星 SGH-E800 手机，2004

Samsung Electronics Co., Ltd.,
Seoul, Korea
Werksdesign: Woo-Seung Han,
Nam-Mi Kim
www.samsung.com

SGH-E800有着流线型的滑盖设计，并且包含创新型的清晰语音功能。它可将周围所有的噪音降低到最小程度。可变的高音、低音以及音量的大小都可以用此功能来控制，这样就能很清晰地听到对方的声音且音质非常优秀。这种滑盖手机内置附带闪光灯的VGA数码照相机，64和弦铃声，以及设计得非常人性化的操作面板。手机的内置天线使其外形显得小巧玲珑，整个机身尺寸仅为87 × 43 × 23.5毫米。

With a streamlined "slide-up" design, the SGH-E800 includes an innovative voice clarity function. All ambient noise is reduced to a minimum. Varying treble, bass and volume are controlled in such a way that the caller's voice can be heard with a sound quality unknown up to now. The clamshell mobile phone features a VGA camera with flashlight, 64 polyphonic ring tones and a user-friendly operating panel. The integrated antenna contributes to the compact shape, measuring just 87 x 43 x 23.5mm.

三星 YP-T7 MP3 播放器，2004

Samsung Electronics Co., Ltd.,
Seoul, Korea
Werksdesign: Seog-Guen Kim,
Goang-Tae Kim
www.samsung.com

YP-T7 MP3播放器色彩鲜艳，外观新颖。铝镁合金的机身动感十足，却也有如大家闺秀般的雅致。它小巧的外型和重量进一步提升了其自身形象，而外形尺寸仅为37 × 62 × 13.3毫米，机身重量为35.5克。该播放器有一个可调节的挂绳，把它当成时尚饰品来佩戴也是再好不过的了。大大的功能键上有五个菜单键，操作起来极其容易，只用一个手指就能控制整体75%的功能。该播放器还配有电子书，数码唱片功能，自动歌曲文本显示，以及可调节音质的图像均衡器。此外，这种播放器还很环保，因为在生产过程中避免了有毒物质例如镉的使用。

With its colourful design, the YP-T7 MP3 player has a fresh appearance. The aluminium-magnesium housing yields the impression of sportive elegance. This impression is enhanced by its compact size of 37 x 62 x 13.3mm and a weight of just 35.5 grammes. With an adjustable lanyard, the player can also be worn as a fashionable accessory. A large function button with five integrated keys allows easy handling and control of 75 per cent of all functions with just one finger. The player features an eBook and digital album functions, an automatic song text display and a graphic equaliser for clean sound. Toxic substances such as cadmium have been abandoned during the manufacturing process; thus, the player is environmentally friendly in its construction.

三星 HD941 HD DVD 播放器, 2005

Samsung Electronics Co., Ltd.,
Seoul, Korea
Werksdesign: Han Kim, Won-Gab Byun
www.samsung.com

HD941是一款外观线条清晰的DVD播放器。它的机身是由可回收的白色银铝制成的。机器的特色在于其前面的白色LCD显示屏。该播放器内设有DVD音频和SACD功能以及HDMI。HD941的尺寸仅为45×430×250毫米，能很简便地与其他设备进行组合。它的安装系统分为两个部分，前面板可以调换，这样就能魔术般地实现颜色上的变化。

The HD941 is a video and audio DVD player with a clear design. The housing is made of recyclable bright silver aluminium. A particular feature is the white LCD display on the front side of the unit. The technical features include a DVD audio and SACD function as well as HDMI. With 45 x 430 x 250mm, the DVD player allows easy combination with other devices. A two-part mounting system allows the exchange of the front portion, thus making variation of colours possible.

三星 DVD-R121 DVD 录像机, 2005

Samsung Electronics Co., Ltd.,
Seoul, Korea
Werksdesign: Hyun-taek Lim,
Won-Gab Byun
www.samsung.com

DVD–R121是一款外观设计高雅的并能与HDTV兼容的DVD录像机。它能够记录、储存并回放HD转换和摄像视频。该机器可以播放所有平常的录音和视频格式。它的功能面板结构清晰，手感舒适。DVD–R121的高度仅为55毫米，小巧纤细，几乎在任何地方都能安装它，而且，生产所用的材料很容易分解并可循环使用。

The DVD-R121 is an elegant HDTV-compatible DVD recorder. It can record, store and play back HD transmissions and camcorder videos. The unit plays all customary disc and video formats. The clearly structured function panel allows easy handling. With a height of just 55mm, the DVD-R121 is very slim and can be placed nearly everywhere. The materials used for manufacture can easily be separated and recycled.

三星 DVD-P355 DVD 播放器, 2005

Samsung Electronics Co., Ltd.,
Seoul, Korea
Werksdesign: Ju-Won Cho,
Hyun-taek Lim
www.samsung.com

DVD–P355的设计是以阴阳的对立统一思想为基础而设计的，它将柔软的线条设计与清晰的结构和实用的把手协调地组合在一起。在前侧控制板上的功能键清楚地排列着，轻轻一按便反应很灵敏。所有的功能和装置能够清楚地显示在位于前侧面板中心的FLT屏上。该播放器高度仅为37毫米 、宽度为430毫米 、厚度为210毫米，因此几乎可以安放在任何地方。

The design of the DVD-P355 is based on the idea of the dichotomy of Yin and Yang: a soft line management combines harmonically with a clear structure and practical handling. The function buttons on the edged front panel are clearly arranged and respond swiftly to a light touch. All functions and settings can be read easily on the FLT screen positioned in the centre. With a height of just 37mm, a width of 430mm and a depth of 210mm, the player will fit in nearly every space.

三星 LT46G1 LCD 电视, 2004

Samsung Electronics Co., Ltd.,
Seoul, Korea
Werksdesign: Jun-Ho Yang,
Young-Jun Kim
www.samsung.com

LT46G1的设计基于一种角度的设计理念，突出了其46英寸的LCD面板。面板区的黑色液晶突出更凸现了16：9的宽屏模式。该电视内设HDTV、DNIE，自动调光功能和半圆形扬声器。两侧均倾斜的扬声器盖使得该电视显得非常雅致。嵌入式的功能按键让这款电视的纯光学效果更加突出。无论是挂在墙上还是安置在桌上，LT46G1看起来都非常典雅大方。

The design of the LT46G1 is based on an angular concept with emphasis on the 46-inch LCD panel. The black glass in the panel area accentuates the 16:9 format display. The technical equipment includes HDTV, DNIE, automatic brightness adjustment and semi-dome speakers. The speaker covers, slanted on both sides, give the unit an elegant impression. The puristic optics are enhanced by immersible function buttons. The LT46G1 is suitable for both wall mounting and tabletop.

三星 VP-M102 迷你数码摄像机, 2004

Samsung Electronics Co., Ltd.,
Seoul, Korea
Werksdesign: In-Shik Kim,
Yeon-Moo Chung
www.samsung.com

VP-M102这款数码摄像机的尺寸为92.5 × 26.5 × 61毫米，与一个香烟盒大小差不多。尽管其外形小，重量轻（仅为150克），VP-M102仍包括了多项综合的技术特征：就移动娱乐而言，它有录像和影像稳定的功能，并且配有一个MP3播放器和PC照相机。该摄像机设有十倍光学变焦，100倍数码变焦的镜头。能支持65K色的两寸屏幕和LED背景灯，使用户能够舒适地监控所有的功能。

With 92.5 x 26.5 x 61mm, this small camcorder is not larger than a cigarette packet. Despite the small format and the low weight of just 150 grammes, the VP-M102 includes comprehensive technical features: for mobile entertainment there are video and freeze image functions, an MP3 player and a PC camera. The camcorder lens features a tenfold optical and a 100-fold digital zoom. The two-inch display with 65K colour capacity and LED backlight allows comfortable monitoring of all functions.

三星 SyncMaster 720T LCD 显示器, 2004

Samsung Electronics Co., Ltd.,
Seoul, Korea
Werksdesign: Jeong-Hoon Ha,
Tae-Yeon Won
www.samsung.com

SyncMaster720T有17英寸和19英寸两种款式，该显示器设计线条清晰，毫无累赘之感。根据TCO'03认证对其结构进行了调整，调整后的外形不仅符合人体工程学的要求，并且很环保。该显示器可以旋转180度，因此可以选择最佳观看角度，它可以向下倾斜3度，也可以向上倾斜35度。另外，1000：1的对比度保证了最佳的图像质量，可以让使用者观看时感觉非常放松。ABS是该显示器使用的唯一材料，因此SyncMaster显示器可以很容易拆卸并可循环使用。

The SyncMaster 720T, available as 17-inch or 19-inch version, is clearly designed without superfluous details. The construction is geared to the TCO '03 certification and is thus conceived ergonomically and environmentally friendly. Many alignment options for optimum view are possible due to the display being rotatable by 180 degrees. It can be tilted down by -3 and up by +35 degrees as well. In addition, a 1000:1 contrast guarantees best picture quality and relaxed working. Due to ABS being the only material used for the unit, the SyncMaster is easily dismountable and recyclable.

三星 Q30 笔记本电脑, 2004

Samsung Electronics Co., Ltd.,
Seoul, Korea
Werksdesign: Seung-Hyun Paek,
Myung-Jung Kim
www.samsung.com

Q30是一款极轻薄的笔记本电脑，显示屏为12英寸，重量竟然不到1千克（999克）。它支持数码电视和3D音效，可让你尽情享受顶级的娱乐效果。针对LAN和WLAN的集成网络界面卡使通讯变得非常简便。尽管其尺寸很小，仅为287.7 × 197 × 21.3毫米，但它键盘的大小却和常规的键盘一样，这样使用起来更舒适，也更富有人性化。

The Q30 is a slim notebook with a 12-inch display and a weight of less than 1 kg (999 grammes). The support of digital TV and a 3D audio sound guarantee a high level of entertainment. The integrated network interface card for LAN and WLAN allows easy communication. Despite the small measurements of just 287.7 x 197 x 21.3mm, the size of the keypad is adapted to the regular keypad dimensions, thus comfortable and user-friendly.

三星 SIT200EM SOHO 办公电话, 2004

Samsung Electronics Co., Ltd.,
Seoul, Korea
Werksdesign: Tai-Hyung Ju,
So-Yoon Jeoun
www.samsung.com

SIT200EM是一款WLAN电话，它有多达八种的外部手柄接口可进行选择。该设计为微微倾斜状，易于操作，具有很强的实用性。可更换的表面使用户可以自由选择自己喜欢的颜色，透明的ABS机身能够保护手柄和充电基座以防刮伤。精密的3.9英寸显示屏和清晰排列的键盘也让这款电话整体透露出一种时尚和高雅。除此之外，安装的简便性让该电话的使用更加人性化。

The SIT200EM is a WLAN telephone with connection options for up to eight external handsets. The design is slanted, optically and functionally, towards a straightforward concept: an exchangeable front cover allows a selection of preferred colours, and a transparent ABS housing protects the handset and the charging station from scratches. The unit features a concise 3.9-inch display and a clearly arranged keypad. Thanks to an easy installation, the phone is user-friendly as well.

三星 X50 笔记本电脑, 2004

Samsung Electronics Co., Ltd.,
Seoul, Korea
Werksdesign: Seung-Wook Jeong,
Myung-Jung Kim
www.samsung.com

X50是一款极为轻薄的15.4英寸宽屏笔记本电脑。它的重量仅为2.3千克，尺寸为357 × 267 × 25.9毫米。它的机身为坚固的镁合金制成的，方便耐用，还很坚固，同时也是外出商务时的理想选择。该电脑的可充电电池能保证长达12个小时的使用时间。该电脑使用英特尔迅驰处理器，设有WLAN界面及多媒体接口。一个特别的技术处理就是将集成指纹识别器与系统启动时的登陆步骤绑定在一起，直到系统通过指纹扫描识别出该用户是合法用户后，系统才能启动。

The X50 is a slim 15.4-inch widescreen notebook. With a weight of 2.3kg, measurements of 357 x 267 x 25.9mm and a solid magnesium alloy housing, it is handy, robust and ideal when being out on business. The rechargeable battery guarantees an operating time of up to twelve hours. The unit features an Intel Centrino processor, a WLAN interface and multimedia connections. A special technical feature is the integrated fingerprint reader coupled with an inquiry step at system start: the system does not start until a legitimate user identifies himself or herself by fingerprint scan.

SoundDock 数字音乐系统, 2004

Bose Corp., Framingham, USA
Werksdesign: Bose Corp. Design Team
Vertrieb: Bose GmbH, Friedrichsdorf
www.bose.de

SoundDock数字音乐系统是一款外形设计充满活力的带有遥控器的音响系统。它是与第三代便携式苹果iPod（包括iPod mini）音乐播放器组合使用的。方方正正的外形下的一种特殊装置把iPod放置在了该设备前端的中间位置上，这样，该设备连同iPod播放器就组成一套外形美观，性能卓越的音响系统，让人们在厨房、卧室、办公室等场所都能欣赏到动听的音乐。

The SoundDock digital music system is an active speaker system with remote control. It works in conjunction with the third generation of portable Apple iPod music players, including the iPod mini. The slim rectangular design provides for "docking" the iPod in centre at the front side, using a special mechanism. In this way, the unit with attached iPod player turns into a shapely, highly functional speaker system with excellent sound quality for kitchen, living room, bedroom or workroom.

东芝 DMR-P1 数字录音机, 2004

Toshiba Corporation, Tokio, Japan
Werksdesign: Toshiba Design Center (Masao Isshiki)
www.toshiba.co.jp

DMR-P1数字录音机设计得像支票卡一样的轻薄。它可以被灵活地随身携带，可将其折叠夹进用户的笔记本里，甚至是商务卡片盒和西服口袋里。这款机器的正面没有任何按键，而背面为铝制的面板，这样一来，其清晰的卡片形状一览无余，并且避免了随身携带时的误操作。尽管该设备非常薄，它仍能与带有USB的PC相连接。

The DMR-P1 digital memory recorder is designed as flat as a cheque card. It can be carried around smartly by folding it into the user's notebook or business card case or sliding it into a suit pocket. With no buttons on the front and rear aluminium panels, this design both clearly expresses the card shape and prevents accidental use while carrying it around. Although the device is thin it can be connected to a PC using USB.

Sonos 数字音乐系统, 2005

Sonos, Inc., Santa Barbara, USA
Werksdesign: Mieko Kusano
www.sonos.com

Sonos数字音乐系统是一个外形设计美观的连接多房间的音乐中心。该系统提供了多种选择，可以在不同的房间里播放储存在Mac或者PC上的音乐。为达到这个目的，所谓的ZonePlayer通过无线网络与单独的音乐存储单元连接起来。多达32个ZonePlayer能够与该系统进行连接，并且安装在房间内的不同地方，使用着相同或多样化的音乐程序。ZonePlayer是由一个PDA状的遥控器来操作的，该遥控器配有一个外置的3.5英寸的彩色LCD屏幕。

The Sonos digital music system is a multi-room music centre with an aesthetic design. The system offers the option to play music, stored on a Mac or PC, in different rooms. For this purpose, the so-called ZonePlayers are connected with the respective music storage unit via a wireless network. Up to 32 ZonePlayers can be connected to the system and set up in various parts of the house, fed with the same or diverse music programmes. The ZonePlayers are triggered by a PDA-like remote control, equipped with a clearly laid-out 3.5-inch colour LCD display.

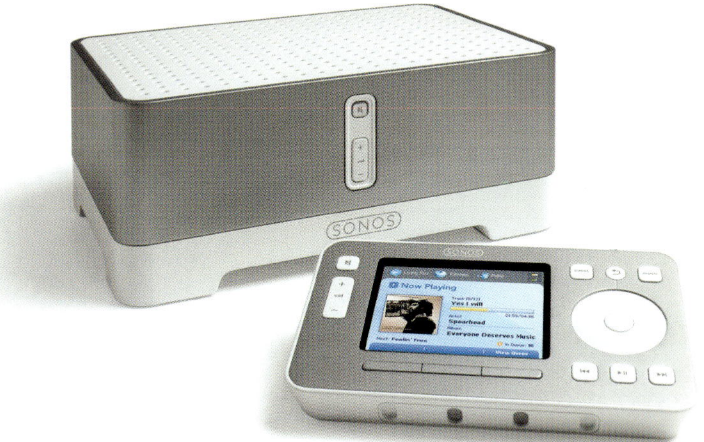

东芝 V601T 手机, 2004

Toshiba Corporation, Tokio, Japan
Werksdesign: Toshiba Design Center
(Hiroko Nakano, Taihei Miyaji, Nobuhiro Yamane)
www.toshiba.co.jp

V601T是专为年轻用户设计的。对于这些用户来说，打电话已经远远不够了，他们还想在手机上玩游戏和卡达OK。因此，歌曲接收模块、移动卡拉OK服务以及3D游戏都成为了该手机的内置功能。V601T可以与外部显示器连接起来，例如电视；并且可以播放包括文本和动画视频在内的卡拉OK歌曲。手机通过电视机的扬声器或是集成在手机上的扬声器都可以播放音乐；如果不和电视机相连的话，该手机用其屏幕也能发挥它的功能。通过由Vodafone控制的动态无线上网服务，就可以随时下载付费新歌。另外，V601T还拥有内置200万像素和两倍光学变焦的镜头。它的重量接近119克，有白色、橙色和深蓝色可供选择。

The V601T is designed for young customers who don't just want to use their mobile phone for calls, but who also want to have fun gaming and doing some karaoke. Part of the set is a song receive mode, a mobile karaoke service as well as various 3D games. The V601T can be connected to an external display like a TV set and play karaoke songs including text and video animations over it. The music itself can be played over the TV set speakers or over the integrated mobile phone speaker; the unit also functions all by itself without a TV set, using the phone display. New songs can be downloaded anytime for a fee, using the Live Mobile Internet Service operated by Vodafone. In addition, the V601T features a two-megapixel camera and a twofold optical zoom. It weighs approx. 119 grammes and is available in white, orange and dark blue.

Lepus 拍照手机, 2005

Asmobile Communication Inc., Taipei, Taiwan
Werksdesign: Asmobile Industrial Design Team
www.asmobile.com.tw

Lepus是一款将数码相机与多媒体电话组合的设计。它是为那些对新事物感兴趣并愿意与朋友一起分享的人士所设计的，使用这款机器可以方便地拍照以及发送照片。它有一个内置的200万像素相机，还有闪光灯和两个3D环绕立体声扬声器。此外，这款手机的拍照功能和数码相机一样简单：只需把底部旋转180度，就会在1.9英寸LCD面板上出现一个客户引导菜单，实现拍照功能。这种特殊的功能使得用户能够给自己拍照而没有任何困难。当使用这种拍照功能时，用户打开镜头盖就会露出连接主件和旋转部分的锁定装置，在旋转镜头时，只需简单的两步用户就可以开始进行随心所欲的拍照了。符合人体工程学设计的键盘与五个方向的控制杆组合在一起，为发SMS和MMS的快速文本输入提供了便利。

Lepus is a digital camera combined with a multimedia phone. It is for people who are interested in new things and sharing things with their friends, helping them to take pictures, and sending them in one handset. It is composed of a two-megapixel camera, a flashlight and two 3D surround speakers. Its excellent function in photographing is as simple as using a digital camera; after rotating the bottom part of the handset by 180 degrees, users will be led through the menu showing up on the 1.9-inch LCD panel and can then enjoy taking pictures. This special function enables users to take pictures of themselves without hassle. When using the scenario function, opening the lens cover will release the locked mechanism which connects the main part with the rotating part, and users can start to take pictures – just two easy steps while rotating the lens to meet individual preferences. The ergonomically designed keypad is combined with a five-way joystick facilitating rapid text inputs for SMS and MMS.

戴尔新型键盘系列, 2004

Dell Inc., Round Rock, USA
Werksdesign: Dell Industrial Design and Usability Group
Design: C10 Design & Development (Robert Sluijter), Haarlem, NL; NPK Industrial Design (Aernout Dijkstra), Leiden, NL
Vertrieb: Dell GmbH, Langen
www.dell.com
www.c10.nl
www.npk.nl

戴尔新型键盘系列的显著特征就是其外形设计有所缩小。狭窄的边缘打破了键盘的方形外形特征，几乎包围了整个键盘。这也同时突出了该设备的基本组成部分以及其标准的功能键。机身在尺寸上有所缩减，但节省了桌面空间，并且由于减少了对合成材料的使用，从而更加环保。

Characteristic feature of the Dell New Keyboard Family is a reduced design. The rectangular shape, typical for keypads, has been opened up with a narrow edge merely engulfing the keypad. This results in an emphasis on the essential component parts of the unit, the standard function keys. Reduced in size, the housing saves space on the desktop and has an environmentally positive effect due to reduced use of synthetic materials.

戴尔 540照片打印机，2004

Dell Inc., Round Rock, USA
Werksdesign: Dell Industrial Design and Usability Group
Design: Herbst LaZar Bell Inc. (Greg Holderfield, Elliot Hsu, Mike Zhang), Chicago, USA
Vertrieb: Dell GmbH, Langen
www.dell.com
www.hlb.com

戴尔540照片打印机的表面是金属制成的，外形设计得很紧凑，巧妙地适应了数码相机的外形。所有的接口和功能键都安装在该设备的六个面上并清楚地排列着，很容易找到。甚至在不理想的照明条件下，2.5英寸的集成显示器也能够呈现出明亮而清晰的图像，使用户能在打印和编辑之前对照片进行挑选。屏幕上所提供的用户指导步骤更便于引导客户，进行直观操作。

With its metallic surface and compact shape, the design of the Dell Photo Printer 540 adapts itself aesthetically to the look of digital cameras. All ports and function buttons are placed, clearly arranged and easily accessible, on the six faces of the unit. The integrated 2.5-inch monitor displays a bright and clear picture, even under difficult or poor lighting conditions, allowing the selection of photos prior to printing and editing. A screen-supported user guidance facilitates intuitive operation.

戴尔 Axim x50v 掌上电脑, 2004

Dell Inc., Round Rock, USA
Werksdesign: Dell Industrial Design and Usability Group
Design: M3 Design, Inc. (Jeff Mulhausen, Taka Okai, Paul Nobel-Campell), Round Rock, USA
Vertrieb: Dell GmbH, Langen
www.dell.com
www.m3designinc.com

Axim x50v掌上电脑的曲面造型及U型外形使其便于携带。键盘的结构是符合人体工程学的，只需一个大拇指就可以非常便利地操作所有的功能。内置3.7英寸的VGA显示屏和集成天线构成了其小巧玲珑的外形。这款掌上电脑包括了所有的连接个人或商务网络设备的无线界面。

With its rounded and implied U-shape, the handheld computer Axim x50v is very handy. The structuring of the keypad is well thought out ergonomically, allowing convenient operation of all functions with just the thumb. The unit features a clearly arranged 3.7-inch VGA display and an integrated antenna, supporting the compact shape. The pocket PC includes all wireless interfaces for connecting the device up to private or business networks.

Rio Carbon MP3 播放器, 2004

Whipsaw, Inc., San Jose, USA
Werksdesign: Dan Harden
www.whipsawinc.com

Rio Carbon是一款走位适中几乎适应各个年龄段的MP3 播放器，容量为5千兆（2500首歌曲），电池能够持续播放20个小时。播放器纤细时髦的外形带来舒适的手感，很容易就能将其滑入口袋中。一个弹性保险杠沿着该设备的边缘延伸，为使用者带来愉悦的触觉感受，也与它那光滑的不锈钢底部外壳和聚碳酸酯顶端形成了相比。当该播放器通电和使用时，控制面板和Rio标识就会用红色的LED照亮。从它的外形就可以表现出机器的功能性和实用性，机身上每一个零件都是银质的或者是白色的，重量仅为90克。它的外观尺寸很小，仅为63 × 83 × 15毫米，因而非常便于携带。

The Rio Carbon is a mid range MP3 player with a 5GB capacity (2,500 songs) and a 20-hour battery life for urbanites of all ages. The slim, sleek design of the player feels good in the hand and slips easily into a pocket. An elastomer bumper runs around the edge of the unit and provides a pleasing tactile contrast to the slick polished stainless steel bottom housing and the glossy polycarbonate top. The navigation panel and the Rio logo light up with a red LED when the unit is powered on and in use. The appearance emanates functionality and usefulness. Every unit is silver or white and weighs only 90 grammes. With its small format of 63 x 83 x 15mm, the Rio Carbon is very handy.

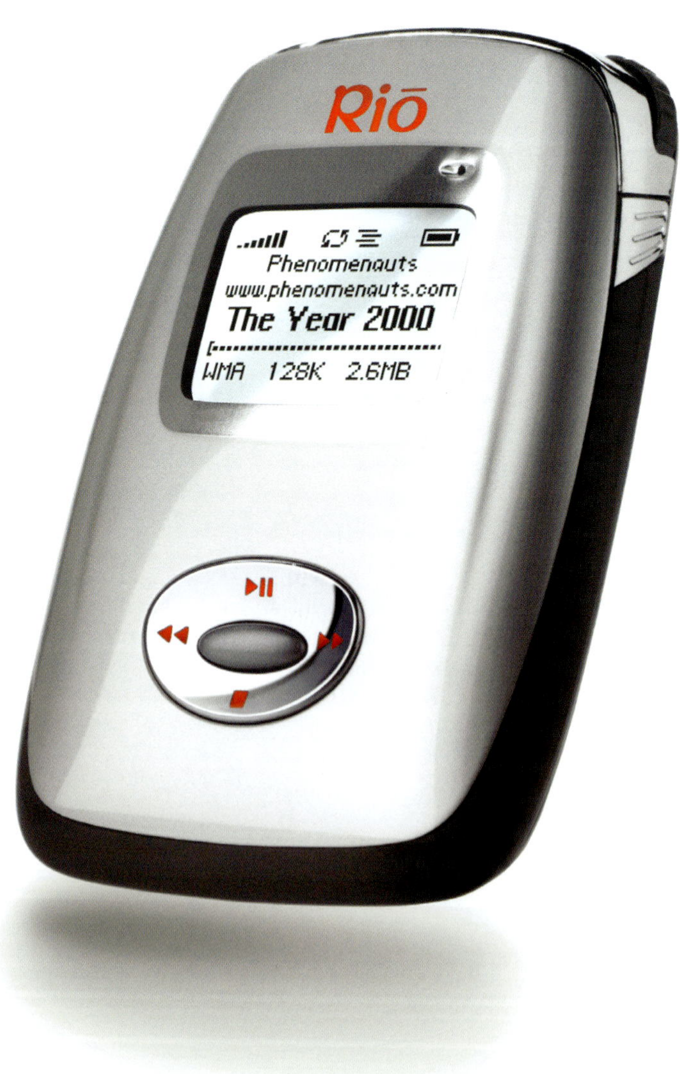

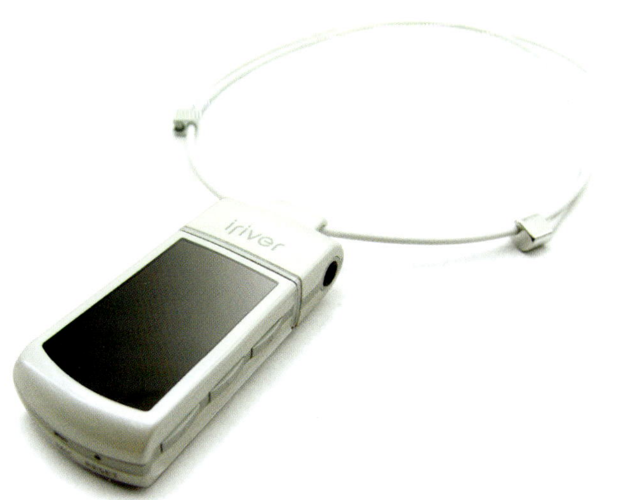

iRiver N10 MP3 播放器, 2004

Innodesign Inc., Palo Alto, USA
Werksdesign: Young Se Kim
www.innodesign.com

iRiver N10的创新型设计是基于这样一种理念，即开发一种能够像首饰一样佩戴的MP3播放器。为了满足数字化生活方式的新一代人的需要，这款多功能的MP3播放器不仅配有挂绳，还配有LCD显示屏以及SAD支持的内置麦克风。该播放器仅重22克，但却有高达1GB的存储量。它的锂离子电池可供连续播放12个小时，从而可以让你享受到无穷的音乐乐趣。蓝色的OLED屏幕下有黑色背光，16级灰度，易于阅读且耗电量非常少。iRiver N10的外观是黑白的，颜色比较中性，可以说它是以不变应万变，以适应多样化的时尚趋势。该播放器尺寸为62×27×13毫米，便于携带，可轻松放置于衣袋之内。

The innovative design of the iRiver N10 is based on the concept of developing an MP3 player, which can be worn as a trinket. Conceived for the digital lifestyle generation, this multi-functional lanyard is equipped with an LCD display and an SAD-supported microphone. The player weighs only 22 grammes and features a memory capacity of up to 1GB. The lithium-polymer cells with an operating time of twelve hours guarantee long-time listening fun. The bright-blue OLED display with backlight and 16 grey scales is well readable and consumes very little energy. In its black-and-white appearance, the iRiver N10 is neutral in terms of colour and thus adapts itself to the most diverse fashion trends. With 62 x 27 x 13mm, the MP3 player is handy and can be tucked away in any pocket.

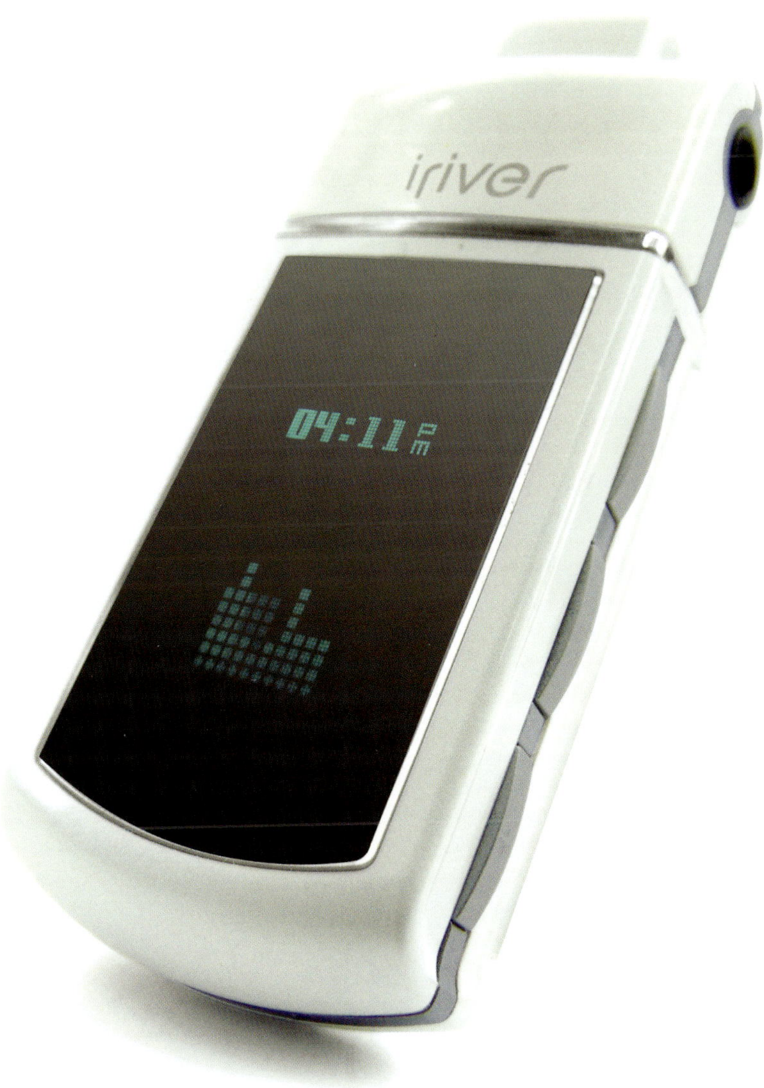

Spirit 吊扇遥控器，2005

Spirit Design LTDA., Rio de Janeiro, Brasilien
Design: Indio da Costa Design (Indio da Costa, Martin Birtel, Jaakko Tammela, Felipe Rangel), Rio de Janeiro, Brasilien
www.spiritdesign.com.br
www.indiodacosta.com

Spirit吊扇遥控器的创新型外形设计的出发点是为了让人们可以非常直观地使用它。该遥控器外形设计清晰直观，且使用简便，甚至可以在黑暗中都可以使用。向右旋转表盘就会加快风扇吸气的速度，而向左转就会加快风扇排气的速度。中间按钮控制着光的强度，其红外线技术并不会干扰其它电子设备。配合吊扇的颜色，该遥控器有九种不同的颜色可供用户选择，它甚至也能应用于市场上出售的大多数吊扇。

The innovative shape of the Spirit ceiling fan remote control was specifically designed for intuitive use. The unit is self-explanatory, intuitive and easy to use, one could operate it even in the dark. Turning the dial rightwards increases fan ventilation speed. Turning the dial leftwards increases fan exhaustion speed. The central button controls light intensity. Its infrared technology doesn't interfere with other electronic equipment. The remote control is available in nine different colours to match the ceiling fan colour. It can also be adapted to the majority of ceiling fans on the market.

Tension Pen 硬盘, 2004

Duck Image Co. Ltd., Taichung, Taiwan
Werksdesign: Rung-Ya Hsieh
www.duckimage.com.tw

Tension Pen硬盘是一款2.0介面的USB移动硬盘。它的设计很具有创新性，小巧的USB插头被安置在防水、防震、且由一个有弹性橡胶环围绕的塑料盖中。该产品原材料的组成部分中含有抗静电物质以便保护其免受静电的干扰。这种保护盖的设计使得它可以挂在钥匙串或项链上，还可把它用作别针简便地别在衬衣上或衣服的翻边上。Tension Pen硬盘有多种时髦的颜色可供选择，可以与不同外套随心所欲地搭配。

The Tension Pen Drive is a USB stick with a 2.0 interface. Innovative in design, the small stick is housed in a water-proof and shock-resistant plastic cover surrounded by an elastic rubber ring. Part of the material composition are anti-static substances so as to protect the unit from electrostatic charge. The protection cover was designed in such a way that the stick can be hooked to a bunch of keys or a necklace. As clip it can be easily attached to a shirt or revers. The Tension Pen Drive is available in many fashionable colours, thus suiting many outfits.

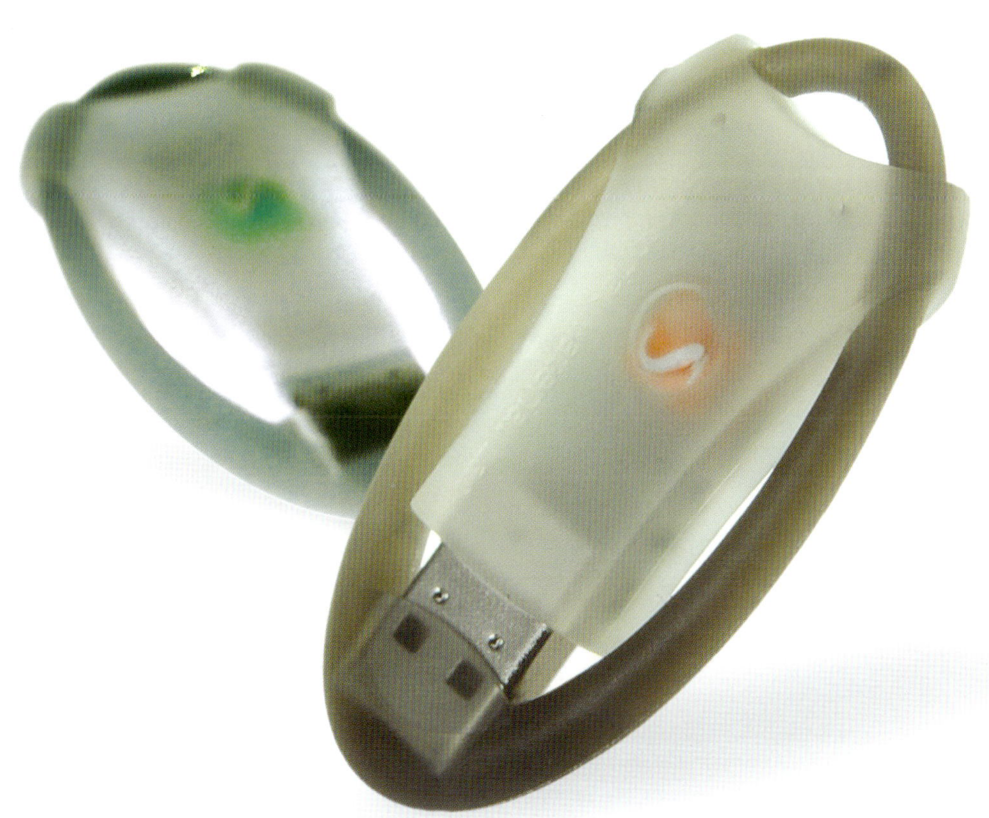

Pen Drive 蓝牙耳机, 2004

Add-On Technology Co., Ltd.,
Taipei, Taiwan
Design: Pilotfish Inc., Taipei, Taiwan
Pilotfish GmbH, München
Vertrieb: Maxfield GmbH, Düsseldorf
www.addontech.net
www.pilotfishproducts.com
www.maxfield.de

Pen Drive蓝牙耳机把美观和人性化设计与先进的通讯和传输技术融合在了一起。它的外壳构造符合人体工程学原理，机身仅仅12克的重量使得即使长达数小时地佩戴也不会有任何地不适。手机和耳机之间的传输半径达10米，因此该耳机使用户可以在工作，休息或驾车时充分享受到活动自由。耳机上的两个按键可以舒适地操作电话的管理、接听和挂机。该耳机还具备手机的语音拨号功能，能够重复所拨过的最后一个号码。耳机由内置的可充电电池为其提供电量，电池容量足够手机使用五个小时或是待机100个小时。LED屏会显示用户电池的充电状态、传输范围及总体操作情况。即便是电池没电了，耳机也不会断电，一般是从包含在传输过程中的电源调节器，车载的12伏充电站或者通过USB接口而供给的。电池充电大概需要两个小时。麦克风和耳机使用了高档零件从而保证了最好的声音质量。另外，处在最理想位置的麦克风能有效地过滤掉环境中的干扰声音及轻微的噪音。

The Pen Drive Bluetooth headset combines aesthetic and user-friendly design with state-of-the-art communication and transmission technology. The ergonomic construction of the housing and the low weight of just twelve grammes allow comfortable and hassle-free wearing of the MobileEar for hours. With a transmission radius of up to ten metres between transmitter and headset, the unit provides generous freedom of movement during work, leisure time activities or while driving. The phone management, call receipt and -ending are comfortably handled with two buttons on the headset. The unit also supports voice dial functions of mobile phones and can repeat the last number dialled. A built-in rechargeable battery serves as power supply for the MobileEar. The battery capacity is sufficient for operating the phone up to five hours or for a standby period of 100 hours. An LED display informs the user of the battery charging status, transmission range and general operating conditions. If the battery is flat, the headset can be supplied with power via the mains adaptor included in delivery, a twelve-volt charging station for the car or via a USB port. Recharging the battery takes about two hours. The use of high-grade components for microphone and earphone guarantees best speech quality for the MobileEar. In addition, an optimised directional microphone filters out disturbing environmental sounds and breeze noise effectively.

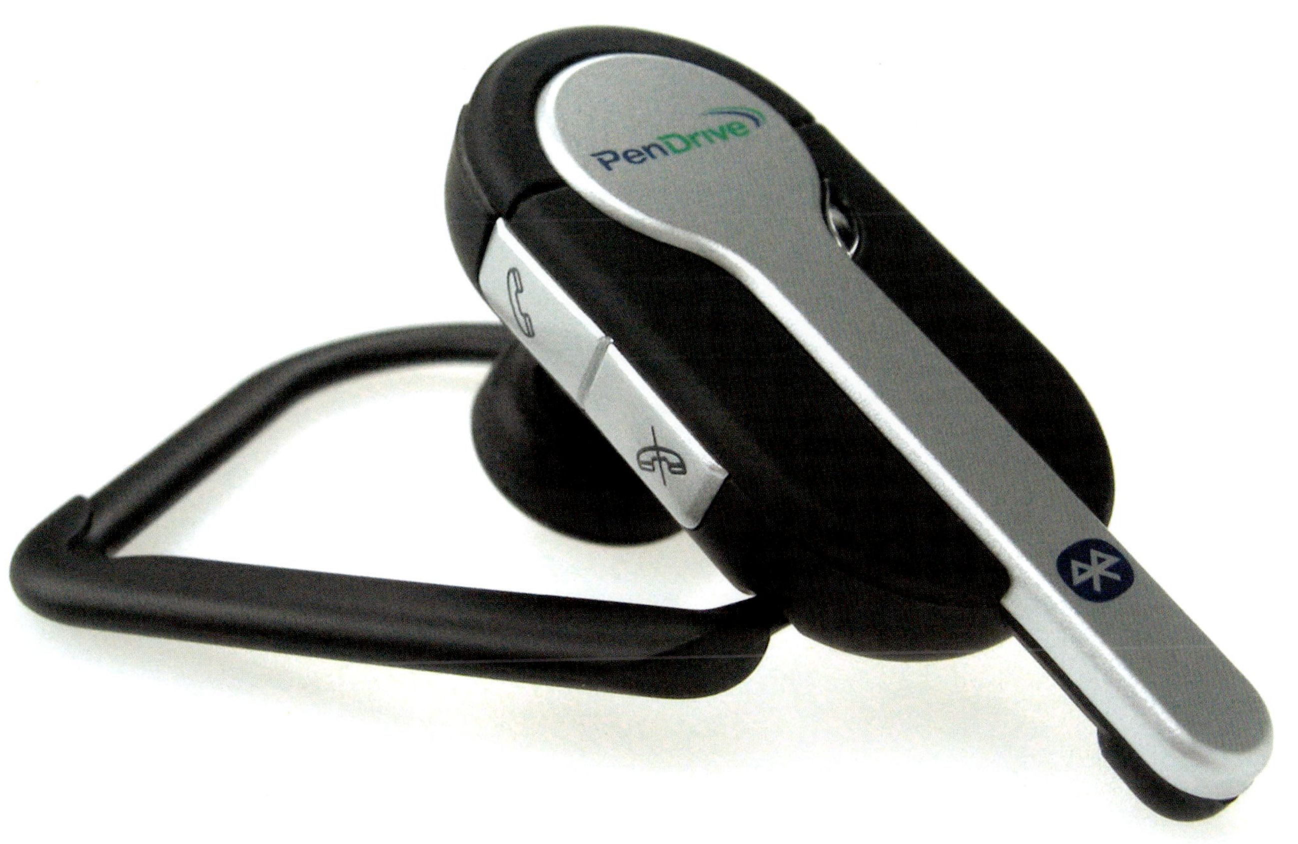
PenDrive

WACOM

Wacom Intuos3 智能数码手写板, 2004

Wacom Co., Ltd., Saitama, Japan
Design: Ziba Europe (Alf Hackenberg, Martin Langkau, Andreas Schüßler), München
Vertrieb: Wacom Europe GmbH, Krefeld
www.wacom.com
www.ziba-europe.com

Intuos3是一款专业的智能数码手写板。它使用户产生一种虽使用着传统工具例如笔和纸，却在数字化领域中工作的感觉。人体工程学因素在设计中发挥了特别的作用：通过集成在手写板上的单独的按键，就不再需要在手写板和键盘之间进行缓慢的来回转换了。在使用例如Photoshop或者Painter这样的程序时，根据程序的需要而垂直设计的触摸带可以上下滚动或放大或缩小Internet文本。为了满足右手和左手使用者的不同需求，手写板上的按键对称分布在工作台面的两侧。为了给键盘旁边的台面节省空间，电线装在手写板下面。这样，只要把插头简单一换，就可以拔掉光缆，然后将其连到它的侧面或背面了。没有连接绳的手写笔也不需要使用电池，它也是该产品中的一部分，拥有三种不同的笔尖，这样就使一支笔便可基本满足用户多样化的需求，笔座可以将手写笔水平或垂直放置。总体来说，Intuos3的设计清晰而干练。它还有多种颜色和外形可供选择，可以完全与PC和苹果的用户需要做最完美的匹配。

The Intuos3 is an intelligent digitiser tablet for professional users. This system simulates the feeling of working in the digital world with traditional tools such as pen and paper. Ergonomic aspects play a particular role here: due to the integration of individually programmable keys on the tablet, a cumbersome switch back and forth between tablet and keypad is not required any longer. A vertically arranged touchpad serves, according to programming, to scroll up and down Internet pages, or to zoom in and out when working with programmes such as Photoshop or Painter. To meet the different demands of right- and left-handers, the keys are arranged symmetrically on both sides of the active work surface. For space-saving work next to the computer keypad, the wire ducts have been placed under the tablet. Thus, with a simple change of the plug, the cable can be led away from the pad to the side as well as to the back. The cordless and battery-less pen belonging to the system is conceived with three exchangeable tips so that only one pen can be used for a wide variety of applications. The pen holder enables vertical and horizontal placement. In its design, the Wacom Intuos3 is clear and concise. Thus, it adapts itself seamlessly to the world of PC- and Apple Macintosh users with its many colours and shapes.

宏基"商务伴侣" 3000 笔记本电脑, 2005

Acer Incorporated, Hsichih, Taiwan
Werksdesign: Acer Design Team
www.acer.com

"商务伴侣"3000笔记本电脑重量仅为1.4千克，厚度仅为25毫米，据称其电池能持续使用达4.5个小时，它专为总是出差的商务人士而设计的。它那令人叹服的图像处理能力是由其12.1英寸的TFT宽屏液晶屏实现的，也确保了该笔记本电脑的一个较长的、富有生命力的生命周期。另外，"商务伴侣"3000的USB接口设在电脑两侧，便利了右手及左手使用者进行简便地操作。该电脑还有丰富的扩展接口选择，例如LAN，WLAN，PAN，拨号和FIR。另外，宏基精巧而有品位的对开底盘设计了独特的防滑提手，使其移动性大大增加，也增加了它的稳固性。

Weighing only 1.4kg, measuring just 25mm thin, and boasting up to 4.5 hours of battery life, the TravelMate 3000 is designed for business users on the move. This notebook promises a long and productive life cycle thanks to impressive processing capability, complemented by integrated graphics seen on a 12.1-inch widescreen TFT display. In addition, the TravelMate 3000 provides ample connectivity options in the form of LAN, WLAN, PAN, dial-up and optical (FIR), while USB ports are considerately positioned on both sides of the unit, facilitating easy operation for right- as well as left-handers. The final touch, Acer's smart and stylish Folio chassis design features a unique non-slip carry grip, adding to this notebook's dependable, take-anywhere mobility.

CyMotion Pro 无线桌面键盘, 2005

Cherry GmbH, Auerbach/Opf.
Werksdesign: Günter Vogl
Design: marwin productdesign
(Marcus Wiedemann), München
www.cherry.de

CyMotion Pro无线桌面键盘的设计紧凑，并且很符合人体工程学原理。这套装置包括了一个无线键盘和无线鼠标，无论是习惯用右手或是和左手的使用者都能够舒适地操作这些设备。64个可调式通道允许同时在多套设备上进行操作。每一套设备都可达到20米的无线范围。防止敲击的数据加密系统提供了必需的保护措施。2.4千兆赫兹的无线技术保证了较低的电量消耗。如果必须要充电的话，电源调节器可使其在充电的同时仍能保证键盘和鼠标的正常运转。该套设备能够通过USB界面简便地与任何一台IBM或者兼容PC相连接。

The ergonomic and compact CyMotion Pro Wireless Desktop consists of a wireless keypad and a wireless mouse that can be comfortably operated by both right- and left-handers. 64 adjustable channels allow simultaneous operation of several sets. A wireless range of 20 metres is intended for each unit. A tap-proof data encryption system provides the security required. The 2.4GHz wireless technology guarantees low power consumption. If units have to be recharged the mains adaptor allows doing so while keypad and mouse are in operation. They can be easily connected to any IBM-type or compatible PC with USB interface.

华硕 S-presso 台式电脑, 2004

AsusTek Computer Inc., Taipei, Taiwan
Werksdesign: Asus Design
www.asus.com

Der im Retro-Look gestaltete Asus

华硕S-presso的外观设计为一种饶有趣味的后倾的形状。它可使用户无须进入Windows操作系统就能够播放DVD，CD，MP3音乐或FM广播节目，从而节省了时间和电量。以上这些的实现是由于采用了Easy Touch控制面板，它采用了在业界领先的独特的触控式面板，代替了对灰尘、泥土和磨损很敏感的机械装置。

Designed in an appealing retro-look, the Asus S-presso allows users to play DVDs, CDs, MP3 music or listen to FM radio programmes without entering the Windows operating system, thus saving time and energy. This is made possible with the Easy Touch Control Panel featuring an industry-first touch-sensitive front surface, eliminating mechanical parts that are sensitive to dust, dirt and wear.

华硕 SDRW-0804P-D DVD-RW 刻录机, 2005

AsusTek Computer Inc., Taipei, Taiwan
Werksdesign: Asus Design
www.asus.com

Asus SDRW-0804P-D是一款铝制机身的超薄外置式DVD刻录机。轻薄而坚固的构造使其非常适合与笔记本电脑或台式机相连接。在刻录过程中，机身的凹入部位可以用来储存原DVD。其线条清晰的设计与放置CD的钻石研磨面、控制按键及螺丝盖在视觉上形成极大的反差。

The Asus SDRW-0804P-D is a slim external DVD burner in an aluminium housing. Its flat, light and robust construction makes it suitable for operation with a notebook or a desktop computer. An indentation in the housing serves as storage space for the original DVD during the burning process. The clear design sets a visual contrast with the diamond grinding of the CD storage, operation buttons and screw covers.

华硕 V6 笔记本电脑, 2005

AsusTek Computer Inc., Taipei, Taiwan
Werksdesign: Asus Design
www.asus.com

华硕V6是一款小巧轻便的15英寸商务笔记本电脑，厚度仅为2.4厘米，重量仅为2.5千克。它将领先的技术与奢华的外观设计融合在一起，堪称是一款高端的笔记本电脑。为了使其更加坚固，机身是由镁铝合金材质制成的，内部的铝制表面提高了其导热性并大大减轻了总重量。内置的超纤细DVD驱动器使其能发挥很好的多媒体功能，并降低了机身的整体高度。

The Asus V6 is a lightweight 15-inch business notebook that is only 2.4cm thick. The high-end machine weighs only 2.5kg and combines leading-edge technology with a luxurious design. The screen housing is made of a magnesium-aluminium alloy for improved stiffness, and the inner aluminium skin improves heat conduction and reduces the overall weight considerably. A built-in ultra-slim DVD drive allows a good multimedia performance and reduces the height.

华硕 W3 笔记本电脑, 2005

AsusTek Computer Inc., Taipei, Taiwan
Werksdesign: Asus Design
www.asus.com

华硕W3笔记本电脑的合叶和电池进行了独特组合，这个灵感来自于打开中国竹简的过程。当打开Asus W3笔记本电脑时，它的流线型边缘曲线与坚硬的金属部件形成对比。14英寸的屏幕对于工作和游戏而言都很完美；它的并排显示功能使其可能同时处理多项工作。隐藏式快捷键，无缝触控面板和集成的音频系统提高了处理速度和娱乐效果。此外，华硕W3的外形也非常轻薄，并且采用了最新的英特尔Dothan CPU。

The motion of opening a Chinese bamboo scroll inspired the unique combination of hinge and battery pack. When opening the Asus W3 notebook, its flowing curves contrast with the hard metal parts. The 14-inch screen is perfect for work and gaming; simultaneous multitasking is possible with the dual display function. Hidden instant keys, a gapless touchpad and an integrated audio system allows enhanced productivity and entertainment. The Asus W3 is a thin, lightweight notebook equipped with the latest Intel Dothan CPU.

华硕 W5 笔记本电脑, 2005

AsusTek Computer Inc., Taipei, Taiwan
Werksdesign: Asus Design
www.asus.com

华硕W5笔记本电脑重量仅为1.6千克，机身高度为2.8厘米，非常轻便纤薄。该笔记本电脑12.1英寸的屏幕造就了其小巧精致的外形，非常便于在路途中携带使用。最新的英特尔Sonoma CPU使其运算速度惊人并且具备了卓越的多媒体功能，同时可旋转180度的相机为130万像素配置，可拍到多角度的完整图像。

With a weight of just 1.6kg and a housing height of 2.8cm, the Asus W5 notebook is extremely light and slim. The 12.1-inch screen creates a compact form that is ideal for use on the road. The latest Intel Sonoma CPU delivers impressive computing power and superior multimedia capabilities, while the 1.3-megapixel camera, rotatable through 180 degrees, allows capturing of images.

罗技 io2 数字笔, 2004

Logitech USA, Fremont, USA
Werksdesign: Niall White
Design: Design Partners (Mathew Bates, Peter Sheehan, Diarmuid MacMahon, Stephen Montgomery), Bray, Irland
Vertrieb: Logitech GmbH, Germering
www.logitech.com
www.designpartners.ie

罗技io2数字笔使得用户能够直接由使用墨水过渡到软件。它使用了Sync技术，这种技术能直接在Microsoft Word，Outlook 和Lotus上转化手写或打印的文本。该笔也含有免费软件，学习用户的笔迹并且将其转化为数字文本。图片和草图也能以任何重要的图形格式输出。该笔内设一个微型摄像头和内存，一次最多储存量可达40页。这种第二代产品比上一代款式更小巧，但性能却丝毫不逊色于其他任何书写工具。

The Logitech io2 digital pen allows users to go from ink to software directly. It incorporates Write Sync technology, which integrates handwritten or typed text directly in Microsoft Word, Outlook and Lotus notes. The pen also incorporates free software that learns user's handwriting and converts to digital text. Drawing and sketches can be exported in all major graphical formats. The pen incorporates a miniature camera and a memory, which can store up to 40 pages at a time. This second generation product is now significantly smaller than previous versions and behaves exactly like any other quality writing instrument.

MD 42125 家庭影院 DLP-投影仪, 2004

Medion AG, Essen
Design: Indx-Design (Yorgo Liebsch, Andre Hanisch, Ulrike Peter), Mülheim
www.medion.com

MD 42125家庭影院DLP – 投影仪设计得比较匀称，清楚地表现出该设备的多种功能，并且保证用户能够直观地进行操作。虽然该投影机集成了大量的高技术设备，但用户还是可以轻松地将其与录像机，数码相机，PC，DVD播放器，游戏控制器或者电视机连接起来。由于采用了垂直的镜头转换功能，图像就能够向上或向下移动50%而不会降低图像的质量。当投影射向有颜色的表面时，颜色上的失真可使用Wall Colour Correcting功能加以调节。

The MD 42125 home cinema DLP projector has a well-balanced design that clearly delineates the numerous functions of the device and ensures intuitive user operation. The projector also provides a multitude of technical equipments. It is child's play to connect video recorders, digital cameras, PCs, DVD players, games consoles or TV sets. Using the vertical lens shift function, the picture can be moved up to 50 per cent upwards or downwards without any loss of picture quality. When projecting onto coloured surfaces, colour distortion can be corrected using the integrated Wall Colour Correction function.

Cara PC 电脑, 2004

Medion AG, Essen
Design: Spannagel.Design (Uwe Spannagel), Köln;
GeisenDesign (Bernhard Geisen), Essen
www.medion.com

考虑到PC要承担越来越多的功能，Cara PC的应用领域不再仅仅限于办公室。由于它功能强大，设计美观，当然也被纳入了日常生活空间范围之内。该PC能监视并控制一些家庭功能，例如发送和接收通讯，播放CD、DVD、接收电视节目，或是可以和朋友一起欣赏上个假期的照片。Cara PC包括一个TFT面板和一个键盘。所有设计元素都互相协调，几乎可以与所有的生活空间相匹配。

Considering the fact that PCs take over more and more functions, the field of application for the Cara PC is not any longer restricted to the office exclusively: due to its many functions and aesthetic design, the everyday living space is included in its operational area as well. This PC can monitor and control household functions, send and receive communications, play CDs, DVDs, receive TV programmes, or you can view photos from your last vacation with your friends. The Cara set includes a TFT panel and a keypad. The design of all elements is harmoniously coordinated, adapting themselves smoothly to any living environment.

Digiframe 数字相框, 2004

Medion AG, Essen
Design: GeisenDesign (Bernhard Geisen, Lidan Liu, Zhen Xie), Essen; Indx-Design (Yorgo Liebsch, Andre Hanisch), Mülheim
www.medion.com

数字相框能将数字图像和MPEG-4录像文件在LCD屏上显示出来。图像可以使用内置的多卡阅读器来下载，并且可按照个人喜好进行变换。就像传统的图框一样，数字相框也能安装在墙上或者桌上。

The Digiframe allows the display of digital pictures and MPEG-4 video files on an LCD screen. The pictures can be loaded with the built-in multi-card reader and can be exchanged as one wishes. Just like a classic picture frame, the Digiframe can be placed on the wall or on a table.

电视导航器, 2004

Medion AG, Essen
Design: GeisenDesign (Bernhard Geisen, Christoph Thauern, Stewart Sandham, Susanne Sievers, Zhen Xie, Lidan Liu), Essen
www.medion.com

电视导航器采用了多部件组成的屏幕，来显示集成的视觉效果。该设备设计为流线型，清晰的线条和连续的压克力玻璃将人的视线引向显示屏和用户操作范围之内。屏幕和开关的圆状外形让它的操作界面看起来很有质感，极富吸引力。当电视导航器启动之后，会显示出它的蓝色标识。由于它的外形设计紧凑，它的外壳看起来要比传统设备要小巧很多，并且能够安放在任何地方。

Using a multi-part screen, the TV Pilot SAT receiver displays an integrated visual language. Its flowing, yet concrete lines and a continuous acrylic glass element directs the eye to display and user field. The form is soft and attractive due to the round shape of the screen and switch. When activated, the TV Pilot displays its blue logo. As a result of compact technology, it is much smaller than traditional units in rack format, and space can be found for it anywhere.

佳能 IXUS 40 数码相机，2004

Canon Deutschland GmbH, Krefeld
Werksdesign: Canon Inc. (Ito Hideki), Tokio, Japan
www.canon.com

IXUS 40数码相机将高雅的外形与先进的数码照相技术融合在了一起，它还采用了最新UA镜头技术的三倍变焦镜头。该相机结构紧凑。高度仅为21毫米，不计充电电池的机身重量仅为130克。IXUS 40镜头为400万像素，且内设一个高性能的九点AiAF自动对焦系统。相机背面的两寸TFT屏可提供清晰、明亮的图像。集成DIGIC II影像处理器可以说是所有影像处理的发动机，能保证在拍照或作为背景墙时极快的反应次数。由于采用了适当的存储媒介，无论是带声音的视频和或是多达1千兆（取决于内存条的速度和型号）的图像，这款相机都能够把它们拍摄下来，并且能以慢动作进行回放。如果再加上相机附加的防护套，那么它几乎在任何天气条件下都可使用，甚至在水下三米处都能进行拍照。

The IXUS 40 digital camera combines an elegant impression with state-of-the-art digital photo technology. The threefold zoom lens, featuring the newest UA lens technology, allows a compact construction: the camera is just 21mm in depth and weighs only 130 grammes without the rechargeable battery. The IXUS 40 is equipped with 4.0 megapixels and features a high-performance nine-point AiAF autofocus system. The two-inch TFT display at the back of the camera provides a clear, bright picture. The integrated DIGIC II image processor is the motor for all image processing, guaranteeing extremely fast response times when taking pictures or playing back images. With the appropriate storage medium, video clips with sound and a size of up to 1GB can be shot (depending on speed and size of the memory card) and played back in slow motion as well. As an additional option, an all-weather housing is available, allowing underwater shots down to three metres in depth.

佳能 PIXMA iP5000 喷墨打印机，2004

Canon Deutschland GmbH, Krefeld
Werksdesign: Canon Inc.
(Naoki Tashiro), Tokio, Japan
www.canon.com

PIXMA iP 5000是一款为有特定需求的用户而设计的新型喷墨打印机。该打印机线条设计清晰，机身被优雅的亮黑色所包围，满足了办公室设备对美观的不断增长的需求。从技术上来说，该打印机的新型打印头质量很高，所谓的“FINE”技术使其每秒钟可喷射2700万滴墨点，即从许多微型喷嘴里精确地喷到打印纸上，因而可产生超清晰的打印影像。一滴墨点的最小尺寸为1皮升，但这也会对打印速度产生影响：10 × 15厘米的彩色照片只需用36秒钟就能打印完毕。PIXMA5000 iP中也包括了从数码相机中和摄像机里直接打印影像的Pict Bridge标准。该打印机尺寸为418 × 286 × 170毫米，其小巧的尺寸很节省空间。

The PIXMA iP5000 is a futuristically designed ink-jet printer for demanding users. A clear line management and a housing in elegant black meet the steadily increasing demands for aesthetic office equipment. Technically, the ink-jet printer with newly developed print heads offers high-level qualities: the so-called "Fine" technology produces an ultra-sharp print image by feeding about 27 million ink droplets per second from many fine micro nozzles onto the printing paper with high precision. The minimum size of a single droplet is just one picolitre. All this has an effect on the print speed as well: 10 x 15cm colour pictures take only 36 seconds to print. The PIXMA iP5000 includes a Pict Bridge standard for direct image printing from digital cameras and camcorders. With 418 x 286 x 170mm, the printer is space-saving and compact.

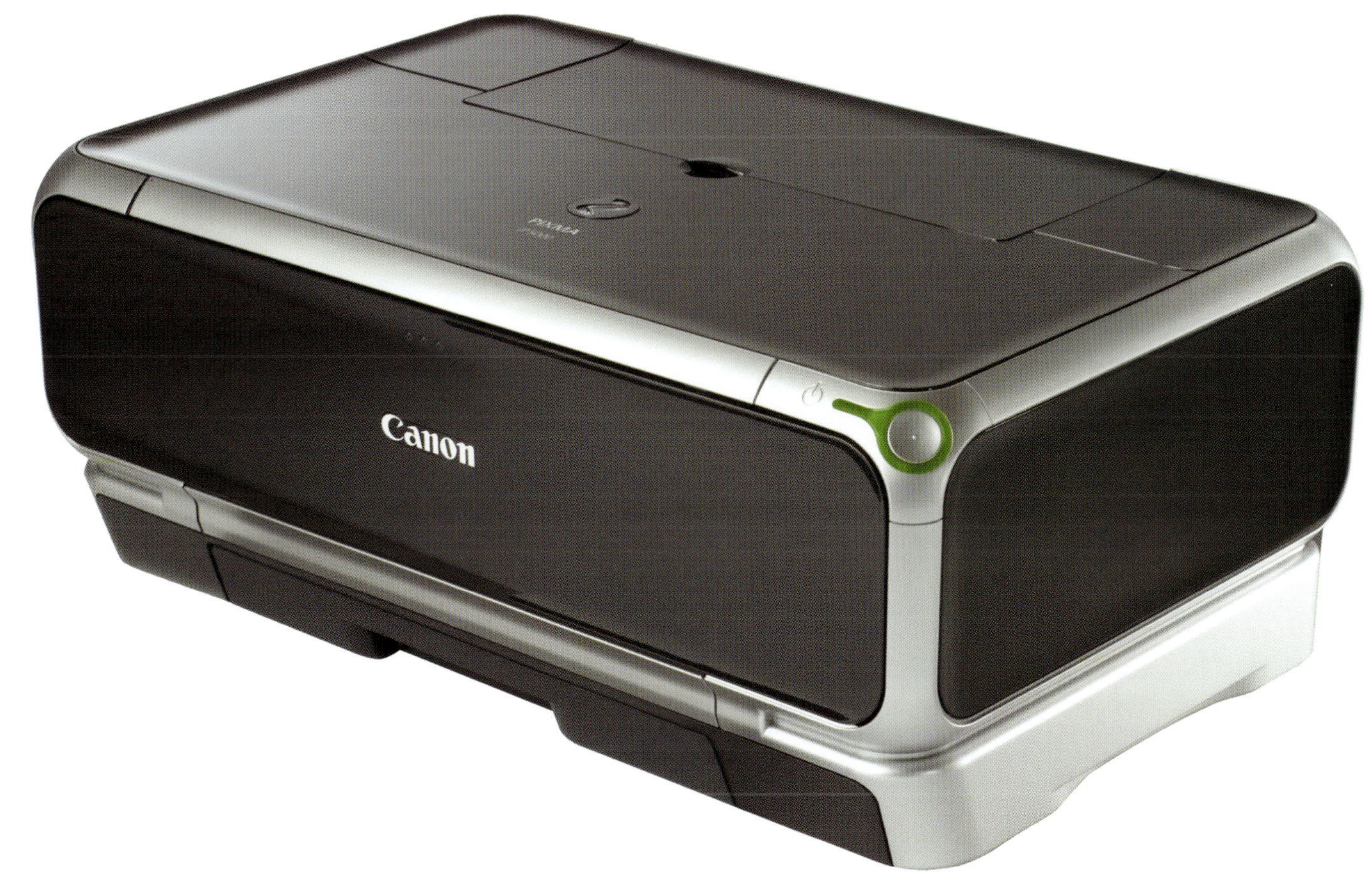

LG GS-9 数码拍照手机, 2005

LG Electronics Inc.,
Corporate Design Center, Seoul, Korea
Werksdesign: Myung Hoon Lee,
Ji hoon Shin
Vertrieb: LG Electronics Deutschland
GmbH, Willich
www.lge.com

GS-9数码拍照手机的外形小巧可爱，为滑盖式设计且配有内置天线。该手机的尺寸为45.5×87×23.9毫米，其流线型的边缘处设计使其能够方便地放入口袋里。320k像素的VGA相机安装在手机的背面，不仅可以拍照并且还可用MMS功能方便地将照片发送出去。滑盖上的第二个显示屏使用户在手机合上时能够查看有无来电等情况，明亮的橙色更彰显出其动感十足的外观。

The GS-9 digital camera/mobile phone is a compact device in clamshell format with integrated antenna. With 45.5 x 87 x 23.9mm and soft round edge helps the perfect fit into any pocket which is very handy. A VGA camera with 320K pixels is located on the back side. Picture can be taken and sent conveniently with the MMS function. A second display on the flip cover allows an overview of calls when the unit is closed. Bright orange is also available for sportive look.

LG X-800 台式 PC, 2004

LG Electronics Inc.,
Corporate Design Center, Seoul, Korea
Werksdesign: Byung Mu Huh,
Sun Jung Park
Vertrieb: LG Electronics Deutschland
GmbH, Willich
www.lge.com

X-800是一款小巧而坚固的台式PC。铬合金制成的装饰板加强了这种感觉并将其分成两个部分。95×380×340毫米的外形尺寸看起来感觉很纤细，甚至在比较拥挤的工作环境下使用也很合适，弧形的边缘也与它那纤细的外形相呼应。X-800的L形开关很符合人体工程学的原理，这让机器很容易被触摸到，并从两侧都能进行操作。

The X-800 is a compact and solid desktop PC. Highlighted by a chrome-plated decorative strip, it optically divides the unit in two parts. With 95 x 380 x 340mm, the X-800 is slim in shape and suitable even for tight working environment. Round edge supports the slim appearance. Ergonomically advantageous is the L-shaped on/off switch, making the unit easily accessible and operable from both sides.

LG DF8900 DVD 播放器, 2004

LG Electronics Inc.,
Corporate Design Center, Seoul, Korea
Werksdesign: Yoon Young Cho,
Kang Heui Cha
Vertrieb: LG Electronics Deutschland
GmbH, Willich
www.lge.com

DF8900是一款设计的非常轻薄的DVD播放器，高32毫米，宽430毫米。它的功能键清晰地排列在机器前面，其中还有一个7-in-2的读卡器。特殊功能按键也醒目地排列在机身表面。该播放器是由坚固并可回收使用的ABS制成的。银色的外观熠熠生辉，可轻易地与其他部件完美地融合。

The DF8900 is a slim designed DVD player with just 32mm height and 430mm width. The function elements are clearly arranged at the front of the unit, amongst them a 7-in-2 multi slot. Buttons for special functions are prominently displayed on the housing surface. The player is made of robust and recyclable ABS and can easily be combined with other components due to its aesthetic silver optics.

LG TN-50PY20 等离子电视, 2005

LG Electronics Inc.,
Corporate Design Center, Seoul, Korea
Werksdesign: Tae Bong Kim,
Young Soo Han, Young ho Lee
Vertrieb: LG Electronics Deutschland GmbH, Willich
www.lge.com

黑色的TN-50PY20等离子电视的外形设计非常雅致大方。它的特别之处是其双层的机身结构，使其具有了三维的特征。扬声器集成在机身内部不能直接看到的地方，使其外观显得更为纯粹。该电视机既可挂在墙上，放在桌上或是可以放在铝制的支架上，其厚度仅为38毫米，几乎能适用于所有的起居室。

The elegant black plasma TV TN-50PY20 is truly appealing even when powered off. Special feature is the double-layer housing construction giving the unit a three-dimensional character. The speakers are invisibly integrated into the housing, underlining the puristic design. Mounted on the wall, placed on a tabletop or an aluminium floor stand, the set, with a depth of merely 38mm, adapts itself discreetly to all living room spaces.

LG 55W 液晶电视, 2004

LG Electronics Inc.,
Corporate Design Center, Seoul, Korea
Werksdesign: Jung Hoon Lee,
Hee Su Yang, Young Ah Lee
Design: designafairs GmbH, München
Vertrieb: LG Electronics Deutschland GmbH, Willich
www.lge.com

LCD 55W是一款设计高雅的液晶超薄电视机。它采用了最新的LCD技术，设计目的满足了家庭娱乐爱好者的要求。它配备了55英寸的宽大屏幕和可以使声音能很好地进行转换的HDTV调谐器。这款电视的两侧都装有扬声器，也可拆卸下来安装在房间的任何地方。这款电视既可以挂在墙上，也能放置在桌上，并且使用了100%的可回收环保材料。

The LCD TV 55W is an ultra-flat unit with elegant design. It is for home entertainment enthusiasts with a newest LCD technology. The large panel measures 55 inches; an HDTV tuner supports a good sound reproduction. The speakers, attached to either side, can be detachable and can be placed elsewhere in the room. The unit features fixtures for wall-mounting as well as tabletop set-up and is 100 per cent recyclable materials.

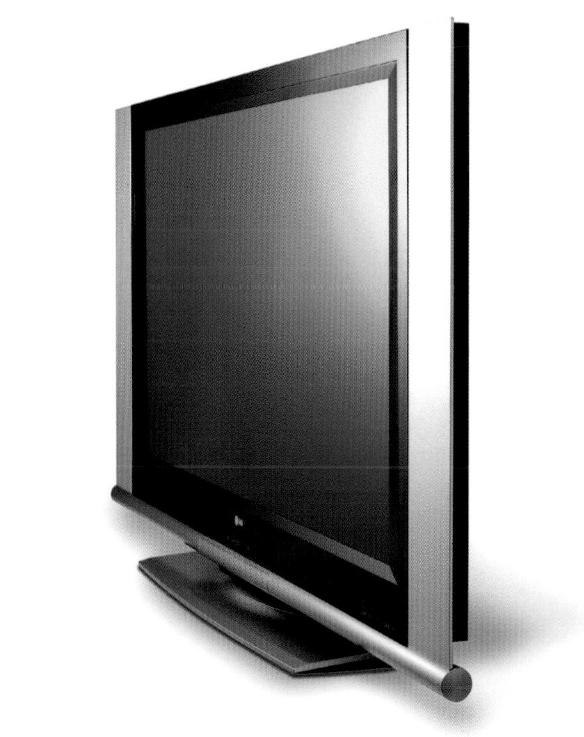

LG L1780U 超薄液晶显示器, 2005

LG Electronics Inc.,
Corporate Design Center, Seoul, Korea
Werksdesign: Myung Seob Jeon,
Wun San Boek, Jung Yeon Hwang
Vertrieb: LG Electronics Deutschland GmbH, Willich
www.lge.com

L1780U是一款非常纤薄的TFT显示器，设计直指对设计和性能的最高需求。为了能获得最佳的观看角度，显示屏可以向前、向后倾斜160度。如果显示器向侧面倾斜的话，自动定位功能会根据新的位置重新排列屏幕的内容。防反射功能阻止了干扰性的反射。此外，L1780U的反应时间很短，仅为12毫秒，厚度仅为20.5毫米，因而可以放置在拥挤的工作间中。

The L1780U is a very slim TFT monitor for highest demands with regard to design and performance. For an optimum positioning of the view angle, the screen can be tilted forward and backward 160 degrees. If the display is turned sideways, the auto-pivot function takes care of rearranging screen contents according to the new position. The anti-mirror effect prevents from disturbing reflections. The LCD display has a short response time of 12ms, measures merely 20.5mm in depth and can thus be placed even in tight working spots.

佳能 CanoScan LIDE 500F 扫描仪，2005

Canon Deutschland GmbH, Krefeld
Werksdesign
www.canon.com

LIDE 500F的高度仅为35毫米，它的外形设计得非常纤薄，但也不失高雅大方。集成的支架使其可竖直放置，从而可以节省空间，并可将模板从顶部轻松插入。一个新发明的盖子可以轻松扫描厚厚的或是超出标准规格的材料。该扫描仪不需要预热就可以直接进行工作，同时机身上的多功能快速扫描功能可以节省很多宝贵的时间。该扫描仪一次可扫描十张照片，并可进行自动修正和单个文件的扫描储存。由于采用了Canon FARE Level 3技术，该扫描仪可自动识别灰尘颗粒及胶片模板上的划痕，并且利用红外线灯将其处理掉。LIDE 500F还配有单独的转换灯装置，可用来扫描底片和无框幻灯片，并且能同步适应所有的PC和Mac的操作系统。

With a height of just 35mm, the LIDE 500F is slim in design and elegant in appearance. An integrated holder allows space-saving upright positioning with easy insertion of templates from the top. With the aid of the newly developed cover, thick or oversized materials can be scanned easily. The unit is ready for operation without a warming-up period, and a Fast Multi Scan function contributes to saving precious time. The scan function allows scanning of up to ten pictures at a time with automatic slope correction and scan saving in separate files. With the Canon FARE Level 3 technology, dust particles and scratches on film templates are automatically identified and removed with the aid of infrared light. The LIDE 500F features a separate transmitted light unit for scanning of negatives and unframed slides and adapts smoothly to all current PC- and Mac operating systems.

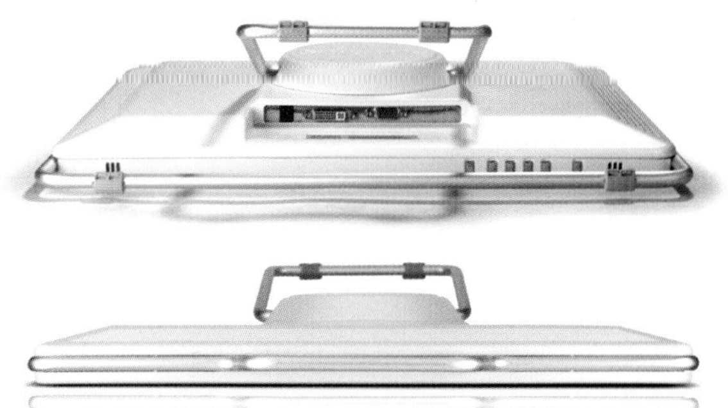

XP17 液晶显示器, 2004

Shuttle Inc., Taipei, Taiwan
Werksdesign: Shuttle ID Team
Vertrieb: Shuttle Computer Handels GmbH, Elmshorn
www.shuttle.com

保持了XPC的特别设计，XP17是一款非常轻薄的TFT显示器。该显示器可以提供最佳的观看角度，1620万色，1280 × 1024像素的分辨率和450：1的对比度以及明亮的图像和华丽的色彩。另外，该面板还设计了D–Sub–和DVI双重模拟输入，可进行不同的播放组合。背面还配有为在桌面安装而设计的实用的铝支架。该支架可进行调整，这样显示器的位置就能够适应每个用户的不同位置。该面板采用了集成的VESA模块，因而能够装在墙上或是放在工作台上。XP17外形设计比例平衡，重量仅为4.3千克，可毫不费劲地将其装在背包里随身携带。

Designed in the special XPC design, the XP17 is a very flat and light TFT panel. With an optimised view angle, 16.2 million colours, a resolution of 1,280 x 1,024 pixels and a 450:1 contrast, the display offers a bright picture and luscious colours. In addition, the panel includes an analogue D-Sub- and a DVI input, allowing different playback combinations. On the back side, the XP17 is equipped with a practical aluminium mounting frame for desktop set-up. The frame is adjustable so that the monitor position can be adapted to the position of the individual user. With the aid of the integrated VESA module, the panel can be mounted to a wall or attached to a worktop. With its balanced format and a weight of merely 4.3kg, the XP17 can be transported easily with the bag included.

索尼 DAV-SR4W 家庭影院系统，2004

Sony Corporation, Tokio, Japan
Werksdesign: Takahiro Tsuge
Vertrieb: Sony Deutschland GmbH, Köln
www.sony.net

DAV-SR4W是一款5.1声道的DVD/SACD家庭影院系统，能够实现影音信号从主机到环绕扬声器的无线传输。传统的家庭影院都是方形的，而且设计元素通常只是集中在前面。相反，DAV-SR4W的理念旨在从外观上找到能够适合任何家庭内部布局的结构。DVD播放器的前表面是倾斜的，这样设计的目的是从实用的角度出发，旨在能轻松地观看显示屏。前端的边缘环绕着形成一个连续的线条，一直延伸到机器的背面。DAV-SR4W配备有S-DIAT系统，该系统能将无线数据传输到环绕扬声器内。这样DAV-SR4W就可以轻松，整洁地安装在房间里而不会有大量的连线。

The DAV-SR4W is a 5.1-channel DVD/SACD home theatre system that achieves wireless transmissions of audio signals from the main unit to the surround speakers. Home theatre systems have traditionally been square, and design elements are usually only found on the front. In contrast, the concept for the DAV-SR4W aimed for a look that would complement any home interior. The front face of the DVD player was sloped for enhanced usability and easy viewing of the display. The front edge was rounded to create a continuous line carrying on to the back. The DAV-SR4W is mounted with an S-DIAT system, which enables wireless data transfer to the surround speakers. The system can thus be installed in a room neatly and easily without messy cables.

索爱 SO213i 迷你手机, 2004

Sony Ericsson Mobile Communications
Japan Inc., Tokio, Japan
Werksdesign: Shigeaki Suzuki,
Tetsuro Sano, Tatsuya Hama
www.sonyericsson.com

SO213i迷你手机的90 x 40 x 19.8毫米的尺寸可谓是几款可供选择的迷你手机中极具吸引力的一款。其重量仅为69克，主要针对喜欢与众不同，彰显个性的用户。这款迷你手机的尺寸比一张名片都小，但其功能却丝毫不打折扣。按键环绕着微微向前倾斜，这保证了快速且连续的按下字母和数字而不会发生错误。TFT显示屏为1.3英寸，可显示多达65，536种颜色。敏感度极佳的话筒，以及i-mode和e-mail功能都使通讯质量达到最佳。该手机的显著特征就是其弯曲的天线，给人带来一种流线型的感觉。SO213i迷你手机有黑色和银白色可供消费者选择。

With 90 x 40 x 19.8mm, the SO213i premini is one of the smallest mobile phones available. Weighing only 69 grammes, it is conceived for users with an appreciation for extraordinary design. The premini is smaller than a business card, yet easily usable. The buttons are slightly rounded and sloped towards the front, allowing typing of letters and numbers in quick succession without erring. The TFT display measures 1.3 inch and displays up to 65,536 colours. An ultra-sensitive microphone and access to i-mode and e-mail contribute to optimum communication. The characteristic feature of this mobile phone is the curved antenna, giving the device a streamlined impression. The premini is available in black and silver.

索尼 QUALIA 004 SXRD 投影仪，2003

Sony Corporation, Tokio, Japan
Werksdesign: Takuya Niitsu
www.sony.net

QUALIA 004 SXRD投影仪将美学需求和强大的功能融合在了一起。投影仪外部的散热片呈展开状，呈现出它那非常稳定牢固的结构。另外，光源、镜头和投影屏排列在一条直线上，为播放无瑕疵的视频图像的回放提供了最佳布局。透明盖由海蓝色的金属聚碳酸酯制成，不仅突出了泡沫铝的可视的内部构造，而且这种材料能够降低噪音，减少热量和电磁波辐射。铝制的功能面板还包括了一个集成制音器，用于移动机械延伸时消除噪音。该投影机可以放在桌上或者安装在天花板上。

The QUALIA 004 SXRD projector combines aesthetic claims with a high degree of functionality. The cooling fins on the outside are deliberately laid out open so as to underline the stable construction of the projector. In addition, light source, lens and projection screen have been arranged in one straight line so that an optimum layout can be generated for the playback of a spotless video picture. The transparent cover made of polycarbonate in metallic marine blue accentuates the foam aluminium visible inside. This material contributes to the reduction of noise and heat as well as electromagnetic waves. The function panel made of aluminium includes an integrated damper for gentle extension of the moving mechanics. The unit can be placed on a table or mounted to the ceiling.

索尼 QUALIA 006 背投电视, 2005

Sony Corporation, Tokio, Japan
Werksdesign: Gen Fujiki
www.sony.net

QUALIA 006背投电视采用了SXRD技术，使其达到高分辨率和像电影一样的清晰影像。为了让用户在面对巨大的70英寸屏幕的时候不会感到压抑，这款电视屏幕通过压克力材料和塑料制成的边框进行了封边处理。显示屏底部的塑料部分很轻便且颜色华丽，总体上给人一种明亮的感觉。此外，针对那些希望电视机像照片一样挂在墙上的用户，或者对于那些希望能把不同的扬声器和电视机相连接的音乐发烧友，这款背投电视左右侧的扬声器都可以拆卸下来。设计美观的地板支架使其也可以放在地面上。插入式设计的底柜可以用来存放一些杂物。

The QUALIA 006 is a rear projection TV that employs SXRD technology to achieve high-resolution, fluid images that resemble movie quality. To eliminate the feeling of sheer overwhelming size experienced when confronting a massive 70-inch screen head-on, the TV screen is framed by clear acrylic material and plastic. The plastic part at the bottom of the display is light and lustrous in colour, creating a bright overall impression. For users who wish to mount the TV on the wall like a picture, or who are sound buffs and wish to connect different speakers to the unit, the left and right speakers are detachable. An aesthetic floor stand allows placement of the QUALIA 006 on the ground. The inserted compartments offer space for additional components.

索尼 QUALIA 005 液晶电视, 2004

Sony Corporation, Tokio, Japan
Werksdesign: Takuya Niitsu
www.sony.net

QUALIA 005是一款外观雅致的超薄液晶电视。一个由高档铝材制成的纤薄的边框，一个透明的压克力玻璃盘设计不仅满足了美学上的较高要求，而且当用户从前面观看电视时，也会有一种轻盈透亮的感觉。机身面板周围的框架在设计上使用了带玻璃珠子的清漆，而与此对比的是电视的表盘则较粗糙，以减少强光，使对显示屏的光学干扰达到最小。此外，显示器的侧面也同样闪亮，清漆所涂部分的多变性带来了颜色的多样化。该系统中的媒体接收器和下面朴素的方形支架与整体设计也都非常协调。不仅如此，显示器的结构设计得很理想，可以把所有的连线都掩盖起来。

The QUALIA 005 is an elegant flat screen LCD TV set for high aesthetic demands. The display is surrounded by a slim frame made of high-grade aluminium extrudate with a transparent acrylic glass plate. This contributes to the impression of lightness and transparency when looking at the unit from the front. For the design of the grill surrounding the panel, a varnish with glass beads has been used. In contrast, the front plate surface is matt, reducing glare and minimising optical interruptions of the screen display. The surface of the side walls is shiny glazed. With variations in the varnished parts, an additional diversity of colour hues is achieved. The media receiver belonging to the system is harmonically adapted to the overall design. The same goes for the floor stand in plain rectangular shape. The well thought-out construction allows cover-up of all disturbing wiring.

索尼 QUALIA 001 影像处理器, 2005

Sony Corporation, Tokio, Japan
Werksdesign: Haruo Oba
www.sony.net

QUALIA 001是一款影像处理器，它能将电视、hi-vision或其他图像信号转换为高清晰度且更真实的影像。在显示器和外部视频设备，如DVD播放器或者调谐器之间连接QUALIA 001能够给用户带来更真实、更漂亮的hi-vision画面影像。QUALIA 001的设计者致力于简约化，以反映其图像纯粹的感觉和设计所产生的透明感。该设备所用材料为人造大理石、压克力和铝，这样的设计可谓是建立在其令人着迷的材质上的完美设计。黑色的主打色下，其余材料与其一同映衬出一种高贵的感觉。为了满足将来可能出现的新的影像标准，在盒子的上半部分安装了扩展终端，以便将来好使其方便升级，只需拿掉顶部的铝制面板，便可与该终端连接起来。

The QUALIA 001 is a device to convert TV, hi-vision and other picture signals to images with higher definition and more realistic quality. Connecting the QUALIA 001 between a display device and external visual equipment such as a DVD player or tuner brings the user more real and beautiful hi-vision images. To reflect the sense of picture purity of the device and the transparency it creates in its design, the designer of the Creation Box aimed for a minimalist simplicity. The materials used are artificial marble, acrylic and aluminium to create a design that is built on the appeal of the materials. The colour is black which is given a rich expressiveness by the surrounding materials. To meet new imaging standards that may appear in the future, extension terminals are mounted on the upper part of the case with the idea of taking the hardware itself to a higher evolutionary stage in the future. The terminals can be connected by removing the aluminium top panel.

AVC Sign Si-300 数码音频播放器，2004

AVC Technology Limited, Hongkong
Werksdesign: Patrick Mak
Vertrieb: AVC Germany GmbH, Hamburg
www.signstyles.com

Sign Si-300是一款设计小巧但却功能性很强的数码音频播放器。该设备上包含了“拖放”功能，能直接从便携式CD播放器上把音乐复制到Sign Si-300上。它还配备了FM广播，可单独调节的有十个预调整按键的均衡器和SRS WOW声音支持系统。还有可以用来录音的内置话筒。Sign Si-300仅重38克，其超轻、符合人体工程学的设计一定是外出携带的理想伙伴。

The Sign Si-300 is a compact designed and functional digital audio player. Equipment components include a drag-and-drop function allowing to copy music directly from a portable CD player to the Sign Si-300. An FM radio, an individually adjustable equaliser with ten presets and SRS WOW sound support are also included. Functional as well is the built-in microphone, which can additionally be used for recording. With 38 grammes, the ergonomically designed Sign Si-300 is ultra-light and the ideal outdoor companion.

AVC Sign Si-120 数码音频播放器，2005

AVC Technology Limited, Hongkong
Werksdesign: Patrick Mak
Vertrieb: AVC Germany GmbH, Hamburg
www.signstyles.com

像Sign Si-300的其他同类产品一样，Sign Si-120也是一款设计小巧，具备多项功能的数码音频播放器。除了能简便进行数据转换的拖放功能，FM广播，和SRS WOW声音支持系统之外，Sign Si-120的技术设备中还包括可单独调节的有十个预调整按键的均衡器和内置话筒。此外还有一个菜单指引操纵杆，它进一步使侧面的操作按键变得完整丰富。几乎从任何角度都能清楚地看到它的OLED屏，它所消耗的电量却很少。

Like its brother Sign Si-300, the Sign Si-120 is a compact designed digital audio player with many functions. Aside from the drag-and-drop function for easy data transfer, an FM radio, SRS WOW sound support, an individually adjustable equaliser with ten presets and a built-in microphone are part of its technical equipment. The operating buttons located to the side are supplemented by a joystick for menu navigation. The OLED display is clearly visible from any view angle and consumes minimal power.

Stelton i:cons 私人配饰，2005

Stelton A/S, Kopenhagen, Dänemark
Werksdesign: Mads Surel
Design: Designit
(Anders Geert-Jensen, Simon Kalmer, Emil Wegger Jensen),
Aarhus, Dänemark
Vertrieb: Stelton Verkaufsbüro Deutschland, Meinerzhagen
www.stelton.com
www.designit.com

Stelton i:cons的设计源于这样一种想法，即设计一种精致的挂在脖子上就可以方便携带的U盘，还能够满足不同人的风格。于是，全新Stelton i:cons系列诞生了。它是由一系列个人配饰组成的，可谓是一种新颖时尚的设计。这一系列不仅非常轻便，而且外观上稍显未来主义色彩，相信其精致的设计一定会吸引时尚人士的眼光。目前该系列包括四个部分：钱夹、名片夹、挂带和U盘。采用的材料包括纤维复合材料、钢，以及在挂带需要的地方使用坚硬而柔软的硅材料。i:cons设计的重点在于它周身透露出来的实用性和简约性、毫无累赘，一定会受到崇尚简约人士的欢迎。

The Stelton i:cons are based on the idea to carry the USB memory stick around the neck in a smart design that completes the individual style. The new i:cons line is made up of a series of personal accessories expressed in an entirely new and refreshing design. The line is light with a slightly futuristic look, made quite deliberately to appeal to the design-conscious person. For the time being, the line comes in four parts: a money clip, a card holder, strap and a USB memory stick. The materials are fibre composites, steel, and where the strap is concerned, a strong but supple silicone material. The keywords for i:cons are functionality and simplicity without superfluous details.

Concept L 42 等离子电视，2004

Loewe AG, Kronach
Design: Design 3 (Wolfgang Wagner, Till Kobes), Hamburg
www.loewe.de
www.design3.de

Concept L 42是一款外观设计简约大方的等离子（PDP）电视。机身的高级铝制圈环绕着IR眼，带给人一种严谨的高雅的感觉，同时也体现出其产品外观上的同一性。这款电视厚度为9.4厘米，对角线长106厘米，直白的设计理念中也映衬出细细的光感，相信会带给人以无与伦比的视觉享受，机身两侧的扬声器更进一步加强了这种形象。该设备配有等离子显示器，能够显示16：9和4：3格式，也能为全景、电影或者快镜头的展示提供平台。便捷的用户引导便利了所有技术功能和选择菜单的安装。Concept L 42能够挂在墙上，如果选择地板支架放置的话，还能掩盖所有必不可少的缆线。

The Concept L 42 is a large-format PDP TV with a minimalistic design. A high-grade aluminium ring around the IR eye creates a discreet elegance and shows the affiliation to the product family. With a depth of 9.4cm and a diagonal of 106cm, the straightforward design concept features slim optics and superior comfort. This impression is further enhanced by the speakers to either side of the screen. The unit features a plasma display capable of showing 16:9 as well as 4:3 formats, Panorama, Cine or Zoom. A comfortable user guidance facilitates the setting of technical functions and options. The Concept L 42 can be mounted on a wall, but is also available with floor stand. The latter also helps to conceal all wires and cables that cannot be dispensed with.

Xelos A 42 等离子电视，2005

Loewe AG, Kronach
Design: Phoenix Design, Stuttgart
www.loewe.de
www.phoenixdesign.de

Xelos A 42是一款高分辨率的等离子电视，其面板上包含有电子元件。它的设计去掉了不必要的元素，体现出了一种纯粹的设计风格，同时也把用户的注意力集中在了其宽大的显示屏幕上，它的对角线宽度为106厘米。该系列中所有的产品都采用了新的显示技术，对角线超过26英寸。与该系列中的其它电视一样的是，Xelos A 42也能够显示高质量的HDTV（高清晰电视），同样也包括单独的界面。这款电视除了模拟方式以外，还有采用了集成数字地面调谐器的Xelos A 42也可供选择。该设备有多种颜色，而且可以挂在墙上或是放置在桌上或地板上。设计别致的电视架有插入式的玻璃架，能够为组合的部件提供放置空间。

The Xelos A 42 is a high-resolution plasma TV set with electronics on board. It is designed in a puristic style, dispensing with superfluous details. Thus, the attention focuses on its large-surface display with a diagonal screen width of 106cm. Like all TV sets of the product family with new display technologies and a diagonal of more than 26 inches, the Xelos A 42 is capable of producing the high quality of High Definition Television (HDTV) and includes the respective interface as well. Aside from the analogue version, the Xelos A 42 Digital is also available with an integrated digital terrestrial tuner (DVB-T). The unit is available in different colours and can be either mounted on a wall or placed on a table or the ground. An elegant rack system with insertable glass shelves offers additional space for assembly of components that can be combined.

Xelos SL 32 HD/DR+ 液晶电视, 2004

Loewe AG, Kronach
Design: Phoenix Design, Stuttgart
www.loewe.de
www.phoenixdesign.de

Xelos SL 32 HD/DR+是一款时尚的液晶电视，它采用了高清晰度显示技术。这款电视的一大特色在于其内置的硬盘录像机，使用户一按键就能延时观看，从而不会错过自己喜欢的节目。除了其清晰而独立的设计之外，孔状外形的扬声器更加突出了该款电视的美观外形，其厚度仅为8.3厘米。屏幕四周的黑色边框增加了图像质量的对比度，而且使机身框架显得异常纤细。它有多种安装方式：既可以把这款电视放在桌上，也可放在支架上，或是放在地板支架上，当然也可以挂在墙上，无论哪一种方式效果都是一样的漂亮。Xelos SL 32 HD/DR+的屏幕对角线长为80厘米，可提供16：9的观看格式。它有几种颜色可供选择：白金色、烟黑色、黑白单色，几乎能与任何地起居室环境相搭配。

The Xelos SL 32 HD/DR+ is a modern LCD TV set featuring high-definition display technology. A built-in harddisk recorder enables deferred viewing at the touch of a button. In addition to the clear and independent design, the extraordinary speaker perforation pattern characterises the pleasing look of this TV set, measuring just 8.3cm in depth. The black frame around the screen area adds contrast in terms of picture quality and gives the housing frame an exceptionally slim look. Four attractive set-up options are available: table stand, rack, floor stand and wall bracket. The Xelos SL 32 HD/DR+ screen diagonal measures 80cm and features a 16:9 format. Available in the discreet colours platinum, anthracite or platinum monochrome, it adapts itself stylishly to any living room ambience.

中道 VU50HD 等离子电视, 2004

Nakamichi Corporation Limited, Singapur
Werksdesign: Brian Ling
www.nakamichi.com

VU50HD外形美观，其设计灵感来自于包豪斯风格。该设计不仅在技术上与用户需求紧密联系在了一起，也体现在了情感和精神层面里。该电视能提供高层次的颜色精确度，其对比率为3000：1，没有过滤时的亮度为1000坎德拉/每平方米。不管是水平方向还是垂直方向，VU50HD 50英寸的屏幕都可提供超过160度的最佳可视角度。它还配有四个内置立体声扬声器，从而显著地改善了声音效果。此外，SRS WOW™提供的三维立体声能显著改善用户的听觉体验，不需要低音炮就能创造出饱满而丰富的低音的感觉。此外，配备了HDTV的VU50HD等离了电视还可提供720p的原初分辨率，接收所有主要DTV格式的输入。VU50HD不仅仅是一台电视机，它还有内置的DVI（数字视频界面）和D-sub 15VGA输入，当用户把电脑和用作显示器的屏幕连接起来时，它就成了一台高质量的电脑显示器。

The VU50HD's aesthetic form is inspired by Bauhaus style. The design is connected with the user – not only on the technical, but on the emotional and spiritual level as well. The TV is providing superior colour accuracy, with a contrast ratio of 3,000:1 and brightness of 1,000cd/m² without filter. The VU50HD's 50-inch screen provides an optimal viewing angle of more than 160 degrees, both horizontal and vertical. It is equipped with four built-in stereo speakers significantly enhancing sound dynamics. SRS WOW™ improves the audio experience by providing three-dimensional sound, creating the perception of deep, rich bass without need for a subwoofer. Equipped with HDTV capability, it provides 720p native resolution and accepts inputs in all major DTV formats. Not just a television set, the VU50HD includes a built-in Digital Visual Interface (DVI) and a D-sub 15 VGA input, thus turning into a high-quality computer display when the user connects a computer to the screen as a monitor.

Grundig Vision 26 LXW 液晶电视, 2005

Beko Elektronik A.S., Istanbul, Türkei
Werksdesign: Beko Industrial Design Team
Vertrieb: Grundig Multimedia, Nürnberg
www.bekoelektronik.com.tr
www.grundig.de

Vision设计系列中的26 LXW不仅包含了许多技术性特征，其外观设计也非常时尚雅致。黑色高光的机身和前半部的玻璃表面在视觉上很具有冲击力。相反，银白色的地板支架使得该设备外表显得轻快，有一种流动的感觉，机身后部滚动的轮廓更加深了这种印象。屏幕上的EPG（电子节目向导）和对话式屏幕手动用户指导给用户操作带来极大的方便。由于它的表面是黑色的，Vision 26 LXW在颜色上并不显眼，但也能使它协调地与任何一种居室环境相搭配。

The 26 LXW of the Vision design line includes many technical features and has an elegant appearance. The black high-gloss coating and a glass surface along the entire front portion contribute to an optically appealing effect. In contrast, a silver-coloured floor stand gives the unit a light and "floating" appearance. The gently rolling silhouette of the back side adds to this impression. An Electronic Programme Guide (EPG) and the Easy Dialogue on-screen user manual guarantee a high degree of user comfort. With its black optics, the Vision 26 LXW is unobtrusive in colour, thus adapting itself harmonically to virtually any living room ambience.

TV
TV Guide
MyTV
Music
Film
Kids
Active
Ent
OK
Skip
Pg
Txt
Ch

HomeChoice 机顶盒和遥控器

Video Networks Ltd., London, GB
Werksdesign: Marco Giusti
www.videonetworks.com

HomeChoice机顶盒和遥控器的设计来源于一套单独针对HomeChoice设计的方案。HomeChoice是一款多频道的通讯平台，它能够按照需要传递80+和数字电视频道，并且可即时点播电影和音乐视频，所有这些都根据用户的电视，以及与PC的高速宽带连接而决定的。小型的机顶盒设有集成的DSL调制解调器，一个软件解码器，两个Scart插座和两个Ethernet接口。其一大特点在于该设计既能垂直放置也可以水平放置。该机顶盒唯一的视觉焦点是当盒子打开时，被蓝色LED照亮的Perspex白色中央显示屏。该显示屏的独特之处在于将红外线接收器和能够感光的蓝灯显示屏集成为了一个单元。它在白天光照条件好的时候很明亮，但是当周围灯光减弱时则会逐渐变暗，以避免干扰观众。该机顶盒完全是用金属制成的，侧面是有柔软涂层的合金钢，而前面是由磨压过的，弯曲的3毫米磨砂铝板制成。遥控器与机顶盒采用了同样的设计，也采用了同样的铝质板面，其塑料底座被包围在同样柔软的黑色漆面中。它可以单独编程，并与HomeChoice用户界面和机顶盒很好地集成在一起。这套设备向顾客传达了一种清晰的设计理念，即不仅它的外观极具吸引利率，且非常简单实用。

The HomeChoice set-top box and remote control are an integrated original design solution created uniquely for HomeChoice, a multichannel and communication platform that delivers 80+ on-demand and digital TV channels, with instant access to movies and music videos, all to the customers' TV, plus super-fast broadband connection for the PC. The diminutive set-top box features an integrated DSL modem, a software decoder, two Scart sockets and two Ethernet ports and, importantly, is designed to be placed either vertically or horizontally. The only key visual focus of the set-top box is a white Perspex central display lit by blue LEDs when the box is on. The unique feature of this display is the integration of the infrared receiver and photosensitive blue light display into a single unit – which retains brightness in daylight conditions but dims as the ambient light reduces, avoiding irritation to the viewer. The set-top box is constructed entirely out of metal – the sides are mild steel with a black soft-feel paint coating, while the front surround is formed from an extruded, curved 3mm brushed aluminium fascia. The remote control retains the same design as the set-top box, with an aluminium fascia and its plastic base coated in the same black soft-feel paint finish. It is individually programmable and integrates perfectly with the HomeChoice user interface and set-top box. Both products deliver a clear design message to customers that the units are attractive, simple and usable.

PV1 Active 低音炮, 2004

B&W Loudspeakers Ltd, Worthing, GB
Design: Native Design Ltd, London, GB
www.bwspeakers.com
www.native.com

PV1 active低音炮的曲线外形设计是基于音响工程原理，即那些与压力容器有关联的原则。球状外形是容纳音箱内外部之间压力差异的最佳形状。铝质的构造真正消除了机箱共振，并能产生比传统低音炮更强大的重低音，这是因为驱动单元把能量用于排出空气，而不是机箱。机箱也可作为扩音器的散热器，而驱动单元这样的特别设计也避免了使用格栅。

The PV1 active subwoofer owes its curved shape to sound engineering principles – those pertaining to a pressure vessel. The spherical form is an optimised shape to accommodate pressure differences between the inside and outside of the enclosure. The aluminium construction virtually eliminates cabinet resonance and produces a cleaner bass sound than a conventional subwoofer, because the drive units devote their energy to driving air, not the cabinet. The cabinet also acts as heat sink for the amplifier, and the drive units are specifically designed so as not to require an extra grill.

HD 485 高保真立体声耳机, 2005

Sennheiser electronic GmbH & Co. KG, Wedemark
Design: Brennwald Design, Kiel
www.sennheiser.com
www.brennwald-design.de

HD 485是一款专门为在家中使用而设计的立体声耳机，其外形设计十分动感。最新涡轮型震膜保证了高清晰立体声，而较轻的铝制传感器则保证了更强大的动力范围，这一切都可以让它的使用者享受到高质量的音乐。较轻的重量，低摩擦接口，以及高品质的耳垫延长了它的使用时间。此外，HD 485还集成了一个音量控制器和在一个可以在桌子放置的耳机架。它那简单却别具匠心的外形，外壳上大大的音响开口，无一不显现出其经典的设计形象，同时也具有很高的品牌识别价值。

The HD 485 is an open, dynamic stereo headphone developed for use at home. Newest membrane geometry for highly detailed stereo sound and lighter aluminium transducers for higher dynamic range are the guarantor for clear music pleasure. The small weight as well as the low-friction joints and high-quality ear cushions enable a long-time use. The HD 485 features an integrated volume control and headphone holder for table or shelf. The formally reduced appearance shows the classic image of a headphone, enhanced by the large acoustic openings in the shell. This detail has a high identification value.

Traffic Pro 7945
高保真汽车音响导航系统，2004

Harman/Becker, Filderstadt
Werksdesign
www.harmanbecker.com

Traffic Pro 7945是一款将创新型技术和纯粹的设计融合在了一起的汽车音响导航系统。简单的设计保证了用户能够快速而安全地进行操作。在其技术上值得强调的一点是其互动多模式的声音对话功能使该系统操作起来更加简便，从而增加了行车的安全性。引领潮流的无线蓝牙技术为与其他设备之间进行通讯和数据交换提供了一种新的方式。它使得用户能够自动接通手机，不用手的参与便可打电话，安全而方便。另外它还能够在Traffic Pro和蓝牙设备上进行地址交换。高分辨率的显示屏占据了该系统的主要位置，呈现出高对比度和结构化图表的特征，易于阅读。白天和夜间在设计上的区别使得用户在任何时间都能很容易地读出设备上的显示。整体说来，这套系统在视觉语言上还是传承了简单大方的设计观点，以便能在多种车型上应用。

The Traffic Pro 7945 is a car audio and navigation system combining innovative technology with puristic design. The design has been kept simple to allow fast and secure user operation. As a technical highlight, its interactive multimodal voice dialogue capability makes the unit even easier to use, adding to road safety. The trendsetting Bluetooth wireless technology provides up-to-date functionality for communication and data exchange with other devices. It enables the user to automatically connect a mobile phone, allowing safe and convenient handsfree phone calls. Additionally, addresses can be exchanged between the Traffic Pro and Bluetooth-enabled equipment. The high-resolution display dominates its appearance, guaranteeing high contrast, structured graphics and outstanding readability. The distinction between day and night design makes it easy to read the device at all times. The visual language of the unit has been kept simple to facilitate installation in a wide range of vehicles.

Verve Serie 高保真/AV 设备、扬声器系列设备, 2004

agile Unterhaltungselektronik GmbH, Wetter/Amönau
Design: Held + Team (Fred Held), Hamburg
www.agile.eu.com
www.heldundteam.de

高保真、AV设备、扬声器以及Verve系列中的一些附件之间衔接得非常和谐。这套设备的特点在于为看不见的封闭端口连线提供了可能。这样，所有的部件都可以放置在房间内的任何地方。当然也可以选择开放的端口，这样就可以安装多维高端连线。整个机身外形与其他传统hi-fi系统的产品相似，组装也很简便。

Hi-fi- and AV devices as well as loudspeakers and accessories of the Verve Series are harmoniously coordinated with one another. The characteristic element of the units is the possibility of an "invisible" wiring with closed cutbacks. In this way, all components can be placed freely anywhere in the room. Optionally, open cutbacks are available so that larger-dimensioned high-end wirings are installable. The shape of all housings resembles that of other conventional hi-fi system manufacturers so as to allow easy combination.

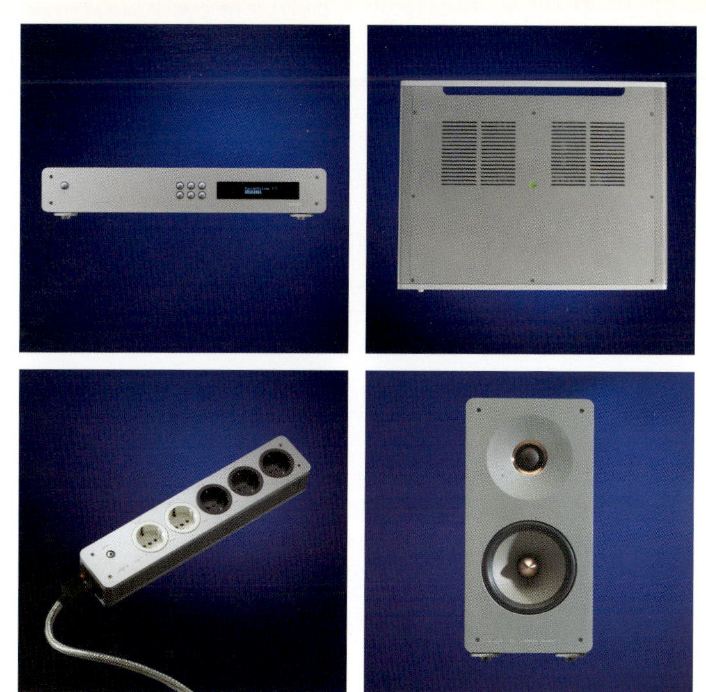

Body Glove Earglove Apex
手机耳机, 2005

Readymade, Pretoria, Südafrika
Werksdesign: Frederick Kruger
www.readymade.co.za

Body Glove Earglove Apex是一款非常轻便舒适的手机用耳机，它采用了先进的扬声器技术和高科技的话筒。可弯曲的材料便于调节话筒杆到正确的位置，且十分结实耐用。控制盘包括一个回答/结束按键，还有弱音功能、音量控制以及绳绕功能。该耳机可以进行调节以适合左右耳的不同形状。其整体的设计进一步强化了Body Glove的商标所透露出来的含义，即“像手套一样合适”。

The Body Glove Earglove Apex is a light and comfortable mobile phone headset with an advanced speaker technology and a high-tech microphone. The materials are flexible, yet durable so that the microphone boom can be adjusted to the correct position. The control pod includes an answer/end button, mute function, volume control and a cord winder feature. The headset adjusts to fit the right and left ear. Its design enhances the Body Glove trademark "fits like a glove".

古董的精致和高雅

Precision and the grace of the archaic

在"珠宝、服装、首饰、纺织品设计和新材料"这一系列中，**对我们所熟悉的造型重新塑造表明了一种潮流**。例如，古典的木屐（即一种木制鞋），经过了重新创造后，采用先进生产技术和新材料而生产出来的鞋子符合人体工程学原理，还非常人性化。对于评委而言，"制造时间" 时采用的新的手表工作技术也呈现出多维性。评委会被这些非常精密的物品吸引住了，无论是每一个细节，还是整体的设计，每一个技术上的创新都是精巧手工艺的表现。另一个趋势便是新事物的出现，例如进行三维设计的手提包。"非常有趣"是评委会做出的评价，这些产品使它们的拥有者变得与众不同、个性十足。这些产品的目标群似乎是清晰界定的，就像太阳镜在设计中巧妙地传递出一种品牌信息一样。在珠宝部分里，这些产品成功地与新型材料之间达成了实用性及简约化的共生。那么，以前的物品重新获得其重要地位了吗？至少对于评委来说，对过去时代里的财富重新进行清楚地评价是一个非常重要的开端，因为它们能够从这里走向未来。

The re-modelling of familiar forms describes one trend in the *"jewellery, fashion, accessories, textile design and new materials" category. For instance, the classical "clog" – a wooden shoe – has been re-invented. Thanks to advanced production techniques and new materials, the resultant shoe is ergonomic and user-friendly. "Making time" also takes on new dimensions for the jurors when interesting new watch work technologies are involved. The jury was very taken by these high-precision pieces: thought out down to the last detail, and sovereign in design, such technological innovations are also an expression of handicraft expertise. Another trend: new forms such as three-dimensionally designed handbags. "Extremely interesting" was the jury's verdict on such products which turn their owners into conscious individualists. The target groups for such products appear to be clearly defined – and likewise for the sunglasses, whose design skilfully transports a brand message. In the jewellery sector, the products successfully create a symbiosis of innovative materials, functionality and minimalism. Are bygone forms regaining importance? For the jurors at least, a clear-eyed re-examination of the riches of past eras is an important starting point – and things can be taken forward from there.*

马尔切罗·莫然迪尼
Marcello Morandini
意大利
Italien

弗莱明·汉森
Flemming Bo Hansen
丹麦
Dänemark

海伦·亚勒
Helen Yardley
英国
Großbritannien

珠宝、服装、首饰、纺织品设计和新材料
Jewellery, fashion, accessories, textile design and new materials

Sotos 珍珠项链卡扣, 2004

Sotos:Kollektion, Köln
Design: Terrumanum, Frechen
www.sotos-jewellery.com

这款珍珠项链的卡扣是由两个具有弹性的夹子一样的金属制作而成的。在加工这件首饰的同时，中间留了一个圆孔，卡扣只和项链的一端相连。在戴项链时，只需把另一端的最后一颗珍珠穿过卡扣的开口处并旋转一下，这样一来，项链就戴上了。卡扣可以用不同材质的稀有金属合成，例如银、黄金、白金或是铂金。所用珍珠共有三种规格，分别为直径5–8毫米、9–12毫米和13–16毫米。

The clasp for pearl necklaces consists of two metal elements functioning as a spring catch. The mechanism, constituting the piece of jewellery at the same time, has a round opening in the centre. The pearl or jewel necklace has a single-side connection to the clasp. When closing the necklace, the last pearl on the open side of the necklace is pulled through the opening of the clasp. With a rotary motion, the necklace is pulled through the metal elements and is closed. The clasp is available in different precious metal combinations: silver, gold, white gold, platinum. It is manufactured in three different sizes for pearls with a diameter of 5-8, 9-12 and 13-16mm.

Meister 太阳罗盘装饰品, 2004

Meister GmbH,
Radolfzell am Bodensee, Deutschland
Meister + Co. AG,
Wollerau am Zürichsee, Schweiz
Werksdesign: Meister-Designteam
www.meisterschmuck.com

太阳罗盘，大小如硬币，是用罗盘和黄金制成的不可折叠的日冕式罗盘。它的设计特征可以说是一切具有动感美的东西的代表，是形式与功能的完美结合。不论把它是作为饰品戴在身上，还是放在口袋里，这件工艺品都可以靠日光和地磁学来判断时间。无论在哪儿，它总是人们目光追随的焦点，因为它凭借自己的完美在告诉人们，智慧和“阳光般的想法”是永远都有生命的。它既是在人类与机械原理之间的交互中所产生的工具，也是由智者传承给人类的饰品中最完美无暇的信使。这种收藏品中几乎包括了人们所珍爱的一切——不仅有可以激发人无限想象的尖端技术，还包含了人类与生俱来的那种“好玩”的想法。

Sundisc, the sundial in coin-size with unfoldable shadow caster made from gold and integrated compass, represents everything that features a dynamic design: a self-contained combination of form and function. Worn as pendant or carried in the pocket, the Sundisc determines the time by means of sunlight and geomagnetism. And as an eye-catcher, it conveys the idea that it is never too late for wit and "sunny ideas". The interplay between man and mechanics results in a tool, which is an unmistakable messenger of men's accessories from Meister. The collection contains everything men hold dear – technical valuables inciting high-flying thoughts and the spirit of play.

Smarts 衬衫纽扣, 2004

Gebr. Niessing GmbH & Co., Vreden
Werksdesign: Susanne Winckler,
Timo Küchler
www.niessing.com

Smarts链扣包括两个椭圆球：大点的做装饰，小点的做纽扣。两个椭圆球被一根横杆结实地连接着，其连接处十分圆滑。由于其设计非常简单，故根本不需要任何接缝。它最基本的部分是不锈钢制成的，起装饰作用的扣子的表面涂有多层不同颜色的稀有金属，也有全钢制成的。这种链扣的特色在于其设计极为简约却功能性突出，它们没有突出的边角，这样就避免了穿着的不适和对衬衫面料的损坏。令一个显著的特征便体现在对稀有金属颜色的选择上：铂金、黄金、不锈钢，这些精心挑选的颜色可以与人们的衬衫做完美的搭配，人们可以随意挑选任何三种暖色调来与它们搭配。

The Smarts cufflinks consist of two ellipsoids; a larger one as decorative element and a smaller one used as a button for fastening. Both elements are linked together firmly by a crosspiece; the links are smooth and rounded. Thanks to the simple button solution a joint was not necessary. The basic part always consists of stainless steel. The decorative button is coated with differently coloured layers of noble metals. An all-steel version is also available. The cufflinks have a reduced and functional design. They have no edges or corners, which could make them less comfortable to wear or could damage valuable fabrics. A special feature is the choice of colours of the noble metals. The sensitively chosen range of colours matches the assortment of men's shirts. Platinum, grey gold, stainless steel, and three warm hues of gold can be chosen individually in combination with these finely matched colours.

Ulla 耳环, 2004

Ulla u. Martin Kaufmann, Hildesheim
Werksdesign: Marit Bindernagel
ulla-martin-kaufmann@t-online.de

这款耳环无论是在设计上还是功能上都有亮点。内部的拉力使耳环可以很容易地戴到耳垂上，同时里面的短绒能够确保最大程度的安全。相信这样的耳环戴起来一定特别的舒服。

Earrings with lightness in design and function. Due to their inherent tension, they attach to the ear lobe easily, while the integrated nap guarantees maximal security. Thus, the earrings will be worn with great comfort.

罗敦司德 R 5191 ff. 时尚眼镜, 2005

Rodenstock GmbH, München
Werksdesign: Christian de Bruyn
www.rodenstock.de

由于它与众不同的双向维度，再加上其超薄的轮廓设计，使得这款罗敦司德时尚眼睛架具有一种神秘而独立的美感，也呈现出一种轻巧的整体视觉效果。此外，此款镜架采用了塑料代替了普通的金属部件，这一先进的改进使其铰链更具聚合力。没有采用普通金属加固的眼镜架给人以持久的透明感。塑料镜架上的薄薄的镜片和透明的光感第一次地在一款特别纤细的镜架上体现出来。玻璃与镜架之间的相互作用就好比视觉系统的展示，不经意间便塑造出一种一体化融合的效果来。

With its distinctive two-dimensionality, interplayed against a minimalised depth profile, the new Rodenstock trend frames concept creates a suspenseful independent aesthetic impression. This in turn creates a very light overall optical and factual effect. Innovative solutions with plastics replacing the ordinary metal components lead to an integrated cohesive concept in the hinge technology as well. The absence of the usual metal reinforcements in the earpiece provides for a continuous transparency. For the first time, a particularly slim frame profile can visually accentuate light and thin glasses in a plastic frame. The interplay of glass and frame as sight-system spectacle can create a self-contained integrative effect.

P'1026 保时捷设计太阳镜, 2005

Rodenstock GmbH, München
Design: Peter Kövari, München
www.rodenstock.de

P'1026钛金架太阳镜是根据一个新型原理制作而成的。一种特制外形的闭合式镜架，直接深入玻璃的外部边缘（沿曲线式地）把它从前到后依次固定住。使用高弹性钛材料可以让镜架张开的更宽，且里面不需要安装其它的螺丝。镜架上边的弧度与镜片的弧度做到了平行一致，这样一来，这款眼镜给人的整体印象就是干净利索，引人注目，并且展示了以技术为导向的品牌外延。

The glass fixing of the titanium sunglasses model P'1026 is accomplished with an innovative principle: a closed frame, made from a specially formed profile, penetrates the glass at its outer rim and fixates it (meander-like) alternately at the front and the rear. The usage of high-flexible titanium materials provides for a wide opening of the frame; no further openings (screws, etc.) are necessary so as to fit in the glasses. The consistently tight curve of the upper part runs parallel to the visible parts of the glass fitting. Thus, the model conveys a tight, striking and markedly reduced overall impression, coherently reflecting the technically oriented brand profile.

OWP Mod. 7574,
男士眼镜, 2004

OWP Brillen GmbH, Passau
Werksdesign: Dagmar Hagen
www.owp.de

专为男性设计的高品质OWP在制造过程中把塑料和抗过敏的钛原料结合到了一起。从脸颊到镜腿的上的延伸面更加突出了这款眼睛的漂亮的方形镜片。与镜框颜色一致的塑料材料被安置在了镜腿的顶端，形成了一对小垫，不仅令佩戴者感觉更加舒适，还在延伸了镜架的线条的同时避免了任何冗赘的设计，使其形成了一个统一的整体。T–槽形状的加工技术可以允许在结实的镜腿上安置一种高级弹簧铰链，这种铰链由不含镍的原料制成，线条平滑、品质过硬。

The high-quality OWP design model for men follows the concept of combining plastic and anti-allergenic titanium material. The expressive square form of the glass is emphasised by a facet that extends via the surface of the cheek into the earpiece. A plastic part, which matches the main frame in colour, is let into the tip of the earpiece and forms a pleasant-to-wear pad. It consistently continues the line of the earpiece and avoids interruption by any attached cell ends. The T-groove milling allows integrating an extra fine, super-flat spring hinge made of nickel-free material into the solidly worked earpiece.

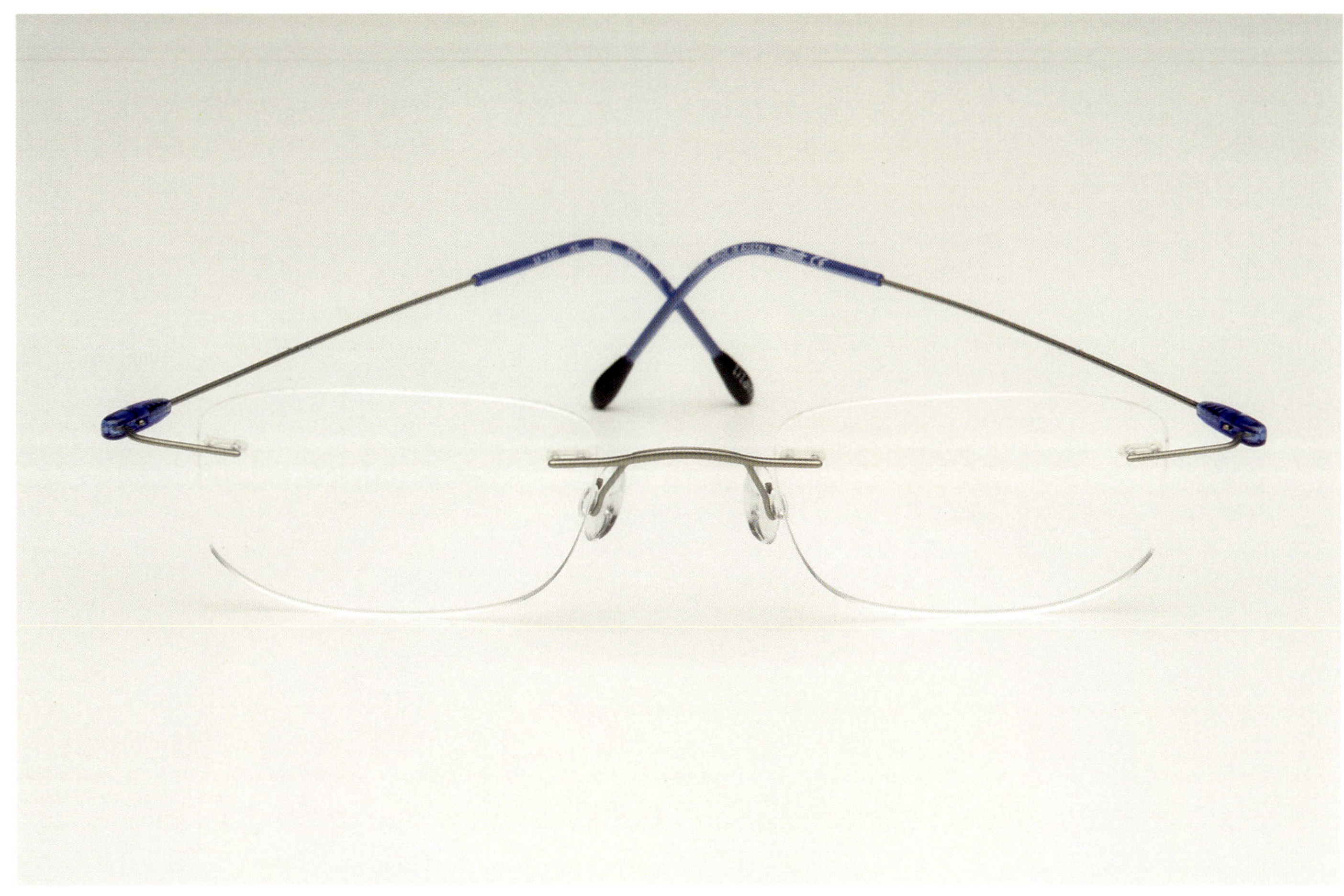

Mod. 7440/15 6080 泰坦无框眼镜, 2004

Silhouette International Schmied AG, Linz, Österreich
Werksdesign: Gerhard Fuchs
Vertrieb: Silhouette Vertriebs GmbH, Ludwigsburg
www.silhouette.com

泰坦新一代无框眼镜给偏爱运动生活方式的人们带来了一个崭新的空间。超细的脚丝采用高科技原料贝他钛制成，质地轻巧，对皮肤无刺激，佩戴舒适。脚丝及镜框被固定在U型的勾状弯曲处，此款镜架所采用的特殊技术可以保证不使用螺丝就可以让铰链活动自如。凭借着其美观大方的外观设计，精致而透明的细部处理，这款眼镜与人们的日常生活和谐地融为了一体。

Titan Translucent is a generation of glasses with frameless design, opening up new dimensions for a sportive lifestyle. Extremely thin temples, made from the high-tech material beta titanium, offer, next to a high degree of lightness and skin tolerance, a high wearing comfort. The temples and trims are fixed in the decorative drop in U-hook form – a special technique allowing for a stepless hinge movement without having to resort to screws. Charming and casual in appearance, these models with their subtle translucent details are unobtrusive partners in everyday life.

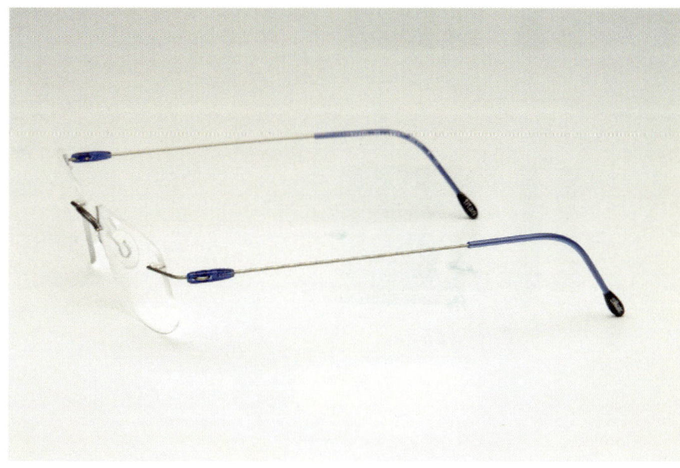

材料组合和新型灯具
Material combinations, and new typologies of light

光的本质是什么？应该说，这个最基本的问题是所有与“光和灯”有关的革新事物的基础。对于解决工作场所的照明问题来说，对光原理的基础性研究显得尤为重要。产品类型组合以及新产品的外观设计是建立在对现有的各种灯具的适用性和功能性价值进行的仔细研究基础之上的。无论在什么情况下，设计首先考虑的是办公室等工作场所里的人。评委毕勇·达尔斯特姆、马汀·克莱森和路易吉·发拉拉说，这些灯具产品都是在“移动”中被感知的。经过多年来的精心实验，人们发现了新的解决办法和形式。这种革新的产品技术在许多同类的灯具上也可得以应用。例如，电脑辅助3-D技术，已经给人们带来了新的设计方案，产品在外观上采用新颖的三维技术，而且由于采用了新的生产方法，价格也有所下调。利用新原料进行的大胆实验又引导了新的流行趋势，新的原料包括塑料、纸张、皮毛和纺织品等自然原料，将它们结合在一起生产出的产品又带来了新奇的美感。在评委们看来，灯具的设计最终不是取决于现有的材料，而是一个面对未来发展的研究。新的材料就会带来新的外形设计，而新的形式却又是新型灯具所要张显的个性的物质基础。

What is the nature of light? *This fundamental question underlies all innovation related to "lighting and lamps." An elementary approach to the principle of "light" is playing an important role for workplace lighting in particular. Critical scrutiny of the suitability and functional value of existing lamps is leading to product-type combinations and the appearance of new genres. In either case, design considerations focus on the individual in the workplace. According to the jurors Björn Dahlström, Mårten Claesson and Luigi Ferrara, the lighting product group is palpably "in motion," with new solutions and forms emergent after long years of experimentation. Innovative production techniques were deployed in the case of a number of lamps likewise. Computer-assisted 3-D techniques, for instance, have opened up new design methods. The products take on a new, three-dimensional appearance, and thanks to the new production methods the prices are dropping. Bold experimentation with materials accounted for a further trend, with plastics and natural materials like paper, furs and fabrics being combined to create an interesting new aesthetic. In the eyes of the jurors, however, the designs of the lamps were ultimately determined not by the existing materials, but by an examination of prospective developments. New materials were resulting in new shapes, and these in turn were the basis of a new formal language of light.*

路易吉·发拉拉
Luigi Ferrara
加拿大
Kanada

毕勇·达尔斯特姆
Björn Dahlström
瑞典
Schweden

马汀·克莱森
Mårten Claesson
瑞典
Schweden

照明与灯具
Lighting and lamps

太阳二代舞台聚光灯，2004

Zumtobel Staff GmbH, Dornbirn, Österreich
Design: Massimo Iosa Ghini, Bologna, Italien
Vertrieb: Zumtobel Staff Deutschland Vertriebs GmbH, Lemgo
www.zumtobelstaff.com
www.iosaghini.it

太阳二代是新一代的舞台聚光灯系统，它将优雅并富于表现力的设计和创新的科技巧妙地结合了起来，构成了一个密不可分的整体设计。由于其外观极具表现力，因此它看上去没有丝毫的刻板与平庸；它的线条也非常柔和，因此这种有着鲜明特色的设计并不给人以突兀的感觉。聚光灯显得极为轻巧，完全是为外露的舞台灯光而设计的，相信它一定能与观众达到美感与情感上的精妙融合。

Solar II is the new generation of a spotlight system, which connects an organic design with expressive elegance and innovative technology. Due to its expressive use of forms, Solar II is anything but rigid or anonymous. The design is distinctive, but at the same time soft with flowing lines. The spotlight seems almost weightless, created for applications in which the lights are not hidden, but shall convey beauty and emotion.

ZUMTOBEL STAFF

ZUMTOBEL STAFF

Evio 吊灯, 2004

Zumtobel Staff GmbH,
Dornbirn, Österreich
Design: Rupert Kopp, Berlin
Vertrieb: Zumtobel Staff Deutschland
Vertriebs GmbH, Lemgo
www.zumtobelstaff.com
www.greige.de

Evio吊灯的最显著特点就是其质地，采用了山毛榉、坚果木材或是石棉水泥质地的灯罩不仅使它那流线型的外表更加突出，而且让它显得格外新颖，与众不同。一方面，由于采用了建筑上常用的木质及石棉水泥材料，它已成为高级私人办公室、会客室、样板间、剧场休息室的主要亮点。另一方面，Evio吊灯将自身定义为建筑中不可或缺的一部分，将空间与灯光直接联系了起来。直接的灯光形式和朴素的天花板照明的统一体使它的形式语言更加突出，而且凸现了灯光以及其优秀的质地。独创的蜂巢百叶窗技术在微型百叶窗照明领域可谓达到了领先水平。蜂巢百叶窗是用注模机生产的，因而尺寸精确、质地结实且均匀。

The most striking feature of the Evio pendant lamp is its material. The flowing form is emphasised by a body made of beech or nut wood, respectively or Eternit. This makes it highly original and different from other systems. On the one hand, the materials wood and Eternit, which are familiar due to their use in architecture, are design features for high-quality single offices and chambers, representative rooms and foyers. On the other hand, Evio defines itself as an integral part of the architecture and creates a direct connection between space and lighting. Evio's direct light version and the version with discreet indirect light for ceiling illumination impress with their striking language of forms, which shows to advantage the lighting as well as the material. An innovative cell louvre technology sets standards in the field of miniaturising louvre luminaires. The cell louvre has been produced by injection moulding and is exact, robust and even.

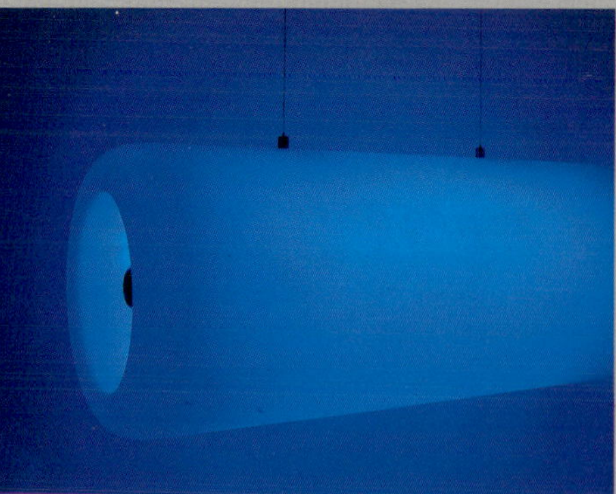

D2V2 照明设备, 2004

Dark NV, Maldegem, Belgien
Design: Venlet Interior Architecture (Danny Venlet), Brüssel, Belgien
www.dark.be

相信凭借D2V2看起来很结实的外形和其独特的造型立刻会牢牢吸引人们的注意力。灯的形状使人联想到飞机的引擎——修长、优雅并且是半透明的，其材料采用了聚乙烯。由于使用了彩色灯管或色彩过滤器，灯光可以随着整体色调的变化而变化。更为神奇的是TL灯光不会碰触到灯罩的侧边。灯光还能够变暗；灯的类型是54瓦的TL5款。采用了滤光器或/和彩色电灯泡的D2V2能够变换各种不同的颜色。

D2V2 is a strong-shaped, very present object that attracts attention. The light shape is reminiscent of an airplane engine – it is long, elegant and translucent. The material is polyethylene, and because of the use of coloured light tubes or colour filters, the light changes tones. Remarkable is the fact that the TL lights are not touching the sidewalls of the fitting. The light is dimmable; the lamp type is TL5 54 watts. D2V2 is available in different colours due to the use of colour filters and/or colour bulbs.

LT01 Seam One 台灯, 2003

e15 Design und Distributions GmbH, Oberursel
Design: Mark Holmes, London, GB
www.e15.com

LT01 Seam One台灯突破了传统的台灯样式，显得更为雅致与现代。它是一个照明灯系列的一部分，这一系列的灯具将高超的设计工艺与优质的材料结合在了一起。该设计的目标就是尽可能地减少其组成部件，使其结构尽可能简单，比例尽可能协调，灯光尽可能明亮。LT01 Seam One台灯的表面有粉末涂层的铝。这款灯有六种不同的颜色可供选择。

The LT01 Seam One lamp is an elegant-looking, modern interpretation of the classical table lamp. It is part of a series of aluminium lamps, which combines a top design with high-quality materials. The aim of the design was to minimise the number of components, keep the construction as simple as possible, the proportions as balanced as possible and to make the light as strong as possible. The surface of the LT01 Seam One lamp is made of powder-coated aluminium. It is available in six different colours.

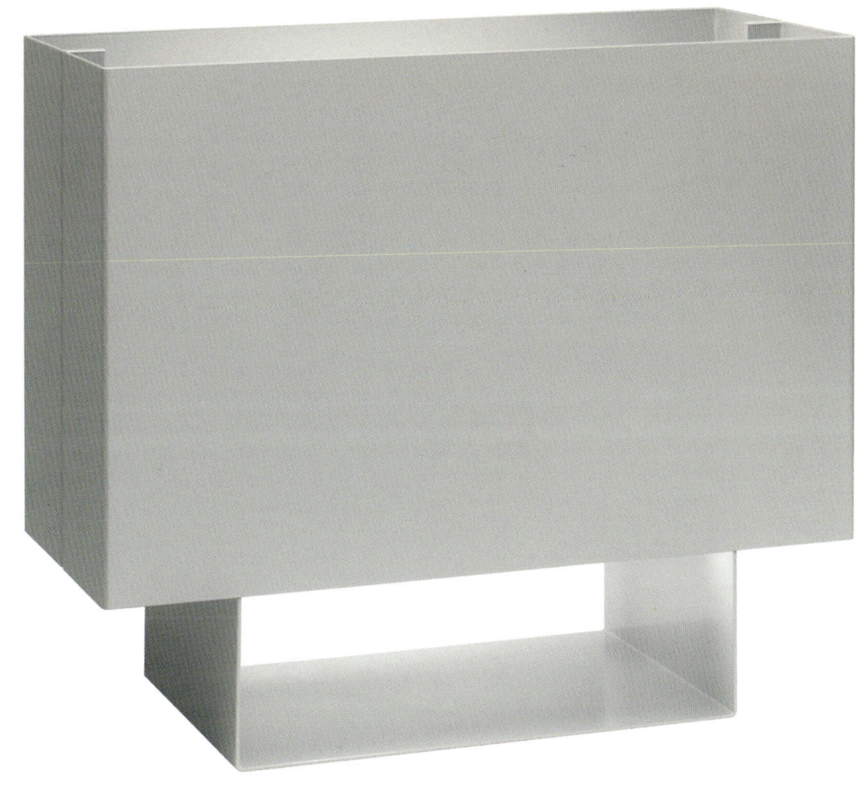

LT02 Seam Two 台灯, 2004

e15 Design und Distributions GmbH, Oberursel
Design: Mark Holmes, London, GB
www.e15.com

LT02 Seam Two台灯也是e15铝灯系列的一部分。灯的表面棱角分明。它由铝金属薄片制成的两个完全相同的部分组成，其表面有粉末涂层，也有很多颜色可供选择。

The LT02 Seam Two is part of the e15 series of aluminium lamps as well. The body of the light is decidedly sculptural with its clear shape and accurate folds. The casing consists of two identical components made of folded sheet aluminium. The surface is powder-coated and available in a range of colours.

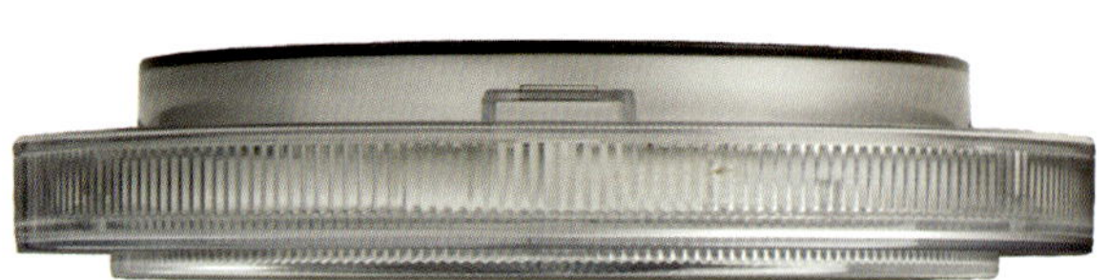

Fresco 灯, 2005

Lumiance B.V., Haarlem, NL
Werksdesign: Raymond Berg, Fritz v. d. Laar
Vertrieb: SLI Lichtsysteme GmbH, Erlangen
www.sylvania-lighting.com

Fresco灯主要可以满足节能的要求，可以应用在诸如公共场所以及天花板上或墙壁上潮湿的环境里（镶嵌或者半嵌壁式表面），并且可以安装不同的荧光灯，包括流行的T16环形灯。管线漫射器使灯光发散到前方和周围，因此就形成了一个平滑和柔和的光圈，如果有附带的悬吊装置的话，Fresco灯便可变成一个具有装饰性的挂件。

Fresco luminaires are designed for general energy-saving light applications in public areas and humid environments on ceilings (surface-mounted and semi-recessed) or walls and take various compact fluorescent lamps including the popular T16 circular. The diffusor distributes the light forward and sideward, thus creating a smooth and soft halo of light. With the pendant set (available as an accessory) Fresco can be transformed into a decorative pendant.

Kometa 灯, 2004

Concord:marlin, Feltham, GB
Werksdesign: Mike Jankowski, Oliver Shakespeare, Jorgé Davis Quinones, Martin Cooper
Vertrieb: SLI Lichtsysteme GmbH, Erlangen
www.sylvania-lighting.com

Kometa灯光设备为办公场所的照明提供了一种很巧妙的方法，它解决了只由一个发光设备便可为大面积房间提供照明的技术难题。同时，其新颖的设计打破了中规中矩的办公室传统的美学结构。Kometa以它独具特色的环形外观，将环绕照明与下端照明有机地结合了起来，并且符合当前的灯光设计思路，同时又使房间的各个表面的光产生协调的环绕。Kometa符合时下广为流行的办公室灯光配备要求，同时又提供了一种非常灵活的灯光处理方案。它的灯泡能够独立地开关——或由电动开关控制变暗——以此来产生不同的灯光效果。

The Kometa lighting fitting offers an innovative approach to workplace lighting, which answers the technical challenge of illuminating the major room surfaces from one luminaire. At the same time, its original design breaks the mould of linear, angular office aesthetics. Combining ambient lighting and downlighting within its distinctive, circular form, Kometa complies with contemporary lighting design thinking, but throwing a balanced rotation of light on all the main room surfaces. Kometa meets current office lighting recommendations and also offers a very flexible light solution. Its lamps can be independently switched on and off – or dimmed with the integrated electronic gear – to create a variety of lighting effects.

Hertz 2 HQI 聚光灯, 2004

Flos S.p.A., Bovezzo (Brescia), Italien
Design: Konstantin Grcic, München
Vertrieb: Flos GmbH, Langenfeld
www.flos.com

优雅的Hertz2 HQI聚光灯能够提供更强的光效和卓越的视觉效果。设计简洁并选用了透明可反光材质的Hertz2 HQI聚光灯可以与任何室内环境自然搭配。墙式或天花板聚光灯以及三相聚光灯电轨都使用的是功率为35瓦的CDM-R111，同时配有GX8.5灯罩和一个2 x 35瓦的恒亮双灯电子压载。

The refined Hertz 2 HQI model offers a high light performance and excellent visual qualities. With its simple design and the choice of transparent, reflecting materials, the lamp fits naturally into any architectural environment. The mounted version as wall or ceiling spotlight or for a three-phase spotlight rail has been equipped with a CDM-R111 mains voltage lamp with 35 watts and a GX8.5 cap, and with a twin-lamp non-dimmable electronic ballast for 2 x 35 watts.

45 墙灯 / 顶灯 / 地板灯, 2004

Flos S.p.A., Bovezzo (Brescia), Italien
Design: Tim Derhaag, Amsterdam, NL
Vertrieb: Flos GmbH, Langenfeld
www.flos.com

45墙灯 / 顶灯 / 地板灯设计利用直射或非直射的照明设备来散光。只需简单地将散光器倾斜45度角，便可达到照明效果。灯具主要用压延铝制成，其他的部件由高技术聚合的钢材和木料制成。所有的组件都采用了特殊的连接方法，便于简单，快速的安装。这一灯具有铝制和柚木两种质地可供选择。

The wall and floor lamp 45 is conceived for diffuse light with direct or indirect illumination. The light selection is accomplished simply by turning the diffusor 45 degrees sideways. The lamp is made from extruded aluminium and consists of component parts and accessories made from techno-polymer, steel and wood. A special joint connecting both lamp elements allows an easy and immediate adjustment. The lamp is available in an aluminium or teakwood version.

Fort Knox 聚光灯, 2004

Flos S.p.A., Bovezzo (Brescia), Italien
Design: Philippe Starck, Paris, Frankreich
Vertrieb: Flos GmbH, Langenfeld
www.flos.com

Fort Knox是一款精心设计的聚光灯，其设计更加注重细节，更适合安装在三相导电轨上。灯体、封边和可调节支架都是由印模压铸铝制成。聚光灯有多种样式可供选择：手工打磨型、清漆保护膜型、电抛光型、黑色镀镍型、白色闪亮型和黑白交叉涂层型。

Fort Knox is a carefully designed new spotlight concept with particular attention to details, suitable for mounting on three-phase current conductor rails. The lamp, the closure flap and the adjustable lamp holder are made from die-cast aluminium. The spotlights are available in different versions: hand-polished and coated with a transparent protective lacquer; polished and galvanic-shining, nickel-plated black; shining-white; or opal-black powder-coated.

施华洛世奇巢状枝形吊灯，2004

Swarovski, London, GB
Design: fuseproject (Yves Behar, Pichaya Puttorngul, Michael Hammers), San Francisco, USA
www.swarovskisparkles.com
www.fuseproject.com

设计这款枝形吊灯旨在体验一种设计的创新，即将无瑕的水晶和现代灯艺融合为一体。它的设计采用传统的水晶切割方法，将其雕刻成了富有怀旧色彩的鸟巢结构的枝形吊灯。于是，施华洛世奇投入了一条新生产线，并决定进行连续的系列化生产。巢形结构中的镂空似乎在等待人们去探索那闪耀的水晶世界。由折射光构成的茧状中心是电致发光胶片。从胶片上放射出的光线由安装在灯盖上的动力系统供给能源，但也可被其减弱光线。这款水晶枝形吊灯体现了二十一世纪现代生产技术与传统产品的完美结合。该款枝形吊灯有大、小、迷你等三种型号可供选择。

The aim in designing these chandeliers was the innovative fusion of an extraordinary design, flawless crystals and modern light technology. It was designed using crystals with a traditional cut, combined with a chandelier with an organic form that is reminiscent of a nest. The result is a new product line by Swarovski, who decided to go into series production. The hollow inside of the nest allows a glance into a sparkling crystal world. In the centre of this cocoon of refracted light is an electroluminescent film. The light emanating from it can be dimmed and is powered by a power supply unit located in the upper hood. Thus, this crystal chandelier represents a modern and poetical integration of manufacturing methods of the 21st century in the traditional chandelier production. The chandelier is available in three sizes – large, small and mini.

Empty 灯, 2004

DAB, Barcelona, Spanien
Werksdesign: Josep Lluís Xuclà
www.dab.es

Empty是一种户外灯，它是一系列不同规格的产品中最先问世的一款。金属结构的外形有锈斑型或是银质的，可根据用户喜好而进行选择。Empty的光源来自于一个提供非直射光源的TC-F 1 × 36W 2G 10的灯。Empty不仅仅是个简单的灯源，说它还是一系列的雕刻作品也不为过。它既可以单独用作座椅供人休息，而成组使用时，它还可当作餐桌使用，别忘了它还能提供令人舒适的灯光呢！此外，该灯光还可以进行不同颜色的过滤，用来强调一些特殊的区域或是服务，也就是用作指向灯。它从设计之初就定位在自然的环境中使用，所以，它那锈渍斑斑的外表可以与花园的整体风格相协调。

Empty is an outdoor light and the first in a series of lamps in different sizes. It has a metal structure and is available in rust or silver. The light source is a TC-F 1x36W 2G10, which provides indirect light. Empty is more than a simple light source, it is a sculpture with a variety of applications, which can be used as a seat to relax or in a group as a table. As such, it has a very pleasant light. Furthermore, the light can be filtered by different colours to emphasise certain zones or serve as a guiding light. Empty has been designed for use in a natural surrounding. The rust variant integrates completely into all kinds of gardens.

百合 MGX 台灯, 2004

Materialise NV, Leuven, Belgien
Design: FOC Freedom Of Creation
(Janne Kyttanen), Amsterdam, NL
www.materialise-mgx.com
www.freedomofcreation.com

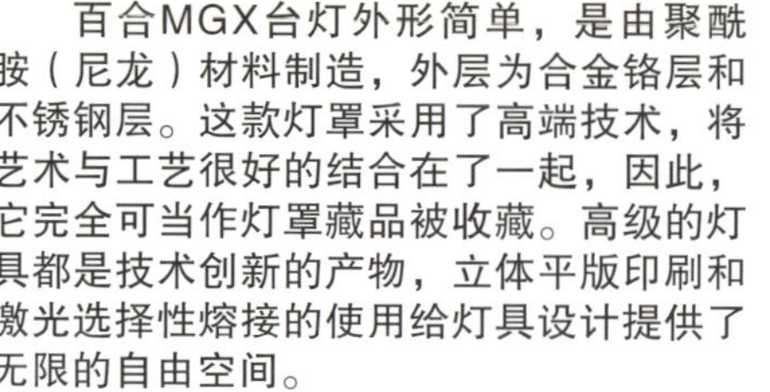

百合MGX台灯外形简单，是由聚酰胺（尼龙）材料制造，外层为合金铬层和不锈钢层。这款灯罩采用了高端技术，将艺术与工艺很好的结合在了一起，因此，它完全可当作灯罩藏品被收藏。高级的灯具都是技术创新的产物，立体平版印刷和激光选择性熔接的使用给灯具设计提供了无限的自由空间。

The lamp Lily.MGX has an organic shape and is made of the materials polyamide (nylon) and chrome-coated, stainless steel. It is part of a collection of lampshades that combines art and technology by using a high-tech background to produce exceptional lampshades. The exclusive lamps are created through innovative prototyping techniques – stereolithography and selective laser sintering – that offer almost unlimited freedom of design.

芦苇室外照明灯, 2004

DZ LICHT – Gruppe Artemide, Fröndenberg
Design: Artemide GmbH
(Klaus Begasse), Fröndenberg
Vertrieb: Artemide GmbH, Fröndenberg
www.artemide.com

芦苇灯是一个柱式灯具，高150厘米，可用作装饰灯或指示灯。七根又细又轻、富于韧性的玻璃纤维灯丝安装在灯的圆形底座上，一个白色的LED（发光二极管）连接在灯丝的末端，形成灯柱的上半部分的光源。阵阵微风轻轻地拂动根根灯丝，在氤氲光线的交错下，如同在玩一个非常有趣的灯光游戏。

Reeds is a bollard lamp with a height of 150cm for decorative illumination and signalation. Seven thin, very light and flexible filaments made of glass fibre are installed on the lamp's circular base. A white LED has been attached to the tip of these filaments, which lights the upper part of the brace. The fine filaments move in the slightest breath of wind, thus creating an interesting play of light.

线条灯, 2004

LRG. Licht + Raum AG, Ittigen, Schweiz
Design: Lichtprojekte Christian Deuber, Luzern, Schweiz
www.lichtraum.ch
www.christiandeuber.ch

用钢缆悬挂起的线条灯是一个小型的照明工具。由于它的横截面仅为38 × 40毫米，所以这一设计简洁的灯具可以和建筑物的背景和谐地搭配在一起。它甚至可以不断的进行360度的扭转，进而通过固定在墙面上或是天花板上而直接直射或是间接地照到任何地方。线条灯是由侧面为38 × 40毫米压延铝制成，长度为110厘米到350厘米的部分都经过阳极电镀处理，其对T5的光源的EVG或EVG模糊度为14 – 54瓦。

Line is a minimal light solution suspended by steel cables. Thanks to its small cross section of 38 x 40mm, this simple and clear lamp remains unpretentiously in the background in relation to the architecture. The profile can be continuously rotated by 360 degrees and illuminates the space either directly or indirectly via wall and ceiling. Line is made of extruded aluminium profile 38 x 40mm, colourlessly anodised in lengths from 110 to 350cm, EVG or EVG dimmable for T5 illuminants from 14 to 54 watts.

Devio 泛光灯, 2004

Hess Form + Licht GmbH, Villingen-Schwenningen
Design: Karsten Winkels, Dortmund
www.hess-form-licht.de

Devio泛光灯能够为处于围墙之间的街道和广场提供十分柔和的照明效果。如果需要，它同样能够加强建筑正面的照明效果。流线型的外观使整个灯源都几乎隐藏起来，不易引起人们的注意，而它的照明效果却是十分显著的。Devio使得城市中光斑分裂技术的应用范围得到进一步扩大，并且它采用了Bartenbach Lichtlabor——奥地利的专业光学公司——的专利的放映和反光系统。

The Devio luminaire provides glare-free lighting of streets and squares from a wall-mounted position. When desired, it also performs the added function of façade illumination. The streamlined form makes the luminaire barely noticeable; remarkable is its lighting. Devio expands the realm of application for the innovative light spot splitting technique in urban areas and utilises the Bartenbach Lichtlabor's patented projector and reflector system.

Elle 室外照明灯, 2004

DZ LICHT – Gruppe Artemide, Fröndenberg
Design: Artemide GmbH (Klaus Begasse), Fröndenberg
Vertrieb: Artemide GmbH, Fröndenberg
www.artemide.com

Elle是为公园、广场和人行道设计的照明设施。3.5米长的杆子的顶部是一个长方形的灯体，光源就安置在其中。安装灯具使用的带子能够根据不同环境的具体要求来进行调节。Elle内配备了高强度的荧光灯，在提供高强度灯光的同时耗电量很少。同时，它还能耐零下20摄氏度的低温。

Elle has been designed for lighting public parks, squares and pedestrian precincts. The 3.5 metres long mast ends in a rectangular luminaire, which also houses the light source. The strap for mounting the lamp allows it to be positioned according to the specific requirements of the environment. Elle is equipped with compact fluorescent lamps with a high light output, which use little energy, and it is resistant to temperatures of down to –20 degrees centigrade.

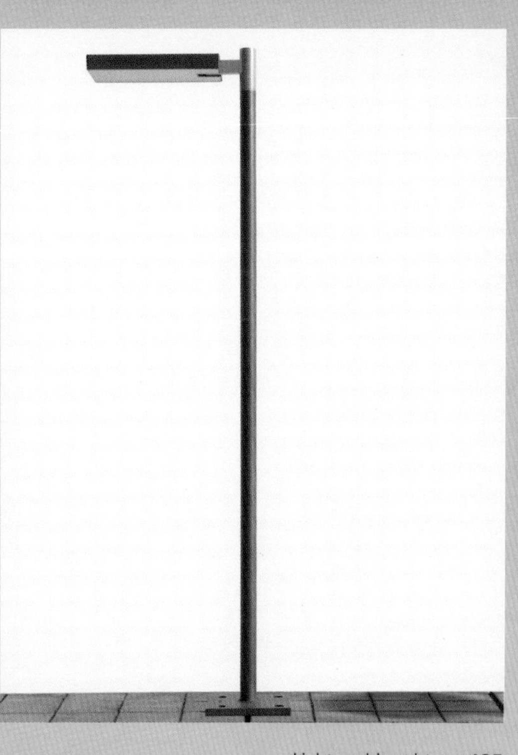

评审标准

- 创新程度
- 功能性
- 外形品质
- 人体工程学
- 耐用性
- 象征性与情感涵义
- 产品外围
- 简明使用程度
- 生态性

Assessment criteria

- *Degree of innovation*
- *Functionality*
- *Formal quality*
- *Ergonomics*
- *Durability*
- *Symbolic and emotional content*
- *Product peripherals*
- *Self-explanatory quality*
- *Ecological soundness*

国际导向与客观性
International orientation and objectivity

“红点奖：产品设计”评委会的所有成员都是在独立和公正的基础上被任命的。他们分别是独立设计师、设计机构里的专家、国际设计事务所里的代表和设计新闻记者。评委在组成上是国际化的，且每年都有一定的变化。这样可以确保最大的客观性。今年的评委会委员名单在随后的部分中将按字母顺序排列。

All members of the "red dot award: product design" jury *are appointed on the basis of independence and impartiality. They are independent designers, academics in design faculties, representatives of international design institutions, and design journalists. The jury is international in its composition, which changes every year. These conditions assure a maximum of objectivity. The members of this year's jury are presented in alphabetical order in the following pages.*

“红点奖：产品设计”的评委
The jury of the "red dot award: product design"

华纳·艾司令格
Werner Aisslinger
(德国/Germany)

生于1964年
Born in 1964

经营着柏林的艾司令格工作室,并在卡尔斯鲁厄的乌尔姆造型学院的产品设计占据一席之位。

华纳·艾司令格教授生于1964年。早先在柏林HdK大学学习设计。而后,从1989年到1992年为伦敦贾斯柏·莫里森和隆·阿拉德、米兰的卢基工作室做自由撰稿人。1993年,他成立了柏林艾司令格工作室,主要涉猎范围有产品研发、概念设计、品牌建筑。他的客户包括interlübke、Cappellini、stilwerk、Porro、Magis、zanotta、戴姆勒–克莱斯勒、捷豹、贝塔斯曼，以及德国电视公司ZDF等。1994年至今，华纳·艾司令格一直是柏林HdK大学和芬兰拉提设计学院的客座讲师。1998年，他被任命为卡尔斯鲁厄乌尔姆造型学院产品设计的教授。

华纳·艾司令格教授在国际设计竞赛中获得诸多褒奖，包括“设计和荣誉”、“邦德斯普里斯产品设计奖”、“红点设计奖”、“金罗盘”奖和“100%蓝图设计奖”。他的作品还在多家著名博物馆展出并被收藏，例如维特拉设计博物馆、维尔莱茵园艺展览馆、慕尼黑的新Sammlung和巴黎的乔治蓬皮杜中心，以及在MoMA和纽约的大都会美术馆。

Runs Studio Aisslinger in Berlin and has a chair in product design at the Hochschule für Gestaltung in Karlsruhe.

Professor Werner Aisslinger was born in 1964. After studying design at HdK, Berlin, he freelanced from 1989 to 1992 for Jasper Morrison and Ron Arad in London and Studio De Lucchi in Milan. In 1993, he founded Studio Aisslinger in Berlin, focusing on product development, conceptual design and brand architecture. His clients include interlübke, Cappellini, stilwerk, Porro, Magis, zanotta, DaimlerChrysler, Jaguar, Bertelsmann, and the German television corporation ZDF. Werner Aisslinger was a visiting lecturer at HdK, Berlin, and the Lahti Design Institute in Finland since 1994. In 1998, he was appointed professor of product design at the Hochschule für Gestaltung in Karlsruhe.

Werner Aisslinger has received numerous awards in international design competitions, including the Design Plus Award, Bundespreis Produktdesign, red dot design award, Compasso d'Oro Selection, and the Blueprint 100% Design Award. His works are on display in various prestigious museums and collections, such as the Vitra Design Museum, Weil am Rhein, the Neue Sammlung in Munich and the Centre Georges Pompidou in Paris, and the permanent collections of the MoMA and Metropolitan Museum in New York.

华纳·艾司令格
Werner Aisslinger

“在经济学领域里，受到全球化的影响，越来越多的生产过程和土木工程被转移到了低工资国家，而设计，作为延续了几个世纪的文化革命的精粹，则成为了全球范围内公司形象和市场竞争的重要因素。”

"In an economic phase in which, due to globalisation, more and more production and parts of civil engineering are sourced out into low-wage countries, design, as distillate of a cultural evolution stretching over centuries, is a key factor in worldwide competition over corporate identity and markets."

阿部真代
Masayo Ave
(意大利/Italy)

生于1962年
Born in 1962

建筑师和设计师。对自己的设计精品进行收藏和展览
"阿部真代创造" 东京和米兰。

阿部真代，1962年生于日本东京，是东京法政大学工程学院的一名建筑学毕业生。曾在I.Ebihara建筑协会工作了一段时间。1990年她从东京搬到米兰，在米兰Domus学院学习工业设计并取得硕士学位。1992年，她在东京和米兰都创立了她自己的设计工作室"阿部真代设计公司"。1996年，她获得德国的德国艺术家基金会资助。2000年她开始了自己的收藏"阿部真代设计系列"。

她的设计项目分布范围很广，从日常生活用品到建筑设计，现代手工艺品到大规模生产的产品，都在她的设计范围之内。这些设计品基于对原材料内在的情感潜在价值的艺术研究，是对传统、先进的技术、天才的独创性的完美结合。她在建筑学、园艺设计、家具、照明、服装和包装以及产品设计领域里已经取得了瞩目的成绩，得到了国际上的认可。除了她自己的收藏品之外，她也是奥坦蒂克、都彭和Industrielle等设计公司的设计师。

自2001年以来，阿部真代利用几十年来在国际领域里的设计经验，正在积极地带领一个国际设计工作室"材料的声音"——其生动的设计以对艺术的鉴赏和感受为基础——和那些年轻的设计者、手工艺者、还有各国各个领域里的专家们共同进行设计。2003年以来，她被提名为ADI国际委员。

Architect and designer. Creates her own design collection
"MasayoAve creation" in Tokyo and Milan.

Born in Tokyo in 1962, Masayo Ave is a graduate of architecture from the engineering department of Hosei University in Tokyo. After working at I. Ebihara Architect and Associates, in 1990 she moved from Tokyo to Milan where she completed a master's degree in industrial design at the Domus Academy. In 1992, she established her own design studio "Ave design corporation" based in Tokyo and Milan. In 1996, she received a grant of Akademie Schloss Solitude, Germany, and in 2000, she established her own collection "MasayoAve creation."

Her design projects, widely ranged from daily objects to architecture, from modern handicraft to mass production, have been developed in a perfect harmony of tradition, advanced technology and her ingenious originality based on her artistic research on the intrinsic potential value of emotion in materials. She has received international acclaim in the field of architecture, garden design, furniture, lighting, textile, and package as well as product design as winner of international competitions. Beside her own collection, she works also as product designer for design companies such as Authentics, DuPont and Industrielle.

Making the most of her decade-long creative experiences in the international field, since 2001 Masayo Ave is also active to lead international design workshop "sound of materials" - a live design workshop based on the sensitivity - for and with young creators, craftsmen as well as the professionals of the various fields in the various countries. Since 2003, she is also nominated as one of the commissioners for ADI International.

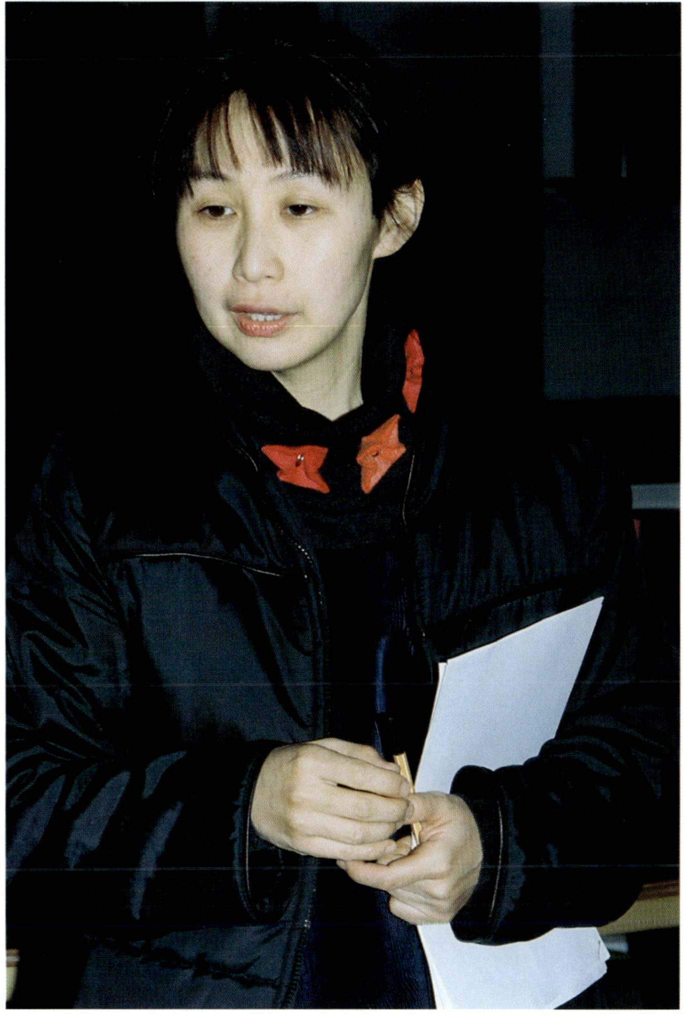

阿部真代
Masayo Ave

"这可能是一个发展方向——在合理的原材料的组成下，
在变化中达到平衡，以满足使用者的需求。"

"It could be a direction – the balance to make a variation out of a good combination of the material to satisfy the user."

马丁·伯格曼
Martin Bergmann
(奥地利/Austria)

生于1963年
Born in 1963

设计公司EOOS创始成员。

马丁·伯格曼于1963年生于奥地利蒂罗尔州的利恩茨。在克谐尔的木材设计和木材管理职业学校完成学业之后，他又在维也纳应用美术学院学习，在1988年到1994年间，他一直在该校的硕士班里学习工业设计。1995年，马丁·贝格曼、Gernot Bohmann和Harald Gründl一起创立了设计公司EOOS，主要关注“旗舰店”、“家具”和“研究”。除了设计家具之外，公司也为一些品牌制造商在理念，或者在当下公司的公共形象方面提供创意。其设计包括奥地利Partner A1/Vodafone的形象设计、德国的阿迪达斯、法国和意大利的Giorgio Armani化妆品，以及德国的沃尔特·科诺。家具和研究领域里的制造商客户包括意大利的阿莱西、德国的杜拉维特和意大利的Matteograssi。此外，马丁·伯格曼和他的EOOS团队已经获得30多个荣誉奖项,其中包括2001和2003年度the Adolf Loos Staatspreis design、2004年的“金罗盘奖”、2004年的iF设计奖，还有2005年伦敦设计周的"设计界闪亮之星 "奖。

Founder member of the design company EOOS.

Martin Bergmann was born in Lienz/East Tyrol in 1963. After completing his education at the Holzkaufmännische Fachschule für Sägewerk und Holzwirtschaft (Vocational School for Wood Design and Wood Management) in Kuchl he studied at the Hochschule für Angewandte Kunst (College for Applied Arts) in Vienna, in the master class for Industrial Design, between 1988 and 1994. In 1995 Martin Bergmann founded, together with Gernot Bohmann and Harald Gründl, the design company EOOS, focusing on the fields "Flagship stores," "Furniture" and "Research." Besides designing furniture, the company also develops, amongst others, concepts for stores of brand manufacturers or ideas for temporary public appearances of companies. Amongst the projects realised are appearances of A1/Vodafone Partner Austria, Adidas Germany, Giorgio Armani Cosmetics France/Italy, and Walter Knoll Germany. Clients in the field Furniture and Research include manufacturers such as Alessi Italy, Duravit Germany, or Matteograssi Italy. Martin Bergmann and his group EOOS have already received more than 30 outstanding awards, amongst them the Adolf Loos Staatspreis Design, 2001 and 2003, the Compasso d'Oro, 2004, the iF design award, 2004, and most recently the award "The Brightest Light in Design" at the Design Week Awards in London, 2005.

马丁·伯格曼
Martin Bergmann

“这个世界需要的产品是可以促使人们说，‘这就是我要拥有的，这才是我想要的’——是‘必备品’。”

"The working world needs products that prompt people to say, 'this is what I´ve got to have, this is what I want to have' – the 'must-have´s'."

马汀・克莱森
Mårten Claesson
(瑞典/Sweden)

生于1970年
Born in 1970

建筑师和设计师。
瑞典设计公司克莱森・卡依威图・茹恩的主要合伙人。

马汀・克莱森于1970年生于瑞典的利丁粤。他先后在斯德哥尔摩的瓦萨技术大学的建筑工程学院和纽约的帕森斯设计学院的建筑和产品设计系学习，1994年他毕业于斯德哥尔摩工业艺术与技术学院并获得MFA学位。

1995年，克莱森・卡依威图・茹恩建筑工作室成立了，它吸收了传统的斯堪的纳维亚国家的多学科齐头并进的风格，也就是说他们不仅涉猎建筑，而且涵盖了设计。他们完成的项目包括最近在日本京都新开的Sfera建筑文化馆、柏林的瑞典大使馆、Ingegerd Raman house和工作室、Kjell A.Nordstrom住宅、索尼音像的斯德哥尔摩总部、快乐云朵饭店、古姿斯德哥尔摩、路易斯威登斯德哥尔摩、斯堪的纳维亚航空公司国际零售业展览会、还有横滨松坂屋店等建筑。

目前，他们的工程主要包括几家瑞典的私人住宅。由马汀・克莱森，艾罗・科伊维斯托和欧拉・朗设计的家具主要是由瑞典爱美达公司、横滨松坂屋店、意大利的博非公司、卡佩里尼公司、大卫设计、沙丘、E et Y、日本Franc franc、Iren Uffici、Living Divani、诺拉、Offecct、Stera Products、Skandiform 和Swedese 等公司生产。

马汀・克莱森是一位自由撰稿人，也是建筑和设计领域的讲师。他曾经获得多项大奖，其中包括1994年的Forsnaspriset奖、1998瑞典设计新人奖，并多次获得最佳瑞典设计奖。

Architect and Designer.
Co-founder of the Swedish design partnership Claesson Koivisto Rune.

Mårten Claesson was born in 1970 in Lidingö, Sweden. After studying at the Vasa Technical College in Stockholm (in the department of Construction Engineering) and at the Parsons School of Design in New York (in the departments of Architecture and Product Design), he graduated in 1994 with an MFA degree from Konstfack, the University College of Arts, Crafts and Design in Stockholm.

In 1995, the Swedish design partnership Claesson Koivisto Rune was founded as an architectural office but is, in the classic Scandinavian way multi-disciplinary, which means that they practise both architecture and design. On the list of completed architectural projects are: the recently opened Sfera Building culture house in Kyoto, the Swedish Ambassador's residence in Berlin, Ingegerd Råman house and studio, Kjell A. Nordström residence, Sony Music headquarters Stockholm, One Happy Cloud restaurant, Gucci Stockholm, Louis Vuitton Stockholm, Scandinavian Airlines Euroshop, and Asplund shop.

Current projects include several private houses in Sweden. Furniture designs by Mårten Claesson, Eero Koivisto and Ola Rune are produced by companies such as Almedahls, Asplund, Boffi, Cappellini, David design, Dune, E & Y, Franc franc, Iren Uffici, Living Divani, Nola, Offecct, Sfera Products, Skandiform, and Swedese, among others.

Mårten Claesson is also a freelance writer and lecturer in the field of architecture and design. He has obtained numerous awards; among them are Forsnäspriset 1994, Young Swedish Design 1998, and several times the award Excellent Swedish Design.

马汀・克莱森
Mårten Claesson

"我认为，作为一名设计师：
永远要做自己，永远不能思想保守！"

*"From my point of view as a designer:
always be yourself and always be open-minded."*

毕勇·达尔斯特姆
Björn Dahlström
(瑞典/Sweden)

生于1957年
Born 1957

平面、工业和产品设计师
瑞典工业设计师协会成员

毕勇·达尔斯特姆，1957年生于斯德哥尔摩，他的职业生涯始于二十世纪七十年代中期，为电影和电视作品进行平面和动画设计，之后他在PR事务所做布景师。1982年他成立了自己的公司，主要为客户做平面设计，他的客户包括爱立信、斯堪尼亚和阿特拉斯·科普柯。二十世纪九十年代起，他开始和其它公司一样在家具领域里为CBI公司成功地进行了项目开发。从那个时候开始，他就越来越注重产品设计。可以说，今天的创造有80%都取材于这个部分。除了建筑行业上的客户，比利时的阿特拉斯·科普柯公司、玩具业的公司Aquaplay and Playsam或者是自行车制造商Skeppshult都是他的客户。从1999年到2001年期间，他在斯德哥尔摩的艺术、手工艺和设计大学做教授。此外，他也在Beckmans设计学院讲学。毕勇·达尔斯特姆凭借他的作品参加过无数次工业展览会和艺术展览会。他设计的产品还获得了多种奖项，其中包括iF设计奖，其中在1991到1998年期间还12次获得了瑞典最佳设计奖。今天，他的一部分作品已经被收藏在哥德堡的卢斯卡博物馆和伦敦的维多利亚艾明达博物馆。另外，他还是瑞典工业设计协会（SID）的会员。

Graphic, Industrial and Product Designer.
Member of the Society of Swedish Industrial Designers.

Björn Dahlström, born 1957 in Stockholm, started his professional career in the mid-1970's with graphics and animations for film and TV productions. After working as an art director for a PR agency he founded his own business in 1982, focusing on graphic design for clients such as Ericsson, Scania, or Atlas Copco. In the 1990's he started the successful development of projects in the field of furniture, amongst others for Consultants & Builders, Inc. (CBI). Since then, he focused more and more on product design. Ca. 80 percent of his creations originate from this sector today. Besides clients from the building and construction industry such as Atlas Copco, companies in the toys segment such as Aquaplay and Playsam or bike manufacturers such as Skeppshult are amongst his customers. From 1999 to 2001 he held a chair as professor at the University of Arts, Crafts and Design in Stockholm. In addition, he taught at Beckmans School of Design. With his works Björn Dahlström was present at numerous trade shows and exhibitions. His designs received several awards, amongst others the iF design award and twelve times the Excellent Swedish Design Award between 1991 and 1998. Today his works are part of the collections of the Rööhska Museet in Göteborg as well as the Victoria and Albert Museum in London. Dahlström is a member of the Society of Swedish Industrial Designers (SID).

毕勇·达尔斯特姆
Björn Dahlström

“对顾客的尊重对于设计质量是至关重要的一个因素。
一定要时刻把消费者放在心上。”

*“Respect is an important matter regarding quality of design.
Always keep the user aspects in mind.”*

约西姆·H.浮士德
Joachim H. Faust
(德国/Germany)

生于1954年
Born in 1954

德国杜塞尔多夫的HPP公司高级合伙人和高层管理团队主要成员
约西姆·H.浮士德，生于1954年，在柏林技术大学和亚琛技术大学学习建筑，师从Böhm教授并取得了学位。同期在德意志学术交流中心(DAAD)获得奖学金。而后他跟随美国建筑师协会的E. J. Romieniec教授学习，并于1981年取得了德克萨斯A&M大学的建筑学硕士学位。约西姆·H.浮士德在美国德克萨斯州休斯敦的SOM设计所的设计部门担任建筑师，并且在美茵茨的Faust咨询建筑工作室担任项目建筑师。1984年到1986年期间，他一直在为纽约的KPF集团工作，并且在纽约的SOM设计所办事处做项目建筑师。1987年他开始经营梅恩的法兰克福HPP办事处。1997年他成为了杜塞尔多夫的HPP公司的大股东和综合管理主要成员。约西姆·H.浮士德在许多专业期刊杂志上发表了许多文章，并在建筑和室内设计方面进行了很多的讲演。2002年，他获得了德克萨斯A&M大学的杰出校友奖，并且他还是德国城乡规划学院DASL的资助人。

Senior partner and member of the general management of HPP Hentrich-Petschnigg & Partner KG in Düsseldorf.
Joachim H. Faust, born in 1954, studied architecture at the Technical University of Berlin and the Technical University of Aachen. He took his degree under Prof. Böhm and received a scholarship from the Deutscher Akademischer Austausch Dienst (DAAD). He then studied with Prof. E. J. Romieniec, FAIA, USA, receiving his Master of Architecture degree from Texas A&M University 1981. Joachim H. Faust worked as an architect in the design department of Skidmore, Owings & Merrill in Houston, Texas, and as a project architect in the architectural studio of Faust Consult GmbH in Mainz. 1984 to 1986 he has also worked for KPF Kohn, Pedersen, Fox/Eggers Group in New York and as a project architect at the Skidmore, Owings & Merrill office in New York. In 1987, he managed the HPP office in Frankfurt/Main. In 1997 he became a senior partner and member of the general management of HPP Hentrich-Petschnigg & Partner KG in Düsseldorf. Joachim H. Faust has published many articles in professional journals and lectures on topics of architecture and interior design. In 2002 he received the Distinguished Alumni Award from Texas A&M University. He is a sponsoring member of the German academy for town and country planning DASL.

约西姆·H.浮士德
Joachim H. Faust

"今天，设计变得越来越吸引人，通过外形和颜色的变化，设计让日常用品显得不再那么普通。但是，只有在材料和技术都具备直观操作性，而且设计出来的产品真正地迎合了人们内心需求的时候，创新才得以实现。"

"Today, design lifts everyday objects with form and colours out of the ordinary in a provocative manner. However, innovation takes place only when material and technology enable intuitive operation, and when the products appeal to the soul of man."

路易吉 ·发拉拉
Luigi Ferrara

“在当前的设计中，最重要的事情就是把设计看成是一个不断发展的过程。甚至家具的线条和各个组成部分都可以用一种全新的方式来重新塑造。”

“The most critical thing in design at this moment is to think of design as an evolutionary process. Even lines and elements of furniture can build upon themselves over time in an evolutionary way.”

路易吉 ·发拉拉
Luigi Ferrara
(加拿大/Canada)

生于 1961年
Born in 1961

多伦多乔治布朗大学设计学院主任
建筑文学论坛主席

路易吉·发拉拉于1985年在多伦多大学获得建筑学学士学位，并以优异的成绩从该校毕业，在校期间他还荣获诸多奖励、奖学金和研究基金。刚一毕业，他就进入国内和国际的建筑公司工作。1989年，他成立了FerCon Architect建筑工作室。

目前，路易吉·发拉拉是多伦多乔治布朗大学设计学院的主任，也是建筑文学论坛的主席。这个论坛是非盈利性组织，是以经营艺术、建筑、设计和数字媒体为主的机构。他是加拿大工业设计师协会的会员。此外，他还担任加拿大设计中心、设计交流处的副院长，也是负责宽带网络设计的DXNe的院长。此外，发拉拉还是安大略省建筑协会和加拿大皇家建筑研究院的成员。2003年以来，他一直是国际工业设计协会 (ICSID)的主席。

多年来，他组织和设计的展览有很多，包括了多伦多大学、建筑学院、the Joseph D. Carrier画廊、安大略遗产基金会、渥太华城市广场、建筑文学论坛、设计交流等。同时，路易吉·发拉拉身兼多职，是国际公认的作家、讲师、发言人。他在设计和设计管理、建筑和城市规划、信息技术、电信和网络协会方面都有很深的造诣。

Director of the School of Design at George Brown College in Toronto
and Chairman of the Architectural Literacy Forum.

Luigi Ferrara obtained a Bachelor of Architecture degree from the University of Toronto in 1985. He graduated with honours and distinction and received a number of prizes, scholarships and fellowships during his tenure at the school. Upon graduation, he was employed by both national and international architectural firms. In 1989, he founded the architectural office of FerCon Architects Inc.

Luigi Ferrara is currently the Director of the School of Design at George Brown College in Toronto and the Chairman of the Architectural Literacy Forum, a non-profit organisation which operates the Realtime Centre for Art, Architecture, Design and Digital Media. He is also a member of the Board of the Association of Canadian Industrial Designers, and he was Vice President of Design Exchange, Canada's centre for design, and President of the DXNet, a broadband network for design. Ferrara is a member of the Ontario Association of Architects and the Royal Architectural Institute of Canada. Since 2003, he has been President of the International Council of Societies of Industrial Design (ICSID).

Over the years, he has curated and designed exhibitions for the University of Toronto, Faculty of Architecture, the Joseph D. Carrier Gallery, the Ontario Heritage Foundation, Ottawa City Hall, the Architectural Literacy Forum, and Design Exchange. Luigi Ferrara is an internationally recognised author, lecturer and speaker on design and design management, architecture and urban planning, information technology, telecommunications and the network society.

安德里亚·芬克–安劳夫
Andrea Finke-Anlauff
(德国/Germany)

生于 1966年
Born in 1966

不伦瑞克的Mango设计和芒果艺术品的创立者和经理

安德里亚·芬克–安劳夫于1966年出生在不伦瑞克。1992年毕业于不伦瑞克的不伦瑞克造型艺术学院，专业是工业设计师。然后她继续出国深造，在巴塞罗那大学(Facultat de Belles Arts)学习和赫尔辛基的工业艺术大学学习(研究生课程“设计领先”硕士学位)。当她还是个学生的时候，就已经在芬兰和日本的诺基亚移动电话营销部门实习，积累了她人生的第一个工作经验。1992她在做自由职业者的同时，也在诺基亚移动电话咨询部门工作。

1994年，安德里亚·芬克–安劳夫在不伦瑞克创立了自己的Mango设计工作室。迄今为止，她一直在用心经营着。这个工作室主要涉猎的项目有：界面设计、产品设计、3D视觉效果和一些培训的课程。最近几年来，她一直在和诺基亚图形设计师合作，有规律地开展一些研讨会和培训课程。

Mango设计所完成的项目有：用户界面、显示字形、头像和动画、UI随机模拟、移动电话、耳机、扬声器、遥控器、电子管家、儿童电话、移动展览系统等。

2003年，她紧接着成立了Mango艺术品设计工作室，这个工作室是用来生产和销售她自己的产品的。

Mango设计凭借它优秀的作品获得了多项大奖，其中包括红点奖、红点：智慧设计奖、iF奖和iF银奖。

安德里亚·芬克–安劳夫
Andrea Finke-Anlauff

“对于设计师来说，这个时期是令人兴奋的，因为它告诉我们怎么样才能更好地去定位产品。”

“These are exciting times for designers, answering the question how to formally position things.”

Founder and manager of Mango Design
and of Mango Objects in Braunschweig.

Andrea Finke-Anlauff was born in Braunschweig in 1966. In 1992, she graduated as industrial designer from the Hochschule für Bildende Künste in Braunschweig, after she had also studied abroad at the Universidad de Barcelona (Facultat de Belles Arts) and at the University of Industrial Arts in Helsinki (graduate course “MA in Design Leadership”). While still being a student, she gained first work experiences e.g. in the marketing department of Nokia Mobile Phones in Finland and Japan. Since 1992 she is self-employed, and since then is also working under a consultancy contract with Nokia Mobile Phones.

In 1994, Andrea Finke-Anlauff founded the Studio Mango Design in Braunschweig. She has been managing it until today, putting an emphasis on interface design, product design, 3D visualisation and the conduct of training courses. In recent years, for instance, workshops and training courses have been given on a regular basis in co-operation with graphic designers from Nokia.

Among the projects realised by Mango Design are, e.g., user interfaces, display fonts, icons and animations, UI simulations, mobile phones, headphones, loudspeakers, universal remote controls, an electronic butler, baby phones, and mobile exhibition systems.

In 2003, the foundation of Mango Design Objects followed, a company intended to produce and distribute its own products.

Mango Design received important awards for its works, among them are red dot, red dot: intelligent design, iF award, and iF silver award.

深泽直人
Naoto Fukasawa
(日本/Japan)

生于 1956年
Born in 1956

东京深泽直人设计的拥有者，
“±0”品牌的创始人。

深泽直人于1956年生于日本的山梨县。1980年毕业于著名的多摩艺术学院产品设计系。在1980年到1988年期间，深泽直人在精工爱普生公司做设计师。1989年，他转到美国加入了ID Two（IDEO公司的前身）。1996年，深泽直人回到日本，创立了IDEO东京办事处。2003年一月，他单枪匹马地开创了深泽直人设计工作室，但作为IDEO的成员，他仍然和IDEO保持着联系。同年，他创立了一个新的品牌“±0”(加减零)，主要介绍他自己设计的电子产品和室内装饰品。深泽直人的设计已经获得了40多个著名奖项，其中包括在日本很著名的“Mainichi设计奖”。深泽直人现在是东京武藏野美术大学和日本多摩艺术学院的教授。他还是MUJI质量设计顾问团的成员。

Owner of Naoto Fukasawa Design in Tokyo
and founder of the new brand "±0".

Naoto Fukasawa was born in the Yamanashi prefecture, Japan, in 1956. He graduated from the Tama Art University's Product Design Department in 1980. From 1980 to 1988, Fukasawa worked as a designer at Seiko Epson Corp. In 1989, he travelled to the United States, where he joined ID Two, the predecessor to IDEO. In 1996, Fukasawa returned to Japan and set up the IDEO Tokyo office. In January 2003, he went independent and established Naoto Fukasawa Design, while maintaining his ties with IDEO as an IDEO Fellow. In the same year, he has founded a new brand "±0" (plusminuszero) introducing his design of the electrical appliances and interior accessories. Fukasawa's designs have won more than 40 renowned design awards such as the prestigious Japanese "Mainichi Design Award." Currently, Fukasawa is professor at the Musashino Art University and Tama Art University in Tokyo. He is also a member of the MUJI advisory board for quality design.

深泽直人
Naoto Fukasawa

“红点设计奖是高层次的设计大赛，它所推崇的不是那种只停留在情感和感官上的漂亮设计。在设计趋同化的潮流中，评委们所关注地并不是所谓的流行趋势，也不是个性，而是融入到我们日常生活中的产品外形，能否与我们的生活完美和谐的融为一体。”

"The red dot design award is a top-ranking design competition that brings into question the quality of emotional, intuitive, beautiful designs. From a trend towards similar featured designs, what judges were concentrating on wasn't trends or pronounced individuality but shapes that melted into everyday life, achieving harmony and balance with it."

肯尼斯·格兰奇
Kenneth Grange
(英国/Great Britain)

生于1929年
Born in 1929

肯尼斯·格兰奇设计有限责任公司的创始人。
五角设计的创立者和长期合作伙伴。

肯尼斯·格兰奇于1929年出生在英国伦敦。早先在Willesden艺术和工艺学校学习。他先是做了几年的建筑助手，而后他又和皇家工程师一起工作，担任工程制图师。

1958年，他成立了肯尼斯·格兰奇设计有限责任公司。1972年到1999年，他与人合伙建立了五角设计。格兰奇的专业是产品设计和公司形象。他所完成的工程包括：国家特快列车、柯达傻瓜相机、威尔金森剃须刀以及派克自来水笔等。不仅如此，他还为很多日本顾客设计过许多产品，为建伍公司设计了100多种产品，还负责设计了最后一台伦敦出租车。

此外，肯尼斯·格兰奇还获得了多项大奖，其中包括爱丁堡伯爵奖的最佳设计、设计委员会奖、工业皇家设计师。此外，他还荣获皇家艺术学院(1985年)和德蒙特福特大学(1998年)的名誉博士学位、飞利浦王子设计师奖(2001年)。1984年，肯尼斯·格兰奇被授予不列颠帝国勋爵士勋章。

Founder of Kenneth Grange Design Ltd.
Co-founder and long-standing partner of Pentagram.

Kenneth Grange was born in London in 1929. After his education at the Willesden School of Arts and Crafts, he worked as an engineering draughtsman with the Royal Engineers, followed by working as an architectural assistant for a number of years.

In 1958, he founded Kenneth Grange Design Ltd. He was a co-founder and partner of Pentagram from 1972 to 1999. Grange specialises in product design and corporate identity. Among his projects are for example the National High Speed Train, the Kodak Instamatic Camera, Wilkinson shavers and Parker fountain pens. On top of that, there have been many jobs for Japanese customers, more than 100 products for Kenwood and the design of the last London taxi.

Kenneth Grange has received a number of important awards, among which are the Duke of Edinburgh's Prize for Elegant Design, the Design Council Award and the Master of Faculty of Royal Designers for Industry.

Among others, he obtained honorary doctorates from the Royal College of Art (1985), DeMontfort University (1998) and through the Prince Philip Designers' Prize (2001). In 1984, Kenneth Grange was appointed Commander of the British Empire.

肯尼斯·格兰奇
Kenneth Grange

"设计奖在当今社会占有很重要的地位。
它们就好比是生活的一部分。"

*"The design awards have an important position in society today.
They are like a slice of life."*

弗莱明・汉森
Flemming Bo Hansen
(丹麦/Denmark)

生于1955年
Born in 1955

金匠和设计师。
弗莱明・汉森，1955年生于哥本哈根。1979年，从他在哥本哈根的Georg Jensen当一名金匠学徒的那一刻起，他的职业生涯就开始了。1983年毕业后他直接到该公司在纽约和东京的分部去实习。当他再次回到哥本哈根的时候，他本人已经具备做艾伦・夏银匠教员的资格。而后，他又继续在丹麦珠宝银匠学院进行深造。1988年,他成立了自己的工作室。从1991年到1995年，他是Eleven Danes design A/S的合伙人，并在1993年到1995年和金匠Vagn Drachmann一起经营一个精品店。1995年到1997年间，他一直在丹麦设计学院担任导师和教授。弗莱明・汉森出席了不计其数的展览，其中包括巴黎的装饰艺术博物馆，汉堡的艺术及手工艺博物馆，俄国圣彼得堡的“Mikhailovsky Manege”展览中心，还有最近在2004年，哥本哈根的Danske Kunstindustri博物馆。除此之外，许多著名的博物馆还把他的作品列入永久收藏的范围。其中包括柏林的工艺美术博物馆、国立普鲁士古典艺术博物馆、日内瓦的the Musée d'Emaillerie et de l'Horlogerie、纽约的现代艺术博物馆、慕尼黑Die Neue Sammlung、慕尼黑应用艺术博物馆。此外，弗莱明・汉森还获得了多个奖项，赢得了公众的认可。例如：1989年纽约Accent奖、1990年哥本哈根的the Sankt Loye奖，还有近期2004的日本年度优秀设计奖。

Goldsmith and Designer.
Flemming Bo Hansen was born in Copenhagen in 1955. He started his professional career in 1979 when he began an apprenticeship as goldsmith at Georg Jensen in Copenhagen, graduating in 1983 and subsequently working in the company's branch offices in New York and Tokyo. Back in Copenhagen he qualified for the educational position of silver smith at Allan Scharff and later continued his studies at the Danish College of Jewellery and Silversmithing. Finally, in 1988, he opened up his own studio. From 1991 to 1995 he was partner of Eleven Danes Design A/S and the goldsmith Vagn Drachmann with whom he ran a boutique between 1993 and 1995. From 1995 to 1997 he was active as tutor and instructor at Danmarks Designskole. Flemming Bo Hansen was present at numerous exhibitions, such as those in the Musée des Arts Décoratifs, Paris, in the Museum für Kunst und Gewerbe, Hamburg, in the Manege, Saint Petersburg, or most recently, in 2004, in the Danske Kunstindustrimuseum in Copenhagen. In addition, some of his works have been adopted to permanent collections of renown museums such as the Kunstgewerbemuseum Berlin, Staatliche Museen Preußischer Kulturbesitz, the Musée d'Emaillerie et de l'Horlogerie in Geneva, the Museum of Modern Art, New York, and Die Neue Sammlung, Staatliches Museum für angewandte Kunst, Munich. Flemming Bo Hansen also received public recognition for numerous design awards such as the Accent Award, New York 1989, the Sankt Loye Award, Copenhagen 1990, and most recently the Good Design Award, Japan 2004.

弗莱明・汉森
Flemming Bo Hansen

“很多东西都有这样的趋势：
以一种独有的前瞻方式把已经过去的东西再次带入流行中。”

*“This is probably a trend in lots of things:
it is now looking backwards to bring things forward again
– in its own way a way of looking forward.”*

塔帕尼・海万恩
Tapani Hyvönen
(芬兰/Finland)

生于1947年
Born in 1947

芬兰特库ED设计有限公司创始人和总经理
塔帕尼・海万恩，1947年出生，芬兰人。1974年，塔帕尼・海万恩毕业于赫尔辛基的艺术设计大学工业设计专业。他于1973年在Salora Oy开始了自己的专业设计生涯，并创立了自己的设计公司。1976年创立了代斯特姆有限责任公司。1990年，他在芬兰特库与人联合创立了ED-设计有限责任公司。如今，海万恩本人已经是这家公司的总经理，也是北欧国家中最大的产品设计公司之一。

塔帕尼・ 海万恩在芬兰曾经荣获过多个大奖：1981年芬兰艺术委员会年度基金、1984年芬兰艺术委员会国家艺术设计奖、1991年度TKO工业设计师奖、1992年 Buscom有限责任公司的Pro芬兰设计奖。他还为芬兰电子工业公司包括Finlux、诺基亚、Polar电子这样的大公司做产品设计。

塔帕尼・海万恩曾经多次担任要职：1989-2000年赫尔辛基艺术和设计大学的设计领先项目顾问委员会成员；1998-2002年芬兰设计论坛协会会员；1999-2003年ICSID（工业设计协会国际委员会）理事会理事；从2003年起芬兰瑞典设计学院成员。他还曾经多次在国际和芬兰的一些设计比赛中担任评委，例如：1992年芬兰设计管理奖、1999年和2001年Pro芬兰设计奖、2003年Fennia奖、2003年印度NID商业世界设计最佳奖、2003年日本大阪设计竞赛、2003年奥地利阿道夫・路斯国家设计奖、2000年、2003年和2004年德国红点设计奖。

Managing director of ED-Design Ltd in Turku, Finland.
Born 1947, Finland, Tapani Hyvönen graduated as industrial designer from the University of Art and Design Helsinki UIAH in 1974. He started his professional career in Salora Oy in 1973 and founded his own design agency, Destem Ltd, in 1976. In 1990, he was co-founder on establishing the company ED-Design Ltd in Turku, Finland. Today ED-Design Ltd, which Hyvönen runs as a managing director, is one of the biggest product design agencies in Nordic countries.
Hyvönen has been honoured with several awards in Finland: Finnish Arts Council, one-year grant 1981; Finnish Arts Council, The National Art & Design Award 1984; Industrial Designers TKO, The Industrial Designer of the Year 1991; Pro Finnish Design for Buscom Ltd 1992. He has made his major professional work for Finnish electronic industry including Finlux, Nokia, and Polar Electro.
Hyvönen has had several confidential posts: Design Leadership Program in University of Art and Design Helsinki UIAH, member of the Advisory Board 1989-2000; Design Forum Finland, member of the council 1998-2002; ICSID, International Council of Societies of Industrial Design, member of the Executive Board 1999-2003; Finnish Swedish Design Academy, member from 2003. He has also acted as a jury member in several Finnish and international design competitions: Finnish Design Management Award 1992; Pro Finnish Design Award 1999, 2001; Fennia Prize 2003; NID Business World Design Excellence Award, India, 2003; Osaka Design Competition, Japan, 2003; Adolf Loos Staatspreis Design, Austria, 2003; red dot design award, Germany, 2000, 2002, 2003, and 2004.

塔帕尼・海万恩
Tapani Hyvönen

“如果产品变得更加复杂的话，比如把照相机和电话结合到一起，那么设计必须能够迎合这种新功能。”

“When the product turns more complex, such as combining a camera with a telephone, the design should correspond with this new function.”

金哲昊
Chul-ho Kim
(韩国/Korea)

韩国工业设计促进研究所所长和首席执行官。
1974年，金哲昊博士毕业于韩国弘益大学并取得工业设计专业的BFA，他还曾在韩国汉阳大学深造过。2002年获得日本千叶大学的工程学、工业设计的博士学位。金哲昊以他多年丰富的设计经验，在很多设计公司担任过设计师：1974年到2003年间，他是LG电气公司设计中心的副执行总裁。1998年到2000年，他担任韩国工业设计师协会(KAID)的主席。2001年，金哲昊负责协助工业设计协会(ICSID)的国际组织委员会的工作。现在，他是韩国设计发展所(KIDP)的代理总裁和首席执行官，同时也是首尔设计论坛的成员。他的作品经常在韩国工业设计展览上展出，已经获得了无数的奖项，例如韩国工业成就银奖、韩国设计品牌大奖等。

President and CEO of the Korea Institute of Design Promotion.
In 1974 Dr. Chul-ho Kim graduated from Hongik University in Korea with a BFA in Industrial Design. In addition, he further studied at the Hanyang University in Korea, and in 2002 he attained the title of Doctor of Engineering, Industrial Design, at the Chiba University in Japan. Chul-ho Kim incorporated his long-time experience as designer into different design organisations: from 1974 to 2003 he was Executive Vice-President of the LG Electronics Corporate Design Center, and from 1998 to 2000 he held the position of President of the Korea Association of Industrial Designers (KAID). In 2001 Kim supported the organisation committee of the International Council of Societies of Industrial Design (ICSID); today he is Acting President and CEO of the Korea Institute of Design Promotion (KIDP) as well as member of the Seoul Design Forum. His works, regularly on display at the Korean Industrial Design Exhibition, have received numerous awards, amongst others the Silver Order of Industrial Achievement, Korea, and the Grand Prize of the Korea Design & Brand Award.

金哲昊
Chul-ho Kim

“评委们所关注的是人们怎么才能通过这些产品来体验一种新的生活——这些产品是人们可以直接感受到的，并且可以把它们融入到自己生活中的产品。”

"The jury was focussing on how people can have a new lifestyle with these products – products people can experience firsthand and integrate into their lifestyles."

奥杜・克洛斯
Odo Klose
(德国/Germany)

生于1942年
Born in 1942

奥杜・克洛斯教授及其合伙人和能力中心（CC254）总经理

奥杜・克洛斯教授在慕尼黑科技大学学习机械工程和技术形态学专业，毕业后在西门子公司担任设计师。他在德国伍伯塔尔大学和台湾大叶大学担任工业设计专业的讲师。

他的设计工作室主要从事座椅、交通工具、医疗技术、机械工具、管道装置等方面的设计工作。他的研究方向针对工具和用户界面的人机工程学设计，设备的美学优化设计及科技生态等领域。

此外，奥杜・克洛斯教授还出版了多部作品，并在杂志上发表过多篇文章。

Managing director of Prof. Odo Klose & Partner and Competence Center CC254.

Professor Odo Klose studied mechanical engineering and technical morphology at the Technical University of Munich, and then worked as a designer for Siemens AG. As a lecturer in industrial design, he taught at the Bergische Universität in Wuppertal and the DAYEH University in Taiwan.

His activities in the design studio focus on seating, vehicles, medical technology, machine tools and plumbing. His research is aimed at the ergonomic design of tools and user interfaces, the aesthetic optimisation of equipment and technical morphology.

Prof. Odo Klose is the author of several books and numerous magazine articles.

奥杜・克洛斯
Odo Klose

"在产品设计中，事物的语义逐渐成为其自身的品质特色，而正是语义体现了事物复杂的重要性。"

"In product design, the semantics of things become increasingly a quality feature. Semantics as complex significance of things."

安妮特・朗
Annette Lang
(德国/Germany)

生于1960年
Born in 1960

在威斯巴登经营自己的设计工作室。

安妮特・朗，生于1960年，在斯图加特艺术学院学习工业设计专业。毕业后她来到米兰，1985年到1988年间，她是一位自由职业者，在马蒂奥・瑟恩、安东尼奥・奇特里奥和索特萨思公司从事设计工作。

1988年到1993年期间，她担任斯图加特艺术学院理查德・沙伯教授的助理，1988年她在威斯巴登创建了自己的设计工作室。

她主要从事家居用品、桌子、办公室、家具、照明设备、医疗技术等领域内的生活消费品设计与发展工作。安妮特・朗曾多次参加国内及国际举办的作品展览，同时，她设计的作品也获得过多次大奖。从1994年到1999年她在斯图加特艺术学院任教。

Runs her own design studio in Wiesbaden.

Annette Lang, born in 1960, studied industrial design at the Academy of Art in Stuttgart. She then moved to Milan, and worked freelance from 1985 to 1988 for Matteo Thun, Antonio Citterio and Sottsass Associati.
From 1988 to 1993, she was Prof. Richard Sapper's assistant at the Academy of Art in Stuttgart, and has run her own design studio in Wiesbaden since 1988.
Her work focuses on the development and design of consumer goods in the fields of household utensils, tableware, offices, furniture, lighting and medical technology.
Annette Lang has taken part in many national and international exhibitions, and has received numerous awards for her work. She lectured at the Academy of Art in Stuttgart from 1994 to 1999.

安妮特・朗
Annette Lang

"我认为，在任何产品的设计中都忽略了老年人，我们的人口越来越老龄化，我们应该为这一目标群体设计出适合的产品。"

"In my opinion, in every category there is missing design for elderly people. With our population increasingly over-aging, we should design attractive products particularly for this target group."

克瑞斯汀娜·拉萨斯
Kristiina Lassus
(意大利/Italy)

生于1966年
Born in 1966

克瑞斯汀娜·拉萨斯工作室所有者
克瑞斯汀娜·拉萨斯，1966年生于赫尔辛基。1992年毕业于赫尔辛基工业艺术大学（UIAH），并获得设计领导专业硕士学位。而后，她继续在赫尔辛基综合技术学院攻读产品开发专业的硕士学位，并于1995年在赫尔辛基工业艺术大学获得了室内设计及家具设计专业的第二硕士学位。她曾在芬兰和澳大利亚多家著名公司从事室内设计工作。之后，她分别在芬兰的Silva Wetterhoff公司和ArtekOy公司担任生产部经理及设计助理。1988年，克瑞斯汀娜·拉萨斯来到意大利的阿莱西公司担任设计部经理，并在那儿一直工作到2004年。1993年她成立了自己的第一家公司"D'Imago"，并于2003年在意大利开办了自己的第一个设计工作室——克瑞斯汀娜·拉萨斯工作室。拉萨斯的作品曾多次在各种展览会展出，其中包括2000年的赫尔辛基设计论坛和2001年米兰三年展，并在冰岛Gardaboer的应用艺术与设计博物馆及意大利甘都城的Galleria del Design e dell'Arredamento进行长期展出。她曾被"金罗盘"奖提名并荣获了"设计师荣誉"大奖，并因她的设计理念获得"公正对待自然环境奖"（铜奖）。另外，"设计21世纪"和"设计和未来设计名人录"等多家商业报刊曾刊登过她的作品。克瑞斯提那·拉萨斯因其专业的学识成为深受欢迎的评委，并在阿莱西公司担任总负责人。

Owner of Kristiina Lassus Studio.
Born in Helsinki in 1966, Kristiina Lassus graduated from the University of Industrial Arts of Helsinki (UIAH) with an MA in Design Leadership in 1992. She continued with postgraduate studies in product development at the Helsinki Polytechnic, graduating with a second MA in Interior Architecture and Furniture Design at the UIAH in 1995. After working in several well-known agencies for interior design in Finland and Australia, Lassus worked as product manager for Silva Wetterhoff as well as design coordinator for Artek Oy, both Finland, before changing to Alessi, Italy, as design manager in 1998. She held this position until 2004. In 1993 she founded her first company, "D'Imago," and in 2003 her first design studio "Kristiina Lassus Studio" in Italy. Lassus' works could be seen, not just at various exhibitions such as the Design Forum Helsinki, 2000, or at the Triennale in Milan, 2001; they can also be found in permanent collections of the Museum of Design and Applied Art in Gardabœr, Iceland, as well as in the Galleria del Design e dell'Arredamento in Cantù, Italy. She was nominated for the Compasso d'Oro and awarded with the Design Plus Award and the Fair to Nature Environmental Prize (bronze) for her design concepts. In addition, her works are documented in various trade journals such as Designing the 21st Century, Who's Who in Design or Furniture Design. Kristiina Lassus passes on her expert knowledge as a sought-after jury member and head of design workshops for Alessi.

克瑞斯汀娜·拉萨斯
Kristiina Lassus

"设计有一项重要的任务：即解决问题，
找到最佳解决方案，节约并给生活增加价值。
新产品的开发需要在这些方面'找到感觉'。"

"Design has an important task: to resolve problems, to offer better solutions, to save and add value to our lives. Development of a new product should always 'make sense' in these terms."

斯坦梵·伦吉尔
Stefan Lengyel

"现今，电子产品已不在以特殊的结构和外观吸引人们的眼球，人们更趋向于返璞归真。"

"Nowadays, electronics as such does not have any particular form or appearance. Thus, people resort to archaic things."

斯坦梵·伦吉尔
Stefan Lengyel
(德国/Germany)

生于1937年
Born in 1937

德国设计委员会执行董事成员和
德国设计协会（北威设计中心）管理委员会成员。
自由设计师。

斯坦梵·伦吉尔教授，1937年生于布达佩斯，从1981年至2003年在埃森大学工业设计专业担任全职教授。并于2002年在布达佩斯艺术与设计大学的工业设计专业担任教授。从1986年到2000年间，在德国工业设计师协会（VDID）担任会长，并从2000年起担任其荣誉会长。

他毕业于布达佩斯工业设计学院。1964年在乌尔姆造型学院担任研究助理，继续着他的学术生涯。1969年他开始在埃森的福克旺学校工作，并担任工业设计系的院长。他还曾在在美国、芬兰、意大利、匈牙利、西班牙和日本等国家进行学术交流、学术座谈与研讨。同时，斯坦梵·伦吉尔作为自由设计师还从事设计工作，并荣获过很多奖项。

他还是德国设计委员会执行董事成员和德国设计协会（德国北威设计中心）管理委员会成员。

Member of the Executive Board of the German Design Council
and of the Governing Board of the Design Zentrum Nordrhein Westfalen.
Works as a freelance designer.

Professor Stefan Lengyel, born in Budapest in 1937, was a full professor for industrial design at Essen University from 1981 to 2003. Since 2002, he has had a professorship of industrial design at the Budapest University of Art and Design. From 1986 to 2000, he was President of the Association of German Industrial Designers (VDID), and since 2000, he has been their Honorary President.

He is a graduate of the Academy of Industrial Design in Budapest. In 1964, he continued his academic career as a research assistant at the Design Academy in Ulm. In 1969, he started working at the Folkwang School in Essen, where he was head of the industrial design department. Visiting professorships, lecture tours and workshops have taken him to the USA, Finland, Italy, Hungary, Spain, and Japan. Stefan Lengyel also works as a freelance designer, and has received numerous awards.

He is a member of the Executive Board of the German Design Council and a member of the Governing Board of the Design Zentrum Nordrhein Westfalen.

沃弗岗・K・梅尔–亥兹
Wolfgang K. Meyer-Hayoz
(瑞士/Switzerland)

生于1947年
Born in 1947

梅尔–亥兹设计工程团队的创始人。
设计师及顾问，并担任圣加仑大学的客座讲师。
专题研讨会的发言人和国际设计评委会的评委。

沃弗岗・K・梅尔–亥兹，生于1947年，毕业于斯图加特国家美术学院的机械工程、视觉通讯及工业设计专业。他现今的设计理念深受克劳斯・雷曼教授、科特・威德曼教授、哈特姆特・西格教授和马克斯・本泽教授的设计观点影响。

1985年，他同时在瑞士（温特图尔）和德国（康斯坦茨）成立了梅尔–亥兹设计工程小组。该公司为处在起步阶段的、中小型企业及全球的市场的领先者提供多方面的咨询服务，其中包括品牌策略、创新发展、设计规划、工业设计、用户界面设计、临时建筑设计、通讯设计及新媒体等。

1987年，沃弗岗・K・梅尔–亥兹成为瑞士工业设计协会的会长（SID），并在这个令人尊敬的职位上一直工作到1993年。同时，他还是德国工业设计师协会（VDID）成员和职业人机工程学及安全性国际团体（ISOES）的成员。

作为设计师和咨询顾问，沃弗岗・K・梅尔–亥兹还是圣加仑大学的客座讲师，并是国际设计评委会评委。梅尔–亥兹设计工程团队的工作重点就是要实现“技术品牌化”这一新术语，该团队通过领导多个国际设计团体，荣获过很多具有影响力的奖项，其中还包括在中国上海及深圳得到的最高设计奖。

Founder of the Meyer-Hayoz Design Engineering Group.
Works as a designer and consultant, and as a visiting lecturer at the University of St. Gallen. Serves as a speaker on symposiums and as a juror on international design panels.

Wolfgang K. Meyer-Hayoz, born in 1947, studied mechanical engineering, visual communication and industrial design, and graduated from the State Academy of Fine Arts in Stuttgart. His current design philosophy draws on the ideas of Professors Klaus Lehmann, Kurt Weidemann, Hartmut Seeger and Max Bense.

In 1985, he founded the Meyer-Hayoz Design Engineering Group with offices in Switzerland (Winterthur) and Germany (Konstanz). The company now provides consultancy services to start-ups, small and medium sized enterprises and global market leaders in the fields of brand strategy, innovation development, design research, industrial design, user interface design, temporary architecture, communication design and new media.

In 1987, Wolfgang K. Meyer-Hayoz was elected President of the Swiss Association of Industrial Designers (SID), and occupied this honorary position until 1993. He is also a member of the Association of German Industrial Designers (VDID) and the International Society for Occupational Ergonomics and Safety (ISOES).

Together with his work as a designer and consultant, he is also a visiting lecturer at the University of St. Gallen and serves as a juror on international design panels. The works of the Meyer-Hayoz Design Engineering Group, for which he coined the term "technology branding," have received a large number of prestigious awards from leading international design institutions, amongst others, the highest design awards in China, awarded in Shanghai and Shenzhen.

沃弗岗・K・梅尔–亥兹
Wolfgang K. Meyer-Hayoz

“毫无疑问，市场总是欢迎新鲜而刺激的设计，因此，产品应体现出新颖性、智能化和观念上的新尝试。”

"Certainly, the market is in urgent need of sustainable stimulation and thus new, intelligent and conceptual approaches."

弗朗塞斯科·米拉尼
Francesco Milani
(瑞士/Switzerland)

生于1937年
Born in 1937

米拉尼设计与咨询公司的联合创办人。
意大利瑞士设计综合技术学院学术委员会成员。

弗朗塞斯科·米拉尼，生于1937年。1953年到1957年在巴塞尔艺术与工艺学院学习平面艺术，曾作过一年的摄影学徒。在米兰Franco Grigniani工作的四年期间，他担任过建筑师、产品设计师和平面设计师，并从那时起他对产品设计领域开始充满了浓厚的兴趣。

从1963年起，米拉尼开办了自己的设计工作室，主要从事工业设计、咨询服务、广告和视觉设计方面的工作。米拉尼的设计领域主要涉及有：高科技产品、医疗技术、薄金属板所应用的电子工具、机械工程、控制设备及照片动画系统等。

1997年，他与人联合开办了米拉尼设计与咨询公司。除了提供以上系列服务外，该机构还负责处理市场、文化咨询及产品工程的方便性能等方面事宜。

从1998年起，弗朗塞斯科·米拉尼成为意大利瑞士设计综合技术学院学术委员会成员。

Co-founder of Milani design & consulting AG.
Member of the academic commission of the Design Polytechnic of Italian Switzerland.

Francesco Milani, born in 1937, attended the School of Arts and Crafts in Basle and trained as a graphic artist from 1953 to 1957, then serving a one-year apprenticeship with a photographer. During his first four years of employment with the architect, product designer and graphic artist Franco Grigniani in Milan, his enthusiasm for product design grew.

From 1963 onwards, Milani managed his own studio for industrial design, consultancy, advertising and visual design. His fields of activity have always been those of high-tech products, medical technology, electrical tools for sheet metal working, mechanical engineering, control systems and photo flash systems.

In 1997, he was a co-founder of the Milani design & consulting AG. Over and above the previous portfolio of services, the agency deals with marketing and cultural consultancy, and engineering up to product readiness.

Francesco Milani has been a member of the academic commission of the Design Polytechnic of Italian Switzerland since 1998.

弗朗塞斯科·米拉尼
Francesco Milani

“我所一直期望的是如何在较低的预算下为人们设计产品。”

“What I was missing were goods for people with a low budget.”

裘连诺・莫利那瑞
Giuliano Molineri
(意大利/Italy)

生于1942年
Born in 1942

设计管理领域专家。
Frimark Srl公司总裁，ICSID董事会成员。
裘连诺・莫利那瑞，1942年生于格瑞西奥，现居住在都灵附近的蒙卡列里。1968年毕业于都灵大学并获得哲学学士学位。而后从1974年到1981年，他成为乔治亚罗公司媒体关系及工业设计部门的总负责人。在1981年到1999年期间，他在乔治亚罗设计公司担任总经理，并在2000年到2004年期间，在都灵与皮德蒙特（ITP）分部担任国内销售经理。现在，他是Frimark Srl公司的总裁，他已经执掌该职位六年了。裘连诺・莫利那瑞的专业学识在各种设计组织都派上了用场：1989年到1992年期间，他是意大利工业设计协会的会员（ADI）；此外，1991年到1992年间他在筹划指导委员会积极工作，并从2002年之后的两年继续担任ADI董事会成员。从1998年到1999年，莫利那瑞作为都灵冬奥会的总经理参与了即将在都灵举办的2006年冬奥会的推广活动。从2003年起，他成为设在都灵的欧洲设计协会（IED）的技术指导及工业设计团体国际委员会（ICSID）的成员。

Expert in the Field of Design Management.
President of Frimark Srl and Board Member of the ICSID.
Giuliano Molineri was born in Garessio in 1942 and lives in Moncalieri near Torino today. After graduating from the University of Torino with a degree in philosophy in 1968 he worked as Head of Media Relations and Industrial Design at Italdesign-Giugiaro from 1974 to 1981. From 1981 to 1999 he held the position of General Manager at Giugiaro Design. Between 2000 and 2004 he held the position of Internal Marketing Manager of Invest in Torino and Piedmont (ITP). Today he is the President of Frimark Srl, a position he has held for the past six years. Giuliano Molineri's expert knowledge is in demand in various design organisations: from 1989 to 1992 he was a member of the Italian Association for Industrial Design (ADI); in addition, he was active for the steering committee from 1991 to 1992 and acted as ADI board member for two years from 2002 on. In 1998 and 1999 he participated as Managing Director of the Torino Bid Committee in the promotion of the 20th Olympic Winter Games 2006 in Torino. Since 2003 he is Scientific Director of the European Institute of Design in Torino (IED) as well as board member of the International Council of Societies of Industrial Design (ICSID).

裘连诺・莫利那瑞
Giuliano Molineri

“设计正经历着非常激动人心的阶段，在这一阶段中，我们要进一步关注‘设计为先’的观念，并协同设计以及所涉及的服务和非物质性领域。所有这些因素都说明了设计绝非仅仅是个装饰品，而是要赋予设计‘成熟’的角色来提升产品。”

“Design is going through a rather stimulating phase, in which closer attention is paid to the ‘design for all’ concept, to interaction design and to the areas covering services and the immaterial. All these elements contribute to giving design a ‘mature’ role, which goes well beyond the cosmetic upgrading of a product.”

马尔切罗·莫然迪尼
Marcello Morandini

“鉴于不同的观点，明显可以看出现今竞争激烈的市场形势促使了生产商更倾向于在绝大多数产品及相关物品上强化设计水平——基于不必投资的情况下，这种决定使市场形势更为复杂化。”

“Assuming different viewpoints, it becomes evident that the current difficult market situation prompts the producers to prefer mostly objects and/or products of codified design – a decision complicating their market situation due to the fact that they are doing without investments.”

马尔切罗·莫然迪尼
Marcello Morandini
(意大利/Italy)

生于1940年
Born in 1940

艺术家、设计师。2001年成立了“centro editoriale di design Marienza”。

艺术家及设计师马尔切罗·莫然迪尼，1940年生于曼图瓦。当他还在布雷拉美术学院学习的时候，就已经在米兰的一家设计工作室工作了。在那期间，创作出了他的第一幅雕刻作品。1964年，他在瓦雷兹成立了一家平面设计工作室。

1968年，他被邀请到威尼斯的XXXIVth公司工作。一年后，他在瓦雷兹设计并创建了他的工作室。

他的第一次作品回顾展览在汉诺威的凯思特纳协会举行，从此在德国开始了与博物馆、展览馆及工业企业活动富有成效的合作，特别是与塞尔普的Rosethal公司的合作。1997年，他参加了第六届卡塞尔文献展。

二十世纪八十年代初，他与位于瓦雷兹的Miraglia建筑公司和新加坡的Ong&Ong建筑公司有着持久的合作关系。其营造出的重要观念在建筑和城市发展领域起到了重要的作用。在慕尼黑Neue Sammlung举行的回顾展览中，第一次展出了莫然迪尼的设计及美术作品。2001年，他创建了centro editoriale di design Marienza。

莫然迪尼在瓦雷兹艺术学院任教多年，并从1995年到1997年，分别担任萨尔茨堡夏季学院及普劳恩夏季学院艺术与设计专业的讲师。1997年，他成为洛桑州立学校艺术专业的讲师及位于达拉维诺的Cerro国际博物馆陶瓷设计部的负责人。

从1964年起，马尔切罗·莫然迪尼的设计作品就曾在多家国际美术展览馆、文化中心、大学、博物馆、设计中心及两年一次的美术历史特殊博览会进行了多达97次的个人展览。他的美术作品和设计物品也在很多家博物馆进行长期的展出。2004年，莫然迪尼获得由伦敦皇家美术协会颁发的“皇家荣誉工业设计师”称号。

Artist and designer. Founded the “centro editoriale di design Marienza” in 2001.

Marcello Morandini, artist and designer, was born in 1940 in Mantua. While still a student at the academy of Brera, he had already been working for a design studio in Milan. His first sculptures originated around that time. In 1964, he opened a graphic studio in Varese.

In 1968, Morandini was invited to the XXXIVth Biennial in Venice. In the following year, he designed and realised his living studio in Varese.

The first retrospective exhibition of his work was held at the Kestner Gesellschaft in Hanover – the beginning of a productive co-operation with museums, galleries and industrial enterprises in Germany, in particular with the company Rosenthal in Selb. In 1977, he participated in the documenta 6.

At the beginning of the 1980s, a long-lasting co-operation developed with the architectural firms Miraglia in Varese and Ong&Ong in Singapore. The outcome was important concepts for the fields of architecture and urban development. The retrospective exhibition in the Neue Sammlung in Munich was the first one to show Morandini’s design as well as artistic work. In 2001, he founded the “centro editoriale di design Marienza.”

Morandini taught at the art college in Varese for some years and from 1995 to 1997 he had been lecturer on art and design at the summer academy in Salzburg and the summer academy in Plauen. Since 1997, he is a lecturer on art at the canton school of Lausanne and director of the International Museum for Ceramic Design in Cerro, Laveno.

Since 1964, Marcello Morandini has been showing his works in up to 97 individual exhibitions in international galleries, cultural centres, universities, museums, design centres, biennials and special fairs on art history. His artistic works and design objects are also part of permanent collections at numerous museums. In 2004, Morandini was awarded the title of “Honorary Royal Designer for Industry” by the Royal Society of Arts, London.

朗・纳巴罗
Ron Nabarro
(以色列/Israel)

生于1946年
Born in 1946

工业设计教授

朗・纳巴罗教授，生于荷兰，从1970年起就从事设计工作。他在得尼安以色列科技学院担任工业设计专业教授，并负责工业设计及设计管理专业的研究生项目。在1998年到2001年的头几年间，他负责管理Holon理工学院的设计美术学院。从1999年到2003年，他是工业设计协会的国际咨询部（ICSID）的执行董事会成员，并作为ICSID的大使协助该机构的工作。在纳巴罗教授的众多设计作品中，他特别注重在生态学设计、设计管理、老年人设计、设计教育、跨学科设计等领域的研究。为了实现他的设计理念，他开办了创新设计责任有限公司（1973年）并主管Design 4all（2001年）；另外，他还与人合伙成立并共同经营高级接触有限责任公司（2003）和森特康有限责任公司。从他获得的20多个奖项中，体现出他有着丰富的设计经验。不仅如此，通过参加国际性会议、工作室、研讨会等活动，他还成为了深受欢迎的演说家、作家和老师。

Professor of Industrial Design.

Professor Ron Nabarro, born in the Netherlands, has been active as a designer since 1970. He works as professor of Industrial Design at the Technion Israel Institute of Technology, heading the graduate program for Industrial Design and Design Management. In the preceding years between 1998 and 2001 he headed the School of Design and Art at the Holon Academic Institute of Technology. He was an executive board member of the International Council of Societies of Industrial Design (ICSID) from 1999 to 2003 and assists the organisation as ICSID Ambassador. In his activities as a designer Nabarro focuses in particular on topics in the fields Ecological Design, Design Management, Design for the Elderly, Design Education and Interdisciplinary Design. For the purpose of realising his ideas, he founded companies like Innovation Design Ltd. (1973) and Design4all (2001) which he is heading; in addition, he is co-founder and co-director of Senior-Touch Ltd. (2003) and Scentcom Ltd. His experience doesn't only reflect in the more than 20 awards he has received, but also at numerous congresses, workshops and seminars he is accompanying as sought-after lecturer, author and coach.

朗・纳巴罗
Ron Nabarro

“设计师能带给这个世界的最大好处便是避免失误。”

“Avoiding mistakes is one of the strongest points that designers can bring into this world.”

丹尼·维勒特
Danny Venlet

“这是个不错的机会，让设计可以更上一层楼——
它确实是个绝佳的时刻。”

"This is a very good moment to take further steps in design – actually the best moment."

丹尼·维勒特
Danny Venlet
(比利时/Belgium)

室内设计师。
维勒特室内设计公司所有者。
丹尼·维勒特出生在澳大利亚，1983年他以优异的成绩毕业于圣卢卡斯建筑与视觉艺术学院，而在此之前，他在布鲁塞尔大学学习计算应用技术专业。此后，他在彼得·桑兹、Inarc设计、documentation NZI，Raine、Horne NAB、阿拉伯的澳大利亚NAB，Rice和Daubney建筑等公司从事设计工作并获得了很多专业的经验。通过他与尼尔·布鲁雷（1988年）及马克·纽森（1998–1990年）的合作，他在1991年成立了自己的工作室——维勒特室内设计工作室。他的设计项目从个人住宅、阁楼、酒吧及酒店到天木蓝和西门子等这些大公司的商品陈列室及办公室。丹尼·维勒特的设计作品曾多次在米兰家具博览会、汉诺威工业博览会、布鲁塞尔voor Kunst en Geschiedenis博物馆、国家设计艺术节及墨尔本的法兰德斯设计节等多次展销会和展览会中展出。维勒特在2003年比利时的Henri van de Velde Prijs等不同的设计竞赛中获得了众多的奖项并提升了知名度。在过去的多年中，丹尼·维勒特作为室内设计师，他还在悉尼大学、悉尼澳大利亚皇家建筑学院和布鲁塞尔的根特市的圣卢卡斯建筑学院等多家澳大利亚和比利时的大学和学院从事教学工作，把自己的经验传授给他的学生们。

Works as interior designer.
Owner of Venlet Interior Architecture.
Danny Venlet, born in Australia, studied applied computer sciences at the University of Brussels before changing to the St. Lucas Institute of Architecture and Visual Arts from which he graduated with distinction in 1983. Thereafter, he gained his professional experience e.g. at Peter Sands, Inarc design and documentation NZI, Raine and Horne NAB, Arab Australia NAB and Rice and Daubney Architects. Following his cooperation with Neil Burley (1988) and Marc Newson (1998 to 1990) he eventually opened up his own studio, Venlet Interior Architecture, in 1991. His design projects range from private mansions, lofts, bars and restaurants all the way to showrooms and offices of large companies such as Timberland or Siemens. Time and again, Danny Venlet can be found with his works at trade shows and exhibitions, such as the Milano Furniture Fair, the Hannover Messe, in the Museum voor Kunst en Geschiedenis in Brussels, or at the State of Design Festival, Design from Flanders, in Melbourne. Venlet received recognition and awards at various design contests – such as the Henri van de Velde Prijs in Belgium 2003. In the past, Venlet passed on his experience as interior architect to students at several schools and universities in Belgium and Australia, such as the University of Sydney, the Royal Australian Institute of Architects in Sydney as well as the St. Lucas Institute of Architecture, Gent and Brussels.

海伦·亚勒
Helen Yardley
(英国/Great Britain)

生于1954年
Born in 1954

在伦敦有自己的工作室。

海伦·亚勒曾在普利茅斯艺术学院学习，她于1973年来到曼切斯特综合技术学院，并在1976年以优异的成绩获得了印刷及纺织专业的文凭。而后又通过两年在皇家艺术学院的学习，海伦·亚勒于1978年获得了纺织专业的硕士学位。

1983年，海伦·亚勒在伦敦成立了自己的工作室。从那时起，她的作品就在不同的展览会及展销会上进行展出，其中包括伦敦当代艺术博览会、纽约国际家具博览会、米兰国际家具博览会、巴黎家具博览会、克隆家具博览会、汉诺威国际地面铺装材料展览会、日本东京国际室内纺织品博览会、伦敦邦汉姆当代装潢艺术展览会，和伦敦皇家学院Spectrum展览会等。

她的设计作品曾被很多有影响力的设计出版物刊登过，其中包括国际设计年鉴、设计21世纪、当代地毯和特伦斯·考伦和麦斯·弗兰斯的设计与设计师。

Has her own design studio in London.

After studying at the Plymouth College of Art, Helen Yardley went to Manchester Polytechnic in 1973, and took her degree with distinction in the field of printed and woven textiles in 1976. She then studied for two years at the Royal College of Art, where she gained her M.A. in textiles in 1978.

Helen Yardley founded her own design studio in London in 1983. Since that time, her works have been shown at numerous exhibitions and fairs, including the Contemporary Arts Fair in London, the New York International Furniture Fair, the International Furniture Fair in Milan, the Paris Furniture Fair, the International Furniture Fair in Cologne, the Domotex in Hanover, the Japantex in Tokyo, Bonhams Decorative Arts Today in London, and Spectrum at the Royal College of Art in London.

Her work is also documented in various prestigious design publications such as the International Design Yearbook, Designing the 21st Century, Contemporary Rugs, and Designers on Design from Terence Conran & Max Fraser.

海伦·亚勒
Helen Yardley

"仅仅有创新是不够的，我们还需要更多。"

"It is not enough to be innovative, it needs to have something more."

评选结果揭晓了！“红点奖：产品设计”

The selection has been made! The “red dot award: product design”

评委：公正的专家意见和评判

“红点奖：产品设计”大赛的国际评委会对来自世界各大洲的产品设计进行了评估。从评估的举办地点就可以很明显地看出大赛的重要性。红点设计博物馆是由诺曼·福斯特爵士设计改建，是2002年被联合国科教文组织列入世界文化遗产工业建筑纪念物的前矿业同盟煤矿的宏伟建筑的一部分。红点设计博物馆是设计和设计文化领域的众多赛事和活动的主要场所。

“红点奖：产品设计”的评委一共由24位资深的在国际上享有盛名的产品设计师、业内记者还有国际设计文化研究所的代表组成。

公正和扎实的专业知识是选拔评委会成员的基础。一年中的绝大部分时间，红点设计奖的组织者们都在密切关注国际设计舞台，希望能够吸纳那些具有新颖的观点和想法的人加入到评委的队伍中来。无论这个人是谁，只要他在国际设计舞台上具有一定的影响力都可以成为我们的评委。可以说，“红点奖：产品设计”的评委都是具备独立和敏锐的判断力以及丰富的专业知识的。

经过长达一个星期的艰难的决定，比赛的最终结果终于揭晓了。正如“红点奖：产品设计” 把获奖的产品传递给整个世界一样，对评委的选拔也体现了对产品设计质量的极大尊重。每位国际评委要对他选择的最佳设计做出清楚地裁定。每种获奖产品都可以说是设计中的精品。

The jury: impartial expertise and judgement

The international jury of the “red dot award: product design” competition appraises current product design from every continent of the world. The setting in which the assessment takes place underscores the importance of this competition. Remodelled by Lord Norman Foster, the red dot design museum is part of the imposing architecture of the former Zollverein colliery listed in 2002 by UNESCO as a World Cultural Heritage industrial monument. The red dot design museum is the venue for numerous events and activities in the field of design and design culture.

The jury of the “red dot award: product design” consists of 24 experienced and internationally reputed product designers, trade journalists and representatives of international design and cultural institutions.

Independence and established expertise are the principles on which the members of the jury are selected. For the best part of a year the organisers of the red dot design award observe the international design scene with an eye to including new jurors with fresh views and ideas. Whoever plays a significant part in the international design scene can be appointed to the competition jury. The jury of the “red dot award: product design” combines independence with extraordinary judgement and expertise.

At the end of a week of frequently long and difficult decisions the final results come in. Just as the “red dot award: product design” communicates the award winning products to the entire world, the selection of the jury is an expression of the highest esteem for the design quality of a product. An international jury delivers a clear verdict in its choice of the best design. Each award winning product constitutes a plea for good design.

“红点奖：产品设计” 和 “红点奖： “媒体设计” 的国家名单
The nations in the "red dot award: product design" and "red dot award: communication design"

竞赛： 国际化并且评选标准十分严格

“红点奖：产品设计”是为目前产品设计而设立的面向国际的大赛。一些媒体活动，比如在国际设计行业和普通报刊上刊登大量的广告就已经强调了大赛的重要性。

经过几十年的发展，“红点奖：产品设计”已经牢牢地立足于国际设计舞台上，近几年它的国际影响力变得愈发突出了。今年，有来自36个国家的1857个参赛选手，他们带来了高质量的产品，体现出“红点奖：产品设计”在评选和产品创新方面在世界五大洲的权威地位。

虽然大赛规则严格：只有上市不到两年的产品才有资格提交和参赛，且产品必须具备创新的特征，这些特征能使它们明显区别于市场上同行业的产品。这正是“红点奖：产品设计”的评委们的专业知识发挥重要作用的地方：只有对某个特殊市场有充分了解的评委，才能做出有创新价值的判断。

评委们把产品分为12个产品组进行评估：起居室和卧室——厨房用具、休闲、运动、医疗器械和度假用品——建筑和室内设计——工业和手工业——交通——浴室、取暖、卫生设备和空调——生命科学和医药——办公室和行政——媒体和家用电器——珠宝、时尚、装饰品、服装设计和新原料——照明设备和灯具等。参赛者可以自己选择自己的产品归属组，这种选择的本身也就暗示了产品的用途。除了那些无法移动的建筑，产品都要原封不动地被提交到“红点奖：产品设计”大赛之上。

通过红点设计奖，可以追溯到竞赛组织中的一个长期传统。“红点奖：产品设计”的组织也是积累了多年的经验，并应用了先进的技术。所有提交到大赛的参赛作品都必须备有两份产品说明，一份德文的和一份英文的。大赛的独立、公平和国际化的原则也同样适用于参赛的作品。

The competition: international and subject to strict criteria of selection

The "red dot award: product design" is an internationally oriented competition for current product design. Its importance is underscored by media activities such as advertising campaigns in the international design trade and general press.

Already firmly established in the international design scene for decades, the "red dot award: product design" has heightened its international significance even more in recent years. This year saw entries of high-quality products from 1,857 competitors from 36 countries, reflecting the status of the "red dot award: product design" as a major authority with regard to the selection and qualification of innovative products from all five continents of the world.

And that despite the strictest competition rules. Only products that have been on the market for no longer than two years may be submitted. The products must also possess innovative characteristics that set them apart from others in their particular branch of industry. This is where the specific know-how of the jurors in the "red dot award: product design" plays a major part: only jurors who are thoroughly familiar with the particular markets involved can judge the merit of an innovation.

The products are divided for assessment into twelve product groups: Living rooms and bedrooms – Households and kitchens – Leisure, sports, wellness and caravaning – Architecture and interior design – Industry and crafts – Transports – Bathrooms, heatings, sanitary installations and air-conditioning – Life science and medicine – Offices and administration – Media and home electronics – Jewellery, fashion, accessories, textile design and new materials – Lighting and lamps. As the entrant chooses the group in which his product is to be judged, this choice itself is indicative of the various uses the product can be put to. With the exception of immovable architecture, products are always submitted in the original to the "red dot award: product design" competition.

The red dot design award can look back on a long tradition of competition organisation. The organisation of the "red dot award: product design," too, is based on years of experience and the use of state-of-the-art technology. All entries are submitted to the jury in their product groups together with a product description in German and English. The competition principles of independence, equity and internationality also apply to the presentation of the products.

“红点奖：产品设计”大赛的评选标准

怎样才能做到大赛中的每种产品的独特的创新品质都能得以公正的评判？这里的关键词是：区别性。评判是在极其严格的标准下做出的。评委的判断是以大赛的规则和标准所提供的参考框架为基础；对这个标准的准确应用确保了每种产品的个性化设计品质都能得到恰如其分地评判。“红点奖：产品设计”的评委是在这9条严格的放之四海而皆准的标准下做出最后决定的。它们是：

The criteria of the “red dot award: product design” competition

How can justice be done to the particular innovative quality of each product in the competition? The key word here is differentiation. Assessment is assisted by firmly established criteria. The jury's judgement is aided by the frame of reference provided by the competition rules and criteria; a finely tuned application of these criteria ensures that the individual design quality of each product is properly assessed. The jury of the “red dot award: product design” reaches its decisions in accordance with nine strict and unfailing criteria. These are as follows:

- 创新程度
- 功能性
- 外形品质
- 人体工程学
- 耐用性
- 象征性与情感含义
- 产品外围
- 简明使用程度
- 生态兼容性

- *DEGREE OF INNOVATION*
- *FUNCTIONALITY*
- *FORMAL QUALITY*
- *ERGONOMICS*
- *DURABILITY*
- *SYMBOLIC AND EMOTIONAL CONTENT*
- *PRODUCT PERIPHERALS*
- *SELF-EXPLANATORY QUALITY*
- *ECOLOGICAL SOUNDNESS*

红点优秀设计质量奖和“红点：精品中的精品”最高设计质量奖都是在这些标准的基础上颁发的。每组最多能有三种产品可以获得“红点：精品中的精品”嘉奖。平均分到12个产品组的话，每年最多有36种产品能获得此奖项。除此之外，评委还会颁发两个特别奖：“红点：智慧设计”奖。这两个奖项都代表着“红点奖：产品设计”大赛的最佳设计。

The red dot for high design quality and the “red dot: best of the best” for highest design quality are awarded on the basis of these criteria. The “red dot: best of the best” seal of quality can be awarded to a maximum of three products in each group. Given twelve product groups, this distinction can be conferred on no more than 36 products each year. In addition, the jury may confer two special “red dot: intelligent design” awards. Both distinctions stand for the best design in the “red dot award: product design” competition.

红点——质量的保证
国际交流的工具

红点奖的卓越之处还体现在它对国际评委的高度尊重上。红点设计奖和它的标志现在已经得到了广泛认可并具有特殊的价值。对于产品的设计师和制造商来说，大赛获奖本身就是对他们长期的研发和为设计献身的精神的一种肯定。

从逻辑上讲，下一步要做的就是有效地宣传这个奖项，并且促进品牌的市场曝光率。我们要打开所有的沟通渠道，这是与之有关公司的营销和沟通能力的问题。红点设计奖有多种传播途径选择，并支持公司制订的可能的传播策略。平面媒体、交易会、零售销售点以及红点设计奖官方网站都为红点设计的所有获奖者建立了一个沟通平台。尤其是网站，是现在设计行业、规划师、建筑师、设计师和那些对设计感兴趣的人的固定搜索媒介。还有许多公司充分利用红点编辑的各种刊物。

*The red dot – seal of quality
and tool of international communication*

The distinction of a red dot is an expression of high esteem on the part of an international jury. The red dot design award and the label that goes with it have now become a globally acknowledged sign of special merit. For the designers and manufacturers of the products an award in the competition represents recognition for an often long process of development and for their commitment to design.

The logical next step is to communicate this award effectively and to promote market exposure of the brand. All communication channels should be exploited. This is partly a question of the marketing and communication capability of the companies concerned. The red dot design award implies a wide variety of communication options and supports companies in devising possible communication strategies. An effective communication platform is available to all winners of the red dot design award, integrating communication tools in print media, trade fairs and point of sale and the red dot design award website. The website, in particular, is now an established research medium for industry, planners, architects, designers and those interested in design. Many companies also make use of the publications in the red dot edition.

红点设计奖将自己置于铺天盖地的媒体评判的中心地位，目的是要在公众眼里和国际设计舞台上建立起其获奖作品的权威地位。红点设计奖通过频频在各种媒体曝光来提高和扩大它的影响力。比如它经常出现在诸如汉莎航空杂志、设计行业报刊、设计评论，还有以美国ID杂志为代表的国际设计刊物上。从最近重要的与设计有关的行业展览里得出详细的趋势报道，几乎是所有行业当前流行趋势的信息来源。这些资源一般是全球共享的。这些消息在www.red-dot.de上都可以查到，并且做成新闻简报定期传阅。红点设计奖的义务之一就是关注全球化和国际化，发掘年轻人才。尤其是在亚洲地区。最近有一个典型的例子便是“红点奖：设计理念”通过新加坡红点，在世界范围内找到最能引起人们兴趣的未来理念。

The red dot design award itself is at the heart of a wide variety of communication measures and is aimed at establishing the award winning products more firmly in the public eye and the international design scene. The red dot design award extends and increases its international significance through its presence in media such as the Lufthansa magazine, the design trade papers form and design report and the international design press as represented, for instance, by America's ID magazine. Detailed trend reports directly from the most important design-relevant trade shows are sources of information about current trends in all industrial sectors, often utilised internationally. They are available under www.red-dot.de and are circulated regularly as newsletter. A strong commitment of the red dot design award focuses on globalisation and internationalisation, centering around the promotion of young talents in, amongst others, the Asian region. A current example is the "red dot award: design concept," identifying, via red dot Singapore, the most interesting concepts worldwide for the future.

红点设计博物馆
展览和陈设的地方

博物馆是由诺曼·福斯特爵士改建的，座落在宏伟的前矿业同盟煤矿上。这个当代设计的博物馆永久收藏了大概1000多种设计新品，占地面积达4000多平方米。此外，红点设计奖的获奖者还可以在持续数周的特别展览上做广告。红点设计博物馆举办的这些展览和重要活动向来自全世界的参观者展示了最新的创新和设计趋势。

所有红点设计的获奖产品都被列入永久收藏的范围。通过这种方式，它们取得了文化遗产的地位。每年都有超过12万的参观者来到这个博物馆，他们或是同行业的从业者、或是普通参观者。不论是红点设计博物馆的展览，还是德国或是国外的一些巡回展览，红点设计对设计质量的关注，永远不会停止。

The red dot design museum
A place for exhibitions and presentations

Remodelled by Lord Norman Foster in the imposing architectural setting of Zollverein, this museum of contemporary design houses a permanent exhibition of approximately 1,000 design innovations on a floorspace of more than 4,000 square metres. In addition to this, the current red dot design award winners are featured every year in special exhibitions lasting several weeks. The exhibitions and events held at the red dot design museum inform visitors from all over the world about the latest innovations and trends.

All red dot design award winning products are included in the permanent exhibition. In this way they acquire the status of cultural assets which are constantly accessible to the over 120,000 annual visitors from the trade and the general public at the red dot design museum. Throughout the entire year the red dot design award focuses attention on design quality in events ranging from exhibitions in the red dot design museum to travelling exhibitions in Germany and abroad.

德国设计协会的赞助商

The Sponsors of the Design Zentrum Nordrhein Westfalen

任何一个机构或组织，像德国设计协会，想让它很好地发挥服务社会的作用，就需要依靠许多资助者的赞助。我们对如下的公司和个人深表谢意，他们通过自己积极地工作，无论是在组织者的理事会上，还是以捐赠或是其他方式的帮助，都为德国设计协会做出了特殊贡献。

彼得・柴克教授
总裁
德国设计协会

An institution like the Design Zentrum Nordrhein Westfalen is particularly dependent on the support of numerous sponsors if it is properly to fulfil its functions which serve the public.
Our sincere thanks are due to the individuals and companies named below, who have made a special contribution to the work of the Design Zentrum in the form of active honorary work on the board of governors, or by the donations and other means of assistance.

Prof. Dr. Peter Zec
President
Design Zentrum Nordrhein Westfalen

董事会
The Governing Board

主席
Chairman

Markus Ferstera

副主席
Deputy Chairman

Klaus Beckmann

Reinhard Jammers

Prof. Stefan Lengyel

Vito Oražem

Dr. Oliver Scheytt

Prof. Dr. Peter Zec

赞助商
Sponsoring Companies and Institutions

Ahrend, Amsterdam, The Netherlands

alfi Zitzmann GmbH, Wertheim

Artemide GmbH, Fröndenberg

Da Daniele, Essen

Gira Giersiepen GmbH & Co. KG, Radevormwald

Halbe-Rahmen GmbH, Kirchen

LK Aktiengesellschaft, Essen

nya nordiska GmbH, Dannenberg

Porzellanfabrik Arzberg Zweigniederlassung der Hutschenreuther AG, Selb

Privatbrauerei Jakob Stauder, Essen

Sparkasse Essen

Stiftsquelle Johann Spielmann GmbH, Essen

Top Event, Dortmund

Vorwerk & Co. Teppichwerke GmbH & Co. KG, Hameln

WMF AG, Geislingen/Steige

A

Accademia srl
Via Indipendenza 4
I-33044 Manzano (UD)
Seite / *page* 160

Acer Incorporated
8F, No. 88, Section 1, Hsin Tai Wu Road
Hsichih, Taipei Hsien 221
Taiwan
Seite / *page* 432

Add-On Technology Co., Ltd.
1F, No. 11, Lane 206, Da-An Rd., Sec. 1
Taipei 106
Taiwan
Seite / *page* 428, 429

adidas-Salomon AG
Adi-Dassler-Str. 1
D-91074 Herzogenaurach
Seite / *page* 246-248

AEG Hausgeräte GmbH
Muggenhofer Str. 135
D-90429 Nürnberg
Seite / *page* 198, 199

AFG Arbonia-Forster-Riesa GmbH
Heinrich-Schönberg-Str. 3
D-01591 Riesa
Seite / *page* 346

agile Unterhaltungselektronik GmbH
Am Bach 11a
D-35083 Wetter/Amönau
Seite / *page* 461

aha Kunststofftechnik GmbH
Industriestr. 4
D-64407 Fränkisch-Crumbach/Odenwald
Seite / *page* 295

Koninklijke Ahrend NV
Laarderhoogtweg 12
NL-1101 EA Amsterdam
Seite / *page* 378, 379

Airflow Developments Ltd.
Lancaster Road
GB-High Wycombe HP12 3QP
Seite / *page* 350

Alape
Am Gräbicht 1-9
D-38644 Goslar
Seite / *page* 337

alfi GmbH
Ernst-Abbe-Str. 14
D-97877 Wertheim
Seite / *page* 230

American Standard Europe BVBA
Chaussee de Wavre 1789
B-1160 Brüssel
Seite / *page* 334, 335

Amor Manufacturing Corporation
8th Fl., No. 137, Jen Ai Rd.
Taipei 106
Taiwan
Seite / *page* 252

Apple
1 Infinite Loop
Cupertino, CA 95014
USA
Seite / *page* 90, 91, 392-399

Arcelik A.S.
Altinordu Cad. No. 5
Organize Sanayi Bölgesi
TR-06931 Ankara
Seite / *page* 194

Artemide Group S.p.A.
Via Bergamo 18
I-20010 Pregnana Milanese
Seite / *page* 102-105

Asmobile Communication Inc.
No. 11, Lane 120, Li-Te Rd., Peitou
Taipei 112
Taiwan
Seite / *page* 422

AsusTek Computer Inc.
No. 150, Li-Te Road
Peitou, 112, Taipei
Taiwan
Seite / *page* 434, 435

Attika Feuer AG
Brunnmatt 16
CH-6330 Cham
Seite / *page* 347

Audi AG
D-85045 Ingolstadt
Seite / *page* 323

Auerhahn Bestecke GmbH
Im oberen Tal 9
D-72213 Altensteig
Seite / *page* 221

AVC Technology Limited
6/F., Enterprise Square Three, 39 Wang Chiu Road
Kowloon Bay
Hongkong
Seite / *page* 450

B

B&W Loudspeakers Ltd
Dale Road
GB-Worthing, West Sussex BN11 2BH
Seite / *page* 458

Balay BSH Electrodomésticos España, S.A.
Avenida de la industria 49
E-50016 Montañana (Zaragoza)
Seite / *page* 178-180

Basta France S.A.S.
Usine de Beaulieu
F-58502 Clamecy
Seite / *page* 252

Becherer Möbel + Innenausbau GmbH
Telfer Str. 6
D-79215 Elzach
Seite / *page* 172

Gebr. Becker GmbH & Co. KG
Hölker Feld 29-31
D-42279 Wuppertal
Seite / *page* 308

Beckhoff Industrie Elektronik
Eiserstr. 5
D-33415 Verl
Seite / *page* 308

Beko Elektronik A.S.
Beylikduzu
TR-34901 Istanbul
Seite / *page* 455

BenQ Corporation
18 Jihu Road, Neihu
Taipei 114
Taiwan
Seite / *page* 400-405

Bessey & Sohn GmbH & Co.
Mühlenwiesenstr. 40
D-74321 Bietigheim-Bissingen
Seite / *page* 298

Bette GmbH & Co. KG
Heinrich-Bette-Str. 1
D-33129 Delbrück
Seite / *page* 333

Birkenstock
P.O. Box 6140
Novato, CA 94948
USA
Seite / *page* 100, 101

BMW Group
D-80788 München
Seite / *page* 68, 69, 320, 321

Boblbee AB
Vintergatan 12
Box 4039
S-20311 Malmö
Seite / *page* 261

Bodenschatz Lederwaren GmbH & Co. KG
Buschaplatz 3
D-95355 Presseck
Seite / *page* 295

Bodum AG
Bodum Design Group
Kantonsstr. 100
CH-6234 Triengen
Seite / *page* 209, 211

Boehringer Werkzeugmaschinen Vertriebsgesellschaft mbH
Stuttgarter Str. 70
D-73033 Göppingen
Seite / *page* 308

Bombardier Recreational Products Inc.
565, Mountain Street
Valcourt, QC J0E 2L0
Kanada
Seite / *page* 324

Bombardier Recreational Products Inc.
Florida Technology Center
111, J.-A. Bombardier Blvd. SW
Cogan Lake, Palm Bay, FL 32908
USA
Seite / *page* 324

Robert Bosch Hausgeräte GmbH
Carl-Wery-Str. 34
D-81739 München
Seite / *page* 181, 186-189, 224, 242, 243

Bose Corp.
The Mountain
Framingham, MA 01701-9168
USA
Seite / *page* 86, 87, 420

Braun GmbH
Frankfurter Str. 145
D-61476 Kronberg
Seite / *page* 368

BREE Collection GmbH & Co. KG
Gerberstr. 3
D-30916 Isernhagen
Seite / *page* 94, 95

Brüel & Kjær Sound & Vibration Measurement A/S
Skodsborgvej 307
DK-2850 Naerum
Seite / *page* 297

Busch-Jaeger Elektro GmbH
Freisenbergstr. 2
D-58513 Lüdenscheid
Seite / *page* 277

C

Canon Deutschland GmbH
Europark Fichtenhain A10
D-47807 Krefeld
Seite / *page* 260, 438, 439, 442

Canyon Bicycles GmbH
Koblenzer Str. 236
D-56073 Koblenz
Seite / *page* 251

Carpet Concept Objekt-Teppichboden GmbH
Bunzlauer Str. 7
D-33719 Bielefeld
Seite / *page* 84, 85, 381

Chef'n Corp
1520 4th Ave., 3rd Floor
Seattle, WA 98101
USA
Seite / *page* 222

Cheoy Lee Shipyards Ltd.
89 & 91 Hing Wah Street West
Lai Chi Kok
Kowloon
Hongkong
Seite / *page* 70, 71

Cherry GmbH
Cherrystr.
D-91275 Auerbach/Opf.
Seite / *page* 433

Concise Living Co., Ltd.
No. 2, Lane 28, Chung Mei St.
Taichung
Taiwan
Seite / *page* 258, 259

Concord:marlin
Hanworth Trading Estate
Hampton Road West
GB-Feltham, Middx. TW13 6DR
Seite / *page* 480

Conmoto GmbH & Co. KG
Schlossallee 7-9
D-33442 Herzebrock-Clarholz
Seite / *page* 279

Crown Equipment Corporation
14 W. Monroe St.
New Bremen, OH 45869
USA
Seite / *page* 325

D

DAB
C/Conflent, 46. P.I. Pomar de Dalt. Badalona
E-08915 Barcelona
Seite / *page* 483

DaimlerChrysler AG
Epplestr. 225
D-70546 Stuttgart
Seite / *page* 318, 319

Damixa a/s
Ostbirkvej 2
DK-5240 Odense
Seite / *page* 333

Dark NV
Vliegplein 43
B-9991 Maldegem
Seite / *page* 478

DASGIP AG
Rudolf-Schulten-Straße 5
D-52428 Jülich
Seite / *page* 368

De'Longhi S.p.A.
Via L. Seitz 47
I-31100 Treviso
Seite / *page* 237

Decathlon Sportartikel GmbH
Holsterhauser Str. 200
D-44625 Herne
Seite / *page* 56, 57

Dell Inc.
One Dell Way
Round Rock, TX 78682
USA
Seite / *page* 423

Derungs Licht AG
Hofmattstr. 12
CH-9200 Gossau
Seite / *page* 364, 365

Deutsche Telekom AG
T-Com Division
Hochstadenring 50
D-53119 Bonn
Seite / *page* 414, 415

Dietiker Switzerland
Dietiker AG
Hofwisenstr. 2
CH-8260 Stein am Rhein
Seite / *page* 147

DORMA GmbH + Co. KG
Breckerfelder Str. 42-48
D-58256 Ennepetal
Seite / *page* 281

Duck Image Co. Ltd.
1st Fl., No. 22, Lane 321, Sec. 1, Hsingan Rd.
Taichung
Taiwan
Seite / *page* 427

Duravit AG
Werderstr. 36
D-78132 Hornberg
Seite / *page* 340, 341

DZ LICHT – Gruppe Artemide
Hans-Böckler-Str. 2
D-58730 Fröndenberg
Seite / *page* 484, 485

E

e15 Design und Distributions GmbH
Hospitalstr. 4
D-61440 Oberursel
Seite / *page* 479

Elco Kunststoffe GmbH
Osnabrücker Landstr. 154
D-33335 Gütersloh
Seite / *page* 173

AB Electrolux
S:t Göransgatan 143
S-10545 Stockholm
Seite / *page* 236, 238

Electrolux Home Products S.A.
Belgicastraat 17
B-1930 Zaventem
Seite / *page* 191

elmarflötotto GmbH
Am Ölbach 28
D-33334 Gütersloh
Seite / *page* 146

EMS-GRIVORY
Reichenauerstr.
CH-7013 Domat/Ems
Seite / *page* 225

Emsa Werke Wulf GmbH & Co. KG
Grevener Damm 215-225
D-48282 Emsdetten
Seite / *page* 235

Esselte Leitz GmbH & Co KG
Siemensstr. 64
D-70469 Stuttgart
Seite / *page* 389

Hermann Eule Orgelbau GmbH
Wilthener Str. 6
D-02625 Bautzen
Seite / *page* 268, 269

Eva Denmark A/S
Maaloev Teknikerby 18-20
DK-2760 Maaloev
Seite / *page* 231

Extremis NV
Weegschede 39 B
B-8691 Gijverinkhove
Seite / *page* 279

F

C. & E. Fein GmbH
Leuschnerstraße 43
D-70176 Stuttgart
Seite / *page* 302

Fennel GmbH & Co. KG
Unterer Sundern 11
D-32549 Bad Oeynhausen
Seite / *page* 173

Festo AG & Co. KG
Ruiter Str. 82
D-73734 Esslingen
Seite / *page* 62-65, 286-292

Fiskars Brands Finland Oy Ab
East Building
FIN-10330 Billnäs
Seite / *page* 263

Fissler GmbH
Harald-Fissler-Str. 1
D-55743 Idar-Oberstein
Seite / *page* 212

Fjällräven
Lilienthalallee 40
D-80939 München
Seite / *page* 261

Flos S.p.A.
Via Angelo Faini 2
I-25073 Bovezzo (Brescia)
Seite / *page* 481

Frank Europe GmbH
Bosenheimer Str. 233-237
D-55543 Bad Kreuznach
Seite / *page* 278

Gebrüder Frei GmbH & Co.
Borsigstr. 15
D-72461 Albstadt
Seite / *page* 311

Porzellanmanufaktur Fürstenberg
Meinbrexener Str. 2
D-37699 Fürstenberg/Weser
Seite / *page* 223

G

Gaba International AG
Emil-Frey-Str. 100
CH-4142 Münchenstein
Seite / *page* 368

Geka Brush GmbH
Division Victoria Cosmetics
Schulweg 3
D-91572 Bechhofen/Königshofen
Seite / *page* 295

Georg Jensen
Søndre Fasanvej 7
DK-2000 Frederiksberg
Seite / *page* 222

Gioel
Via Brennero 260/G
I-38100 Trento
Seite / *page* 239

Le Groupe GO inc.
103-291, rue De St. Vallier Est
Quebec, G1K 3P5
Kanada
Seite / *page* 250

W.L. Gore & Associates GmbH
Aiblinger Str. 60
D-83620 Feldkirchen-Westerham
Seite / *page* 254

Gorenje d.d.
Partizanska 12
SLO-3503 Velenje
Seite / *page* 182

Gebr. Graef GmbH & Co. KG
Donnerfeld 6
D-59757 Arnsberg
Seite / *page* 233

Grimmeisen Vertriebs GmbH
Äußere Lohe 2
D-83512 Wasserburg a. Inn
Seite / *page* 380

Grohe Water Technology AG & Co. KG
Industriepark Edelburg
D-58675 Hemer
Seite / *page* 343

H

Hamberger Sanitary
Postfach 10 03 53
D-83003 Rosenheim
Seite / *page* 351

Hansa Metallwerke AG
Sigmaringer Str. 107
D-70567 Stuttgart
Seite / *page* 48, 49, 232

Hansaton Akustik GmbH
Stückenstr. 48
D-22081 Hamburg
Seite / *page* 363

Hansgrohe AG
Auestr. 5-9
D-77761 Schiltach
Seite / *page* 74-77, 342

Harman/Becker
Raiffeisenstr. 34
D-70794 Filderstadt
Seite / *page* 460

Holzprojekte Härtenberger HKH GmbH
Hauptstr. 39
D-94336 Hunderdorf
Seite / *page* 171

Haworth GmbH
Von-Achenbach-Str. 21-23
D-59229 Ahlen
Seite / *page* 262

Heineken Beer Systems
Stadhouderskade 79
NL-1072 AE Amsterdam
Seite / *page* 205

Henkel KGaA
Henkelstr. 67
D-40191 Düsseldorf
Seite / *page* 387

Hensoldt AG Carl Zeiss Gruppe
Gloelstr. 3-5
D-35576 Wetzlar
Seite / *page* 261

Hess Form + Licht GmbH
Schlachthausstr. 19-19/3
D-78050 Villingen-Schwenningen
Seite / *page* 485

Hilti AG
Feldkircher Str. 100
FL-9494 Schaan
Seite / *page* 300, 301

Hirschmann Laborgeräte GmbH & Co. KG
Hauptstr. 7-15
D-74246 Eberstadt
Seite / *page* 370

I

I-House Incorporadora LTDA.
R. Ezequiel Freire, 51 - 13° Andar - Cj. 136
BR-02034-000 São Paulo, SP
Seite / *page* 330, 331

Ikea of Sweden AB
P.O. Box 702
S-34381 Älmhult
Seite / *page* 221, 235

Imaje AB
Säterigatan 20
S-41764 Göteborg
Seite / *page* 306

Innovativ Vision AB
Attorpsgatan 7
S-58273 Linköping
Seite / *page* 309

Inotech Medizintechnik GmbH
Boschstr. 3
D-92507 Nabburg
Seite / *page* 294

Interflex Datensysteme GmbH & Co. KG
Zettachring 16
D-70567 Stuttgart
Seite / *page* 276

interstil Diedrichsen GmbH & Co. KG
Liebigstraße 1-3
D-33803 Steinhagen
Seite / *page* 161

J

JAB Teppiche Heinz Anstoetz KG
Dammheider Str. 67
D-32052 Herford
Seite / *page* 156

Jacob Delafon Paris (Kohler France)
60, rue de Turenne
F-75139 Paris cedex 03
Seite / *page* 337

Jado
Paul-Ehrlich-Str. 5
D-63322 Rödermark
Seite / *page* 280, 336

Jordan AS
Haavard Martinsens vei 30
N-0978 Oslo
Seite / *page* 351

Jura Elektroapparate AG
Bahnhofstr. 135
CH-4626 Niederbuchsiten
Seite / *page* 203

K

möbelbau kaether & weise
Dammstr. 43
D-31195 Lamspringe
Seite / *page* 42, 43

KAHLA/Thüringen Porzellan GmbH
Christian-Eckardt-Str. 38
D-07768 Kahla
Seite / *page* 50, 51, 217

Franz Kaldewei GmbH & Co. KG
Beckumer Str. 33-35
D-59229 Ahlen
Seite / *page* 332

Alfred Kärcher GmbH & Co. KG
Alfred-Kärcher-Str. 28-40
D-71364 Winnenden
Seite / *page* 304

Ulla u. Martin Kaufmann
Goslarsche Landstr. 54
D-31135 Hildesheim
Seite / *page* 467

Kellogg Company
One Kellogg Square
P.O. Box 3599
Battle Creek, MI 49016-3599
Seite / *page* 207

Kenwood Ltd.
New Lane
GB-Havant, Hampshire PO9 2NH
Seite / *page* 230

Keramag AG
Kreuzerkamp 11
D-40878 Ratingen
Seite / *page* 337

Kermi GmbH
Pankofen-Bahnhof 1
D-94447 Plattling
Seite / *page* 344, 345

Kesseböhmer GmbH
Mindener Str. 208
D-49152 Bad Essen
Seite / *page* 170

Keuco GmbH & Co. KG
Oesestr. 36
D-58675 Hemer
Seite / *page* 348

Klafs Saunabau GmbH & Co. KG
Erich-Klafs-Str. 1-3
D-74523 Schwäbisch Hall
Seite / *page* 256, 257

Klöber GmbH
Bürositzmöbel
Rauensteinstr. 18
D-88662 Überlingen
Seite / *page* 388

Walter Knoll AG & Co.KG
Bahnhofstr. 25
D-71083 Herrenberg
Seite / *page* 148, 154

Krups
Groupe SEB Moulinex
Immeuble Le Monge
22, place des Vosges
La Défense 5
F-92979 Paris La Défense
Seite / *page* 205

Küppersbusch Hausgeräte AG
Küppersbuschstr. 16
D-45883 Gelsenkirchen
Seite / *page* 185

KWC AG
Hauptstr. 57
CH-5726 Unterkulm
Seite / *page* 233

L

C. Josef Lamy GmbH
Grenzhöfer Weg 32
D-69123 Heidelberg
Seite / *page* 384, 385

Laufen Ceramconsult AG
Wahlenstr. 46
CH-4242 Laufen
Seite / *page* 338, 339

Lehnen edel:stahl GmbH
Zum Rachtiger Wald 3
D-54516 Wittlich
Seite / *page* 366

Leicht Küchen AG
Gmünder Str. 70
D-73550 Waldstetten
Seite / *page* 169, 173

Leolux Meubelfabriek BV
P.O. Box 3076
NL-5902 RB Venlo
Seite / *page* 146

LG Electronics Inc.
Corporate Design Center
15Fl, LG Gangnam Tower, 679 Yeoksam-dong,
Gangnam-gu, 15Fl
Seoul 135-985
Korea
Seite / *page* 194, 195, 440, 441

Lignum arts GmbH
Kapellenstr. 2
D-82256 Fürstenfeldbruck
Seite / *page* 232

Linde AG
Schweinheimer Str. 34
D-63743 Aschaffenburg
Seite / *page* 66, 67

LiTraCon Bt.
Tanya 832
H-6640 Csongrád
Seite / *page* 60, 61

Loewe AG
Industriestr. 11
D-96317 Kronach
Seite / *page* 88, 89, 451-453

LoeweVonAppen GmbH
Bugdahnstr. 5
D-22767 Hamburg
Seite / *page* 264

Logitech USA
6505 Kaiser Drive
Fremont, CA 94555
USA
Seite / *page* 435

LRG. Licht + Raum AG
Hinterer Schermen 44
CH-3063 Ittigen
Seite / *page* 485

Lumiance B.V.
Oudeweg 155
P.O. Box 6310
NL-2001 HH Haarlem
Seite / *page* 480

M

Machalke Polsterwerkstätten GmbH & Co. KG
Burkheimer Str. 20
D-96272 Hochstadt
Seite / *page* 152, 153

Materialise NV
Technologielaan 15
B-3001 Leuven
Seite / *page* 484

mayer und thiele gbr
Hofaue 53
D-42103 Wuppertal
Seite / *page* 223

Medion AG
Gänsemarkt 16-18
D-45127 Essen
Seite / *page* 436, 437

Meister + Co. AG
Hauptstr. 66
CH-8832 Wollerau am Zürichsee
Seite / *page* 465

Meister GmbH
Kasernenstr. 85
D-78315 Radolfzell am Bodensee
Seite / *page* 465

Melitta Haushaltsprodukte GmbH & Co. KG
Ringstr. 99
D-32427 Minden
Seite / *page* 202

Miele & Cie. KG
Carl-Miele-Str. 29
D-33332 Gütersloh
Seite / *page* 192, 193

Miele & Cie. KG
Werk Warendorf
Mielestr. 1
D-48231 Warendorf
Seite / *page* 46, 47

Molteni & C
Via Rossini 50
I-20034 Giussano
Seite / *page* 40, 41, 162, 163

mono-Metallwarenfabrik Seibel GmbH
Industriestr. 5
D-40822 Mettmann
Seite / *page* 155, 210

monopezzo
Klein + Gärtner GbR
Vespasianstr. 16
D-68526 Ladenburg
Seite / *page* 240

Royal Mosa
P.O. Box 1026
NL-6201 BA Maastricht
Seite / *page* 274, 275

N

Nakamichi Corporation Limited
146 Robinson Road
Singapur 068909
Seite / *page* 454

Naturquell S.A.
Carreira de Puigcerdá
km 139,2
E-25719 Estamariu
Seite / *page* 267

Neff
B/S/H/ Markendesign Constructa Neff
Carl-Wery-Str. 34
D-81739 München
Seite / *page* 190

NEOMAN Bus GmbH
Heinrich-Büssing-Str. 1
D-38239 Salzgitter
Seite / *page* 326

NEOMAN Bus GmbH
Vaihinger Str. 118-122
D-70567 Stuttgart
Seite / *page* 326

Nestlé Nespresso SA
Route du Lac 3
CH-1094 Paudex
Seite / *page* 200, 201

Gebr. Niessing GmbH & Co.
Butenwall 117
D-48691 Vreden
Seite / *page* 466

Normann Copenhagen
Strandboulevarden 98
DK-2100 Kopenhagen
Seite / *page* 208

nya nordiska textiles gmbh
An den Ratswiesen
D-29451 Dannenberg
Seite / *page* 149-151

O

OG Invent
Snap Alarm
P.O. Box 5108
S-10243 Stockholm
Seite / *page* 216

Olympus Deutschland GmbH
Wendenstr. 14-18
D-20097 Hamburg
Seite / *page* 369

Olympus Diagnostica Lab Automation GmbH
Bötzinger Str. 31
D-79111 Freiburg
Seite / *page* 371

Olympus Winter & Ibe GmbH
Kuehnstr. 61
D-22045 Hamburg
Seite / *page* 82, 83

Adam Opel AG
D-65423 Rüsselsheim
Seite / *page* 316, 317

OSIM International Ltd
65 Ubi Avenue 1
Singapur 408939
Seite / *page* 265

OTAG Vertriebs GmbH & Co. KG
Zur Hammerbrücke 9
D-59939 Olsberg
Seite / *page* 347

Otto Bock HealthCare
Utah Design and Manufacturing Center
3820 West Great Lakes Drive
Salt Lake City, UT 84120
USA
Seite / *page* 374

Otto Bock HealthCare GmbH
Max-Näder-Str. 15
D-37115 Duderstadt
Seite / *page* 80, 81, 362, 372, 373, 375

OWP Brillen GmbH
Spitalhofstr. 94
D-94032 Passau
Seite / *page* 470

P

P2 Group
Leidsevaartweg 1
NL-2106 AH Heemstede
Seite / *page* 283

Pantech & Curitel
Peungwha Seocho Bldg., 1451-34
Seocho-Dong, Seocho-Gu
Seoul 137-070
Korea
Seite / *page* 410-412

Pelikan Vertriebsgesellschaft mbH & Co. KG
Werftstr. 9
D-30163 Hannover
Seite / *page* 266, 386

Pfeiffer Vacuum Technology AG
Berliner Str. 43
D-35614 Asslar
Seite / *page* 309

Pinc AB
Kungsborgsbacken 1
S-13146 Nacka
Seite / *page* 58, 59

Plan Creations Co., Ltd.
114/1 Soi Sathorn 10
North Sathorn Road
Bangkok 10500
Thailand
Seite / *page* 266

Poggenpohl Möbelwerke GmbH
Poggenpohlstr. 1
D-32051 Herford
Seite / *page* 166, 167

Pommerening Armaturenwerk GmbH & Co. KG
Böcklerstr. 11
D-31789 Hameln
Seite / *page* 354

Dr. Ing. h.c. F. Porsche AG
Porscheplatz 1
D-70435 Stuttgart
Seite / *page* 72, 73

Porsche Lizenz- und Handelsgesellschaft mbH & Co. KG
Porschestr. 1
D-74321 Bietigheim-Bissingen
Seite / *page* 272, 273

PSA Marine (Pte) Ltd
7B Keppel Road
Tanjong Pagar Complex #09-07
Singapur 089055
Seite / *page* 70, 71

R

Readymade
341B 21st Ave., Villieria
ZA-0186 Pretoria
Seite / *page* 461

Renz GmbH
Hanns-Klemm-Str. 35
D-71034 Böblingen
Seite / *page* 388

Resol GmbH
Heiskampstr. 10
D-45527 Hattingen
Seite / *page* 309, 354

Rodenstock GmbH
Isartalstr. 43
D-80469 München
Seite / *page* 98, 99, 468, 469

Rolf Benz AG & Co. KG
Haiterbacher Str. 104
D-72202 Nagold
Seite / *page* 144, 145

Rosenthal AG
Philip-Rosenthal-Platz 1
D-95100 Selb
Seite / *page* 218, 219

Roset S.A.
B.P. 9
F-01470 Briord
Seite / *page* 44, 45

Rösle GmbH & Co. KG
Johann-Georg-Fendt-Str. 38
D-87616 Marktoberdorf
Seite / *page* 228

RoyalVKB
Zilverstraat 40
NL-2718 RK Zoetermeer
Seite / *page* 226, 227

RWE Mechatronics GmbH
Friedrich-Wilhelm-Str. 14
D-53894 Mechernich
Seite / *page* 52, 53

S

Sahm GmbH + Co. KG
Westerwaldstr. 13
D-56203 Höhr-Grenzhausen
Seite / *page* 230

Sam-Electronics GmbH
Behringstr. 120
D-22763 Hamburg
Seite / *page* 327

Samsung Electronics Co., Ltd.
14th Fl., Joong-Ang Ilbo Bldg. 7
Soonhwa-Dong, Chung-Ku
Seoul 100-759
Korea
Seite / *page* 196, 197, 416-419

Arkitekterne maa Schmidt, Hammer & Lassen K/S
Clemensborg
Aaboulevarden 37, 5.
DK-8000 Aarhus C
Seite / *page* 159

Hermann G. Schütte & Co GmbH
Zum Achimer Bahnhof 16
D-28832 Achim
Seite / *page* 294

Sennheiser electronic GmbH & Co. KG
Am Labor 1
D-30900 Wedemark
Seite / *page* 459

Severin Elektrogeräte GmbH
Röhre 27
D-59846 Sundern
Seite / *page* 203

Shimano, Inc.
77 Oimatsu-cho 3-cho
Sakai
Osaka 590-8577
Japan
Seite / *page* 264

Shur-Line
A Newell-Rubbermaid Company
4051 S. Iowa Ave.
St. Francis, WI 53235
USA
Seite / *page* 303

Shuttle Inc.
No. 30, Lane 76, Rei-Kuang Rd., Nei-Hu Dist.
Taipei 114
Taiwan
Seite / *page* 443

SieMatic Möbelwerke GmbH & Co. KG
August-Siekmann-Str. 1-5
D-32584 Löhne
Seite / *page* 223

Siemens AG
Henkestr. 127
D-91052 Erlangen
Seite / *page* 360, 361

Siemens AG
Haidenauplatz 1
D-81667 München
Seite / *page* 406-409

Siemens AG
Rupert-Mayer-Str. 44
D-81359 München
Seite / *page* 293

Siemens AG
L&A PA
Bücklestr. 1-5
D-78467 Konstanz
Seite / *page* 305

Siemens AG
Medical Solutions
Siemensstr. 1
D-91301 Forchheim
Seite / *page* 359

Siemens Electrogeräte GmbH
Carl-Wery-Str. 34
D-81739 München
Seite / *page* 174-177, 183, 184

Siemens Medical Solutions USA
2501 North Barrington Road
Hoffman Estates, IL 60195
USA
Seite / *page* 78, 79, 358

Silhouette International Schmied AG
Ellbognerstr. 24
A-4021 Linz
Seite / *page* 471

Silit-Werke GmbH & Co. KG
Neufraer Str. 6
D-88499 Riedlingen
Seite / *page* 214

Simplon Fahrrad GmbH
Oberer Achdamm 22
A-6971 Hard
Seite / *page* 250

Sirona Dental Systems GmbH
Fabrikstr. 31
D-64625 Bensheim
Seite / *page* 367

Solo Cup Company
1700 Old Deerfield Rd.
Highland Park, IL 60035
USA
Seite / *page* 206

Sonos, Inc.
506 Chapala
Santa Barbara, CA 93101
USA
Seite / *page* 421

Sony Corporation
6-7-35 Kitashinagawa, Shinagawa-ku
Tokio 141-0001
Japan
Seite / *page* 92, 93, 444, 446-449

Sony Ericsson
Mobile Communications Int. AB
Fritz-Vomfelde-Str. 26
D-40547 Düsseldorf
Seite / *page* 413

Sony Ericsson Mobile Communications Japan Inc.
Konan Minatoku
Tokio 108-0075
Japan
Seite / *page* 445

Sotos:Kollektion
Landgrafenstr. 36
D-50931 Köln
Seite / *page* 464

Spirit Design LTDA.
Rua Riachuelo 239/SL 209
BR-20230-010 Rio de Janeiro, RJ
Seite / *page* 426

stawert Mühlenbau GmbH & Co. KG
Tilsiter Str. 142
D-22047 Hamburg
Seite / *page* 202

Steelcase Werndl AG
Georg-Aicher-Str. 7
D-83026 Rosenheim
Seite / *page* 382, 383

Stelton A/S
Christianshavns Kanal 4
DK-1406 Kopenhagen K
Seite / *page* 231, 450

Stiebel Eltron GmbH & Co. KG
Dr.-Stiebel-Str.
D-37603 Holzminden
Seite / *page* 355

Andreas Stihl AG & Co. KG
Badstr. 115
D-71336 Waiblingen
Seite / *page* 298

A. & J. Stöckli AG
Ennetbachstr. 40
CH-8754 Netstal
Seite / *page* 215

Sunwave Corporation
2-6-10, Sarugaku-cho, Chiyoda-ku
Tokio
Japan
Seite / *page* 168

Swarovski
14-15 Conduit Street 2nd Floor
GB-London W1R 9TG
Seite / *page* 482

T

TAG Heuer
4, rue L.J. Chevrolet
CH-2300 La Chaux de Fonds
Seite / *page* 96, 97

Tai Ping Carpets
Bilkerstr. 5
D-40213 Düsseldorf
Seite / *page* 157

Tampoprint AG
Lingwiesenstr. 1
D-70825 Korntal-Münchingen
Seite / *page* 307

Team 7 Natürlich Wohnen GmbH
Braunauer Str. 26
A-4910 Ried
Seite / *page* 146

Tente-Rollen GmbH
Herrlinghausen 75
D-42929 Wermelskirchen
Seite / *page* 296

tesa AG
Quickbornstr. 24
D-20253 Hamburg
Seite / *page* 241

Thermoplastik Erich Müller GmbH
Gewerbestr. 1
D-64807 Dieburg
Seite / *page* 255

Topeak, Inc.
8F-4, No. 20, Ta-Long Road
Taichung
Taiwan
Seite / *page* 54, 55, 264

Toshiba Corporation
1-1, Shibaura 1-Chome, Minato-ku
Tokio 105-8001
Japan
Seite / *page* 237, 240, 350, 420, 421

Toucan-T Carpet Manufacture GmbH
St. Töniserstr. 84
D-47803 Krefeld
Seite / *page* 388

Trelock GmbH
Harkortstr. 17
D-48163 Münster
Seite / *page* 252

Trere s.r.l.
Via Modena 18
I-46041 Asola (MN)
Seite / *page* 249

Tupperware France S.A.
Route de Monts
F-37300 Joue-les-Tours
Seite / *page* 234

U

Uhlmann Pac-Systeme GmbH & Co. KG
Uhlmannstr. 14-18
D-88471 Laupheim
Seite / *page* 310

V

Vaillant GmbH
Berghauser Str. 40
D-42859 Remscheid
Seite / *page* 352

Vermop Salmon GmbH
Kiesweg 4-6
D-97877 Wertheim
Seite / *page* 312, 313

Video Networks Ltd.
205 Holland Park Avenue
GB-London W11 4XB
Seite / *page* 456, 457

Volkswagen AG
Berliner Ring 2
D-38440 Wolfsburg
Seite / *page* 322

Vorwerk Elektrowerke GmbH & Co. KG
D-42270 Wuppertal
Seite / *page* 213

W

Wacom Co., Ltd.
2-510-1, Toyonodai, Otone-machi,
Kitasaitama-gun
Saitama 349-1148
Japan
Seite / *page* 430, 431

Max Weishaupt GmbH
Max-Weishaupt-Str. 14
D-88475 Schwendi
Seite / *page* 353

Weitz-Möbelmanufaktur GmbH
Leutersdorfer Str. 51
D-02782 Seifhennersdorf
Seite / *page* 172

WERMA Signaltechnik GmbH + Co. KG
Dürbheimer Str. 15
D-78604 Rietheim-Weilheim
Seite / *page* 299

Whipsaw, Inc.
434 South First Street
San Jose, CA 95113
USA
Seite / *page* 424

William Levene Ltd
Bridge House
Eelmoor Road
GB-Farnborough, Hampshire GU14 7UE
Seite / *page* 229

WM-Logistik GmbH & Co. KG
Am Gut Baarking
D-46395 Bocholt
Seite / *page* 299

WMF Württembergische Metallwarenfabrik AG
Eberhardstr.
D-73309 Geislingen/Steige
Seite / *page* 204, 220

X

X-Technology Swiss GmbH
Kantonsstr. 146
CH-8807 Freienbach
Seite / *page* 249

Z

Zumtobel Staff GmbH
Schweizer Str. 30
A-6850 Dornbirn
Seite / *page* 474-477

Zweibrüder Optoelectronics GmbH
Kronenstr. 5-7
D-42699 Solingen
Seite / *page* 253

Zwilling J.A. Henckels AG
Grünewalder Str. 14-22
D-42657 Solingen
Seite / *page* 222, 349

Zyliss AG
Eggbühlstr. 28
CH-8032 Zürich
Seite / *page* 229

索引——经销商（按字母顺序）

Alphabetical address-index distributors

A

AEG Hausgeräte GmbH
Muggenhofer Str. 135
D-90429 Nürnberg
Seite / *page* 191

Ahrend GmbH & Co. KG
Frankfurter Straße 39
D-63303 Dreieich
Seite / *page* 378, 379

Airflow Lufttechnik GmbH
Kleine Heeg 21
D-53359 Rheinbach
Seite / *page* 350

Alno AG
Heiligenberger Str. 47
D-88630 Pfullendorf
Seite / *page* 171

Artemide GmbH
Hans-Böckler-Str. 2
D-58730 Fröndenberg
Seite / *page* 102-105, 484, 485

AVC Germany GmbH
Schopenstehl 22
D-20095 Hamburg
Seite / *page* 450

AVD Videoproduktion GmbH
Burgstr. 17
D-53842 Troisdorf
Seite / *page* 52, 53

B

Basta Deutschland GmbH
An der Silberkuhle 1
D-58239 Schwerte
Seite / *page* 252

BenQ Deutschland GmbH
Weidestr. 122a
D-22083 Hamburg
Seite / *page* 400-405

Blomberg Vertriebsgesellschaft mbH
Voltastr. 50
D-59229 Ahlen
Seite / *page* 194

Peter Bodum GmbH
Feldstr. 3b
D-24559 Kaltenkirchen
Seite / *page* 209, 211

Bose GmbH
Max-Planck-Str. 36
D-61381 Friedrichsdorf
Seite / *page* 86, 87, 420

Brucker Loft
Kapellenstr. 2
D-82256 Fürstenfeldbruck
Seite / *page* 232

C

CarbonFunctions Vertriebs GmbH
Hachelallee 7
D-75179 Pforzheim
Seite / *page* 255

Crown Gabelstapler GmbH & Co. KG
Moosacher Str. 52
D-80809 München
Seite / *page* 325

D

DaimlerChrysler Vertriebsorganisation Deutschland
D-10878 Berlin
Seite / *page* 318, 319

Damixa Armaturen GmbH
Köbbingser Mühle 7
D-58640 Iserlohn
Seite / *page* 333

De'Longhi Deutschland GmbH
Am Reitpfad 20
D-63500 Seligenstadt
Seite / *page* 230, 237

Dell GmbH
Monzastr. 4
D-63225 Langen
Seite / *page* 423

E

ECC Efficient Cycle Concepts GmbH
Dr.-Carlo-Schmid-Str. 93a
D-90491 Nürnberg
Seite / *page* 250

Eva Deutschland
Pinneberger Chaussee 99
D-25436 Moorrege
Seite / *page* 231

F

Fiskars Brands Germany GmbH
Oststr. 23
D-32051 Herford
Seite / *page* 263

Flos GmbH
Elisabeth-Selbert-Str. 4a
D-40764 Langenfeld
Seite / *page* 481

G

Gorenje Vertriebs GmbH
Garmischer Str. 4-6
D-80339 München
Seite / *page* 182

Grundig Multimedia
Beuthener Str. 43
D-90471 Nürnberg
Seite / *page* 455

I

Ideal Standard Deutschland
Euskirchener Str. 80
D-53121 Bonn
Seite / *page* 334, 335

Imaje GmbH
Schockenriedstr. 8c
D-70565 Stuttgart
Seite / *page* 306

J

Jura Elektrogeräte Vertriebs-GmbH
Postfach 99 01 44
D-90268 Nürnberg
Seite / *page* 203

K

Kohler GmbH
Holtgarde 30
D-45739 Oer-Erkenschwick
Seite / *page* 337

KWC Deutschland GmbH
Rigipsstr. 15
D-71083 Herrenberg
Seite / *page* 233

L

Laufen GmbH
Feincheswiese 17
D-56424 Staudt
Seite / *page* 338, 339

Leolux Möbelfabrik GmbH
Postfach 111303
D-47814 Krefeld
Seite / *page* 146

LG Electronics Deutschland GmbH
Jakob-Kaiser-Str. 12
D-47877 Willich
Seite / *page* 194, 195, 440, 441

Logitech GmbH
Streiflacher Str. 7
D-82110 Germering
Seite / *page* 435

Lurch AG
Schinkelstr. 6
D-31137 Hildesheim
Seite / *page* 222

M

Mahlkönig Vertriebsgesellschaft mbH
Rungedamm 22
D-21035 Hamburg
Seite / *page* 202

Maxfield GmbH
Kaistr. 2
D-40221 Düsseldorf
Seite / *page* 428, 429

N

Naturquell Mineralwasser Vertriebs GmbH
St.-Apern-Str. 26
D-50667 Köln
Seite / *page* 267

O

Olympus Diagnostica GmbH
Wendenstr. 14-18
D-20097 Hamburg
Seite / *page* 371

R

Roset Möbel GmbH
Industriestr. 51
D-79194 Gundelfingen
Seite / *page* 44, 45

RTI Sports GmbH
Rudolf-Diesel-Str. 21
D-56220 Urmitz
Seite / *page* 54, 55, 264

S

Hans Schwarzkopf & Henkel GmbH & Co KG
Hohenzollernring 127-129
D-22763 Hamburg
Seite / *page* 294, 295

Shimano Germany Fishing GmbH
Diessemer Bruch 114f
D-47805 Krefeld
Seite / *page* 264

Shuttle Computer Handels GmbH
Fritz-Strassmann-Str. 5
D-25337 Elmshorn
Seite / *page* 443

Silhouette Vertriebs GmbH
Schwieberdinger Str. 56
D-71636 Ludwigsburg
Seite / *page* 471

SLI Lichtsysteme GmbH
Graf-Zeppelin-Str. 9-12
D-91056 Erlangen
Seite / *page* 480

Sony Deutschland GmbH
Hugo-Eckener-Str. 20
D-50829 Köln
Seite / *page* 92, 93, 444

Stelton Verkaufsbüro Deutschland
Volmestr. 1
D-58540 Meinerzhagen
Seite / *page* 231, 450

Stihl Vertriebszentrale AG & Co. KG
Robert-Bosch-Str. 13
D-64807 Dieburg
Seite / *page* 298

T

Trere s.r.l.
Via Modena 18
I-46041 Asola (MN)
Seite / *page* 249

Tupperware Deutschland GmbH
Praunheimer Landstr. 70
D-60488 Frankfurt/Main
Seite / *page* 234

V

Van Laar Agentur
Himmelgeister Landstr. 167
D-40589 Düsseldorf
Seite / *page* 159

Vorwerk & Co. Thermomix GmbH
D-42270 Wuppertal
Seite / *page* 213

W

Wacom Europe GmbH
Europark Fichtenhain A9
D-47807 Krefeld
Seite / *page* 430, 431

Herbert Waldmann GmbH & Co. KG
Peter-Henlein-Str. 5
D-78056 Villingen-Schwenningen
Seite / *page* 364, 365

WM-Logistik GmbH & Co. KG
Am Gut Baarking
D-46395 Bocholt
Seite / *page* 299

WoodEye Scannersysteme GmbH
Schachtweg 11
D-57080 Siegen
Seite / *page* 309

Z

Zumtobel Staff Deutschland Vertriebs GmbH
Grevenmarschstr. 74-78
D-32657 Lemgo
Seite / *page* 474-477

索引——设计师（按字母顺序）

Alphabetical address-index designers

A

Acer Design Team
Acer Incorporated
Seite / *page* 432

Christian Ågren
AB Electrolux
Seite / *page* 236, 238

Airflow Design Team
Airflow Developments Ltd.
Seite / *page* 350

Jochen Allard
Grohe Water Technology AG & Co. KG
Seite / *page* 343

Alno AG
Heiligenberger Str. 47
D-88630 Pfullendorf
Seite / *page* 171

Jan Andersen
Normann Copenhagen
Seite / *page* 208

Apple Design Team
Apple
Seite / *page* 90, 91, 392-399

Calum Armstrong
Electrolux Home Products
Electrolux Industrial Design Centre Europe
Seite / *page* 191

Matthias Arnold
DASGIP AG
Seite / *page* 368

Firat Arnt
NEOMAN Bus GmbH
Seite / *page* 326

Artefakt Industriekultur
Achim Pohl und Tomas Fiegl
Liebigstr. 50-52
D-64293 Darmstadt
Seite / *page* 280, 334-336, 345

Artemide GmbH
Hans-Böckler-Str. 2
D-58730 Fröndenberg
Seite / *page* 484, 485

Alexander von Ascheberg
Otto Bock HealthCare GmbH
Seite / *page* 80, 81

Asmobile Industrial Design Team
Asmobile Communication Inc.
Seite / *page* 422

Asus Design
AsusTek Computer Inc.
Seite / *page* 434, 435

Les Ateliers du Nord
Place du Nord 2
CH-1005 Lausanne
Seite / *page* 200, 201

Audi Design Team
Audi AG
Seite / *page* 323

Eduardo Azevedo
Indio da Costa Design
Seite / *page* 330, 331

B

Byung-Kook Baek
Samsung Electronics Co., Ltd.
Seite / *page* 196

Martin Ballendat
Maximilianstr. 15
D-84359 Simbach
Seite / *page* 146

Felix Ballerstedt
Carsten Gollnick product design
& interior design
Seite / *page* 202

Klaudia Bartsch
Alerdsweg 4
D-38118 Braunschweig
Seite / *page* 295

Mathew Bates
Design Partners
Seite / *page* 435

Jessica Battram
Glittenbergstr. 5
D-26676 Reekenfeld
Seite / *page* 210

Peter Bäurle
Wiesentalstr. 43
D-73312 Geislingen-Eybach
Seite / *page* 220

Rochus Becherer
Becherer Möbel + Innenausbau GmbH
Seite / *page* 172

Christoph Becke
Siemens Electrogeräte GmbH
Seite / *page* 177

Cornelius Becker
Siemens AG
Henkestr. 127
D-91052 Erlangen
Seite / *page* 360

Martin Becker
Gebr. Becker GmbH & Co. KG
Seite / *page* 308

Martin Beeh
Electrolux Home Products
Electrolux Industrial Design Centre Europe
Seite / *page* 191

Klaus Begasse
Artemide GmbH
Seite / *page* 484, 485

Yves Behar
fuseproject
Seite / *page* 100, 101, 482

Beko Industrial Design Team
Beko Elektronik A.S.
Seite / *page* 455

Detlef Belter
Delta Form Industriedesign
Seite / *page* 233

BenQ Lifestyle Design Center
BenQ Corporation
Seite / *page* 400-405

Raymond Berg
Lumiance B.V.
Seite / *page* 480

bgp design
Lindenstr. 10
D-70563 Stuttgart
Seite / *page* 307

Felippe Bicudo
Indio da Costa Design
Seite / *page* 330, 331

Marit Bindernagel
Ulla u. Martin Kaufmann
Seite / *page* 467

Jens Bingenheimer
Am Horn 6
D-38667 Bad Harzburg
Seite / *page* 294

Martin Birtel
Indio da Costa Design
Seite / *page* 426

Jonas Blanking
Boblbee AB
Seite / *page* 261

Claudia Blum
Studio Matteo Thun
Seite / *page* 272, 273

Thomas Blümel
designafairs GmbH
Seite / *page* 367

Designteam der BMW Group
BMW Group
Seite / *page* 321

Designteam der BMW Group
Designteam Motorrad
BMW Group
Seite / *page* 68, 69, 320

Bodum AG
Bodum Design Group
Kantonsstr. 100
CH-6234 Triengen
Seite / *page* 209, 211

Prof. Michael Boehm
Sahm GmbH + Co. KG
Seite / *page* 230

Wun San Boek
LG Electronics Inc.
Corporate Design Center
Seite / *page* 441

Brian Bone
Metaphase Design Group, Inc.
Seite / *page* 303

Christoph Böninger
designafairs GmbH
Seite / *page* 281

Reinhard Boos
WMF AG
Seite / *page* 204

Per Börjesson
Electrolux Home Products
Electrolux Industrial Design Centre Europe
Seite / *page* 191

Bose Corp. Design Team
Bose Corp.
Seite / *page* 86, 87, 420

Moritz Böttcher
LoeweVonAppen GmbH
Seite / *page* 264

Ronan & Erwan Bouroullec
12, rue Roussel
F-93200 St. Denis
Seite / *page* 44, 45

John Boye
Langergårdsvej 3 Resen
DK-7600 Struer
Seite / *page* 297

Knut Braake
bgp design
Seite / *page* 307

Jörg Brennwald
Brennwald Design
Feldstr. 133
D-24105 Kiel
Seite / *page* 459

Stefan Brodbeck
Brodbeck Design
Schillerstr. 40c
D-80336 München
Seite / *page* 351, 366, 383

Philip Brook
Le Groupe GO inc.
Seite / *page* 250

BRP Design Team
Bombardier Recreational Products Inc.
Seite / *page* 324

Bernd Brüssing
Prodesign
Seite / *page* 277

Christian de Bruyn
Rodenstock GmbH
Seite / *page* 468

Christian Bunse
Tesign
Seite / *page* 309

Achim Burmeister
NEOMAN Bus GmbH
Seite / *page* 326

busse design ulm GmbH
Nersinger Str. 18
D-89275 Elchingen
Seite / *page* 298, 301

Won-Gab Byun
Samsung Electronics Co., Ltd.
Seite / *page* 417

C

C10 Design & Development
Zijlweg 76
NL-2013 DK Haarlem
Seite / *page* 423

Antoine Cahen
Les Ateliers du Nord
Seite / *page* 200, 201

Philippe Cahen
Les Ateliers du Nord
Seite / *page* 200, 201

Canon Inc.
30-2, Shimomaruko 3-chome, Ohta-ku
Tokio 146-8501
Japan
Seite / *page* 438, 439, 442

Nikolaï Carels
Vrijburglaan 56
NL-2051 LD Overveen
Seite / *page* 226

Werner Carl
DASGIP AG
Seite / *page* 368

Kang Heui Cha
LG Electronics Inc.
Corporate Design Center
Seite / *page* 440

Yong-Hun Chang
LG Electronics Inc.
Corporate Design Center
Seite / *page* 195

Dennis Chiang
Topeak, Inc.
Seite / *page* 264

Yukie Chiba
Toshiba Design Center
Toshiba Corporation
Seite / *page* 240

Keiji Chikuma
Toshiba Design Center
Toshiba Corporation
Seite / *page* 350

Ju-Won Cho
Samsung Electronics Co., Ltd.
Seite / *page* 417

Kyeong-Chul Cho
LG Electronics Inc.
Corporate Design Center
Seite / *page* 195

Yoon Young Cho
LG Electronics Inc.
Corporate Design Center
Seite / *page* 440

Je-Seung Choi
LG Electronics Inc.
Corporate Design Center
Seite / *page* 195

Kyu Kwan Choi
LG Electronics Inc.
Corporate Design Center
Seite / *page* 194

Louis Chuang
Topeak, Inc.
Seite / *page* 264

Yeon-Moo Chung
Samsung Electronics Co., Ltd.
Seite / *page* 418

Antonio Citterio
Via Cerva 4
I-20122 Mailand
Seite / *page* 76, 77

Hilary Clark
Virgin Atlantic Airways
Seite / *page* 282

Martin Cooper
Concord:marlin
Seite / *page* 480

David Crafoord
Ergonomidesign AB
Seite / *page* 221

D

DaimlerChrysler AG
Bereich Design
Benzstr., HPC X800
D-71059 Sindelfingen
Seite / *page* 318, 319

Denis Dammköhler
Alfred Kärcher GmbH & Co. KG
Seite / *page* 304

Jorgé Davis Quinones
Concord:marlin
Seite / *page* 480

de Gast deSign
Viale Lambardia 66
I-20131 Mailand
Seite / *page* 214

De'Longhi Industrial Design Center
De'Longhi S.p.A.
Seite / *page* 237

Decathlon
4, boulevard de Mons
F-59650 Villeneuve d'Ascq
Seite / *page* 56, 57

Manfred Deffner
Leicht Küchen AG
Seite / *page* 169, 173

Dell Industrial Design and Usability Group
Dell Inc.
Seite / *page* 423

Delta Form Industriedesign
Wiehengebirgsstr. 34
D-49328 Melle
Seite / *page* 233

Tim Derhaag
Kloveniersburgwal 16-2
NL-1012 CT Amsterdam
Seite / *page* 481

Simon Desanta
Industrial Design
Schloss Holtfeld
D-33829 Borgholzhausen
Seite / *page* 262

Design 3
Schaarsteinwegsbrücke 2
D-20459 Hamburg
Seite / *page* 241, 415, 451

Design AG
Neupförtner Wall 21
D-33378 Rheda-Wiedenbrück
Seite / *page* 161, 308

Design Partners
IDA Business Park
Southern Cross Route
IRL-Bray, Co. Wicklow
Seite / *page* 435

designafairs GmbH
Konrad-Zuse-Str. 12
D-91052 Erlangen
Seite / *page* 359-361, 367

designafairs GmbH
Tölzer Str. 2c
D-81379 München
Seite / *page* 281, 293, 305, 408, 409, 441

Designit
Klosterport 4E
DK-8000 Aarhus C
Seite / *page* 450

Designkontor
Stresemannstr. 374
D-22761 Hamburg
Seite / *page* 241

Lichtprojekte Christian Deuber
Postfach 6330
Bürgenstr. 9
CH-6000 Luzern 6
Seite / *page* 485

Stefan Diez
Geyerstr. 20
D-80469 München
Seite / *page* 146, 218, 219

Aernout Dijkstra
NPK Industrial Design
Seite / *page* 423

Peter Distler
Siemens AG
Henkestr. 127
D-91052 Erlangen
Seite / *page* 361

Han Young Doh
LG Electronics Inc.
Corporate Design Center
Seite / *page* 195

Stefan Domalski
Siemens AG
Henkestr. 127
D-91052 Erlangen
Seite / *page* 361

Heath Doty
Metaphase Design Group, Inc.
Seite / *page* 303

DTC
Zeppelinstr. 5-7
D-64625 Bensheim
Seite / *page* 367

Fredy Dubach
Dubach Design
Schürlistr. 11
CH-8344 Bäretswil
Seite / *page* 215

E

Wolfgang Eiff
Sirona Dental Systems GmbH
Seite / *page* 367

Anke Eigenbrodt
Goslarsche Str. 97
D-38118 Braunschweig
Seite / *page* 295

Frank Eisele
Eisele Kuberg Design
Oderstr. 1
D-89231 Neu-Ulm
Seite / *page* 186, 187

Electrolux Home Products
Electrolux Industrial Design Centre Europe
Corso Lino Zanussi 30
I-33080 Porcia (PN)
Seite / *page* 191

EOOS
Theresiengasse 11/15
A-1180 Wien
Seite / *page* 154

Kenan Erdinc
NEOMAN Bus GmbH
Seite / *page* 326

Ergonomidesign AB
P.O. Box 14004
Missionsvägen 24
S-16714 Bromma
Seite / *page* 216, 221

Boje Estermann
3, rue Jean Beausire
F-75004 Paris
Seite / *page* 208

F

Wolfgang Fabian
Relaisstr. 183
D-68219 Mannheim
Seite / *page* 384, 385

Preben Fabricius
Walter Knoll AG & Co.KG
Seite / *page* 148

Fachhochschule Hannover
Fachbereich Design und Medien
Kurt-Schwitters-Forum
Expo-Plaza 2
D-30539 Hannover
Seite / *page* 264

Feder Design
Produkt- und Graphikdesign
Roddestr. 5
D-48153 Münster
Seite / *page* 203

Shaun Fernandes
Jump Studios
Seite / *page* 283

Fido industridesign as
Rådhusgata 5b
N-0151 Oslo
Seite / *page* 351

Maja Finke
Carsten Gollnick product design
& interior design
Seite / *page* 202

Camila Fix
Indio da Costa Design
Seite / *page* 330, 331

Oskar Fjellman
AB Electrolux
Seite / *page* 236, 238

Bianca Fleischer
designafairs GmbH
Seite / *page* 409

FOC
Freedom Of Creation
Hobbemakade 85 hs
NL-1017 XP Amsterdam
Seite / *page* 484

Peter Fornoff
Sirona Dental Systems GmbH
Seite / *page* 367

Herbert Forrer
A. & J. Stöckli AG
Seite / *page* 215

fpm factor product münchen
Comeniusstr. 1 RGB
D-81667 München
Seite / *page* 254

Christiane Frank
Neumeister + Partner
Industrial Design
Seite / *page* 276

Manfred Frank
Manfred Frank Systems Ltd.
P.O. Box 47947 Ponsonby
Auckland
Neuseeland
Seite / *page* 278

Arch. Enrico Franzolini
Via Girardini 20
I-33100 Udine
Seite / *page* 160

frog design europe gmbh
Kalkofenstr. 51
D-71083 Herrenberg
Seite / *page* 194

Gerhard Fuchs
Silhouette International Schmied AG
Seite / *page* 471

Gen Fujiki
Sony Corporation
Seite / *page* 447

Frank Fulgoni
Severin Elektrogeräte GmbH
Seite / *page* 203

Samuel Furrer
Derungs Licht AG
Seite / *page* 364, 365

fuseproject
123 South Park
San Francisco, CA 94107
USA
Seite / *page* 100, 101, 482

G

Marcus Gabrielsson
Ergonomidesign AB
Seite / *page* 216

Sven Gaedtke
NEOMAN Bus GmbH
Seite / *page* 326

Mike Gallagher
Crown Equipment Corporation
Seite / *page* 325

Frank Gärtner
monopezzo
Klein + Gärtner GbR
Seite / *page* 240

Anders Geert-Jensen
Designit
Seite / *page* 450

Bernhard Geisen
GeisenDesign
Schloßstr. 256
D-45359 Essen
Seite / *page* 436, 437

Deert Gellner
Siemens AG
Henkestr. 127
D-91052 Erlangen
Seite / *page* 361

Jason Germany
Chef'n Corp
Seite / *page* 222

Massimo Iosa Ghini
Studio Iosa Ghini
Via Castiglione 6
I-40124 Bologna
Seite / *page* 474, 475

André Gilli
Design by Gilli
Feldweg 5
CH-6415 Arth
Seite / *page* 215

Marco Giusti
Video Networks Ltd.
Seite / *page* 456, 457

Michael Glanz
DORMA GmbH + Co. KG
Seite / *page* 281

gneiss group
Frederikssundsvej 2
DK-2400 Kopenhagen
Seite / *page* 333

Nils Göbel
Leopoldstr. 7
D-38100 Braunschweig
Seite / *page* 295

Carsten Gollnick
Carsten Gollnick product design
& interior design
Bülowstr. 66
D-10783 Berlin
Seite / *page* 84, 85, 202, 381

Wolfgang Gößwein
Siemens AG
Henkestr. 127
D-91052 Erlangen
Seite / *page* 360

Michael Grasshoff
Königsstieg 19
D-38118 Braunschweig
Seite / *page* 295

Konstantin Grcic
Industrial Design
Schillerstr. 40 RGB
D-80336 München
Seite / *page* 481

Frank Greiser
Design AG
Seite / *page* 161, 308

greutmann bolzern Designstudio
Sihlquai 268
CH-8005 Zürich
Seite / *page* 147

Gerhard Grimmeisen
Grimmeisen Licht
Äußere Lohe 2
D-83512 Wasserburg a. Inn
Seite / *page* 380

Stefan Grobe
bgp design
Seite / *page* 307

Tassilo von Grolman
Tassilo von Grolman Design GmbH
Feldbergstr. 27
D-61440 Oberursel
Seite / *page* 230

Rickard Grönstedt
OG Invent
Seite / *page* 216

Karsten Großhauser
Siemens AG
Henkestr. 127
D-91052 Erlangen
Seite / *page* 361

Frederik Gundelach
Someones Design
Seite / *page* 231

H

Jeong-Hoon Ha
Samsung Electronics Co., Ltd.
Seite / *page* 418

Britta Hachenberg
NEOMAN Bus GmbH
Seite / *page* 326

Andreas Hackbarth
Siemens Electrogeräte GmbH
Seite / *page* 175, 184

Alf Hackenberg
Ziba Europe
Seite / *page* 430, 431

Regina Hadersbeck
KAHLA/Thüringen Porzellan GmbH
Seite / *page* 50, 51

Dagmar Hagen
OWP Brillen GmbH
Seite / *page* 470

Tatsuya Hama
Sony Ericsson Mobile Communications Japan Inc.
Seite / *page* 445

Nicolas Hamoignon
Decathlon
Seite / *page* 56, 57

Peter Hamm
Siemens Electrogeräte GmbH
Seite / *page* 175, 184

Michael Hammers
fuseproject
Seite / *page* 482

Woo-Seung Han
Samsung Electronics Co., Ltd.
Seite / *page* 416

Young Soo Han
LG Electronics Inc.
Corporate Design Center
Seite / *page* 441

Andre Hanisch
Indx-Design
Seite / *page* 436, 437

Ineke Hans
Dijkstraat 105
NL-6828 JS Arnheim
Seite / *page* 227

Dan Harden
Whipsaw, Inc.
Seite / *page* 424

Stephan Härtenberger
Holzprojekte Härtenberger HKH GmbH
Seite / *page* 171

Hartmann + Hartmann
Industriedesign und Werbeagentur GmbH
Bürgermeister-Fischer-Str. 9-11
D-86150 Augsburg
Seite / *page* 308

Peter Hartwein
Braun GmbH
Seite / *page* 368

Anthony Hatter
Dr. Ing. h.c. F. Porsche AG
Seite / *page* 66, 67

Erwin Hauenstein
Attika Feuer AG
Seite / *page* 347

Hauer & Ege GmbH
Schwieberdinger Str. 62
D-70435 Stuttgart
Seite / *page* 389

Hawa AG
Untere Fischbachstr. 4
CH-8932 Mettmenstetten
Seite / *page* 169

Karl-Leo Heitlinger
heitlinger form und technik
Tannenweg 9
D-73525 Schwäbisch Gmünd
Seite / *page* 370

Fred Held
Held + Team
Rehmstr.3a
D-22299 Hamburg
Seite / *page* 82, 83, 369, 461

Gerd Helmreich
designafairs GmbH
Seite / *page* 360, 361

Henkel Design Team
Henkel KGaA
Seite / *page* 387

Sören Henssler
LoeweVonAppen GmbH
Seite / *page* 264

Henssler und Schultheiss
Fullservice Productdesign GmbH
Weissensteiner Str. 28
D-73525 Schwäbisch Gmünd
Seite / *page* 256, 257, 302

Herbst LaZar Bell Inc.
355 North Canal Street
Chicago, IL 60606
USA
Seite / *page* 423

Bruno Herren
William Levene Ltd
Seite / *page* 229

Ito Hideki
Canon Inc.
Seite / *page* 438

Jan Hoekstra
RoyalVKB
Seite / *page* 226

Henrik Holbæk
Tools Design
Seite / *page* 231

Greg Holderfield
Herbst LaZar Bell Inc.
Seite / *page* 423

Carldieter Hollmann
Gebr. Becker GmbH & Co. KG
Seite / *page* 308

Mark Holmes
c/o The Lane
55 Leather Lane
GB-London EC1N 7TJ
Seite / *page* 479

Kirsten Hoppert
Studio Vertijet
Seite / *page* 94, 95

Christian Hosse
RWE Mechatronics GmbH
Seite / *page* 52, 53

Duck Hsieh
1st Fl., No. 22, Lane 321, Sec. 1, Shingan Rd.
Taichung
Taiwan
Seite / *page* 258, 259

Rung-Ya Hsieh
Duck Image Co. Ltd.
Seite / *page* 427

Elliot Hsu
Herbst LaZar Bell Inc.
Seite / *page* 423

Byung Mu Huh
LG Electronics Inc.
Corporate Design Center
Seite / *page* 440

Thorsten Huth
Lignum arts GmbH
Seite / *page* 232

Jung Yeon Hwang
LG Electronics Inc.
Corporate Design Center
Seite / *page* 441

Kap Sun Hwang
Am Markt 4
D-25548 Kellinghusen
Seite / *page* 223

I

IDEO
100 Forest Avenue
Palo Alto, CA 94301
USA
Seite / *page* 229

Indio da Costa
Indio da Costa Design
R. Pinheiro Guimarães 101
BR-22281-080 Rio de Janeiro, RJ
Seite / *page* 330, 331, 426

Indx-Design
Wiescher Weg 100
D-45472 Mülheim
Seite / *page* 436, 437

Innodesign Inc.
577 College Avenue
Palo Alto, CA 94306
USA
Seite / *page* 425

Institut für Verbundwerkstoffe GmbH
Erwin-Schrödinger-Str., Gebäude 58
D-67663 Kaiserslautern
Seite / *page* 251

Tomiaki Ishihara
Toshiba Design Center
Toshiba Corporation
Seite / *page* 350

Masao Isshiki
Toshiba Design Center
Toshiba Corporation
Seite / *page* 420

Yoichi Ito
Sunwave Corporation
Seite / *page* 168

Masakazu Iwabuchi
Shimano, Inc.
Seite / *page* 264

J

Martin Jahnke
müller/romca Industrial Design Hamburg
Seite / *page* 327

Mike Jankowski
Concord:marlin
Seite / *page* 480

Hans-Reinhart Janssen
Robert Bosch Hausgeräte GmbH
Seite / *page* 188

Peter Jaritz
LoeweVonAppen GmbH
Seite / *page* 264

Jehs + Laub
Markus Jehs und Jürgen Laub
Römerstr. 51a
D-70180 Stuttgart
Seite / *page* 388

Thomas Jeltsch
EMS-GRIVORY
Seite / *page* 225

Rok Jenko
Gorenje d.d.
Seite / *page* 182

Claus Jensen
Tools Design
Seite / *page* 231

Ho il Jeon
LG Electronics Inc.
Corporate Design Center
Seite / *page* 194

Myung Seob Jeon
LG Electronics Inc.
Corporate Design Center
Seite / *page* 441

Se Min Jeon
Pantech & Curitel
Seite / *page* 411

Sei-Ill Jeon
Samsung Electronics Co., Ltd.
Seite / *page* 197

Seung-Wook Jeong
Samsung Electronics Co., Ltd.
Seite / *page* 419

So-Yoon Jeoun
Samsung Electronics Co., Ltd.
Seite / *page* 419

Carsten Joergensen
c/o Bodum AG
Bodum Design Group
Seite / *page* 211

Lennart Johansson
Electrolux Home Products
Electrolux Industrial Design Centre Europe
Seite / *page* 191

Tai-Hyung Ju
Samsung Electronics Co., Ltd.
Seite / *page* 419

Jump Studios
35 Britannia Row
GB-London N1 8QH
Seite / *page* 283

Tobias Jung
Lignum arts GmbH
Seite / *page* 232

Manfred Junker
Poggenpohl Möbelwerke GmbH
Seite / *page* 166, 167

K

Wolfgang Kaczmarek
Siemens Electrogeräte GmbH
Seite / *page* 176

Helmut Kaiser
Robert Bosch Hausgeräte GmbH
Seite / *page* 224, 242, 243

Michael Kaiser
Institut für Verbundwerkstoffe GmbH
Seite / *page* 251

Simon Kalmer
Designit
Seite / *page* 450

Georg Kaluza
Emil-Schniewind-Str. 10
D-42553 Velbert
Seite / *page* 281

Rino Kappler
kapplerdesign
Hof
CH-9620 Lichtensteig
Seite / *page* 300

Maria Sofia Karanthaki
Hohestieg 9
D-38118 Braunschweig
Seite / *page* 295

Jørgen Kastholm
Walter Knoll AG & Co.KG
Seite / *page* 148

Klaus Keichel
Küppersbusch Hausgeräte AG
Seite / *page* 185

Thoralf Keipert
NEOMAN Bus GmbH
Seite / *page* 326

Michael Keller
KMS Team GmbH
Seite / *page* 272, 273

John Kelly
Airflow Design Team
Airflow Developments Ltd.
Seite / *page* 350

Uwe Kemker
Vorwerk Elektrowerke GmbH & Co. KG
Seite / *page* 213

François Kergoet
Jacob Delafon Paris (Kohler France)
Seite / *page* 337

Hiroyuki Kikuchi
Sunwave Corporation
Seite / *page* 168

Morten Kildahl
Fido industridesign as
Seite / *page* 351

Goang-Tae Kim
Samsung Electronics Co., Ltd.
Seite / *page* 416

Han Kim
Samsung Electronics Co., Ltd.
Seite / *page* 417

In-Shik Kim
Samsung Electronics Co., Ltd.
Seite / *page* 418

Jeong-Min Kim
Samsung Electronics Co., Ltd.
Seite / *page* 197

Ji-Ho Kim
Samsung Electronics Co., Ltd.
Seite / *page* 197

Kyung Yun Kim
Pantech & Curitel
Seite / *page* 412

Myung-Jung Kim
Samsung Electronics Co., Ltd.
Seite / *page* 419

Nam-Mi Kim
Samsung Electronics Co., Ltd.
Seite / *page* 416

Seog-Guen Kim
Samsung Electronics Co., Ltd.
Seite / *page* 416

Seon-Kyu Kim
LG Electronics Inc.
Corporate Design Center
Seite / *page* 195

Sung Jae Kim
Pantech & Curitel
Seite / *page* 411, 412

Tae Bong Kim
LG Electronics Inc.
Corporate Design Center
Seite / *page* 441

Tae-Hong Kim
LG Electronics Inc.
Corporate Design Center
Seite / *page* 195

Young Se Kim
Innodesign Inc.
Seite / *page* 425

Young-Jun Kim
Samsung Electronics Co., Ltd.
Seite / *page* 418

Robert Kipry
Fasanenstr. 40
D-38102 Braunschweig
Seite / *page* 294

Henrik Kjellberg
Sweedish Designstudio
Seite / *page* 235

Elke Klar
JAB Teppiche Heinz Anstoetz KG
Seite / *page* 156

Jan Kleffmann
Festo AG & Co. KG
Seite / *page* 62-65, 286-292

Armin Klein
monopezzo
Klein + Gärtner GbR
Seite / *page* 240

Klöber Design-Team
Klöber GmbH
Seite / *page* 388

KMS Team GmbH
Deroystr. 3-5
D-80335 München
Seite / *page* 272, 273

Tomoyuki Kobayashi
Suwada
Seite / *page* 349

Till Kobes
Design 3
Seite / *page* 451

Claudia Köhler
Mocca Design
Seite / *page* 220

Rupert Kopp
Greige / Büro für Design
Raumerstr. 40
D-10437 Berlin
Seite / *page* 476, 477

Peter Kövari
Beethovenstr. 14
D-82049 München
Seite / *page* 98, 99, 469

Dirk Koy
KMS Team GmbH
Seite / *page* 272, 273

Dorothee Krause
LoeweVonAppen GmbH
Seite / *page* 264

Steffen Kroll
Studio Vertijet
Seite / *page* 94, 95

Frederick Kruger
Readymade
Seite / *page* 461

Christian Kruse
EMS-GRIVORY
Seite / *page* 225

Alexander Ksoll
Design 3
Seite / *page* 415

Timo Küchler
Gebr. Niessing GmbH & Co.
Seite / *page* 466

Klaus W. Kugler
Deutsche Telekom AG
T-Com Division
Seite / *page* 414, 415

André Kunzendorf
Kunzendorf Design
Ludwigstr. 25
D-42105 Wuppertal
Seite / *page* 308, 349

Mieko Kusano
Sonos, Inc.
Seite / *page* 421

Kenichi Kwasaki
Shimano, Inc.
Seite / *page* 264

Soon Uk Kwon
LG Electronics Inc.
Corporate Design Center
Seite / *page* 194

Janne Kyttanen
FOC
Freedom Of Creation
Seite / *page* 484

L

Fritz v. d. Laar
Lumiance B.V.
Seite / *page* 480

Prof. Bodo W. Lambertz
X-Technology Swiss GmbH
Seite / *page* 249

Martin Langkau
Ziba Europe
Seite / *page* 430, 431

Hea-Me Lee
Samsung Electronics Co., Ltd.
Seite / *page* 197

Jung Hoon Lee
LG Electronics Inc.
Corporate Design Center
Seite / *page* 441

Myung Hoon Lee
LG Electronics Inc.
Corporate Design Center
Seite / *page* 440

Young Ah Lee
LG Electronics Inc.
Corporate Design Center
Seite / *page* 441

Young ho Lee
LG Electronics Inc.
Corporate Design Center
Seite / *page* 441

Alois Lehnen
Lehnen edel:stahl GmbH
Seite / *page* 366

Leolux Produktentwicklungsabteilung
Leolux Meubelfabriek BV
Seite / *page* 146

Jan-Michael von Lewinski
Design 3
Seite / *page* 415

Yorgo Liebsch
Indx-Design
Seite / *page* 436, 437

Hyun-taek Lim
Samsung Electronics Co., Ltd.
Seite / *page* 417

Kim Lim
AB Electrolux
Seite / *page* 236, 238

Olavi Lindén
Fiskars Brands Finland Oy Ab
Seite / *page* 263

Mattias Lindqvist
Sweedish Designstudio
Seite / *page* 235

Brian Ling
Nakamichi Corporation Limited
Seite / *page* 454

Andrea Lipp
NEOMAN Bus GmbH
Seite / *page* 326

Designstudio Lippe
Lüderichstr. 2-4
D-41105 Köln
Seite / *page* 267

Lidan Liu
GeisenDesign
Seite / *page* 437

Loewe Design
Loewe AG
Seite / *page* 88, 89

Áron Losonczi
LiTraCon Bt.
Seite / *page* 60, 61

Ross Lovegrove
21 Powis Mews
GB-London W11 1JN
Seite / *page* 96, 97

Prof. Glen O. Löw
Andreasstr. 27
D-22301 Hamburg
Seite / *page* 382

M

M3 Design, Inc.
575 Round Rock W. Dr., Suite 100
Round Rock, TX 78681
USA
Seite / *page* 423

ma design
Düvelsbeker Weg 12
D-24105 Kiel
Seite / *page* 414

Diarmuid MacMahon
Design Partners
Seite / *page* 435

Poul Madsen
Normann Copenhagen
Seite / *page* 208

Detlev Magerer
Zeug Designgroup
Seite / *page* 364, 365

Sebastian Maier
designafairs GmbH
Seite / *page* 360

Hubert Maître
Jacob Delafon Paris (Kohler France)
Seite / *page* 337

Patrick Mak
AVC Technology Limited
Seite / *page* 450

Peter Maly
Oberstr. 46
D-20144 Hamburg
Seite / *page* 84, 85, 279

Simone Mangold
Festo AG & Co. KG
Seite / *page* 288, 289

marwin productdesign
Schraudolphstr. 2a
D-80799 München
Seite / *page* 433

Christian Marx
rosenthal design
Seite / *page* 252, 309, 354

Thomas Märzke
Held + Team
Seite / *page* 82, 83

Michael Mauer
Dr. Ing. h.c. F. Porsche AG
Seite / *page* 66, 67

Franz Maurer
Streichergasse 7/Atelier
A-1030 Wien
Seite / *page* 155

Sarah McCarvill
Otto Bock HealthCare
Utah Design and Manufacturing Center
Seite / *page* 374

Steve McGugan Industrial Design
Mortonsvej 21
DK-2800 Lyngby
Seite / *page* 297

Meister-Designteam
Meister GmbH
Meister + Co. AG
Seite / *page* 465

Rainer Mendler
AEG Hausgeräte GmbH
Seite / *page* 199

Metaphase Design Group, Inc.
12 S. Hanley Rd.
St. Louis, MO 63105
USA
Seite / *page* 206, 207, 303

Meyer en Van Schooten Architecten
P.O. Box 2737
NL-1000 CS Amsterdam
Seite / *page* 378, 379

Nico Michler
designafairs GmbH
Seite / *page* 409

milani d&c
Seestr. 78
CH-8703 Ertenbach/Zürich
Seite / *page* 212

Taihei Miyaji
Toshiba Design Center
Toshiba Corporation
Seite / *page* 421

Shin Miyashita
Sony Corporation
Seite / *page* 92, 93

MM Design
Via Vittorio Veneto 73
I-39042 Brixen (BZ)
Seite / *page* 239

Mocca Design
Bülowstr. 66 – D2
D-10783 Berlin
Seite / *page* 220

Cecile Mohr
Siemens AG
Henkestr. 127
D-91052 Erlangen
Seite / *page* 360

.molldesign – reiner moll & partner
Turmgasse 7
D-73525 Schwäbisch Gmünd
Seite / *page* 348

Bernd Montag
Siemens AG
Henkestr. 127
D-91052 Erlangen
Seite / *page* 360

Stephen Montgomery
Design Partners
Seite / *page* 435

Ollie Moore
Electrolux Home Products
Electrolux Industrial Design Centre Europe
Seite / *page* 191

Design Team Mosa
Royal Mosa
Seite / *page* 274, 275

Bernard Mosset
Basta France S.A.S.
Seite / *page* 252

Nadjaf Mougoni
DTC
Seite / *page* 367

Andreas Mühlenberendt
Otto Bock HealthCare GmbH
Seite / *page* 375

Jeff Mulhausen
M3 Design, Inc.
Seite / *page* 423

Alexander Müller
designafairs GmbH
Seite / *page* 360, 361

Tim Müller
BSH Bosch und Siemens Hausgeräte GmbH
Seite / *page* 180

müller/romca Industrial Design
Bei den Mühren 88
D-20457 Hamburg
Seite / *page* 327

Roger Münstermann
designafairs GmbH
Seite / *page* 408

N

Hiroko Nakano
Toshiba Design Center
Toshiba Corporation
Seite / *page* 421

Native Design Ltd
2a Tabernacle Street
GB-London EC2A 4LU
Seite / *page* 458

Jessica Nebel
Hagenring 3
D-38106 Braunschweig
Seite / *page* 294

Merete Nes
Fido industridesign as
Seite / *page* 351

Neumeister + Partner
Industrial Design
Liebigstr. 8
D-80538 München
Seite / *page* 276

Stephan Niehaus
Proform Design
Seite / *page* 300

Andreas Niessner
KMS Team GmbH
Seite / *page* 272, 273

Takuya Niitsu
Sony Corporation
Seite / *page* 446, 448

NOA
Bismarckstr. 106
D-52066 Aachen
Seite / *page* 232, 233

Paul Nobel-Campell
M3 Design, Inc.
Seite / *page* 423

Åke Nordin
Fjällräven
Seite / *page* 261

Jean Nouvel
10, cité d'Angoulême
F-75011 Paris
Seite / *page* 162, 163, 222

NPK Industrial Design
Noordeinde 2d
NL-2311 CD Leiden
Seite / *page* 205, 423

Gerhard Nüssler
Neff
Seite / *page* 190

Design-Team nya nordiska
nya nordiska textiles gmbh
Seite / *page* 149-151

O

Haruo Oba
Sony Corporation
Seite / *page* 449

OCO-Design
O.K. Nüsse
An der Kleimannbrücke 79
D-48157 Münster
Seite / *page* 202, 368

octopus productdesign
Ligsalzstr. 31
D-80339 München
Seite / *page* 48, 49

Taka Okai
M3 Design, Inc.
Seite / *page* 423

Michael Olsson
OG Invent
Seite / *page* 216

Harald Opolka
Zweibrüder Optoelectronics GmbH
Seite / *page* 253

Rainer Opolka
Zweibrüder Optoelectronics GmbH
Seite / *page* 253

Ora-Ïto
c/o Artemide Group S.p.A.
Seite / *page* 102, 103

Ottenwälder und Ottenwälder
Büro für Industrie Design
Sebaldplatz 6
D-73525 Schwäbisch Gmünd
Seite / *page* 312, 313, 371

Otto Bock HealthCare Products GmbH
Kaiserstr. 39
A-1070 Wien
Seite / *page* 362

P

Seung-Hyun Paek
Samsung Electronics Co., Ltd.
Seite / *page* 419

Markus Paloheimo
Fiskars Brands Finland Oy Ab
Seite / *page* 263

Palomba Serafini Associati
Via Zambonina 68
I-37068 Vigasio (VR)
Seite / *page* 338, 339

Kyung Soo Park
LG Electronics Inc.
Corporate Design Center
Seite / *page* 195

Sun Jung Park
LG Electronics Inc.
Corporate Design Center
Seite / *page* 440

Pearl Creative
Rheinlandstr. 10
D-71636 Ludwigsburg
Seite / *page* 304

People on the Move
Beckersweg 10
NL-5915 PB Venlo
Seite / *page* 146

Ulrike Peter
Indx-Design
Seite / *page* 436

Burkhard Peters
Held + Team
Seite / *page* 369

Florian Petri
Erich-Weinert-Str. 1
D-10439 Berlin
Seite / *page* 42, 43

Roberto Pezzetta
AEG Hausgeräte GmbH
Seite / *page* 198

Phoenix Design
Kölner Str. 16
D-70376 Stuttgart
Seite / *page* 88, 89, 342, 406, 407, 452, 453

Ralph Pietruska
BSH Bosch und Siemens Hausgeräte GmbH
Seite / *page* 178, 179

Pilotfish GmbH
Schleißheimer Str. 6
D-80333 München
Seite / *page* 363, 428, 429

Pilotfish Inc.
2F, No. 74, Zhou-Zi Street
Nei-Hu, Taipei
Taiwan
Seite / *page* 428, 429

Pinc Designteam
Pinc AB
Seite / *page* 58, 59

Elisabeth Piper-Mäkitalo
AB Electrolux
Seite / *page* 236

Warunee Piyawannawong
Plan Creations Co., Ltd.
Seite / *page* 266

Robin Platt
Clements Yard
Iliffe Street
GB-London SE17 3LJ
Seite / *page* 218

Jens Plewa
Designkontor
Seite / *page* 241

Brigitta Podobrin
OCO-Design
O.K. Nüsse
Seite / *page* 368

Dr. Ing. h.c. F. Porsche AG
Porscheplatz 1
D-70435 Stuttgart
Seite / *page* 72, 73, 268, 269

Dr. Ing. h.c. F. Porsche AG
Porschestr. 1
D-71287 Weissach
Seite / *page* 66, 67

Porsche Design GmbH
Flugplatzstr. 29
A-5700 Zell am See
Seite / *page* 224, 337

PPS International
Schwarzkopf Professional
Hohenzollernring 127-129
D-22763 Hamburg
Seite / *page* 294

Andreas Preussner
designafairs GmbH
Seite / *page* 293, 305

Lidija Pritržnik
Gorenje d.d.
Seite / *page* 182

Prodesign
Bernd Brussing
Turmstr. 39
D-89231 Neu-Ulm
Seite / *page* 277

Proform Design
Seehalde 16
D-71364 Winnenden
Seite / *page* 300

Britta Pukall
milani d&c
Seite / *page* 212

Pichaya Puttorngul
fuseproject
Seite / *page* 482

R

Felipe Rangel
Indio da Costa Design
Seite / *page* 426

RazorBite Design Studio
6 Arlington Place
GB-Porthcawl CF36 3DD
Seite / *page* 235

Etienne Redouin
Decathlon
Seite / *page* 56, 57

reform design
Industriestr. 25
D-70565 Stuttgart
Seite / *page* 311

Pelle Reinius
Ergonomidesign AB
Seite / *page* 216

Frank Rieser
Siemens Electrogeräte GmbH
Seite / *page* 174

Robert Allan Ltd.
Suite 230 – 1639 West 2nd Avenue
Vancouver, B.C. V6J 1H3
Kanada
Seite / *page* 70, 71

Hwa Joon Roh
Pantech & Curitel
Seite / *page* 410

rosenthal design
Vöcklinghauser Str. 10
D-45130 Essen
Seite / *page* 252, 309, 354

Marc Ruta
WILDDESIGN
Seite / *page* 347, 368

Bryce Rutter
Metaphase Design Group, Inc.
Seite / *page* 303

Joo-Hee Ryu
Samsung Electronics Co., Ltd.
Seite / *page* 196

索引——生产厂商（按字母顺序）

Alphabetical address-index manufacturers

A

Accademia srl
Via Indipendenza 4
I-33044 Manzano (UD)
Seite / *page* 160

Acer Incorporated
8F, No. 88, Section 1, Hsin Tai Wu Road
Hsichih, Taipei Hsien 221
Taiwan
Seite / *page* 432

Add-On Technology Co., Ltd.
1F, No. 11, Lane 206, Da-An Rd., Sec. 1
Taipei 106
Taiwan
Seite / *page* 428, 429

adidas-Salomon AG
Adi-Dassler-Str. 1
D-91074 Herzogenaurach
Seite / *page* 246-248

AEG Hausgeräte GmbH
Muggenhofer Str. 135
D-90429 Nürnberg
Seite / *page* 198, 199

AFG Arbonia-Forster-Riesa GmbH
Heinrich-Schönberg-Str. 3
D-01591 Riesa
Seite / *page* 346

agile Unterhaltungselektronik GmbH
Am Bach 11a
D-35083 Wetter/Amönau
Seite / *page* 461

aha Kunststofftechnik GmbH
Industriestr. 4
D-64407 Fränkisch-Crumbach/Odenwald
Seite / *page* 295

Koninklijke Ahrend NV
Laarderhoogtweg 12
NL-1101 EA Amsterdam
Seite / *page* 378, 379

Airflow Developments Ltd.
Lancaster Road
GB-High Wycombe HP12 3QP
Seite / *page* 350

Alape
Am Gräbicht 1-9
D-38644 Goslar
Seite / *page* 337

alfi GmbH
Ernst-Abbe-Str. 14
D-97877 Wertheim
Seite / *page* 230

American Standard Europe BVBA
Chaussee de Wavre 1789
B-1160 Brüssel
Seite / *page* 334, 335

Amor Manufacturing Corporation
8th Fl., No. 137, Jen Ai Rd.
Taipei 106
Taiwan
Seite / *page* 252

Apple
1 Infinite Loop
Cupertino, CA 95014
USA
Seite / *page* 90, 91, 392-399

Arcelik A.S.
Altinordu Cad. No. 5
Organize Sanayi Bölgesi
TR-06931 Ankara
Seite / *page* 194

Artemide Group S.p.A.
Via Bergamo 18
I-20010 Pregnana Milanese
Seite / *page* 102-105

Asmobile Communication Inc.
No. 11, Lane 120, Li-Te Rd., Peitou
Taipei 112
Taiwan
Seite / *page* 422

AsusTek Computer Inc.
No. 150, Li-Te Road
Peitou, 112, Taipei
Taiwan
Seite / *page* 434, 435

Attika Feuer AG
Brunnmatt 16
CH-6330 Cham
Seite / *page* 347

Audi AG
D-85045 Ingolstadt
Seite / *page* 323

Auerhahn Bestecke GmbH
Im oberen Tal 9
D-72213 Altensteig
Seite / *page* 221

AVC Technology Limited
6/F., Enterprise Square Three, 39 Wang Chiu Road
Kowloon Bay
Hongkong
Seite / *page* 450

B

B&W Loudspeakers Ltd
Dale Road
GB-Worthing, West Sussex BN11 2BH
Seite / *page* 458

Balay BSH Electrodomésticos España, S.A.
Avenida de la industria 49
E-50016 Montañana (Zaragoza)
Seite / *page* 178-180

Basta France S.A.S.
Usine de Beaulieu
F-58502 Clamecy
Seite / *page* 252

Becherer Möbel + Innenausbau GmbH
Telfer Str. 6
D-79215 Elzach
Seite / *page* 172

Gebr. Becker GmbH & Co. KG
Hölker Feld 29-31
D-42279 Wuppertal
Seite / *page* 308

Beckhoff Industrie Elektronik
Eiserstr. 5
D-33415 Verl
Seite / *page* 308

Beko Elektronik A.S.
Beylikduzu
TR-34901 Istanbul
Seite / *page* 455

BenQ Corporation
18 Jihu Road, Neihu
Taipei 114
Taiwan
Seite / *page* 400-405

Bessey & Sohn GmbH & Co.
Mühlenwiesenstr. 40
D-74321 Bietigheim-Bissingen
Seite / *page* 298

Bette GmbH & Co. KG
Heinrich-Bette-Str. 1
D-33129 Delbrück
Seite / *page* 333

Birkenstock
P.O. Box 6140
Novato, CA 94948
USA
Seite / *page* 100, 101

BMW Group
D-80788 München
Seite / *page* 68, 69, 320, 321

Boblbee AB
Vintergatan 12
Box 4039
S-20311 Malmö
Seite / *page* 261

Bodenschatz Lederwaren GmbH & Co. KG
Boschaplatz 3
D-95355 Presseck
Seite / *page* 295

Bodum AG
Bodum Design Group
Kantonsstr. 100
CH-6234 Triengen
Seite / *page* 209, 211

Boehringer Werkzeugmaschinen Vertriebsgesellschaft mbH
Stuttgarter Str. 70
D-73033 Göppingen
Seite / *page* 308

Bombardier Recreational Products Inc.
565, Mountain Street
Valcourt, QC J0E 2L0
Kanada
Seite / *page* 324

Bombardier Recreational Products Inc.
Florida Technology Center
111, J.-A. Bombardier Blvd. SW
Cogan Lake, Palm Bay, FL 32908
USA
Seite / *page* 324

Robert Bosch Hausgeräte GmbH
Carl-Wery-Str. 34
D-81739 München
Seite / *page* 181, 186-189, 224, 242, 243

Bose Corp.
The Mountain
Framingham, MA 01701-9168
USA
Seite / *page* 86, 87, 420

Braun GmbH
Frankfurter Str. 145
D-61476 Kronberg
Seite / *page* 368

BREE Collection GmbH & Co. KG
Gerberstr. 3
D-30916 Isernhagen
Seite / *page* 94, 95

Brüel & Kjær Sound & Vibration Measurement A/S
Skodsborgvej 307
DK-2850 Naerum
Seite / *page* 297

Busch-Jaeger Elektro GmbH
Freisenbergstr. 2
D-58513 Lüdenscheid
Seite / *page* 277

C

Canon Deutschland GmbH
Europark Fichtenhain A10
D-47807 Krefeld
Seite / *page* 260, 438, 439, 442

Canyon Bicycles GmbH
Koblenzer Str. 236
D-56073 Koblenz
Seite / *page* 251

Carpet Concept Objekt-Teppichboden GmbH
Bunzlauer Str. 7
D-33719 Bielefeld
Seite / *page* 84, 85, 381

Chef'n Corp
1520 4th Ave., 3rd Floor
Seattle, WA 98101
USA
Seite / *page* 222

Cheoy Lee Shipyards Ltd.
89 & 91 Hing Wah Street West
Lai Chi Kok
Kowloon
Hongkong
Seite / *page* 70, 71

Cherry GmbH
Cherrystr.
D-91275 Auerbach/Opf.
Seite / *page* 433

Concise Living Co., Ltd.
No. 2, Lane 28, Chung Mei St.
Taichung
Taiwan
Seite / *page* 258, 259

Concord:marlin
Hanworth Trading Estate
Hampton Road West
GB-Feltham, Middx. TW13 6DR
Seite / *page* 480

Conmoto GmbH & Co. KG
Schlossallee 7-9
D-33442 Herzebrock-Clarholz
Seite / *page* 279

Crown Equipment Corporation
14 W. Monroe St.
New Bremen, OH 45869
USA
Seite / *page* 325

D

DAB
C/Conflent, 46. P.I. Pomar de Dalt. Badalona
E-08915 Barcelona
Seite / *page* 483

DaimlerChrysler AG
Epplestr. 225
D-70546 Stuttgart
Seite / *page* 318, 319

Damixa a/s
Ostbirkvej 2
DK-5240 Odense
Seite / *page* 333

Dark NV
Vliegplein 43
B-9991 Maldegem
Seite / *page* 478

DASGIP AG
Rudolf-Schulten-Straße 5
D-52428 Jülich
Seite / *page* 368

De'Longhi S.p.A.
Via L. Seitz 47
I-31100 Treviso
Seite / *page* 237

Decathlon Sportartikel GmbH
Holsterhauser Str. 200
D-44625 Herne
Seite / *page* 56, 57

Dell Inc.
One Dell Way
Round Rock, TX 78682
USA
Seite / *page* 423

Derungs Licht AG
Hofmattstr. 12
CH-9200 Gossau
Seite / *page* 364, 365

Deutsche Telekom AG
T-Com Division
Hochstadenring 50
D-53119 Bonn
Seite / *page* 414, 415

Dietiker Switzerland
Dietiker AG
Hofwisenstr. 2
CH-8260 Stein am Rhein
Seite / *page* 147

DORMA GmbH + Co. KG
Breckerfelder Str. 42-48
D-58256 Ennepetal
Seite / *page* 281

Duck Image Co. Ltd.
1st Fl., No. 22, Lane 321, Sec. 1, Hsingan Rd.
Taichung
Taiwan
Seite / *page* 427

Duravit AG
Werderstr. 36
D-78132 Hornberg
Seite / *page* 340, 341

DZ LICHT – Gruppe Artemide
Hans-Böckler-Str. 2
D-58730 Fröndenberg
Seite / *page* 484, 485

E

e15 Design und Distributions GmbH
Hospitalstr. 4
D-61440 Oberursel
Seite / *page* 479

Elco Kunststoffe GmbH
Osnabrücker Landstr. 154
D-33335 Gütersloh
Seite / *page* 173

AB Electrolux
S:t Göransgatan 143
S-10545 Stockholm
Seite / *page* 236, 238

Electrolux Home Products S.A.
Belgicastraat 17
B-1930 Zaventem
Seite / *page* 191

elmarflötotto GmbH
Am Ölbach 28
D-33334 Gütersloh
Seite / *page* 146

EMS-GRIVORY
Reichenauerstr.
CH-7013 Domat/Ems
Seite / *page* 225

Emsa Werke Wulf GmbH & Co. KG
Grevener Damm 215-225
D-48282 Emsdetten
Seite / *page* 235

Esselte Leitz GmbH & Co KG
Siemensstr. 64
D-70469 Stuttgart
Seite / *page* 389

Hermann Eule Orgelbau GmbH
Wilthener Str. 6
D-02625 Bautzen
Seite / *page* 268, 269

Eva Denmark A/S
Maaloev Teknikerby 18-20
DK-2760 Maaloev
Seite / *page* 231

Extremis NV
Weegschede 39 B
B-8691 Gijverinkhove
Seite / *page* 279

F

C. & E. Fein GmbH
Leuschnerstraße 43
D-70176 Stuttgart
Seite / *page* 302

Fennel GmbH & Co. KG
Unterer Sundern 11
D-32549 Bad Oeynhausen
Seite / *page* 173

Festo AG & Co. KG
Ruiter Str. 82
D-73734 Esslingen
Seite / *page* 62-65, 286-292

Fiskars Brands Finland Oy Ab
East Building
FIN-10330 Billnäs
Seite / *page* 263

Fissler GmbH
Harald-Fissler-Str. 1
D-55743 Idar-Oberstein
Seite / *page* 212

Fjällräven
Lilienthalallee 40
D-80939 München
Seite / *page* 261

Flos S.p.A.
Via Angelo Faini 2
I-25073 Bovezzo (Brescia)
Seite / *page* 481

Frank Europe GmbH
Bosenheimer Str. 233-237
D-55543 Bad Kreuznach
Seite / *page* 278

Gebrüder Frei GmbH & Co.
Borsigstr. 15
D-72461 Albstadt
Seite / *page* 311

Porzellanmanufaktur Fürstenberg
Meinbrexener Str. 2
D-37699 Fürstenberg/Weser
Seite / *page* 223

G

Gaba International AG
Emil-Frey-Str. 100
CH-4142 Münchenstein
Seite / *page* 368

Geka Brush GmbH
Division Victoria Cosmetics
Schulweg 3
D-91572 Bechhofen/Königshofen
Seite / *page* 295

Georg Jensen
Søndre Fasanvej 7
DK-2000 Frederiksberg
Seite / *page* 222

Gioel
Via Brennero 260/G
I-38100 Trento
Seite / *page* 239

Le Groupe GO inc.
103-291, rue De St. Vallier Est
Quebec, G1K 3P5
Kanada
Seite / *page* 250

W.L. Gore & Associates GmbH
Aiblinger Str. 60
D-83620 Feldkirchen-Westerham
Seite / *page* 254

Gorenje d.d.
Partizanska 12
SLO-3503 Velenje
Seite / *page* 182

Gebr. Graef GmbH & Co. KG
Donnerfeld 6
D-59757 Arnsberg
Seite / *page* 233

Grimmeisen Vertriebs GmbH
Äußere Lohe 2
D-83512 Wasserburg a. Inn
Seite / *page* 380

Grohe Water Technology AG & Co. KG
Industriepark Edelburg
D-58675 Hemer
Seite / *page* 343

H

Hamberger Sanitary
Postfach 10 03 53
D-83003 Rosenheim
Seite / *page* 351

Hansa Metallwerke AG
Sigmaringer Str. 107
D-70567 Stuttgart
Seite / *page* 48, 49, 232

Hansaton Akustik GmbH
Stückenstr. 48
D-22081 Hamburg
Seite / *page* 363

Hansgrohe AG
Auestr. 5-9
D-77761 Schiltach
Seite / *page* 74-77, 342

Harman/Becker
Raiffeisenstr. 34
D-70794 Filderstadt
Seite / *page* 460

Holzprojekte Härtenberger HKH GmbH
Hauptstr. 39
D-94336 Hunderdorf
Seite / *page* 171

Haworth GmbH
Von-Achenbach-Str. 21-23
D-59229 Ahlen
Seite / *page* 262

Heineken Beer Systems
Stadhouderskade 79
NL-1072 AE Amsterdam
Seite / *page* 205

Henkel KGaA
Henkelstr. 67
D-40191 Düsseldorf
Seite / *page* 387

Hensoldt AG Carl Zeiss Gruppe
Gloelstr. 3-5
D-35576 Wetzlar
Seite / *page* 261

Hess Form + Licht GmbH
Schlachthausstr. 19-19/3
D-78050 Villingen-Schwenningen
Seite / *page* 485

Hilti AG
Feldkircher Str. 100
FL-9494 Schaan
Seite / *page* 300, 301

Hirschmann Laborgeräte GmbH & Co. KG
Hauptstr. 7-15
D-74246 Eberstadt
Seite / *page* 370

I

I-House Incorporadora LTDA.
R. Ezequiel Freire, 51 - 13° Andar - Cj. 136
BR-02034-000 São Paulo, SP
Seite / *page* 330, 331

Ikea of Sweden AB
P.O. Box 702
S-34381 Älmhult
Seite / *page* 221, 235

Imaje AB
Säterigatan 20
S-41764 Göteborg
Seite / *page* 306

Innovativ Vision AB
Attorpsgatan 7
S-58273 Linköping
Seite / *page* 309

Inotech Medizintechnik GmbH
Boschstr. 3
D-92507 Nabburg
Seite / *page* 294

Interflex Datensysteme GmbH & Co. KG
Zettachring 16
D-70567 Stuttgart
Seite / *page* 276

interstil Diedrichsen GmbH & Co. KG
Liebigstraße 1-3
D-33803 Steinhagen
Seite / *page* 161

J

JAB Teppiche Heinz Anstoetz KG
Dammheider Str. 67
D-32052 Herford
Seite / *page* 156

Jacob Delafon Paris (Kohler France)
60, rue de Turenne
F-75139 Paris cedex 03
Seite / *page* 337

Jado
Paul-Ehrlich-Str. 5
D-63322 Rödermark
Seite / *page* 280, 336

Jordan AS
Haavard Martinsens vei 30
N-0978 Oslo
Seite / *page* 351

Jura Elektroapparate AG
Bahnhofstr. 135
CH-4626 Niederbuchsiten
Seite / *page* 203

K

möbelbau kaether & weise
Dammstr. 43
D-31195 Lamspringe
Seite / *page* 42, 43

KAHLA/Thüringen Porzellan GmbH
Christian-Eckardt-Str. 38
D-07768 Kahla
Seite / *page* 50, 51, 217

Franz Kaldewei GmbH & Co. KG
Beckumer Str. 33-35
D-59229 Ahlen
Seite / *page* 332

Alfred Kärcher GmbH & Co. KG
Alfred-Kärcher-Str. 28-40
D-71364 Winnenden
Seite / *page* 304

Ulla u. Martin Kaufmann
Goslarsche Landstr. 54
D-31135 Hildesheim
Seite / *page* 467

Kellogg Company
One Kellogg Square
P.O. Box 3599
Battle Creek, MI 49016-3599
Seite / *page* 207

Kenwood Ltd.
New Lane
GB-Havant, Hampshire PO9 2NH
Seite / *page* 230

Keramag AG
Kreuzerkamp 11
D-40878 Ratingen
Seite / *page* 337

Kermi GmbH
Pankofen-Bahnhof 1
D-94447 Plattling
Seite / *page* 344, 345

Kesseböhmer GmbH
Mindener Str. 208
D-49152 Bad Essen
Seite / *page* 170

Keuco GmbH & Co. KG
Oesestr. 36
D-58675 Hemer
Seite / *page* 348

Klafs Saunabau GmbH & Co. KG
Erich-Klafs-Str. 1-3
D-74523 Schwäbisch Hall
Seite / *page* 256, 257

Klöber GmbH
Bürositzmöbel
Rauensteinstr. 18
D-88662 Überlingen
Seite / *page* 388

Walter Knoll AG & Co.KG
Bahnhofstr. 25
D-71083 Herrenberg
Seite / *page* 148, 154

Krups
Groupe SEB Moulinex
Immeuble Le Monge
22, place des Vosges
La Défense 5
F-92979 Paris La Défense
Seite / *page* 205

Küppersbusch Hausgeräte AG
Küppersbuschstr. 16
D-45883 Gelsenkirchen
Seite / *page* 185

KWC AG
Hauptstr. 57
CH-5726 Unterkulm
Seite / *page* 233

L

C. Josef Lamy GmbH
Grenzhöfer Weg 32
D-69123 Heidelberg
Seite / *page* 384, 385

Laufen Ceramconsult AG
Wahlenstr. 46
CH-4242 Laufen
Seite / *page* 338, 339

Lehnen edel:stahl GmbH
Zum Rachtiger Wald 3
D-54516 Wittlich
Seite / *page* 366

Leicht Küchen AG
Gmünder Str. 70
D-73550 Waldstetten
Seite / *page* 169, 173

Leolux Meubelfabriek BV
P.O. Box 3076
NL-5902 RB Venlo
Seite / *page* 146

LG Electronics Inc.
Corporate Design Center
15Fl, LG Gangnam Tower, 679 Yeoksam-dong,
Gangnam-gu, 15Fl
Seoul 135-985
Korea
Seite / *page* 194, 195, 440, 441

S

Bruno Sacco
Wendelsteinstr. 14
D-71067 Sindelfingen
Seite / *page* 48, 49

Robert Sachon
BSH Bosch und Siemens Hausgeräte GmbH
Seite / *page* 178–180

Stewart Sandham
GeisenDesign
Seite / *page* 437

SANI
Sani Saksuwan
77/89 Phayathai Rd., Tanonphayathai
Ratchathewi, Bangkok 10400
Thailand
Seite / *page* 158

Tetsuro Sano
Sony Ericsson Mobile Communications
Japan Inc.
Seite / *page* 445

Steffen Sawatzki
Otto Bock HealthCare GmbH
Seite / *page* 375

Sven Schaarschmidt
busse design ulm
Seite / *page* 298

Christina Schäfer
Potthofstr. 3
D-58455 Witten
Seite / *page* 210

Dirk Schäfer
Gebr. Becker GmbH & Co. KG
Seite / *page* 308

Lutz Scheffer
Canyon Bicycles GmbH
Seite / *page* 54, 55, 251

Steven Schilte
Schilte Industrial Design B.V.
Hoiserstraatweg 71
NL-1411 GM Naarden
Seite / *page* 152, 153

Michaela Schleypen
Tai Ping Carpets
Seite / *page* 157

Barbara Schmidt
KAHLA/Thüringen Porzellan GmbH
Seite / *page* 50, 51, 217

Karoline Schmidt
Festo AG & Co. KG
Seite / *page* 64, 65, 286, 288–292

Jörn Schmoldt
Imaje AB
Seite / *page* 308

Sabine Schober
Design 3
Seite / *page* 241

Stephan Schönherr
NEOMAN Bus GmbH
Seite / *page* 326

Jörg Schröter
Siemens Electrogeräte GmbH
Seite / *page* 183

Wolfgang Schüller
Hamberger Sanitary
Seite / *page* 351

Dirk Schumann
Büro für industrielle Formentwicklung
Hiltruper Str. 39
D-48167 Münster
Seite / *page* 355

Andreas Schüßler
Ziba Europe
Seite / *page* 430, 431

Christian Schwamkrug
Porsche Design GmbH
Seite / *page* 224

Augusto Seibel
Indio da Costa Design
Seite / *page* 330, 331

Woon-Kyu Seo
LG Electronics Inc.
Corporate Design Center
Seite / *page* 195

Kun-Jun Seok
LG Electronics Inc.
Corporate Design Center
Seite / *page* 195

Oliver Shakespeare
Concord:marlin
Seite / *page* 480

Chris Sharples
Virgin Atlantic Airways
Seite / *page* 282

Peter Sheehan
Design Partners
Seite / *page* 435

Gwan-Woo Shin
Samsung Electronics Co., Ltd.
Seite / *page* 196

Ji hoon Shin
LG Electronics Inc.
Corporate Design Center
Seite / *page* 440

SHL Design
Arkitekterne maa Schmidt Hammer & Lassen K/S
Seite / *page* 159

Shuttle ID Team
Shuttle Inc.
Seite / *page* 443

Michael Sieger
Sieger Design GmbH & Co. KG
Schloss Harkotten
D-48336 Sassenberg
Seite / *page* 279, 337, 340

Susanne Sievers
GeisenDesign
Seite / *page* 437

Hyun-Joo Sim
Samsung Electronics Co., Ltd.
Seite / *page* 196

Shawn Sinyork
fuseproject
Seite / *page* 100, 101

Björn-Åke Sköld
Sköld Design AB
Box 7043
S-60007 Norrköping
Seite / *page* 309

Robert Sluijter
C10 Design & Development
Seite / *page* 423

Hans-Christian Smolik
Canyon Bicycles GmbH
Seite / *page* 251

Someones Design
Njalsgade 19D, 6. Sal.
DK-2300 Kopenhagen S
Seite / *page* 231

Sven Sonnendorfer
KMS Team GmbH
Seite / *page* 272, 273

Sony Ericsson
Mobile Communications Int. AB
Nya Vattentornet
S-22188 Lund
Seite / *page* 413

Sottsass Associati
Via Melone 2
I-20121 Mailand
Seite / *page* 332

Uwe Spannagel
Spannagel.Design
Rubensstr. 15
D-50676 Köln
Seite / *page* 436

speziell produktgestaltung
Sybille Fleckenstein / Jens Pohlmann /
Thilo Schwer
Luisenstr. 30b
D-63067 Offenbach
Seite / *page* 50, 51

Squareone GmbH
Talstr. 66
D-40217 Düsseldorf
Seite / *page* 296

Ralph Stand
Robert Bosch Hausgeräte GmbH
Seite / *page* 188

Philippe Starck
Agence Starck
18/20, rue du Faubourg du Temple
F-75011 Paris
Seite / *page* 74, 75, 341, 342, 481

Starczewski Design Team
Thomas Starczewski
Heimstr. 29
D-89073 Ulm
Seite / *page* 310

Stefan Stark
Dr. Ing. h.c. F. Porsche AG
Seite / *page* 66, 67

Thomas Steuri
zed AG
Seite / *page* 261

Michael Streicher
NEOMAN Bus GmbH
Seite / *page* 326

Rolf Strohmeyer
Vorwerk Elektrowerke GmbH & Co. KG
Seite / *page* 213

Andreas Struppler
Struppler Associates Design GmbH
Senftlstr. 7
D-81541 München
Seite / *page* 346

Heinrich Stukenkemper
Am Förderturm 8
D-44575 Castrop-Rauxel
Seite / *page* 228

Ragnar Sturm
LoeweVonAppen GmbH
Seite / *page* 264

Mads Surel
Stelton A/S
Seite / *page* 231, 450

Suwada
1332, Koanji, Sakaemachi, Minamikanbara
Niigata 959-1114
Japan
Seite / *page* 349

Shigeaki Suzuki
Sony Ericsson Mobile Communications
Japan Inc.
Seite / *page* 445

Esbjörn Svantesson
AB Electrolux
Seite / *page* 236, 238

Øyvar Svendsen
Fido industridesign as
Seite / *page* 351

Sweedish Designstudio
Brännkyrkagatan 56
S-11822 Stockholm
Seite / *page* 235

T

Satoshi Taguchi
Sunwave Corporation
Seite / *page* 168

Hideyuki Takaku
Sunwave Corporation
Seite / *page* 168

Jaakko Tammela
Indio da Costa Design
Seite / *page* 426

Naoki Tashiro
Canon Inc.
Seite / *page* 439

Teams Design
Kollwitzstr. 1
D-73728 Esslingen
Seite / *page* 214, 353

Prof. Georg Teodorescu
Tesign
Seite / *page* 309

Terrumanum
Hauptstr. 124–126
D-50226 Frechen
Seite / *page* 464

Tesign
Burg Sülz
Haus 8
D-53797 Lohmar
Seite / *page* 309

Christoph Thauern
GeisenDesign
Seite / *page* 437

Dieter Thomas
Zwilling J.A. Henckels AG
Seite / *page* 349

Klaus Thormann
designafairs GmbH
Seite / *page* 359

Andrew Thornton
William Levene Ltd
Seite / *page* 229

Matteo Thun
Studio Matteo Thun
Via Appiani 9
I-20121 Mailand
Seite / *page* 272, 273

Michael Tinius
busse design ulm
Seite / *page* 298, 301

Eskil Tomozy
fuseproject
Seite / *page* 100, 101

Tools Design
Rentemestervej 23A
DK-2400 Kopenhagen NV
Seite / *page* 231

Topeak Design Team
Topeak, Inc.
Seite / *page* 54, 55

Prof. Martin Topel
Squareone GmbH
Seite / *page* 296

Toshiba Design Center
Toshiba Corporation
Seite / *page* 237, 240, 350, 420, 421

Jörg Tragatschnig
Porsche Design GmbH
Seite / *page* 224

Byron Tsai
Topeak, Inc.
Seite / *page* 264

Peggy Tsai
1st Fl., No. 22, Lane 321, Sec. 1, Shingan Rd.
Taichung
Taiwan
Seite / *page* 258, 259

Takahiro Tsuge
Sony Corporation
Seite / *page* 444

Tupperware Global Design Group
Tupperware France S.A.
Seite / *page* 234

U

Patricia Urquiola
Via Morgagni 6
I-20125 Mailand
Seite / *page* 40, 41

V
Ulrika Vejbrink
Ergonomidesign AB
Seite / *page* 221

Danny Venlet
Venlet Interior Architecture
Lakensestraat 88
B-1000 Brüssel
Seite / *page* 478

vertical pre-production management GmbH
Hebbelplatz 5
A-1100 Wien
Seite / *page* 362

Studio Vertijet
Harz 5a
D-06108 Halle
Seite / *page* 94, 95

Roland Vetter
Robert Bosch Hausgeräte GmbH
Seite / *page* 186-189

Virgin Atlantic Airways
02 Manor Royal
GB-Crawley RH10 2NU
Seite / *page* 282

Vistapark GmbH
Viehhofstr. 119
D-42117 Wuppertal
Seite / *page* 352

vitamin d
Hofaue 53
Kolkmannhaus
D-42103 Wuppertal
Seite / *page* 223

Günter Vogl
Cherry GmbH
Seite / *page* 433

W
Helmut Wagner
Otto Bock HealthCare GmbH
Seite / *page* 80, 81

Mathias Wagner
reform design
Seite / *page* 311

Wolf Udo Wagner
Wagner:Design
Hanauer Landstr. 161-173
D-60314 Frankfurt/Main
Seite / *page* 255

Wolfgang Wagner
Design 3
Seite / *page* 241, 451

Emil Wegger Jensen
Designit
Seite / *page* 450

Weinberg & Ruf
Produktgestaltung
Ludwigstr. 8
D-70794 Filderstadt
Seite / *page* 298

Yvonne Weisbarth
Robert Bosch Hausgeräte GmbH
Seite / *page* 181

Erwin Weitgasser
Zeug Designgroup
Seite / *page* 364, 365

Silke Wendt Product Design
Dorfstr. 71
D-29362 Hohne
Seite / *page* 242, 243

Christian Werner
Am Aarbach 14
D-21279 Hollenstedt/Appel
Seite / *page* 144, 145, 156

Kathrin Westkämper
Königsstieg 19
D-38118 Braunschweig
Seite / *page* 295

Niall White
Logitech USA
Seite / *page* 435

Marcus Wiedemann
marwin productdesign
Seite / *page* 433

Markus Wild
WILDDESIGN
Leithestr. 39
D-45886 Gelsenkirchen
Seite / *page* 347, 368

Ulrich Wilkesmann
Gebr. Becker GmbH & Co. KG
Seite / *page* 308

Jean-Michel Wilmotte
c/o Artemide Group S.p.A.
Seite / *page* 104, 105

Irmy Wilms
Mocca Design
Seite / *page* 220

Gerd E. Wilsdorf
Siemens Electrogeräte GmbH
Seite / *page* 174, 175, 184

Susanne Winckler
Gebr. Niessing GmbH & Co.
Seite / *page* 466

Karsten Winkels
bauwerkstadt
Leibnizstr. 8a
D-44147 Dortmund
Seite / *page* 485

Tae-Yeon Won
Samsung Electronics Co., Ltd.
Seite / *page* 418

Dirk Wynants
Extremis NV
Seite / *page* 279

X
X-Technology Swiss GmbH
Kantonsstr. 146
CH-8807 Freienbach
Seite / *page* 249

Zhen Xie
GeisenDesign
Seite / *page* 437

Josep Lluís Xuclà
DAB
Seite / *page* 483

Y
Masato Yamamoto
Bodum AG
Bodum Design Group
Seite / *page* 209

Nobuhiro Yamane
Toshiba Design Center
Toshiba Corporation
Seite / *page* 421

Toshiyuki Yamanouchi
Toshiba Design Center
Toshiba Corporation
Seite / *page* 237

Hee Su Yang
LG Electronics Inc.
Corporate Design Center
Seite / *page* 441

Jun-Ho Yang
Samsung Electronics Co., Ltd.
Seite / *page* 418

yellow design | yellow circle
Georgstr. 5a
D-50676 Köln
Seite / *page* 266, 386

Cairn Young
Clements Yard
Iliffe Street
GB-London SE17 3LJ
Seite / *page* 221

Z
Matthias Zäh
Attika Feuer AG
Seite / *page* 347

zed AG
Seefeldstr. 303
CH-8008 Zürich
Seite / *page* 261

Zemp + Partner Design
Pfingstweidstr. 30
CH-8005 Zürich
Seite / *page* 203

Reinhard Zetsche
octopus productdesign
Seite / *page* 48, 49

Zeug Designgroup
Morzger Str. 4
A-5020 Salzburg
Seite / *page* 364, 365

Mike Zhang
Herbst LaZar Bell Inc.
Seite / *page* 423

Ziba Europe
Am Tucherpark 4
D-80538 München
Seite / *page* 430, 431

Agnes Zuber
Wasserfederring 49
D-38446 Wolfsburg
Seite / *page* 295

Sonia Zvirbulis
Hafenstr. 4a
D-38442 Wolfsburg
Seite / *page* 294